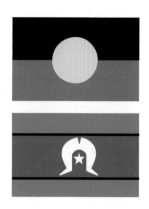

Aboriginal Australia
& the Torres Strait Islands

guide to Indigenous Australia

Sarina Singh
David Andrew
bryan Andy
Monique Choy
Hugh Finlay
Paul Greenway
Kath Kenny
Philip Morrissey
Denis O'Byrne
Belinda Scott

LONELY PLANET PUBLICATIONS
Melbourne | Oakland | London | Paris

2 Contents – Text

NORTHERN TERRITORY   188

QUEENSLAND   254

Contents – Text

Aboriginal Australia & the Torres Strait Islands
1st edition – July 2001

Published by
Lonely Planet Publications Pty Ltd ABN 36 005 607 983
90 Maribyrnong St, Footscray, Victoria 3011, Australia

Lonely Planet Offices
Australia Locked Bag 1, Footscray, Victoria 3011
USA 150 Linden St, Oakland, CA 94607
UK 10a Spring Place, London NW5 3BH
France 1 rue du Dahomey, 75011 Paris

Photographs
Many of the images in this guide are available for licensing from
Lonely Planet Images.
email: lpi@lonelyplanet.com.au

Front cover image
Sky and Country by Donna Brown

Photographic index
Phylis Thomas at work on *Hole in the Rock*; Bradley Byquar in Ivan
Senn's *Wind*; Sea of Hands installation (Sydney, NSW); Wandjina rock
painting (Gibb River, WA); Kakadu National Park (NT); Uluru-Kata
Tjuta National Park (NT); Prime Minister Gough Whitlam hands back
Gurindji lands to Vincent Lingiari (NT, 1975); Torres Strait Islander
festive headress; Aboriginal Tent Embassy, Canberra (ACT); Manuel
with stringy bark for making a didjeridu (Arnhem Land, NT).

ISBN 0 86450 114 6

text & maps © Lonely Planet 2001
photos © photographers as indicated 2001

Printed by The Bookmaker International Ltd
Printed in China

AIATSIS LANGUAGE GROUP MAP

Every part of Australia is on the traditional land of Indigenous tribal societies, or
nations. The language groups depicted on the AIATSIS map, reproduced at the start of
this book, are not necessarily distinct nations with firm boundaries. This map is based
on information derived from many sources, including the early records of non-Indigenous people, which was sometimes incorrect. Boundaries can be negotiable and can
change over time; boundary areas may have been shared. All these factors contribute
to the difficulty in mapping traditional boundaries in the Western sense and this map,
like all other attempts to map Indigenous Australia, is disputed by many Indigenous
people. For these and other reasons, AIATSIS has stipulated that the map should not be
used for land claims. However, we have reproduced it here because it powerfully expresses (in a way that words can't) the sheer number and great diversity of traditional
Indigenous societies in Australia.

A poster-sized edition of the map, which was produced for *The Encyclopedia of Aboriginal Australia* (David Horton, General Editor) is widely available at map shops
throughout Australia, or you can purchase it directly from AIATSIS. Check out their Web
site at www.aiatsis.gov.au/rasp.htm, or fax them on (02) 6249 7310.

'If you are born black you are born political'
The events, movements and activists that have shaped Indigenous politics (page 36)

Special Events
Where to find the stomping grounds, footy fields, theatres and story circles (page 134)

Land Bridge to Land Rights
A summary of Australian history and the Indigenous struggle to the present day (page 22)

approach

Beyond Jedda
Indigenous people on both sides of the camera lens (page 59)

The Sacred Rock
Explore Uluru with the Anangu, whose ancestors created it (page 247)

Island Home
Meet the other Indigenous people of Australia – Torres Strait Islanders (page 335)

SOUTH AUSTRALIA

TASMANIA

TORRES STRAIT ISLANDS

VICTORIA

WESTERN AUSTRALIA

GLOSSARY   429

INDEX   437

MAP LEGEND   back page

METRIC CONVERSION   inside back cover

Contents – Maps

MAP INDEX

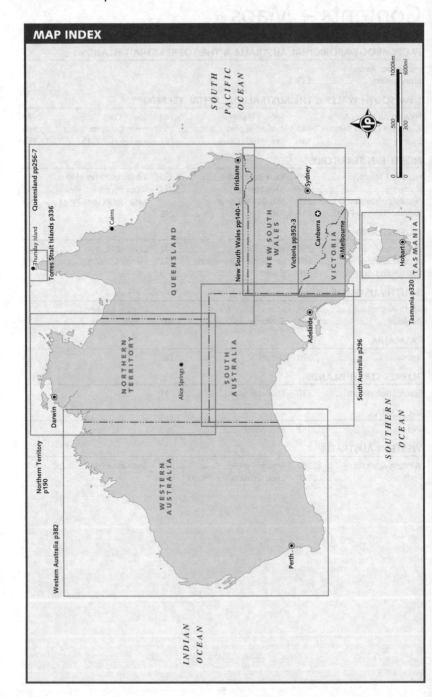

SOUTH PACIFIC OCEAN

INDIAN OCEAN

SOUTHERN OCEAN

1000km
600mi
500
300
0
0

Queensland pp256-7

Torres Strait Islands p336

New South Wales pp140-1

Victoria pp352-3

South Australia p296

Northern Territory p190

Western Australia p382

Tasmania p320

QUEENSLAND

NEW SOUTH WALES

VICTORIA

NORTHERN TERRITORY

SOUTH AUSTRALIA

WESTERN AUSTRALIA

TASMANIA

Thursday Island

Cairns

Brisbane

Sydney

Canberra

Melbourne

Adelaide

Alice Springs

Darwin

Perth

Hobart

The Authors

Sarina Singh

After finishing a business degree in Melbourne, Sarina bought a one-way ticket to India where she completed a corporate traineeship with Sheraton Hotels, but later worked as a freelance journalist and foreign correspondent. After four years she returned to Australia, completed post-graduate journalism qualifications and wrote two TV documentary scripts. Other Lonely Planet books she has worked on include three editions of *India*; two editions of *Rajasthan*; *Mauritius, Réunion & Seychelles*; *North India*; *Africa*; *Sacred India* and the *Out to Eat* restaurant guides to Melbourne and Sydney. She is also the author of *Polo in India* and has contributed to international publications, including *National Geographic Traveler*.

Sarina was the coordinating author of this book. She wrote part of the Victoria and introductory chapters and was also involved in training many of the Indigenous writers. Her hope for the future is to see a prime minister who acknowledges the First Australians beyond the rhetoric of reconciliation.

David Andrew

After his father was mauled by a gorilla at Howletts Zoo, David and his family were dragged off to live somewhere safer than the wilds of England and fled to Australia. There David revolutionised the face of birdwatching by creating *Wingspan* and *Australian Birding* magazines, did a stint as editor of *Wildlife Australia* then worked as an in-house editor at Lonely Planet. But in his view there are few things in life more worthwhile than travel and natural history, and he now writes Lonely Planet books. He has worked on LP's *Northern Territory* and *Malaysia, Singapore & Brunei*; wrote most of *Watching Wildlife East Africa*; and contributed extensively to *Watching Wildlife Australia*. He researched the Queensland chapter for *Aboriginal Australia & the Torres Strait Islands*. When not writing for LP David spends much of his time amassing a bird list to bequeath to the nation.

bryan Andy

bryan is a proud Yorta Yorta man from the Aboriginal village of Cummeragunja. At the age of 18 he moved to the 'big smoke' (that'd be Melbourne) where he bided his time studying before getting out of that chicken outfit and finding real work. This work has almost always revolved around Aboriginal affairs – one could define it as a kind of 'calling'. He was among the first four Indigenous people to address the Victorian parliament and dreams of spending a winter in Iceland, canoeing the entire Murray River and witnessing the day his mob's land aspirations are recognised. While he lives in Melbourne, he still calls Cummeragunja home.

Donna Brown

Gumbainggir artist Donna Brown painted the image on the cover.

Donna has been involved in the arts for more than a decade in various media, her favourite being painting and designing. During this time she has worked and exhibited with many artists at major public and private galleries across Australia. She's kept busy being mum to little Aretha Stewart Brown and by being active in the arts community.

Monique Choy

Born in Canada to Anglo-Australian and Chinese parents, Monique had lived in four different cities and on a farm before she turned six years old. The last move was to Sydney, where the family stayed, but she's never been able to shake the nomad lust.

Over the years Monique has found herself in jobs promoting safe sex, the preservation of elephant habitats and decent housing for intellectually disabled people. She worked in Hong Kong, Sri Lanka and the Maldives before settling down to life as an editor in Lonely Planet's Melbourne office. When the opportunity to coordinate *Aboriginal Australia & the Torres Strait Islands* came up she jumped at the chance and is now writing full time.

Monique supports a treaty between Indigenous and non-Indigenous Australia so that we can get on with the big job of facing the truth about our history.

Hugh Finlay

After an unsuccessful foray into academia in Melbourne, Hugh first hit the road in 1976, on a trail that eventually led him to Africa via Asia, Europe and the Middle East in the early '80s.

Since joining Lonely Planet in 1985, Hugh has coauthored with Geoff Crowther the LP guides to *Kenya*; *East Africa*; and *Morocco, Algeria & Tunisia*. Other LP books he has been involved with include *Africa*; *Australia*; and *Malaysia, Singapore & Brunei*.

Hugh currently lives in central Victoria with Linda and their two daughters, Ella and Vera, trying to juggle the demands – and pleasures! – of family life, restoring an old farmhouse, writing, raising sheep, gardening and lengthy phone calls from Lonely Planet editors!

Paul Greenway

Gratefully plucked from the blandness and security of the Australian public service, Paul has worked on about a dozen Lonely Planet books, including *Mongolia*; *Iran*; *Jordan*; *Madagascar*; and *Bali & Lombok*. During the rare times that he's not travelling – or writing, reading and dreaming about it – Paul relaxes to (and pretends he can play) heavy rock, eats and breathes Australian Rules Football, and will go to any lengths (eg, staying in Mongolia and Iran) to avoid settling down.

Kath Kenny

Kath Kenny has worked as a journalist, media officer and events organiser. She has written opinion pieces, music and arts criticism, and book reviews for a wide range of publications including the *Australian*, *Sydney Morning Herald* and *Rolling Stone Magazine*. From writing about the Spice Girls and the significance of their platform shoes to a 2½ year stint as a media officer for the Liquor, Hospitality & Miscellaneous Workers Union, Kath Kenny has now joined the giddy ranks of LP authors.

Philip Morrissey

Philip Morrissey is an Aboriginal writer, originally from northern New South Wales. Philip wrote all the history sections in this book. He's worked in a range of jobs – fettler, flyhand, doorman etc, and, inevitably, the public service. For the last few years he's taught in Australian universities.

Philip has travelled extensively in Australia – some of his most memorable travel experiences include a tropical storm over Wyndham in the Kimberley, the lush vegetation of central Australia after rain, the wild flowers of south-west Western Australia and a visit to Wybalenna on Flinders Island. Philip writes regularly for a range of academic and popular journals. He particularly wants to thank the Lonely Planet team and his friends and family for support while writing his sections.

Denis O'Byrne

Denis was born in country South Australia, where he attended school with Aboriginal children from the Coorong. He has spent more than 20 years living in central and northern Australia, during which time he has visited numerous remote Aboriginal communities and learned many lessons in cross-cultural awareness. He says that he has learned enough to realise that he is definitely no expert! Currently a travel writer most of the time, Denis lives in Darwin in the Northern Territory. He wrote Lonely Planet's *South Australia*, coauthored *Outback Australia* and *South Pacific*, and updated *Australia* and *Vanuatu*.

Belinda Scott

Born in the early '60s, Belinda grew up surrounded by natural bushland, part of which is now Bellbird Corner, in Mt Waverley. Her early years saw much exploration, finding bull-ants, snakes, spawning frogs, and nurturing wounded birds sling-shot by the boys.

Belinda was introduced to 'other' cultures from an early age through her father's frequent travels to the Far East from which he brought dolls in national costumes, postcards, slides, textiles and the occasional visitor. Her father also introduced her to photography and many of her images have since been published in books on Aboriginal Art.

Belinda currently works as a consultant having studied Anthropology and Art History. She has worked with Indigenous peoples since she joined the staff of the Northern Land Council in 1985. Then she lived and worked with the Yolngu of Ramingining, Central Arnhem Land for four years. Her publications include NATSIVAD: The National Aboriginal & Torres Strait Islander Visual Artists Database.

FROM THE AUTHORS

Sarina Singh This book would not have been possible without the support and input of the Aboriginal and Torres Strait Islander contributors – thank you all for your time, inimitable insights and ardent enthusiasm.

I am also deeply grateful to the following people who so generously gave me their time and assistance: Lionel Harradine (Chairman Framlingham Aboriginal Trust); Neil Martin (Framlingham Aboriginal Trust); Dr Ian D Clark; Toby Heydon; Mick Dodson (Chair of the Australian Institute of Aboriginal and Torres Strait Islander Studies – AIATSIS); Les Ahoy (Aboriginal Tourism Product Manager, Australian Tourist Commission); Trevor Edwards (CEO, Wathaurong Aboriginal Cooperative); Lyn McInnes (Chairperson, Wathaurong); Allan Browning (Tourism Officer & Inspector, Wathaurong); Reg Abrahams (Cultural Officer, South West and Wimmera Cultural Heritage Program/Wathaurong Aboriginal Co-operative); Tim Chatfield & Kaye Harris (Brambuk Aboriginal Cultural Centre); Alan Burns (Goolum Goolum Aboriginal Cooperative); Stuart Harradine; Jeffrey Hood; Joe Chatfield (Regional Coordinator, South West and Wimmera Cultural Heritage Program); Denise Lovett (Cultural Heritage Officer, South West and Wimmera Cultural Heritage Program); Chris Allen (CEO, Moogji Aboriginal Council); Peter Ryan (Community Manager, Lake Tyers Aboriginal Trust); Ray Madden; Brendan Edwards (Aboriginal and Torres Strait Islander Commission – ATSIC regional councillor); Ivan Couzens (ATSIC regional councillor); Richard Fry (ATSIC regional councillor); Diet Simon; Ray Thomas; David 'Buzzy' Hewat; Brendan O'Kane (CEO, Ninde Dana Quarenook Aboriginal Cooperative); Jason Eades (CEO Ramahyuck District Aboriginal Corporation); Barbara Tilley (Ramahyuck District Aboriginal Corporation); Ken Fisher (Anthropologist, Mirimbiak Nations Aboriginal Corporation); Esmai Manahan (Aboriginal Affairs Victoria); Steven Avery (Aboriginal Affairs Victoria); and Antoinette Smith (Victorian Aboriginal Corporation for Languages).

Many thanks also to the phenomenal team at Lonely Planet who worked so passionately on this project: to the incredible Monique Choy for being the best coordinating editor a coordinating author could ever wish for; to Peter Cruttenden and Martin Heng for their invaluable insights and ongoing encouragement; to Anne Mulvaney for so brilliantly editing this challenging new book; to Allyson de Fraga, Sarah Northwood and Fiona Siseman for doing a sterling job of keeping pace with everything; to the talented bryan Andy for being such a vibrant trainee; and to all the LP regional authors for their commendable efforts on this first edition. Thanks also to the proofers, cartos and designers at LP who worked on this project long after my submission. Last, but by no means least, I'd like to extend a special vote of thanks to Sue Galley, whose open-mindedness, knowledge, encouragement and dedication played a paramount role in the making of this book.

David Andrew David would like to thank Ken Isaacson (Kalkadoon Tribal Cultural Keeping Place), Bob Forysth in Mt Isa, Mary Alderman and Ross Logan (Cooktown Travel Centre)

bryan Andy Principal thanks go to the Yorta Yorta nation and all at Cummeragunja; in particular my Nan & Pop (Faye & Colin Walker) for advice, accommodation and breakfast. Thanks to my brother Charles (the world's funniest guy) and cousin Jarrod for cruising around the northern parts with me. If I hear that name (Destiny) again I'll scream! Also, love and thanks to Aunty Hilda, Aunty Monica, Aunty Greta and to Dhoma Nyini gana (my dear Mother). Thanks also to Tanya Lamb for the consistent writings!

In the Kulin nation huge thanks to my Aunty Joy Murphy, Sid Spindler, Esmai Manahan, Matty D & Leanna (for proofreading, computer use and pancakes) and also to Kim Kruger (City of Port Phillip). Sincere thanks to George, Christine and John for doing the city with me; also to Bree, Gene, Jen and Dr Liz Reed. Thanks also to Dangers & Hangers (it's in print now!), Kelle, Nolan, Soph and Andrew Carter for insights, patience and ongoing inspiration. Also totally worthy of a mention are Maty C (for research and editorial assistance) and John Foss. Thanks to the amazing Ilsa Colson for advice and that ultra-handy WA pack you let me use for my additional research (priceless!) and to Dr Greg Gardiner (CAIS) for that lecture from way back. Sincerest love and thanks to Damian Frank.

Thanks to Trev and David at Allinjarra, Rodney at NW Nations, Georgina at Swan Hill Information, Bruce Pascoe from down Katabanut way and Aunty Alma Cupper, Uncle Brian and Marie Pettit from Robinvale. Also to Kylie Jones from Tourism Albury-Wodonga.

A paragraph of thanks to all of Victoria's Aboriginal cultural officers who dealt with my pestering: thank you, thank you, thank you…

Huge thanks to the mob at LP – Monique, Peter, Martin and Sue. However, my most sincere thanks must go to Sarina Singh for guidance, patience and persistence – I've had a ball and hope that I didn't prove to be too much of a headache.

Thanks also to the people from WA who helped me with the extra research – Phil Matsumoto at Beagle Bay, Susan Main from the Western Desert and to all the helpful others.

Finally, to all my brothers, sisters, Uncles and Aunts mentioned in this book, may I wish you all the best of luck. Let the world know that we have survived!

Monique Choy I'd like to pay my respects to the Indigenous Elders of Cape York, the Torres Strait and Tasmania and acknowledge the traditional owners of those lands. In particular, for Tasmania, I'd like to thank Greg Lehman for proofreading the text. Thanks also to Rosey Smith and TAC; Daryl Medcraft, Merv Gower and MLAC; John Clarke and FIAAI Jillian Mundy, John Dickson and TALC; Leonie Dickson; Caleb Peder and the Aboriginal Unit of the PWS; Clyde Mansell and ALCT; Darlene Mansell; Hank Horton; the Aboriginal Elders Council of Tasmania; DACA; SETAC; Mick Q; Bobby Wilson for the songs; Jim Everett; Ellen Greenberg; Steve Thomas; and Constable Matt Massie from Lady Barron Police for tracking down my camera.

In Cape York, thanks to Leigh Harris and the CYLC for proof-reading the text; Bill Snider, Linda Craig and the Indigenous Joint Management Unit of the QPWS; Terry Hogan and the Pormpuraaw Aboriginal Community Council; Gary Drewien, Vol Norris and the Kowanyama Land and Natural Resource Management Office; Aurukun Shire Council; the Napranum Aboriginal Community Council; and the Napranum Aboriginal Corporation; Lawry Booth and the Mapoon Aboriginal Council; Wayne Butcher and the

Lockhart River Aboriginal Council; Rosella Namok and the Art Gang; the Coen Regional Aboriginal Corporation; Mr Gordon Pablo; the Injinoo Community Council; the New Mapoon Council and Art Centre; Linda Wapau, Alan Wattridge and the Seisia Island Council; Dalassa Yorkston and the Bamaga Island Council; Bob Jacobs and the Umagico Aboriginal Council; and special thanks to Gloria Fletcher Thancoupie, Mary Ann Coconut, Stuart and Kate.

In the Torres Strait, thanks to Garrick Hitchcock from the TSRA for proofreading the text; Councillor Pedro Stephen and the Torres Shire Council; Andrew Plate, Nikie Kormendy and the TSRA; the ICC; Don Mosby and the Yorke Island Council; Ida May and the Coconut Island Council; Fred Gela and the Hammond Island Council; and the chairs and staff of all the other island councils. Thanks also to Vanessa Seekee from the Torres Strait Heritage Museum; and Ugarie Mene and Christine from Peddell's.

I'd also like to thank everyone who worked so hard on this book, especially Sarina, who remained serene through crazy obstacles and revealed to me the secret of the yellow highlighter; Pete, Martin, Sue, Anne and Lachie; Waa Waa Immakan for adopting me; Nicky, Dan and Matt for putting me up and putting up with me; and mountain man Clint for driving me up the falls.

Hugh Finlay I would like to thank the following people who assisted me with my research: Alan & Emma Withers, Yidumduma Bill Harney, Alan James, Kelvin Leitch (Dhimurru Land Management), Leon Morris & Rosemary Cadden (NLC), Will Stubbs & Andrew Blake (Buku-Larrngay Mulka).

Paul Greenway I would like to thank the following tourist officials who were particularly helpful: Katherine Grebneff at Wilpena Pound; June Kain, Mt Gambier; Rod Hand, McLaren Vale; and Paul Donnellan at the SA Tourism Commission. Also, thanks to the staff at the State Department of Aboriginal Affairs in Adelaide; and Jo Gorman at NPWS, Buronga.

From the Aboriginal communities, thanks to Kevin Bromely at Parakeelya; Terry Coulthard at Iga Warta; Mike Gray at Tauondi; and Geoff du Toit at Tandanya.

Kath Kenny Thanks go to Tess McLennan, Keith Gleeson, Yvonne Jackson, Kyrn Stevens, Allen Madden, David Cooper, Lynn Pollack, Michelle Matthews, John Hobson, Michelle Avery, Daniel Ariel, Summa Naylor, Keith Munroe, Daryl Wright, John Lennis, Maureen Smith, Keith Gleeson, Vic Simms, Nick Brack, Roy Barker, Phill Khan, Rusty Worsman, Vicky at the Aboriginal Culture & Resource Centre (Katoomba), Bob Sutor, Wayne Brennan, Anne Schuhmacher, Mark Intervera, Wilay Bijarr and Kirsten, Harry Brandy, the Miimi Mothers, Wiruungga Dunggiirr and friends, Carol Conte, Glenny Naden, Graham Emzin, Dee Murphy, Lisa Appo, Ngulingah LALC, Patricia Laurie, Wally Davies, Magpie and Jock from Minjungbal, Sue Green (Valma), Colin Newsome, John Summerland, Patti Ainsworth, Fay Ball, Ellen Draper, the Bingara Information Centre, Daryl Tighe, Dallas Dodd, Nambucca Heads LALC, Nambucca Heads Visitors Centre, Deidre Randall, Laurie Perry, Kay Smith, Kerry Robinson, Grafton Visitors Centre and the National Parks and Wildlife Service.

And thanks to all those many others who I have neglected to mention here, but who provided invaluable assistance along the way.

Denis O'Byrne A lot of people and organisations provided information and assistance during this project and I'm very grateful to them all. Special thanks go to Susan Graham (Keringke Arts, Ltyentye Apurte), David Ogilvie (Warlukurlangu Artists, Yuendumu), Libby Larsen (Uluru-Kata Tjuta National Park), Zahra Shirazee (Heritage Council of WA), Noel Nannup and his team of Nyoongar tour guides (Department of Conservation & Land Management, Perth), the Noongar Language & Cultural Centre, Perth), Yamaji News (Geraldton) and Patrick Mullaley (Mid-West Development Commission, Geraldton).

Thanks also to the helpful staff of the Aboriginal Affairs Department (WA), ATSIC, and the Central Land Council and the Institute for Aboriginal Development (both in Alice Springs). Last but by no means least, I can't forget the generosity of Phil & Kerry Smyth of Perth and Max Kleiner of Alice Springs for providing me with a home away from home during my travels.

Belinda Scott Thanks to all those Indigenous and non-Indigenous people who assisted with my research and endless questions. These people ranged from CEOs of Aboriginal land councils to the local publican at a country pub or people in the street. Each gave me interesting leads and advice on my quest about Indigenous tourism. To those not listed below, please accept my apologies, you were all wonderful!

Thanks to 2 Cuz FM, Bourke; Ann and Professor Ian Thornton; ATSIC: Norm Wilson & Maria Tsirimokos; Australian Heritage Commission; Australian Institute of Aboriginal & Torres Strait Islander Studies: Barry Cundy, Patrick McConvell, Nick Thieberger, Pat Turner, Mick Dodson and Toni Bauman; Australian National Botanical Gardens; Avis Rent A Car; Avril Quaill; Barry's Bush Tucker Tours; Bega Local Aboriginal Land Council; Boomanulla Oval; Boree Aboriginal Land Council; Brewarrina Aboriginal Cultural Museum; Brewarrina Local Aboriginal Land Council; Centacare, Bourke; Cobar Aboriginal Land Council; Coonabarabran Local Aboriginal Land Council; Coonamble Aboriginal Land Council; Djon Mundine, Curator & Writer; Dubbo Museum & History Centre; Ellimata CDEP; Gamilaroi Aboriginal Land Council; Gilgandra Cultural Heritage Centre; Goolgowie Tourism Office; Great Western Hotel Motel, Cobar; Gundabooka Aboriginal Corporation; Kathy Barnes; Katrina Fanning; Kejole Koorie Studio; Laddie Timbery's Aboriginal Arts & Crafts; Merrimans Local Aboriginal Land Council; Muda Aboriginal Land Council; Nangana Home Care; Ngunnawal Aboriginal Land Council; Ngunnawal Community Care; Nindethana Association; North West Regional Aboriginal Land Council; NSW Aboriginal Land Council, Bateman's Bay; Nulla Nulla Aboriginal Land Council; Pejarr Local Aboriginal Land Council; Pulkurru Aboriginal Corporation, Gilgandra; Queen Jean Collidge; Red Earth Gallery; Sandhills Artefacts; South Coast Aboriginal Cultural Centre; The Great Cobar Outback Heritage Centre; Ulladulla Local Aboriginal Land Council; Umbarra Cultural Tours; Wagga Wagga Local Aboriginal Land Council; Wagona Land Council, Narooma; Waiwa Aboriginal Land Council; Walgett Local Aboriginal Land Council; Warrana Aboriginal Corporation; West Wyalong Aboriginal Land Council; Wiradjuri Regional Land Council.

This Book

This is the 1st edition of a book that started as a bright idea back in 1998. The plans were ambitious, and despite being told we were crazy by everyone we asked for advice, we went ahead and secured funding from the helpful folk at the Regional Tourism Program, Department of Industry Science and Resources.

We advertised for writers in the Indigenous press and on e-networks, and were overwhelmed with the response from interesting folk. One of our main goals was to present a diverse range of voices, so we signed up Indigenous writers from many different backgrounds – the book in your hand is the hard work of 51 Aboriginal and Torres Strait Islander contributors.

But at that stage the finished product was a long way off – most of the writers had not written professionally before so we set up an extensive feedback and training process, working with inexperienced authors until they had polished their work to a dazzling shine. In return Indigenous contributors provided invaluable feedback and advice on cultural issues throughout the production process. Wherever possible, we plan to recruit writers, production staff and the coordinating author for the next edition from this group of Indigenous contributors.

Next, we brought together a team of experienced Lonely Planet authors and Aboriginal experts who headed out to uncover Indigenous Australia from the perspective of travellers. They focussed on ventures owned or operated by Indigenous people and included only the places they felt they could recommend. They took care not to include any information that is secret or private, places that don't have the infrastructure to handle visitors, or communities that simply don't welcome unexpected guests.

Gumbainggir artist, Donna Brown provided original artwork for the cover. We asked Larrakia artist Gary Lee, Gurindji artist Brenda L Croft and Budjiti artist Elizabeth McNiven to recommend museums, galleries and shops that work in cooperation with Indigenous communities and carry good collections in the 11 major Indigenous centres around Australia. They covered Adelaide, Alice Springs, Brisbane, Cairns, Canberra, Darwin, Fremantle, Kuranda, Melbourne, Perth and Sydney. Meanwhile, it was up to the other Aboriginal and Torres Strait Islander authors to cover historical and cultural issues.

During the project, production training was conducted for a number of Indigenous people. Yorta Yorta writer bryan Andy hit the road to learn guidebook writing. He covered sections of the Kulin Nation, the Cape Otway region and the Murray River in the Victoria chapter. Meanwhile, Richard I'Anson, photographic manager of Lonely Planet Images, went north to train in the art of photography Jason Davidson in the Kimberley and Hopie Managku in Arnhem Land. Jason also wrote the piece 'The Lucky

DIVERSE VIEWS

Indigenous Australians are a diverse group of people, living vastly different lifestyles in each corner of the country. There is no homogenous 'Indigenous viewpoint'. We have attempted to represent a small part of this diversity by inviting around 50 Indigenous people from around Australia to contribute to this guide. However, each writer's individual views and opinions are not necessarily those of Lonely Planet.

There are up to 700 traditional societies in Australia and only a small number of these are covered, or even mentioned, in this book. We have focussed on areas where there are facilities for visitors.

Population statistics given in this book are based on the 1996 census data from the Australian Bureau of Statistics.

NAMING THE DEAD

Please be aware that mentioning the personal name of someone who has died recently can cause offence, anguish and grief in some Aboriginal cultures. While we have avoided doing this, readers should be aware that there are entries in this book that do feature the names of deceased people. Where appropriate we have inserted a warning. However, there may be deaths we were unaware of, and cases where people have died since publication. Please be tactful.

Country?' in the Facts about Aboriginal Australia & the Torres Strait Islands chapter. Denise Goodfellow (Lawungkurr Maralngurra) and Miriam Nganjmirra provided invaluable assistance on this trip, and thanks also to Stephanie Thompson, Michael Stott and Amber Goodfellow for their help. Back in Melbourne Joseph Kennedy, an editor of Trawlwoolway descent, came in house to learn guidebook editing – cutting his teeth on the South Australia chapter. Joseph also wrote the Books section and a number of boxed text entries.

Tamara Watson contributed photographs for the 'Ngarrindjeri Weaving' section.

Philip Morrissey wrote brief Indigenous histories for each state and the Torres Strait Islands, as well as the national history section. Other Indigenous writers' names and biographies appear alongside their main contribution, which includes most of the introductory section and boxed texts throughout the book.

Once the text had passed through the standard Lonely Planet production process we sent the entire book to the gracious Mick Dodson (Australia's first Aboriginal and Torres Strait Islander Social Justice Commissioner) and the gregarious Les Ahoy (Aboriginal Tourism Product Manager at the Australian Tourist Commission) to double check that all the text was appropriate, and to provide advice from an Indigenous perspective on cultural issues.

At the end of the project we had accumulated an enormous collection of information and advice from Indigenous contributors and advisers. This will be fed back into Lonely Planet's long list of other Australia titles to ensure Indigenous issues are covered accurately.

And so, after three years in the pipeline, we present you with *Aboriginal Australia & the Torres Strait Islands*. Happy travels.

Researchers

Coordinating author Sarina Singh researched Gippsland, Around Melbourne and the western region of Victoria. Sarina also wrote sections of the Facts for the Visitor chapter. David Andrew covered most of Queensland – the central and western regions and the east coast. Monique Choy covered Cape York in Queensland and wrote the Tasmania and Torres Strait Islands chapters. Hugh Finlay researched the Top End of the Northern Territory (NT). Paul Greenway covered South Australia (SA), and Outback regions of Victoria and New South Wales (NSW). Kath Kenny wrote Sydney and north-east NSW. Denis O'Byrne covered central Australia (NT and SA) and southern Western Australia. Belinda Scott covered southern and Outback NSW. Joyce Connolly, bryan Andy, Anne Mulvaney and Monique Choy put together the northern WA section, based on information supplied by Trudi Ridge.

Sandra Bardwell and Matt Fletcher provided the short walks sections: Yankee Hat Walk, Red Hands Hat Cave and Barrk Bushwalk.

Many people contributed to the Language sections, which were compiled by Vicki Webb. Jenny Tindale (Institute for Aboriginal Development) provided the information on central

Australian languages; Denise Angelo (Diwurruwurru-jaru Aboriginal Corporation) wrote the section on Top End languages with Carolyn Coleman and Melanie Wilkinson (Northern Territory Education Department); Julian Barry contributed to the sections on Western Desert and South Australian languages; Alan Dench (Centre of Linguistics, University of Western Australia) wrote the Western Australia language section; Barry Blake and Peter Austin wrote the language sections for Victoria and New South Wales; and Dana Ober wrote the Torres Strait language section.

In-house writers also contributed to the text, Graham Fricke (currently an Adjunct Professor at the School of Law, Deakin University) prepared the boxed text asides 'Terra Nullius', 'The Battle of Mabo' and 'Wik, Four Judicial Elders and Sammy Davis Junior' in the Facts about Aboriginal Australia & the Torres Strait Islands chapter, as well as 'Batman Went a' Robbin': The Tale of a Failed Private Adventurer' in the Victoria chapter. Joseph Kennedy, Justin Flynn and Joyce Connolly also contributed boxed text asides, and we pulled some other entries from existing Lonely Planet guides.

Indigenous writers are credited in the main text.

TRADITIONAL COUNTRY

Where practical, the traditional Indigenous country names and cultural information offered in this text have been checked by local Elders, Indigenous organisations or land councils. However, in many cases, the traditional country is based on language groups defined by published sources such as those produced by the Australian Institute of Aboriginal and Torres Strait Islander Studies (AIATSIS). They do not represent exclusive traditional ownership or occupation of the land. The boundaries used are not suitable for Native Title or other land claims. See also the entry 'AIATSIS Language Group Map', on the imprint page.

Aboriginal land is marked on maps throughout this guide according to the *Australia Land Tenure* map, *Edition 1*, *AUSLIG (1993)*.

From the Publisher

A long list of wonderful people joined the production team to make this book possible.

The screeching beast of a manuscript (put together from the work of 71 different authors) was coaxed into a well-behaved read by coordinating editor Monique Choy and the miracle-working Anne Mulvaney. Coordinating author, Sarina Singh, went far beyond the call of duty to train writers, research protocols and steer the project when the in-house staff were on the road. Sarina also worked closely with Indigenous authors through many drafts. Russ Kerr and Cathy Lanigan painstakingly proofed the book. Joseph Kennedy and Joanne Newell compiled the index and assisted with editing, along with Bridget Blair and George Dunford.

Coordinating cartographer, Lachlan Ross developed a special cartographic style and symbols, as well as drawing the maps for the book. Paul Piaia assisted and also created some of the base maps and symbols.

Indra Kilfoyle developed a new design for the book and Tim Uden smoothed over the technical complications and laid it out. Martin Harris drew the illustrations and Matt King, Val Tellini and Kerrie Williams worked on image selection.

Peter Cruttenden was the Publishing Manager for the project, seeing it through a maze of complex twists and turns until authoring work took him overseas, when Martin Heng took his firm grip on the reins.

Associate Publisher Sue Galley established and oversaw the project, keeping it afloat even when things looked grim. Sue pulled together the original team including Bethune Carmichael, Matt King and Monique Choy to get it off the ground. Bethune shaped the book at the start of the project, preparing the book and funding proposals.

Sally Steward took over as publisher in the final stages of production. Martin Heng, David Kemp, Martine Lleonart and Jane Hart checked the text.

Anna Bolger coordinated the launch, Paul Clifton supervised the mapping and David Kemp supervised the design.

A team of editors helped put the skeleton manuscript together from Indigenous information in existing LP guidebooks, including Martine Lleonart, Sarah Mathers, Vicki Webb and Arabella Bamber.

An in-house team including Allyson de Fraga, Fiona Siseman, Sarah Northwood and Elissa Coffman worked hard on administering the project. Thanks also to Richard I'Anson, Greg Herriman, Nikki Anderson, Leonie Mugavin, Louise Poultney, Des Ford, Chaman Sidhu, Gabrielle Green, Natasha Velleley and Charles Rawlings-Way for their invaluable assistance.

Special thanks to Jeff Beeston and everyone at the Regional Tourism Program of the Office of National Tourism; Toni Bauman for her sound advice; Bruce Simms from Magabala Books; Heather Zeppell, author of Aboriginal Tourism in *Australia: A Research Bibliography*; Jenny Pender from CAAMA; Beverley Knight from Alcaston Gallery; Jemima & Jonas Wood and Wesley, Leslie & Dean Williams.

In Western Australia, thanks to Bruce at Kimberley Land Council and Christine Robinson at Kimberley Aboriginal Law and Cultural Centre.

Thanks also to the following people for their letters of support: Laurie Berryman (Anangu Tours); Tim Chatfield (Brambuk); Mia Lacy (Tjapukai); Marilyn McPherson (Minjungbal Cultural Museum); Ursula Raymond (Northern Land Council); John Morse & Rhett Lego (Australian Tourist Commission); Elisbeth Allen (Tourism NSW); Andrew Clark (NT Tourist Commission); Shane Crockett (WA Tourism Commission); Jane Foley (Tourism Tasmania); Glen Miller (Queensland Tourist and Travel Corp); Rebecca Somerfield (SA Tourism Commission); Debbie Kearns & Rolf Dülks (YHA Australia); Esmai Manahan (Arts Victoria); W. Gary Grimmer (Melbourne Convention & Marketing Bureau).

And finally, very special thanks to Mick Dodson and Les Ahoy for their expert guidance, and to all the other contributors for sharing their stories, art, insights and advice.

Acknowledgements

INDUSTRY
SCIENCE
RESOURCES

Lonely Planet gratefully acknowledges the assistance of the Regional Tourism Program, Department of Industry Science and Resources, who partly funded this project.

The Aboriginal Australia map (General Editor, D Horton) is reproduced with the kind permission of the Australian Institute of Aboriginal and Torres Strait Islander Studies © 1999.

The Aboriginal flag © Harold Thomas, is reproduced with kind permission of its designer.

The Torres Strait Islands flag, designed by Bernard Namok, is reproduced with the kind permission of the Island Co-ordinating Council.

Foreword

ABOUT LONELY PLANET GUIDEBOOKS

The story begins with a classic travel adventure: Tony and Maureen Wheeler's 1972 journey across Europe and Asia to Australia. Useful information about the overland trail did not exist at that time, so Tony and Maureen published the first Lonely Planet guidebook to meet a growing need.

From a kitchen table, then from a tiny office in Melbourne (Australia), Lonely Planet has become the largest independent travel publisher in the world, an international company with offices in Melbourne, Oakland (USA), London (UK) and Paris (France).

Today Lonely Planet guidebooks cover the globe. There is an ever-growing list of books and information in a variety of forms and media. Some things haven't changed. The main aim is still to help make it possible for adventurous travellers to get out there – to explore and better understand the world.

At Lonely Planet we believe travellers can make a positive contribution to the countries they visit – if they respect their host communities and spend their money wisely. Since 1986 a percentage of the income from each book has been donated to aid projects and human rights campaigns.

Updates Lonely Planet thoroughly updates each guidebook as often as possible. This usually means there are around two years between editions, although for more unusual or more stable destinations the gap can be longer. Check the imprint page (following the colour map at the beginning of the book) for publication dates.

Between editions up-to-date information is available in two free newsletters – the paper *Planet Talk* and email *Comet* (to subscribe, contact any Lonely Planet office) – and on our Web site at www.lonelyplanet.com. The *Upgrades* section of the Web site covers a number of important and volatile destinations and is regularly updated by Lonely Planet authors. *Scoop* covers news and current affairs relevant to travellers. And, lastly, the *Thorn Tree* bulletin board and *Postcards* section of the site carry unverified, but fascinating, reports from travellers.

Correspondence The process of creating new editions begins with the letters, postcards and emails received from travellers. This correspondence often includes suggestions, criticisms and comments about the current editions. Interesting excerpts are immediately passed on via newsletters and the Web site, and everything goes to our authors to be verified when they're researching on the road. We're keen to get more feedback from organisations or individuals who represent communities visited by travellers.

Research Authors aim to gather sufficient practical information to enable travellers to make informed choices and to make the mechanics of a journey run smoothly. They also research historical and cultural background to help enrich the travel experience and allow travellers to understand and respond appropriately to cultural and environmental issues.

Lonely Planet gathers information for everyone who's curious about the planet – and especially for those who explore it firsthand. Through guidebooks, phrasebooks, activity guides, maps, literature, newsletters, image library, TV series and Web site we act as an information exchange for a worldwide community of travellers.

Authors don't stay in every hotel because that would mean spending a couple of months in each medium-sized city and, no, they don't eat at every restaurant because that would mean stretching belts beyond capacity. They do visit hotels and restaurants to check standards and prices, but feedback based on readers' direct experiences can be very helpful.

Many of our authors work undercover, others aren't so secretive. None of them accepts freebies in exchange for positive write-ups. And none of our guidebooks contains any advertising.

Production Authors submit their raw manuscripts and maps to offices in Australia, USA, UK or France. Editors and cartographers – all experienced travellers themselves – then begin the process of assembling the pieces. When the book finally hits the shops, some things are already out of date, we start getting feedback from readers and the process begins again...

WARNING & REQUEST

Things change fast in the travel industry – prices go up, schedules change, good places go bad and bad places go bankrupt – nothing stays the same. Things also change on the political front (although sometimes not fast enough). Each year land is handed back to its traditional owners and Indigenous people gain more control over the information that should and should not be published. This is the first attempt to cover Indigenous Australian tourism experiences comprehensively in a guidebook. We have made every effort to get it right with this edition, but if we didn't, we want to get it right in the next one.

So, if you find things better or worse, recently opened or long since closed, please let us know. If you come across inappropriate or outdated background information, tell us and help make the next edition even more accurate and useful. We genuinely value all the feedback we receive and especially encourage members of the Indigenous community to write to us with comments and suggestions.

Julie Young coordinates a well-travelled team that reads and acknowledges every letter, postcard and email and ensures that every morsel of information finds its way to the appropriate authors, editors and cartographers for verification.

Everyone who writes to us will find their name in the next edition of *Planet Talk*, our quarterly printed newsletter, or *Comet*, our monthly email newsletter. Subscriptions to both newsletters are free. The best contributions will be rewarded with a free guidebook.

Excerpts from your correspondence may appear in new editions of Lonely Planet guidebooks, the Lonely Planet Web site, *Planet Talk* or *Comet*, so please let us know if you don't want your letter published or your name acknowledged.

Send all correspondence to the Lonely Planet office closest to you:

Australia: Locked Bag 1, Footscray, Victoria 3011
USA: 150 Linden St, Oakland, CA 94607
UK: 10A Spring Place, London NW5 3BH
France: 1 rue du Dahomey, 75011 Paris

Or email us at: talk2us@lonelyplanet.com.au

For news, views and updates see our Web site: www.lonelyplanet.com

HOW TO USE A LONELY PLANET GUIDEBOOK

The best way to use a Lonely Planet guidebook is any way you choose. At Lonely Planet we believe the most memorable travel experiences are often those that are unexpected, and the finest discoveries are those you make yourself. Guidebooks are not intended to be used as if they provide a detailed set of infallible instructions!

Contents All Lonely Planet guidebooks follow roughly the same format. This guide is a companion to the *Australia* guide. So it doesn't double up on information that is covered there. Turn to *Australia* if you're looking for a starting point for researching travel to and from Australia. The Getting Around chapter of *Australia* gives an overview of the transport options when you arrive.

Some places to stay and places to eat are covered in this book, but only if they are owned or run by Indigenous people. You'll find plenty of other options in *Australia* for cities and towns across the country, as well as more information on how to get to and from the destinations in this book, and how to get around once you're there.

Reflecting other Lonely Planet guides, this book contains a Facts about Aboriginal Australia & the Torres Strait Islands chapter giving background information ranging from history to sport. Facts for the Visitor gives practical information on issues like permits and special events.

These are followed by chapters covering the Indigenous attractions in each state and the Torres Strait Islands. The chapters are divided into sections following the traditional language group regions, as far as we've been able to determine them (see also the boxed text 'Traditional Country', earlier).

Heading Hierarchy Lonely Planet headings are used in a strict hierarchical structure that can be visualised as a set of Russian dolls. Each heading (and its following text) is encompassed by any preceding heading that is higher on the hierarchical ladder.

Entry Points We do not assume guidebooks will be read from beginning to end, but that people will dip into them. The traditional entry points are the list of contents and the index. In addition, however, this book has a complete list of maps and an index map illustrating map coverage. Entries by Indigenous contributors are indexed by name, including their short biographies. You can also turn to the index if you're looking for the page of a section indicated by a cross-reference.

Maps Maps play a crucial role in Lonely Planet guidebooks and include a huge amount of information. A legend is printed on the last page of the book. We seek to have complete consistency between maps and text, and to have every important place in the text captured on a map. Map key numbers usually start in the top left corner.

Although inclusion in a guidebook usually implies a recommendation we cannot list every good place. Exclusion does not necessarily imply criticism. In fact there are a number of reasons why we might exclude a place – sometimes it is simply inappropriate to encourage an influx of travellers.

Introduction

All of us at Lonely Planet would like to pay our respects to the Elders and other traditional owners of the lands now called Australia. We are grateful to the Aboriginal and Torres Strait Islander people who shared their stories and allowed Lonely Planet researchers to visit their countries.

Australia originally contained at least 600 different societies, each with its own dialect, culture and traditions. Outsiders, from the first invasion forces to the latest waves of new migrants, have introduced an entirely new way of seeing Australia – just take a look at the two maps at the start of this book. Today, two centuries after the first massacres and battles, the outsiders are beginning to take a much greater interest in what Indigenous people have to say.

Aboriginal and Torres Strait Islander people are facilitating this process by making films, writing books, creating music and art, setting up businesses, building Web sites and inviting visitors to learn something about Indigenous culture. In this book we present you with a selection of these access points. You'll also find an introduction to history and culture, and the various issues affecting Aboriginal and Torres Strait Islander people today.

Whether you are interested in tasting bush foods or learning to speak Nyoongar, in listening to Anangu creation *stories* in the desert or live Indigenous pub rock in Sydney, you'll find out about it here. Or perhaps you're a non-Indigenous Australian curious to find out more about the people whose traditional land your house is built on.

Indigenous cultures are rich and varied and non-Indigenous people often have a skewed impression of Australia's First Nations. The time has come to debunk the cliches, and the only way to do this is by meeting and spending time with Indigenous people themselves.

At its best, tourism is education, enabling Indigenous people to teach outsiders about their culture in a way in which they can control the access to and interpretation of their information, and also make a living out of it. That's not to say that the book is full of cheesy tourist stuff. There are plenty of off-the-beaten-track places and thought-provoking personal stories included here. With this guide in your backpack or glovebox, you'll find a very different Australia from the one most often presented to the world.

Facts about Aboriginal Australia & the Torres Strait Islands

History

Philip Morrissey

Australian Aboriginal society has the longest continuous cultural history in the world. Depending on who you talk to, its origins date back at least 50,000 years, possibly 70,000 years, or since the beginning of time in the Dreaming. The word Aborigine comes from the Latin, meaning 'from the beginning' or 'origin'. Indigenous – the other word used to designate both Aborigines and Torres Strait Islanders – means 'native to a place'.

Specific histories relating to each state, territory and the Torres Strait Islands can be found at the start of the regional chapters.

Pleistocene Period

The arrival of the people who became known as Aborigines took place during an exciting period in the earth's history known as the Pleistocene. Those early travellers used a combination of land bridges and sea-crossings to make their way to the continent of Sahul – a landmass made up of Australia and New Guinea. How many people were involved in that crossing? It's been suggested that three to five couples would have been enough to populate Australia! Other theories suggest that there was a series of arrivals over a longer period of time. Many Aborigines reject the superficial analogy between these ancient journeyings and the modern concept of migration.

Much of Australia's ancient history is a matter of scientific controversy and conjecture. Very slender 'gracile' skeletons, dated at 48,000 years, have been found at Lake Mungo in south-western New South Wales (NSW) and heavier-boned 'robust' skeletons, dated at 13,000 years, have been found at the Kow Swamp site on the Victoria–NSW border. These skeletal remains have led some Europeans to hypothesise that there were two distinct peoples living in Australia and that one group replaced another. Others have suggested that they represent genetic differences that occur in any one population.

The debate continues – one consequence has been a challenge to the theory that all modern peoples originate from a common ancestor in Africa. For the lay person it's hard sifting plausible theories from pseudo-scientific 'bright ideas' – an illustration of the fact that when it comes to Aborigines, some things don't change much.

Although much of Australia is arid today, the first arrivals found a much wetter continent, with large forests and numerous inland lakes teeming with fish. The fauna included giant marsupials – known appropriately as megafauna. These included species such as kangaroos that were 3m tall, huge flightless birds and giant reptiles. The environment was relatively nonthreatening – only a few carnivorous predators existed. Because of these favourable conditions, archaeologists suggest that within a few thousand years Aborigines had populated much of Australia, although the central parts of the continent were not occupied until about 24,000 years ago.

Holocene Period

The last ice age came to an end 15,000 to 10,000 years ago. During this period, called the Holocene, the sea level rose and large areas of land were inundated in just a few decades. Coastal Aboriginal groups in some regions retain traditions about areas of their traditional land now covered by the sea. Many of the inland lakes dried up and vast deserts formed. In consequence, coastal Australia became more densely occupied. The stabilisation of the sea level led to more fixed patterns of settlement and social organisation. For Aborigines, the connection with the land was generated over this long period of intimate contact with the changing continent, and it continues today. What seems to some a hostile wilderness was nurtured and known with a thoroughness Europeans have not yet been able to approach.

Aboriginal society was a 'knowledge-based society' which survived enormous changes in climate and environment. Trade routes crossed the length of the continent and ceremonial innovations travelled just as widely as commodities like red ochre. This stable but delicately balanced way of life was radically disrupted with European settlement.

Contact

Portuguese navigators had probably come within sight of the Australian coast in the first half of the 16th century and Chinese junks, which were active in the seas around Timor in the 15th century, may well have visited Australia. In fact a Chinese book, the *Classic of Shan Mai*, written before 338 BC,

apparently notes kangaroos and dark-skinned people using boomerangs in a land to the south. No archaeological evidence has been found to confirm Portuguese and Chinese contact with Aborigines, though both are historically probable. In 1606 the Spaniard Luis Vaez Torres sailed through the strait between Cape York and New Guinea that still bears his name, though there's no record of his actually sighting the southern continent. Dutch and English mariners also came into contact with Australia at this time. It seems that the first visits of Macassans

TERRA NULLIUS

Graham Fricke

According to the international codes of conduct prevailing in the 18th century, as interpreted by imperial powers such as Britain, a nation could acquire new territory by peaceful settlement (as distinct from conquest), providing the land was previously unoccupied. To deal with the fact that there were Aborigines living in Australia (up to an estimated one million in the Sydney area alone), the British extended the idea of *terra nullius* (unoccupied land) by saying that the Aborigines were not really in occupation of the land. The fiction was that the land was really an uninhabited desert.

This approach was patronising and arrogant. It was based on preconceptions about the way land can be occupied, by tilling the soil and other traditional British agricultural techniques, and failed to recognise the land management practices of Aboriginal tribes and Torres Strait Islanders (whose territory was later annexed by the Australian government).

But it was enough to support the imperial claim to sovereignty over the entire continent. The fact that it clashed with historical truth, and the brutality of the invaders, was brushed aside. It formed part of the received legal framework throughout the 19th century and indeed into the 1970s when the Gove Land Rights claim *(Milirrpum v Nabalco)* was rejected on the basis of terra nullius.

The fiction was given its last rites in 1992, in the case of *Mabo (No 2)*, when the High Court upheld a claim brought by a group of Mer Islanders in the Torres Strait (see the boxed text 'The Battle of Mabo' in this chapter). In burying the doctrine, Justices Deane and Gaudron used language that was uncharacteristically emotive in a legal judgment. They referred to historical racial strife in terms of a conflict that was to spread across the continent 'to dispossess, degrade and devastate the Aboriginal peoples and leave a national legacy of unutterable shame'. They added:

The acts and events by which that dispossession in legal theory was carried into practical effect constitute the darkest aspect of the history of this nation. The nation as a whole must remain diminished unless and until there is an acknowledgment of, and retreat from, those past injustices... The lands of this continent were not terra nullius or 'practically unoccupied' in 1788.

They also said that the official endorsement of the terra nullius notion 'provided the environment in which the Aboriginal people of the continent came to be treated as a different and lower form of life' than the settlers, and a people 'whose very existence could be ignored'.

from Sulawesi in modern-day Indonesia, date from the 17th century and there was on-going contact between the Torres Strait Islanders, Australia's other Indigenous people, and the mainland.

During western Europe's colonisation drive of the 18th century, French and British explorers began to take a stronger interest in the land they came to know as 'New Holland'. Captain James Cook 'discovered' the fertile eastern coast that earlier explorers had overlooked, and the British government, to head off French claims, established a penal colony there in 1788 under the name of New South Wales.

Invasion

When Sydney Cove was first colonised by the British, it is believed the Aboriginal population in the region was between 500,000 and 1,000,000 people. Around 250 distinct languages were spoken across the continent, many as distinct from each other as English is from Chinese, and there were around 700 dialects. Tasmania alone had eight languages, and tribes living on opposite sides of present-day Sydney Harbour spoke distinct languages.

Despite the presence of Aborigines, the newly arrived Europeans considered the continent to be *terra nullius* – a land belonging to no-one. Conveniently, they saw no recognisable system of government, no commerce or permanent settlements and no evidence of land use or land ownership. If the opposite had been the case – or they had been met by large-scale, coordinated resistance – they might have been forced to legitimise their colonisation and enter into a treaty with the Aboriginal landowners. This happened in New Zealand with the Treaty of Waitangi. Instead, what resulted was an undeclared war between Aborigines and settlers.

The dispossession of Aborigines was a gradual process, only completed in the late 19th century. It was marked by numerous local skirmishes and massacres, including the use of poison, as European settlement expanded on several fronts. The settlers also had an unusual weapon – germ warfare. The diseases they introduced, such as smallpox, leprosy, influenza, whooping cough and measles, had immediate effects. Others, such as forms of venereal disease, contributed to the radical decline in the

Aboriginal population in the longer term. Each of Australia's states and territories has its 'secret history' of dispossession, dispersal and massacre. Massacres continued into the 20th century. Other than the men convicted and punished for the Myall Creek massacre of 1838 (see History at the start of the New South Wales chapter), very few Europeans were ever brought to justice.

Resistance

The delicate balance between Aboriginal people and the environment was broken as the settlers cut down forests and introduced domestic animals – by 1860 there were 20 million sheep in Australia. Sheep and cattle destroyed waterholes and turned grassland into semidesert – ruining the habitats that had for tens of thousands of years sustained the Aborigines' food resources. Competition for water and food inevitably led to warfare between Aborigines and settlers. Starving Aborigines speared sheep and cattle and then suffered bloody reprisal raids. Settler men often raped Aboriginal women and when Aborigines speared the rapists in retaliation, they suffered genocidal retribution.

In many parts of Australia, Aborigines defended their lands with desperate guerrilla tactics. Many of these people are anonymous but warriors including Pemulwuy in NSW, Yagan, Calyute and Jandamarra (also known as 'Pigeon') in Western Australia (WA) and Nemarluk in the Northern Territory (NT) have become publicly known. In Tasmania the Aborigines, though vastly outnumbered, were winning the war until they were persuaded to lay down their arms. But whatever resistance Aborigines mounted, Europeans kept arriving in ever greater numbers. The discovery of gold in any particular region could lead to an influx of tens of thousands of diggers, and anywhere there was fertile land, settlers flooded in. By 1900 traditional Aboriginal society survived only among relatively small groups in central and northern Australia.

Stolen Generations

By the early 1900s, legislation designed to segregate and 'protect' Aboriginal people had been passed in all states. The legislation generally imposed restrictions on the Aborigines' rights to own property and seek employment,

WHEN I WAS AWAY

Lorraine Mafi-Williams

I was 12 years old when we were stolen from our parents. Brother John was 14, Bell 16, Lucy was nine, Elaine seven and Cid, the baby, three. There was no warning. The white welfare officer came in his truck with two white policemen. It was early in the morning. Dad had gone to work… The last time I saw my mum she was crying. I never saw mum cry like this before, only at funerals. Her whole body heaved with sobs. I remember saying, 'It's alright mum, we're only going down town'. I thought we'd be back soon enough. I was wrong.

I was put onto the open-air back of a truck with my brothers and sisters. By the time we got to Armidale (New South Wales), we were caked in red dirt from the road and looked truly neglected. By this time I was in a state of confusion. Cid and John were taken straight to Kinchella Boys Home. Bell was taken to work at a cattle station 100 miles away. Elaine, Lucy and I were taken to the Armidale Children's Orphanage. I was there for about a year and during that time I was very rebellious. My young mind didn't register that I was confined to an institution, separated from my parents. And why? Because I was an Aboriginal child… What made these people do such things? I was lost and lonely and tried everything to escape – even suicide – but that came later.

My little sister Lucy was a sickly child and she wet the bed nearly every night. When the orphanage matron found out, she began beating Lucy with a strap every morning. I would tell Lucy to wake me up in the night so I could swap her bed sheets with my dry ones and put my dry nightdress on her. When the matron inspected the beds in the morning she would find mine wet, so I took the beatings instead.

Several months later I was sent away to Cootamundra Girls Home to be trained as a domestic servant. I'd wash filthy clothes, scrub dirty floors and wipe shitty babies' bums. I worked from dawn to dark in return for a bed and three feeds a day. I was 13 years old.

When I was 18, I finally made it to freedom. I was released from Cootamundra Girls Home and I got a job in Sydney. I would ask other Kooris if they knew my mum and dad. One day a tall, well-built, handsome black man approached me and said, 'You're Lorraine Turnball?… I'm your cousin Darcy'. He told me where mum and dad were living.

It didn't take me long to pack and board the train for Taree, where my parents were living on Purfleet Mission – the place I was born. That early morning meeting with my parents will stay in my heart forever. Mum and dad were on the station when I got off the train. I was now a woman, no longer the child they knew. The three of us clung together and cried. I was 19 and I was the last to make it home.

Lorraine Mafi-Williams

My father is Bundjalung man and my mother is Dainggatti. I was born near a billabong at dawn in 1940 and was one of the last babies to be born in the traditional way. I married a Githraubaul man and now have three sons and 12 grandchildren. My dream is for my grandchildren to be treated equally in society but at the same time to retain their Aboriginality.

During my 20s I became a filmmaker, producer, writer and director. My short documentary film *Eelemarni* won an award in the 1988 Melbourne Film Festival.

In 1970 I established the Aboriginal Community Health Service (which is now national) under the late Dr Nugget Coombs.

I am the caretaker, keeper and carrier of the Knarkbaul clan knowledge. This clan is almost extinct. I deplore the Northern Territory's legal law of mandatory sentencing. I believe the Howard Government should say sorry to the survivors of the Stolen Generations – this would ease a lot of our hurt.

SORRY SEEMS TO BE THE HARDEST WORD

It might seem the quickest way to destroy a society would be to take the children, put them into foreign institutions and homes and raise them to despise their own people and culture. It would also seem an inhuman and unthinkable thing to do. Yet, for almost 100 years, this is what happened to Aboriginal and Torres Strait Islander people. These people, many of whom are now adults, make up the Stolen Generations.

Nationally, it has been estimated that between one in three and one in 10 (around 100,000) Indigenous children were forcibly removed between 1910 and 1970. Cases have been recorded where three generations in the one family were taken. Non-Indigenous children were generally removed for 'neglect' or 'abuse'. But Indigenous children could be removed from anywhere, at any time, without a court order. Indigenous children could be placed in an institution, fostered or adopted, without the knowledge or consent of their parents. Unlike non-Indigenous people, Indigenous parents had no legal rights to their children. Indigenous children – some within days of their birth – were taken into a foreign culture. Many had to learn English for the first time, and adapt to different ways of being, living and thinking. Many were told their parents were 'no good', had abandoned them or were dead. It's clear from the records of churches and governments that the purpose was to take Indigenous children, train them to live like whites – and put them into the service of whites as domestics and labourers – with the aim of 'breeding out their Aboriginality'.

In 1995, after years of lobbying by Aboriginal organisations and individuals, the National Inquiry into the Separation of Aboriginal and Torres Strait Islander Children from Their Families began. The inquiry travelled to every state and territory of Australia, recorded over 700 personal stories, held extensive public and private hearings, and consulted widely with individuals, families, communities, churches and government and nongovernment agencies. Its report, *Bringing Them Home*, was released in May 1997. Its findings shocked the nation. One in five people who gave evidence had been sexually abused while in an institution. Almost a quarter of witnesses who were fostered or adopted reported being sexually abused. One in six witnesses spoke of excessive physical punishment. Despite claims it was for their own good, they were not better educated, not more likely to be employed and not receiving significantly higher incomes than people who were raised in their communities. The consequences of forced removal – suicide, alcohol and substance abuse problems, an inability to form relationships, mental ill-health, shattered families and communities, and poor parenting skills – have created ongoing trauma for the Stolen Generations, their families and the rest of the Indigenous community. This cycle of dysfunction means that removals are still happening under current child welfare laws. Indigenous children are six times more likely to be removed for child welfare reasons, and 21 times more likely to be removed for juvenile justice detention, than non-Indigenous children.

The inquiry found that removal was a form of genocide. Genocide is not only the mass killing of a people. The *Convention on Genocide*, ratified by Australia in 1949, includes in its definition 'forcibly transferring children of a group to another group' with the intention of destroying the group. The Inquiry made 54 recommendations. To date, fewer than nine have been implemented by the federal government. In fact, the government has heavily criticised *Bringing Them Home*. In early 2000 the government released its own report claiming

and in most states an official, usually known as the Protector of Aborigines, who had far-reaching powers, was the legal guardian of all Aboriginal children. Children could be taken from Aboriginal mothers if it was suspected that the father was non-Aboriginal. The intention was, in the first instance, to stop the development of a 'half-caste' population, and, in the second, to assimilate them into Australian society. This practice continued

there was no Stolen Generation, that only 10% of Indigenous children were taken, but it does not explain how it reached such a figure. This statement has caused a great deal of pain and hurt for Indigenous people. To us, it's akin to denying the Holocaust.

State and territory governments have made formal apologies to Aboriginal and Torres Strait Islander people. But the federal government says it will not. Prime Minister John Howard has expressed his personal 'sincere regret' but firmly refuses to apologise on behalf of the nation, believing that no-one should be held responsible for the actions of the past. His critics point out that saying 'sorry' does not imply you are guilty of a crime, it just means you are capable of recognising that an injustice was suffered by Indigenous people, many of whom are still living, and that an apology can begin the healing process.

But the Stolen Generations can't just 'get over it' and move on. Apart from acknowledgment and apology, they need counselling, family reunion services, access to records, and other programs to address the damage that forced removal continues to do to our families and communities. And many, many Australians agree. At 'Corroboree 2000' (26–28 May 2000), the 10th anniversary of the beginning of the Reconciliation process, about 250,000 people marched across the Sydney Harbour Bridge in support of a national apology and Reconciliation. The turnout was extraordinary: on one cold and windy Sunday morning, a quarter of a million people – old, young, black, white – walked together, talked, shared jokes and ideas, and united to show their commitment to making a lasting peace with the first peoples of this country. And as the seemingly endless sea of people crossed the bridge, a sky-writer spelled out, in the clear blue winter sky, the one word this government is unable to say: Sorry.

See also the boxed text 'When I Was Away'.

Lorena Allam

Lorena Allam comes from the Kamilaroi and Yawalarai peoples of north-west New South Wales. Lorena has been a journalist and radio producer for over 12 years, having worked for (among others) the news department of the Australian Broadcasting Corporation (ABC), Triple J youth radio station and Radio National, where for six years she was the presenter and producer of *Awaye!*, Australia's only national Indigenous arts and culture program. She also helped organise the Second World Indigenous Youth Conference in 1993, an enormous gathering of over 2000 Indigenous people from every continent on the planet.

Lorena was the media/policy officer for the National Inquiry into the Separation of Aboriginal and Torres Strait Islander Children from Their Families. She feels privileged to have been involved in raising awareness of the inquiry in the Indigenous and non-Indigenous communities, as well as managing its public profile in the media here and overseas.

Lorena has a small son, Lewis. She is currently producing features and documentaries for the ABC's social history unit.

until the early 1970s and those people who were taken from their families have become known as the Stolen Generations. A comprehensive report on the removal of Aboriginal children from their families, titled *Bringing Them Home*, was released in 1997. It's now accepted that the trauma of this separation from family and culture has had wideranging impacts on Aboriginal society and been passed on down the generations.

Social Change

The processes of social change were accelerated by WWII, and after the war 'assimilation' became the stated aim of the federal and most state governments. In theory it was aimed at helping Aborigines achieve a standard of living comparable to settler Australians but in practice the rights of Aborigines were subjugated even further – governments controlled everything, from where Aborigines could live to whom they could marry. In some states, Aborigines were encouraged to apply for exemption from the constraints of the various laws that controlled them – if they could prove that they were able to live like Europeans and break off contact with other Aborigines. Exemption certificates, known as 'dog-tags' were issued to those Aborigines who complied. Not many did and the policy was a dismal failure.

In the 1960s Australia's treatment of Aborigines came under greater scrutiny, and settler Australians became increasingly aware of the inequity of their treatment of Aborigines. Some churches and socialist groups played a role in supporting Aborigines in their bid for social justice, and Aboriginal-settler organisations were formed to lobby for Aboriginal rights. In a 1967 referendum, settler Australians voted (with an unprecedented 90% majority) to count Aborigines in the census and, importantly, gave the federal government power to legislate for Aborigines in all states.

THE BATTLE OF MABO

The *Mabo* case, decided by the High Court in 1992, was one of the most sensational cases in recent Australian history. It involved a full frontal attack on the principle of *terra nullius* – the idea that Australia was uninhabited at the time of British colonisation.

Those who sought to overcome terra nullius (which had been used to dismiss the Gove land rights claim as recently as 1971) faced a formidable set of hurdles. In selecting the case of Eddie Koiki Mabo and four other Mer (Murray) Islanders, they chose a strong test case, for it was clear that the Meriam people had been in uninterrupted occupation of the Mer Islands – even by European standards of cultivating the soil – for many years. Even so, it took the Mabo legal team 10 years of struggle to achieve victory in the High Court.

The road to victory was not only long, but convoluted. An early obstacle was raised by the Queensland government, which passed a timely law (the Queensland Coast Islands Act, 1985) declaring that the Queensland government had owned the Mer Islands since their annexation in 1879.

Fortunately, a Wiynchanam man from northern Queensland, who recognised injustice when he saw it, had already taken on the Queensland government for discrimination. The case of Koowarta v Bjelke-Petersen (1982) had established the validity of the Whitlam government's 1975 Racial Discrimination Act, and the fact that it ousted inconsistent state legislation. So in the first venture into the High Court (*Mabo No 1*, 1988), the Mer Islanders' lawyers could argue that the 1985 Queensland act was invalid. That argument just made it through with a four to three majority.

In the meantime there had been lots of legal skirmishes in the *Mabo* litigation, as the Queensland government raised objections to the Mer Islanders' documents defining issues. There were also housekeeping problems, since the High Court is mainly a court of appeal and is not equipped to hear evidence (there is not even a witness box in the current High Court complex).

In 1986, four years after the proceedings had begun, Chief Justice Gibbs of the High Court ordered that the evidence in the case was to be taken by Justice Moynihan, a judge of the Queensland Supreme Court. That judge heard evidence for a couple of months. When problems raised by the 1985 Queensland act began to recur, he adjourned the hearing to enable the High Court to deal with them.

On Australia Day, 26 January 1972, Aborigines erected a 'Tent Embassy' on the lawns of Parliament House in Canberra. The Aboriginal Embassy became a great symbol of resistance and also signalled that a younger generation of Aboriginal activists had appeared. The reformist Whitlam Labor government took office later in 1972 and the assimilation policy was replaced by the policy of self-determination, which for the first time enabled Aborigines to identify their needs and priorities and the best ways of meeting them. The federal government established the Department of Aboriginal Affairs (DAA) to meet the special needs of Aborigines, and important Aboriginal organisations in the areas of health, legal services and housing were established. In the 1990s the DAA evolved into the Aboriginal and Torres Strait Islanders Commission (ATSIC), a statutory authority with increased Indigenous control. This has not always meant greater efficiency or accountability, however, and there has been increasing awareness of the need to find alternative ways of meeting Aboriginal needs.

The Northern Territory land rights legislation was enacted by the federal government in 1976. Large areas of land were returned to Aboriginal communities in the NT and a process set up which enables them to make claims for crown land. In South Australia (SA) in 1981, the Pitjantjatjara Land Rights Act gave Pitjantjatjara communities rights to

---

continued...   Graham Fricke

When the High Court decided that the Queensland act was invalid, Justice Moynihan resumed the hearing of evidence. He sat on occasions in Brisbane and at other times on Thursday Island and Mer. After a total of 67 sitting days, he prepared a three-volume set of findings for the High Court.

There had been many evidentiary problems in the course of the hearing. Whenever a witness began his historical account by saying 'My father told me that…' (for example, 'when he died, this land would be mine'), counsel for the Queensland government would object. Even when Justice Moynihan began to rule on these objections, the defence counsel would argue that he had no authority to make such rulings, since he was not a High Court judge. Eventually the barristers had to appear before Justice Toohey of the High Court to sort that one out.

At long last the High Court heard legal argument based on the factual findings of Justice Moynihan. By the time the High Court gave its decision in June 1992, Eddie Mabo and two other members of the original quintet had died. But six of the seven members of the court were persuaded by the painstaking but creative advocacy of Ron Castan QC to produce an array of powerful precedents.

They made the revolutionary finding that there was such a thing as native title which might, in appropriate circumstances, survive the advent of European colonisation.

The decision had huge implications for Aboriginal and Torres Strait Islander land rights claims throughout the country, but much work remained to be done before any mainland people could benefit from the decision. The 1993 Native Title Act had to be passed by the Commonwealth government under Paul Keating to establish the machinery for determining land rights claims. The Wik case needed to be fought to establish that native title might even survive the granting of pastoral leases in Queensland. Politicians had to be lobbied to resist the 'bucket loads of extinguishment' of native title that the Howard Government sought to achieve with its 10-Point Plan. However, there is no doubt that *Mabo* was a landmark case in Australian history, finally interring the dreaded doctrine of terra nullius.

See also the boxed text 'Terra Nullius' earlier, and '*Wik*, Four Judicial Elders & Sammy Davis Junior'.

large areas of their traditional lands and Aboriginal land rights legislation was passed in 1983 in New South Wales. Elsewhere in Australia, recognition of Aboriginal rights to land met with resistance.

Terra Nullius Rejected

In May 1982 a group of Torres Strait Islanders led by Eddie Mabo commenced a legal action to have traditional title to their land on Mer (Murray Island) recognised. They argued that the legal principle of terra nullius disregarded the fact that for thousands of years Mer Islanders had maintained a relationship with their land that included a concept of ownership. In June 1992 the High Court of Australia rejected the principle of terra nullius and accepted that the Mer Islanders did indeed own their lands prior to their annexation. This had far reaching implications and led to the Native Title Act of 1993.

The High Court's judgment became known as the *Mabo* decision, possibly the most revolutionary decision ever handed down by an Australian court. The decision was ambiguous, as it didn't outline the extent to which native title existed in mainland Australia. However, it was hailed by Aborigines and the then prime minister Paul Keating as an opportunity to create a basis for Reconciliation between Aboriginal and non-Aboriginal Australians.

Just as activists such as Kath Walker, Faith Bandler, Bill Ferguson, William Cooper and Jack Patten had carried on the fight against racism and discrimination in earlier times, a new generation of activists, including Michael and Patrick Dodson, Noel Pearson and Marcia Langton, played major roles in developing Reconciliation and native title legislation in the 1990s. Just as importantly, they explained what these developments were about to the Australian public.

Wik

To define the principle of native title, the federal parliament passed the Native Title Act in December 1993. Its intention was to limit the application of native title to land which no-one else owned or leased, and with which the Indigenous claimants have continued to have a physical association. The act stated that native title was extinguished by existing freehold title, but it did not adequately address the issues of native title and pastoral leases. It also stated that where Aborigines successfully claimed land under the act, they would have no veto over developments including mining.

Several months prior to the Native Title Act becoming law, the Wik and Thaayorre peoples had made a claim in the federal Court for native title to land on Cape York Peninsula. The area claimed included two pastoral leases. Neither had ever been permanently occupied for grazing purposes, but the Wik and Thaayorre peoples had been in continuous occupation of them. They argued that native title coexisted with the pastoral leases.

In January 1996 the Federal Court decided that the claim could not succeed, as the granting of pastoral leases under Queensland law extinguished any native title rights. The Wik people appealed that decision in the High Court, which subsequently overturned it.

The *Wik* decision caused an uproar among pastoralists across Australia, who claimed that the security of their leases was under threat. They demanded that the federal government step in to protect them by legislating to limit native title rights, as was intended in the original act. Aboriginal leaders were equally adamant that native title must be preserved. John Howard's Liberal government developed a controversial '10-Point Plan' to resolve ambiguities in native title legislation, and the Native Title Amendment Act was passed in 1998, after wheeling and dealing among Australian politicians and amendments to the original 10-Point Plan.

The Late 1990s

Reconciliation has been a powerful concept in contemporary Australia. Though initially viewed by some Indigenous people with scepticism, it's been one positive element in the climate of racism which developed following the election of the Howard Government in 1996. Pauline Hanson's One Nation Party, which attracted support from some voters because of its race-based policies, also appeared during the first term in office of the Howard Government. The party faltered in the 1998 federal election because of its own ineptness – not necessarily because its policies were rejected as anti-Aboriginal.

WIK, FOUR JUDICIAL ELDERS & SAMMY DAVIS JUNIOR

Graham Fricke

The *Mabo* decision was certainly the cause of much celebration for overturning *terra nullius* throughout Australia, but when it came to determining specific land claims, the decision upheld only the Meriam people's native title claim over their land on Mer. Native title land claims in other parts of Australia remained to be determined.

Many observers thought that the grant of freehold land or leases extinguished native title. The decision of 'the European Elders of Australia' (the High Court) in the *Wik* case shows that, in the words of the song popularised by Sammy Davis Junior, 'It Ain't Necessarily So'.

Following the *Mabo* decision, the Wik people brought proceedings seeking a declaration that they were the owners (by virtue of Aboriginal or native title) of about 30,000 sq km of their traditional lands on the western side of the Cape York Peninsula, south of Weipa and between the Embley and Edward Rivers. There were a number of procedural steps, including the joining of the Thaayorre people in the proceedings, but eventually the case was heard by the High Court in June 1996, and a decision was given six months later.

By a four-to-three majority, the High Court decided that the mere granting of a pastoral lease does not necessarily extinguish native title. It is important to note that although pastoral leases had been granted earlier in the century for two relevant parcels of land, the lessees had never actually occupied that land. They never put cattle on the land; they never fenced it; nor did they seek to interfere with the Aboriginal people who continued to live on the land. One lease was surrendered by the pastoralist shortly after the end of WWI. The other lease was, at about the same time, forfeited due to nonpayment of rent.

But it was argued that a lease involved the grant of exclusive possession of land to the lessee, so that the mere fact of the grant, whether or not it was followed up by the taking of possession, automatically extinguished native title. That, so the argument ran, was the characteristic nature of a lease.

The majority of the High Court rejected that argument. They said that a pastoral lease is not the same thing as a common law lease – the sort of lease that British lawyers are used to – which does involve the grant of exclusive possession. To determine whether a pastoral lease (or a mining lease, for that matter) gives the lessee exclusive possession, you need to conduct a case-by-case examination of the overall circumstances. You need to examine the precise terms of the legislation setting up the scheme for such so-called leases. Did parliament intend that the lessees should have exclusive possession of these large pieces of land? Or did it intend that Aborigines should continue to exercise their ancient rights to gather and hunt on these lands while the lessees grazed cattle on them? When you analysed the Queensland legislation, the court said, it did not emerge that pastoral leases contemplated by the legislation were meant to convey exclusive possession. So native title could coexist with Queensland pastoral leases.

The High Court did not decide that native title did in fact exist over the Wik traditional lands. That was left for later courts and tribunals to determine on the basis of the evidence to be presented before them. In October 2000, after five years of negotiations, the Federal Court ratified an agreement that recognised the Wik people's native title over 6000 sq km of land in Cape York, although another 24,000 sq km remain to be determined.

See also the boxed text 'The Battle of Mabo'.

In many ways contemporary Australia is a nation of contradictions – combining idealism and generosity with regressive attitudes towards Aborigines. The contempt of some settler Australians for Aborigines has its origins in the massacres which mar modern

Australia's history and those who hold these attitudes can aptly be described as 'the children of violence'. Unfortunately, these attitudes have often been uncritically absorbed by later migrants. This, combined with a cynical denial of wrongdoing, has continued to hold back any fundamental improvement in relations between Aborigines and settlers. On the world stage, settlers perpetuated a vast confidence trick for many years – the myth of peaceful settlement in a land that belonged to no-one: terra nullius.

The Future

The 2000 Sydney Olympics was a celebration of the positive spirit of Australia.

In an important symbolic gesture, Aboriginal athlete Cathy Freeman lit the Olympic torch. In the same year hundreds of thousands of settler Australians marched in support of Reconciliation with Aborigines. In many ways it was the largest protest vote in Australia's history. Many of those marching were fed up with Prime Minister John Howard, and right-wing organisations, presenting their narrow views as those of 'ordinary Australians'. On most of the indices that measure quality of life, Aborigines still fall below the standards of many Third World nations. Yet there is also a spirit of optimism and an obvious commitment from many in settler and Aboriginal communities to rectify the wrongs of the past.

More historical information can be found at the start of each regional chapter; see also Politics.

The Land & Indigenous Peoples

Barry Hunter

Australians generally refer to this vast land as the 'sunburnt county', and this may give rise to the notion that it is one of the driest continents on earth. However, there are contrasting landscapes throughout Australia. If I were able to traverse the country from east to west and north to south, in a relatively fast time, I would witness a changing landscape – rich, lush wet tropical rainforest, towering eucalypt forests, spectacular mountain ranges made up of rugged sandstone and jagged granite outcrops, grassy savanna plains, tropical islands and a dry red heart known as the central desert region.

For more than 50,000 years Aboriginal and Torres Strait Islander peoples have occupied the full range of environments within Australia. Indigenous people have successfully utilised and renewed the country, using an accumulated intimate knowledge of the land, and have implemented innovative management regimes with traditional customs to keep the country healthy and productive.

Importance of Land

Through this long-term use and occupation, Indigenous people developed an intimate understanding of the environment, including the flora and fauna, and the environmental conditions. This knowledge was crucial for long-term survival in a land that can be harsh and uninviting at the best of times. The land has always nurtured and provided for Indigenous people, through foods like kangaroo and emu, or vegetables like yams and sweet potatoes. However, the land means a great deal more than that – it also provides spiritual strength. Through *story* places (where special Dreaming events occurred) and Dreaming tracks throughout the landscape, our attachment to land provides us with our identity – where we come from as Aboriginal people, who we are, where our land is, our languages and our social structure.

The land is all-important. However, with invasion, many Aboriginal people were denied access to their land – they were killed, dispersed or taken away to Aboriginal missions. This has had a variety of effects on Aboriginal people, including separation from family, loss of identity and the myriad of social problems that accompany these things, such as alcohol abuse and unemployment (which is five times the national average in some Aboriginal communities).

Land & Culture

For traditional people, life centred on the health of their country and was determined by the type of environment they lived in. For instance, in the past Aborigines of the central desert region maintained a nomadic lifestyle, moving periodically to access seasonal water, food and resources. In the resource-rich tropical rainforests of north Queensland, Aboriginal people maintained semipermanent dwellings, only moving from lower to higher ground during the annual Wet season. On the islands of the Torres Strait, people lived in villages and relied heavily on the sea for their resources.

Aboriginal Land Management

Aboriginal occupation and day-to-day use have been, and in many places continue to be, significant factors in maintaining the landscape. Firestick farming (burning off), is a well-documented technique Aboriginal people used to renew and manage the land. In most areas burning off the country with fire was, and in some areas continues to be, an annual occurrence. In the north of Australia it is carried out at the beginning of the cool Dry season. Firestick farming serves two main purposes. One is to decrease the chance of a wildfire by reducing the vegetation build-up after a Wet season. This vegetation could be fuel for a major fire. Secondly, fire is used to clear the country and encourage new growth. This new growth attracts wildlife, like kangaroos and other species, which are drawn to nibble on the soft new shoots sprouting after the fire.

Sites & Special Places

Archaeological evidence suggests that Aboriginal people first arrived in Australia around 50,000 to 70,000 years ago. Australia's landscape bears both physical and oral evidence of this ancient occupation and use by Aboriginal people, providing us with a special connection to the land that can be heard in stories and seen at archaeological sites.

Story Places Stories from the past are tales of the Dreaming, a time of world creation according to Aboriginal religion and spirituality. Many of the stories recount times when the landscape formed; for instance, there are oral accounts of volcanic activity, and of the rising and falling of the sea level during the ice age. The stories also tell of Aboriginal peoples' connection to animals and how they relate to Aboriginal spirituality.

Rock art sites depict the storytelling of the past by conveying messages on the rocks. However, many places were also told of in oral accounts connected to story

Barry Hunter

I am 29 years of age and I'm a descendant of the Tjapukai-speaking people of the Cairns hinterland in north Queensland.

I joined the Australian Conservation Foundation after being employed as a cultural liaison officer with the Great Barrier Reef Marine Park Authority in Townsville for four years. I have also spent time working for the Australian Heritage Commission in Canberra and with the Tjapukai Aboriginal Cultural Park in Cairns.

My main areas of work and interest are Aboriginal land, and natural and cultural resource management.

places. These places are recorded in the oral histories of different Aboriginal peoples as places where special events – such as accounts of the creation of the world – took place. These places are highly significant. They may include Dreaming tracks where the Rainbow Serpent travelled, or the doings of other story-time creators. They may be where renewal ceremonies are carried out – where people conduct ceremonies for gratification and to ensure the ongoing presence of animals and food resources. There are also places where different speaking groups would gather for times of ceremony and other social gatherings.

Cultural Places The physical landscape also tells its own stories through the archaeological evidence that Aboriginal people have left behind, including sites such as artefact scatters, rock art sites and shell middens. The accumulation of shellfish and other leftover camp refuse deposited at some middens is thousands of years old. These places are areas where Aboriginal people hunted, lived and gathered their tools, such as rock quarries, or are special ceremonial places, such as men's and women's initiation sites. Aboriginal people call these places cultural sites.

ARCHAEOLOGICAL SITES

Monique Choy

Following are some of the sites archaeologists use to study the occupation of Australia over the last 50,000 years. Indigenous people sometimes call these cultural sites.

Sites of even greater importance are those linked to oral history and Dreaming *stories*, although there is often no physical evidence of occupation at these sites. Cultural sites are protected by strict conservation legislation.

Camp Sites Popular camping areas or meeting places often contain evidence of thousands of years of occupation, such as charcoal from fires or discarded tools and materials (sometimes called artefact scatters).

Ceremonial Grounds Created particularly in New South Wales and south-east Queensland, ceremonial sites are often stone arrangements or *bora* grounds (areas ringed with banked earth). These areas are sacred places, seek permission from the local Aboriginal community before visiting.

Fish Traps Simple and complex fish traps have been built along the coast in many places (particularly in the tropics). The basic concept behind a fish trap is a barrier or dam of rocks or vegetation. Fish swim into the area at high tide and become trapped behind the barrier when the tide goes out. Complex fish traps used with woven baskets can also be seen in some rivers.

Grinding Grooves & Surfaces Often made near rivers (where the water has been used for lubrication), grinding grooves are places where tools have been sharpened over many generations. In many cases, tools made of hard igneous rock have been rubbed onto soft sandstone. Grinding surfaces, for grinding seeds into flour or paste, can also be seen, usually in arid areas.

Middens Like an ancient compost heap, middens are the remains of camp refuse. Usually they are mainly composed of the discarded shells of edible crustaceans, but can also include animal bones, stone tools and charcoal from fires. Often middens have accumulated over thousands of years.

Quarries Places where stone for tools (or ochre for ornamentation) has been mined can be seen throughout Australia. Hard rock makes the best stone tools, and sandstone was also quarried to use as a portable sharpening stone. Mined materials were valuable trade commodities and welcomed gifts, and stones have been found hundreds of kilometres from the site where they were quarried. The distribution of mined materials provides archaeologists with evidence of trade and exchange routes.

Rock Art Sites These can include paintings or rock carvings (sometimes called petroglyphs). Rock art sites are usually sacred places, depicting Dreaming stories and beings, and should be treated with the proper reverence. Rock art is very fragile – never touch or disturb the art or the environment around the site. Even dust stirred up from visitors' feet can damage rock paintings.

Rock Shelters Caves and other good sheltering places often contain well-preserved evidence of occupation, such as the remains of meals and discarded tools.

Scarr Trees Trees all over Australia have scars where bark has been cut away to make canoes, dishes, shields or other items. Sometimes a small notch can be seen below a long scar, which the cutter has used as a toehold to reach the top of the cutting.

Wells Natural wells (particularly in dry areas) have often been deepened or modified. Some wells were also covered with a lid to prevent evaporation. Wells in rock are sometimes called rockholes.

See also the boxed text 'Aboriginal Sites in Western Australia' for more information.

Places such as Kakadu National Park in the Northern Territory and Laura's Quinkan Reserve on Cape York Peninsula in Queensland have some of the most spectacular rock art in the world. Many of these sites date back thousands of years and present a graphic insight into past Aboriginal societies. Aboriginal people used ochre colours (including red and orange), black charcoal and white clay to paint. Much art represents significant symbols or tells a story, some is spiritual and other works depict day-to-day activities such as hunting trips. Other archaeological sites that can be found in national parks such as Kakadu and Uluru include camp sites and rock quarries where stone tools where made. Ku-ring-gai Chase National Park, close to Sydney, has a wide array of sites called pictographs – where symbols have been carved out of the sandstone. Nearby are axe-grinding grooves where people sharpened stone axes. It should be noted that many of these places are protected in some way, and certainly Aboriginal people themselves play a major role in protecting these places and ensuring their integrity. In the Torres Strait Islands, many old fish traps that have a long history of use are still catching fish for local villagers. The traps made of rocks and coral high on the shore would trap fish in the outgoing tide. There are also great extended fish traps in waterways in western New South Wales.

Managing the Future

Although much of the special knowledge of the environment has been lost due to the various impacts upon traditional culture, a great deal still exists. It is important to note that Aboriginal people hold a special attachment to land which, as explained earlier, is tied into the social, cultural and economic wellbeing of the Aboriginies. Understanding this attachment can provide a good insight into the way Aboriginal people used and continue to use the land, and their aspirations for looking after their 'country'. Many Aboriginal and Torres Strait Islander people want to play a role in managing their country. Since invasion, Australia has lost a large percentage of its native vegetation and many native species are in danger of extinction. For Australia to maintain its unique environmental

credentials, it needs Aboriginal people and their knowledge to play a role in environmental management.

See also 'Spirituality'. For more information on art sites, see individual entries in the regional chapters.

Flora & Fauna

Barry Hunter

Australia has a wide variety of animal species, from marsupials, including kangaroos, wallabies, potoroos, possums, gliders and wombats, to reptiles such as the large monitor lizard and freshwater and estuarine crocodiles. Australia also has some of the deadliest snakes in the world including the inland taipan, the eastern taipan and the king brown. Historically, Australia was once home to megafauna which included giant 3m kangaroos, giant wombats and 4m pythons. All of these species are now extinct – controversially, the extinction of these species has been attributed to the inhabitancy of Australia by Aboriginal people, but there is no firm scientific evidence to confirm this. Australia is also now home to unwelcome introduced visitors such as the cane toad from South America, rabbits and domestic cats gone wild and the feral fox, which thrive with no natural predators and have an enormous impact upon native fauna.

Plant species found in Australia include banksia, eucalyptus, hakea and melaleuca. Many of these species have associations with similar vegetation types found in South America, New Zealand, New Guinea and other Pacific islands. Australia is also home to the unusual boab tree.

Many of these species always have been used in some form by Indigenous people, to make the tools from the raw materials and sometimes also animal products. For instance, the sinew of the tail of a kangaroo can be used as an effective binding agent after it is has been wet, twined and then applied to dry. Some chemical agents of plants can be used – such as the leaves of the cocky apple which can be crushed, then released into a slow-flowing stream where their juices will temporarily stun fish, enabling the people to collect the fish for meals. Other plants have useful resins, such as the xanthorrhoea, which is used as a very effective glue. Many different plants and animals have been utilised and have played important roles in the survival of Aboriginal and Torres Strait Islander people.

Politics

Dr Anita Heiss

Readers should be aware that the names of deceased members of the Aboriginal community are cited in this section. Mentioning the personal name of someone who has died recently can cause offence, anguish and grief in some Aboriginal cultures.

Although Aborigines and Torres Strait Islanders have long been denied an official say in the politics that affect us, we have as a people been politically motivated and active since resistance fighters, like the Yura warrior Pemulwuy, fought against the takeover of Aboriginal land as far back as the 1780s. Since then a number of government policies – including assimilation, self-determination and Reconciliation – have lead to political activism becoming part and parcel of being an Indigenous Australian. It is often said that if you are born Black, you are born political.

Events & Movements

There have been a number of significant political events and grass-roots movements that have highlighted the increasing political activity of Indigenous people, and indeed the political awareness of non-Indigenous people, to the issues facing Indigenous Australia.

Aboriginal peoples' ability to protest has been our main form of political activity, and one of the first protests saw Aborigines boycott the centenary of colonisation celebrations on 26 January 1888, the anniversary of the day when British Captain Arthur Philip landed the First Fleet at Sydney Cove.

Day of Mourning Fifty years later the Aboriginal civil rights movement began. Sydney Aborigines boycotted the 1938 sesquicentennial (150 years of colonisation) celebrations, instead holding the Aboriginal Day of Mourning and Protest

Dr Anita Heiss

Anita Heiss is from the Wiradjuri nation and lives in Sydney. She is the author of a book of social commentary, *Sacred Cows*, and a poetry collection, *Token Koori*. In 2000 Anita completed her PhD in Communication and Media at the Nepean campus of the University of Western Sydney with a thesis on publishing Aboriginal literature in Australia.

Anita has been published widely in journals, anthologies and newspapers, and in 1998 she was the first Aboriginal author to be elected to the management committee of the Australian Society of Authors.

on 26 January. This protest saw an 'Aboriginal-only' conference held at Australia Hall in Sydney, attended by 1000 people calling for citizenship rights, voting rights and equal pay for Aborigines. The conference was the first Aboriginal civil rights gathering, and served to further motivate political activism.

The 1950s and '60s saw the establishment of Aboriginal organisations around the country working towards the same aims: equal rights, civil rights and land rights. They also fought against discriminatory legislation that prevented Aboriginal communities from attaining even basic levels of social and economic achievement.

The Freedom Ride With South African and Black American civil-rights movements in the international news, a more active attitude towards protest flowed into Australia. In 1965 Dr Kumantjayi Perkins brought together a bus-load of university students who travelled throughout country NSW with the aim of increasing public awareness of racial intolerance, and exposing the apartheid-like segregation operating in swimming pools, theatres and restaurants. This famous political trip became known as the Freedom Ride.

The Wave Hill Strike This famous strike in 1966 at Wave Hill cattle station was supported nationally by Aboriginal communities and unions. The strike and walk-off by the Gurindji people was led by Vincent Lingiari and highlighted the Aboriginal struggle for justice in central Australia. The protesters were demonstrating against poor wages and the deplorable living conditions that the Aboriginal stockmen and their families were enduring.

The Tent Embassy In 1972 a group of Aboriginal people established the Tent Embassy on the lawns of the then parliament house in Canberra as a further protest against the denial of land rights.

Around the same time Harold Thomas designed the Aboriginal flag. The flag, with its distinctive black, red and yellow design, still flies at the site in Canberra and was at the temporary site erected in Victoria Park, Sydney, during the 2000 Olympic Games.

WE ARE THE INVISIBLE AUSTRALIANS   Dr Rosemary van den Berg

Did you know that Aboriginal people are an invisible race in Australia? Although Aborigines have lived in this country for around 60,000 years and are from the oldest living culture in the world, they were not considered citizens in Australia until 1967. While the Australian people voted overwhelmingly for Aborigines to be counted in the census in the federal government's referendum of 1967, Aborigines are still excluded and marginalised in their own country. There are still people from all strata of society in multicultural Australia who refuse to acknowledge Aboriginal existence.

Aborigines became invisible in 1770. The English explorer, Captain James Cook 'discovered' Australia and sent reports back to England claiming that this country was *terra nullius*, a land belonging to no-one. This fallacy was compounded for over 200 years and it was only in 1992 that the *Mabo* High Court decision ruled that Australia was never terra nullius; Aborigines were its first people. It is incredible that it was only 10 years ago that Indigenous people were finally recognised as being the original owners of their land. Sadly, this decision did not stop the colonial practice of treating Aboriginal people as an invisible race. In fact, if anything, it promoted more friction with Aborigines in Australia, because non-Aborigines felt threatened by the possible takeover of their lands by land rights claims. It is a paradox, really. On the one hand, white Australians treat Aboriginal people as invisible yet, on the other, they are fighting these same 'invisible' people in court over their rightful ownership of land.

I am an Elder of the Nyoongar people of the south-west of Western Australia and I, along with many of my friends and relations, have found that there are white and other Australians who will not talk to an Aboriginal person unless it is absolutely necessary. Others are afraid of us and there are still others who have never met an Aboriginal person. I have even come across some people who will speak through my Dutch husband because they think I cannot understand English! I have found that only the most 'daring' will sit next to an Aboriginal person on public transport. Shopkeepers and their assistants usually ignore an Aboriginal person waiting to be served. Public hospitals, especially those in country towns, make Aboriginal people wait longer than others to see the doctor. Aborigines also find it very difficult to obtain private rental accommodation and they face more obstacles when seeking employment, especially by the private sector.

Admittedly, times have changed. Australia has laws that prohibit discrimination against minority groups. Yet, from my experiences, white Australians now use more subtle and covert forms of exclusion and marginalisation against the Aboriginal peoples. I hope the day comes when Aboriginal people will be acknowledged and accepted on a par with other cultures living in Australia. Why should we, the original inhabitants of Australia, be treated as the invisible people of this country?

THE ROYAL COMMISSION INTO ABORIGINAL DEATHS IN CUSTODY

bryan Andy

Tabled in Australia's federal parliament in May 1991, the Royal Commission into Aboriginal Deaths in Custody (RCIADIC) investigated the deaths of 99 Aboriginal people who died while they were incarcerated between the years 1980 and 1989. The RCIADIC highlighted the fact that Aboriginal people were being imprisoned, and dying, in custody at disproportionately high rates compared to non-Indigenous Australians. The report proposed some 339 recommendations to Australian governments in the hope that measures could be taken to cease these injustices in the Australian legal system.

Some of the findings of the report were:

• While Aboriginal people (aged 15 years and above) make up 1.1% of the general Australian population, Aboriginal people constituted a staggering 29% of those held in custody in Australia
• Figures from the report show that between 1980 and 1988 Aboriginal people were 23 times more likely to die in custody than non-Indigenous Australians
• During the time of the investigation, Aboriginal people were 20 times more likely to be arrested than non-Indigenous people. Many of the charges laid against Aboriginal people were for minor offences (like offensive language and behaviour); these charges made up 63% of the overall charges laid against Aborigines

Overall, the report made broad recommendations that demanded policy changes in the areas of health, education, housing, drug and alcohol dependence and Aboriginal self-determination. The entire report (and other links) can be seen at www.atsic.gov.au/issues/rciadic. Also worth viewing is the documentary *Who Killed Malcolm Smith?* (1992, Titus Films), a case study of a young Aboriginal artist who died while in custody after being imprisoned, initially, for stealing a bike. It's available in any good Australian research or university library.

You'll find that many of the deaths investigated during the Royal Commission were of Aboriginal people who had been institutionalised from a young age under paternalistic assimilation policies. Eleven of the 99 deaths investigated in the RCIADIC were of women.

While governments have publicly supported the 339 recommendations, Aboriginal people continue to die in custody; and their families and communities still ask for justice.

The Bicentennial of Invasion A wave of emotion and unity swept across Sydney in 1988 when 40,000 people – including people from as far away as Arnhem Land – participated in the March for Freedom, Justice and Hope, protesting against the bicentennial celebration of the invasion of Australia by Europeans 200 years before.

Reconciliation In 1991 the Council for Aboriginal Reconciliation (CAR) was formed as a government initiative with the vision of 'A united Australia which respects this land of ours, values the Aboriginal and Torres Strait Islander heritage, and provides justice and equity for all'. The government's process of Reconciliation came to an end in 2000, culminating in Corroboree 2000, when 250,000 people joined in the Peoples' Walk for Reconciliation across the Sydney Harbour Bridge and the Reconciliation document was handed to Prime Minister John Howard by CAR, in a ceremony at the Sydney Opera House. This was matched later in the year by similar marches around the country.

THE LUCKY COUNTRY?

Jason Davidson

This country is built on lies, massacres, genocide, imprisonment, poison, stolen children, and the ongoing bullshit of Western politics. To me, the history of Australia is a white man's portrayal, which focuses on non-Indigenous milestones such as Captain Cook's 'discovery' of Australia. I vividly remember my school history classes – all revolved around the 'great' white explorers, such as Captain Cook, who brought 'civilisation' to Australia. Swagmen, pioneers, shearers and convicts were also a big part of our history lessons. We learnt all about the joys and hardships of the white invaders, yet there was little if any mention of Australia's first peoples, the Aborigines and Torres Strait Islanders. It was as if they never existed at all. This denial of our history saddens me to this day. Although today there are more and more non-Indigenous Australians who share our grief, the government is still holding back this crucial healing process. They are dividing a nation that is finally striving to acknowledge the real history of Australia and move towards Reconciliation.

Time cannot be recaptured. All the willpower in the world cannot undo the devastation that European settlers have inflicted on our people. White settlement in Australia was built on sly and cruel criminal tactics against the traditional Indigenous owners. Not only did the white settlers slaughter our people, they also destroyed much of the bush tucker that our ancestors depended on, such as emu, kangaroo and bush turkey. Robbed of their food source, many Aboriginal people had no choice but to kill a whitefella's cow so they could feed their families. In their quest to save their children from starvation, many Aboriginal people were killed or imprisoned – the life of a cow was more precious than the life of a blackfella.

It seems ironic to me that the white people who died fighting in wars for Australia were automatically classed as heroes. However, although my ancestors had their homeland callously stolen away from them and died fighting to preserve their country and culture, they were never, and still are not, given the same honour... Our battle is not over. Today we still struggle for equality. My dream is to one day see the same level of respect given to us, the first Australians of this 'lucky country' of ours.

Jason Davidson

My family was assimilated by the government through the Stolen Generations process. My grandmother's country is at Kalkaringi, also known as Wave Hill (Gurindji Country), my grandfather's country is at Ngukurr, also known as Roper River (Ngalakan Country).

I moved down to Adelaide with my parents after Cyclone Tracy hit Darwin in 1974. I was educated at TAFE college and at the Centre for Aboriginal Studies in Music (CASM) at the University of Adelaide.

I worked for the dole, also known as CDEP, in my grandmother's country at Kalkaringi, doing carpentry, welding and mechanics. My interest in photography started when I was going out hunting with my uncles in the Northern Territory.

I have just completed my Batchelor of Visual Arts, having already achieved my Diploma of Fine Art.

For more information on the stories of the East Kimberley, check out the Web site at www.anat.org.au/Aboriginal_Ancestors/index.html.

A number of community groups also formed nationally during the late 1990s, supporting the growing political protest against the federal government's failure to say 'sorry' to the Stolen Generations and its '10-Point Plan', a plan to limit native title over pastoral leases, developed by the Howard Government after the High Court's *Wik* decision that pastoral leases did not necessarily extinguish native title.

The Sea of Hands One new group was Australians for Native Title and Reconciliation (ANTaR), responsible for the Sea of Hands. By 2000, 250,000 Australians had signed 120,000 plastic hands that make up the Sea of Hands to show their support for native title and Reconciliation, and to prove that Reconciliation was truly a peoples' movement. The hands are planted in the ground on wire stems in a pattern designed by a local Indigenous artist. This installation has been to every major city as well as regional locations, with many local organisations holding small Sea of Hands events.

The Preamble Debate In 1999 Australia voted at a referendum on whether the country should become a republic, independent of Britain. During the lead-up to the referendum there was much controversy over the preamble for a potential new Australian constitution. The proposed document did not state that the land was originally owned by Aboriginal people, instead it 'honour(ed) Aborigines and Torres Strait Islanders, the nation's first people, for their deep kinship with their lands and for their ancient and continuing cultures which enrich the life of the country'.

The nation voted on two questions at the referendum: the first was whether the country should be a republic or not; the second was whether to include the proposed preamble in a new constitution.

Both questions received 'no' votes – 54.87% and 66.66% respectively. Many still feel the preamble to the constitution should be rewritten to acknowledge Aboriginal people as traditional owners with land and sea rights.

Mandatory Sentencing During 1999 and 2000 there was national outrage over mandatory sentencing laws in the Northern Territory and Western Australia, as these laws served to increase the incarceration rates of Indigenous people in particular, and went against the recommendations of the 1991 Royal Commission into Aboriginal Deaths in Custody. This royal commission was established to investigate the disturbingly high number of Indigenous people who die in Australian prisons. On top of these laws, 'zero-tolerance policing' was also promoted in areas such as the Northern Territory, which would have increased the jailing of Aboriginal people for trivial offences and would also be in breach of 19 recommendations of the royal commission.

Indigenous Organisations
ATSIC In 1990 the Aboriginal and Torres Strait Islander Commission (ATSIC) was set up as a commonwealth statutory authority as a way of including Indigenous people in the political decisions affecting our lives. ATSIC works to improve the legal, economic, social, cultural and political rights of Indigenous Australians by working at both a community level, through elected regional councils, and on a national level through a fully elected board.

ATSIC has advisory, advocacy and monitoring roles. It works for all levels of government, as well as Indigenous people nationally and organisations servicing Indigenous people. ATSIC also has a number of programs to assist community, social and economic development, and community housing. It also aims to promote and protect heritage, culture, land and sea rights.

Experienced Aboriginal administrator and bureaucrat, Yankuntjatjara woman Lois O'Donoghue, was nominated by the former minister for Aboriginal Affairs, Gerry Hand, to act as chair of the new ATSIC in 1990, and it wasn't until 1999 that the organisation enjoyed its first elected national chair in Djapwurrung man Geoff Clark. He was elected by the ATSIC board of commissioners after being re-elected for a second term as the ATSIC commissioner for Victoria. Mr Clark has travelled extensively throughout Australia and overseas in his role as commissioner with native title and land rights responsibilities.

State Government Bodies Aside from the federal body ATSIC, there are also state and territory departments that advise their own governments on issues and policies affecting their own Aboriginal communities. These include the Aboriginal Affairs Department (WA), Aboriginal Affairs Victoria, the Department of Aboriginal Affairs

(NSW), the Department of Aboriginal and Torres Strait Islander Development (Queensland), the Department of State Aboriginal Affairs (SA), the Office of Aboriginal Affairs (Tasmania) and the Office of Aboriginal Development (NT).

Each state and territory also has Aboriginal land councils representing particular communities. For example, the Central Land Council is a statutory body representing Aboriginal people in the central Australia region (approximately 780,000 sq km), which grew out of the 1966 Wave Hill walkout.

There are also organisations like the Indigenous Land Corporation, designed to assist Indigenous peoples to acquire and manage land in a sustainable way to provide cultural, social, economic or environmental benefits for themselves and for future generations.

Political Activists & Politicians

The political history of Indigenous Australia since invasion has seen a number of key people in leadership roles, beginning in the 1780s when Bennelong acted in a conciliatory manner to begin communications with the colonisers, and Pemulwuy led the war of resistance. Modern-day Aboriginal 'warriors' have come from all over Australia, and have been men and women, young and old.

Pearl Gibbs, Jack Patten & Bill Ferguson At the beginning of the civil rights movement, political motivators and activists came to the fore in the 1930s, largely in NSW with Sydney as the focal point. People like Pearl Gibbs, Jack Patten and Bill Ferguson were an integral part of the Aboriginal struggle and were members of the historic deputation to the prime minister following the Day of

THAT 'T' WORD
bryan Andy

Considered a dirty word by many white officials, 'treaty' is a term that should be celebrated, discussed and placed on Australia's social, legal and political agenda. After all, a treaty is an agreement between two peoples – a negotiated document of conduct, recognition and respect.

Of the world's Commonwealth countries, Australia is the only nation that hasn't entered into, or formalised, any form of treaty (let alone agreement) with its Indigenous occupants – how embarrassing! Countries such as Canada and New Zealand have acknowledged the Indigenous occupation of their lands prior to European invasion. When it came to Australia, Indigenous peoples were ignored in the hope that they'd go away.

By formalising a treaty, Indigenous occupation prior to the invasion would be acknowledged; Australia would become a more just society; and Indigenous people would secure constitutional recognition of their inherent rights within the Australian nation. This in turn would allow Indigenous Australians to inform governments in Australia – meaning real self-determination, not just the pseudo-sincere concepts that have been bandied around throughout Australia's history.

Fortunately, you'll now find that many people in support of Reconciliation are warming to the idea of a treaty between Indigenous and non-Indigenous Australians. Many who took part in the nation's Peoples' Walk for Reconciliation events made known their desire for a treaty by getting vocal and talking about the issue, carrying banners in support of a treaty, and wearing stickers demanding 'Treaty Now!'. These informed people are realising that the 'unfinished business' of the past should be dealt with; with a treaty spearheading their aspirations to 'get it right'.

So, next time you are fortunate enough to hear Yothu Yindi's *Treaty*, clear your throat and sing it loud: 'Treaty yeah, treaty now!'.

For more information check out www.treatynow.org, the Web site of Australia's National Treaty Support Group.

See also the Reconciliation section earlier in this chapter.

POLITICAL WEB SITES

Aboriginal and Torres Strait Islander Commission The ATSIC site has comprehensive information on ATSIC's corporate plan, structure, programs, policies, regional councils and resources, plus links to other sites.
www.atsic.gov.au

Apology Australia Tells you where you can sign a petition saying 'Sorry'.
www.apology.west.net.au

Australian Electoral Commission With information on past elections, referendums, voting, parliamentary committees and electoral education.
www.aec.gov.au

Australians for Native Title Includes information about the organisation, information on native title, lobbying and campaigns.
www.nativetitle.aust.com

Australians for Native Title and Reconciliation (ANTaR) Here you'll find information on events, articles, an on-line shop and information on the Sea of Hands.
www.antar.org.au

Central Land Council The CLC Web site gives information about the CLC, land acquisition, mining, policy and permits to visit Aboriginal land.
www.clc.org.au

City of Sydney Includes an Aboriginal section called Barani that documents the Aboriginal history of central Sydney and includes information about the political movements that developed in the city. It also includes a timeline and an information section on how and where to research Aboriginal history.
www.cityofsydney.nsw.gov.au

Indigenous Land Corporation The ILC site includes information about the organisation and the land fund, land management, land acquisition and land purchase. It has links to other sites, newsletters and a mailing list.
www.ilc.gov.au

National Aboriginal and Torres Strait Islander Education Website Use keywords and maps to explore the cultural and educational issues of Aboriginal and Torres Strait Islander peoples.
www.natsiew.nexus.edu.au

Mourning and Protest in 1938. As members of the Aboriginal Australian Fellowship, Patten and Ferguson also published the manifesto *Aborigines Claim Citizenship Rights* and the newspaper the *Australian Abo Call*, a political tool to voice issues of concern to Aboriginal Australians. (Note that 'Abo' is now considered an offensive term.)

Dr Kumantjayi Perkins Arrernte and Kalkadoon man Dr Kumantjayi Perkins, from Alice Springs, passed away in 2000 and was given a state funeral because of his contribution to Australian political life, and his continual struggle for basic rights for Indigenous people. Dr Perkins is best remembered for his leadership in the 1965 Freedom Ride.

Kevin Gilbert Wiradjuri activist and author Kevin Gilbert was one of the founders of the Tent Embassy in Canberra in 1972 and was also an advocate for a sovereign treaty between Aboriginal and non-Aboriginal Australia. In 1988 he published a draft treaty that has yet to be adopted by an Australian government.

Michael Mansell Lawyer and land rights activist Michael Mansell, from northern Tasmania, played a prominent role in the discussions leading up to the drafting of the 1993 *Mabo* legislation by the federal government. He was also a founder of the Aboriginal Provisional Government (APG). The APG was established in 1990 to seek self-determination for Aboriginal people

continued...   Dr Anita Heiss

Northern Land Council This site has information on how the permit system works when visiting Aboriginal land, how the NLC operates, the battle for land and sea rights, the importance of land in Aboriginal culture and how to care for it, and commercial operations on Aboriginal land.
www.nlc.org.au

Reconciliation Australia This site gives information about the organisation that took over after the Council for Reconciliation disbanded in 2000.
www.reconciliation.org.au

State Departments
Many of the state government bodies maintain useful Web sites.

Aboriginal Affairs Department The Western Australian government site has contacts, news, publications and links.
www.aad.wa.gov.au

Department of Aboriginal Affairs This site includes information on native title in New South Wales and links.
www.daa.nsw.gov.au

Department of Aboriginal and Torres Strait Islander Policy and Development The Queensland government site includes a kids' area and links page.
www.indigenous.qld.gov.au

Department of State Aboriginal Affairs This site has information on Aboriginal communities in South Australia and a digital library.
www.dosaa.sa.gov.au

Office of Aboriginal Affairs This Tasmanian government site has information on legislation, resources and contact numbers.
www.dpac.tas.gov.au/divisions/oaa

Office of Aboriginal Development The site of the Northern Territory government has publications and links.
www.nt.gov.au/oad

For more reviews of Web sites, see the Internet Resources section.

through a government system, independent of the Australian government.

Lois O'Donoghue Lois O'Donoghue, aside from being the first chair of ATSIC, was Australian of the Year in 1984 and played an important role in CAR.

Noel Pearson As executive director of the Cape York Land Council, Bama Bagarrmugu man Noel Pearson, from Cooktown in northern Queensland, is an adviser to a number of organisations and outspoken on issues of economic and social development for Aboriginal people, particularly in his own community.

Pat & Mick Dodson The Dodson brothers from the Kimberley region of WA have been a dynamic political team in the past decade. Patrick Dodson was appointed a commissioner of the Royal Commission into Aboriginal Deaths in Custody and became chair of CAR in 1992. Mick Dodson was Aboriginal and Torres Strait Islander social justice commissioner for the Human Rights and Equal Opportunity Commission between 1993 and 1998.

Neville Bonner In terms of Aboriginal people in mainstream politics, we have had little representation. The late Neville Bonner became Australia's first federal Aboriginal parliamentarian and Liberal Party senator in 1971, remaining in government until 1983. The Jagera Elder from Queensland died in 1998.

Aboriginal protestors at the opening of Parliament House, Canberra, in the bicentennial year – 1988

Aden Ridgeway It was 15 years before we would see another Aboriginal person in parliament when Aden Ridgeway, a Gumbainggir man from the north coast of NSW, became a NSW senator for the Australian Democrats in 1998. Ridgeway was given the role of spokesperson for Recreation, Industry, Arts, Tourism, Financial Services and the Centenary of Federation.

See also the History section, earlier, and History sections at the start of each regional chapter.

Economy
Dr Anita Heiss

All the economic and social indicators suggest that Indigenous Australians are still the most disadvantaged group within Australian society.

Indigenous incomes are approximately two-thirds the Australian average. In 1996 the median income for Indigenous Australians was $190 per week, but the median was $292 for all Australians.

Education

Obviously, the role education plays in the lives of Indigenous people affects their employment opportunities as well as their income earning potential. However, it was not until the 1940s that Indigenous children were provided with teachers in government reserves. This is an example of historical disadvantage that is, in some areas, only being addressed today.

The 1996 census found that Indigenous Australians were less likely to be attending an education institution full-time than other Australians. The census also found that 73.7% of Indigenous people 15 years and over were in full-time education compared with 91% of others in this age group.

At 19 years of age, the standard tertiary level age, only 12% of Indigenous people were in full-time education, compared to 33% of the rest of the population.

In 1996 only 13.6% of Aborigines and Torres Strait Islanders had post-school qualifications, compared to 34.4% of the total population. Most of those Indigenous people with post-school qualifications came from larger urban centres.

Education Programs Education programs specifically targeting Indigenous people were established by the federal government in 1969 to encourage Indigenous people to take advantage of educational opportunities. Such programs include ABSTUDY, which provides financial assistance for Indigenous people in approved secondary and tertiary education courses. In 1998 ABSTUDY assisted over 50,000 students in full-time, part-time or correspondence study.

Other programs include the Aboriginal Tutorial Assistance Scheme, Aboriginal

Student Support and Parent Awareness Program, and Vocational and Educational Guidance for Aborigines Scheme. It is obvious that these programs are assisting the enrolment of Indigenous people – Indigenous enrolments in higher education were negligible in the late 1960s but by 1997 they had risen to 7460. However, Indigenous students' success and retention rates are about 20% lower than other Australians'.

Employment
The unemployment rate for Indigenous people is an estimated 26%, as against about 8% for the general Australian community. That's three times the national average!

In terms of the areas in which Aboriginal people are employed, the 1996 census found that the largest sector was in health and community services (19.5%), then government administration and defence (15.3%), education (7.9%), retail trade (7.5%), manufacturing (7%), property and business services (6%), right down to mining (1.5%) and finance and insurance (1%).

Government Initiatives
CDEP ATSIC's Community Development Employment Program (CDEP) has been successful since 1977 as a means of providing employment and community development to more than 260 Indigenous communities around Australia. CDEP accounts for about one quarter of Indigenous employment, and without CDEP, the unemployment rate would be more than 40%. In remote areas CDEP is often the only alternative to unemployment. Essentially it is a work-for-the-dole scheme.

Identified Positions The introduction of identified Indigenous positions within many government departments and organisations has also seen an increase in employment of Aboriginal people. Such strategies are supported by Section 14 of the Anti-Discrimination Act that says race is a genuine qualification for some positions.

Welfare As a large number of Aboriginal people remain within their rural and remote communities, where unemployment levels are high generally, welfare forms the main income for the communities. This is also the case for communities in urban centres that suffer high levels of unemployment, regardless of race.

Indigenous Business
At the other end of the spectrum, the 21st century has seen the rise of individual Indigenous people establishing their own businesses and acting as consultants for government departments, private research companies and community organisations.

Much of the work being generated in these areas includes the evaluation and review of government programs, cross-cultural awareness training, researching and writing Indigenous policy, historical and cultural learning, as well as promotion and media-related work. Tourism is another industry in which many Indigenous people have started small businesses, with services such as walking tours, harbour cruises and cultural entertainment.

Even with the new influx of consultants and Aboriginal businesspeople, there is a real employment crisis in the Indigenous community. This crisis remains because large numbers of Indigenous people reside in remote and rural communities that don't have established labour markets. There are still comparatively low participation rates for Indigenous people in the education system, and there is still lingering prejudice on the part of non-Indigenous employers.

For more information on education, see the Education section, later in this chapter.

People & Population
Dr Anita Heiss

Aborigines and Torres Strait Islanders are the traditional owners of Australia, having been custodians of the land for over 50,000 years. Australia's *Macquarie Dictionary* (1997) defines 'Aborigine' as 'one of a race of tribal peoples, the earliest known inhabitants of Australia' and 'Indigenous' as 'originating in and characterising a particular region or country'. These are still European definitions of Australia's first peoples, and suggest that we are a homogenous group. Terms such as 'tribe' or 'clan' can also be problematic; some Indigenous people like to use them, and some do not. Because of the implications of these definitions, we have moved towards using our own generic terms to define who we are. In this way we distinguish ourselves from other nations and highlight the diversity of the one 'Aboriginal community'. Our own terms also show that while we are united by a shared history of invasion and a continued struggle, we are also unique in our cultures and experiences.

Who We Are

In New South Wales, Aboriginal people like myself generally call ourselves Koori (except on the mid-north coast and in north-western regions of NSW, where some people use Goori). Victorians also use Koorie (spelt differently). Murri is used in Queensland (and parts of NSW around Moree), Nunga in South Australia, Palawa in Tasmania and Noongar (with various spellings) in south-western Western Australia. It would be offensive to call someone in Broome or Kununurra a Noongar, for example, as it is seen very much as an urban definition. In the Northern Territory people generally define themselves by their nation, *skin* group or language group, for example, Eastern Arrernte people around Alice Springs, Warumungu around Tennant Creek and Jawoyn around Katherine.

It is also common for Aboriginal people to define themselves by their mob (family). For example, I might say I am a Williams from Cowra. Williams is the family name, Cowra is in Wiradjuri country. The Wiradjuri nation are the traditional owners of the land at Cowra and much of south-western NSW. So I have been located by family and country.

How Many Aboriginal Nations Are There?

Indigenous people in Australia belong to Aboriginal 'nations' (otherwise known as tribes). Prior to European invasion in 1788, there were between 600 and 700 distinct nations in Australia, speaking between 200 and 250 languages. Each nation was made up of communities, clans and individuals who lived in and owned an area of country that was usually strictly defined. Each had a particular language or dialect, was known by a distinct name and possessed customs and lores which varied from those of their neighbouring nations. Each nation also had their own rites and

beliefs, which often differed from those people around them.

If you imagine the map of Europe with all its different countries, each with their own distinct cultures, you can imagine the map of Australia before electoral, state and territory boundaries were introduced by Europeans. It was a mosaic of hundreds of different societies.

The Tindale map commonly referred to as the basis for identifying Aboriginal nations around Australia is riddled with problems, as many nations shared boundaries and land ownership distinctions were sometimes blurred. The same problems arose when AIATSIS mapped traditional language groups in 1994.

Defining Aboriginality

Historically, the need to define Aboriginality has never come from within Aboriginal communities. We have never been advocates of, or accepted, titles like half-caste, quarter-caste, quadroon and so on, unlike our Native American sistas and brothers who choose blood quantum to measure Indigeneity.

Definitions of Aboriginality have historically been designed by white governments to 'water down' Aborigines, and to force assimilation of Black people into white society. Being defined as 'half-caste' or 'part-Aboriginal' not only detracted from someone's Aboriginality but forced even Aboriginal people to question their own identity.

Defining and declaring Aboriginality is something that the Australian government has imposed on Aboriginal communities, having to fulfil government requirements in some instances, where an individual is required to provide a certificate of Aboriginality by an incorporated Aboriginal body under its common seal. Applying for the recently released Aboriginal Label of Authenticity requires an artist to supply two letters or certificates confirming their Aboriginality.

Many Aboriginal organisations also require certificates or confirmation of Aboriginality. They, however, do so for other reasons. In the case of publishing, for example, a 'Proof of Aboriginality' form is used as protection from exploitation by white frauds in light of the 1997 outing of

BEING A BLACK WOMAN IN 2001

Karen Milward

I am a 31-year-old Aboriginal woman. I am neither black nor white in colour. I have never had a problem with my identity, but I constantly have to justify myself to everyone around me, from taxi drivers to work colleagues.

Even when I had my baby, Kayn, the midwives at hospital found it hard to believe that I was a Koorie. They said things like, 'What nationality are you? Where do you come from?'. When I told them I was of Aboriginal descent, they looked at me in disbelief. Many insisted I couldn't possibly be a Koorie. Some even argued that I must be Greek, Italian or even Chinese! Once they knew I was of Aboriginal descent, they talked to me in a condescending tone: 'Now dear, this is how you change a nappy – make sure you're clean all over before you do... Do you understand?'. Then, when they saw the Mongolian blue spot (a birthmark most Indigenous babies are born with), they said, 'Your son has bruises on his back!'. I replied, 'Not bruises, that's his Mongolian blue spot!'. They scoffed in disbelief.

Recently, when I had some professional photos taken of my son, the photographer asked my mother and I what nationality we were. When I told him we were Koories, he laughed and said, 'You've got to be pulling my leg!'. Then, when we had the photos taken outside, he gave my son a piece of bark and a pine cone and said, 'Here you go, you would be used to this!'. At the end of the photo session he kept repeating the fee. Did he think I couldn't afford it because of my Aboriginal background?

Aboriginal people have to deal with racist attitudes at many levels. I have even encountered racism from a former office boss who told me that I was 'not bad looking for a *boong*' (derogatory word for Aboriginal people). According to him I am 'very clean, dress well', and gee my 'teeth are very white!'. Later, he sarcastically said, 'Nice scarf you're wearing, did you steal it?'!

Although my climb up the corporate ladder has not been easy, my commitment to bridging the cultural gap between Indigenous and non-Indigenous Australians has paid off. In my last job, I worked with white men over the age of 50 to change attitudes and improve the relationships between Aboriginal people and local government councils. After six years, my perseverance for acceptance has been acknowledged. I am now constantly invited to represent Aboriginal people on important committees which seek to improve life for my people and for the broader community.

No matter what happens around me, I will continue to prove that we can make it in this country so that, hopefully, more people will think just a little more positively about Aboriginal Australia.

Karen Milward

I am a Yorta Yorta woman, as well as being a director within Aboriginal Affairs Victoria, an ATSIC Binjirru regional councillor, a Masters student of Business Administration and single mother of my two-year-old son, Kayn Tarloo.

I have worked in public relations/advertising at Melbourne City Council and the Municipal Association of Victoria. I am also the author of various newsletters and *Wurreker*, a good-practice guide promoting successful joint initiatives between local councils and Aboriginal communities.

I believe I am very fortunate to have been given the strength to fight for my cultural beliefs (no matter how hard, and sometimes depressing) by the same black women who have fought against the injustices that still haunt Aboriginal people today. These women are, most notably, my mother Daphne and my work colleague Lorraine – for believing in my ability to make a difference for Victorian black women.

FACING MY IDENTITY

Donisha Duff

I remember growing up on Thursday Island in the Torres Strait. My mother is a Torres Strait Islander woman and my father is an Englishman. However, this was never an issue – most other Torres Strait Islander families were like us too. It wasn't until we moved to the mainland of Australia that the difference became apparent and my cultural identity was challenged.

When I was seven years old one of my white classmates – assuming I was white because of my light skin – asked why my mother was a black woman. How was I supposed to answer that? As the years went by, I found that I often had to justify my heritage and place in society. I grew up with questions and dismissals from many white people: 'You're not like other Aboriginal or Torres Strait Islander people. You should pretend to be Maori, Italian or someone (white) with a really good tan! You don't have to be part of *them*.'

At university I became more anxious and angry, and I was always on the defensive. I found that I was often the only black face in a sea of questions, and expected to be an expert on all things black – unemployment, appalling health conditions, crime, incarceration and welfare. If I couldn't answer these questions, then I was not considered to be a *real* Aborigine or Torres Strait Islander. On top of that, I had to work harder and excel in my studies to defend my place in higher education and to break the stereotypes.

But my identity was not only questioned by white people; some Aboriginal people were quick to label me as someone after a free ride because of my light skin...someone who didn't know her roots. I remember once being excluded from an Aboriginal and Torres Strait Islander women's meeting. Being excluded by your own people leaves a painful and lasting impression. I became even more angry.

It took a number of years for me to realise the problem people had with my identity did not necessarily stem from prejudice or bigotry. Over 200 years of white colonisation have left unhealed scars on thousands of people searching for family, culture and a place in society. I realised that most of these people, black and white, were just misinformed or completely lacking insight into my heritage and culture. Many who questioned my identity were actually searching for an affirmation of their own heritage and culture.

Donisha Duff

Donisha was born and grew up on Thursday Island, in the Torres Strait. She is of Torres Strait Islander descent, from St Paul's and Kubin on Moa, and also of Aboriginal descent, from Yadhaigana in Shelbourne Bay, Cape York, through her mother's side.

During her school years her family moved to the mainland of Australia, where they settled in Brisbane. Donisha went on to university, where she excelled, becoming the first Torres Strait Islander woman to graduate with Honours from her degree program. In 1999 she moved to Canberra to begin work within the public service.

In her spare time Donisha likes travelling around Australia (and overseas when she can afford it), playing basketball, painting, reading and spending time with her partner.

Leon Carmen as 'Wanda Koolmatrie'. This white male taxi driver from Sydney posed as an Aboriginal woman from the Pitjantjatjara people of South Australia and wrote the life story *My Own Sweet Time*, going on to win a literary award for women writers.

For the purposes of federal government requirements, a 'working definition' of

Aboriginality was accepted in 1978. The definition states:

An Aboriginal or Torres Strait Islander is a person of Aboriginal or Torres Strait Islander descent who identifies as an Aboriginal or Torres Strait Islander and is accepted as such by the community in which s/he is associated.

This definition is supported and endorsed by many other organisations 'outside' Aboriginal communities, such as the Australia Council for the Arts – the major sponsor of Aboriginal arts in Australia – who use the government's definition as part of their daily practice of administering grants to artists.

While you might hear phrases like 'Black and White Australia', the term 'Black Australian' is not used as often as it would be in the US, for example. You might also hear the terms 'whitefellas' and 'blackfellas' used by Indigenous people, and these are not used offensively.

There has also been a shift from the negative to the positive in the use of the word 'Black' in Australia. Aboriginal people have embraced the terms and often capitalise the first letter as a political statement of self-defining and importance.

Defining Whitefellas

There are also commonly used terms for non-Indigenous Australians which change across geographical regions, for example in NSW, Kooris use the word *gubbah* and in Queensland, Murris use *migloo*. These terms are not used as commonly as the term *pakeha* is for Europeans in Aotearoa (the original name for New Zealand), and depending on the tone used when saying them, they can be derogatory.

How Many Aboriginal People Are There in Australia Today?

Indigenous people currently make up approximately 2% of the overall general Australian population, a growth of 2.3% between 1991 and 1996. This means the resident Aboriginal and Torres Strait Islander population in June 1996, when the census was taken, was 386,000 (out of the 18,310,000 general Australian population).

The estimated resident population of Indigenous people in each state and territory, according to the 1996 census, shows that

NSW has the highest Indigenous population with 109,925; then, in decreasing order, Queensland (104,817), Western Australia (56,205), Northern Territory (51,876), Victoria (22,598), South Australia (22,052), Tasmania (15,322) and the Australian Capital Territory (3058). It is commonly believed that the Indigenous population of greater Sydney is around 36,000 – the largest concentration of Indigenous people in Australia.

...And How Many Were There?

While there are no accurate estimates of the population of Australia before European settlement, recent studies have changed the estimate of Aboriginal people living in Sydney in 1788 from 300,000 to one million. However, they also suggest that by 1888, the year of Centenary celebrations, only 60,000 Aboriginal people existed. It wasn't until the 1967 referendum that Aborigines were given citizenship rights and then counted on the Commonwealth census, so anything before then was based on individual anthropological research.

To show the effects of disease on the Aboriginal population, consider that there were an estimated 1500 Yura people living in Sydney at the point of invasion in 1788. By the end of 1789, it is believed that only two Yura had survived the smallpox epidemic. Disease, alongside the consequences of dispossession, dislocation, attempted genocide (poisoned watering holes, for example) and the modern-day realities of Black deaths in custody, have all contributed to the loss of Aboriginal life and the decline in population figures.

There are also a number of political and social issues affecting the population figures of Indigenous Australians in the 21st century. Firstly, as a result of government policies of the past that 'took' Aboriginal and Torres Strait Islander children from their parents, there are many people still unaware of their family roots and heritage. For this reason they may not identify as Indigenous in census counts. As the 'Stolen Generation' actually included many generations, population figures could be greatly altered.

Secondly, the census only asks respondents if they 'identify as Indigenous' to determine the Indigenous population, while the Commonwealth government and many Aboriginal agencies have three criteria to define who is and who is not Aboriginal. This too could greatly affect population figures.

In recent years, with changing social attitudes and political developments, as well as broader definitions of what it is to be Indigenous, the likelihood of people identifying as Indigenous has increased and this has been reflected in the population figures.

See also the Responsible Tourism section for information on stereotypes, and the Aboriginal Language map at the start of this book.

Education

Davina Woods

In order to maintain our culture, Indigenous Australians need an education system that supports our Aboriginality (Indigenous identity) in all its diversity, and provides us with the skills to participate in modern Australian society as a whole.

A number of attempts have been made to bring the different requirements of Indigenous people and the wider community together in the education system, including employing traditional teaching techniques and using Aboriginal languages in schools.

Building on Traditional Education Practices

The traditional cultures of Australia see learning as bestowing the gift of knowledge and skills from one person to another. The stories and songs of a particular Dreaming are used to pass on wisdom, beliefs and values. These strong oral traditions have enabled the archives of our knowledge to be passed on from one keeper to the next for approximately 2000 generations.

There are many parallels between traditional teaching practices and those used in modern classrooms and lecture theatres. For example, we still tell stories to explain a point. Storytelling is an age-old way of teaching and learning.

Another example is demonstration. People usually learn best when they are shown something and then asked to demonstrate what they have been shown. This method of showing and doing was used in this

Davina Woods

Davina Woods is a Murri woman who has been living with her immediate family in Koorie country, namely Melbourne, for the last decade. Originally a primary school teacher in Queensland, Davina established Clever Women Consultants in 1998.

For her millennium challenge, Davina has decided to undertake a Master of Arts in Australian Indigenous Studies at Monash University and learn Spanish in her spare time. Over the years, Davina has had opportunities to travel to all the capital cities of Australia as well as a few far-flung places such as Thursday Island and Aurukun in far north Queensland, St Helens in Tasmania and Albany in Western Australia. Her overseas travel has included places as far apart as Stockholm and the Solomon Islands, Albuquerque and Auckland. She is a mother of three and has published several articles and chapters in journals and books of an academic nature. Davina looks forward to the day her poetry is published and is contemplating her first novel.

country long before 1788 and is still in use today.

Whether learning through doing or learning through listening, it is easier to learn as a member of a group. The group allows for the sharing of knowledge, skills and support through peer tutoring. Group activities have been the preferred methods of learning for many thousands of years and, again, this technique is still in practice today.

Teaching Language

It's important for teachers to understand their students' cultural identity, and language is an important marker of culture. Indigenous students respond well when they are able to learn their 'home' language, which may be Aboriginal English or another Indigenous language that is spoken at home. Education in a student's home or first language is a valuable strategy for the student's overall success in education. For this reason, the preferred language for students during cooperative work with other children is usually their home language.

Teachers need to respect a student's home language; however, they must also ensure that the features of Standard Australian English are clearly taught and, where relevant, the differences from the students' home language must be plainly defined and explained. For example, students need to know when it's appropriate to use Aboriginal English or Torres Strait Islander Kriol and when it's not.

Two-Way Schooling

To achieve our goals, Indigenous Australians need the skills afforded us through formal education. In the Australia of the third millennium it is absolutely necessary for us to be able to read and write in Standard Australian English. Although we had, and in some places still do have, our own mathematic systems, being able to use the maths of contemporary Australia is also an imperative.

In recognising the key link between culture and obtaining skills, Indigenous Australians have set up new schools such as the Koorie Open Door Education (KODE) school within the Victorian state education system, and Yipirinya, a private Aboriginal school in Alice Springs. Yipirinya and KODE are just two examples of schools put in place by Indigenous Australians for our children. In these schools we use two-way schooling, which brings together the best of Indigenous and non-Indigenous ways of teaching and learning.

Good relationships between teacher and student are crucial. In the process of developing a relationship of mutual respect, teachers need to get to know not only the student but also the student's Indigenous community. School staff need to be taught about Indigenous cultures generally, and Indigenous cultures in their local school area in particular.

Education that respects and builds on the traditions of a child's Indigenous heritage is the best education for Aboriginal and Torres Strait Islander children.

For further information on Indigenous participation rates in education, see the Economy section earlier.

Health

Marcelline Burns

Health statistics highlight some of the most shocking disparities between the Indigenous and non-Indigenous populations of Australia. The average life expectancy for non-Indigenous Australians is 78.3 years, while Indigenous people can expect to live for 60 years. Around 53% of Indigenous men and 41% of Indigenous women die before the age of 50, compared with 13% of men and 7% of women in the non-Indigenous population.

The statistics for infants and children are even more distressing. Indigenous babies are three times more likely to die in their first year than their non-Indigenous compatriots.

Two Australias

Australia is forever being promoted as 'the lucky country', but this is not the case for the Aboriginal and Torres Strait Islander peoples who have inhabited the land since time immemorial.

To understand the appalling rates of disease and mortality among Indigenous peoples, any analysis must be framed within the historical, social and economic context of invasion.

At the beginning of the 21st century, basic needs such as clean water, proper sewerage, access to decent health services, education and housing are still far from a reality for many Aboriginal and Torres Strait Islander communities. The loss of traditional lands, displacement, loss of language and the enforced separation of families has resulted in a Fourth World nation within a First World nation – such is the state of Indigenous health in Australia. Diseases that are taking many lives in Aboriginal and Torres Strait Islander communities include diabetes, eye health/trachoma, chronic illness, ear infections, heart disease, mental health and respiratory/asthma problems.

Changes in Lifestyle

In stories handed down through many generations, Indigenous children are told of their ancestors who lived off the land and the sea before invasion. The responsibility of getting food was shared between men and women, the men hunting and the women gathering.

However, with invasion people were forced off their lands and away from their traditional food sources. In many places, previously unknown diseases such as smallpox, typhoid, influenza and measles, spread through the population along trade routes and caused many deaths even before the Europeans arrived in an area.

People were forcibly removed from their homelands and traditional ways and compelled to live in institutions run by the government or the church until well into the 20th century. In these institutions, a diet consisting mainly of fresh meat, nuts and berries was replaced with a diet consisting of rations of sugar and flour, syrup and, on the odd occasion, tinned meat. The new diet was high in fats, carbohydrates and sugars, leading to heart disease and other health conditions.

Community-Controlled Services

In many cases mainstream health services have not been appropriate service providers for communities in isolated locations. In addition, mainstream services have often been set up to cater for people in a Western cultural context and not to meet the needs of Indigenous Australians.

While there has been progress in the last few decades, there has not been enough. In comparison, much progress has been made in Canada and New Zealand. However, the formation of Aboriginal community-controlled health services more than 30 years ago ensures that Indigenous Australians can now access good health care. It was a long struggle for those involved in setting up these health services, which were often established through donations from supporters.

These services are administered by Aboriginal and Torres Strait Islander communities, and the funding comes from the government and donations. They are staffed by Indigenous and non-Indigenous medical workers. There are 80 Aboriginal community-controlled health services from Broome to Hobart to Alice Springs. It is not unusual to find doctors from all corners of the globe filling the professional medical positions.

The establishment of community-controlled health services ensures that Indigenous people are involved in the delivery

Marcelline Burns

My mother is from the Kuku-Yalangi people, the traditional owners of the region around Daintree National Park. She's from the coastal Yalangi – the Sunrise people – rather than the mountain Kuku people – the Sunset people. My father's family is Kuku-Djundan.

I have a first-class honours degree in Communications from the University of Technology, Sydney. Since then I've worked in media and PR in organisations such as ABC Radio and the NSW Premier's Office. I've also worked for state and federal government agencies in the areas of arts and health.

I've worked as a subeditor for the *Aboriginal Law Bulletin* at the University of New South Wales (NSW) and as a research assistant at the NSW Health Department looking at family violence and sexual assault in the Koori community.

I'm a travel-lover and a terrible cook. I also like reading, off-beat films and doing crossword puzzles, and I'm a huge Sydney Swans supporter.

of primary health care services and policy-making. According to the National Aboriginal Health Strategy, under community control, 'communities become active participants rather than passive recipients… community control rids the system of paternalism and promotes self-esteem'.

Through promotion and education, there has been progress, but there is still a lot of work to be done. Unfortunately, Indigenous Australians remain in the high-risk categories for many health problems.

With the implementation of new programs across Australia, there is a glimmer of light. However, it will only be through promotion, education and collaboration between communities and government – and the provision of basic services such as clean water, sewerage, housing, education and employment – that we will see the grim statistics fall.

For more information on diet, see Food – Bush Tucker.

Dance

Leonora Adidi

There was an arresting moment in the opening ceremony of the Sydney 2000 Olympics which encapsulates Indigenous dance today. The performance represented a nationwide gathering of tribes, smoothly performing their respective traditional dances in harmony to the strains of the didjeridu from the north, *clapsticks* from the south, *kulups* (hand-shakers) from the Torres Strait, and a songman from Arnhem Land.

Dance is integral to Aboriginal and Torres Strait Islander culture, a physical and spiritual expression of our norms, religion and stories. An essential part of our ceremonies, it incorporates music, song and art.

A dance performance will tell a story of the Dreaming, an ancestor spirit or the passing down of a law. As most spirit ancestors were animals or birds, dancers imitate the movements and sounds of these creatures.

Cycles of Dance

Dance is a communal event, every member of the clan participates. Children learn dance and song at an early age and are expected to perform during certain ceremonies. Some dances are gender-based – men and women will perform separately as they tell a story that is significant to each group.

Sacred dances and songs are performed in seclusion during special rituals. These dances include the initiation ceremonies of young boys and girls, and fertility rituals for women and for the earth, to increase the foods available for gathering by some tribes.

An initiation ceremony is also a time of great communal celebration, of singing, dancing and music. Dancing is also a part of death rituals.

Regional Styles

Dancing styles vary across regions and tribes. Most dances are accompanied by singing, percussion instruments such as clapsticks and boomerangs, or the clapping of hands and thighs. The *yidaki* (didjeridu) provides music to the fast moving 'shake-a-leg' dance of Cape York Peninsula and the rhythmical stomp of Arnhem Land.

In the Torres Strait the energising militaristic style is categorised into three forms: social dances, ceremonial dances and war

Leonora Adidi

Leonora comes from Bamaga in Cape York, in far north Queensland and she belongs to the Sui-Baidham Clan of Saibai Island, Torres Strait.

She works as a freelance cultural performing artist and teacher and is co-director of Bibir Torres Strait Islander Dance Troupe. Leonora has performed across the country, including at the Laura Aboriginal Cultural Festival, the Sydney Opera House and as performing artist-in-residence at the Art Gallery of New South Wales. Her performance skills include traditional dance, singing, drumming and costume design.

She is also currently involved in scriptwriting and Web design and is actively involved in the Indigenous community.

dances. There is a strong Polynesian influence in Islander dance, music and song.

Unfortunately, in NSW, Victoria and Tasmania many of the dance practices, along with languages and songs, were lost during colonisation.

Contemporary Dance

Contemporary Aboriginal and Torres Strait Islander dance combines traditional and Western dance styles. It draws on traditional and contemporary themes in movement, stories, costume and body art, and fuses music and song.

This unique and mesmerising blend of dance is expertly performed by Bangarra Dance Theatre (☎ 02-9251 5333), the country's premier Indigenous dance company, based at The Wharf, Pier 4–5, Hickson Rd, Walsh Bay, Sydney. Credited with international and Olympic performances, Bangarra has collaborated with the Australian Ballet in *Rites*, an acclaimed work blending two different cultural expressions in movement. Its Web site is at www.bangarra.com.au. Contact them for details of their highly recommended performances.

The award-winning Tjapukai Aboriginal Cultural Park (☎ 07-4042 9900) on Kamerunga Rd, Smithfield (a 15-minute drive north of Cairns) showcases the highly entertaining and informative traditional dance and culture of the Tjapukai people of north Queensland. Its Web site is at www.tjapukai.com.au.

The successful establishment of the National Aboriginal and Islander Skills Development Association (NAISDA; ☎ 02 9252 0199) College of Dance in Sydney has led to the formation of companies like Bangarra and many small troupes specialising in both traditional and contemporary styles. NAISDA give performances during November and December in the Sydney area. You can drop into their office at 3 Cumberland St, The Rocks, or visit their Web site at www.naisda.com.au.

The future of Aboriginal and Torres Strait Islander dance is assured by the increasing demand – from both participants and audiences – for an entertaining and educational tool for Indigenous and non-Indigenous people in Australia and abroad.

See also the Music section. For details on festivals featuring dance, see the Special Events section.

Body Art

Leonora Adidi

Body art is an important form of creative expression, often combined with dance. Within the tribes, each clan has its own dance, and body paintings depicting the story of its ancestral totems. For instance, the Gunwinggu men of west Arnhem Land use a design of intricately patterned crisscross lines on their torsos, given to them by their giant ancestor Luma Luma. The decaying body of Birrkilli, the sacred whale of the Girrkirr clan, gave them the colours and diamond patterns used in their rituals.

Music

Bunna Lawrie

Song and dance have always been in the culture of Aboriginal Australia and the Torres Strait Islands. The basic instruments of Aboriginal culture in historical times included hitting the ground with hunting sticks, clapping boomerangs together or using hands or the stomping of feet to keep the beat or time.

Many coastal and inland tribes have different musical instruments because of the different natural resources in their tribal areas. All tribes have selected woods, shells, stones and natural ochres (earth paints) that are used to decorate the body and musical instruments.

Many tribes travel great distances to ceremonies or special *corroborees* where tribes come together on neutral ground to gather these special resources and to trade or barter with other tribes.

Traditional Aboriginal Music

Clapsticks Today Aboriginal tribes still use percussion with different shaped clapsticks or message sticks, which are hit together to make different pitches – whether high or low – just like music notes.

Clapsticks are usually made of hardwood

Didjeridu The didjeridu is created from a tree or tree trunk that has been eaten out by white ants or termites, leaving the tree hollow inside. It is cut down to about a metre or more in length and then carved and shaped so it fits into the palm of your hand. When the didj is blown it creates a rhythmic droning sound; expert players can make bird and animal sounds as well.

The didjeridu comes from the top end of the Northern Territory and its Yolngu name is yidaki. Today it has become a recognised Aboriginal instrument throughout Australia. It has been used in different traditional song and dance ceremonies (tribal group dancing) from the beginning of time and is now being incorporated into contemporary music by Aboriginal artists to express their origin and identity in modern Indigenous music.

Didjeridus have a wax mouth-piece
to give a good lip grip

Bunna Lawrie

My name is Bunna Lawrie, lead singer of Coloured Stone, the longest surviving Indigenous band in Australia, and I have 22 years' experience in the music business. Unfortunately, I have only managed to scrape the surface of the Indigenous music industry, which is very strong in Australia. My latest CD albums *Best of Coloured Stone Volume One* and *Rhythm of Nature*, and my CD single 'Australia' are all available through the Central Australian Aboriginal Media Association on the Internet.

Australia has up to 150 professional recording artists and many artists working in the fields of traditional dance and dance theatre, with many professional dancers and producers creating their own shows. All these artists are thriving in Indigenous Australia, but we are all just competing and surviving in the mainstream Australian music industry. I was once introduced on a television show by a well-known personality who said, 'It's hard enough being in a band but it's much harder if you're in a band and you're Aboriginal, trying to break into the music industry in Australia'.

I have received many awards in the course of my career. Most recently, in 1999 I was awarded the Deadly Sounds National Aboriginal & Torres Strait Islander Music Award for the most outstanding contribution to Aboriginal Music in Australia. In 2000 I received the Australia Council's Don Banks Music Fund Award for 2000, the first time this award has gone to a rock musician.

Gong Stones In the Great Australian Bight my tribe, Yirkala Mirning (a coastal tribe from the Nullarbor Plain at the bottom of Australia), uses *gong stones* – musical stones that are from the caves and cliff faces of the area.

The gong stones come in all shapes and sizes. Different pitches of sound are made by hitting the gong stones with smaller stones. This creates a means of communication to call the southern right and sperm whales into the Great Australian Bight. The gong stones are used in certain song and dance ceremonies between the Yirkala Mirning and the whales.

The language version of my song, 'Mouydjengara Whale Dance Song', is on my album *Rhythm of Nature* by Coloured Stone, and you can hear the gong stones throughout the song. All Indigenous artists like to incorporate the different instruments, such as didjeridu, clapsticks, animal sounds and especially Aboriginal language to give us our own identity and grassroots sounds.

Traditional Torres Strait Music

Like other people from the different tribes around Australia, including the Torres Strait, I cannot speak about another tribe's business. We all have our own stories and songs. Being a non-Islander, I can only speak about the Torres Strait in certain basic terms, and go by what is common knowledge.

Just as the Aboriginal cultures are different in many cultural ways, the many islands in the Torres Strait have their own special stories with songs and dances for their islands. But what they all have in common throughout the Torres Strait is the beautiful harmonies of the men and women singing in English or traditional languages.

On 1 July the Coming of the Light Festival is celebrated when missionaries brought Christianity to the Islanders.

Island Drum The Torres Strait island drum has a deep sound and is held in one hand while the palm of the other hand is used to create a rhythmic pounding sound with a hypnotic echoing.

The drum is made from a special tree and is hollow. It is decorated with carvings from the particular island or painted with their stories. The top of the drum has animal skin stretched over the top to give it the deep echoing sound of the natural wood.

Kulups are a special kind of island rattle

Island drums can be very simple or elaborately decorated with island designs

Kulup The kulup is a hand-shaker made up of black seeds and is tied together with special twine from the islands to make a sound of shells being shaken.

Contemporary Music

Modern Australian Indigenous music is the music that has developed over the years by artists and bands from the communities, towns and cities. We have created our own unique style with traditional instruments included in the modern band of today. All the political concerns of the Aboriginal and Torres Strait Islander peoples – whether it's land, health, education, the Stolen Generations or Reconciliation issues – can be heard in the songs. These are the messages that artists are trying to get across to the rest of the Australian community and the world. The messages in our music will help to heal and overcome the problems within our own Aboriginal and Torres Strait Islander communities, as well as in the wider community.

The Australian music industry has labelled Australian Indigenous music 'Aboriginal music', lumping contemporary and traditional styles together into one category in the music shops around the country. They always scrutinise the product to see how political it is for the Australian mainstream public. For example, to purchase a CD by my band, you have to know my record company name and the distribution company handling the orders for the record shops, and then hope that the store you're in is aware of how to access information on that record company. As an artist I would like to walk into a store and find my CDs in alphabetical order along with the other artists.

So if you find that you are having a hard time finding a CD of an Aboriginal or Torres Strait Islander artist, don't give up, but get yourself on the Internet and access the Web site (www.caama.com.au/music/music.cfm) of Australia's only Indigenous record company, the Central Australian Aboriginal Media Association (CAAMA) in Alice Springs, or email the CAAMA Music Shop (**e** c.shop@caama.com), where you will be able to buy directly.

LISTEN UP
Monique Choy

Contemporary Indigenous music is thriving across the country. Indigenous artists are creating sounds as varied as hip hop, metal, country, reggae and spoken word, much of it with a strong political message.

Yolngu band Yothu Yindi's 'Treaty' (1991) became an international success, calling for a 'Treaty Now!' between black and white Australia – a call that remains unanswered. Gunditjmara artist Archie Roach's moving song 'Took the Children Away' (from his 1990 album *Charcoal Lane*) highlighted the issue of the Stolen Generations.

Performers like Yothu Yindi and Saibai Islander Christine Anu have made international names in mainstream music, but contemporary Indigenous music is as diverse as its performers.

Bands like Coloured Stone and the Warumpi Band have been drawing loyal crowds on the Australian pub circuit for many years (as well as winning prestigious music awards), as have folk-rock musicians like Ngarrindjeri artist Ruby Hunter, Murri singer/storyteller Kev Carmody and Frank Yamma (whose lyrics are often in his home language of Pitjantjatjara).

Country music legend Jimmy Little was the first Aboriginal performer to achieve mainstream success in the 1960s, and in 2000 Troy Cassar-Daley won the Australian Record Industry Association (ARIA) award for Country Album of the Year with *Big River*.

The all-girl band Tiddas (which means 'Sisters') earned a reputation for beautiful harmonies before they split up in May 2000. The Sydney-based Stiff Gins and Leah Purcell have also made names as female singer/songwriters.

The Indigenous music scene keeps evolving – lately Arrernte band NoKTuRNL have introduced Australia to their brand of political rap-metal, and in August 2000 Yothu Yindi launched their new sound in alternative dance music with their latest album *Garma*.

Each year the Deadly Sounds Aboriginal and Torres Strait Islander Music Awards ('the Deadlys') recognise excellence in black Australian music. Check out its Web site at www.vibe.com.au/deadlys.htm. For Indigenous gig listings, look for the monthly *Deadly Vibes* magazine, available from many Indigenous organisations.

See also Yothu Yindi lead singer Mandawuy Yunupingu's boxed text 'Maintaining Culture'.

CAAMA also has a recording studio and a radio station with a footprint (broadcast area) stretching throughout the Top End and middle part of Australia.

For information on Indigenous radio stations, see the Radio & TV section.

Literature
Philip Morrissey

One of the easiest and most pleasant ways to learn about Australia's Indigenous cultures is to read some of the literature produced by Aborigines and Torres Strait Islanders. The book may now be an old-fashioned technology, but it's still a durable and rewarding companion on the road and one of the best ways of preparing yourself for travelling.

Most of the big issues in Indigenous Australia are covered in Indigenous writing. A good introduction is James Miller's *Koori: A Will to Win*. It's a history of European settlement in Australia from a Koori perspective and it combines personal insights with historical analysis. Philip McLaren, another writer who is based in Sydney, has produced politicised but absorbing crime fiction. Through the genre of crime fiction, McLaren covers many of the aspects of contemporary Aboriginal life. One of his books, *Scream Black Murder*, is set mainly in Sydney, although it also takes you to Aboriginal communities in north Queensland and the central coast of New South Wales.

Ruby Langford's *Don't Take Your Love to Town* covers many things – the struggle of an Aboriginal woman trying to raise a large family by herself and the drift of rural Aborigines to the cities. It also deals with the impact of urban life on young Aborigines, police harassment, the continuing importance of Aboriginal spirituality for city Aborigines; the list goes on... Be prepared to make notes as you read – this is a dramatic life, set in many locations with lots of characters.

Crossing the border into Queensland, you may want to read Rita and Jackie Huggins' *Auntie Rita*. Jackie is Rita's daughter and complements her mother's narrative with her own story. *Aunty Rita* is much more than a story of an individual life. It tells how Aborigines were rounded up and moved on to missions and government reserves and gives a rich account of Aboriginal lives in post-war Queensland. Other life narratives worth looking at include Ida West's *Pride against Prejudice* and Ellie Gaffney's *Somebody Now*.

The University of Queensland Press (UQP) has been a leader in publishing Indigenous writing. Aboriginal writers who've been published by UQP include Bill Rosser and Herb Wharton. Rosser has written on Palm Island in his book *This Is Palm Island*. His other books include the award-winning *Dreamtime Nightmares* and *Up Rode the Troopers: The Black Police in Queensland*. In books like *Cattle Camp* and *Unbranded*, Wharton tells stories of life in the tough cattle country of western Queensland.

Two especially significant books published under the UQP label are *Paperbark* and *The Honey-Ant Men's Love Song*. Edited by Jack Davis, Adam Shoemaker, Mudrooroo and Stephen Muecke, *Paperbark* is an anthology of Aboriginal writing going back to 19th century. It includes a petition from the Kaurna people of South Australia to Governor Gawler, a traditional story dealing with the Myall Creek massacre and contemporary writing by Aborigines. Bob Dixon and Martin Duwell have edited a superb collection of Aboriginal song-poems in *The Honey-Ant Men's Love Song*. As well as being great literature, these song-poems provide the reader with insights into often unsuspected dimensions of Aboriginal traditional life.

Black Hours is the story of Wayne King, an Aboriginal man growing up gay in Ipswich – at one time the headquarters of Pauline Hanson's One Nation Party, whose race-based policies have tended to polarise communities. King escapes and makes an exciting life for himself as he travels overseas, but when he comes home he finds he has unfinished business – many others besides himself have been scarred by Australian racism. Sam Watson's *The Kadaitcha Sung* is one of those books best described as 'gripping'. Combining science fiction, crime fiction, fantasy, social analysis and historical references, it's not a book for the faint-hearted but has enjoyed something approaching 'cult status' among Australian readers.

Gagadju Elder Bill Neidjie's book *Story about Feeling* has been described as narrative philosophy and provides an Aboriginal perspective on stars, trees, rocks, animals and people. It's a message about connectedness for all people, including city folk. In *Gularabalu*, Paddy Roe, a Broome Elder, tells stories which illustrate the power of the Aboriginal *clever man* – sometimes in relation to settlers and their law, sometimes in relation to law breakers in the Aboriginal community. Both books use Kriol – a poetic language which draws on both traditional Aboriginal languages and English. It may seem a little difficult to understand at first but it's worth persevering. If you get the chance to hear anyone speaking Kriol, you'll be able to re-create the sounds in your head as you read.

In terms of 'classics', the poetry of Oodgeroo Noonuccal (Kath Walker), written in the early 60s, still makes great reading – outliving the unfortunate critic who argued that she was not a 'real poet'. You may not be able to find copies of *We Are Going* and *The Dawn Is at Hand* but Kevin Gilbert's *Inside Black Australia* has remained in print. It's long been one of Australia's most popular anthologies of Aboriginal poetry. In particular look for poems by Mary Duroux, Rex Marshall and Frank Doolan from NSW, Eva Johnson from SA and Jim Everett from Tasmania.

One of the success stories of Aboriginal publishing is Magabala Books. It's based in

Broome, WA, and achieved early success with *Wandering Girl* by Glenyse Ward. It's continued to publish strong works such as Magdalene Williams' *Ngay Janijirr Ngank – This Is My Word*. It's a senior woman's testimony with its own charm. It makes use of bilingualism and weaves the narrator's Christian spirituality with traditional Aboriginal spirituality and history.

Jinangga, the autobiography of Monty Walgar, is in most respects quite a different story. Walgar tells of his love affair with alcohol – but he's no victim. He liked to work, and work hard, and speaks with pride of the various jobs he has done. But he also liked to drink and when drunk liked to fight. In fact he started his street-fighting career at the same time as his drinking career. Monty has since reformed and given up his fighting and drinking. What's unexpected is that the author always comes across as a decent and ethical person in spite of his wild excesses.

Sally Morgan's *My Place* is one of the most popular books ever written by an Aborigine – it's been translated into numerous languages and sold thousands of copies. It's the story of Morgan's mother and grandmother, who try to pass Sally and her brother and sisters off as 'Indian' – anything but Aboriginal – in an attempt to evade the government policy of removing 'part-Aboriginal' children from their families and institutionalising them. As such it anticipated the inquiry and report on the Stolen Generations by over a decade. Morgan sets out to uncover and reclaim her repressed identity as an Aborigine.

Two other authors are essential reading. Jack Davis and Kim Scott are probably Australia's finest Aboriginal writers. Any reading of one of Davis' plays (such as *No Sugar* or *In Our Town*) is amply rewarded and if you ever have the chance to see his work performed, don't miss it. Scott shared the prestigious Miles Franklin award for *Benang* in 2000 and this, along with his earlier novel *True Country*, are books which are fundamental to Australia's self-understanding. They're complex but you'll find them dense with feeling and intelligence if you persevere.

See also 'Cultural Tourism – Can It Help Create Paradise on Earth?' by Herb Wharton.

Film & Cinema – Camera Obscura

Wal Saunders

Australia has amassed an enormous hoard of images of colonialism since the European invasion just over 200 years ago. For Indigenous Australians, this colonialism persists, and images of them are still largely manufactured by the dominant invasive culture.

Early Ethnographic Film

Australia's introduction to cinema came with the projection of films in Sydney in late 1894. The first film about Aboriginal and Torres Strait Islander Australians was made on Mer (Murray Island), off the Queensland coast, by a visiting British academic, AC Haddon, in 1898. Haddon's film was the first use of the motion picture camera as an aid to ethnographical field work (ethnography is a branch of anthropology concerned with the scientific description of a human society). Thus began a tradition of film-making that has lasted almost as long as cinema itself – and the cameras have been rolling ever since!

Vast ethnographical projects based on photographic records were undertaken from the 1920s onwards, reflecting the containment of Indigenous Australians on remote reserves. As the government increased its involvement with the administration of these peoples, its partnership with ethnography was secured and the discipline was often, albeit occasionally reluctantly, the handmaiden of colonialism.

These projects were most often concerned with establishing a racial typology (study to determine the nature of types) of the continent. This typology often reflected the scientific concerns of its day and influenced the decisions of government, as well as contributing to the construction of the popular racial stereotypes that are still so prevalent today. Examples include the noble savage staring wistfully into the distance; the fringe-dwelling victim of society; the shiftless drunk; and, more recently, the happy working 'aborigine', proving that 'they can do it if only they try'.

Documentary Film

The second great colonial expansion coincided with the spread of cameras and the development of the documentary form, which attempted to provide an 'objective' and 'factual' representation of the truth.

By the 1850s the camera was ubiquitous, and by 1895 the Pocket Kodak had been introduced to Australia, placing photography within reach of all. Meanwhile, the frontier was moving relentlessly inland as the rush for gold and pastoral land dispossessed the Indigenous landowners.

The mere name of Grierson's Empire Film Unit suggests the close link between documentary and colonialism (John Grierson coined the term 'documentary'). From that time onwards this genre became intertwined with colonialist and primitivist discourses. The symbiosis spread throughout the Commonwealth, prevailing in India, Canada and Australia. In Africa, films from those of Jean Rouch to some of those made by today's Granada and National Geographic teams show the 'disappearing world' of the colonised 'other', rather than the emergent worlds that in fact exist, having grown in response to colonialism and post-colonialism.

Feature Film

In Australia the fiction or feature film industry has only ever been peripherally interested in Indigenous people. Gaston Merlies visited Australia and used them as exotic subjects in such titles as *The Black Trackers*, *Captured by Aboriginals* and *Cast amid Boomerang Throwers* (all released in 1913). From this period on, Indigenous Australians were generally cast as the 'Indians' in Outback westerns. If a role called for a more central character, this was usually played by a white actor in 'blackface' make-up. A notable exception was Australia's first colour feature film, Charles Chauvel's *Jedda*, which cast Aboriginal actors in leading roles. However, on all other levels, the Outback western remained a standard piece of exotic melodrama with Aboriginal characters trapped by their supposedly savage and primitive nature.

This situation has changed little in recent times. The 'quintessential Aborigine' is often played by the same actor. For example, the same actor appeared in Nicholas Roeg's *Walkabout* (1971) and Peter Weir's *The Last Wave* (1977), while Ernie Dingo has appeared in many television programmes, as well as in *Crocodile Dundee* (1985).

Wal Saunders

Wal Saunders is from the Kilcarer/Gilger clan of the Gunditj-mara tribe. His traditional country is the south-western district of Victoria on Australia's mainland.

Wal has been involved in the film and television industry since early 1980, when he worked in the film archive of the Australian Institute of Aboriginal and Torres Strait Islander Studies (AIATSIS). Since then his involvement has increased to a level that has seen him direct, write and produce for a television series (SBS TV's *First in Line*, 1988) and co-write for a 1995 episode of the Australian television drama *Blue Heelers* (episode 69, 'The Collector').

Wal was the inaugural director of the Indigenous Branch of the Australian Film Commission in 1993, where he created five Indigenous initiatives for film and television (From Sand to Celluloid, NIDF 1 & 2, Shifting Sands and Crossing Tracks).

In 1999 Wal was awarded a Fellowship from the Australia Council, which he is using to write for film and television. He is currently working on a feature film that is planned to be filmed in his home town of Portland in late 2001.

Wal is a keen raconteur who loves sports of all sorts, especially fishing.

These films do little to present a real understanding of Aborigines or their cultures. Some of the larger and more commercially oriented productions have taken this distortion to new heights. For example, *Quigley Down Under* (1989) used blackened, life-size, cardboard cut-outs to represent Indigenous people in the distance. In *Crocodile Dundee*, Mick (Paul Hogan) used an Indigenous men's initiation tool, a *bullroarer*, as a long-distance communication device. In some Indigenous cultures the bullroarer should only be used by initiated men, and under no circumstances are women allowed to hear its sound. One feature film which did present a more realistic picture was *Wrong Side of the Road* (1981). Here Ned Lander directed a group of musicians who played themselves, and this virtually unscripted film presents a most evocative portrayal of the life of young urban Aborigines.

Indigenous Film-Makers

Today, Indigenous people have shown clearly that they wish to control their own representations in all forms of media, but particularly in film. As individuals or as community groups, Indigenous people now produce paintings, photographs, films, video, radio, television, theatre, popular music, newspapers and magazines about themselves and their cultures. At the same time, they have developed a critique of mainstream media representations, calling for change.

Cinema Organisations Since the early 1980s a number of Aboriginal community organisations have been formed. These are regionally based, such as the Central Australian Aboriginal Media Association and the Townsville Aboriginal and Islander Media Association; or located in individual communities, such as the Warlpiri Media Association at Yuendumu or the Pitjantjatjara/Yankunytjatjara Media Association at Ernabella. Other Indigenous-owned, independent production houses have also emerged. Together, these represent a concerted effort by Indigenous people in their quest for self-representation.

Government Support The call for change has been heard by federal screen-culture institutions and government broadcasters. In 1993, the Australian Film Commission (AFC) established an Indigenous Branch, whose primary responsibility was to improve the rate of Indigenous participation in all

COURTESY OF THE AUSTRALIAN FILM INSTITUTE

David Ngoombujarra as Shane Francis in Richard Frankland's film *No Way to Forget*, exploring the life of an investigator on the 1991 Royal Commission into Aboriginal Deaths in Custody

areas of the film industry. Another function of the branch was to implement a national employment strategy covering three other federal film institutions: the Australian Film Finance Corporation; the Australian Film, Television and Radio School; and Film Australia. The only federal film agency that failed to heed this call was the National Film and Sound Archive (currently known as ScreenSound Australia).

While implementing the national employment strategy across the participating federal agencies, the Indigenous Branch also created a series of initiatives that led to the development, production and broadcast of what are arguably the most successful series of short fiction films in Australia's history. Between 1993 and 1999, the Indigenous Branch created an atmosphere in each state and federal government agency and the two government broadcasters – the Special Broadcasting Service (SBS) and the Australian Broadcasting Corporation (ABC) – in which Indigenous film-makers

were creatively free. They were provided with access to the 'wealth' and the 'power' to be free from the broadcast imperatives that plague current filmic representations of Indigenous people. Each of the fictional dramas had a theatrical release in two capital cities and premier release on SBS and ABC. Under these circumstances, new Indigenous film-makers produced a total of 35 films: one feature film, 18 documentaries and 16 short dramas. The initiatives – From Sand to Celluloid, Shifting Sands and Native Titles (broadcast as 'Crossing Tracks') – launched the cinematic careers of a plethora of new Indigenous Australian visual storytellers and enabled partnerships to form between black and white film-makers.

Recent Films The films themselves are as evocative as they are eclectic. Ivan Senn made two wonderful films under the Indigenous Branch initiatives, *Tears* and *Wind*. As with all his films, these two have

COURTESY OF THE AUSTRALIAN FILM INSTITUTE

Rima Tamou's *Saturday Night/Sunday Morning* won Best Original Concept at the 2000 Tudawali Awards, an Indigenous screen award named after Robert Tudawali, who played the lead role of Marbuck in 1954's *Jedda*. Foreground: Alyssa McClelland; left–right: Luke Carroll, Sam O'Dell, Jie Pittman.

a cinematic quality and style that belies their length. *Wind* (1999) deals with post-colonial contact in the late 1880s through the eyes of a young black tracker who is torn between his sense of duty and his culture. *Tears* (1998) shows the ironic choice that mission life offers young Indigenous people in rural NSW.

Another successful film-maker who used the AFC initiatives to great success is Richard Frankland. *No Way to Forget* (1996) and *Harry's War* (1999) deal with war – the inequality felt by Indigenous army personnel who enlisted for WWII in *Harry's War*, and the combat zone that is the life of an Indigenous investigator on the Royal Commission into Aboriginal Deaths in Custody in *No Way to Forget*. In these films, Frankland uses David Ngoombujarra to portray Harry Saunders in *Harry's War* and Shane Francis in *No Way to Forget*.

Another new talent unearthed by these initiatives is Rima Tamou (*Round Up*, 1996, and *Saturday Night, Sunday Morning*, 1999). Tamou's *Round Up* is a poignant exploration of the relationship between two hard-headed 'cowboys' who, after having a brawl, find themselves thrown together in a big city hospital. It is full of humour and sad moments as they begin to realise that they are not so different after all.

Sally Riley takes a different look at the life of an Indigenous Australian. In her first film, *Fly Peewee Fly* (1995), she analyses family life through the eyes of a young Koorie boy called Robbie who lives with his father and grandmother in the country. After a series of minor crises, which end with the death of his friend the Peewee bird, he decides he will stay up in his favourite tree. This proves to be a challenge for Nan and Dad who are forced to see the world from Robbie's point of view. In *Confessions of a Headhunter* (1999) Riley explores the world of two modern-day headhunters who are on an Australia-wide rampage, taking trophies in every state and continually eluding the authorities. They don't collect just any head – they need famous heads!

Unfortunately, there has been only one feature film made during this same dynamic period of Indigenous film-making. *Radiance* (1998), by Rachel Perkins, deals with the relationship between three sisters who meet again when they come together on the death of their mother. The oldest sister is a successful opera singer based in London, the youngest lives a carefree life on the streets of Sydney, while the remaining sister is the one who stayed home and looked after their mother. Deborah Mailman's wonderful performance as the youngest sister steals the show.

These are just a few of the new and exciting Indigenous film-makers who are quietly practising their craft. Their films and those of others are available through the National Film Lending Collection, accessed through local municipal libraries, the Australian Film Institute (in Melbourne ☎ 03-9696 1844, Web site: www.afi.org.au) and RONIN Films (in Canberra ☎ 02-6248 0851).

Theatre

Romaine Moreton

Indigenous theatre emerged from the vigorous politics of Indigenous existence during the 1970s. Redfern's Black Theatre was born during the same period as the Aboriginal Medical Service and the Aboriginal Housing Group, organisations that were developed to cater specifically to the needs of Indigenous Australians.

The Black Theatre was the first of its kind, and was the vision of a few individuals who saw the necessity of developing theatre tailored to the needs of Indigenous society. At the time, the originators felt that there were no literature or theatre productions to which Indigenous people could relate within a cultural and community context. One of the first plays staged by the Black Theatre was *Here Comes the Nigger*, written by Gerry Bostock.

The theatre developed a policy that had a resounding influence on all Indigenous stage and film productions that were to follow. Aboriginal actors played Aboriginal parts, and at no time was an actor's appearance 'blackened' by the application of make-up. The result of this artistic policy can be seen in contemporary theatre productions, as well as in film. It is now the protocol to use Indigenous actors for Indigenous parts in any Indigenous production, be it theatre or film.

Street Theatre

The works developed by Black Theatre were inspired directly by the politics of the day. The plays were devised as a response to the social and political climate. Bostock claims that the real theatre took place in the streets. This 'street theatre' began with the artfully political positioning of the actual theatre building. Middle-class white folk were confronted with the task of accessing the theatre through the mostly black neighbourhood of Redfern before entering the site itself.

With the location of the physical building informing the audience before a Black Theatre production, it is interesting to compare contemporary Indigenous theatre and its concerns.

Contemporary Theatre

Black theatre today looks at the issues that define Indigenous existence within this country. Deborah Cheetam's *White Baptist ABBA Fan* discusses the author's experience of being adopted by a white family, growing up without her spiritual, emotional and intellectual existence being informed by Aboriginal culture and identity. *Box the Pony*, a one-woman show that toured Britain, is an autobiographical tale of an Aboriginal woman trapped and frustrated by her life in a small and limited town who decides, after considering suicide, to head for the city.

The Sunshine Club, written by Wesley Enoch, discusses the duplicity of nationalism that is experienced by Aborigines who fought for Australia during WWII. When they returned from the war, they found themselves occupying the margins of a racially segregated country. *Stolen*, a stage play recently directed by Enoch, is an Indigenous play dealing with the Stolen Generations. This production assumes the audience has some background information on the theme of Aboriginal children being forcibly removed from their families to promote assimilation and the White Australia policy (a government policy operating from the 1850s to the early 1970s that attempted to exclude or severely limit the rights of non-white races).

All contemporary productions deal with issues intrinsic to past and contemporary Indigenous existence, offering different

Romaine Moreton

Romaine is a freelance writer and performance artist belonging to the nations of Bundjalung and Goernpil of Northern NSW and Stradbroke Island. She has an MA in Scriptwriting, which she completed at the Australian Film Television and Radio School in 1997.

Romaine's main interests are Indigenous social and cultural issues, writing and performance. She participated in the 1997 Festival of the Dreaming as a performance poet and writer and has since continued with both the performing and written aspects of her craft.

Romaine's script *Redreaming The Dark* was produced by Charlotte Seymour and included in the Australian package presented in the 1999 Cannes and New York Film Festivals. It explores notions of blackness and how language perpetrates symbolic racism with its usage. Another of Romaine's scripts *Cherish* tells the story of a man trying to get on with his life after losing a friend to AIDS. It was directed by Stephen Jones and was shown at the 1998 Cannes Film Festival.

perspectives on experiences such as being stolen and placed in government institutions or white foster homes, or living with the morbid and mortal effects of racism. They explore the consequences of the various policies that have been implemented during the history of Australia – policies that have manufactured a myriad of Indigenous experiences – while paying homage to the strength of Indigenous cultures and their survival.

With the majority of contemporary productions with Indigenous story lines being staged in mainstream venues such as the Sydney Opera House, the 'street theatre' that informed the early Black Theatre productions of the '70s is now rarely available to today's audiences.

See also the Film & Cinema – Camera Obscura and Literature sections.

edited by B R E N D A L C R O F T

visual ART

Visual imagery is a fundamental part of Indigenous life, a connection between past and present, between the supernatural and the earthly, between people and the land. The early forms of Indigenous artistic expression were rock carvings (petroglyphs), body painting and ground designs, and the earliest engraved designs known to exist date back at least 30,000 years.

While it has always been an integral part of Indigenous culture, Indigenous art, with some notable exceptions, was either largely ignored by non-Indigenous people or simply seen as an anthropological curiosity. Then, in 1971 an event took place that changed non-Indigenous perceptions of Indigenous art. At **Papunya**, north-west of Alice Springs, a group of senior men from the community, led by Kaapa Mbitjana Tjampitjinpa (from the Anmatyerre/Arrernte people; 1925–89), along with Long Jack Phillipus Tjakamarra (Pintupi/Luritja/Warlpiri) and Billy Stockman Tjapaltjarri (Anmatyerre), all Elders of the community and employed as groundsmen at the Papunya school, were encouraged to paint a mural on one of the school's external

Rock engraving near Rock Holes Loop Walk, Mutawintji National Park, NSW

ROSS BARNETT

walls. Shortly after work commenced, other members of the community became enthused by the project and joined in creating the mural named *Honey Ant Dreaming*. Government regulations later saw the mural destroyed, but its effect on the community was still profound. Images of spiritual significance had taken on a permanent and very public form. Notwithstanding the debate the mural caused at Pupunya, other members of the community expressed a desire to paint. Initially the paintings were executed on smallish boards, but within a short time canvases were used.

From this quiet beginning in a remote Aboriginal community one of the most important art movements of the late 20th century grew and spread. That it developed in Papunya is not without irony. Papunya was established in 1960 under the auspices of the Australian government's cultural assimilation policy – a policy designed in combination with others, such as the forced removal of Indigenous children from their families, to undermine Indigenous culture. *Honey Ant Dreaming* and the creative and cultural energy this painting unleashed helped to strengthen Indigenous culture and contributed to the abandonment of assimilation as the foundation stone of non-Indigenous social policy.

Right and title page: George Wallaby working on a painting that represents his country, Barragoo (Lake Gregory)

While paintings from the Aboriginal communities in central Australia are among the more readily identifiable, and probably most popular, forms of modern Indigenous art, there's a huge range of material being produced across the country. The long list includes bark paintings from Arnhem Land in the Northern Territory, ironwood carvings and silkscreen printing from the Tiwi

JASON DAVIDSON

Islands north of Darwin, batik and wood carvings from central Australia, *didjeridus/yidakis*, film, video and digital media.

Of particular importance is the strength of artistic expression emanating from Indigenous artists living in the cities and rural townships of southern Australia whose ancestors felt the full brunt of colonial occupation. The level of brutality the Indigenous peoples of southern Australia endured through the 19th and well into the 20th century is difficult for non-Indigenous Australians to imagine, to the point that some in government refuse to utter the word 'sorry'.

While the art of the more traditional communities differs in style from urban works, a common theme that appears to run through all the works, be it a painting by Rover Thomas (Wangkajungka/Kukatja; 1926–98) or Trevor Nickolls, is the strong and ancient connection Indigenous people have with the land, mixed with a deep sense of loss occasioned by the horror of the last 200-plus years. Ultimately, however, the viewer is left with a sense of Indigenous cultural strength and renewal.

ART IS CULTURE

Dr Irene Watson

Many Indigenous people have experienced a history of colonisation which resulted in our removal from traditional lands and the separation from our families. However, it is our Indigenous art forms that link us in our commonality of ancestral connections, history and experiences as survivors. Whether the artist lives in a remote location or in the city; whether they are a painter, dancer, or singer – the themes of our artists are the same: connection to the land, and the feelings of Indigeneity and identity. Observing Indigenous art, the viewer gets a strong sense of what is Indigenous, whatever the sources or origins of the artist.

While Indigenous art is often labelled either contemporary or traditional, it is nevertheless Indigenous in its form and essence, by virtue of the artist(s)' heritage. Any work that is created today is contemporary, regardless of its medium or content. From an Indigenous perspective art is an integral part of our culture, for it is not seen as being separate. The commercialisation of Indigenous art has brought to us another way of viewing art. However, from an Indigenous perspective, art is culture, it is law, it is Dreaming, it is the land, and it is also who we are. It is part of the whole circle of Indigenous being.

Some of the traditional forms Indigenous art takes are in rock art, ceremonial body paintings, ground designs, rock engravings, and wood-burnt design. Many of these arts are still practised, being regenerated and reshaped into newer forms. It is through art that Indigenous people have found a way of voicing identity and the renewal of Indigenous culture and the spirituality of the Dreaming.

ROCK ART

Arnhem Land & Kakadu

Arnhem Land, in Australia's tropical Top End, is an area of rich artistic heritage. Recent finds suggest that rock paintings were being produced as early as 60,000 years ago, and some of the rock art galleries in the huge sandstone Arnhem Land plateau are at least 18,000 years old.

The rock art of Arnhem Land depicts Dreaming *stories* literally, with easily recognisable (though often stylised) images of ancestors, animals and Macassans – Indonesian mariners from Sulawesi who regularly visited the north coast until their visits were banned by government regulations in 1906.

The paintings contained in the Arnhem Land rock art sites range from hand-prints to paintings of animals, people, mythological beings and European ships, constituting one of the world's most important and fascinating rock art collections. They provide a record of changing environments and lifestyles over the millennia.

The Lightning Brothers of Wardaman Country, near Katherine (NT), pictured here with Bill Harney, a Wardaman Elder who runs Jankangyina Tours

In some places they are concentrated in large galleries, with paintings from more recent eras sometimes superimposed over older paintings. Some sites are kept secret – not only to protect them from damage, but also because they are private or sacred to the Aboriginal owners. Some are believed to be inhabited by malevolent beings, who must not be approached by those who are ignorant of the Indigenous customs of the region. However, two of the finest sites have been opened up to visitors, with access roads, walkways and explanatory signs. These are **Ubirr** and **Nourlangie** in Kakadu National Park.

The rock paintings show how the main styles succeeded each other over time. The earliest hand- or grass-prints were followed by a 'naturalistic' style, with large outlines of people or animals filled in with colour. Some of the animals depicted, such as the thylacine (Tasmanian tiger), have long been extinct on mainland Australia.

HUGH FINLAY

X-ray art examines the internal structure of its subject – this fish is in Kakadu National Park

After the naturalistic style came the 'dynamic', in which motion was often depicted (a dotted line, for example, to show a spear's path through the air). In this era the first mythological beings appeared, with human bodies and animal heads.

The next style mainly showed simple human silhouettes, and was followed by the curious 'yam figures', in which people and animals were drawn in the shape of yams (or yams in the shape of people and animals!). Other painting styles, including the 'x-ray' style, which displays the internal organs and bone structure of animals, also appeared around this time.

By about 1000 years ago many of the salt marshes had turned into freshwater swamps and *billabongs*. The birds and plants that provided new food sources in this landscape appeared in the art of this time.

ART & THE DREAMING

All early Indigenous art was based on the various clans' and nations' ancestral Dreamings – the Creation – when the earth's physical features were formed by the struggles between powerful supernatural ancestors such as the Rainbow Serpent, the Lightning Men and the Wandjina. Codes of behaviour were also laid down in the Dreaming and these laws remain the foundation for most Indigenous communities today, even those that have felt the greatest effects of colonisation. Ceremonies, rituals and visual representations of specific totems and stories are interrelated elements of Indigenous culture, known as the Dreaming.

The Dreaming can relate to a person, an animal or a physical feature, or it can be more general, relating to a region, a group of people, or natural forces such as floods and wind. A vast network of Dreamings exists among Indigenous clans throughout Australia, with neighbouring groups often sharing certain aspects such as stories and totems.

From around 400 years ago, Indigenous artists also depicted the human newcomers to the region – Macassan traders and, more recently, Europeans – and the things they brought, or their modes of transport such as ships and horses.

North Queensland

In North Queensland rock art again predominates. The superb Quinkan galleries at Laura on the Cape York Peninsula, northwest of Cairns, are among the best known in the country. Among the many creatures depicted on the walls are the **Quinkan** spirits, which are shown in two forms – the long and stick-like Timara, and the crocodile-like Imjim with their knobbed, club-like tails.

The Kimberley

The art of the Kimberley is perhaps best known for its images of the **Wandjina**, a group of ancestral beings who came from the sky and sea and were associated with fertility. They controlled the elements and were responsible for the formation of the country's natural features.

Wandjina images are found painted on rock as well as on more recent contemporary media, with some of the rock images being more than 7m long. They generally appear in human form, with large black eyes, a nose but no mouth, a halo around the head (representative of both hair and clouds) and a black oval shape on the chest.

The Wandjina are ancestral spirits with the power to summon the great storms of the Wet season – here their images are photographed at Gibb River in the East Kimberley

One of the other significant styles of painting found in the Kimberley is that of the **Bradshaw figures** (named after the first non-Indigenous person who saw them). The Bradshaw figures are generally small and seem to be of ethereal beings depicted

MITCH REARDON

engaged in ceremony or dance. It is believed that they predate the Wandjina paintings though little is known of what significance or meaning they have.

PAINTING

Western Desert Painting

Following the developments at Papunya (see earlier) and with the growing importance of art, both as an economic and a cultural activity, an association was formed to help the artists sell their work. The Papunya Tula company in Alice Springs is still one of the relatively few galleries in central Australia to be owned and directed by Indigenous people.

Painting in central Australia has flourished to such a degree that it is now an important source of income for communities. It has also been an important educational tool for children, through which they can learn different aspects of religious and ceremonial knowledge. More recently women have played a much greater role in the visual arts movement.

Western Desert painting, also known as 'dot' painting, partly evolved from 'ground paintings', which formed the centre-piece of dances and songs. These were made from pulped plant material, and the designs were made on the ground using dots of this mush. Dots were also used to outline objects in rock paintings, and to highlight geographical features or vegetation.

While these paintings may look random and abstract, they depict Dreaming stories, and can be read in many ways,

Bushbean *by William Sandy (1998); acrylic on canvas*

Photo from Warumpi Arts, courtesy of Desart

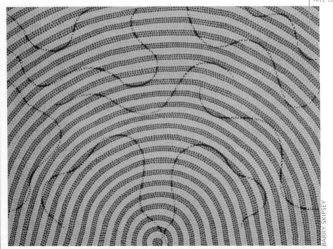

BARRY SKIPSEY

including as aerial landscape maps. Many paintings feature the tracks of birds, animals and humans, often identifying the ancestral beings. Subjects may be depicted by the imprint they leave in the sand – a simple arc depicts a person (as that is the print left by someone sitting), a *coolamon* (wooden carrying dish) is shown by an oval shape, a digging stick by a single line, a camp fire by a circle. Men or women are identified by the objects associated with them – digging sticks and coolamons for women, spears and boomerangs for men. Concentric circles usually depict Dreaming sites, or places where ancestors paused in their journeys.

While these symbols are widely used, their meaning in each individual painting is known only by the artist and the people closely associated with him or her – either by clan or by the Dreaming – since different clans apply different interpretations to each painting. In this way sacred stories can be publicly portrayed, as the deeper meaning is not revealed to uninitiated viewers.

TIWI ISLAND ART

Due to their isolation, the Indigenous people of the Tiwi Islands (Bathurst and Melville islands, off the coast of Darwin) have developed art forms – mainly sculpture – not found anywhere else, although there are some similarities with the art of Arnhem Land in the use of natural pigments, feathers and wood, for carvings and baskets.

The *pukumani* burial rites are one of the main rituals of Tiwi religious life, and it is for these ceremonies that many of the art works are created – *yimwalini* or *tunga* (bark baskets), spears and *tutini* (burial poles). These carved and painted ironwood poles, up to 2.5m long, are placed around the grave, and represent features of the deceased person's life.

In the last 50 or so years the Tiwi have been producing sculptured animals and birds, many of these being Creation ancestors (the Museum and Art Gallery of the Northern Territory in Darwin has an excellent display of sculpture). More recently, bark painting, textile design, sculpture, ceramics and print-making have become popular, and there are art centres on both islands where these items are produced.

Pukumani poles at Milikapiti, Melville Is
Photo courtesy of Jilamara Arts & Crafts

Bark Painting

Bark painting is an integral part of the cultural heritage of Arnhem Land's Indigenous people. It's difficult to establish when bark was first used, partly because it is perishable, so very old pieces don't exist. The paintings were never intended to be permanent records. Non-Indigenous visitors in the early 19th century noted the practice of painting the inside walls of bark shelters, and the trade in examples of bark paintings brought them to the notice of museums around the world.

The bark used is from the stringy-bark tree *(Eucalyptus tetradonta)*, and it is taken off the tree in the Wet season when it is moist and supple. The rough outer layers are removed and the bark is dried by placing it over a fire and then under weights on the ground to keep it flat. In a couple of weeks the bark is dry and ready for use. A typical bark painting made today has sticks across the top and bottom of the sheet to keep it flat.

The pigments used in bark paintings are mainly red and yellow (ochres), white (kaolin) and black (charcoal). The colours are gathered from special sites by the traditional owners, and traditionally they were traded with other clans. An amazing range of colours can be mixed from the four pigments available and many artists are identified by their choice of a particular tone. These natural pigments give the paintings their superb soft and earthy finish. Binding agents such as egg yolks (from native birds), wax and plant resins were added to the pigments. Recently some of these materials have been replaced by synthetic agents such as wood glue. Similarly, the brushes used in the past were obtained from the bush materials at hand – twigs, leaf fibres, feathers, human hair and the like – but today artists sometimes choose commercial brushes.

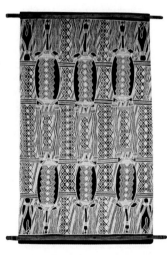

Arnhem Land cross-hatched bark paintings

Top: Minhala at Gangan *by Nawurapu Wunungmurra; earth pigments on bark*

Bottom: Wuyal *(detail) by Wolpa Wanambi; earth pigments on bark*

Photos courtesy of Buku Larrngay Arts (Yirrkala)

One of the main features of Arnhem Land bark paintings is the use of rarrk designs (cross-hatching). These designs identify the particular clans, and are based on body paintings handed down through generations. The paintings can also be broadly categorised by their regional styles. In the region's west the tendency is towards naturalistic images and plain backgrounds, while to the east the use of geometric, abstract designs is more common.

ALBERT NAMATJIRA

Australia's most renowned Indigenous artist was arguably Albert Namatjira (Western Arrernte; 1902–59). He lived at the Hermannsburg Lutheran Mission, about 130km west of Alice Springs, and was introduced to European-style watercolour painting by a non-Indigenous artist, Rex Batterbee, in the 1930s.

Namatjira successfully captured the essence of central Australia using a strongly non-Indigenous-influenced style. At the time they were created, his paintings were seen solely as picturesque landscapes. However, his work has been reassessed in recent times and it is now understood that his landscapes depicted important Dreaming sites to which he had a great cultural bond.

Like many later Indigenous artists with strong kinship ties, Namatjira supported many of his people on the income from his work, as was his obligation under traditional law. In 1957 he became the first Indigenous person to be granted Australian citizenship (a particular irony!). Due to his fame and the granting of citizenship, he was permitted to buy alcohol. However, this was at a time when it was illegal for all other Indigenous people to do so. By remaining true to his kinship responsibilities, he broke non-Indigenous laws and in 1958 he was jailed for six months for supplying alcohol to his community. Released from jail, he died the following year aged only 57.

Although Namatjira died from a broken spirit due to his ill-treatment by white society, he did much to overturn some of the extremely negative views of Indigenous people that prevailed back then. At the same time, he was instrumental in paving the way for the Papunya Tula painting movement, which emerged just over a decade after his death. Namatjira continues to influence and inspire many contemporary Indigenous artists, both through his art and the obstacles he faced in his lifetime.

WENDY HART

Previously unpublished photograph of Albert Namatjira (1952)

The art reflects themes from the Dreaming that vary by region. In the eastern Arnhem Land area the most prominent ancestor beings are the Djang'kawu Sisters, who travelled the land with their elaborate *dilly* bags (carry bags) and digging sticks (for making waterholes), and the Wagilag Sisters, who are associated with snakes and waterholes. While in western Arnhem Land Yingarna, the Rainbow Serpent, is the significant being (according to some clans), as is one of her offspring, Ngalyod. Other groups paint Nawura as the principal ancestral being – he travelled through the rocky landscape creating sacred sites and giving people the attributes of culture.

Untitled, *Douglas Abbott (1998); watercolour on board – Abbott draws artistic inspiration from Albert Namatjira's style*

The Mimi spirits are another feature of western Arnhem Land art, both on bark and rock. These mischievous spirits are attributed with having taught the Indigenous people of the region many things, including hunting, food gathering and painting skills.

It's worth visiting the Buku-Larrngay Mulka Centre at Yirrkala (☎ 08-8987 1701), Bulabula Arts at Ramingining (☎ 08-8979 7911) and Maningrida Arts and Culture (☎ 08-8979 5946), although the latter two are difficult to visit unless you make special arrangements. You can also buy locally made crafts at the Nambara Arts & Crafts Aboriginal gallery at Yirrkala (☎ 08-8987 2811).

Contemporary Painting

The Kimberley

Contemporary art in the eastern Kimberley sometimes features elements of the works of the Indigenous people of central Australia, a legacy of the forced relocation of people during the 1970s. The community of Warmun, at Turkey Creek on the Great Northern Hwy, has been particularly active in ensuring that Aboriginal culture, through painting and dance, remains strong. Renowned artists from this region include Rover Thomas (Wangkajungka/Kukatja; 1926–98), Queenie McKenzie (Kija (Gija)/Gurindji; 1930–99) and Paddy Tjamintji (Kija(Gija); 1912–86), among others. Other important art centres in the Kimberley are the Mangkaja Arts Resource Agency at Fitzroy Crossing (☎ 08-9191 5272) and Warmun Arts (☎ 08-9168 7496) at Turkey Creek.

Balgo

On the edge of the Great Sandy Desert, Balgo was established as a Catholic mission in 1939. While the community is a fair distance from the communities of Papunya and Yuendumu, there are strong cultural connections with the two communities, as there are with the Kimberley to the north. It wasn't until the mid-1980s that Balgo artists embraced painting for people outside the community with gusto. Balgo art is characterised by the vivid use of colour, as best seen in works by Kukatja artists such as Peter Sunfly 'Sandfly' Tjampitjin (1916-96), Susie Bootja Bootja Napangarti, Donkeyman Lee Tjupurrula (1921–93), Eubena Nampitjin, Wimmitji Tjapangarti (1925–2000) and Lucy Yukenbarri, who are (or were) represented by the Warlayirti Artists Aboriginal Corporation at Balgo Hills (☎ 08-9168 8960).

Driving to Iltjiltjari by Bessy Liddle (2000); acrylic on linen – some Aboriginal artists choose to express traditional stories in a figurative style that can appear similar to naïve European art

Photo from Jukurrpa Artists, courtesy of Desart

STEVE STRIKE

Utopia

This community north-east of Alice Springs came into existence in 1977 when the Anmatyerre and Alyawarre people re-established their community on traditional land taken from them to create what had been Utopia Station for 50 years. The service centre for the Utopia community is Arlparra. Initially, batik was produced following, like other communities, the influence of the women batik artists of Ernabella. Batik was introduced by art coordinator Jenny Green in the early 1980s. In the late 1980s, members of the community started to paint on canvases with acrylics, largely abandoning batik. While some men in the community paint, Utopia is best known for the work produced by its women artists, in particular Emily Kame Kngwarreye (Anmatyerre; 1910–96), Ada Bird Petyarre (Anmatyerre), Kathleen Petyarre (Anmatyerre/Eastern Alyawarre) and Gloria Tamerre Petyarre (Anmatyerre).

Of this group of extremely talented artists Emily Kame Kngwarreye holds a special place. Her life as an artist only commenced when she was in her late 70s, first with batik and then in the late 1980s with acrylic paints. Thematically, Kngwarreye's paintings are closely connected to her people's relationship with the land. This is evident throughout, though simultaneously her paintings, with their beautiful use of textured colour, are reminiscent of expressionist paintings of the non-Indigenous art world. Another startling feature of her work was the number of stylistic changes made over her painting life of a mere eight years. The National Gallery of Australia in Canberra, the Art Gallery of New South Wales in Sydney and the National Gallery of Victoria in Melbourne (set to move to the Museum of Australian Art in 2002) hold particularly fine examples of Kngwarreye's paintings.

My Country by Samantha Napurrula Napanangka (1999); acrylic on canvas

Photo from Jukurrpa Artists, courtesy of Desart

Devil Devil Corroboree by Djambu Barra Barra (1999); 167x100cm; acrylic on linen; Ngukurr NT – Barra Barra combines x-ray and cross-hatching techniques with the distinctive bright palette made famous by the Ngukurr artists

Photo courtesy of Alcaston Gallery, Melbourne

Ngukurr

Since the late 1980s the artists of Ngukurr, a settlement near Roper Bar in south-eastern Arnhem Land (NT), have been producing works using acrylic paints on canvas. People from a number of language groups live at Ngukurr. This is reflected stylistically in the art emerging from this community, as can be seen in paintings by Ginger Riley Munduwalawala (Mara), Amy Johnson, Willie Gububi/Gudapi (Mara; 1916–96) and Gertie Huddleston (Nameratjara). Although ancestral beings feature very prominently, there are many other subjects including bush tucker and reference to missionaries. The works of these artists are contemporary in their use of vibrant palettes, and differ markedly from the bark painting and associated art of their contemporaries in other regions of Arnhem Land.

Metropolitan & Rural Artists

The quantity of work being produced in the desert and Arnhem Land communities has sometimes resulted in the work of Indigenous artists based in metropolitan and rural regions being somewhat overshadowed. However, the work of these latter artists is thought-provoking and at times deeply confronting.

Notable artists include Queenslanders Fiona Foley (Badtjala), Judy Watson (Waanyi) and Gordon Bennett. From New South Wales there is HJ Wedge (Wiradjuri), Michael Riley (Wiradjuri), Rea (Gamilaroi/Wailwan), Richard Bell (Gamilaroi) and Lin Onus (Wiradjuri; 1948–96). South Australian artists include Trevor Nickolls, Yvonne Koolmatrie (Ngarrindjeri) and Ian Abdulla (Ngarrindjeri). Julie Dowling (Badimaya) and Sally Morgan (Palyuku) are working in WA. Others are based in places outside their traditional regions, such as Destiny Deacon (Kuku/Erub/Mer) in Victoria, Brenda L Croft (Gurindji) in WA, or travel frequently for work, like Palawa artist Julie Gough from Tasmania. These artists, and many others, are gaining a reputation for their work.

Content often focuses on the terrible injustices of the past 200-plus years while raising issues of dispossession; access to language, cultural practices and land; contemporary Indigenous culture and the artist in the modern post-colonial world. By their very creation, the paintings speak of the strength, unity and also diversity of contemporary Indigenous culture.

Taking God for a Walk by Julie Dowling (2000); acrylic, oil and red ochre on canvas – much of Dowling's work explores the tension between her Aboriginality and her Catholic education

Photo courtesy of Artplace

ARTEFACTS & CRAFTS

Objects traditionally made for practical or ceremonial uses, such as weapons and musical instruments, often featured intricate and symbolic decoration. In recent years many communities have also developed non-traditional craft forms that have created employment and income, and the growing tourist trade has seen demand and production increase steadily.

BETHUNE CARMICHAEL

Didjeridus

The most widespread craft objects seen for sale these days are didjeridus. There has been a phenomenal boom in their popularity and they can be found in outlets around the country.

Originally they were (and still are in many communities) used as ceremonial musical instruments by Indigenous people in Arnhem Land (where they are known as yidaki). The traditional instrument was made from particular eucalypt branches that had been hollowed out by termites. The tubes were often fitted with a wax mouthpiece made from sugarbag (native honeybee wax) and decorated with traditional designs.

Although they may look pretty, many didjeridus made these days bear little relation to traditional ones: they may be made from the wrong or inferior wood, have been hollowed out using mechanical or other means, have poor sound quality, and may have never had an Indigenous person anywhere near them, since many have been manufactured overseas or by visiting backpackers!

Boomerangs

Boomerangs are curved wooden throwing sticks used for hunting and also as ceremonial *clapsticks*. Contrary to popular belief, not all boomerangs are designed to return when thrown – the idea is to hit the animal being hunted! Returning boomerangs were mostly used in southeastern and western Australia. Although they all follow a similar fundamental design, boomerangs come in a huge range of shapes, sizes and decorative styles, and are made from a number of different wood types.

Didjeridu by Djambu Barra Barra; private collection – Didjeridus come from the Top End of the Northern Territory, where the Yolngu know them as yidaki

Photo courtesy of Alcaston Gallery, Melbourne

Wooden Sculptures

Traditionally, most wooden sculptures were made to be used for particular ceremonies. Arnhem Land artists still produce soft-wood carvings of birds, fish, animals and ancestral beings. The lightweight figures are engraved and painted with intricate symbolic designs. Tiwi artists create impressive carvings from the other end of the wood spectrum – ironwood, which is said to be impossible for termites to bore through.

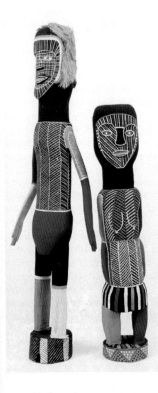

Early in the 20th century, missionaries encouraged some communities and groups to produce wooden sculptures for sale.

Scorched Carvings

Also very popular are the wooden carvings that have designs scorched into them with hot fencing wire. These range from small figures, such as possums, up to quite large snakes and lizards. Many are connected with Dreaming stories from the artists' country. In central Australia one of the main

Top: Carved figures by Andrew Freddy Puruntatameri (1999); natural ochre and coconut fibre on ironwood (105cm and 88cm)

Photo courtesy of Alcaston Gallery, Melbourne

Bottom: Scorched wood carvings are one of the most popular items for sale at the Maruku Gallery in the Uluru-Kata Tjuta Cultural Centre (NT)

Photo courtesy of Maruku Arts & Crafts

BARRY SKIPSEY

outlets for these is the Maruku Arts & Crafts centre (☎ 08-8956 2153) at the Uluru-Kata Tjuta National Park Cultural Centre, where it's possible to see the crafts being made. Although much of the artwork is usually done by women, men are also involved at the Maruku centre. The Mt Ebenezer Roadhouse, on the Lasseter Hwy (the main route to Uluru), is another Indigenous-owned enterprise and one of the most inexpensive places for buying sculpted figures.

DAVID PATERSON

Spearthrowers by Reggie Jackson – these tools, often called woomeras, have a spike at one end that fits into a notch in the spear giving greater leverage
Photo courtesy of Maruku Arts & Crafts

Ceremonial Weapons

Around the country many types of weapons were traditionally produced, including spears, *woomeras* (spear-throwers), *nulla-nullas* and *bundis* (names for clubs) and shields. The shields were made from timber or bark in different shapes and sizes, and were often richly decorated with carved and painted surfaces showing the owner's ancestry or Dreaming. They were mainly used for ceremonial purposes, but they were also put to practical use when fighting between clans occurred.

HOLLOW-LOG COFFINS

Hollowed-out logs are often used for reburial ceremonies in Arnhem Land, and are also a major form of artistic expression. They are highly decorated, often with many of the Dreaming themes, and are known as *dupun* in eastern Arnhem Land and *lorrkon* in western Arnhem Land.

In 1988 a group of Arnhem Land artists were commissioned to create the Aboriginal Memorial, highlighting the continuing injustices against Indigenous people. This was, of course, the year when non-Indigenous Australians were celebrating 200 years of European settlement – the Bicentennial. The artists painted 200 hollow-log coffins, commemorating the Indigenous people who had died in the 200 years since colonisation had begun in 1788, with traditional clan and Dreaming designs. These now form a permanent display in the Australian National Gallery in the ACT.

JASON DAVIDSON

Fibre Craft & Weaving

Articles made from fibres are a major art form among women, although in some regions men also made woven objects as hunting tools. String or twine was traditionally made from bark, grass, leaves, roots and other materials, hand-spun and dyed with natural pigments, then woven to make dilly bags, baskets, garments, fishing nets and other items. Strands or fibres from the leaves of the pandanus palm (and other fibrous palms or grasses) were also woven to make dilly bags and mats. While all these objects have utilitarian purposes, many also have ritual uses. Exquisite contemporary fibre works are sold by many art centres and represented in numerous public galleries and museums.

Top: Paddy Bedford, a member of the Juwulinypany community in the east Kimberley, painting a boomerang

Bottom: Pandanus baskets woven by Esther Managku at Kudjekbinj in Arnhem Land

RICHARD I'ANSON

Other Crafts

The Ernabella Presbyterian Mission, in northern South Australia (SA), was another place where craft work was encouraged. A 1950 mission report stated that 'A mission station must have an industry to provide work for and help finance the cost of caring for the natives'. As the mission had been founded on a sheep station, wool craft techniques of spinning, dyeing and weaving were introduced. The Pitjantjatjara women made woollen articles such as rugs, belts, traditional dilly bags and scarves, using designs incorporating aspects of *yawilyu* (women's law). With the introduction of batik fabric dyeing in the 1970s, weaving at Ernabella virtually ceased.

Eeritja by Carol Rontji (2000); 38x36cm; terracotta and underglaze – a piece from the Hermannsburg School

Photo courtesy of Alcaston Gallery, Melbourne

While probably better-known for their traditional watercolour artists, in particular Albert Namatjira, the Western Arrernte community of Hermannsburg has recently begun to work with pottery, a craft that is not traditionally Indigenous. They have incorporated moulded figures and surface treatments adapted from Dreaming stories.

Another art form, from the western Kimberley, is the engraved pearlshell pendants that come from the Broome area. It is believed that the Aboriginal people of the area were using pearlshell for decoration before the arrival of Europeans, but with the establishment of the pearling industry in Broome in the late 19th century, the use of pearlshell increased markedly. The highly prized shells were engraved and used for ceremonial purposes, as well as for personal decoration and trade – examples of this art have been found as far away as Queensland and South Australia.

The designs engraved into the shells were usually fairly

Ceramic Vase by Dora Taylor
Photo from Walkatjara Art, courtesy of Desart

ROSE WALLIS

simple geometric patterns. The practice of pearlshell engraving is now quite rare, although the decorated shells are still highly valued.

BUYING INDIGENOUS ART & ARTEFACTS

One of the best and most evocative reminders of your trip is an Indigenous artwork or artefact. By buying authentic items you are supporting Indigenous culture and helping to ensure that traditional and contemporary expertise and designs continue to be of economic and cultural benefit for Indigenous individuals and communities. Unfortunately, much of the so-called Indigenous art sold as souvenirs is ripped-off, consists of appropriated designs illegally taken from Indigenous people or is just plain fake, usually made overseas by under-paid workers. Admittedly it is often difficult to tell whether an item is genuine, or whether a design is being used legitimately, but it is worth trying to find out. In 2000 the 'Label of Authenticity' was launched by the National Indigenous Arts Advocacy Agency to help protect the intellectual property and copyright of Indigenous artists. You can look for the swing tag on merchandise to determine its authenticity and support Indigenous people.

The best place to buy artefacts is either directly from the communities that have art and craft centres or from galleries and outlets that are owned and operated, or supported by Indigenous communities. This way you can be sure that the items are genuine and that the money you spend goes to the right people. There are many Indigenous artists who get

Anangu arts and crafts are sold at the Uluru-Kata Tjuta Cultural Centre

Photo courtesy of
Maruku Arts & Crafts

BARRY SKIPSEY

paid very small sums for their work, only to find it being sold for much higher prices in commercial galleries in cities that do not have the interest of the communities producing the art as their priority. There are also many reputable galleries that have long supported the Indigenous arts industry – usually members of the Australian Commercial Galleries Association (ACGA).

Didjeridus are the hot item these days, and you need to decide whether you want a decorative piece or an authentic and functional musical instrument. The didjeridus sold are not always made by Indigenous people, and there are many stories of backpackers in Darwin earning good money by making or decorating didjeridus. From a community outlet

Wulukarritji Waterhole by Narputta Nangala Jugadai

Photo from Ikuntji
Arts Women's Centre,
courtesy of Desart

such as Manyallaluk in the Northern Territory you could expect to pay $100 to $200 for a functional didjeridu that has been painted with ochre paints/natural pigments, and you may even get to meet the maker, although do not always expect to do so. On the other hand, from a non-supportive souvenir shop in Darwin or Cairns you could pay anything from $200 to $400 or more for something that looks pretty but is really little more than a painted bit of wood.

If you're interested in buying a painting, possibly in part for its investment potential, then it's best to purchase the work from a community art centre, Indigenous-owned gallery or reputable non-Indigenous-owned gallery. Regardless of its individual aesthetic worth, a painting purchased without a certificate of authenticity from either a reputable gallery or community art centre, in most cases, will not be easy to resell at a later time – even if the painting is attributed to a well-known artist. Be guided by your own eye and heart in determining what is 'good' Indigenous art – remember you have to live with it when you get home!

For more information, see the boxed text entries 'Why Dots?'; 'Kunwinjku Painting'; 'A Tradition Carved in My Mind'; 'Pandanus Weaving' and 'Ngarrindjeri Weaving'. See also the Shopping section and the Galleries, Museums & Shops sections in major capital cities.

BRENDA L CROFT

Brenda is from the Gurindji people in the Northern Territory on her father's side and Anglo-Australian heritage on her mother's. Born and now living in Perth, she works as curator of Indigenous art at the Art Gallery of Western Australia. For most of her life Brenda has been based in the south-eastern states, and she has written extensively on contemporary Indigenous visual art and culture for a decade.

She is also an artist and feels fortunate that her work has enabled her to travel extensively in Australia and overseas. Brenda has participated in exhibitions and cultural exchanges in Britain, Germany, South Africa, Norway, Japan, Italy, Canada and the USA, to name a few.

She owes many thanks to Steven Gilchrist for his assistance with research on the Perth Galleries, Museums & Shops section. Living close to some of the best beaches in the world, Brenda wants to find time to learn how to surf.

Sport – Connected to Culture

Michael Long

I was born in Darwin. My mother Agnes was born in Daly River, south-west of Darwin, and my father Jack was from central Australia, a little desert town called Ti Tree.

My parents came from two different Aboriginal tribes, thousands of kilometres apart. Perhaps under a traditional Aboriginal community lifestyle, they would never have met.

However, due to the government policy of the day, they were both stolen as toddlers – forcibly removed from their parents and put on a Catholic mission on Melville Island, north of Darwin.

My mother and father, being part of the Stolen Generations, had little information about their past and the history of their family. Family members died and information went with them.

My parents grew up on Melville Island, later married and moved to Darwin in search of work. Here they brought up their children, seven boys and two girls!

My father Jack played Australian Rules football for St. Mary's Football Club in Darwin – sport was something that dominated our everyday lives.

Following in my father's and older brother's footsteps, my six brothers and I played footy, but I was lucky to pursue other sports as well – like cricket and basketball. My mother was the person who washed the jumpers for the footy teams and took us to the games. Looking back, it was her commitment to us which exposed us to more sports, especially the discipline of sport.

My mother died when I was 13. I would like to think she saw my natural ability. I was so young at the time and it is only now that I appreciate how important she was in my life. She has stayed with me through my whole career.

As a teenager I loved basketball. I played with the local team called the Rebels. At one time I gave up playing footy to pursue basketball, but in the end, I knew my mother saw my future as a footballer.

I am sure she knew that football at the elite level gave Aboriginal people an opportunity to have a financial and healthy,

Michael Long

Michael was born in 1969. In 1988, at 18, he was drafted into the Essendon Football Club and began a career with many milestones. In 1989 he won Best First-Year Player. In 1993 he won the Norm Smith medal for Best and Fairest in a winning Grand Final. In 1995 he changed the face of Australian Football League (AFL) football forever when he campaigned for the AFL to introduce Rule 30, the Racial and Religious Vilification Rule. It is now an offence for any player or official to vilify another person for their race, religion, ethnic background or the colour of their skin.

In 1998 he was awarded life membership of the Essendon Football Club. He was co-captain in 1999 and played in another winning Grand Final in 2000. Michael was also a torch-bearer for the Sydney 2000 Olympic Games.

In early 1999 after having observed and befriended acclaimed artists Ginger Riley Munduwalawala, Barney Ellaga and Kathleen Petyarre (through his close friendship with Essendon Football Club and Alcaston Gallery director Beverly Knight), he began to paint. Painting has given Michael contact with family and country through his mind's eye, which would have been impossible due to his elite athletic commitments.

Michael was appointed to the inaugural Reconciliation Australia board in December 2000. This board will carry forward the work of Reconciliation from the former Council for Aboriginal Reconciliation, that disbanded in 2000.

He enjoys a happy life with his three children and partner Lesley Turner. A man of quiet dignity and proven leadership qualities, Michael sets himself challenges and goals where nothing but high performance is acceptable.

A SPORTING CHANCE

When Cathy Freeman crossed the finish line to win gold in the 400m sprint at the 2000 Sydney Olympics, an entire nation celebrated one of Australia's greatest sporting moments.

In less than 50 seconds this young, modest Aboriginal athlete had sent nearly 19 million people into a frenzy of fist-thumping patriotic bliss.

It was easy to get caught up and swept away in the jubilant scenes that followed. Freeman running a victory lap to the delight of 110,000 adoring people at Stadium Australia with the Aboriginal and Australian flags entwined in one hand. Many observers felt Freeman's win did more for Reconciliation than some of the more official efforts, and Freeman said she was happy for it to be recognised that way.

The question is: Was it the greatest sporting triumph by an Indigenous Australian? It's an argument that could be debated forever but in the end it probably doesn't matter. Aboriginal people have always performed well when it comes to sport and always will. Indeed, some of Australia's best athletes have been Indigenous Australians, who have brought joy to a nation of self-confessed sports lovers.

Lionel Rose won an Australian bantamweight boxing title in 1966 and a world title two years later. In 1968 he was the first Aborigine to be crowned Australian of the Year. His name is synonymous with boxing in this country.

Who could forget the exploits of Evonne Goolagong? The shy tennis player, raised in Barellan New South Wales, won four Australian Open tennis titles, won Wimbledon twice (1971 and 1980) and emerged victorious in the French Open in 1971. Now known as Evonne Goolagong-Cawley, she is an inspiration to young Aboriginal people to this day.

Nova Peris-Kneebone won gold at the Atlanta Olympics in 1996 as one of Australia's best women's hockey players and then turned her attention to running. She competed in the Sydney 2000 Olympics with distinction, underlining her tremendous capacity to adapt to new challenges.

Rugby Union had the Ella boys – Mark, Gary and Glen – while Rugby League fanatics have marvelled over the talents of Mal Meninga (a South Sea Islander Australian), as well

independent lifestyle. She had seen Maurice Rioli, another great Darwin player who was a Tiwi from Melville Island. I am sure my mother wanted the same for me, so I chose to try my luck.

Maurice was a great player for Richmond and achieved a Norm Smith Medal in the 1982 Grand Final. This is the highest award possible in my eyes.

Essendon Football Club

In 1988, when I was 18, I was drafted by the Essendon Football Club in Melbourne. The football club was established in 1873 and is now part of the Australian Football League (AFL). Our playing jumper (jersey), originally red and black stripes, was changed in 1875 to our current and famous black jumper with a red sash coming over the left shoulder. The 'sash' wearers, as they were commonly known in those days, excited their supporters, who were mainly local traders and their families. They were the first team to kick 10 goals in a match and by 1897 the Victorian Football League (VFL) was founded, so Essendon broke away from the Victorian Football Association to join the big league. That year they won the very first VFL premiership and have gone on to win another 15, over the past 100 years or so.

Australian Football League

By 1990 the competition was truly national and the AFL was official. The sport is the most popular game played in Australia and dominates the media and the workplace during the season from March to September each year. Australia stops for the last Saturday in September, the AFL Grand Final at the Melbourne Cricket Ground (MCG).

Teams come from most states of Australia, and the clubs turn over about $20

as Lionel Morgan, Larry Corowa, Sam Backo and Anthony Mundine, who has also turned his attention to boxing with some success. The Aboriginal Rugby League Knockout (held annually in October) is the highlight of the NSW Aboriginal calendar.

Probably the best example of Aboriginal talent can be seen in the uniquely Australian game of Australian Rules Football, arguably the country's favourite sport. Aboriginal and Torres Strait Islander people have excelled at this sport for a century, exciting millions with their uncanny evasive skills and an almost sixth sense when kicking for goal. Of the dozens of brilliant Indigenous footballers, the ones to really stand out have been Michael Long, Maurice Rioli, Gavin Wanganeen, Graham 'Polly' Farmer, Barry Cable, Sid Jackson, Jim and Phil Krakeour, Nicky Winmar, David Wirrpunda, Chris Lewis, Jeff Farmer and Michael O'Loughlin. Doug Nicholls played for Fitzroy and went on to become the governor of South Australia. Nicholls was also a great sprinter, winning the Nyah and Warracknabeal Gifts.

Bobby Kinnear (1883), Tom Dancey (1910) and Lynch Cooper (1928) were all winners of the Stawell Easter Gift, a foot race for amateur athletes in country Victoria. Richard McCarthy was a champion jockey who won the Newcastle Gold Cup in 1962; the Stradbroke Handicap in 1963, 1964 and 1966; and the Brisbane Cup, AJC Derby and AJC Epsom in successive starts at Randwick in Sydney in 1969.

Aboriginal people have also excelled in more obscure sports. Steve Mangiri Bowditch won a squash world championship in Sweden in 1981, May Chalker was Australia's only professional Aboriginal golfer and Steve Tutton captained Australia's volleyball team.

Eddie Gilbert remains Australia's most successful Aboriginal cricketer. A tearaway fast bowler from Queensland, Gilbert troubled the best batsmen in the country in the 1930s, including Sir Donald Bradman. And how many people would know that Australia's first ever touring cricket team in 1868 was an Aboriginal team?

For more information on Australia's first touring cricket team, see Edenhope in the Victoria chapter.

million annually. There is a salary cap system to pay the players, to keep the competition even. Recruiting is annual and players come from all over Australia, usually as 18-year-olds.

Aboriginal footballers, while small in numbers, have an 80% success rate to go on after recruitment to play a substantial number of games, compared with non-Aboriginal players, with a success rate of about 40%.

Recruited

In 1989 I travelled to Melbourne with my older brother Chris, leaving family and friends to pursue a career in Australian Rules football.

The pressure of failing to fulfil my family's dreams was immense. Not many Aboriginal players have succeeded at the elite level, but I wanted to follow in the footsteps of Maurice Rioli.

My first year was lonely, adjusting to the cold winter climate compared to Darwin's 32°C heat, but I was named Essendon's best first-year player in 1989 and in 1990 I played in a losing Grand Final.

In 1993 I played in another Grand Final with our young team and won. My mother was my inspiration in this game, and to my great surprise and pride I was awarded the Norm Smith Medal. To my delight, it was presented by my childhood hero, Maurice Rioli.

Racial Vilification

One thing I did not count on when I came to Melbourne was racial vilification.

There is an unspoken bond between Aboriginal athletes. We are possibly likened to Afro-Americans but in reality we are more like Native Americans or New Zealand Maori.

It was an easy tactic on and off the field to racially vilify another person. It appeared that coaches would instruct a player to try to trigger some anger or put you off your game. For me, even in the 1993 Grand Final, I had to use all my will power to avoid feeling vilified. I had to constantly remind myself that it was only a tactic and try not to react like I had earlier in the year, when I was suspended twice for rough play after I reacted to racial taunts.

In 1995 I was once again racially taunted on the field. This had happened many times over the six years I had been playing, so I decided I had had enough. The support I had from my Aboriginal counterparts at other clubs gave me the courage to tackle the issue once and for all. An Aboriginal network has evolved, drawn from the Murris in Queensland, the Nungas from South Australia, the Kooris from south-east NSW and Victoria, together with my own mates from the Northern Territory. They symbolically joined me and said the time was right to fight this soul-destroying aspect of the sport I love.

The Essendon Football Club and the AFL gave me their full support, as did all my Aboriginal and non-Aboriginal colleagues when I asked for help.

Also I was playing very well in 1995, in fact I was runner-up to the Brownlow Medal, so I suppose the media wanted to talk to me and fully supported me too. Essendon had many players from Italian backgrounds at the time and they also knew too well that I was standing up for all ethnic or marginalised people.

We did succeed and the AFL introduced Rule 30, the Racial and Religious Vilification Rule, governing all people connected with the sport. It is now an offence for any player or official to vilify another person for reasons of race, religion, ethnic background or the colour of their skin.

Retired Aboriginal St Kilda player Nicky Winmar had symbolically tried to do the same in 1993, by holding up his shirt to show off (and be very proud of) his black skin, during a St Kilda–Collingwood game, but it really took another four years for all clubs to adopt the racial vilification rules and to provide ongoing education.

However, even now whenever I am out of my comfort zone, away from my club environment, I feel people looking at, and sometimes distrusting me.

Olympic Recognition

Being part of the Australian Torch Relay in 2000 for the Sydney 2000 Olympic Games, especially carrying the flame that was passed on to me by so many Australians from all walks of life, made me very proud.

However, there must be many people who visited our great country and especially went on to visit the Northern Territory, during and after the Olympics who wondered why Aboriginal people are so poorly represented in our Olympic sports. Cathy Freeman is my hero but I know there are lots of great young Aboriginal men and women all over Australia just wanting a chance.

Positive Change

There are many positives happening all over Australia and sport is certainly a great starting point. The Yorta Yorta people in a large country town called Shepparton, in far north Victoria, have released a book called *The Story of the Rumbalara Football and Netball Club*. 'The sporting achievements,' says Paul Briggs, Club President, 'have played an important role within the community. For it was on this front and this front only that the Yorta Yorta people were able to front, challenge and compete against white people in a semi-acceptable forum.'

The club is based on Koorie philosophies of sport, culture and community, with a purpose – to strengthen the spiritual and emotional wellbeing of our people, promote recreation, enhance public understanding of, and Reconciliation with, our culture.

The Northern Territory Football League (NTFL) operating from Darwin is the body in charge of Australian Rules development in the Northern Territory. In recent years, the AFL and mining giant Rio Tinto, with the NTFL, have jointly funded development of young teams, mainly Aboriginal players from all over the Territory.

Their Kickstart Program is reaching out to isolated communities and towns, including Alice Springs and Darwin. The distance many young players travel to play in their communities' league is astounding. In central Australia, the Central Australian Football League have large community carnivals. The Yuendumu Sports Day is the most famous.

Yuendumu is a desert community hundreds of kilometres from Alice and literally truck-loads of young people from as far as 1500km away come to compete. The long dusty tracks, north, south, east and west of the community are alive come that special weekend.

The eventual winner, history says, needs to get away quickly to avoid community rivalry and retribution. Offensive behaviour on the field, they say, is dealt with by the senior Elders of the community at each quarter break. 'A tribunal, bush style' deals with misdemeanours harshly, often *nulla-nullas* (hunting and fighting clubs) being used for serious indiscretions.

The whole community joins in and there is much singing, dancing and fun. It is usually around the first week in August and well worth a visit. No permits are required on this weekend. Just come and have fun, and bring your own swag.

Traditional Sports

Football is also a part of our culture, as years ago, before the white man came, tribes came together to compete in hunting, fishing, running, spear throwing and also football – kicking a ball, often made of an animal skin filled with mud or animal dung. It would be like a mini Olympics.

Ginger Riley, a great Australian Aboriginal artist, can remember how tall, strong and agile the men were. They did not play on fields of grass, they played on hard red earth. The football game was seen as a show of strength, that one tribe was stronger than the other, but it was also played in fun.

For it was a time that families came together and travelled hundreds of miles on foot to join in the fun. Many celebrations took place, dancing, singing, telling stories about their Dreaming to the young children, but the football game would determine who was the most skilled and strongest clan of all. Ginger says they played naked, while all the families sat around the edge in their makeshift *humpies* (huts). All the old men would sit around and talk while watching the footy.

These days Aboriginal gatherings or carnivals take place at communities throughout the country. All states of Australia compete against each other, and not only men compete but also the women in sports like netball and basketball.

Role Model

One of the many things I have tried to do during my last few years of football is pass on my knowledge of how important it is for my people to learn and enjoy a healthy lifestyle. I suppose being able to earn a good living from football does help to make you realise that education is so important for us to enjoy and make the most of our lives – something I didn't appreciate as a kid.

My people are trapped in many instances in a lifestyle of low self-esteem, high unemployment and quick fixes like alcohol and drugs to ease their pain.

Maybe through sport and art there is a light at the end of the tunnel where the wider community can recognise Aboriginal talents and accept we are different but the same. As Ginger Riley says 'we are all one people, one blood, God made us the same, we need to love one another as we love ourselves'.

I have three beautiful children, Jessie aged 10, Jake aged five and Michaela aged four. My family and close friends are very precious to me and maybe through my sport and my personal achievements, my kids will have the chance to be part of a reconciled Australia. The trauma that their grandparents and great grandparents went through will hopefully be acknowledged by our government and we can all move forward together.

For more information on the Stolen Generations, see the boxed text 'Sorry Seems to Be the Hardest Word' and 'When I Was Away'. See also the Yuendumu Festival section.

Food – Bush Tucker

Dr Rosemary van den Berg

Australia's bush food, or bush tucker as it is widely called, has sustained Indigenous people for millennia. The countryside was like a huge supermarket where Aboriginal people could browse at will, picking and choosing what to eat and when to eat it. Everything they ate and drank was beneficial for the body and rarely did one see an obese Aboriginal person. With age and maturity – the middle-aged spread – perhaps some people gained weight, but the majority were fit and healthy. Old photos of Aborigines, like those in *Patterns of Life* by ME Lofgren (1975) and many other texts, show that the men's and women's physiques were well toned and trim without any excess fat. This was due to their dietary intake and natural outdoor living, an alfresco lifestyle.

Preparation

Following a long tradition, Aboriginal game is freshly caught, cooked and eaten. Edible vegetables are dug from the earth (such as yams and other tubers), cooked in the coals and eaten, or picked from a bush or tree (such as berries, nuts and honey). Seeds are collected, ground between stones and made into a type of flour which, when water is added, becomes a dough. This type of bread, or *damper*, is placed in the ashes to cook. Kangaroo stew and damper was, and still is, a gourmet's delight for Aboriginal people.

Nothing is wasted. Traditionally, leftover damper and meat were taken along if the people were in transit, or eaten at the next meal if they remained in one place for any length of time. Kangaroo meat lasts for a day or two without becoming rancid. Aborigines used to (maybe still do in remote areas) hang a leg or shoulder of a roo in a tree (out of reach of their dogs) to cook for the next meal. The kangaroo meat would form a transparent membranous coating that protected it from flies and other insects and prevented it from becoming infected or going bad.

Knowing the Country

Aborigines only take from the bush what they need for their immediate hunger. They always ensure edible plants and game can regenerate. They never pull anything up by the roots, except for edible tubers, and they always catch just enough kangaroos and other animals for their immediate needs. In this way, the food chain and the cycle of life continue to be replenished. Fresh water from rivers, lakes and springs can always be found and Aborigines know where to find it, especially the springs in desert areas.

For traditional people, knowing these locations is a matter of survival. Different regional groups have different kinds of foods which are particular to their areas and subject to seasonal availability. For example, very

Dr Rosemary van den Berg

I am married, and my husband and I have five adult children and 22 grandchildren. I live in Armadale, Western Australia (WA) and am considered an Elder among the Nyoongar and other Aboriginal people. I am also a writer, historian, editor and researcher.

I have recently completed my Doctorate of Philosophy in the School of Communication and Cultural Studies at Curtin University of Technology in Bentley.

My book *No Options No Choice!: The Moore River Experience* was published in 1994 and I have published academic papers and short stories in journals and anthologies in Australia as well as overseas. My PhD thesis, titled *Nyoongar Perspectives of Racism and Multiculturalism*, has also been submitted for possible publication.

I am co-editor of an anthology of Aboriginal writers and poets called *Those Who Remain Will Always Remember* (2000), which was launched by Fremantle Art Centre Press.

I'd like to thank Brendon Ah Chee, who so kindly supplied me with information on traditional bush foods of the Kimberley, WA.

different foods are to be found in the temperate and semitemperate climates of southern Australia, the inland desert regions and the tropical and subtropical areas of the north. Generally bush tucker is found only in specific local areas, but there are sources of food, like kangaroos and emus, which can be found in many regions.

Aborigines (traditionally a hunter-gatherer and forager society) know where to find these sources of food at each particular time of the year. The dietary range includes meat, fish and other marine life, edible vegetation, bush fruits and nuts and the fresh water so vital to existence.

GARDENING

Joseph Kennedy

Unlike the Indigenous people of Australia's mainland, Torres Strait Islanders traditionally derived much of their food from gardening. The eastern islands, with their rich, volcanic soil, were particularly bountiful. Among the crops grown were yam, taro, banana and coconut. Later, sweet potato, corn and cassava were introduced from the Americas by Europeans.

Gardening was important not only for subsistence but also to provide food for ceremonies and festivals, and as a medium of exchange with other Islanders. Considerable ritual was associated with gardening. A person's prestige could be measured by their ability to produce enough surplus for local consumption or trade, or by their ability to produce 'show' gardens, with fruits and vegetables of prodigious size. Gardening techniques were carefully preserved and passed on. Young people would observe their Elders at work and mimic techniques, thereby mastering them.

Today, as with so much else, reliance upon the cash economy has disrupted this age-old lifestyle.

The Temperate & Semitemperate Zones

I grew up in Pinjarra, a small country town in the south-west of WA, about 85km south of the capital city, Perth. Pinjarra is situated on the coastal plains, between the Indian Ocean and the Darling Ranges. Prior to European occupation, and for many years after, this area was rich in bush foods and fresh water. Aborigines who lived around the Murray River area of WA lived well. They not only had access to the food sources of the coastal plains and the Darling Ranges, but also to the bountiful marine life that inhabited the waters of the Murray River, its estuary and the Indian Ocean.

Seasonal Change In the south and southwest of WA (the Nyoongar people's territory), there are six seasonal changes to the climate and the Nyoongar people gauged the climatic change by the food sources available.

The warm to hot months from October to April were the time for movement, hunting, gathering and foraging, as well as attending to trade, cultural business and socialising (such as going to corroborees and arranging marriages).

During winter, they lived in *mia-mias* (small hut-like buildings, also called humpies) and clad themselves in kangaroo skins to keep warm. These cape-like garments were threaded together for warmth and tied over the shoulders or around the neck, keeping the arms free for unhindered movement.

During the winter months Aborigines from these regions of Australia did not shift camp as often as they did in the summer months. They were content to keep their fires burning at a regular base.

In the harsh months of winter, the people separated into small family groups for economic purposes because it was harder to find enough food to cater for a large group.

These groups contained a *nyoongar* (man), his *yorgas* (wives), *culungas* (children) and the Elders for whom he was responsible. In all, the group would comprise approximately eight to 10 people (depending on the number of children the man and his wives had, and if they had any old parents to look after).

This nuclear group would hunt, gather and forage, always keeping in mind that there was less food available during the cold months than in the warm to hot days of summer. During the winter months, game became scarcer and the edible vegetation became dormant. It was a time when nature rested. Yet there was always food available, and Aborigines still know where to find it. So contrary to European concepts of Australia's Aborigines being undernourished, they had a diet that was both healthy and nutritious; it was just very different to what the Europeans conceived of as a civilised way of living.

MY BOOMERANG WON'T COME BACK
bryan Andy

Borrow something of value from an Aussie and you could be told that the book (CD, whatever...) is a 'boomerang', obliging you to return it, swiftly mate! But not all boomerangs come back. Made from hardwood, often mulga, they can do much more than kill a few recreation hours. Why? Smaller boomerangs are used to kill small animals like birds, possums and wallabies. Larger, non-returning boomerangs are used like clubs to hunt big animals like kangaroos and emus. Smaller ceremonial boomerangs are used as instruments (tapping two together); these ceremonial types are often beautifully decorated with ochre and/or burnt engravings.

If you're buying one (as they make great, if somewhat unoriginal gifts), make sure it's a genuine, Aboriginal-made piece.

See also the Shopping section.

Temperate Foods During the warm to hot months, this area abounds in fish, shellfish, crabs, turtles, mussels and other marine food, including freshwater crustaceans like *marron* and the smaller *djilkies*, or *jilgies* (the Western Australian name for *yabbies*, or crayfish). The countryside teems with wildlife. Nyoongar foods include *yongka* (kangaroos), *waitj* (emus) and *coomarl* (possums), snakes, many types of lizards including the long-tail *kaarder* (goanna), turtles and their eggs, edible birds like bronze-wing pigeons, rosellas, ducks, duck eggs and *bardi grubs* (found in wattle and the blackboy, or grass, tree), these are all in plentiful supply. Bardi grubs can be eaten raw or cooked in the coals.

Wild honey, fruit from the quandong tree, berries, edible tubers and nuts are collected, and grain can be crushed and made into a flour from which damper is made. Some wildflowers like grevillea and banksia are sucked for their sweetness, and the tips of the WA orange Christmas trees are chewed as gum. Wattle gum and manna gum are also chewed and eaten. Fruit called *boyoo* from the toxic zamia palm can be treated with salt water and left to stand for several weeks, then eaten. Further inland from Pinjarra, Aboriginal people enjoy much the same dietary intake, except for the saltwater varieties of marine life.

The Desert Regions
The desert peoples live a different lifestyle to those in the southern and northern parts of the country. Food sources are scarcer and traditionally these Aborigines had to travel for miles at times before they found any kangaroos or emus. The inland regions of Australia suffer extremes in temperature. The summer months maintained a constant heat, but during the winter months people experience bitterly cold nights and warm to hot days. These changes in climate and the harsher environment (compared to that of the temperate zones) make hunting and gathering much more difficult. The distances between water sources also make surviving in the desert regions much more hazardous. Yet the desert Aborigines know how to utilise the desert's resources to the best advantage.

Desert Foods Some of the desert foods, or bush foods from the inland areas, are the staple kangaroo, emu and bush turkey. Aborigines have become adept at hunting down and killing these animals. Reptiles, like snakes, small lizards and the larger *bungarras* (the Yamitji name for goannas) are other game that help fill an empty spot in the stomach. In the desert regions, game is thrown on a campfire and cooked whole. Yams or *cunmanggu* (wild potatoes), which taste like sweet potatoes, can be cooked in the coals or eaten raw. *Wamulu* (bush tomatoes), *minyarra* (wild onions), honey, wild grain and seeds from the woolly butt tree (which is winnowed, crushed and made into a flour for damper) are collected. Nuts and berries, bush turkeys, honey ants, turtles and jilgies, and (if the rivers and creeks have permanent waterholes), fish like mullet and bream are added to the diet. But, of course, the main source of life is water.

Traditionally, Aborigines use water with care. Not a drop is wasted and they make sure that they learn the sites of waterholes, springs and natural wells.

Most of the time, Aboriginal people did not use any alcohol or drugs; only the clever men, or shamans, had access to trance-inducing substances used in certain rites and ceremonies.

Subtropical & Tropical

The northern parts of Australia enjoy a totally different lifestyle to that of the desert peoples and the communities further south. Although the Kimberley (the top end of WA), the NT and North Queensland have areas of lush growth and tropical rainfall, in the lower regions there are areas of dry country where it is difficult to survive. The Kimberley and other subtropical and tropical areas have their Wet and Dry seasons. During the cyclonic Wet, huge areas of land are subject to flooding and some parts look like an inland sea. This makes it difficult for Aboriginal people to hunt, gather and forage. However, marine life abounds and Aborigines have survived on these delicacies.

Tropical Foods The main bush foods of Aborigines in this region come from the rivers, land and sea. The rivers and lagoons supply *cherrabun* (the Kimberley word for yabbies) and mussels, catfish, barramundi, turtle and crocodile, besides the wild ducks and other edible bird life. In the lakes and swamps are also water reeds or rushes that one can eat. On land there is a plentiful supply of *barni* (goanna), *gunanunja* (emu), *bingajuooi* (wild turkey), *niminburr* (flying fox), *nyilli nyilli* (bush bubblegum), *mukabala* (bush banana), *gubinge* (bush fruit), wild passionfruit, *lulguoi* (boab nut), *kilu* (wild tomato), bush honey (also from flowers of the *jigul* tree) kangaroo and snake. There are also some introduced fruits from Asia which now grow wild, such as mango, cashew nut and tailor fruit. From the sea, Aborigines eat *gulbudigdo* (mud crabs), *jinyp*, (stingrays), *gulil* (sea turtles), dugongs, oysters and chinaman hats, a type of shellfish. There is nothing as

tasty as fresh oysters baked in the oven and served with a slice of lemon. It is so delicious and makes the mouth water just thinking about it.

Changes to Diet

Over the 200-plus years of European habitation, Aboriginal diets have undergone a drastic change. Fats, sugars and alcohol have been added, much to the detriment of Aboriginal health. In these contemporary times, Aborigines eat a wide range of junk food, in keeping with modern trends. While Aboriginal people living in remote and rural areas of Australia still maintain a semblance of their traditional diets, many urban Aborigines (in the main) have adopted the multicultural diets now available in Australia. Yet, there are many Aborigines living the urban lifestyle who will go out in the bush and hunt kangaroo. The kangaroo flesh (legs, shoulders and tail) make a delicious stew when onions, carrots, potatoes, salt and pepper are added. My mother used to make the meat of the kangaroo tail into a type of brawn. I never did learn the recipe, but when eaten cold, it was a gourmet's delight.

Health Issues Over the years, Aboriginal people have suffered dire health problems with the change from their traditional diet of bush foods to the more fatty, sugar-orientated Western diet. Foods cooked in fat and refined sugar products (sweets, cakes and ice cream) were unknown in traditional diets and unfortunately, many have paid the price for eating foods alien to their system. Obesity, diabetes and heart problems are just some of the illnesses that cause many untimely deaths in Aboriginal people. Unfortunately, many Aboriginal people are not in the position to pursue their traditional ways of catching or gathering food. Nowadays it is much easier to shop at supermarkets where all sorts of food products are at hand and within easy reach. They do not have to walk for miles to hunt, gather or forage for food.

Contemporary Times

In these contemporary times, Aborigines can indulge in any type of food they like, especially those living in an urban situation. They have truly become Europeanised in their

BUSH MEDICINE

Esther Managku
with the assistance of Lawungkurr Maralngurra

We still use that bush medicine sometimes. We go in that forest to pick *mangumberre* (acacia) leaves, flowers and seeds. Break them up and cook in little bit water till they turn soapy. Then you rub that soap on your sores many times a day. For skin rash you can use *mangol* (cocky apple, or *Planchonia careya*) and mandjalem (woollybutt, or *Eucalyptus miniata*). That mangol you can take skin (inner bark) from anywhere, but with mandjalem you cut hairy skin low down. You break (shred) the skin in little pieces and boil in water. Then it turn soapy and when it's cool you can use it for sores like prickly heat. I boil this in a milk tin and use for sore finger and sore hand when I was scratching. My auntie taught me that. Mangol also good for bandage. Just break it up and put it on. Or you heat that leaf for mosquito bite. One old lady tell me that. Then there's that other tree in the rocks, *manbulara* (emu apple). We cut off that skin and sometimes that fruit and put it all in the billycan to boil. We won't let the kids take that medicine – it very strong, but number one bush medicine for skin.

Gabo (green ant) is good bush medicine too. They build nests in trees. If we have bad cold and coughing or ache a little bit, we can use that ant. First put that nest in cold, fresh water. Smash them like that (rubbing hands together) or squeeze him tight. I been watching my grandmother, my mother – they been drinking those ants. Eggs and new green ants coming in November. And then we eat those eggs and those new ants too. That's the strongest medicine. Gabo too strong for me now. Gabo also good for headache, or we tie *mandjol* (bush string) around our head.

We go look around for sugarbag (native bee's nest), just watching to see if those little bees go into a cave or maybe a tree. They cut that nest when it fat (has lots of wax), clean it and put that fat one in billycan. Drink the sugarbag eggs for tummyache. All the old people they been taste 'em and drink. Oh good! When we used to live in bush – I seen them, all those old people drinking that sugarbag.

One old man he been broke his leg long time ago while hunting with other men. Maybe him jumping or been chasing kangaroo out in the bush. They didn't have any doctor. They been thinking, 'What we do?' Then they remember that timber skin (bark) of *manlara* (native cypress). They been cut that skin and put it around that old man's leg high up (around the femur) and tie it with mandjol. They leave it on for many weeks until it got healed.

If people have diarrhoea you can use *mandjodmi* (*Grewia retusifolia*). You dig up many roots and take off that skin. Then you wash it, smash it up and boil it and you drink.

Esther Managku

Esther Managku was born Esther Maralngurra at Kudjekbinj about 1928, and she is the oldest living member of the Nalangbali clan of the Kunwinjku people. She went to school for a few years in the settlement of Gunbalanya about 150km away.

Esther was married three times, but is now widowed. She lives with her sister Miriam, daughter Hopie and her little grandson Kyle at Kudjekbinj. This country is the home of Yawk Yawk or Baby Dreaming, little spirits which live in the waterways. Esther knows those spirits well and intercedes with them for young women who want to become pregnant.

In some ways Esther's life goes on as it always has, cooking meals over an open fire, wandering into the bush to collect pandanus and other plants for her weaving, and trying to look after her country.

culinary intake. Yet there are still those living in rural and remote areas who maintain links with their land and practice traditional food gathering. These people continue to hunt kangaroo and emu; catch snakes, lizards and goannas; fish in the seas, rivers, lakes and lagoons; and gather and forage for delicacies from the bush. The only difference now is that these food sources supplement items that they buy from the supermarkets (flour, sugar, tea and coffee, tinned food, alcohol, fresh vegetables and frozen goods). It is a far cry from the traditional food that Aboriginal people ate prior to European civilisation arriving on these shores.

Many older Aboriginal people yearn for the times when their ancestors walked through the bush, seeking sustenance and keeping fit in the bargain. In some cases, government policies of conservation and land management have forbidden Aborigines to practise their ancestral way of food gathering and hunting, unless they are living in their own communities in their traditional lands. Even so, the spear and boomerang have often been replaced by guns and reel fishing. Bush foods and drink are seen on television shows, but cooking these foods over a barbecue is not the same as chucking them on the coals or cooking them in the ashes. Nevertheless, the old way of life, inherent to Aboriginal people, has all but vanished into another time and place.

For more information, see the Health section and the boxed text 'Is This the Death of Our Ancient Fishing Tradition?'

Society
Dr Irene Watson

Aboriginal societies are diverse. We are not one large homogeneous group but hundreds of different sovereign First Nation peoples. Torres Strait Islanders are a Melanesian people with a completely separate culture to that of Aboriginal Australians. They share many cultural ties with the peoples of Papua New Guinea and their lives focus heavily on the sea.

Aboriginal Identity
There are many common stereotypes of Aboriginal peoples. One is that we are all

the same and conform to the idealised image of the naked Aborigine standing with spear in hand watching the sun set. This is a picture which quickly dissolved into the reality of the 21st century. We are as different as the landscapes of coast, desert, rainforest and snowy mountains. The land is different and so are we, the first peoples of the land.

Another misconception is that our cultures are static. We, like the people of other nations, live in the modern world and we embrace both traditional and contemporary lifestyles.

Traditional & Nontraditional Many Aboriginal people still live in communities where their families and clan members retain the connections to a common Dreaming ancestral being. Spirituality and the land are central to our Aboriginal identity.

However, most Aboriginal families have experienced the government policy of removing young 'mixed-blood' children to place them in non-Aboriginal families or institutions, a group commonly known as the Stolen Generations. This practice has impacted on the wellbeing of communities and has eroded traditional Aboriginal society, especially as the policy was directed at the heart of our culture, the family.

The policy of forced removal of Aboriginal children from their families has created a separation and a difference in culture among Aboriginal peoples. The negative impact of these policies is revealed when Aboriginal identity and culture are constructed as having two categories: traditional and nontraditional.

We Are All Real Aborigines A more positive view of Aboriginal identity is one in which there are no categories or divisions, for we are all traditional as we are all of an Aboriginal culture and tradition. The maintenance of tradition holds greater meaning than the idea of being a 'full-blooded Aboriginal' or 'traditional Aboriginal', living in a remote region of Australia.

The construction and identification of 'traditional Aboriginal' has also led to the creation of other categories: 'nontraditional' Aborigines, 'rural' Aborigines, and 'urban' Aborigines. It is often assumed that these other categories are 'of a lesser quality' or are not authentic; that these people are not 'real Aborigines'. But we are all 'real' and though we identify with a diverse range of lifestyles, skin colours, cultures and languages, we are all equally Aboriginal. We are the descendants of the original ancestors of this place of creation, now known as Australia.

Kinship with Family, Ancestors & Land
Studies of the Aboriginal peoples of Australia frequently make the comment that our kinship and social systems are among the most complicated in the world. That may be so.

The difficulty in understanding how our kinship system works is perhaps because of our special relationship to our country, our kin and our ancestral spirits of the Dreaming. We believe we are related to all things in the natural world. These relationships were formed in the Dreaming, our time of creation.

Family The core of Aboriginal society is the extended family and our relationships to kin and clan members, whether it is in a remote region or a big city. The family clan groups are also connected to a larger collective, which shares a common language, land, culture, history, tradition and customs, sometimes called a nation.

The clan group shares Dreaming ancestors, whose spirits are alive in the land. Our relationships to family and country identify who we are as Aboriginal people. These relationships are spiritual and are recorded in Dreaming stories and songs.

Dreaming Ancestors The Aboriginal relationship to a spirit ancestor is more commonly known as a totem. The idea of a totem is a simple explanation for the very complex and spiritual relationship that Aboriginal people have with their country, the ancestors and the Dreaming.

These beings are our spiritual guides, and one may take the form of a bird, animal or natural feature. Our spirit guide is our connection to both country and the Dreaming and it is our teacher, who teaches us much about our relationship with all things in the natural world.

Land In walking over the land in the steps of the creative ancestors, we are affirming our relationship to the Dreaming. When we

Dr Irene Watson

I am a Tanganekald and Meintangk *mimini* (woman). My ancestors were, and still are, the sovereign peoples of the Coorong and the south-east region of South Australia.

My knowledge in law, Aboriginal culture and history is in the essence of this material, as is the knowledge I have gained from Aboriginal Elders, my mother, uncles and aunties.

return to our sacred places we fulfil our cultural obligations to the ancestors by taking care of the country and protecting the spirit places of our ancestors through ceremony.

Our traditional identity comes from the land, and an important Aboriginal tradition is to introduce ourselves in relation to the country of the grandmothers and grandfathers. We will talk to the spirit ancestors to tell them where we come from, and who our people, kin and family are. It is one of our ways.

Our relationship to country determines how we speak to one another; who speaks about our culture, country and our *laws*; and how we speak about them. These protocols are important to the identity of who is traditional to the country.

The Hunter-Gatherer Lifestyle
Aboriginal society was based on a hunter-gatherer culture. We used the earth's resources in accordance with the ancient teachings of the Dreaming. Foods were hunted or gathered in a way which ensured the continuation of a stable ecology and a quality food supply. The earth's resources were left in their natural state, as we did not engage in agriculture or other farming practices that altered or impacted upon the land.

Fire Management One environmental practice was used (and in some areas continues to be used) to alter the natural environment: the use of fire. This was used to selectively

A CHANGING CULTURE

Hugh Finlay

It cannot be disputed that traditional Aboriginal culture is changing, adapting itself so that it can survive alongside the modern culture which has been imposed upon it. As this happens, traditions change, laws become diluted and skills and stories are adapted.

I heard of an incident which illustrates this situation beautifully:

A couple of young Aboriginal men were driving out in the bush with some white people, when they were asked if they could light a fire the traditional way. 'Sure,' they said, 'We'll do it right here.' They stopped the car and got out, and the visitors waited expectantly for the men to go off into the bush and gather the particular sticks for fire-making. To their surprise, however, the men instead went to the ute, took out an old shirt and ripped a scrap from it. They then removed the fuel cap, shoved the rag in and soaked it. One of the men opened the bonnet and removed a spark plug from the engine, and reconnected it to the spark plug lead. He then held the rag to this and said to his mate, 'Righto, turn 'er over!' With that the key was turned to crank the engine over, and the spark plug ignited the petrol-soaked rag! 'There, fire traditional way!' beamed the young men, very pleased that they had been able to show these whitefellas one of their traditional bush skills.

burn dry grasses and undergrowth to propagate certain plant species, which require heat to germinate. Selective burning was also used to prevent larger-scale bush fires during the drier months by removing the dry kindling. Fires were also lit to assist hunters in the trapping of animals by flushing them out of the undergrowth.

The fires were limited in size and were separated from other burnt areas. This created a mosaic of burnt and green areas, so that a burnt-out area was always next to a green or unburned area. This acted as a reserve for animals and plants which could regenerate the burnt area.

Fires were also used as a weapon in the protection and maintenance of the territory of different nations against invasion by neighbouring groups. Fire was used in the same way as a means of defending the land and resisting the European invasions after 1788.

Nomadic Life As hunter-gatherers, we didn't use agriculture (although in some areas important plants were cared for). The availability of foods and water determined the extent to which a community travelled over the country. Traditionally, some communities remained permanently in locations where there was an abundance of food and water. However, where food resources were scarcer, the community lived a more nomadic lifestyle.

Travelling across country involves cultural obligations and also great respect for the traditional boundaries of neighbouring clan groups. Custom requires visitors to obtain permission to cross the lands of different nations.

Some Aboriginal cultures used ceremonial designs or symbols, painted in ochre onto rock or wood, to serve as boundary markers. These identified the owners of the country.

Environmental Technologies Ancient Aboriginal knowledge of the land enabled our ancestors to live an ecologically sustainable lifestyle. Knowledge of animals and plant species, the climate and the land was handed down by the ancestors from the time of the Dreaming through songs and stories. This knowledge guaranteed our survival against food shortages.

Our ancestors gave us the knowledge to make hunting implements, such as the boomerang and the spear, and the techniques of finding food – how to gather and hunt and the best times to collect seasonal foods.

In coastal and river communities they gave us the technology to weave fishing nets from native grasses. We also wove large baskets from freshwater rushes that were used to catch eels in the rivers of many parts of south-eastern Australia. Fish traps

TRADITIONAL LAW VS MODERN LAW

Contemporary Indigenous Australians originate from numerous unique traditional societies. They still largely adhere to traditional laws, which are the bedrock of their complex societies. However, the inevitable conflict between these traditional laws and the modern Western legal system has had devastating consequences. Indigenous Australians are frequently incarcerated for minor offences, such as drinking alcohol in public places (eg, parks). Traditional laws facilitated communal social activities. Therefore, while drinking in public is an offence in the Western legal system, Indigenous Australians would not regard incarceration as an appropriate penalty. In most cities, they have taken steps to address this through community-based interventionary programs, such as the Murri Watch program in Brisbane. This program is aimed at Indigenous people, who may be at risk of detention for minor offences, by taking diversionary measures such as taking people home (if they have one) or to a shelter. Visitors should be aware that excessive use of alcohol is a problem in many Aboriginal communities and for this reason many are now dry, and it is an offence to carry alcohol into these places. The problem has also led to restricted trading hours and even 'dry days' in some places – in Alice Springs, for instance, takeaway liquor outlets don't open until noon.

Gary Lui

I come from Mackay in north Queensland, but was born in Cairns to a large Torres Strait Islander extended family, which migrated from Erub (Darnley Island) in the eastern Torres Strait. My parents' heritage includes the Torres Strait, as well as Filipino/Malay on my mother's side and New Caledonian on my father's.

I grew up in Torres Strait Islander culture and continue my involvement with the Indigenous community in Brisbane. I am one of the few Indigenous lawyers in private practice but hope that this will soon change. I have worked for Paul Richards & Associates for almost three years and hope to one day return to north Queensland, with my wife Felecia, to whom I am grateful for very many things.

There have been remarkable changes in the law in Queensland with significant consequences for Indigenous people. I hope to see a lot more changes in law and justice for Indigenous people in the future.

---

were built out of rocks in quiet coastal bays and in inland rivers as well.

A Delicate Balance Aboriginal culture is based on the principles of reciprocity. As the people fulfilled cultural obligations by holding ceremonies and protecting the sites of the Dreaming ancestors, the ancestors in return ensured an ecological balance of all things in the natural world.

The impact of colonisation has disrupted our culture and traditions, and in many regions the traditional practices of hunting and gathering are no longer possible due to the occupation of land by farmers, or by damage caused to the environment. The life of the hunter-gatherer is in many regions now replaced by a supermarket or shopping mall culture.

Trade

Aboriginal people are traders, and trade routes criss-crossed the country. We traditionally exchanged ochre, hunting implements, food, stone axes, native tobacco, shell and other artefacts.

The exchange of items would most frequently occur during the time of ceremonies. At these times, songs and dances were shared and marriages were often

continued...   Gary Lui

The 1991 Royal Commission into Aboriginal Deaths in Custody found that imprisonment (especially for minor offences) was 18 times more likely for Indigenous Australians than for any other segment of the Australian community. In 1994 the Australian Bureau of Statistics conducted a National Survey of 197,500 Indigenous people. The survey found that over 20% of the respondents had been arrested in the previous five years. Present statistics indicate that incarceration rates remain disproportionately high for Indigenous Australians. This is largely because of the Western legal system's failure to adequately recognise traditional laws and methods of punishment as more effective and appropriate alternatives for Indigenous Australians.

However, Indigenous customary practices have won some recognition in today's legal system. In Queensland, section 14 of the Juvenile Justice Act allows cautioning or counselling of young Indigenous offenders by respected community members (usually an Aboriginal field officer) who gives a verbal warning for minor offences. This culturally appropriate form of discipline is designed to keep young offenders out of the court system. The Brisbane Aboriginal and Torres Strait Islander Legal Service has a juvenile cautioning program which is highly effective. Indigenous juvenile offenders are often counselled by someone who knows them or their family. The Indigenous community therefore plays a much-needed role in their discipline and this works as a powerful disincentive to reoffend.

At a federal level, the family court has recently taken some steps to recognise the rights of children adopted according to Torres Strait Islander traditional adoption practices known as *kupai omasker* (see the Web site www.familycourt.gov.au/forms/html/rearing.html). Traditionally, children are 'gifted' by one set of parents to another (within the same extended family), often where the second set of parents cannot bear children. However if, for example, the parents died without making a will (commonplace among Indigenous Australians), their traditionally adopted children had traditional rights, but no legal rights under Western law.

The result of integrating traditional Indigenous laws into the Western system has generally been very effective. However, there is still potential for traditional laws to play a greater role. This would heighten non-Indigenous Australians' appreciation and awareness of Indigenous culture, and hopefully result in decreasing the marginalisation of Indigenous Australians.

arranged between young people of the different clan groups.

Some of the trade was not merely for economic purposes but was part of ceremonial exchange cycles. This trade was more symbolic than economic. Frequently the trade of gifts brought with it special relationships and obligations between the giver and the receiver, and during the lifetime of the parties a special spiritual relationship evolved.

Women & Men

In our culture there is a difference between the responsibilities held by men and those held by women in economic, political, spiritual and cultural concerns.

Women and men are both involved in the economic business of hunting and gathering foods. We are also equally involved in the ceremony and law business. Men and women share with each other and, in a traditional political context, no-one is the boss.

Secret Business In the spiritual and cultural realm, women and men develop their ceremonial life separately and keep much of their ceremonial knowledge secret from each other. However, between us we ensure that law and order are in balance and work to maintain peace and harmony in our communities. The distinct laws of Aboriginal women and men are essential to each other and each respects the secret business of the other. Both sets of laws were given to us by the ancestral beings of the Dreaming.

Aboriginal men and women have separate ceremonies, many of which are secret and sacred, where only women attend the women's ceremonies and only the men attend the ceremonies of men. However there are also ceremonies held where the entire community gathers for the teaching of culture, the honouring of law, dancing and the maintenance of songs. Thus there is a balance where the whole community of men, women and children participate together in the business of ceremonies. These ceremonies are an important time for teaching culture to the next generations.

Overcoming the Threats to Culture

Before the invasion of our country in 1788, there were between 600 and 700 dialects spoken across Australia. Today, the number of languages and dialects spoken has been greatly reduced because of the impact of colonisation and the Australian government policies of assimilation of Aborigines.

In the past 200-plus years, many Aboriginal people have been dispossessed of our

OUR INDIGENOUS GAY & SISTERGIRL SCENE

Sistergirl is a word of endearment, which is often used between Indigenous women. In the gay context, sistergirl describes those who identify as transsexual or transgender. The first Indigenous Sistergirl Forum was held on Magnetic Island in Queensland in July 1999 and offered a rare opportunity for Aboriginal and Torres Strait Islander transgender and transsexual people from all over Australia to get together and address various issues including sexual health, identity, community isolation and violence. This gathering fostered a sense of well-being and a greater understanding of sistergirl history.

The Sydney Gay and Lesbian Mardi Gras is one of the biggest international gay events in the world and in 2000 it brought together around 600,000 people (see the Web sites www.mardigras.com.au and www .pinksydney.com.au for more information). The Aboriginal and Torres Strait Islander Community float was selected to lead the procession and was awarded the prize for the best community float. Diversity was the theme and the message was loud and proud. With the support of their Elders, Indigenous gay, lesbian and sistergirl marchers carried placards bearing the language names of their traditional lands. A unique blend of traditional and modern

Sue Wood

Despite identifying as heterosexual, I found warmth and friendship within the gay and lesbian community of the late 1960s. I have remained part of that world ever since, participating in every Sydney Mardi Gras parade since 1993. I am a member of the Indigenous Gay Games committee Black White and Pink and the Indigenous Gay Community Support Group.

I dropped out of an Arts degree in 1974 and spent two years travelling around Australia, working where I could. In 1979 I graduated with a BA (Honours), majoring in English Literature. In the early '80s I worked in Darwin, where I learnt Gumadj, the language of the Yothu Yindi recordings. I travelled throughout the Northern Territory and in 1983 returned to New South Wales (NSW) and gave birth to boy and girl twins in 1985. This absorbed me entirely until 1987, when financial commitments forced me back to work.

I am now a senior Aboriginal project officer with the NSW Department of Education and Training, and secretary of Wirringa Baiya Aboriginal Womens Legal Service.

traditional lands. Our lands have been occupied by farms, mines, towns and other developments. The traditional peoples of the country were relocated to government mission stations, or rural and urban centres.

Our removal from our traditional country has caused trauma and conflict for many Aboriginal people. This impacts on the practice and maintenance of culture, and is further exacerbated by the constant threat to our country by new mines, exploration, farms and other developments. Separation from our traditional lands and the places of our Dreaming contributes to our great sense of loss and longing to return to the country of our Dreaming ancestors.

Under the Australian government's assimilation policies, we were prohibited from speaking our traditional languages, and we were also prevented from practising many of our ceremonies and cultural practices.

However, despite the difficulties we face in retaining a connection with, and control over, our traditional lands, Aboriginal peoples are working on the regeneration of our ancient cultural practices. Our people are affirming the sacredness of the Dreaming and the continuing relevance of the spirituality of the Dreaming ancestors in our lives today. The traditional owners of the country are once again teaching the children their Aboriginal languages.

continued...   Sue Wood

interpretive dance was created and performed by a group of Indigenous gay men in red sequined *lap-laps*.

Black, White and Pink is a community-based organisation which represents gay men, lesbians and transsexual people who are committed to the process of Reconciliation with Indigenous Australians. They came together in 1997 to promote the drafting of a statement of Reconciliation between Aboriginal and Torres Strait Islander people and the Sydney gay and lesbian community. The Black, White and Pink Reconciliation float at Mardi Gras 2000 was one of the biggest in the parade. It was a colourful blend of Indigenous and non-Indigenous marchers, gays, lesbians, and their friends and family. This float powerfully demonstrated the support that the gay community has always shown towards Reconciliation with Indigenous Australians. For more information and a fabulous photo gallery, see www.bwp.org.au.

Many Indigenous gay men, lesbians and sistergirls move to urban environments, but although the urban lifestyle may be very appealing, it's not everything. Sistergirls agree that their cultural identity always comes first and foremost. There is always the pull of family and home and the strong cultural ties that bind Indigenous people to their traditional communities.

For the last decade Indigenous gays, lesbians and sistergirls have been playing a vital role in the front line of sexual health education and in crisis and counselling services. The AIDS Council of New South Wales (ACON) currently employs three Aboriginal project officers to provide culturally appropriate assistance for Indigenous gay men and sistergirls, and to coordinate the Indigenous Gay and Lesbian Support group, which meets regularly for discussions and social gatherings. For more details, contact ACON (☎ 02-9276 2000, fax 02-9206 2069), or see www.acon.org.au, www.afao.org.au, and www.rainbow.net.au.

The next Gay Games, an international event which has been held every four years since 1982, will take place in 2002 in Sydney from 25 October to 9 November. An Indigenous outreach committee has been set up to ensure Aboriginal and Torres Strait Islander people are involved. One of the features of the Gay Games is a week-long cultural festival which is followed by a week of sporting events. Apart from Indigenous sportsmen and women, Indigenous Elders, academics, artists, actors and dancers will also participate in the 2002 games.

This process of cultural and spiritual revival is most difficult for those of our people who have experienced two or three generations of removal from their traditional lands, but there have been many successes and this is particularly evident in the area of the arts.

Aboriginal Culture Today

Colonisation and dispossession from our traditional lands has impacted upon the traditional culture of Aboriginal societies across Australia, damaging some groups more than others. Some Aboriginal peoples living in remote regions have been able to retain their traditional lands, and land-related aspects of their traditional culture. This is often because of their remoteness and the fact that no-one has yet wanted their lands for development or exploration.

However, traditional culture is not only being maintained in remote, northern Aboriginal communities. In the southern areas – including the more settled and densely populated cities and rural towns – languages are spoken, kinship obligations are met, traditional customs are observed and Aboriginal people are caring for their country. It is here that culture and tradition takes on a more contemporary form, where Aboriginal culture coexists with the changed environment.

Aboriginal peoples, like other cultures, embrace different walks of life: from academic professions in big city universities to teaching the law in traditional communities, from nursing in a modern hospital to gathering bush medicines in a remote community.

While our population comprises a very small minority group (2% of the whole population), we have survived as culturally distinct peoples against the brutal colonisation of our territories. In our struggle to survive assimilation, many of our people have retained connections to our culture and are still living on the lands of our ancestors. We have retained many of our traditional customs and many of our ancient ceremonies are being revived throughout Australia.

Aboriginal culture moves in the cycles of the past, present and future: 'always was, always will be'. We are culturally diverse. We are living both a traditional life and a modern one; maintaining traditional cultural beliefs in the middle of populated cities as well as by remote *billabongs* in the Northern Territory.

See also the People & Population section. For information on Torres Strait Islander culture, see the Torres Strait Islands chapter.

Spirituality

Dr Irene Watson

Just as there were hundreds of different languages spoken across Australia, there were also hundreds of different Aboriginal cultures and spiritual beliefs. However, all Aboriginal people have a common belief in the creation, or the Dreaming, which is a time when the ancestral beings travelled across the country creating the natural world and making the laws and customs for Aboriginal people to live by. The Dreaming ancestors take the form of humans, animals or natural features in the landscape.

Law and spirituality are one and the same thing; our laws are also our spiritual beliefs. Spirituality and the land are also one entity, for our spirituality comes from the Dreaming ancestors whose spirits are alive in the land. The land is us, for we are in the land, as is the spirit of creation in all things. All is one, one is all.

The Dreaming

Many Aboriginal people believe that they are born of the creation, a time commonly known as the Dreaming.

Although it is often considered to be a time in the past, or the 'Dreamtime', we believe that it is a continuing time. The Dreaming is in the past, the present and the future. We are always present in the spirit of creation. The Dreaming is a spiritual time, which lives in humanity, animals, birds and the natural environment. The Dreaming spirits are all around us because they entered the earth, taking the form of natural features in the landscape.

The Creation As the Dreaming ancestors travelled over the land, they formed the landscape. The great fish swished its huge tail and splashed the water making the bends in the river as it travelled to where the river meets the sea. The ancestor spirits cried and made the natural springs from their tears, and the great snake travelled all over the land forming the great life-giving underground and inland rivers. The Dreaming stories of the ancestors criss-cross every part of this country, and bring life to the land creating the landscape, rocks, mountains, trees and rivers, travelling everywhere and making the country as we know it now.

Our beginnings came out of the Dreaming, a creative time when spirituality and laws, humanity and the natural environment, songs and stories were created. The Dreaming created a way of life for the ancestors and it is a way of life and spiritual understanding which passed from the ancestors to us with each new generation. We learn of the Dreaming through the ceremonies of dance and song, and are taught how to live in the natural world, as hunter-gatherer people.

Ancestral Spirits We believe that we are descended from the creative ancestral beings of the Dreaming and that our ancestral relations teach us about the unity we share with all things in the natural world. Our ancestral relatives are both human and animal in form.

The ancestors gave us a system of law, in which humans and all other natural species have a moiety, or skin classification. This system provides Aboriginal peoples with a means of organising relationships, for example, 'proper marriage' partners. It is a way of organising properly all things within the universe.

The Dreaming places in the land are our ancestors who entered the earth, and in a real sense they are our relations. As we care for our family we are obliged to care also for the ancestors who are alive in the country. It is these sacred places and the creation songs of the ancestors which hold us in this Dreaming cycle.

Nature Time The time of the Dreaming is not simply an epoch of time in the past but is also a continuing time which forms a part of the ongoing past, present and future cycles of life.

Our Dreaming ancestors teach us about life's cycles. In our culture, unlike European societies which embrace the idea of God giving man dominion over the natural world, there is no hierarchy in which humanity is at the pinnacle. Humanity is rather just one part of the overall circle or cycle of life.

In our way all is one; we are all things of the natural world, all animals and plants are equal to the other. The traditional cultures never left nature time; the old people lived by the seasons and moon cycles, and we still do today.

The Earth Is Sacred

The earth is our sacred relative, it is a relationship that is based on nurturing, caring and sharing. From birth we learn of the sacredness of all living things. Every aspect of the natural world is honoured and respected, and we learn to tread lightly on the earth.

The spirit of creation is in all things, for all life forms are related. The philosophy of respect for all living things is an idea central to Aboriginal spirituality and is an idea which nurtured and kept the land in a pristine state prior to colonisation.

The Spirit in the Land The land is sacred because the essence of our spirituality lies in the earth; our spirit guides are resting in the mountains, in the rocks, in the rivers, and they are everywhere in the land. The land is sacred because it carries the footsteps of our spirit ancestors as they walked every part of it, laying tracks and spiritual songs across the country. The ancestors lie sleeping deep in the earth and we are responsible for the care of their places of rest, for their creative powers are alive and influence all things still in the natural world.

If these spirits are disturbed, so too are the natural order and cycles of life. Where sacred sites are destroyed we believe the ancestors are disturbed and will no longer protect or provide for the people. As a result of damaged or destroyed sacred sites, natural disasters and sickness may occur and afflict communities who have not fulfilled their cultural obligations as custodians. By neglecting our spiritual and cultural obligations we bring disharmony to the country and the community.

Our Land The idea of the land being terra nullius, or a vast empty space across which we range sporadically, is a myth. We know the land intimately, every rock and every river has a name and is remembered in the Dreaming, as it is still remembered today.

TALKING ABOUT COUNTRY

From time immemorial the Ancestral Serpent, a creature larger than storm clouds gathered on the horizon, came down from the stars laden with its own enormity of creative pursuits. Perhaps it moved graciously – if you had been watching with the eyes of a bird hovering in the sky far above the ground, looking down at the serpent's wet body, glistening from an ancient sunlight reflecting off its body, long before man was a creature who could contemplate the next moment in time. Perhaps it moved those billions of years ago, with a speed unknown to measuring devices, to crawl on its heavy belly all around the wet clay soils in the Gulf of Carpentaria.

Picture the creative serpent, scoring deep into – perhaps scouring down through – the slippery underground of the mud flats, leaving in its wake the thunderous sounds of tunnels collapsing behind the tip of its tail, to form deep sunken valleys. Instantaneously, the sea water following in the serpent's wake, swarming in a frenzy of tidal waves, changed colour from ocean blue to yellow mud. The water filled the swirling rocks to form the mighty bending rivers spread across the vast plains of the gulf country. So the serpent travelled over stretches of marine plains, past the mangrove forests, over the salt flats, through the sand ridges and crawled inland. Then it went back to the sea. And it came out at another spot along the coastline and crawled inland and back again.

When it finished creating the many rivers in its wake, it created one last river, no larger or smaller than the others, that offers no apologies for its nature of discontent with people who do not know it. This is where the giant serpent continues

Alexis Wright

Alexis Wright is a member of the Waanyi people of the southern highlands of the Gulf of Carpentaria. Her first novel *Plains of Promise* was shortlisted for the 1997 Commonwealth Writers Prize. Her other book is *Grog War* (nonfiction), and she was editor of *Take Power*, a book of stories and essays on land rights in central Australia. Her short stories can be found in the Oxford University Press book *Australian Women's Stories* and ABC Books' *Across Country*.

Alexis has worked extensively in Aboriginal agencies across four states and territories as a professional manager, educator, researcher and writer. She worked in the 1980s for the former National Aboriginal Conference in Canberra as the senior research officer on land rights, and also in Alice Springs as the Northern Territory (NT) coordinator. In this role she coordinated the preparation of the Aboriginal evidence for the Royal Commission into British Nuclear Tests in Australia.

Alexis was also the coordinator of the NT Aboriginal Constitutional Convention for the NT Land Councils and Legal Services in 1993, and the Kalkaringi Convention on constitutional issues affecting central Australia in 1998. She continues to work on issues of Aboriginal governance and Waanyi land.

to live, deep down under the ground in a vast network of limestone aquifers. They say its being is porous, it permeates everything. It is all around in the atmosphere and is attached to the lives of the river people like skin.

In this tidal river snake of flowing mud, the serpent's body takes in breaths of a size that is difficult to comprehend by a human mind no longer able to dream. Imagine the serpent's

Alexis Wright

continued...

breathing rhythms as the tide flows inland, edging towards the spring waters nestled deeply in gorges of ancient limestone plateaux, covered with rattling grasses dried yellow from the prevailing winds. Then, with the outward breath, the tide turns and the serpent flows back to its own circulating mass of shallow waters in a giant water basin, in a crook of the mainland geography whose sides separate it from the open sea.

The inside knowledge about this river and coastal region is the traditional knowledge of Aboriginal law handed down through the ages since time began. Otherwise, how would one know where to look in the hidden underwater courses of the vast flooding mud-plains, full of serpents and fish in the monsoon season of summer? Can someone who did not grow up in a place that is sometimes under water, sometimes bone-dry, know when the trade winds blowing off the southern and northern hemispheres will merge in summer? Know the moment of climatic change better than they know themselves? Know who fishes in the yellow-coloured monsoonal runoff from the drainages, with sheets of deep water pouring into the wide rivers swollen over their banks, filling vast plains with flood water? Meanwhile, the cyclones linger and regroup, the rain never stops pouring, but the fat fish are abundant.

Previously published in *The Serpent's Covenant, A Sea Change: Australian Writing and Photography* (ed Adam Shoemaker), Sydney Organising Committee for the Olympic Games, 1998; and *Australian Women's Stories* (selected by Kerryn Goldsworthy), Oxford University Press, 1999.

To own the land as a piece of real estate, as a 'property', is an idea remote to Aboriginal people. Our relationship to the land is considerably more complex. The land cannot be treated as a consumable, which can be traded or sold. We believe the land cannot be sold.

We have always lived as a part of the natural world, and we take from the environment only what is needed to sustain life; we nurture the land as we do ourselves, for we are one.

The land is both nurturer and teacher from which all life forms grow; all life is inseparably linked. The Aboriginal relationship to the land carries with it both obligations and rights. The relationship to land is at once one of traditional owner and of custodian. It is a relationship that is difficult to explain in a foreign language, because the term 'owner' has different meanings across cultures. Ownership is not viewed in relation to ownership of material goods, but is more accurately viewed as in possession of other values: knowledge, culture and law business, a relationship, a problem, a dispute, a ceremony.

The idea of Aboriginal ownership is not exclusive, and it does not define the owned object as a commodity. Instead, that which is owned is defined as the concern of a limited group of people who stand in a particular relationship to the owner, and whose various responsibilities depend on that relationship.

Managers & Bosses There are both managers and bosses for country, and each party has a different responsibility or right. The manager is the custodian and the boss is the owner. Naming the parties a manager or a boss is simply a way of discerning between custodian and owner, although in reality these two roles are not always strictly separate and are often merged to become one.

Some of these responsibilities are made known to the members of an Aboriginal community through songs and ceremonies. For example, there may be a particular obligation not to kill the females of a certain animal species, in order to preserve the species.

When traditional custodians and/or owners approach their country they will talk to the spirit ancestor of the place. They will tell them who they are and also who they may have brought with them to the place. When food is taken from the land, thanks are given to the ancestors. Nothing is assumed or taken for granted, not even the next meal. We are always seeking permission from the spirit world for our actions.

The boundaries between different Aboriginal clans or nations are sometimes marked. These boundaries are not straight lines but may be determined by the footsteps and tracks of the ancestors or by bends in the creek or the river, the rain shadow, trees, and rocks. Some regions were shared between different Aboriginal peoples and some were restricted, with strict rules for obtaining permission to travel across the country.

Ceremonies

Ceremonies are an integration of song, dance, art and mime. They are a time when the best dancers and singers become the ancestral beings and they re-enact the activities of the ancestors. Ceremonies regenerate Aboriginal communities and are reminders of our roots and the expected behaviour which has been set down in law by the ancestors.

The ceremonies are Aboriginal law in action, involving the serious business of maintaining the law. Ceremonies serve many purposes. They provide a forum for the settling of disputes which may arise over land, marriages, hunting and gathering rights and a whole range of community conflicts. They are a process of teaching cultural knowledge and the spirituality of the ancestors to the next generations. There are also community forums where information about the best times to hunt and gather are discussed. They may also remind the community of taboos and the correct marriages for their families and children.

The spiritual significance of ceremonies is in their focus on the land. A ceremony is a collective act of the people in honouring and celebrating the ancestors and the Dreaming. At these times we are given the opportunity to reaffirm our connection to the Dreaming and to maintain and protect the spirit places of our ancestors. Ceremonies are also a celebration for the renewal of life, and the changing of seasons.

Songs

With the first steps of the ancestors across the land, country was sung into creation. The creation songs of the ancestors blessed the land. Our spirituality was sung to us then, and is still sung across the country today, by the ancestors with the rising of the sun. Law, culture and spirituality is sung and is alive in all things.

The Purposes of Songs Aboriginal songs are sung into the country, and each song is related to a specific place. There are old songs of the Dreaming, and there are more contemporary songs, which sing of the present.

Songs are about the life of the ancestors from the Dreaming. Songs are sung of creation, our relationship to the Dreaming and our place in the land.

Songs are also like a map of the country and are able to record details in the landscape. A singer can describe the country from the rhythm of a song, which changes to describe hills or lakes and rivers. The beat of the song will tell the singer, and the knowledgeable listener, what is in the land.

Songs are also our medicine; they can be healing. They can be used to bring rain, stop floods, change the direction of the wind, or sing a heat wave.

Our old people sing the songs over and over again with the birth of each new generation. The songs are a record of our history and they lay a path to follow, a path unchanged by time or circumstance.

Singing the Law Some of these songs record the original instructions from the Dreaming. The ancestors created the landscape, the natural world we have inherited. They laid down the law for future generations to follow. The law is sung in song and spoken in stories, sung by the ancestors and passed onto us.

Our laws and spiritual beliefs were not written down; our knowledge is passed on from one generation to the next in our dances, songs, stories, dreams and paintings. The songs are a record of our culture, our history, and our laws.

Songholders The ancestor is responsible for both the law and country, a responsibility which is carried by the traditional owner of the song today. The owner of the song is responsible for the country and particular sacred places, and when the song travels over these sacred places it is sung by the traditional owner of song or country.

Each clan group has its own song of creation, law and religion, and those songs are often the locally relevant parts of more extensive songs. No individual could ever know all the songs or stories of this country, for there are so many to know.

Song is the universal order. Song prevents chaos and the destruction of humanity and the natural environment. The singing of song ensures the continuity of life; the cycle of song provides abundance and harmony. Song expresses the relationship to land, sea and people; it unifies all life.

Secret, Sacred & Secular Knowledge

Aboriginal law and spirituality is a layered system of knowledge. Some knowledge is for the public to know, while other layers of information and knowledge are secret and sacred, and are kept by those initiated in ceremonies and those who have had the knowledge passed on directly to them.

Aspects of Aboriginal law are veiled in secrecy. Some of the men's ceremonial business is not ever revealed to women, and also some of the sacred ceremonial business of the women's law is not ever conveyed to men, or to the public at large. Secrecy provides a means of protecting and maintaining knowledge of the law and spirituality in a way that is 'proper' and in accordance with Aboriginal protocols.

Law travels across the country, and unlike most non-Aboriginal stories, the law has no beginning or end. Communication of law is a complex process of negotiation between 'bosses' who hold the law as it crosses their traditional country. It is not simply a process of telling a story; there are protocols which apply. The traditional boss for a story or song may decide to sanction or not to sanction the teaching of it, in accordance with custom and tradition.

The maintenance of oral tradition is strengthened by passing songs and stories through the 'right line' or the proper relation, and not leaving them open to the public domain for appropriation or misinterpretation.

SO NOW I AM AN ELDER

Lorranie Mafi-Williams

An Aboriginal Elder is a caretaker and keeper of sacred and ancient knowledge that has been passed down many, many generations. An Elder is not necessarily an old person. I began being trained to be an Elder at the age of 35 – it was decided by the Dreaming ancestors. There is no one definition for an Elder – we have so many different roles, which vary from clan to clan. However, there are some elements that all Elders share: we are humble, humane and we are not judgmental. Elders are taught to read the stars, the sun, the moon, the planets and other things that affect the Earth and its people. As Elders, it is our duty to care for Mother Earth, who in turn will nurture all living beings.

Sometimes we Elders have to struggle long and hard to preserve our country and culture. In 1997 I stood up against a powerful mining company which was encroaching on sites of Aboriginal significance. Apart from desecrating a sacred Aboriginal women's gathering place, it was also polluting a small lake, in which lay the remains of two Aboriginal women and a young Aboriginal girl who were slaughtered in a massacre during early European settlement. My efforts paid off – I managed to get the lake and surrounding land placed under government protection. But that was not the end. I am now involved in protecting other sacred sites that are threatened by property development.

Today, a big part of my role as an Elder is to raise awareness about Indigenous Australia and to break the 'noble savage' stereotype that still exists. For instance, I have been invited to give several talks in England and North America, and some of the questions people asked astonish me to this day. One man asked me what sort of clothes I wore; another lady asked me if Aborigines eat the placenta after giving birth! Yet another woman from Cambridge University in England asked me how Aborigines greet each other – I told her to come down from her seat at the back of the lecture hall and when she was in front of me, I shook her hand saying, 'That's how we greet people'. Many people I have met even think that Aboriginal people came to Australia after European settlement! Although more and more people in Australia and around the world are becoming better educated about Indigenous Australia, there is still a long way to go.

Christianity

The impact of Christianity is viewed differently throughout Australia. Some Aboriginal communities have embraced Christianity and integrated it with their own cultural beliefs. Other communities and individuals would argue that the impact of Christianity and the work of early Christian missionaries has contributed to our assimilation and the erosion of our Aboriginal culture and spiritual beliefs.

From the early years of federation, at the turn of the 20th century, Aboriginal people have been expected to assimilate into Australian society. The churches of Australia were instrumental in the implementation of the government's assimilation policy. The churches owned, administered and staffed many of the institutions where Aboriginal children were placed following their forced removal from their families.

Global colonialism has impacted on Indigenous relationships to the natural world. Many Aboriginal nations of Australia now have no land base, and their people live within cities, suburbs, and country towns. However, while many Aboriginal groups have no control over their traditional lands, they continue to have a rich spiritual and cultural life.

There are fundamental philosophical differences between Aboriginal spirituality and Christianity. The Christian religion is based on the idea of a hierarchy and a single god. Aboriginal culture has no hierarchical order of life which sustained the idea of one all-embracing god.

Aboriginal spirituality maintains a belief in the ancestral creative spirits. In this system, humans and animals are the messengers from the Dreaming. These ancestors carry and pass on the knowledge of the law and Aboriginal culture, as well as an understanding of how to live in the natural world as one. They are the teachers and carriers of the law, and through their creative actions the stories are sung and the law 'comes' into being.

We believe that the Dreaming can never be taken away from our people, because it is a spiritual belief that lives deepwithin us. The Dreaming is also alive in the land, whether we are in 'ownership' as defined in Australian property law or not. The Dreaming, unlike the land, cannot be removed from us; you cannot take the Dreaming out of the country. We can never have the knowledge of the Dreaming taken from us, for that is who we are. The Dreaming will always live in the land, it is all over this country. The country is alive with the Dreaming spirit.

See also The Land & Indigenous People section. For protocols on visiting sacred sites, see the Responsible Tourism section.

▌MISSIONS
Joseph Kennedy

'Missions' were government- or church-administered areas of land where Indigenous people were concentrated, regardless of language distinctions or tribal affiliations, from the early 1800s. In the early years, missions were places where some Indigenous people found refuge from settler violence. Later, a policy of forced relocation to missions was employed by the government.

Some missions actively degraded Indigenous culture, while others were more sympathetic. All encouraged assimilation of Indigenous people through the adoption of 'Christian values'.

New Indigenous communities formed on missions. The mission settlement often became a place of permanent residence for people who had previously gathered together in such large numbers only during times of ceremony. New languages and affiliations emerged, as well as distinct styles of music and art.

In the 1960s and '70s, a new policy of self-determination was introduced, and today many former missions are thriving Indigenous communities. Nepabunna, in South Australia, and Hermannsburg (Ntaria), in the Northern Territory, are two examples, the latter's success based in part on monies derived from tourist visits to the old mission buildings. An irony indeed.

Language

Before Europeans arrived in Australia, it's estimated that 600 to 700 dialects of 200 to 250 languages were spoken by the people living here. It's believed that all these languages evolved from the same language family as Aboriginal people gradually moved out over the continent and formed new social groups. For information on the languages spoken in each state, territory and the Torres Strait Islands, see the regional chapters.

A number of words were used throughout the continent, such as *jina*, (foot) and *mala* (hand), and the grammar of different languages also showed similarities. Today, at least 100 distinct Aboriginal languages are still spoken to varying extents, and many have a number of dialects. Some languages are actually gaining speakers as populations expand and dominant languages replace others.

Membership of a particular language group is of great social and cultural significance to Aboriginal people – as in many cultures, land, language and people are intricately bound. Languages 'belonged' to tracts of country and, according to Aboriginal tradition, had often been bestowed by Dreaming creator figures. Aboriginal people living in a particular area are bound to both their country and the languages of their country. Often a group of neighbouring clans would have similar forms of speech, which could be called dialects of the same language. Many Aboriginal people were bilingual or multilingual, speaking their own as well as neighbouring languages, and these days English as well.

As Aboriginal cultures traditionally kept oral records, and Aboriginal languages weren't written until well after European contact, many languages were lost forever when their speakers died out. Today, there are no fluent speakers left of the original languages of Tasmania, Victoria, and most of NSW. The only flourishing languages are to be found in the centre of the continent and along the north coast.

Aboriginal people don't usually expect to speak their languages with non-Aboriginal people, and in most such situations English is the language of choice. However, travellers who choose to try out a few local names for animals, plants or places, will probably be perceived as showing an interest in Aboriginal languages and culture.

Lonely Planet's excellent *Australian phrasebook* gives a detailed account of Aboriginal languages.

Features

Many Aboriginal languages share some features, such as the sounds they use, the types of vocabulary or structural features.

Vocabulary Most Aboriginal languages have about 10,000 words – about the same number of words used by the average speaker of English. Many words reflect the close relationship that Aboriginal people have with their environment. The Western Desert Pintupi dialect of Outback WA has 18 words for 'hole' – an ant burrow, a rabbit burrow, a goanna burrow, a small animal burrow and so on. Traditionally, all Aboriginal adults could identify and name hundreds of plants and animals. This is still the case in many parts of Outback and northern Australia, and one reason why Aboriginal people are central to much contemporary biological research.

Many Aboriginal words don't correspond directly to English words – they often cover a different classification of the natural world and express concepts particular to Aboriginal culture. The Kalkadoon word *kanimayintyirr* means 'policeman' (lit: the-one-who-ties-up). *Kanimayi* is 'tie up' and *-nytyirr* is a suffix like '-er' in English words such as 'driver'.

Dozens of Aboriginal words describing the environment and native species have been incorporated into Standard Australian English, including animals such as barramundi (a fish), dingo (a native dog), kangaroo, perentie (a lizard) and wallaby; birds such as brolga, budgerigar, galah and kookaburra; types of trees, including coolabah, jarrah, mallee and mulga; and the words boomerang, corroboree (a celebration) quandong (a fruit) and *yakka* (work).

Sounds Other similarities between Aboriginal languages include the sounds used and the way these sounds are combined.

All Aboriginal languages have the sound *ng* as in 'sing', while the sound *ny* as in 'canyon' is very common. Other sounds frequently found are 'r-coloured' sounds that are much the same as the *rn* in 'mourner' in a typical American pronunciation, and 'y-coloured' sounds, made by holding the tip of the tongue down behind the lower front teeth while making sounds such as *t*, *n* and *l*.

Some Australian languages have dental consonants, made by placing the tongue against the back of the front teeth.

Aboriginal languages usually don't distinguish between *p/b*, *t/d*, *k/g* and *ch/j*. This is one of the reasons why the names of some languages have several spellings, such as Walbiri/Warlpiri, which is spoken in central Australia.

Structure Aboriginal languages characteristically add different endings to words to indicate the relationship between words in a sentence. In the Kalkadoon language of the Mt Isa area, for example, a particular ending is used to mark who's performing the action in a sentence. In the sentence '*Martuyu ngulurmayi thuku*', which means 'Mother grabs the dog' (literally 'mother-*yu* grab dog'), the ending -*yu* is added to 'mother' to indicate that it's the mother who grabs the dog rather than the dog who grabs the mother.

Across the north of the continent, languages tend to have very complex verbs that seem more like sentences than single words. In Tiwi, the language of the Bathurst and Melville Islands, for instance, the English sentence 'He sent them a message' can be expressed as a single word: *yu-wuni-marri-wa-yangirri* (literally 'he-them-with-words-sent').

Language Shift

The establishment last century of large, permanent communities on missions, reserves, cattle stations and Aboriginal communities has brought changes to the acquisition and use of traditional Aboriginal languages. In many larger communities, one language has become dominant, be it a local Indigenous language, a creole language (a blend of an Indigenous language with English) or a koine (a new local language resulting from contact between traditional languages).

In communities where traditional languages continue to be used, the number of speakers for some languages is increasing while other languages are in decline as speakers shift their language use from one language to another. Formerly, small numbers of people lived in isolated clan groups, and this isolation fostered the maintenance of many distinct language varieties. These days, people tend to live for at least some of the year in large regional communities populated by members of different language groups. In multilingual communities like these, there's a tendency for one language to emerge as a lingua franca. Children growing up in such situations tend to learn the lingua franca, as it's the language they hear most often and the one that enables them to communicate with the largest number of people.

Maintenance

Well over a hundred of Australia's Indigenous languages have died out, and only a few are expected to survive much of this century. However, as traditional languages are an intrinsic part of Aboriginal identity, Aboriginal communities all over Australia are showing a renewed interest in preserving what they can of their languages, and in trying to restore them from materials recorded during past generations.

In many parts of Australia, the present generation of Aboriginal children is being taught the language of their area. A number of bilingual schools teach Aboriginal children in both their own language and in English.

Aboriginal languages are also being kept alive by musicians playing contemporary

FURTHER READING

Vicki Webb

If you'd like to learn more about Indigenous languages, try the following books: *Language and Culture in Aboriginal Australia* (1993), edited by M Walsh and C Yallop, *Australian Aboriginal languages* (1982) by C Yallop and *Macquarie Aboriginal Words* (1994), a dictionary of Aboriginal words edited by N Thieberger and W McGregor.

and more traditional Aboriginal music, including songs in Aboriginal languages. One of the better known is the rock band Yothu Yindi, whose members come from the Yolngu language group. Other bands and church choirs also help maintain traditional languages.

Media such as the CAAMA and Imparja Television, both in Alice Springs, broadcast Aboriginal-language radio and television programs.

A number of community language centres conduct research into Aboriginal languages and produce dictionaries, books, and other language-related materials. They encourage the interest of members of the general public and welcome visitors. (For contact details, see the Language sections in the state chapters.)

Aboriginal English

While many Aboriginal people speak Standard Australian English, in parts of Outback Australia where people seldom have to use English within their communities, and where access to formal secondary education is limited, many Aboriginal people don't speak English regularly or fluently. Others, especially those who speak an Aboriginal language as their first language, may be fluent in an English dialect known as Aboriginal English.

There's an array of varieties of Aboriginal English which range from close to Standard Australian English to varieties very close to Kriol (widely spoken in the NT). Aboriginal English mostly uses English vocabulary, but takes some sounds, features of grammar and many cultural meanings from the Aboriginal languages of its speakers. Accordingly, Aboriginal English isn't always easily understood by speakers of other English dialects, just as, for instance, someone from Texas may have difficulty understanding someone from Newcastle.

Common Features There are many features and styles common to Aboriginal languages that might be heard in Aboriginal English.

Many Aboriginal languages use the same pronoun when referring to either a male or female. When speaking in English, an Aboriginal person may use 'he', 'him' and words like 'fella' when referring to either a man or a woman.

Because of the differences between Aboriginal and English sound systems, many Aboriginal people have difficulty pronouncing some English words. For example, many Aboriginal languages don't have the sounds *s*, *z*, *v*, *sh* or *th* and don't distinguish between *b* and *p*, or *d* and *t*. Conversely, it's difficult for some English-speaking people to roll their '*r*'s, or to distinguish between the retroflexed sounds (made with the tongue curled back on the roof of the mouth) typical of most Aboriginal languages and non-retroflexed sounds.

Conventions of politeness often differ between cultures. Most Australian languages don't have words for greetings like 'hello'. Instead, Aboriginal people often call out a person's skin name or use a relationship term when they meet someone.

However, as Aboriginal people are now accustomed to English speakers using greetings, some languages have adopted greetings based on the English form, which are used mainly to greet non-Aboriginal people.

Some languages don't have words for 'please' or 'thank you'. Although more people are now using the English 'thank you', thanks is traditionally expressed in actions rather than words, such as by doing something for a person at a later date. However, people will appreciate you using these terms as usual, as they show your friendly intentions.

Polite Conversation In many remote areas, the rules for politeness and avoidance reflect those of traditional languages, and special forms and styles of speaking may be used in English or an Aboriginal English dialect.

Traditionally, people would avoid their in-laws and use a special vocabulary in speaking with them. Children would defer to members of their parents' generation, but interaction between members of the same generation, or between grandparents and grandchildren, is more relaxed and often involves a great deal of joking, teasing and innuendo.

Visitors can respect these rules of politeness by treating older people with respect and reserve and by understanding that the reserve they may meet from younger people doesn't necessarily indicate a cool reception. Unless introduced, introduce yourself by first asking from a little distance, 'Can I come and see you?'

The names of people recently deceased are avoided for a period of time, and in general the overuse of personal names is avoided. People address each other by a kin term or by nickname. Some words, especially kin terms, may be borrowed from traditional languages.

Conversational styles differ across cultures and Aboriginal people do not, as a rule, interrogate each other as English speakers tend to do, but rely on each other to be reasonably cooperative in communicating information. Direct questions may be interpreted as rudeness and are more politely phrased as statements of knowledge, eg, 'I'm trying to find my way to the Language Centre'.

Generally, if you want to learn something, give something in return. Tell a story or anecdote to hear a story.

Aboriginal people tend to tolerate more silence in communication than the average Western person. If no-one says anything for a few minutes, don't feel compelled to fill the silence with idle chatter. Be content to wait and to listen.

As in many cultures, some language is restricted and some topics can't be discussed freely with strangers. Certain songs and language styles may be restricted to initiated men.

A visitor attempting to speak Aboriginal English runs the risk of being seen as patronising and insulting. When speaking to people who don't speak English as their first language, it's helpful to speak slowly and clearly, but don't use baby talk or a kind of pidgin language, and don't speak in a voice that's louder than your normal speaking voice.

See also the Education, Music and Responsible Tourism sections.

Facts for the Visitor

Information

Although Indigenous organisations (such as cooperatives, councils and corporations) have been included throughout this book, please be aware that many of these have been set up predominantly to cater to local Indigenous needs, *not* tourists. They can, however, point you in the right direction and some have Indigenous displays and/or tours. Most are already under considerable work pressure so be considerate – a call ahead of your visit, for instance, would probably be greatly appreciated. For general tourism inquiries (such as accommodation, maps etc) check out Lonely Planet's *Australia* guide, or visit the local tourist office/visitor information centre. However, don't expect all non-Indigenous tourist centres to be *au fait* with the local Indigenous attractions, history etc.

USEFUL ORGANISATIONS

Aboriginal Tourism Australia (ATA; ☎ 03-9620 4533, e ataust@ataust.org.au), at Level 2M, North Rialto Tower, 525 Collins St, Melbourne, is Australia's peak Indigenous tourism body. Based in Melbourne, its board has representatives from many of Australia's Indigenous tourism companies. Check out its happening Web page at www.ataust.org.au, which features information on permits, tours, protocol and authenticity.

The national group Australians for Native Title and Reconciliation (ANTaR; ☎ 02-9555 6138, e antar@antar.org.au) is an active, predominantly non-Indigenous, community group dedicated to promoting Indigenous land justice and Reconciliation. ANTaR is responsible for the Sea of Hands, a mobile art installation that records the support of thousands of Australians for Reconciliation in the form of signatures on the back of plastic hands. ANTaR stages events (all welcome), runs campaigns and can provide information on issues of land justice. See the state chapters for state-specific information, or visit its Web page at www.antar.org.au.

The Apology Australia Reconciliation Events Calendar Web site at www.apology.west.net.au/events.html has comprehensive and up-to-date information about seminars, study circles, performances, exhibitions, video and film screenings, festivals, ecumenical services for healing and Reconciliation, rallies and Sea of Hands displays throughout the country, with state-by-state listings.

By the time you read this, the Australian Institute for Aboriginal and Torres Strait Islander Studies (AIATSIS; ☎ 6246 1111) will have relocated to Canberra's Acton Peninsula, next to the National Museum of Australia. AIATSIS is an independent Commonwealth statutory authority and houses a vast library of resources relating to Indigenous peoples (open to the public; closed Tuesday).

The Australian Heritage Commission (☎ 6217 2111) has a Register of the National Estate detailing sites of significance across the country, including the Tent Embassy in Canberra (see Politics in the Facts about Aboriginal Australia & the Torres Strait Islands chapter). Web site: www.ahc.gov.au.

ORGANISED TOURS

Indigenous involvement in the tourism industry has steadily risen over recent years

---

STEREOTYPES

Sarina Singh

There is a plethora of stereotypes which have been promulgated by the media and others in relation to Aboriginal Australia and the Torres Strait Islands (many of these stereotypes have been articulated by Indigenous writers throughout this book, especially in the boxed text sections). If you cast aside any expectations you may have, stay open-minded, and respect requests that Aboriginal and Torres Strait Islander people (as well as tour guides, cultural centres, etc) may make about appropriate behaviour, your visit is bound to be far more rewarding for everyone. For more advice, see the Responsible Tourism section in this chapter.

TOLL-FREE CALLS & MOBILE PHONES

Many businesses and some government departments operate a toll-free service (prefix 1800), so no matter where around the country you are ringing from, it's a free call. Having said that, these numbers may not be accessible from certain areas, or from mobile phones, in which case you'll have to dial the normal number.

Many companies also have numbers beginning with 13 or 1300, and these are charged at the rate of a local call. Often these numbers are Australia wide, or may be applicable to a specific state or STD district only.

Phone numbers with the prefixes 04xx or 04xxx are mobile phones; the caller is charged mobile rates on calls both to and from mobiles.

and as Aboriginal and Torres Strait Islander culture is of escalating interest to tourists, this trend is set to continue. This book aims to direct travellers to tours and places where you can access Indigenous cultural experiences in an appropriate and responsible way. Rather than providing comprehensive background information, this guide provides the details of various tours, cultural centres and other places where you can find out about Indigenous Australia directly from Indigenous Australians.

It is highly recommend that you go on at least one tour, as not only will most of these provide you with accurate Indigenous interpretations and insights, they should also give you the opportunity to meet Aboriginal and Torres Strait Islander people, usually in a relaxed atmosphere. These tours may also offer access to Indigenous sites and information that are off limits to independent travellers. This book focuses on tours which have Indigenous involvement and/or support. Although some tour companies may be Indigenous-owned or -operated, non-Indigenous guides may be hired because of their communication skills and knowledge of Indigenous issues.

Informal Tours

Tour information is provided under the heading 'Organised Tours' in the regional chapters of this book, but please understand and appreciate that not all tours are strictly 'organised' in the conventional sense. Indeed this is often a highlight, as rather than sticking to inflexible itineraries and rehearsed commentary, many Indigenous tours are conducted in a delightfully informal and interactive way, allowing plenty of

time to chat and ask questions. Many tours are run solely by one person.

It's highly advisable to book tours well in advance, as some may need permits (see the Travel Permits section, later in this chapter) and require time to make other necessary arrangements. Also, some tours only operate at certain times of the year and many require a minimum number of people, so advance bookings are vital. Prices often vary depending on the number of people, the time of year and the duration of the tour. Quite a few tour operators can tailor-make itineraries to suit individual requirements (ask when booking). It's wise to ring a couple of days ahead of your tour just to confirm that it will be running as planned (especially if minimum numbers apply). Finally, some tours involve a fair bit of walking, so wear appropriate shoes and carry water (seek advice when booking).

For further related information, see the Responsible Tourism section, following.

Responsible Tourism

Mick Dodson & Toni Bauman

Many travellers are keen to experience and understand the unique worlds of the first Australians – and many Indigenous Australians will be interested in meeting you. You can be a responsible tourist by reading about some of the sensitivities we describe in this section which we hope will help make your visit a happy and memorable one.

The best thing you can do is to *always ask* when in doubt. Act naturally and with respect for privacy, take your time, be flexible in your responses – and enjoy yourself and the company of Indigenous Australians. But remember that your time constraints, sense of urgency and priorities may not always be shared. Many Indigenous people are dealing with serious issues of survival on a daily basis; their lives do not necessarily revolve around photo opportunities or your visit.

You will generally find Indigenous Australians very polite and willing to share their life and culture with you – but it must necessarily be on their terms.

For more information on responsible tourism see the Aboriginal Tourism Australia Web site at www.ataust.org.au. The ATA is the foremost Indigenous tourism body in Australia and you'll find the informative *Welcome to Our Land* on their site.

A Responsible Tourist Is an Informed One

Elite athletes never go into the big race without loads of hard work and training. You, the traveller, have to be travel-ready and information is the key to a rewarding visit. Reading this book and a few brochures just will not do.

Try to familiarise yourself with Indigenous histories and cultural practices prior to your trip. Be aware of the history of colonisation in Australia which continues to shape interactions between Indigenous people and others.

Breaking Stereotypes Check out the local library and Web pages listed in this book. Look for recent books about Indigenous Australians in both urban and remote settings, keeping in mind that the First Australians are not all the same. Picture postcards often show dark-skinned, timeless and primitive 'noble savages' who live idyllic hunting and gathering existences in the Australian Outback. However, Indigenous cultures are dynamic and contemporary and have adapted to the circumstances surrounding them.

Aboriginal and Torres Strait Islander peoples live many and varied lifestyles and have a range of likes and dislikes just like you. Today, Indigenous Australians are traditional hunters, academics, bureaucrats and politicians; some speak numerous traditional languages, others may speak only English; some live in remote areas in the

Mick Dodson

Mick Dodson is a director with Dodson, Bauman & Associates, a legal and anthropological consultancy company. He was recently the director of the Indigenous Law Centre at the University of New South Wales, and is retained by the centre as a special advisor.

Mick was Australia's first Aboriginal and Torres Strait Islander social justice commissioner, serving from 1993 until 1998. He has been a prominent advocate on land rights and other issues affecting Aboriginal and Torres Strait Islander peoples.

Born in the Northern Territory township of Katherine, Mick was educated in Katherine, Darwin and Victoria. He completed a Bachelor of Jurisprudence and a Bachelor of Laws at Monash University. Mick joined the Victorian Bar in 1981 and joined the Northern Land Council (NLC) as senior legal adviser in 1984. He became director of the NLC in 1990.

From 1988 to 1990 Mick was counsel assisting the Royal Commission into Aboriginal Deaths in Custody. He has been a member of the Victorian Equal Opportunity Advisory Council and treasurer of the North Australian Aboriginal Legal Aid Service. He is chair of the Australian Institute of Aboriginal and Torres Strait Islander Studies.

Mick is a vigorous advocate of the interests of the world's Indigenous peoples. He was the co-deputy chair of the Technical Committee for the 1993 International Year of the World's Indigenous People. He also chairs the United Nations Advisory Group for the Voluntary Fund for the Decade of Indigenous Peoples.

Australian bush, some live in country towns and others live in cities. Some are dark-skinned and some are very fair.

Seek out local information on arrival by contacting relevant bodies such as tourism offices, local tour operators, Indigenous councils, cultural centres, art galleries, local government bodies, Indigenous art centres and other local organisations.

Communicating

Some travellers may feel uncomfortable when visiting their first Indigenous community or home or camp. It may take some time to become accustomed to cultural practices and manners which are complex and may differ from yours – just as Indigenous Australians may take some time to get used to you. But if you act normally, take your cues from Indigenous people, say hello, smile or wave, you will generally receive a positive response. Humour is a mainstay of the interactions between Indigenous Australians, so keep it light where appropriate.

Conversation Understand that certain Indigenous behaviour is culturally influenced and is not intended to be impolite. The phrase 'thank you', for example, which is an automatic response for many travellers, may not be used in some areas. Many Indigenous cultures have systems of mutual obligation in place. It is understood that the favour will be eventually returned so there is no need to say thank you. In other areas, greetings such as 'hello' and 'goodbye' may not be used or direct eye contact may be avoided, especially between certain kin who may be in what has been called a *taboo relationship* with each other. This can be the case for a mother-in-law and son-in-law, who may not even be permitted by Aboriginal *law* to be in each other's presence.

Toni Bauman

Toni Bauman is an anthropologist who has worked for over twenty years in Aboriginal Australia in matters relating to land claims, native title and Aboriginal sites of significance, particularly in the Northern Territory but also elsewhere. Toni has been an Aboriginal adult educator and an art and craft adviser for Mimi Aboriginal Arts and Crafts in Katherine. She has served as a member on the Community Living Areas Tribunal in the Northern Territory and has worked in a wide range of consultancies. She has worked as an editor of the Indigenous Law Bulletin and is currently a co-director, with Mick Dodson, of Dodson, Bauman & Associates, a legal and anthropological consultancy.

In some parts of Australia, English is not a first language, in others many people speak English fluently. Take care not to be seen to be the stereotypical tourist, raising your voice and labouring over each word in the hope that you will be understood. You will feel a right idiot when someone responds to you in fluent and highly educated English. Yelling at people is a sure-fire way of killing any hope of meaningful conversation. Speak distinctly, using straightforward English and a normal tone of voice,

WHAT'S NEW?

Sarina Singh

Indigenous tourism is an evolving industry. By the time you read this book, it is very likely that new ventures with Indigenous involvement will be operating. To find out about the latest developments, ask at the relevant local Indigenous organisations, tourist offices or visitor information centres, and other appropriate bodies such as cultural centres. Fellow travellers, the Internet and Indigenous media (see the Internet Resources, Newspapers & Magazines and Radio & TV sections in this chapter) can also be terrific sources of information. For details on developments nationwide, you could also contact the Aboriginal Tourism Product Manager at the Australian Tourist Commission in Sydney (☎ 02-9361 1290, e lahoy@atc.gov.au, or check out their Web site at www.australia.com).

CULTURAL TOURISM – CAN IT HELP CREATE PARADISE ON EARTH?

Herb Wharton

I often wonder how much closer we would be to living in that mythical paradise today if Adam and Eve had been Indigenous... they would have eaten the snake and not the bloody apple! Temptation could have been eliminated on day one because the snake, which watched the naked cavorting couple with a smirk on its mouth, managed to wriggle away.

Cultural tourism run by Indigenous people, or in partnership with non-Indigenous people, is one way of ensuring the survival of our cultural identity in this ever-changing word of economic globalisation. Globalisation brings together more and more people of diverse backgrounds. It means that cultural tourism has the capacity to create positive worldwide benefits for tribal unification. The sharing of cultural diversities helps to break down the world's greatest threats to peaceful coexistence: discrimination and intolerance.

There are also potentially great economic benefits which could flow from cultural tourism. However, it must be remembered that *bungo* (money) was only introduced into Australia around 200 years ago. The arrival of bungo saw most Indigenous people deprived of their self-determination, economic independence, cultural identity, and basic human rights.

Cultural tourism could greatly benefit those at the grass-roots level and provide tourists with an authentic Indigenous experience. It also enables visitors to talk *to* Indigenous people (not *about* them). Yet

Herb Wharton

Herb left home after a couple of years' schooling to travel Outback Australia on horseback as a drover, behind big mobs of horses, cattle and sheep. It took 40 years for Herb to write his first poem, and now he travels Australia and the world, riding in jet aeroplanes to literary festivals and on reading tours of places like Japan, Hong Kong, England, Scotland, Germany, France and Belgium.

He has published four books and has sold the film rights to his novel *Unbranded*, which has also been translated into Dutch. *Cattle Camp* is an oral history of Aboriginal drovers, while *Where Ya' Been Mate?* is a collection of short stories. *Yumba Days* is a factual account of Herb's childhood in an Aboriginal camp in Outback Queensland.

Herb's one great claim to fame is that in his home town of Cunnamulla in Outback Queensland (where there is not a traffic light or McDonald's within 200 miles), his latest book *Yumba Days* out-sells Jeffrey Archer, Harry Potter and the Bible.

no one person or group can talk for all Indigenous people – such is our diversity. As with Europeans, we cannot be defined by language, features or colour. One thing is for sure – there is no such thing as a part-Indigenous person. That is only in the minds of others.

Like the misguided notion that Captain Cook discovered Australia – hence the beginning of history on this continent – the fact is that our history began in the Dreamtime BC (before Cook; before Christ). Our *stories* and histories are written on the landscape. They are imprinted in our minds as well as in books, unlike in many foreign lands where it seems to me that people have imposed a 'cut-off date' for their histories. For example, many countries base the beginning of their civilisation on great man-made monuments. To me, these monuments are nothing but dates in time which are really built on the Dreaming tracks of others who lived before them in the ongoing human process of 'becoming'.

TO BE OR NOT TO BE

bryan Andy

There's more to being an Aborigine than playing the didjeridu and posing in a barren landscape, spear in hand before a mystical dusk backdrop. Yet some unfortunate (misinformed, ignorant, neglectful...) souls – bless 'em – think that these constructs epitomise Aboriginality. For starters my mob didn't even have the didjeridu before the invasion, yet reductionist attitudes would have you think otherwise.

Aboriginality is not just about physical attributes like skin colour, what you wear or where you choose to be situated come sunset. There's so much more to it than what the romanticising media has chosen to filter through to us all. I remember secondary school classes studying (objectifying?) Aborigines – how they were supposed to act, what they were supposed to do and the position they held within Australian society. Of course very little of it had any relevance to how I was an Aborigine and how I existed in my Aboriginal community.

As a south-eastern Aborigine I cringe when non-Indigenous people dichotomise Aboriginal identity and say 'this is traditional and that is not'. Not only does it make me want to thwack them on the forehead with (the spine of!) a book the size of this one, it also makes me want to ask them, 'Well, what is traditional?' and consequently, 'Who are you to define that?'. As an Indigenous person I define myself in accordance with my community and my upbringing. Indigenous identities and their composition don't belong to the paradigm and whims of non-Indigenous legislation and thinking. This naïve fascination with what is 'traditional' is a non-Indigenous construct, and this should be recognised as such.

Many non-Indigenous people need to challenge themselves and the system that encourages homogenisation, objectification and the acceptance of straight-up stupidity as we don't have to put up with being misrepresented. I am not 'part-white' or 'non-traditional'; I am a Yorta Yorta man. I wouldn't define myself as anything else.

remember Indigenous Australians have a range of English language skills.

Paying a Visit In the early days, a visiting group, especially strangers, could be made to sit on the outskirts of a camp for days before being invited in. This allowed time for each to become used to the other's presence and to prepare themselves, as well as to ensure that no bad spirits were around. In urban settings, it may be enough to knock on the door. But whether approaching a group of people in the street or in a camp, in houses in the city or in the bush, take care. Don't be too forceful or direct in your approaches. Instead of barging in, stand a little way off and approach slowly. In remote communities, you might try making some movement or noise – coughing is a typical way by which Indigenous Australians in many areas announce their presence. Once your presence is registered, you may be beckoned over or someone may come up, otherwise, proceed slowly and knock on the door. If this approach does not work in communities, try walking over to the nearest house or shelter and calling out to attract attention. Don't hang around if it's obvious that your presence isn't wanted.

In some areas of Australia, Indigenous Australians don't get straight to the point. Take your time, begin with a few pleasantries to establish your interest in the person you are talking to, and see if they're interested in talking to you. Listen to what's being said and resist the urge to fill pauses in the conversation; the point will be made eventually. Questions that require 'yes' or 'no' answers are not helpful in many situations. Reluctance to offend can result in a 'yes' which really means 'no' since, in some areas of Australia, it may be seen as impolite to refuse requests publicly. If you're unsure, especially in remote communities, check with a third party that 'apparent agreement' does not mean 'no', or raise the issue in a way that encourages discussion. There may be others who need to be spoken to before you can be given an answer.

Differences in Etiquette Body language and etiquette vary across the country, so take note of local practices – take it as it comes and follow the cues. In some Indigenous cultures, it is not acceptable to use the names of deceased people. In some places direct eye contact is avoided, in other places it will be fine. Indeed, in some urban situations, refusal to make eye contact could be seen as rudeness.

In urban situations, it may be fine to dress however you like; in some remote communities, it may be important, especially for women, to dress modestly and not reveal too much. In many remote areas, women may, at times, lead relatively separate and independent lives from men; sitting in their own groups and not freely mixing. It may not be appropriate for a woman to approach a group of males or socialise with them by herself. Learn to appreciate difference; a firm handshake may be a sign of aggression to Indigenous Australians; a soft clasp of hands might be better.

Indigenous practices are based on complex relationships between kin and to be alone can be looked upon with suspicion in some areas. For a start, Indigenous Australians may feel sorry for you if you are camping by yourself and feel that you are placing yourself in a dangerous situation. Shame is a very important emotional force in Indigenous lives. In many areas, it can be a *shame job* to stand out in a crowd, for the social world is one of relationships with each other. Walking alone across a crowded room can cause shame; people may hang their heads and appear shy if singled out in a group. You may cause Indigenous Australians to be shamed if your behaviour is too extroverted or loud.

Inside Knowledge

Access to ritual and cultural knowledge may be restricted to specific individuals or groups and may be secret. Although this may have exotic appeal for travellers, asking about such things may cause offence. Show an interest in local heritage but try to understand the signs when your questions are making Indigenous people uncomfortable. It's better not to be too inquisitive. This will avoid embarrassment on all sides. Senior individuals may volunteer information if they see fit, perhaps about cultural practices and

rituals which are public. But remember that the line between the public and the secret or private is blurred and that such inquiries might be seen by an Indigenous person as a request for secret information.

It takes years of trust, association and friendship before such topics can be talked about. You are a short-term visitor and a stranger and are unlikely to reach that point during your stay. This is one case where it might be better not to ask. Instead, consider supporting local public performances of Indigenous dance and song, which are public celebrations of culture.

Photography & Video

Don't wear out your welcome by taking photographs or videoing all over the place. Indigenous Australians are not objects of curiosity; they are people like you and photography can be highly intrusive. Always ask permission before photographing or videoing a person, group or residence and offer to return copies of photographs or footage (make sure you get an address!). Taking photographs of cultural places, practices and images, sites of significance and ceremonies – and other apparently less significant subjects – may be a sensitive matter. If you have permission to use photographs in reports or publications, it is polite to acknowledge the names of the individuals in the shots.

Always ask and respect the right to say no.

Caring for Country

By reading this book, you will know that Indigenous Australians are the custodians of all of the Australian landscape. They also feel a responsibility for visitors to their lands. There are many different kinds of sites of spiritual or cultural significance to Indigenous Australians.

Some sites are registered under heritage legislation and have special conditions attached. Some may be public and accessed readily; others may only be visited by men or by women. Some may be regarded as sacred and considered too dangerous to enter while the significance of others may not be apparent. Still others might only be visited with permission from their traditional custodians or in their company.

While many sites are open to visitors, the wear and tear of large numbers of visitors

VISITING SACRED SITES

Dr Irene Watson

From the Dreaming the ancestors created women's places and men's places – there are secret, sacred places where only men or women can go alone. In these places it is important to understand that in being respectful and honouring Aboriginal law, a certain code of behaviour is required to avoid violating any Aboriginal laws. This behaviour could involve many things – sitting quietly; not staring too hard at a particular site; restrictions on camping and drinking water; restrictions on the removal of artefacts or stones from a particular country; avoiding climbing particular rocks and mountains; and avoiding certain sites entirely.

Throughout Australia you will find places of significance to men and women, and many of these places are not recognised or protected by Australian law. In these situations, individuals will need to apply their own judgement and discretion. You will need to decide whether or not you will comply with the Aboriginal law of place, and the concerns and wishes of traditional owners and custodians, in respect of the restrictions or special conditions which apply when accessing sacred sites.

Australian law may not restrict access to a popular tourist attraction but the traditional owners may have strong cultural reasons for doing so. For example, the traditional owners may prohibit people from climbing a sacred rock (such as Uluru) and the Australian laws may provide no sanctions or penalties against climbing the rock. The choice is left to the individual to determine whether compliance with Aboriginal culture is more important than the desire to climb the rock for the view and the recreational pleasure of the climb. Aboriginal people have very little power to apply Aboriginal laws and prohibit access to some of the most sacred cultural sites in Australia.

For further information on cultural protocols and appropriate behaviour in relation to accessing sacred Aboriginal sites visitors should contact the traditional owners or local Aboriginal communities and their management.

places enormous pressure on them. Some sites are part of fragile ecosystems and need special protection.

Please respect the wishes of Indigenous custodians by reading signs carefully, keeping to dedicated camping areas, staying on tracks and board walks, not wandering into unauthorised areas, and complying with other requests. Wording on signs has often been settled in cooperation with those Indigenous Australians who have a responsibility under Indigenous laws to care for them. At some sites, it may be sufficient to observe respectful, quiet behaviour. At others, there may be specific rules relating to the surrounding environment. Always ask about appropriate behaviour and take care not to casually kick ant beds or stones, break twigs from (or carve initials into) trees or souvenir earth, leaves or other cultural artefacts you might find.

Remember that Indigenous rock art and engravings are manifestations of beliefs and Indigenous laws.

Keep an eye on your children and never interfere with rock surfaces and cultural artefacts. Resist the temptation to touch artworks and motifs; the skin's natural oils can cause considerable deterioration. Dust also causes problems, so move thoughtfully at rock art sites and leave your vehicle some distance away.

Clambering over rocks beyond designated areas to get that photo opportunity will not win you any friends. At least some sites will have been photographed by professionals so you might like to think about buying postcards instead.

Alcohol

One common stereotype of Indigenous Australians is that they all drink alcohol to excess. But the reality is that a smaller percentage of Aborigines drink alcohol than do other Australians. Nevertheless, Indigenous drinking may be more obvious than that of other Australians because it often takes place in public.

One reason for this is that some Indigenous councils have banned the possession and consumption of alcohol on their communities, declaring them dry areas under relevant legislation. Those who live on such communities may drink irregularly, only when they come to town where they may have no accommodation. Others may simply enjoy the opportunity to socialise with other Indigenous Australians who they would otherwise have little opportunity to meet, since socialising most often occurs amongst groups of extended kin.

Indigenous Australians are actively involved in the fight against alcohol which has had a devastating effect on their people. In some areas, they have persuaded hotels and takeaway outlets not to sell alcohol to Indigenous people or to limit the amount they can purchase and there may be signs requesting visitors not to purchase alcohol for Indigenous Australians.

Before visiting a community, always check whether alcohol-related rules apply and respect these rules. Permit conditions may also include rules relating to the purchase and consumption of alcohol.

On the other hand, local pubs are often the only meeting places where you might get to know Indigenous Australians. Be aware of the problem and don't find yourself loading up with alcohol after the pub closes and turning up with a mob of people on someone's doorstep; you and your friends will generally not be welcome.

See also Polite Conversation in the Language section.

Travel Permits

Mick Dodson & Toni Bauman

Seeking permission to enter the lands of others is a basic courtesy in any society. There are a range of protocols for visiting Indigenous lands, homes or camps, but one thing is the same throughout Australia: It is always courteous to make contact prior to your visit. Some communities encourage visitors, others don't. So don't be foolhardy and just rock up without checking the protocols beforehand.

If you do, in some places, you may find yourself in trouble because it is illegal to enter Indigenous lands without a permit and you could incur a fine. Permits give Aboriginal landowners some administrative control over their land and recognise their rights to manage it. Check with local Indigenous Land Councils and police stations before visiting to ensure that you do not break any rules and apply for permits as required. If you're travelling on organised tours, the tour operators will have made permit arrangements for you. Read the conditions on the permit and respect local landowners by adhering to them.

Plan in Advance

Don't be in a rush; permits sometimes take time to process. Traditional owners have to be contacted and the relevant people in authority may not always be available. Remember that there may be a network of people who have to be consulted; Indigenous authority is not centralised. If your request is not dealt with promptly it may simply mean that not all relevant people have been spoken to.

Timing is important, so make sure that your visit does not conflict with other important events like funerals which can go on for some time. Respect the rights of Indigenous people to say no. There may be ceremonies going on which are private and sometimes secret, just for men or just for women or *sorry business* (funeral rituals) which can sometimes take a long time. Access to some areas may be closed because of such events.

On Arrival

When you arrive at a community, go to the local council office or store, or ask someone in the street about which people you should notify of your arrival. If you're camping, ask where to stay and whether there are any areas in the community that you should avoid. Some areas may not have free access because of ritual activity; some may only be open to women or to men; others may have cultural and spiritual significance which determines their access.

Be self-contained – resources are often scarce in Indigenous communities. Some of you may be looking for an 'authentic' experience of living with an Indigenous family, but be aware that your presence could be a burden on a family and that, even so, many Indigenous people would consider it impolite to refuse such a request.

Permit Applications

To make a permit application, you must fax or write to the appropriate Indigenous land council and/or community. If you write, enclose a stamped, self-addressed envelope. Permits can take time to issue, so apply well in advance. If you are going on an organised tour, the operator should take care of any permits – check when booking. Permit requirements may vary across Australia (specific permit requirements are described in the regional chapters of this book), but some common information that is usually required includes:

- [ ] names of all members of the party
- [ ] dates of travel
- [ ] route details
- [ ] purpose of the visit
- [ ] make, model and registration number of the vehicle
- [ ] contact address and telephone number

Included below is a brief overview of the permit requirements to visit places listed in this guide. For more information (including contact details), see the regional chapters.

New South Wales & the Australian Capital Territory

New South Wales (NSW) While permits are not generally required to visit the vast majority of Aboriginal land councils, museums, and Indigenous cultural or educational centres in NSW, permits are required in some instances. One example is The Willows, a camping and fishing property on the Severn River, just outside of Glen Innes, which is owned and operated by the Ngoorabul Local Aboriginal Land Council.

Australian Capital Territory (ACT) There is no permit requirement for entering onto Aboriginal land in the ACT.

Northern Territory (NT)

Top End Arnhem Land and other northern mainland areas are administered by the Northern Land Council in Darwin.

Permits from the Northern Land Council are required to visit any part of Arnhem Land. This includes Ganbalanya (Oenpelli), across the East Alligator River from Kakadu National Park.

The process rarely takes more than a couple of weeks, the exception being the permit for Oenpelli, which is issued on the spot at the Jabiru Northern Land Council office.

Visitors to Bathurst and Melville islands (the Tiwi Islands) also require a permit from the Tiwi Land Council in Nguiu, Bathurst Island. Visitors on organised tours have their permit included and it is not necessary to make a separate application.

Central Australia The Central Land Council administers all Aboriginal land in the southern and central regions of the Northern Territory, its area extending as far north as Daguragu and the Barkly Tableland.

There are two kinds of permit, transit permits (for passing through) and entry permits (for longer stays).

A transit permit is required for the Yulara-Kaltukatjara (Docker River) road, but not for either the Tanami Rd or the Sandover Hwy where these cross Aboriginal land.

Queensland

It is not necessary to obtain permits to visit Yarrabah or Cherbourg Aboriginal Communities. You can also visit Hopevale without a permit, but note that you must obtain a permit to *pass through* Hopevale (eg, to get to the coast). Permits are also required for a visit to Wujal Wujal or any of the Palm Islands.

Large sections of Cape York Peninsula are on Aboriginal land. You don't need a permit to travel on the main road to the tip of Cape York until you reach the Dulhunty River. Much of the land north of the Dulhunty is Injinoo custodial land and requires a permit.

Travelling across Aboriginal land elsewhere on the Cape may require a permit. Some are easy to obtain while others are difficult – it all depends on the community concerned.

South Australia (SA)

Almost all of the region bordered by the railway line to Perth, the Stuart Highway and the Western Australia and Northern Territory borders is restricted or Aboriginal land. To visit the southern part, ie Maralinga-Tjarutja Aboriginal land, contact the administration office in Ceduna.

Independent tourism is not encouraged in the northern part, ie, the Anangu Pitjantjatjaraku Yankunytjatjaraku lands.

Tasmania

There are no permits issued in Tasmania to visit Indigenous sites or Aboriginal land. However, Aboriginal land is private land and you need to let the relevant community authority know if you want to visit some sites independently.

If you want to go to Wybalenna, inform the Flinders Island Aboriginal Association Inc. At Preminghana on the north-west coast, let the resident caretaker know if you'd like to take a look around.

Torres Strait Islands

At the time of writing a permit was not required to visit Thursday Island or Horn Island, although this may change as more land is handed back to traditional owners. If you want to visit any of the outer islands, you must get permission from the relevant island council. The councils vary in their enthusiasm for tourism, and some don't allow visitors at all.

You'll need to approach the council well in advance, usually four weeks. Often a phone call is enough, but sometimes you'll be asked to put your request in writing. You may be turned down for many different reasons – the guest house may be booked up with health workers, your dates may clash with a tombstone unveiling or it may be a feast day.

Western Australia (WA)

The Aboriginal Affairs Department (AAD) is responsible for the administration of all Aboriginal land trusts in the state, including the Kimberley, Pilbara and eastern desert regions, the Gunbarrel Hwy and the northern end of the Canning Stock Route. You will also need permits from both the AAD and the Central Land Council to traverse the full length of the Great Central Road. For permission to visit Aboriginal freehold land you must apply directly to the owners.

If you wish to visit areas that are on Aboriginal land trusts you need to contact the AAD for an Aboriginal Land Permit in advance. Although this allows you to access some Aboriginal communities, it does not give you any special rights and it is advisable to contact the community directly, prior to arrival, for their permission to visit. At certain times of the year access may be denied due to ceremonial/traditional reasons.

Once you arrive at the community you should report directly to the community office to be advised of specific access limitations. Many areas are not accessible to the general public.

National Park Permits

You sometimes need a permit to camp in a national park or even to visit, and such a permit must usually be obtained in advance. See the regional chapters for details.

Internet Resources

Brett Leavy

There is an abundance of information about Aboriginal Australia and the Torres Strait Islands on the Internet, but there is not a lot of good quality travel information. For general information on travel in Australia see the Lonely Planet Web site at www.lonelyplanet.com.

As well as visiting the Web sites listed below, for new material you should try searching with the words 'Indigenous Australian' or 'Aboriginal Australia'.

Many of these Web sites will contain links to others and this is also a great way of finding new or more recent Web listings about Indigenous Australia.

Information

Aboriginal and Torres Strait Islander Commission (ATSIC) For the facts and figures, visit this Web site. The commission receives funding every year from the federal government for Indigenous programs such as community development, employment, housing, native title, arts and cultural maintenance.
www.atsic.gov.au

Australian Institute of Aboriginal and Torres Strait Islander Studies (AIATSIS) AIATSIS describes itself as the premier institute for information about the culture and lifestyle of Aboriginal people. It's jam-packed full of online newsletters, language dictionaries and discussion papers, and has a comprehensive online library catalogue about Aboriginal Australia.
www.aiatsis.gov.au

KooriNet Run by the University of Sydney's Koori Centre, KooriNet hosts BlackTracka, an Indigenous Australian search engine.
www.koori.usyd.edu.au

Outback Digital Network The design of this Web site may be a little dull, but it does have lots of relevant links to Aboriginal Australia, including links to remote Aboriginal Communities.
www.odn.net.au/links.html

Torres Strait Regional Authority One of the few sites that relates to Indigenous people from the Torres Strait.
www.trsa.gov.au

VICNET Victoria's community Internet network contains many links to Aboriginal sites in Victoria and around Australia. Many of the sites are informative, but visually uninspiring.
vicnet.net.au/aboriginal

Media

Indigenous Australia This is a links portal developed by the National Indigenous Media Association of Australia. At the time of writing it was new and there was not much there, but it should develop into an interesting Internet resource in the future.
www.Indigenousaustralia.com.au

The Koori Mail Australia's only national Indigenous newspaper. Unfortunately the Web site is an online brochure and has yet to include its published stories.
www.koorimail.com.

Land Rights Queensland You will find Land Rights Queensland, a newspaper of Queensland's Indigenous community, online within this Web site.
www.faira.org.au/lrqarc.html

Yahoo Australia Aboriginal News This site has a news service which links to stories on Indigenous issues covered by Australia's mainstream media organisations.
au.fullcoverage.yahoo.com/fc/AUNZ/Aboriginal_News

Art & Culture

Aboriginal Art & Culture Centre A site hosted by the Pwerte Martne Martne Aboriginal Corporation, a southern Arrernte tribal group whose homelands are 100km south of Alice Springs in Central Australia. There is a virtual art gallery and information on the Arrernte people, the Dreaming, the didjeridu and many Aboriginal tours including itineraries and prices.
www.aboriginalart.com.au

Desart The Web site for the Association of Central Australian Aboriginal Art Centres may be useful as a contact point for information on Aboriginal artists in the Northern Territory.
www.desart.com.au

Dreaming Art Centre of Utopia This virtual art gallery exhibits art from the Utopian region of Central Australia.
www.dacou.com.au

GeoClans This portal seeks to promote, market and support various Indigenous-designed surfboards.
www.geoclans.com

Jukurrpa Artists This online gallery of Western Desert art showcases Warlpiri, Pitjantjatjara, Luritja, Anmatyerre, Arrernte and Pertame artists from an Alice Springs-based women's cooperative.
www.ozemail.com.au/~jukurrpa

Kaltjiti Arts & Crafts The Kaltjiti artists specialise in printing and fabric work, such as batik.
pymedia.in-sa.com.au/arts/kaltjiti/index.html

Message Sticks This Web site showcases the artwork of Indigenous inmates in Queensland.
www.messagesticks.com

Language

The World Wide Web Virtual Library There are hundreds of Aboriginal dialects and distinct languages in Australia. This Web site has information on nearly 40 of those languages.
www.dnathan.com/VL/austLang.htm

The Struggle

Cape York Land Council Land councils represent and promote the interests of Aboriginal people throughout Australia. This Web site contains information on the 17 Aboriginal communities of Cape York.
www.cylc.org.au

Central Land Council Information on the communities of central Australia, including a downloadable permit application.
www.clc.org.au

Indigenous Land Corporation The Indigenous Land Corporation, established by the Commonwealth Government in 1995, aims to acquire land for Aboriginal people and to manage Indigenous-held land to provide benefits for Indigenous Australians.
www.ilc.gov.au

Mirrar Online The Web site of the tiny Mirrar Clan of the Kakadu region – who have 27 members – describes their fight against continued uranium mining in Kakadu.
www.mirrar.net/pages/welcome.htm

Northern Land Council The Northern Land Council's confrontational Web site describes the fight for land rights – dealing with developers, miners and government opposition.
www.ozemail.com.au/~nlc95

Native Title

Australians for Native Title and Reconciliation Visit this Web site to see photographs of the colourful Sea of Hands, which has travelled around Australia in support of native title and Reconciliation.
www.antar.org.au

Human Rights and Equal Opportunity Commission The Aboriginal and Torres Strait Islander Social Justice Commissioner has a statutory obligation to report annually to the government on native title – in that report the commissioner is also required to consider human rights implications. You can download the report from this Web site.
www.hreoc.gov.au/social_justice/native_title/index.html

The National Native Title Tribunal Set up to determine native title in Australia. This site contains lots of information on native title including details of recent determinations.
www.nntt.gov.au

Native Title Research Unit This unit of AIATSIS conducts research into native title and publishes the results. You can view their publications on this Web site.
www.aiatsis.gov.au/ntru_abt.htm

Reconciliation

Reconciliation Australia 'A united Australia which respects this land of ours; values the Aboriginal and Torres Strait Islander heritage; and provides justice and equity for all.' This is the vision of Reconciliation Australia, which was formed after the Council for Aboriginal Reconciliation disbanded in 2000. If you want to know about Reconciliation in Australia then this Web site is a good place to start.
www.reconciliation.org.au

Community Sites

Many Aboriginal communities and community organisations maintain Web sites which provide an introduction to history and culture in the local area. Below is a small sample.

Brisbane Stories This collection of related community Web sites, initiated by the Brisbane City Council, is about south-east Queensland. Snippets of Aboriginal history are revealed in many of the stories, which cover the growth of various Brisbane suburbs.
brisbane-stories.powerup.com.au

Nyangatjatjara Aboriginal Corporation The site promotes the aims of three Anangu communities at Imanpa, Kaltukatjara (Docker River) and Mutitjulu, the custodians of Uluru.
www.ozemail.com.au/~nyac

Yorta Yorta Home Page Information on the Yorta Yorta people of the Echuca region of Victoria.
users.mcmedia.com.au/~yorta/yorta.htm

For reviews of political Web sites, see the Politics section in the Facts about Aboriginal Australia & the Torres Strait Islands chapter.

Brett Leavy

Brett lives in Brisbane and is a member of the Kooma people whose traditional lands are in south-west Queensland. He loves teaching people to work with computers and is a strong advocate of communication through the online world. He sees the Internet as a tool not only for building bridges between people, but also for education and growing business. It took Brett 27 years to build his first Web site but today, with the help of a team of nine people, his company CyberDreaming provides world-class online solutions to government, business, community organisations and individuals.

Brett is establishing one of the first Indigenous-owned and -managed Web and multimedia companies in Australia. He is a board member of the Virtual Systems and Multimedia International Society, and former chief executive officer of the National Indigenous Media Association of Australia.

Brett's other claim to fame is that in his younger days he represented Australia in two sports: track and field and Rugby Union, in which he had the opportunity to compete at an international level and visit countries like Britain, France, Germany, Italy, New Zealand, Cuba, Japan, Canada and the United States. Brett is married to Jill and has three sons: Nathanael, Dominic and Sebastian.

Books

Joseph Kennedy

The Little Red, Yellow & Black (and green and blue and white) Book is an invaluable pocket guide to the society, culture and politics of Indigenous Australia. It's published by AIATSIS and you can pick it up for free at many Indigenous organisations. *The*

Encyclopaedia of Aboriginal Australia, published by Aboriginal Studies Press for AIAT-SIS, is two volumes of in-depth information and is one of the most useful Indigenous Australia references around.

Josephine Flood's *The Riches of Ancient Australia* is a traveller's guide to the sacred and material 'prehistory' of Indigenous Australia, from ancient fish traps in NSW to Uluru in the NT. *Burnum Burnum's Aboriginal Australia*, edited by David Stewart, is a cultural travelogue featuring magnificent photographs and the wit of Burnum Burnum, the man who planted the Aboriginal flag at the white cliffs of Dover in 1988, declaring 'I Burnum Burnum, being a nobleman of ancient Australia do hereby take possession of England on behalf of the Aboriginal people', just as Arthur Phillip had done in Sydney in 1788. It's currently out of print so if you see a second-hand copy on sale – grab it!

Bush Food – Aboriginal Food and Herbal Medicine, by Jennifer Isaacs, is a beautifully illustrated and written guide to the bounty of Australia's natural environment, full of good eating and good medicine. Jennifer Isaacs has also written *Australia's Living Heritage*, another lavish, full-colour book focusing on traditional arts and artists from around Australia. Another good introduction to Indigenous art is Wally Caruana's *Aboriginal Art*, which authoritatively covers ancient forms and contemporary movements. For sports fans and others, *Black Gold: The Aboriginal and Islander Sports Hall of Fame*, by Colin and Paul Tatz, features 172 stars of 30 sports, from Australian Rules football to athletics.

Historian Henry Reynolds challenges 'orthodox' post-1788 Australian histories, which often denied an Indigenous presence of any great consequence. His books, which include *The Other Side of the Frontier*, *Black Pioneers* and *Why Weren't We Told*, are highly recommended. Richard Broome's *Aboriginal Australians* presents a good overview of Australian history from the Indigenous standpoint, while Bruce Elder's *Blood on the Wattle* tells the tragic story of depredation and murder suffered by Indigenous people at the hands and guns of Settlers.

For more information on literature by Indigenous Australians, see the Literature section in Facts about the Country. You'll also find entries on further reading recommendations about specific places in the regional chapters.

LONELY PLANET TITLES

This book is a companion to Lonely Planet's *Australia* guide. In that book you will find over 150 maps, plus detailed information on places to stay and eat and how to get around as you explore Indigenous Australia.

Lonely Planet's *Australian Phrasebook* contains an excellent 100-page section on Indigenous languages, including information on cultural life.

For trips into the Outback in your own vehicle *Outback Australia* is the book to get. That guide also contains essential safety information for travelling to many of the remote locations included in this book.

For more detail on particular areas, Lonely Planet has the *New South Wales*, *Northern Territory*, *Queensland*, *South Australia*, *Tasmania*, *Victoria* and *Western Australia* state guides, *Melbourne* and *Sydney* city guides and *Out to Eat* restaurant guides to Melbourne and Sydney.

Lonely Planet's *Walking in Australia* describes walks of different lengths and difficulty in various parts of the country. The *Sydney* CitySync guide allows you to access travel information from your hand held computer. And if you're still not satisfied, other useful Lonely Planet titles include *Cycling Australia*, *Watching Wildlife Australia*, *Healthy Travel Australia, NZ & the Pacific*, the *Australia* road atlas, *Melbourne* and *Sydney* city maps and a selection of diving guides published through the Pisces series – *Australia's Great Barrier Reef*, *Australia: Southeast Coast & Tasmania* and *Victoria, Australia*.

Newspapers & Magazines

Kerryne Liddle

Newspapers

There are a number of newspapers produced by Aboriginal organisations that work to counteract much of the negative information written in mainstream print media. The content and circulation varies from paper to paper, but commonly Indigenous issues are more comprehensively and accurately covered at a local, regional and national level.

The *Koori Mail* is a fortnightly, national newspaper and is considered the peak national newspaper and voice for Indigenous people, covering issues of interest to Indigenous and non-Indigenous peoples. Established in 1991, the *Koori Mail* is based in Lismore in country NSW. Its content is overseen by an Indigenous editor and most staff, including correspondents, are Aboriginal or Torres Strait Islander people.

The *Koori Mail* is 100% Aboriginal owned and is controlled by five Indigenous organisations in NSW. It is self-funding, with profits generated from the sale of advertising and newspapers. The *Koori Mail* is available by subscription or at various newsagents and retail outlets.

ATSIC produces a quarterly publication, *ATSIC News*, as well as radio and video progams which highlight Indigenous issues and ATSIC activities.

Land Rights News is produced by the Central and Northern Land Councils of the NT and is a quarterly publication with a circulation of around 14,000. *Aboriginal Way*, a publication of the South Australian Aboriginal Legal Rights – Native Title Unit, is also a quarterly newspaper, with a circulation of 20,000.

Yamaji News is a fortnightly newspaper produced in WA and *Land Rights Queensland* is published monthly by the Foundation for Aboriginal & Islander Research Action. *Torres News* covers Torres Strait Islander issues and is produced in a magazine/ newsletter style weekly. Publications that are produced by Aboriginal and Torres Strait Islander organisations are usually supported by grant funding.

Kerryne Liddle

I am a media marketing consultant of the Eastern Arrernte people from central Australia. I have worked as a news journalist/ producer in many of Australia's television and radio stations since 1988. Most of my work has been with Australia's commercial television networks.

Some of my employers have included the Australian Broadcasting Corporation, the Seven and Ten television networks, Imparja Television and the Central Australian Aboriginal Media Association.

My work now involves communication and marketing management, which includes desktop publishing and media consultancy. I am especially interested in assisting Indigenous people to obtain more fair and equitable representation in Australia's print, television and radio media.

Living in Adelaide, and a mother of two, I have been studying part-time, and have almost completed a Bachelor of Management through the University of South Australia.

Newsletters

A wide variety and number of newsletters are produced specifically for Indigenous readers. Their content covers a range of topics from health to land rights. These publications are usually distributed by mailing lists or can often be found at places where Indigenous people meet.

Magazines

Deadly Vibes is a monthly magazine, which focuses on Indigenous music, sports, health and lifestyles. Based in Sydney, *Vibes* also produces *Deadly Sounds* – a weekly national top 10 of Indigenous music, which is distributed to 200 radio stations across Australia.

Streetwize creates comics that address a wide range of issues relating to youth, including health, violence and drug abuse.

Producing six million comics since starting up 15 years ago, work for *Streetwize* comics is commissioned – with Aboriginal writers and artists employed on editions produced to target Indigenous readers.

Radio & TV

Kerryne Liddle

The issues that affect Indigenous peoples are extremely complex, and often reported by journalists who have little real understanding of Indigenous peoples or cultures. This often results in the sensational and unbalanced reporting we so often see in the Australian media.

The Australian Broadcasting Corporation (ABC) and Special Broadcasting Service (SBS) are government-funded, national radio and TV broadcasters which strive to accurately report Indigenous issues. Unfortunately the commercial print, radio and television media have a much greater audience reach than ABC and SBS – so the potential for damage done by bad reporting is significant. However, the media was clearly overwhelmed by the Australian population's support during the 2000 Reconciliation marches. Community fears, aspirations and prejudices often direct the angle taken on stories, so we may see an improvement in the quality of reporting on Indigenous issues – although this will take time.

Due to the mainstream media's past treatment of Indigenous issues, Indigenous newspapers, radio and television evolved in an effort to provide more accurate reporting and presentation of information, and to present it in ways that better inform Indigenous audiences.

Many Indigenous media are members of The National Indigenous Media Association of Australia (NIMAA; ☎ 07-3252 1588). Based in Brisbane, NIMAA has the job of advising broadcasters on policy, licensing and funding issues and acts as an advocate and lobbyist for Indigenous media organisations. They have a Web site at www.indigenousaustralia.com.au/nimaa/home_fs.htm.

Television

Imparja is the only fully commercially run, Aboriginal owned and operated television station in Australia. Imparja means tracks or footprints in the Arrernte language – the language of the traditional owners of the Alice Springs region. Their Web site is at www.imparja.com.

Based in Alice Springs, Imparja hit the airwaves in 1988 and has a potential audience of 189,000 people in regional areas of the NT, SA, NSW and Victoria.

Imparja is responsible to its shareholders, but also has social and ethical obligations to the Indigenous community to positively promote Aboriginal cultures and values. It does this by providing Indigenous programming, with some programs made by Indigenous journalists, film-makers and producers. In 1989, Imparja banned all alcohol advertising because of its social impact on Indigenous communities. This was a significant decision, because the protection of Indigenous people from the possible effects of this advertising was given precedence over the potential revenue that could be generated from it.

Radio

Australia's first Aboriginal radio station was 8KIN FM in Alice Springs, which is owned by the Central Australian Aboriginal Media Association (CAAMA). The station hit the airwaves in 1985 and there are now over 120 Indigenous licenses broadcasting in cities, in the country and in remote areas, most of them through the BRACS network.

These radio stations survive mostly on government funding and grant programs, but one wholly commercial Aboriginal radio station, Radio 6LN operates from Carnarvon in WA.

Radio makes up the largest part of Indigenous media but the diversity of Aboriginal and Torres Strait Islander peoples means there is also no single, definitive Aboriginal sound. Play lists on radio stations may include Aboriginal artists singing country, rock, reggae or heavy metal, or songs in an Aboriginal language. Mainstream hip-hop, rock, reggae, pop or country music is also played.

BRACS

In over 100 very remote Aboriginal and Torres Strait Islander communities, viewers have access to the Broadcasting for Remote Aboriginal Communities Scheme (BRACS),

INDIGENOUS RADIO BROADCASTERS

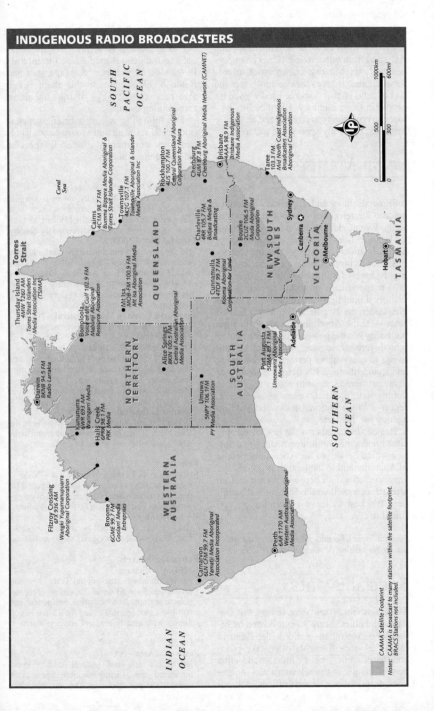

Torres Strait

Thursday Island
4MW 1260 AM
Torres Strait Islanders
Media Association Inc
(TSIMA)

Darwin
8KNB 94.5 FM
Radio Larrakia

Nununurra
8WR 693 AM
Waringarri Media

Halls Creek
6PRK 98.1 FM
PRK Media

Fitzroy Crossing
Wangki Yupurnanupuarra
Aboriginal Corporation

Broome
6GME 99.7 FM
Goolarri Media
Entreprises

Carnarvon
6LN CFM 99.7 FM
Yamatji Media Aboriginal
Association Incorporated

Perth
6AR 1170 AM
Western Australian Aboriginal
Media Association

Borroloola
Voice of the Gulf
Mabunji Aboriginal
Resource Association

Alice Springs
8KIN 100.5 FM
Central Australian Aboriginal
Media Association

Umuwa
5NPY 106.1 FM
PY Media Association

Port Augusta
5UMA 89.1 FM
Umeewarra Aboriginal
Media Association

Adelaide

Cairns
4CIM 98.7 FM
Bumma Bippera Media Aboriginal &
Torres Strait Islander Corporation

Townsville
4K1G 107.1 FM
Townsville Aboriginal & Islander
Media Association Inc.

Mt Isa
MOB-FM 100.9 FM
Mt Isa Aboriginal Media
Association

Cunnamulla
4TOF 99.7 FM
Kooma Aboriginal
Corporation for Land

Rockhampton
4US 100.7 FM
Central Queensland Aboriginal
Corporation for Meura

Charleville
4RR 105.1 FM
Bidjara Media &
Broadcasting

Bourke
2CUZ 106.5 FM
Muda Aboriginal
Corporation

Cherbourg
4UM 97.8 FM
Cherbourg Aboriginal Media Network (CAMNET)

Brisbane
4AAA 98.9 FM
Brisbane Indigenous
Media Association

Taree
603.3 FM
Mid North Coast Indigenous
Broadcasters Association
Aboriginal Corporation

Sydney

Canberra

Melbourne

Hobart

QUEENSLAND

NORTHERN
TERRITORY

WESTERN
AUSTRALIA

SOUTH
AUSTRALIA

NEW SOUTH
WALES

VICTORIA

TASMANIA

INDIAN
OCEAN

SOUTHERN
OCEAN

SOUTH
PACIFIC
OCEAN

Coral
Sea

CAAMA Satellite Footprint

Notes: CAAMA is broadcast to many stations within the satellite footprint.
BRACS Stations not included.

0   500   1000km
0   300   600mi

allowing communities to receive radio and television programs via satellite from the ABC and from Imparja. BRACS is an important tool which assists communities to preserve culture. It gives them control over the sort of material that is sourced and viewed by people in the community. BRACS also provides an opportunity to produce and air locally made and culturally appropriate material.

Legal Matters

Gary Lui

Indigenous laws and customary practices predate Western law by tens of thousands of years. Even today, traditional laws are integral to the lives of Aborigines and Torres Strait Islanders, as they are inexorably linked to a complex network of ancient and highly revered spiritual beliefs. There are laws to specifically protect these beliefs and visitors should be aware of them. For example, under the Northern Territory's Sacred Sites Act, the Aboriginal Areas Protection Authority has the power to prosecute people who disturb sacred sites, which includes entering an area without permission, damaging areas, and littering. It's illegal to disturb or deface a sacred site, or to enter one without permission. If you come across a new site, report it to the national parks and wildlife agency for that state.

Besides being against the law, disturbing sites breaks the continuing history and stories which belong to the Aboriginal people of Australia and to the land. It is not always easy to distinguish between a rock and an artefact, or a shell washed ashore and a midden. It's best to leave everything as you found it.

See the Travel Permits section for more information on visiting Aboriginal land.

Special Events

There is a vibrant and diverse range of festivals and other special events hosted by Indigenous Australians nationwide. Keep in mind that one-off events often take place and therefore may not be mentioned in this book – inquire at the relevant local Indigenous organisations, tourist offices, cultural centres and other appropriate bodies to find out about these. Fellow travellers, the Internet and Indigenous media (see the Internet Resources, Newspapers & Magazines and Radio & TV sections in this chapter) can also be excellent ways of tracking down forthcoming events.

The following is just a brief overview (inquire at relevant state tourist authorities and local community groups for precise dates and more details):

January

Oyster Cove Festival – Tasmania
This is the biggest day on the state's Indigenous calendar. It's held on the Saturday closest to 16 January at Oyster Cove, south of Hobart, and features top Aboriginal acts from around the country.

Survival Day – NSW
On 26 January, when much of Australia is commemorating the day Captain Arthur Phillip invaded Australia (the Australia Day public holiday), the Aboriginal community celebrates its survival at Waverley Oval in Bondi, Sydney, with bands, stalls, and art for sale.

Tamworth Country Music Festival – NSW
Indigenous musicians and singers are invariably on the programme.

Tarerer Festival – Victoria
Held in the Warrnambool area each January, the festival showcases Indigenous and non-Indigenous local musicians. The concert is officially opened by local Elders and has a focus on Reconciliation.

Wybalenna Festival – Tasmania
Celebrated in January on Flinders Island in the Bass Strait at the site which became home to the Aboriginal survivors of the Black War.

February

Sydney Gay & Lesbian Mardi Gras – NSW
Every year large numbers of loud and proud Indigenous participants take part in this huge gay and lesbian celebration on Oxford St, Sydney.

Womadelaide – SA
Held in Adelaide in odd-numbered years, the festival showcases Aboriginal music and dance.

February/March

Golf Day – Victoria
At Warrnambool, the annual Golf Day was established by a group of Aboriginal organisations to promote Reconciliation. Indigenous and non-Indigenous people gather for a friendly golf tournament, usually held in February/March.

March

Festival of Arts – SA
Adelaide's renowned festival held in even-numbered years, includes some Indigenous art and cultural performances. The supplementary

Fringe Festival, however, offers more Aboriginal music and dance.

Moomba Festival – Victoria
The Moomba mob see to it that Indigenous culture is celebrated by incorporating Indigenous dance, art and music into their program.

March/April

East Coast Blues and Roots Festival – NSW
Held in Byron Bay during Easter, there's usually a strong Indigenous line-up.

Easter Lightning Carnival – NT
See 25 Aussie Rules teams fight it out in Alice Springs.

Muttonbirding Season – Tasmania
The season kicks off in Tasmania at the end of March when millions of birds which have nested in the Bass Strait Islands take off on their journey to the Arctic Circle, leaving their plump and delicious chicks behind.

April

Bush Food Festival – Victoria
CERES (in Brunswick, Melbourne) hold this annual festival in April with entertainment, stalls, activities and, you guessed it…bush food.

May

Sorry Day – National
On 26 May 1997 the *Bringing Them Home* report, an inquiry into the removal of Indigenous children from their families, was tabled in parliament. On the anniversary each year, concerned Australians acknowledge the continuing pain and suffering of Indigenous people affected by Australia's child removal practices and policies. Events are held in most cities, for example, in Melbourne there's a procession through the city's streets. Check out the Journey of Healing Web site for details: www.journeyofhealing.com.

May/June

DAR Festival – Queensland
This Brisbane festival of dance, music, storytelling, new media, art and theatre is held between 29 May and 5 June.

Reconciliation Week – National
Held between 27 May and 3 June to commemorate the anniversary of the 1967 referendum which gave Indigenous Australians the vote (27 May) and the anniversary of the High Court's landmark Mabo decision (3 June). For information on events, which are held nationwide, see the Reconciliation Australia Web site: www.reconciliation.org.au.

June

Barunga Wugularr Sports & Cultural Festival – NT
Held over a four-day weekend each June in Barunga, this lively event draws Aboriginal people from all over the Top End and from as far away as WA. While it is mainly a sporting festival, these are also traditional arts and crafts, as well as dancing, spear-throwing competitions and live bands.

International Environment Day – SA
Held in early June in the Belair National Park in the Adelaide Hills, this event boasts strong Aboriginal involvement.

Kowanyama Rugby League and Softball Carnival – Queensland
Players and sports fans gather from Aboriginal communities across Cape York to compete on the Queen's Birthday long weekend.

Laura Aboriginal Dance Festival – Queensland
Held in June of odd-numbered years on the banks of the Laura River a few kilometres south of town. People from all over Cape York get together for three days of dancing, music and crafts.

Merreppen Arts Festival – NT
This festival is held over a Saturday in early June at Nauiya in the Daly River area. Aboriginal communities from around the district display their arts and crafts, and music, dancing and bush tucker are also featured.

June/July

Ruchook Festival – Queensland
In even-numbered years you can see Indigenous dancing and art displays at Napranum, near Weipa.

July

Beanie Festival – NT
Fun event over four days in Alice Springs featuring beanies and anything else made from fibre and fabric. (Beanies are woven hats designed for warmth.) Watch Aboriginal women using traditional spinning techniques, or take in a fashion parade of Aboriginal-made fabrics and batik.

Coming of the Light – Torres Strait Islands
Islanders celebrate the day when Christian missionaries first arrived in the strait on 1 July, with commemorative ceremonies and feasting.

Croc Eisteddfod – Queensland
This cross-cultural festival is held in Weipa on Cape York Peninsula around mid-July, and draws together communities from around the Cape.

NAIDOC Week – National
The National Aboriginal and Islander Day of Celebration has been held since 1957. Communities across Australia celebrate NAIDOC, from the annual Melbourne NAIDOC Ball to local street festivals.

Pormpuraaw Croc Races – Queensland
You can try your luck at picking a winner at these dangerous races, held in western Cape York at the end of July.

Torres Strait Cultural Festival – Torres Strait Islands
Held on Thursday Island in even-numbered years, with cultural performances and local arts and crafts for sale.

Torres Strait Music Festival – Torres Strait Islands

Held in odd-numbered years (alternating with the Cultural Festival).

We Iri We Homeborn – Victoria

This lively little festival attracts Indigenous artists from Melbourne and beyond to show off their knack in producing top-quality film, theatre, art, multimedia and dance productions. Check to see if the festival is happening during this month (rumour has it that it will be moved to September).

July/August/September

Hopevale Show & Rodeo – Queensland

Staged in July, August or September each year, the Hopevale Show includes formal equestrian events as well as novelty races and the more traditional rodeo spectacle.

August

The Art of Place: The National Aboriginal and Torres Strait Islander Heritage Art Award – ACT

Run by the Australian Heritage Commission in Canberra, this award is held in even-numbered years. Indigenous artists from across the country are invited to submit entries depicting a place they nominate for listing on the National Estate.

Barddiy'wanga String Festival – NT

This small, four-day festival, held at the Myilly Point Historic Precinct in the Northern Territory, brings together women from seven different Top End communities. The women are all artists, designers and string makers, and the festival features live music, workshops and exhibitions.

Broome Footy Grand Final – WA

The local football grand final in late August should not be missed, with its colourful atmosphere and all the thrills and spills of Australian country football played at a frenetic pace.

Fortescue Festival – WA

Held in Newman in August each year, this is a float parade and community festival which always features Aboriginal cultural activities.

Gunbalanya Open Day – NT

Held in western Arnhem Land in the Northern Territory, featuring art, craft, bush foods, rock art sites and entertainment.

Yuendumu Festival – NT

Held over the long weekend, this three-day sports carnival at Yuendumu attracts Aboriginal teams from as far away as Alice Springs. Features a 'Battle of the Bands'.

August/September

Bamaga Annual Show – Queensland

This community festival and rodeo at the tip of the state includes an amusement fair and carnival stalls.

September

AFL Grand Final – Victoria

Sporting attention turns to Melbourne with the Grand Final of Aussie Rules football, when a crowd close to 100,000 assembles at the MCG (Melbourne Cricket Ground). It's the biggest sporting event in Australia and every team in the league has Aboriginal players.

Desert Harmony Festival – NT

Eight-day event in Tennant Creek that includes Aboriginal participation in such activities as poetry reading, traditional dance and rock-band performances.

Garma Festival – NT

Held annually in September at Gulkula on the Gove Peninsula, this is a week-long cultural festival organised by the Yothu Yindi Foundation as a celebration of Yolngu culture.

Harold 'Crow' Williams Annual Memorial Rugby League Knockout – ACT

This great Rugby League tournament is held in Canberra in September. Harold Williams (1946–94) was an Indigenous football hero who played mainly in the Canberra region.

Multicultural Carnival – NSW

Walgett has an annual carnival in September.

Shinju Matsuri Pearl Festival – WA

This Broome community festival features Aboriginal stalls, parade floats and activities.

Tauondi Aboriginal College Open Day – SA

Held in Adelaide on the second Thursday of September (during Youth Cultural Week).

September/October

Desert Mob Art Show – NT

Alice Springs event displaying the recent work of over 30 central Australian Aboriginal art centres such as Hermannsburg Potters, Papunya Tula Artists, Keringke Arts and Utopia Awely Batik. Buy fabulous art direct from the centres.

Fringe Festival – Victoria

Held annually in Melbourne around September/October, the Fringe is a lively source of great entertainment with Indigenous events and performances always featuring on the program.

October

Annual Rugby League Carnival – NSW

The NSW Aboriginal Rugby League Association (NARLA) annual knockout is held on the October long weekend, in which approximately 64 teams from across NSW compete. The knockout is hosted in different locations in NSW.

Back to Pinjarra Day – WA

Festival of Nyoongar people at Pinjarra celebrates Nyoongar culture and commemorates the Pinjarra Massacre of 1834. Listen to storytelling and band music, watch theatre and traditional dance, join in the spirit of Reconciliation.

Cooma Cottage Festival – NSW

Each October, this festival is held in Yass with Indigenous participation.

Melbourne Art Fair – Victoria

The capital's biennial fair (from 2002) is held in the first week of October. This leading trade fair takes place in the Royal Exhibition Buildings, Carlton Gardens, and features Indigenous art, with most of it for sale.

Ngarrindjeri Ngrikilun Corroboree – SA

The inaugural corroborree was held in October 1999 (open to the public) at Raukkan, along the shores of Lake Alexandrina. The organisers of this weekend of dancing, music and art hope that it becomes an annual event.

Stompem Ground – WA

This biannual cultural festival in October of even years features Indigenous bands from around the country and traditional foods.

November

Mungabareena Ngan Girra Festival – NSW

This festival takes place during the last week of November at the Mungabareena Reserve, Albury. The festival has been held for at least 20,000 years (!) and continues to celebrate Indigenous culture with dance, bush tucker tasting, storytelling and stalls.

Return of the Sacred Kingfisher – Victoria

CERES (in Brunswick, Melbourne) hold their annual festival, celebrating the return of the bird to the waters of the Merri Creek. The festival originates from local Wurundjeri legend and features stalls, entertainment and activities for all.

December

Risdon Cove Festival – Tasmania

Around 10 December the Aboriginal community celebrates the hand back of 12 parcels of land in 1995, at Risdon Cove in Hobart.

December/January

Woodford Folk Festival – Queensland

Held from 27 December to 1 January annually. With an exciting program of Indigenous performers, musicians, storytellers, artists and craftspeople from around the country.

Courses

Mini 'courses' (such as bush tucker, boomerang throwing etc) which run for half a day or less, are available from a number of Indigenous cultural centres/tour operators around Australia – see the regional chapters for details.

Culture

Adelaide (SA)

Workers' Education Association (WEA; ☎ 08-8223 1979, ✉ wea@ao11.aone.net.au) runs an Introduction to Aboriginal Art online course through the Internet and Aboriginal Art Tours.

Alice Springs (NT)

The Institute for Aboriginal Development (IAD; ☎ 08-8951 1311, ✉ acap@iad.edu.au) runs one-day cultural awareness workshops.

Copley (SA)

Iga Warta (☎ 08-8648 3737, ✉ enquiries @igawarta.mtx.net), an excellent organisation run by Adnyamathanha people, runs courses in Aboriginal art.

Meningie (SA)

The Camp Coorong Cultural Museum & Administration Centre (☎ 08-8575 1557, ✉ nlpa @camtech.com.au), run by the Ngarrindjeri Lands & Progress Association, offers basket weaving lessons.

Lismore (NSW)

Contact the College of Indigenous Australian Peoples at Southern Cross University (☎ 02-6620 3318) for course information.

Perth (WA)

The Noongar Language & Cultural Centre (NLCC, ☎ 08-9202 1261, fax 9202 1262, ✉ nlcc@iinet.net.au) at 23-25 Moore St, in East Perth, runs half and full-day workshops in cultural awareness. These explain Nyoongar values and the balancing act that must be performed by people living in two worlds. Workshops are run according to demand and are very reasonably priced; a minimum of five participants is required. You can write to them at PO Box 6060, East Perth WA 6892.

Sydney (NSW)

For information about short courses, single semester units, degree and diploma courses in Aboriginal studies, contact the Koori Centre (☎ 02-9351 2046) at the University of Sydney, The Jumbunna Centre (☎ 02-9514 1902) at the University of Technology, Sydney and Tranby College in Glebe (☎ 02-9660 3444). Maureen Smith teaches traditional Koori women's knowledge at the Women's Business spirituality camps (☎ 4471 8653).

Tennant Creek (NT)

The Papulu Apparr-Kari Language Centre (☎ 08-8962 3270, ✉ papak@tennant-creek-high .nt.edu.au) runs workshops in cultural awareness.

Language

Adelaide (SA)

Yaitya Warra Wodli Language Centre (☎ 08-8269 3601, ✉ yaityawarra.camtech.net.au) is a new Aboriginal-run centre which plans to offer language courses.

Alice Springs (NT)

The Institute for Aboriginal Development (IAD; ☎ 08-8951 1311, www.iad.edu.au/iad) runs courses in local Indigenous languages.

Perth (WA)

The Noongar Language & Cultural Centre (☎ 08-9202 1261, ✉ nlcc@iinet.net.au), at 25 Moore St in East Perth, runs half and full-day introductory workshops to the Nyoongar language – these are held according to demand. They also offer an intensive language course over three or four days. This one costs $20, and obviously lunch is not included.

Shopping

Mick Dodson & Toni Bauman

The artwork of Indigenous Australians is highly valued internationally. Support the First Australians by purchasing these works if possible and look for Indigenous-run outlets and galleries where you can be sure that the profits are going to benefit the Indigenous community directly. A visit to an Indigenous community presents an ideal opportunity to purchase directly from the artist, or at least from their representative outlet.

If you are buying directly from the artist, remember that while some discussion about price is obviously necessary, bargaining is not generally part of the cultural practices of Indigenous Australians (as you might expect in Asian countries, for example). Try not to be opportunistic and drive the price down. The seller's inherent politeness may force him or her to accept an unfair outcome rather than offend you. On the other hand, Indigenous artists are far more aware of the value of their works than they have been in the past.

Remember that Indigenous weaving, usually produced by women, involves collecting, processing and dying materials as well as weaving them and takes much longer than you would think. Keep this in mind when you are settling on a price. Sometimes a basket can be a week's work.

Most importantly, be aware that every society has the right to respect for their cultural heritage and intellectual property. Designs, songs and the like may have been handed down from generation to generation over many thousands of years and may be accompanied by elaborate systems of ownership which also relate to land and ritual.

Copyright has become a major issue for Indigenous Australians as their designs and motifs have been ripped off and used for the mass production of tourist items. It may be unlawful to copy, publish, sell or otherwise use Indigenous images, artefacts, crafts, music, songs, dances, stories, interpretations, performances, and so on.

If you are buying souvenirs look for authorised Indigenous authenticity labels, including the boomerang shaped national one with the red, black and yellow colours of the Australian Aboriginal flag. In this way you will support Indigenous Australians in their efforts to preserve and protect their heritage.

See individual city entries for details on recommended retailers working in cooperation with Indigenous communities.

▌WOMEN & THE DIDJERIDU

Gary Lee

'Within our culture it is not appropriate for women to play the didjeridu.' So reads the prominent sign at Indigenous-owned and -operated Gavala Shop and Cultural Centre at Darling Harbour. Not only is it inappropriate, but Aboriginal people find it very offensive to even see a woman attempting to play one. However, one shop at The Rocks, apparently driven by profits, actively encourages women to play the didjeridu. While there are no restrictions on women buying or even owning a didjeridu, playing one is a cultural no-no. The didjeridu was the most popular Aboriginal item bought during the Sydney Olympic Games. The didjeridu is exclusively a man's instrument and women should respect Aboriginal cultural law and leave the playing of them to men.

New South Wales & the Australian Capital Territory

New South Wales (NSW), Australia's most populous state, also has Australia's largest Aboriginal population, 109,925. Sydney, its capital and the largest city in Australia, is home to Kooris (as the state's Indigenous people refer to themselves) from NSW and also Aborigines and Torres Strait Islanders from all over Australia, who contribute to a rich artistic and cultural community.

As the point of first contact between the English and Europeans, the state's Indigenous people have shown surprising resilience in maintaining their cultural traditions and developing new forms of cultural expression.

History

Philip Morrissey

EARLY HISTORY

When sea levels rose after the last ice age, the striking harbours and waterways of the Sydney region were created. Sydney and its environs contain superb examples of rock engravings, and to date over 4000 sites have been identified. There are also post-contact paintings and engravings of European sailing ships and animals. Middens occur all along the NSW coast and adjacent waterways. As elsewhere in Australia, Aborigines used controlled burning to manage the environment – ignorant of fire technology, James Cook thought the widely spaced trees and lawn-like grasses he saw occurred naturally.

Bora rings (circular areas of banked earth used for ceremonial purposes) are found throughout NSW – even in densely populated areas. These large circular rings of earth are the sites where secret-sacred initiation ceremonies were carried out to celebrate the journey from childhood into adulthood.

The dry beds of the Willandra Lakes in the arid west of NSW have been a rich source of archaeological information. The strongest evidence for the length of Aboriginal occupation of Australia has been found in this region, and human remains found there have been dated in excess of 48,000 years old.

Telephone code: ☎ 02
Indigenous population: 109,925
Overall population: 6.34 million
Area: 802,000 sq km

- The ancient rock engravings and etchings scattered throughout national parks in the Yura Country region around Sydney

- Cruising on Sydney Harbour on the Eora Star or the Tribal Warrior, providing an Indigenous insight into the Aboriginal occupation of the Sydney basin

- The vibrant community of Indigenous contemporary artists at Forster-Tuncurry

- The moving Myall Creek memorial to honour the memory of more than 28 Wirrayaraay people who were massacred by settlers on 10 June 1838

- The large-scale stone fish traps at Brewarrina, and the excellent Brewarrina Cultural Museum

- Umbarra Cultural Tours' marvellous guided journeys to sites and places of significance in the Wallaga Lake area

QUEENSLAND

Around Sydney p158
Red Hands Cave Walk p162
Yankee Hat Walk p183

CANBERRA p180

Sydney p146
Sydney Harbour p149

VICTORIA

ACT

South Coast p178

FIRST CONTACT

Captain James Cook left England in 1768 with instructions to discover new lands and

NEW SOUTH WALES & ACT

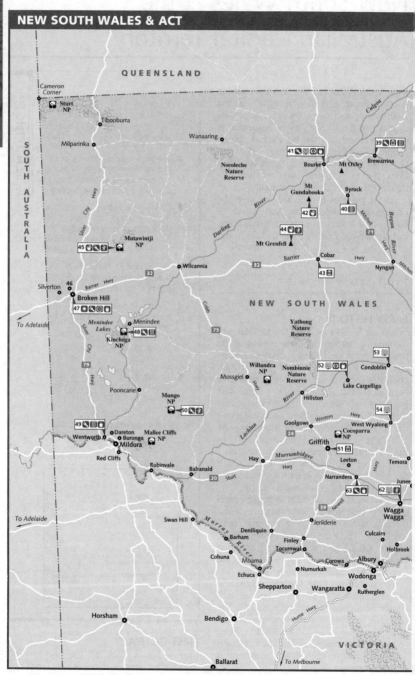

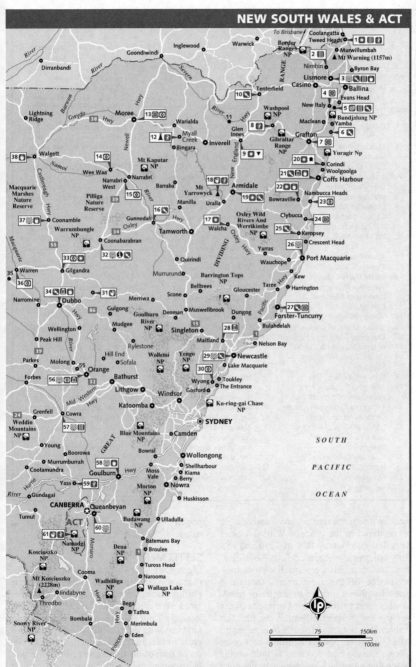

NEW SOUTH WALES & ACT

1   Minjungbal Aboriginal Cultural Centre; Bora Ring; Walking Trail
2   Nimbin Rocks
3   Ngulingah Local Aboriginal Land Council; Organised Tours; Bora Ring; Goobah Goobah Koori Theatre Company; Bundjalung Way
4   Gurrigai Aboriginal Arts & Crafts
5   Middens; Scarr Tree; Discovery Tour
6   Lower Clarence Aboriginal Tourist Site Drive
7   Durahrwa Centre
8   Walking Trails
9   Cooramah Aboriginal Cultural Centre; Koori Cuisine Restaurant
10 Woollool Woollool Aboriginal Culture Tours
11 The Willows
12 Memorial; Walking Trail
13 Moree Plains Gallery; Yurundiali Aboriginal Co-Op; Nindethana Aboriginal Corporation
14 Waiwa Aboriginal Corporation
15 Waiwa Aboriginal Corporation
16 Organised Tours
17 Amaroo Museum & Cultural Centre; Rainbow Serpent Sculpture
18 Rock Art; Walking Trail
19 Aboriginal Cultural Centre; Fable Tours of the Arts
20 Yarrawarra Aboriginal Cultural Centre & Accomodation
21 Gambaarri Tours; Historical Museum; Classic Koori Designs
22 Bawrrung Culture Centre; Ngurrala Arts & Crafts
23 Muurrbay Aboriginal Language Centre

24 Brandybrook Lavender Farm; Art Gallery
25 Wilay Bijarr's Organised Tours; Wijay Cultural Park
26 Biripi Local Aboriginal Land Council & Shop
27 Tobwabba Tours; Tobwabba Art
28 Museum
29 Awabakal Local Aboriginal Land Council; Bush Food Tours
30 Darkingjung Local Aboriginal Land Council
31 The Drip (Rock Paintings)
32 Coonabarabran Local Aboriginal Land Council; Tours & Culture Walks
33 Pulkurru Aboriginal Corporation; Gilgandra Cultural Centre
34 Wirrimbah Direct Descendants Organised Tours; Dubbo Museum & History Centre; Red Earth Gallery
35 Indigenous Carved Pole & Western Road Sign
36 Warrana Aboriginal Corporation
37 North West Regional Land Council
38 Gamilaroi CDEP
39 Walkabout Tours; Brewarrina Aboriginal Cultural Museum; Ngunnhu (Brewarrina Fisheries)
40 Byrock Ancient Waterhole
41 Car Tour; Nulla Nulla Local Aboriginal Land Council; Gundabooka & Muda Aboriginal Corporations; Centacare
42 Cave Art
43 Great Cobar Outback Heritage Centre

44 Rock Art; Ngiyampaa Walk
45 Rock Carvings; Mutawintji Heritage Tours; Discovery Walks
46 Broken Hill Sculptures
47 Thankakali Aboriginal Cultural Centre; Organised Tours; Broken Hill City Art Gallery
48 Organised Tours; Scarr Tree
49 Harry Nanya Tours; Scarr Tree; Harry Mitchell Arts & Crafts
50 Organised Tours; Walking Trails
51 Pioneer Village Museum; Western Riverina Community Library
52 Murrin Bridge Local Aboriginal Land Council; Murrin Bridge Aboriginal Advancement Corporation; Kejole Korri Studio
53 Condoblin Local Aboriginal Land Council
54 West Wyalong Local Aboriginal Land Council
55 Yaranigh's Grave
56 Orange Land Council; Museum; Boree Aboriginal Corporation
57 Wiradjuri Land Council; Lachlan River Bridge Pylons
58 Pejar Aboriginal Land Council; Koori Kullas
59 Ngunnawal Walk
60 Ngunnawal Aboriginal Land Council; Ngunnawal Elders Council
61 Rock Art; Yankee Hat Rock Walk
62 Wiradjuri Regional Land Council; Wiradjuri Walking Track
63 Organised Tours; Sandhills Artefacts

treat with forbearance any natives he encountered in the process. With this brief he sailed into Botany Bay in 1770 and in a first, enigmatic encounter, four Aboriginal men spearing fish from small canoes took no notice of the *Endeavour*, though it passed within a quarter of a mile of them. Cook's perceptions of Aborigines were benign and respectful and drew on then fashionable notions of the 'noble savage'. After he had mapped Australia's east coast Cook reported back to Great Britain on the peaceable nature of Australia's Indigenous people, their small numbers and the fertile nature of the land.

SETTLEMENT

Eight years after Cook's visit a penal settlement was set up under Governor Arthur Phillip. His instructions in relation to Aborigines were to 'conciliate their affections, enjoining all our subjects to live in amity and kindness with them'. Phillip was capable of great forbearance and understanding, but he was a man of his times and ordered the first kidnappings and punitive expeditions against

Aborigines. For their part, Aborigines were horrified by the brutal punishments Europeans imposed on their own people.

RESISTANCE & MASSACRE

The Yura were the first to lose their lands to the invaders. One by one, other tribes suffered as settlement spread and Aboriginal water and hunting lands were taken. When Aborigines tried to survive by eating settler vegetables or livestock, they were shot.

Smallpox also took a devastating toll on Aborigines even before large-scale conflict between Aborigines and settlers had begun. No-one is sure how Aborigines first became infected with smallpox – attempts have even been made to blame the Macassans, but the fact that the disease first appeared in the Sydney region strongly suggests that Europeans introduced it.

After settlers were killed on the Nepean in 1816, a punitive expedition was sent out with the aim of terrifying the Aborigines into submission. Lachlan Macquarie, the colony's governor, also ordered that no Aborigine was to go within a mile of a British farm or town. In 1838 the Kamilaroi were defeated in a series of battles which degenerated into massacres, and three years later the Barkindji resistance was crushed. In the Sydney of the 19th century, Aborigines had become a pariah race, often represented by artists of the day wearing cast-off clothes and drinking alcohol, or sitting in squalor and dejection.

MYALL CREEK

In the history of NSW one particular atrocity and its aftermath stands out. In 1838 a massacre of Aborigines, like many others before and after, took place at Myall Creek. Here, settlers roped at least 28 peaceable Aborigines together and murdered them. In an unprecedented consequence 11 men were tried for the crime and seven were found guilty and executed. In some respects it was a 'cruel and unusual punishment', in that each of the guilty sincerely believed he was doing no more than what others had done elsewhere and that the law would turn a blind eye. In fact it almost did – a first trial produced a not guilty verdict after only 15 minutes, and a conviction was only secured with a second trial.

The verdict and sentence produced outrage among settlers who continued their murders of Aborigines covertly, often using poison. On the north coast of NSW, the Biripi had initial successes in battles against settlers, but were defeated when poisoned flour was left out as bait for them.

ASSIMILATION

What has been referred to as a 'second land grab' occurred in the early part of the 20th century – over half of the lands originally reserved for Aborigines were lost when the NSW Lands Department moved Aborigines off reserved land so settlers could have it.

After WWII, the NSW state government adopted a policy of assimilation. Exemption certificates were issued to Aborigines who proved that they could 'live like Australians'. The exemption certificates were known among Aborigines as 'dog-tags'; those who were exempted were free of the oppressive Aborigines Protection Act in exchange for a

ABORIGINAL RESISTANCE

Philip Morrissey

Bennelong and Pemulwuy illustrate the strategies of accommodation and resistance used by Aborigines in their relations with settlers – and their relative futility. Pemulwuy harassed and raided settlers until they shot him in 1802. Bennelong negotiated a more complex relationship with the settlers and their culture, and even visited England. Notwithstanding this, he died an isolated and broken man.

A similar fate awaited Bungaree, a young man who was an adventurer and circumnavigated Australia with Mathew Flinders. Like Bennelong, he became an object of derision in later years in the colony. More in the mould of Pemulwuy, Mosquito, a warrior from a Broken Bay tribe, was transported to Tasmania, where he became a resistance leader before being captured and hanged in Hobart.

lifestyle of assimilation. Where previously children – particularly Aboriginal girls – had been taken from their families for labour, the Aborigines Welfare Board now removed them in order to be assimilated. The entire scheme was a failure, with only a small number of Aborigines applying for exemption.

Settlers for their part vigorously opposed anything that would break down the barriers between themselves and Aborigines. Treatment of Aborigines could vary from town to town – one town might practise strict segregation to the extent of reserving specific linen and crockery for Aboriginal hospital patients, while another might have relatively tolerant racial attitudes.

Dr Kumantjayi Perkins, who became one of Australia's most influential Aboriginal leaders, was one of a group of NSW university students who, in 1965, made Freedom rides to western NSW towns protesting blatant discrimination and segregation. Since then there have been occasional race-based riots in NSW country towns. There is resentment in many rural areas at benefits to Aborigines, although financial benefits paid by the federal government to farmers and wealthy graziers escape scrutiny.

SESQUICENTENARY & BICENTENARY

The 150th anniversary of European settlement was celebrated in 1938, and Aboriginal leaders proclaimed it a Day of Mourning and issued a manifesto calling for equal rights for Aborigines. In Sydney on Australia Day 1988, thousands of Aborigines from all over Australia took part in a peaceful protest and affirmation of cultural survival.

Language

Today in NSW, only a few fluent speakers remain from a small number of traditional languages, including Bundjalung of the north coast around Lismore, and Barkindji, spoken on the Darling River near Wilcannia.

Some people still speak a traditional language from the NSW area, and efforts are under way in Aboriginal communities to revive and preserve their linguistic and cultural heritage. Dictionaries, tape recordings and grammars of languages of the area have been produced using word lists and materials compiled with the last generations of fluent speakers.

Some words from traditional languages are still in use, especially in country areas. Visitors will see evidence of traditional Aboriginal languages in three areas – in the use of words and expressions from Aboriginal languages, in place names and the names for natural features, and in Aboriginal words that have entered the English language and are commonly used by all members of the community.

Examples of place names taken from Aboriginal languages include:

Boggabilla from **bagaaybila** ('place full of creeks')
Bundarra from **bundaarra** ('place of kangaroos')
Cobar from **gubarr** ('red ochre')
Coonamble from **gunambil** ('full of shit')
Gunnedah from **gunithaa** ('orphan')
Nambucca from **bagabaga** ('knees')
Torrowotto from **thuru-katu** ('snake's windbreak')
Uralla from **urala** ('camp')
Wagga Wagga from **waagan-waagan** ('crows')

Dozens of words from NSW Aboriginal languages are now in general use in Standard Australian English, especially those describing plants and animals that were new to European settlers.

birds
  galah, kookaburra, brolga, currawong, budgerigar
animals
  dingo, koala, wallaby, wallaroo
plants
  mulga, coolabah, gidgee, bindi-eye
landscape
  billabong (river pool), gibber (stone)
artefacts
  coolamon (bark dish), woomera (spearthrower), nulla-nulla (club), gunya (shelter)

USEFUL CONTACTS

Australian Institute of Aboriginal & Torres Strait Islander Studies (AIATSIS; ☎ 6246 1111) GPO Box 553, Canberra, ACT 2601
Aboriginal & Torres Strait Islander Commission (ATSIC; ☎ 6121 4000) Mezzanine Level, Lovett Tower, PO Box 17, Woden, ACT 2606; Web site: ww.atsic.gov.au
Matong Merringanna, NSW Aboriginal & Torres Strait Islander Corporation for Languages & Culture (☎ 4474 4692) PO Box 517, Moruya, NSW 2537

Muda Aboriginal Corporation (☎ 6872 1233)
63 Mitchell St, Bourke, NSW 2840
Muurrbay Aboriginal Language Centre
(☎ 6566 9353) 648 Sherwood Rd, Sherwood,
NSW 2440; (☎ 6569 4294) 465 Bellwood Rd,
Nambucca Heads, NSW 2448

Information

INDIGENOUS ORGANISATIONS

Australians for Native Title and Reconciliation (ANTaR) can be contacted in NSW on
☎ 9555 6138 – see Information in the Facts
for the Visitor chapter for full details. See also
the Facts for the Visitor chapter for other relevant nationwide Indigenous organisations.

NATIONAL PARKS

Entry and camping fees usually apply in national parks. Contact the head office of the
National Parks & Wildlife Service (NPWS;
☎ 9585 6444, 1300 361 967, ⓔ info@npws
.nsw.gov.au); Web site: www.npws.nsw.gov
.au. Alternatively, contact the local NPWS
office in the town you are visiting (contact
numbers are listed in the relevant sections
throughout this chapter).

For information on national park fees in
the ACT, contact ACT Parks & Wildlife on
☎ 6207 2334.

Discovery Programs

The NPWS Discovery program 'Walks,
Talks and Tours' includes a number of tours
that look at Indigenous history, plant usage,
medicine, hunting and/or art techniques.
Many of the tours are run by Aboriginal
rangers, and are often designed in consultation with local Indigenous communities.
Contact local NPWS offices (see the relevant
sections in this chapter) for tour schedules.

BOOKS

*Invasion to Embassy: Land in Aboriginal
Politics in NSW 1770–1972* by Heather
Goodall is an essential read if you wish to
understand the government policies that affected Aboriginal people and their struggles.

The Man Who Sold His Dreamings by
Roland Robinson provides the reader with
Dreaming *stories* from the peoples of NSW.
These intriguing stories explain the creation
of the land and peoples of NSW.

Healing the Land by Judith Monticone
raises serious issues about the background

of the Reconciliation movement. While the
horror of atrocities committed in the battle
for settlement of Australia makes for unpleasant reading, it is nonetheless a very
informative book.

Yura Country

Sydney Area

SYDNEY
Information
Indigenous Organisations Gadigal Information Services (☎ 9564 5090), Web site:
www.gadigal.org.au, is an Aboriginal arts,
media and cultural centre, and the organisation behind Koori Radio (94.5 FM). Check
out its stunning Web page (www.metro
.org.au/indigi/The Koori Radio Web Site)
for information about theatre performances,
profiles of Indigenous writers and musicians, and information about Indigenous arts
and cultural events in and around Sydney.
Gadigal is named after the traditional owners of the inner Sydney area (see also Gadigal Walking Tours under Organised Tours).

The Metropolitan Local Aboriginal Land
Council (☎ 9267 2985), Level 3, The Edge,
13–15 Wentworth Ave, is the elected body
representing the traditional custodians of
the greater majority of the Sydney basin.

University Associations The Koori Centre at
the University of Sydney is one of the leading teaching and research centres in Indigenous Australian studies. The centre maintains
KooriNet (Web site: www.koori.usyd.edu.au)
a directory of Indigenous Web sites, and
Australia's first Indigenous search engine,
BlackTracka. Check KooriNet for the latest
information on tours, galleries and courses.

The Jumbunna Centre (☎ 9514 1902) at
the University of Technology Sydney is
currently developing the Indigenous Learning Centre. You can talk to staff about
courses in Aboriginal history and culture.

Tourist Offices The Sydney Visitors Centre
(☎ 9255 1788, 1800 067 676 toll free), 106
George St, The Rocks, can provide limited
information on Indigenous tours and performances in and around Sydney.

Libraries The State Library of NSW
(☎ 9273 1414) on Macquarie St is more of

NEW SOUTH WALES & ACT

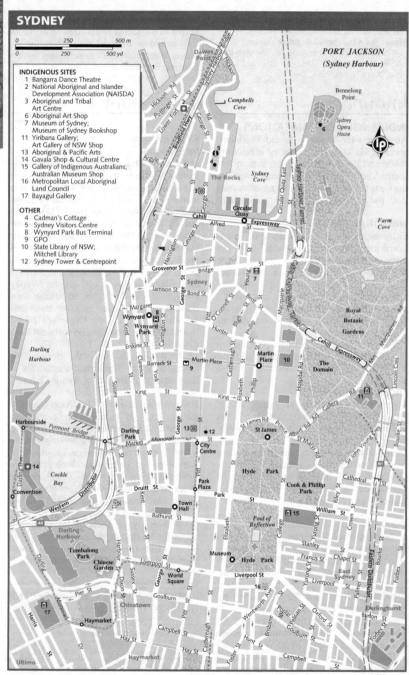

SYDNEY

0 — 250 — 500 m
0 — 250 — 500 yd

INDIGENOUS SITES
1 Bangarra Dance Theatre
2 National Aboriginal and Islander
   Development Association (NAISDA)
3 Aboriginal and Tribal
   Art Centre
6 Aboriginal Art Shop
7 Museum of Sydney;
   Museum of Sydney Bookshop
11 Yiribana Gallery;
   Art Gallery of NSW Shop
13 Aboriginal & Pacific Arts
14 Gavala Shop & Cultural Centre
15 Gallery of Indigenous Australians;
   Australian Museum Shop
16 Metropolitan Local Aboriginal
   Land Council
17 Bayagul Gallery

OTHER
4 Cadman's Cottage
5 Sydney Visitors Centre
8 Wynyard Park Bus Terminal
9 GPO
10 State Library of NSW;
   Mitchell Library
12 Sydney Tower & Centrepoint

PORT JACKSON
(Sydney Harbour)

Dawes Point

Campbells Cove

Bennelong Point

Sydney Opera House

The Rocks

Sydney Cove

Circular Quay

Cahill Expressway

Farm Cove

Grosvenor St

Sydney

Bond St

Royal Botanic Gardens

Margaret St

Wynyard
Wynyard Park

Darling Harbour

Erskine St

Martin Place

Martin Place

The Domain

King St

King St

Harbourside

Pyrmont Bridge

Darling Park Market

St James

St James Rd

Darling Harbour

Cockle Bay

Convention

City Centre

Park Plaza

Hyde Park

Cook & Phillip Park

William St

Druitt St

Town Hall

Pool of Reflection

Darling Harbour

Tumbalong Park

Chinese Garden

Liverpool St

World Square

Museum

Hyde Park

Liverpool St

Chinatown

Goulburn St

Haymarket

Campbell St

Hay St

Haymarket

Ultimo

East Sydney

Darlinghurst

a cultural centre than a traditional library. It houses the Australian Research Collections, covering both Indigenous and non-Indigenous history. The adjacent Mitchell Library (same phone number as the state library) holds one of the largest collections of Aboriginal-related material in the world, including original diaries, manuscripts and records from the enforced Aboriginal missions, pictorial material and original watercolours, as well as all books, CD-ROMs, magazines, and community newsletters published in NSW relating to Indigenous issues. The libraries' Aboriginal liaison officers can assist with inquiries and research. Both are nonlending libraries.

Books *A Field Guide to Aboriginal Rock Engravings* by Peter Stanbury & John Clegg is widely regarded as the most authoritative layperson's guide to sites in and around Sydney.

The Metropolitan Local Aboriginal Land Council's *Footprints on Rock: Aboriginal Art of the Sydney Region* by T & N Popp & Bill Walker looks at the historical and cultural context of various sites.

Organised Tours

Sydney Aboriginal Discoveries (☎ 9568 6880, 9568 5203) offers a variety of interesting tours that look at Indigenous culture, history, spirituality and relationships to the environment. Introductory tours in the Royal Botanic Gardens cost from $18/25. Harbour cruises, camping trips to Jibbon Head at the Royal National Park (see later in this chapter), a walkabout tour and a feast of native Australian foods can also be organised (prices on application).

The black, red and yellow flag of the *Tribal Warrior* (☎ 9699 3491) is one of the most striking sights on Sydney Harbour, but not many people realise that this 1899 vessel, a Gaff rigged ketch, is available for short cruises or charter. The *Tribal Warrior* was last in the spotlight when it transported the national Reconciliation document to the Sydney Opera House during the Corroboree 2000 ceremony (see the Politics section in the Facts about Aboriginal Australia & the Torres Strait Islands chapter for more information). *Tribal Warrior* dancers performed on the forecourt as champion boxer Glen Kelly, dressed in ceremonial ochre, carried the document up the Opera House steps. Up to 20 passengers can sail on the *Warrior* at a time. The cost is $30 per person for four hours, and the emphasis is on an informal meeting between non-Indigenous and Indigenous people. Visitors have a chance to meet with youth from Aboriginal nations around Australia who train for maritime certificates and professional qualifications on the Warrior.

The *Eora Star* (☎ 9318 1496) is available for four-hour cruises around the Harbour, leaving from the Man O' War steps at the Sydney Opera House, and sailing past Fort Denison, Clarke Island, Rose Bay and Cremorne Point, then back under the Sydney Harbour Bridge and across to Balls Head and Berry Island Reserve. Tour guides introduce you to the history and culture of Indigenous Australians and tell stories about the Aboriginal groups that live along Sydney Harbour's shores, eg, Matyewanye (Fort Denison) was an important ceremonial site, and there are many rock shelters at Billongoola (Clarke Island) that were used before the European invasion. Visitors are shown spears and boomerangs, and methods of rock painting and carving are explained. The cruise stops under the Sydney Harbour Bridge for a dance performance and barbecue (you can request traditional tucker such as emu fillets and kangaroo steaks). The cost for a group is $770 (maximum of 50 people).

Koori Connections (☎ 9489 8977) can put you in touch with Aboriginal guides and Elders such as Uncle Max, a community leader who hails from the Yuin nation on the NSW south coast. Koori Connections also offers advice on planning trips and accommodation. Speaking and consultancy fees are available on application.

Gadigal Walking Tours (Web site: www.gadigal.org.au) is a virtual tour through the history of the Gadigal people, the traditional owners of the Sydney city centre area. You can read about resistance leader Pemulwuy, the warrior who lead a 12-year armed war against the British and who escaped from Parramatta Hospital despite being chained and badly wounded (see also the boxed text 'Aboriginal Resistance' earlier in this chapter). A more contemporary leader remembered on the site is 'Mum Shirl', a strong woman who was much loved and admired for

SYDNEY DREAMING

Jenny Munro

From the mountains to the coast there are 29 different clan group areas in the Sydney region, and according to our *laws* the Creator Biame made these places during the Dreaming, by sending the Rainbow Serpent to the land. The Rainbow Serpent travelled the land creating the rivers, lakes and billabongs. Then the ancestral heroes came: gods like Biame in the guise of the Crow, Kangaroo, Emu, Snake, Goanna and human also.

For cultural reasons, images of Biame and Daramulan (Biame's brother/son) are not shown. Biame gave the people laws of life, tradition, art, song cycles, totem cycles and explained how they all came together. When all things had their place, Biame returned to the sky.

Daramulan and Biame are heard through the sound of the sacred bullroarers used to begin the *bora*, or initiation cycles of young boys.

Initiation ceremonies include both Biame and Daramulan and involve large gatherings of clans to prepare their young boys for manhood. This event occurred in different areas of the Sydney basin for 40,000 years.

The large number of whale engravings in the area suggests that a significant figure in the Dreaming for the people of the Sydney region was the whale.

In Aboriginal communities across Australia the creation stories always stress the connection between land, totem and family. Our totems are therefore our brothers and sisters and we cannot harm, eat or deplete their numbers by over-hunting. For our people to survive, our totems must.

All Aboriginal sites have either a totemic or ceremonial significance to Aborigines. To white Australians, in anthropological terms, the Sydney basin as it is presently configured is approximately 20,000 years old. This is relatively young compared to the 120,000 years some scholars are now attributing to Aboriginal occupation of the continent of Australia, although our lore says we have been here since time immemorial.

Geological evidence available today shows that 20,000 years ago the coast was 10km to 15km further east. With the melting of the ice at the end of the ice age, the sea rose to its present level. The Nepean, Hawkesbury, Parramatta and Georges Rivers were deep gorges then; now they are gentle deltas.

Aborigines adapted to these changes, down the countless generations, slowly as the events unfolded. They still fished and hunted and utilised all the resources of the valley from the mangroves to the forest, the mountains and the sea. Aboriginal life did not change drastically – they still used the overhangs for shelter and they still recorded the totemic and ceremonial rituals of significance to each clan by engraving in the sandstone.

Jenny Munro

I was born at 'Erambie' at Cowra into a large family of Wiradjuri people. I moved to Sydney when I was 18 years old, where I worked for many Aboriginal organisations in the Redfern community, as well as around the state.

In 1990 I was elected the chair of the Metropolitan Local Aboriginal Land Council. In this role I am the elected custodian of the lands of the Gadigal, Bidjigal, Wallumattagal, Burramattagal, Wangal, Cammeraigal, Terramerragal, and many more of the clans and traditional owners of the Sydney basin. I have the heavy responsibility of representing and articulating the interests of this diverse group of people.

It is a privilege also to be the custodian of many of the Aboriginal sites in the Sydney basin. The basin represents the largest open-air gallery in the world, with over 5000 sites, containing either art or evidence of occupation within the greater Sydney area.

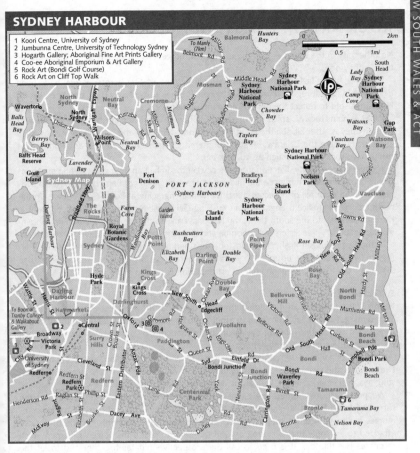

SYDNEY HARBOUR

1 Koori Centre, University of Sydney
2 Jumbunna Centre, University of Technology Sydney
3 Hogarth Gallery; Aboriginal Fine Art Prints Gallery
4 Coo-ee Aboriginal Emporium & Art Gallery
5 Rock Art (Bondi Golf Course)
6 Rock Art on Cliff Top Walk

the care she showed for Indigenous people from the Stolen Generations, and the jailed and displaced people of her community. The virtual tour also looks at political events such as the Redfern Day of Mourning Protest March in 1938, which marked 150 years of invasion, and it celebrates Indigenous football stars with a brief history of the All Blacks Rugby League team.

The **Royal Botanic Gardens** (☎ 9231 8111) has developed a tour named after the Gadigal people. The Cadi-jam-ora ('This is a place called Cadi') tour shows how the land might have looked before the First Fleet colonised the area and tried, often unsuccessfully, to plant European seeds. Aboriginal names of plants are given – *watanggre* (banksia), *budjor* (paperbark

tree) and *mizooboore* (lilly-pilly) – and each plant's use for food, medicine and/or tools is described. Traditional Aboriginal houses are being constructed for the tour, and – depending on availability – Elders will talk to tour groups at a specially constructed meeting place. You need to book a week in advance. Prices are available on application.

Parks, Squares & Gardens

South of the City Centre The site of former prime minister Paul Keating's historic 1992 Redfern speech is **Redfern Park**. This was seen as the first significant admission by an Australian prime minister of wrongdoing by settler Australians towards Indigenous people. The park has long been a focal point for Redfern's Aboriginal community, and

ROCK ART OF THE SYDNEY REGION

No other city in the world enjoys the number of Indigenous art sites within its boundaries that Sydney does.

However, in the last 200-plus years, many important art sites across Sydney have been destroyed by the disregard of white Australians for their sacredness. They should be World Heritage Listed to reflect their importance internationally.

What remains today is still a smorgasbord for anyone interested in Aboriginal history and sites. Sydney is, after all, still the point of first contact. Some of the lesser-known sites, such as Kurnell (where the Dharawal first encountered Captain Cook) are just as significant as the famous rock art sites, such as Ku-ring-gai.

Today if you go in any direction from the city centre, in half an hour you will find an Aboriginal site of some sort. It may be the midden and rock engraving of Berry Island in North Sydney, or (in an example of desecrated art) the whale engraving at Bondi Golf Course. To the north are the magnificent engravings in Ku-Ring-Gai Chase National Park (named after the Kuringai people), to the south the Royal National Park, to the west the mountains containing the beautiful Three Sisters of Katoomba and the magnificent Jenolan Caves further south.

In the Sydney basin itself, the sandstone weathering processes means that the engravings still visible could be up to 1000 years old. There are also engravings that are less than 200 years old – post-European contact art depicting European subjects.

Subject Matter

Normally the subject matter of engravings is as diverse as the life experiences of the artists. Sacred images of the Sky Hero Biame, other sacred beings, their *mundoes* (footprints), and ceremonial cycles, the hunting cycles or totem markings of different animals, and their tracks, all appear in the Sydney area.

The predominance of depictions of whales in engravings in the region suggests that Whale Dreaming is the dominant totemic feature of the area. Other animals include dingoes, stingrays, fish, sharks, emus, kangaroos, wallabies, a koala, lyrebirds, snakes and goannas.

Weapons such as boomerangs, clubs, shields and spears, as well as *dilly* bags (woven carry bags) and fishing lines are shown. A special instrument used in boys' initiation ceremonies is also depicted – the *bullroarer*. This very sacred instrument is made of a strap attached to a handle that is swung around the head to sound the voice of Biame, which resonates like thunder. It is used to call the prospective initiates together and to let the women and children know that they should stay away. Engravings of people – men, women and children, and their mundoes, also dot the landscape.

Aboriginal people believe that not all rock art was made by their ancestors; some was made by the creational ancestral heroes depicting their time on the earth. Later only special people were allowed to redraw these stories associated with ceremonies.

The range of engravings show:

Dreaming stories showing creational ancestral heroes that were used as initiation sites
European contact images

many outdoor music events, rallies and festivals are held here.

Next to the University of Sydney in Chippendale, **Victoria Park** was a Saturday and Sunday night gathering point in the 1960s and 1970s for Aboriginal people after dances at the Foundation for Aboriginal Affairs, an early welfare and social organisation on George St. In 2000 the park was the site of a temporary Aboriginal Tent Embassy and protest site in the lead-up to the Olympic Games.

continued...   Jenny Munro

Human beings in different poses with hunting and ceremonial items
Hunting stories and hunting magic to aid in a hunt
Increase stories or magic such as a shoal of fish or a row of kangaroos
Linking footprints that link one series of engraving sites to another – a storyline (Dreaming Track)
Sacred instruments such as bullroarers (the voice of Biame)
Totemic animals
Travel footprints that show the travels of the creational ancestral heroes during the Dreaming

Technique
The engravings are known as 'pecked petroglyphs' and are made by striking the rock surface with a pointed stone or very strong shell. This technique was used to form a line of punches, or pits, that overlapped to form a groove. It was usually U-shaped, 5mm to 10mm deep and 20mm wide. The outline was achieved by joining the pits with the aid of a stone tool and water.

In the Sydney area variations in technique are evident north and south of the Georges River, which flows into Botany Bay. Kangaroos south of the river have two front legs, two hind legs and two ears, while those north of the river have only one of each feature.

The engravings are presented in one of three ways: plan view (as seen from above), profile view (as seen from the side) and front view (as seen from the front). Human beings are shown in front view. The general rule for animals is the profile.

In depictions of humans, hands are in plan view with the hand in outline or the fingers as single lines. Feet and footprints are shown in plan view. Images of men show penises while women show breasts. Some images have facial features, for example, eyes and mouth, but no nose. Headdress was shown with a single line.

There are many features which can identify engravings with internal markings. For example, eels with lines across their bodies, shields with internal lines (generally one line is down the centre, with two parallel lines across the shield), humans with waistbands, creational ancestral heroes with various markings on their bodies, echidnas with depictions of their spines, and whales with parallel lines across their bodies and/or fins. Another feature is engravings within engravings, for example, a man inside a whale.

The various linguistic/clan groups of Sydney migrated across country called 'clan estates'. This movement was associated with the seasonal harvesting of food, ceremonial obligations and trade. Travel occurred mostly along the ridge-tops and this is also where the Dreaming tracks and art are found. We ask all visitors to respect these special places.

Legislative protection is weak, but it's better than nothing. Most sites in Ku-ring-gai are registered on the NPWS Site Register. Most sites in the Royal National Park are still not registered or recorded. The Blue Mountains area was recently declared a World Heritage Site; however, many Aboriginal sites are still not registered or recorded.

For information on rock art sites in the Sydney region, see the main chapter text, or *Footprints on Rock*, published by the Metropolitan Aboriginal Land Council.

See the Organised Tours section, earlier, for a guided walk through the Royal Botanic Gardens.

Sydney Harbour National Park This beautiful park has been set up to protect the scattered pockets of bushland that remain around the harbour and the many important Aboriginal engravings within them. The information centre for the park is at Cadman's Cottage (☎ 9247 5033), located in The Rocks.

NEW SOUTH WALES & ACT

SYDNEY GALLERIES, MUSEUMS & SHOPS

Readers should be aware that the names of deceased members of the Aboriginal community may be cited in this section. Mentioning the personal name of someone who has died recently can cause offence, anguish and grief in some Aboriginal cultures.

There are far too many places in Sydney that sell or exhibit works by Indigenous artists to list them all here. Below is a selection of recommended outlets. See the Shopping section in the Facts for the Visitor chapter for further information.

Aboriginal & Pacific Arts (☎ 9223 5900) Dymocks Bldg, 8th Floor, 428 George St. This small but excellent gallery with changing exhibitions is geared towards the fine art market. Ask to see some of the older bark paintings, as well as some fine sculptures and beautiful Aboriginal prints by some of Australia's best Indigenous artists, at affordable prices. The gallery has a long and reputable history for dealing directly with Aboriginal artists and arts centres. The gallery is open 10 am to 5.30 pm Tuesday to Friday, and to 2 pm on Saturday (closed Christmas to early January).

AGNSW Bookshop A wide range of Aboriginal art books, posters and postcards is available at this bookshop, which has one of the best selections of books on Aboriginal art and culture in Sydney. There's a plethora of Aboriginal art books available; recommended are *Aboriginal Art* by Wally Caruana and *Dreamings: The Art of Aboriginal Australia* edited by Peter Sutton.

Australian Museum Shop This small shop at the museum, on College St, has an excellent range of Aboriginal and Torres Strait Islander books. Titles cover the arts, social and political issues, history, autobiographies and other contemporary issues. Indigenous products available are of good quality and include weaving and basketry (from $80), pottery and a small range of *didjeridus* and boomerangs. There is a selection of postcards, posters, CDs and cassettes. The Aboriginal T-shirts start at a reasonable $30, with a nice range on offer. All the Indigenous products have been made by Indigenous people, so you are assured of authenticity. The shop is open 9.30 am to 5 pm daily. See also the Gallery of Indigenous Australians.

Bayagul: Contemporary Indigenous Communication Gallery (☎ 9217 0111) Powerhouse Museum, 500 Harris St, Ultimo. Bayagul is the Yura word for 'Speaking up', and this is the inaugural permanent gallery at the museum devoted to Indigenous Australian culture. Situated on the lower level, Bayagul presents aspects of Indigenous identities as expressed through today's technologies and industries. Indigenous achievements in areas such as fashion, textile design, television, radio, tourism, architecture and even surfing are featured. The work of outstanding Indigenous artists and performers such as Jimmy Little, Justine Saunders, Mervyn Bishop, Rachel Perkins and the Bangarra Dance Theatre are documented. Tracey Moffatt's award-winning film *Night Cries* is cleverly screened alongside the 1956 Australian feature film *Jedda*, which it effectively parodies. The interesting exhibits are complemented by fun educational interactives and audiovisual displays. This gallery will show you a different picture of Indigenous Australians and shouldn't be missed. The gallery is open 10 am to 5 pm daily, except Christmas Day; admission is $9 adults, $2 children, with variations for specialised exhibitions.
Web site: www.phm.gov.au

Boomalli Aboriginal Artists Co-operative (☎ 9698 2047) 191 Parramatta Rd, Annandale, a short bus ride from George St. The first NSW Aboriginal art co-operative and gallery, Boomalli showcases the talents of local artists, with regular exhibitions. All profits go back to the artists and prices are reasonable for paintings, prints, ceramics, sculpture, carved emu eggs, and some unusual carved and painted chairs. Buying here means you are supporting Indigenous NSW artists directly. Among the many artists represented are Jeffrey Samuels, Bronwyn Bancroft, Tracey Bostock and Elaine Russell. Boomalli is open 10 am to 5 pm weekdays, and to 4 pm on Saturday; admission is free.
Web site: www.culture.com.au/boomalli

continued... Gary Lee

Gallery of Indigenous Australians (☎ 9320 6000) 6 College St, on the corner of William St. Based at the Australian Museum, this gallery has a display of 10 Tiwi *pukamani* (mortuary) poles acquired in 1981 at its entrance. The exhibition takes the visitor through different Indigenous themes such as spirituality, the Dreaming, Dreaming *stories*, the missions and the Rainbow Serpent. Audiovisual displays feature Indigenous Australians from around the country telling their histories and life experiences as related to the various themes. Contemporary issues are also featured in the informative displays and installations. There are some interesting artefacts on show such as a *dari* (headdress) from the Torres Strait dating from 1907 and Arnhem Land bark paintings from the 1930s. Inside a re-created bush chapel there is a striking acrylic painting by noted Pintubi artist Tjangika Napaltjarri (Linda Syddick), *Three Wise Men/Last Supper*. The gallery is open 9.30 am to 5 pm daily; admission free. See also the Australian Museum Shop. Web site: www.austmus.gov.au

Museum of Sydney (☎ 9251 5988, e info @ho.hht.nsw.gov.au) 37 Phillip St. The museum is an easy stroll east of Martin Place and has several Indigenous displays. Prominently situated at the entrance is the

Gary Lee

Gary was born in Darwin and is a member of the Larrakia people, the traditional owners of the Darwin and Cox Peninsula regions.

After travelling around Australia he went to England when he was 17 to visit an uncle, then spent four years travelling overland back to Australia. He got to Kolkata, or Calcutta as it was called then, and ended up living there for two years. On his return he trained as an anthropologist and also works as an independent Aboriginal arts curator and writer.

Gary is a confirmed Indophile and has returned many times to India, Nepal and other parts of South Asia. He has also backpacked through South East Asia and Europe.

large sculptural installation by Janet Laurence and noted Badtjala artist Fiona Foley, *Edge of the Trees*. Visitors are encouraged to walk between the 'trees', which are a homage to the Yura people of the Sydney area. Concealed speakers evoke the voices, presence and history of the Yura within the sculpture, which also acknowledges the white occupation of Australia since 1788. Given the museum's location on the site of the colony's first government house, this installation is a poignant and fitting tribute to Aboriginal presence and passing. Inside, at the top of the stairs, is an interesting visual display featuring Pemulwuy, the first Aboriginal warrior hero, which is centred around a short film, *Sydney People*, by Aboriginal filmmaker Michael Riley. The film is also an introduction to the other Sydney-area Aboriginal groups such as the Dharug people. On the next level is Gadigal Place, a room with a focus on the Gadigal as well as the Tharawal/Dharawal, Gundunguna and Kuringai peoples. Cabinets with pull-out drawers house historical items such as stone tools, clay pipes and other interesting artefacts. The museum is open 9.30 am to 5 pm daily; admission is $6 adults, $3 children.
Web site: www.hht.nsw.gov.au

Museum of Sydney Bookshop (☎ 9251 4678) The bookshop is to the left inside the museum entrance. Its range of Aboriginal books is small but excellent, covering Aboriginal art, politics, history, language, biography, bush foods and other contemporary Indigenous issues. The illustrated children's storybooks are a good buy at $10.80 and there's a range of interesting postcards depicting early colonial illustrations of Aboriginal people ($1), with Desert Design silk neckties (from $70) by Aboriginal artist Jimmy Pike. The beautiful Outstation Australia silk scarves are good value at $44, designed in Australia by prominent Yolngu and Warlpiri artists. The shop is open 9.30 am to 5 pm daily.

SYDNEY GALLERIES, MUSEUMS & SHOPS

continued...

Walkabout Gallery (☎ 9550 9964, e wvabprog@wva.org.au) 70 Norton St Leichhardt. This initiative of World Vision Indigenous Programs purchases work directly from artists and community art centres in remote Australia, and most of the profits go directly back to them. There's a small but very good range of Western Desert acrylics on canvas, carved emu eggs and baobab nuts, screen-printed fabrics and limited-edition prints. It also has some beautiful coolamons, clapsticks, boomerangs and didjeridus. Prices start at around $60 for small paintings, $200 for didjeridus and up to $1500 for larger paintings. Buying here means you are not only getting something authentic but are also supporting Aboriginal artists and communities in remote Australia. The gallery is open 9 am to 5 pm Monday to Wednesday, 9 am to 10 pm on Thursday, Friday and Saturday. Web site: www.walkaboutart.com.

Yiribana Gallery (☎ 9225 1744) Level 3, Art Gallery of New South Wales (AGNSW), Art Gallery Rd, The Domain. Yiribana (meaning 'This way' in the language of the Yura people) is the world's largest single space devoted to the permanent exhibition of Aboriginal and Torres Strait Islander art. It houses a very significant historic collection of Arnhem Land bark paintings and Tiwi pukamani poles collected and displayed for the first time since the late 1950s. The installation of the poles caused a major furore at the time, and as such was highly influential in Aboriginal art first transcending the 'art or artefact?' divide. Also showcased are contemporary Indigenous arts and artists from around the country in regular changing exhibitions. The gallery is open 10 am to 5 pm daily, with free guided tours at 11 am Tuesday to Friday. There is a worthwhile (free) half-hour cultural dance, song, storytelling and didjeridu performance at noon Tuesday to Saturday. Admission to the gallery is free, except for special exhibitions.

Oxford St Galleries

The following galleries can be found easily on a stroll along Oxford St.

Aboriginal Fine Art Prints Gallery (☎ 9332 1722) 68 Oxford St, Darlinghurst. If an Aboriginal painting is out of your budget or you're looking for something a bit different, consider buying an Aboriginal print. This gallery has Sydney's biggest selection (over 300 works) and at very reasonable prices. Expect to pay from $125 up to $2000 for framed or unframed rare and current limited-edition prints. Beautiful screen-prints, lithographs, etchings, woodcuts, linocuts and mixed-media works are available. Many of Australia's leading Indigenous artists from Arnhem Land, the Central and Western Deserts, the Kimberley and the Tiwi and Torres Strait Islands are represented. Easily accessible on Oxford St between Riley and Crown Sts, the quality and diversity of prints here makes this gallery worth visiting. It's open 9 am to 5 pm Monday to Friday, from 11 am on Saturday and from noon on Sunday. Visit the gallery online to view what's on offer. Web site: www.aboriginalartprints.com.au

Co-ee Aboriginal Emporium & Art Gallery (☎ 9332 1544) 98 Oxford St, Paddington. Although not Aboriginal-owned, this retail outlet with a small exhibiting gallery upstairs has been around a long time and has established links with Aboriginal artists and communities. There's a large range of souvenir and fine art products, with Aboriginal artefacts, fabrics, cards, posters, books and many other gifts from around the country and something to suit most tastes and budgets. Pop upstairs to check out the current exhibition and to see some fine Aboriginal art, sculpture and limited-edition prints. Expect to pay from about $300 upwards. The shop and gallery are open 10 am to 6 pm Monday to Saturday (to 8 pm Thursday), and 11 am to 5 pm on Sunday.

Hogarth Gallery and Aboriginal Art Centre (☎ 9360 6839) 7 Walker Lane, Paddington. This gallery has a fine selection of Aboriginal art, sculpture and prints, and has a long and respected history of dealing with Aboriginal art and promoting Aboriginal artists. There are also some nice didjeridus and bark and acrylic paintings for sale. The emphasis is on quality and this is reflected in the pieces available. This gallery is also

continued...   Gary Lee

renowned for its regular changing exhibitions showcasing some of Australia's most talented Indigenous artists, which means there's always something worth viewing here. Expect to pay from $400 up to $10,000 for exceptional paintings. Beautiful tie-dyed silk fabric lengths are available, or how about a snail-shell dance rattle? There's a small but interesting range of postcards, as well as some handsome boomerangs, didjeridus and other artefacts at reasonable prices. The gallery is tucked a little out of the way off Oxford St – look for the sign on the left opposite the entrance to Victoria Barracks – but is well worth the effort. It's open 11 am to 5 pm Tuesday to Sunday, except public holidays.

Darling Harbour
Gavala Shop and Cultural Centre (☎ 9212 7232) Level 3, Harbourside Plaza. This shop should definitely not be missed. The only Aboriginal-owned and -staffed shop of its kind in the city, Gavala has a wide and interesting range of traditional and contemporary Aboriginal art and craft items at very reasonable prices. Items include killer and hunting boomerangs (both nonreturning) from $50 and $70, and beautiful didjeridus from $300, with attractive 'didj' bags from $55. There's a nice range of bush jewellery made of sea shells and natural (and painted) seed pods and gum-nuts, including the red Ininti seed bean from central Australia, with prices from $25 to $50. The striking T-shirts ($33) by Lindsay Bird are worth checking out, as are the charming wood Dirigun Spirit man and woman dolls ($50) by Bundjalung artist Timothy Ives. There's a fine selection of Aboriginal postcards, books, CDs and cassettes, prints, ceramics and paintings, both framed and unframed. You'd be hard-pressed not to find something to your liking here, and the friendly and helpful Indigenous staff will make your task all the easier. It's open 10 am to 8 pm daily. Ask about the free daily cultural and music performance.
Web site: www.gavala.com.au

Circular Quay & The Rocks
There are possibly more shops selling Aboriginal products in these two areas than in any other part of the city. The following in particular are worth a look.

Aboriginal Art Shop (☎ 9247 4344) Upper Concourse, Sydney Opera House, East Circular Quay. This shop specialises in quality Aboriginal gift and souvenir items, and has a small but interesting range. The carvings are notable, with river red-gum animals ($60 to $150) of burnt, incised (with hot fencing wire) designs made by women from the Central and Western Deserts. Tiwi carvings cost from $60 to $150 and Yolngu carvings from Yirrkala are $50 to $250. Tiny to medium-sized acrylics on canvas by Arrernte artists are reasonably priced at $50 to $120, and framed bark-painting styles on paper cost from $275. There are some nice didjeridus from Arnhem Land at $170 to $220, as well as fine weavings, including tiny dilly bags from Yirrkala ($55) and larger ones from Maningrida ($150). Also from north-central Arnhem Land are seashell and natural seed necklaces from $33. Check out Baghindi/Paakantyi artist David Janganlinji's beautiful painted boomerangs ($50 to $80). The Keringke artists from Santa Theresa have produced impressive painted chairs (from $935). The shop is open 10 am to 6 pm daily.

Aboriginal and Tribal Art Centre (☎ 9247 9625) 1st floor, 117 George St, The Rocks. Opposite the Museum of Contemporary Art, this shop also has a gallery space with a changing exhibition program. Permanent displays include attractive screen-prints by noted artists Djardie Ashley and Roy Burrunyula from Ramingining ($500) and others from north-west Kimberley ($360 unframed, $550 framed). Other items include some nice didjeridus ($200), Arnhem Land basketry ($50 to $300), clap sticks ($25 to $80), carvings ($30 to $60) and Tiwi Prints fabric lengths. This shop deals directly with artists and communities. It's open 10 am to 5 pm daily.
Web site: www.citysearch.com.au/syd/atac

Bondi In the middle of the Bondi Golf Course, next to the towering brick chimney of the sewerage treatment works, you'll find important Aboriginal engraving sites on two rocky outcrops. A large whale with a shark laying over it and a man holding a fish high above his head are two of the main images at this site. A plaque commemorates the 1962 reworking of the site's grooves by Waverley Council, an act the Metropolitan Local Aboriginal Land Council has described as an 'ill-judged conservation attempt' and an 'act of desecration'. Early morning is the best time to visit this site, when the shadows from the rising sun pick out the engraving lines. On the cliff-top walk between Bondi and Tamarama is a large whale carved into the sandstone at the cliff's edge: look to the left of the path as you round Mackenzies Point on your way to Tamarama.

Balls Head Reserve Balls Head Reserve has old rock paintings and carvings, although they're not easily discernible. You'll find a large engraving of a whale with a man inside its body in front of the Environmental and Earth Services Building at the reserve entrance. Enclosed by a low rail fence and outlined in white paint, this engraving is another example of how many Aboriginal sites in large metropolitan centres have been vandalised. The park is two headlands west of Sydney Harbour Bridge. Take a train to Waverton, turn left when you leave the station and follow Bay Rd, which becomes Balls Head Rd, for just over 1km.

Manly The 8km **Manly Scenic Walkway** passes ancient rock carvings on a sandstone platform just off the pathway between the Cutler Rd Lookout and Grotto Point. The walk takes about four hours and follows the shore from Manly to Spit Bridge, where there are buses back to the city centre. The route can be tricky to discern at times, so grab a leaflet from the visitors centre on Manly Wharf. For more information call the NPWS (π 9247 5033) and the Metropolitan Local Aboriginal Land Council (see Information earlier in this section).

Courses

At the Women's Business spirituality camps (π 4471 8653), Web site: www.minmia .com, senior Wiradjuri woman Maureen Smith teaches traditional Koori women's knowledge. Over a weekend, participants learn about the creation and the Dreaming from a Koori perspective, the interconnectedness of land and people, and what *songlines* (Dreaming tracks) are. You need to bring your own camping equipment and food, but you'll learn traditional cooking methods and medicine techniques. The camps are held in south Sydney, 20km south of Batemans Bay in Broulee, and cost is \$130 for the weekend.

Tranby College in Glebe (π 9660 3444), 13 Mansfield St, is a Sydney institution that has been a training ground for hundreds of Indigenous artists, activists, businesspeople and community leaders. It is renowned for the striking circular architecture of the classrooms, reflecting the traditional Aboriginal style of learning and meeting. Non-Indigenous people can enrol in Tranby's two-year Aboriginal studies course (\$2500). Tranby welcomes visitors: contact program director Yvonne Jackson.

Special Events

The Survival Day concert is a big family affair for Sydney's Koori community and its supporters, held at Waverley Oval, Bondi, on 26 January every year. This date is also the Australia Day public holiday, when many non-Aboriginal Australians celebrate the anniversary of European arrival in Sydney in 1788. Survival Day is a celebration of thousands of years of Koori culture, with children's face-painting, information stalls and art, crafts and food for sale. Performers such as Yothu Yindi, Tiddas, Coloured Stone, Christine Anu, Archie Roach and Ruby Hunter have all taken the stage at Survival Day, along with Aboriginal stars from Sydney's football teams and actor Ernie Dingo.

The Annual Rugby League Carnival is held every October, with some 64 teams from across NSW participating. Aboriginal football stars from Sydney teams play for their home towns. For more details contact the NSW Aboriginal Rugby League Association (π 9241 3533).

The City Info – What's On Line (π 9265 9007), Web site: www.cityofsydney.nsw .gov.au, can give you information about current events and festivals such as Bangarra Dance Theatre performances (see Entertainment later) and Indigenous art exhibitions.

Sorry Day is held each year on the 26 May, and Reconciliation Week takes place in the week following. Check the *Koori Mail* and daily papers for festivals, art exhibitions, church services and other activities.

Entertainment

Dance The National Aboriginal and Islander Skills Development Association (NAISDA; ☎ 9252 0199) puts on regular performances at both the Sydney Opera House and its college centre in The Rocks.

The Bangarra Dance Theatre (☎ 9251 5333, Pier 4, Hickson Rd, Walsh Bay) is one of Australia's premier dance companies. Bangarra dancers, who combine both contemporary and traditional styles, have performed at the Olympic Games opening and closing ceremonies, at the Sydney Opera House and in tours overseas.

There's a free half-hour Aboriginal or Torres Strait Islander dance performance or workshop at the Art Gallery of NSW, on Art Gallery Rd, at noon Tuesday to Saturday.

Theatre The Sydney Opera House (☎ 9250 7777) regularly puts on Aboriginal and Torres Strait Islander performances. In late May and early June each year, to coincide with Sorry Day, it hosts two weeks of Aboriginal theatre, dance and music performances, as well as workshops for young people.

Kuringai Country

North of Sydney

INFORMATION

Darkingjung Local Aboriginal Land Council (☎ 4351 2930), in Wyong, covers the central coast region, and the area encompassing Brisbane Water National Park and parts of Yengo National Park. The council asks that local sites be visited with an Indigenous guide; you can contact the council to arrange this.

KU-RING-GAI CHASE NATIONAL PARK

This national park's name commemorates the Kuringai (or Guringai) people that lived here for thousands of years. In 1788 Kuringai clans are said to have warmly greeted Governor Phillip and his small party when they explored the inlets of what is today called Pittwater. But the Europeans left behind them the fatal smallpox disease, and the Kuringai population was devastated by the following year. In the subsequent decades outbreaks of warfare as the Kuringai tried to protect their land meant they were all but decimated within just 50 years of the First Fleet's arrival.

The outcrops of relatively soft Hawkesbury sandstone in the park are smooth, even and relatively easy to engrave, and there are many precious rock artworks here. The best places to see them are on the Basin Track and the Garigal Aboriginal Heritage Walk, both at West Head (see Walking Trails & Rock Art later in this section).

Information

The 15,000-hectare park (NPWS information centre ☎ 9472 8949) abuts the maze of waterways formed by the Hawkesbury and Cowan Rivers and the Pittwater inlet.

Brochures for the walks and maps of the park roadways are available from the Kalkari and Bobbin Head visitors centres on Ku-ring-gai Chase Rd (enter the park from the eastern Mt Colah entrance). The most direct route to the walks, however, is to take the southern Booralie Rd/McCarrs Creek Rd turn-off from Mona Vale Rd.

Walking Trails & Rock Art

The **Basin Track** is one of the best interpreted rock engraving sites within easy reach of Sydney, featuring images of fish, a row of hopping wallabies and life-size human figures in outline with just eyes for details. The first engraving you come to is a group of four figures, and the largest man has raised arms and is holding a boomerang and fish. In the last engraving site is a figure with arms outstretched and wearing a belt and necklet. The walk begins approximately 3km south of the lookout at the end of West Head Rd. It also leads to the only camping area in the park.

The next marked trail (about 500m before the West Head Rd lookout) is the circular **Garigal Aboriginal Heritage Walk** (3.5km). The first site is a shallow rock shelter with red ochre hand stencils. The next site is an engraving of a man without a neck and with no internal details – similar to the style of figures found elsewhere around Sydney.

AROUND SYDNEY

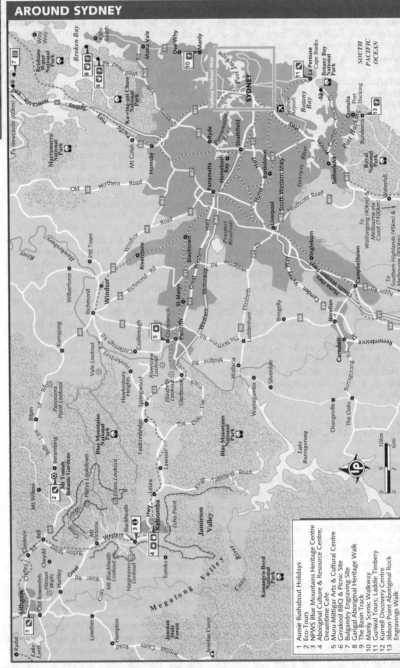

1 Aussie Bushabout Holidays
2 Eco-Tours
3 NPWS Blue Mountains Heritage Centre
4 Aboriginal Culture & Resource Centre;
 Dreamtime Cafe
5 Muru Mittigar Arts & Cultural Centre
6 Girrakool BBQ & Picnic Site
7 Bulgandry Engraving Site
8 Garigal Aboriginal Heritage Walk
9 The Basin Track
10 Manly Scenic Walkway
11 Guriwal Tours; Laddie Timbery
12 Kurnell Discovery Centre
13 Jibbon Point Aboriginal Rock
 Engravings Walk

When a storm almost ran Governor Phillip's ship aground during an exploration of Broken Bay, an old Aboriginal man and a boy helped them to land safely in a Pittwater cove. Evidence suggests that the large cave where they were offered shelter (which they declined) is the final site on the walk.

BRISBANE WATER NATIONAL PARK

This park, north of Ku-ring-gai Chase and abutting the squiggly flame-shaped inlets of the Hawkesbury River and Brisbane Water, contains the **Bulgandry Aboriginal Engraving** site. The most unusual feature of this site is a man depicted wearing an elaborate headdress, carrying a sword and club or small boomerang, and seemingly about to step into a canoe. Another engraving is a kangaroo with what looks like either an octopus or spider over its tail.

Information

There is a good information display about the Bulgandry site and another walk to less easily discernible engravings at the Girrakool barbecue and picnic site. Look for the turn-off to Girrakool on the Pacific Hwy about 9km south-west of Gosford. For more information contact the Gosford NPWS (☎ 4324 4911).

To reach the park, take the turn-off to Woy Woy from the Pacific Hwy and look for a low-lying sign pointing to the Bulgandry car park (about 3km south of the township of Kariong). From there it's a short, easy walk through bushland (about 350m) to the engravings.

Tharawal Country

South of Sydney

BOTANY BAY NATIONAL PARK

Botany Bay National Park encompasses both headlands of the bay where the first recorded contact between Australia's traditional owners and the British was made. At the time of writing, a proposal to change the park's name to Kamay-Botany Bay, in acknowledgment of the Aboriginal name for the region, was being considered by the NSW government. The NPWS Discovery program (☎ 9542 0648) includes tours in the park led by Aboriginal rangers. Costs are usually around $7/5/20 for adults/kids/family.

La Perouse

Organised Tours An Indigenous community has been living here since 'the beginning of time', says Vic Simms, a LaPa man and local Elder. His Guriwal Tours (☎ 9311 2999, 0408 204 506) takes visitors on bushwalks through the area of the national park on north headland, explaining history pre- and post-settlement. He shows plants that were used for bush cures, and he will point out tracks that he used as a boy when the government mission imposed curfews on residents at night. Vic is also a singer who has twice been named Aboriginal Entertainer of the Year, and is sometimes called upon to act as MC of the annual Survival Day concert. Tours need a minimum of 15 people (prices on application).

Just about every Saturday (9 am to 1 pm) and Sunday (to 4 pm), Laddie Timbery can be found demonstrating boomerang throwing and clapstick playing at 'The Loop', at the end of Anzac Parade on the northern headland of Botany Bay. Laddie's people are the Bidjigal clan, and his family are well-known artists, dancers and storytellers based in Huskisson (see also the Shopping section under Yuin Country later in this chapter).

Kurnell

It was the ancestors of today's Tharawal community who first encountered Captain James Cook at present-day Kurnell, on the south headland of Botany Bay, in 1770.

Information The Sutherland Shire Tourism Office (☎ 9544 2144), on Cronulla St next to Cronulla Station on the north side of the national park, can provide up-to-date information on programs of local Aboriginal dance and performances and guided tours.

Kurnell Discovery Centre At the time of writing, the Kurnell Discovery Centre (☎ 9668 9111), just off Captain Cook Drive, was changing its exhibition to emphasise the area's significance as a meeting place between two cultures. A natural amphitheatre in front of the centre is sometimes used by Aboriginal guides for teaching. The centre is open 11 am to 3 pm weekdays, and 10 am to 4.30 pm on weekends. Entry is $5 per car (pedestrians free). From Cronulla train station (10km away), catch Kurnell Bus Co

(☎ 9523 4047) bus No 987 ($6.30/3.10 adult/child under 15 and concession return).

ROYAL NATIONAL PARK

There are many significant sites and Aboriginal engravings in Royal National Park. However, due to vandalism and the sacred nature of many of these sites, visitors are encouraged to visit only the **Aboriginal rock engravings** at Jibbon Point, on the southern shores of Port Hacking.

The engravings include kangaroos, whales and a six-fingered male figure who could be one of the mythical spirits from coastal Aboriginal stories. They are anywhere from 200 to 5000 years old. A message to visitors from the La Perouse Local Aboriginal Land Council reads: 'You will no longer hear the songs of the women as they fish in their bark canoes. Nor will you hear the excited cries of children as they find pipis beneath the sand with their toes. However, we know that you will still feel our people's presence as you approach this beautiful place'. Take care to avoid treading near or on the engravings, as the high level of visitation to this site has caused erosion.

Information

To reach the engravings, enter the park from the north at Farnell Rd; there is a visitors centre with maps and pamphlets 1km in from the entrance. Alternatively, catch a ferry (☎ 9523 2990) from the southern Sydney suburb of Cronulla (Tonkin St Wharf). The ferry crosses Port Hacking, stopping at the Bundeena Bay Wharf. From the wharf proceed through the Bundeena Reserve and along the Lambeth Walk to Jibbon Beach and towards the headland (as the engraving signs are badly deteriorated, take the time to pick up a NPWS leaflet from the cafe above the wharf).

Contact the NPWS Discovery program (☎ 9542 0648) for guided tours.

WOLLONGONG

In the Town Hall forecourt, on the corner of Crown and Kembla Sts, is the **Gurungaty Fountain**. Constructed in 1997 to commemorate the 30th anniversary of the Aboriginal citizenship referendum, it is built on the spot where a freshwater spring once marked a meeting place used by Indigenous communities before they were dispossessed from their lands. Gurungaty is a Creation Spirit that lives underwater, and the mural depicts various creatures and stories from both Aboriginal and non-Aboriginal cultures. The work was a cooperative venture by Jerringha artist Lorraine Brown, non-Indigenous artist Nick Brack and the Coomaditchie artist group.

There is a good collection of Aboriginal paintings at the Wollongong City Gallery (☎ 4228 7500), on the corner of Kembla and Burelli Sts. The Fine room includes bark paintings from Arnhem Land and dot paintings from the Western Desert. At the time of writing, the exhibition included a work by the renowned artist Emily Kngwarreye, and striking black and white lino prints by local Aboriginal TAFE students. The gallery is open 10 am to 5 pm Tuesday to Friday and noon to 4 pm on weekends; entry is free.

AROUND WOLLONGONG

South of Wollongong is Shellharbour, a popular holiday resort named after the number of shell middens found here. The murals of crabs, lobsters, dolphins and seabirds on the Beverley Whitfield Pool's amenities block on the foreshore were designed by Lorraine Brown (see Wollongong earlier).

Shopping

The Warrigal Aboriginal Arts Centre (☎ 4274 9037), on Bakers Lane, Primbee, south of Wollongong, sells didjeridus ($80 to $300), painted emu eggs, clapsticks, motif stationery and T-shirts. Many of the designs reflect the coastal scenes and marine life of the area. A number of Warrigal artists have been shown in exhibitions around the world.

Dharug Country

Blue Mountains

INFORMATION
Tourist Offices

The NPWS Blue Mountains Heritage Centre (☎ 4787 8877), Govetts Leap Rd, Blackheath, has a very good selection of books on the Aboriginal history of the area. The NPWS Discovery program employs a number of Aboriginal rangers, and groups can arrange tours to Aboriginal sites on request.

Books

Blue Mountains Dreaming, edited by Eugene Stockton and published by Three Sisters

Production, is an introductory account of the archaeology, art, history, language and early contact stories of the Dharug people, the custodians of the Blue Mountains.

Christopher Tobin's *The Dhurug Story* traces the history of Dharug people from the relatively amicable first encounters with the British, to the years of war, smallpox and other diseases that devastated the Dharug tribes, through to the era of the Aboriginal Protection Board and the Stolen Generations. It is available from the NPWS centre in Blackheath (see Tourist Offices earlier).

ORGANISED TOURS

Muru Mittigar (☎ 4729 2377), Castlereagh Rd, Cranebrook, is an Aboriginal arts and cultural centre at the foot of the Blue Mountains, adjacent to the Sydney International Regatta Centre. Activities include sampling bush tucker, dance performances, storytelling and a native plants nursery. Most activities require advance bookings. The excellent retail shop is open 9 am to 5 pm weekdays. You can buy cotton T-shirts, silk ties, carved emu eggs, brilliantly coloured emu callers (these pieces of wood, hollow at both ends, make a sound like a male emu calling for a female when they're banged together, and didjeridus from the Wiradjuri region in central NSW, as well as paintings by local artists. There are also children's books, some telling Dreaming stories from the local area, and books about the Dharug people.

Mudla Yupa Mucka Ngurra tours (☎ 0414 45 6550, 4735 7083) are a great way to see many of the most popular Blue Mountains tourist sites and learn about Aboriginal history and spirituality at the same time. Starting at The Three Sisters at Echo Point, where you will hear the story of the beautiful sisters and their medicine man father, you then move on to an Aboriginal cafe and gallery, and visit a scarr tree from which spears and water carriers were made. You'll visit a centre where goods, stories and information were traded, and stop at ancient waterwells for a barbecue lunch. The final stop is a visit to engravings of the Kangaroo Dog at Shores Creek.

At the Mt Tomah Botanic Gardens (☎ 4567 2154), Bells Line of Road, Mt Tomah, you can take an exclusive eco-tour into a closed conservation area (only one group is allowed per day). The tour travels through rainforest onto a ridge of wind-sculpted sandstone with panoramic views. Aboriginal interpretation is given on daily life, plant use and ecology of the Blue Mountains. A range of tours is available, up to a full day ($71.50, including lunch); it's by prior booking only.

KATOOMBA
Organised Tours

The Aboriginal Culture & Resource Centre (☎ 4782 6569), 14 Oak St, conducts 'Kangaroo Dreaming' tours on request to significant Blue Mountains sites. Tours can be adapted to your needs; easy walking tracks and disabled access can be arranged. Bookings (☎ 0404 474 448) are essential. The centre also has artworks for sale.

Entertainment

A woman's dance group, the Coontori Dancers, performs at many of the mountains' regular festivals: call the Aboriginal Culture & Resource Centre for details of upcoming performances.

The didjeridu player, Joomblar, who can be found most fine days entertaining the crowds at Echo Point, is a mountains' institution. He can give you some lessons on the 'didj'; also take the opportunity to ask about his roles in movies such as *Oscar and Lucinda*, and in the opening ceremony of the 1999 World Cup Rugby Union.

Shopping

The Dreamtime Cafe (☎ 4782 9635), 176 Lurline St, sells a range of CDs, from world music to Aboriginal rock, as well as doona covers ($90), leatherwork and artworks ($5 to $300). Groups can ask for clapstick demonstrations or buy painted didjeridus ($120) made from gidgee wood, which has been partly eaten by termites (it improves the sound). The cafe also serves food ranging from sandwiches to emu stir-fries and more traditional bush tucker.

LITHGOW

Aussie Bushabout Holidays (☎ 0408 695 958) specialises in bushwalking eco-tourism, and works with Indigenous guides from Burramadine Aboriginal Corporation, such as Bob Sutor. Visitors are given an Indigenous perspective on local history, culture and archaeology and shown significant

NEW SOUTH WALES & ACT

RED HANDS CAVE

Distance: 9km
Duration: 3 hours
Standard: Easy-medium
Start & Finish: Glenbrook Causeway
Nearest Town: Glenbrook

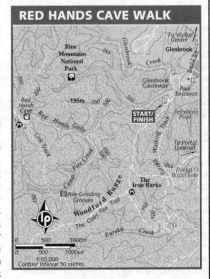

RED HANDS CAVE WALK

As long as 12,000 or 15,000 years ago, the Dharug Aboriginal people lived in the rugged area now protected in the vast Blue Mountains National Park, on Sydney's western doorstep. Stone axes and implements have been found in isolated fertile pockets such as Euroka Clearing near Glenbrook, where food was plentiful – including the fruits of various trees and shrubs such as lilly-pilly, wild cherry and geebung.

In 1913 European settlers searching for a lost child in the Glenbrook Creek area stumbled upon a sandstone shelter adorned with coloured images of human hands, now known as Red Hands Cave. In the form of orange, red and white outlines and filled-in images, they were drawn about 1600 years ago and are one of the best examples of this type of art near Sydney. Ochre was used to create the images. The raw coloured clay or rock was ground to a powder and water added to make a paste, topped off with animal fat to ensure it would last. Today, the wall of the shelter is protected behind a perspex window and there's a viewing platform from where the images are clearly visible; interpretive signs explain their origin.

The ideal way to visit the shelter is an easy-medium walk, starting at Glenbrook Causeway. From here walk up beside Red Hands Creek then climb, not too steeply, to the cave. To vary the return, go on up to a nearby car park, then follow Link Track down to Camp Fire Creek. Along here you'll see some axe-grinding grooves – an interpretative sign describes their formation. Further on, rejoin the track along Red Hands Creek to return to the start. The tracks are clearly defined and there are enough signs to ensure you don't get lost.

You can do this walk using public transport – CityRail runs regular trains from Sydney Central; the off-peak adult return fare to Glenbrook is $8.20. From Glenbrook station, cross the line to a footpath that parallels Burfitt Parade and Bruce Rd to the park entrance. Walk down the road and across Glenbrook Causeway; the walk starts nearby to the right beside Red Hands Creek (about 1.8km from the station).

By road, turn off the Great Western Hwy in Glenbrook along Ross St (signposted to Blue Mountains National Park); at a T-junction turn left along Burfitt Parade and Bruce Rd to the park entrance. There is a park entry fee of $5. There is a car park just down the road on the right, between the entrance and Glenbrook Causeway; from here walk down to cross the causeway – the walk starts close by to the right.

Strong shoes are suitable for this walk; carry a warm jacket and a waterproof, just in case the weather changes.

In Glenbrook, the tourist information centre (☎ 1300 653 408) on the highway has national park information, and there are plenty of cafes nearby.

sites, such as Blackfellas Hands Rock, a 30m overhanging rock decorated with hand stencils and rock art. Tours range from four hours to five days. Prices start at $65 per person (with refreshments) for the half-day tour. Most tours take in either the Wollemi or Blue Mountains National Parks. Accommodation is generally in wilderness cabins.

BLUE MOUNTAINS NATIONAL PARK

The Blue Mountains National Park protects large areas to the north and south of the Great Western Hwy. Many Aboriginal art sites, including stencils, can be viewed in the park. See the boxed text 'Red Hands Cave'. Contact the NPWS (☎ 4787 8877) or see the Organised Tours entries in this section for more information.

Awabakal Country

Newcastle Area

NEWCASTLE

Yamuloong's Bush Food Tours (☎ 4943 6877) boasts the most diverse range of bush tucker plants on the east coast. Guides familiar with both traditional and contemporary horticulture methods take you along a zigzagging trail down a steeply sloping five-hectare site. You pass desert plants such as mulga and prickly wattle, tropical species like lemon myrtle and local Awabakal plants such as water vine and kangaroo apple. The walk finishes with a stroll through a small rainforest valley to a *corroboree* (ceremony) and camp site. Visitors can sample berries, learn how to tell when it's time for kangaroos to give birth to their babies (watch for when the wattles are in flower), and much more. The tour is primarily geared to school groups, but smaller tour groups can ring for quotes (approximately $7 per person; minimum group size of 15).

Keeping Place

The Awabakal Local Aboriginal Land Council (☎ 4965 4532) has a *keeping place* (cultural centre) museum that you can visit, as well as artwork for sale. The museum has artefacts on loan from the Australian Museum, including boomerangs, didjeridus and nulla-nullas, some of which are from the local area and have been returned to the

council for safekeeping by the original custodians. Artworks for sale cost from $24 upwards. It's at 127 Maitland Rd, in the Newcastle suburb of Islington.

METFORD

There is a small **museum** that is rich in artefacts at the Mindaribba Local Aboriginal Land Council (☎ 4934 8511) at Lot 457 Chelmsford Drive, Metford, on the border of Awabakal and Wonnarua country. The land council is just off the New England Hwy on the Newcastle–Singleton Rd.

Displays include boomerangs of all sizes and shapes, a replica bark canoe, a sleeping mat and spears made from old stones, as well as more modern materials such as coloured glass bottles. According to the staff here, Maitland (in the Hunter Valley) was one of the last places in Australia where traditional corroborees were held. The staff can arrange tours to some of the plentiful grinding-rock sites in the area. The land council is usually open 9 am to 4.30 pm weekdays.

Wallamba Country

North of Newcastle

FORSTER-TUNCURRY
Information

You can book Tobwabba Tours (see Organised Tours) at the information centre (☎ 6554 8799), set back from the lake on Little St just south of the roundabout. The centre is open 9 am to 5 pm daily.

Organised Tours

Tobwabba Tours (☎ 6554 5755) has two tours which are conducted by Jan Leon from Tobwabba Art (see the following entry) and Kate Morgan, a local historian and environmentalist. Both tours explain how the Wallamba people lived before European settlement and look at the impact of contact and local environmental issues.

One tour follows a path along the coastal headland, while the other takes in Wallis Lake and the surrounding mangrove wetland systems. Tobwabba means 'place of clay', a reference to the hill on which many descendants of the Wallamba now live. You'll need a minimum of three people to book a tour.

Tobwabba Art

Tobwabba is one of the best-known and largest Aboriginal artistic communities in NSW, and Tobwabba artists' work is regularly exhibited overseas. Many Tobwabba paintings feature marine images and blue shades, reflecting the coastal region. The Tobwabba Art studio-gallery (☎ 6554 5755), 10 Breckenridge St, has paintings and carved wooden figures on display, while the shop (☎ 6555 3871) at the Australia Post Centre on Beach St sells everything from silk-printed umbrellas and intricately painted didjeridus, to silver jewellery and painted pencil holders. The studio-gallery and shop are open 9 am to 5 pm weekdays; the shop is also open 10 am to 4 pm weekends.

Biripi Country

Taree Area

PORT MACQUARIE

The Biripi Local Aboriginal Land Council (☎ 6584 9066), 33 Aston St, has a display of historical artefacts. Two local artists have their studios on site, and their canvas and rock paintings and other artworks are for sale.

TAREE

Radio station Ngarralinyi FM (103.3 FM) broadcasts Indigenous programs. The station is operated by Mid-North Coast Indigenous Broadcasters Aboriginal Corporation (MIBAC, ☎ 6551 3131, e ngarralinyi@yahoo.com.au).

Dhangutti Country

Kempsey Area

ORGANISED TOURS

Wilay Bijarr (☎ 6562 5959), based in Kempsey, runs tours to the surrounding area, ranging from half-day trips to the 17km midden site at nearby Stuarts Point, to 21-day trips to central Australia. A well-known Aboriginal Elder, Wilay performs many traditional ceremonies, including *smoking* (cleansing) and *joining* (marriage) ceremonies. With Australia-wide connections in the Indigenous community, Wilay links up with Aboriginal Elders wherever he goes, so visitors can be introduced to the local knowledge and stories. In the Kempsey region he will demonstrate how Aboriginal people did the 'pipi shuffle' in the sand to find seafood delicacies, and he explains how songs were sung to the dolphins so they would bring in the fish. You can book tours through Wilay Bijarr, PO Box 703, Kempsey, NSW 2440.

WIJAY CULTURAL PARK

Wijay Cultural Park (☎ 6566 2332, fax 6562 1608) at 58 Sea St, Kempsey, west of the showgrounds, is a large Indigenous garden, run by the Djigay Student Association Incorporated. They offer tours of the park on the weekends (bookings essential) that can incorporate a bush tucker lunch, cultural talks, dancing and demonstrations of gum leaf playing and boomerang throwing. Tours cost between $3 and $20, depending on what you'd like to include. The park is also open weekdays 9 am to 3 pm and you can take a look around for free.

CLYBUCCA
Brandybrook Lavender Farm

Brandybrook Lavender Farm (☎ 6565 0000), 2304 Pacific Hwy, is a tearoom, Aboriginal art gallery and lavender plantation 1km north of the Clybucca BP station. You can take a short tour through the gardens and learn about lavender's many uses. In the tearoom you can try lavender scones, blackberry and lavender jam, lavender honey and even lavender ice cream. Aboriginal art is sold by local artists, and you can also purchase ties, scarves, T-shirts, decorated ceramic work, coasters and place mats and a range of lavender cosmetics. Entry is $1 per head for group bookings, including a short tour. As opening hours can vary, ring in advance.

WALCHA
Amaroo Museum & Cultural Centre

The Amaroo Museum & Cultural Centre (☎ 6777 1100), 38 Derby St, is a keeping place with many artefacts from Sydney's Australian Museum collection. The centrepiece is a large wall hanging showing the layout of the old mission, 25km from Walcha, where Indigenous people were sent. Local artists are renowned for their screen-printing designs, and the centre also sells screen-printed material. Entry is by donation.

Amaroo can also arrange tours to Apsley Falls lookouts and axe-grinding groove and scarr tree sites. Prices are available on application.

Sculpture
Overlooking the Apsley River at John Oxley Park in Walcha is a sculpture of the rainbow serpent, by artist Gordon Hookey. Local stories say this is one of the places where the Creator Being surfaced before moving along down the river.

Wonnarua Country
Hunter Valley

ORGANISED TOURS
The highlight of Gringai Aboriginal Cultural Tours (☎ 6572 4935) is a visit to Bulga Mountain and the painted cave of the Aboriginal Creator Spirit, Biame; this is one of the most important sites on the east coast. The tour also takes in Yengo National Park, and includes a history of the Wonnarua people (Wonnarua means 'Hills and plains'). To sample wattleseed truffles and native rainforest punch, and to watch performances by the Yidaki Didg and Dance group, you must book a week or so in advance. Prices are $40 ($80 with food and entertainment), plus GST.

Gumbainggir Country
Mid-North Coast

INFORMATION
Our Land, Our Spirit: Aboriginal Sites of North Coast New South Wales, published by the North Coast Institute for Aboriginal Community Education, is a full-colour pictorial book describing many significant and sacred sites – including bora rings, scarr trees and middens – along the NSW north coast. The authors have gathered together many of the Dreaming stories relating to each region.

NAMBUCCA HEADS
The coastal town of Nambucca Heads marks the southern boundary of Gumbainggir country. Nambucca means 'Crooked knee', and was named after a young warrior whose knees were bent when he was speared to death. This spearing happened at what is now the site of the Bellwood Caravan Park (East Nambucca Heads). There are some trees with detailed carvings of animals and geometric designs in Nambucca, but only local initiated men can visit them.

Information
To find out more about the traditional history of the area, you can visit the Muurrbay Aboriginal Language Centre (☎ 6569 4294) at 465 Bellwood Rd, Bellwood, a suburb of Nambucca Heads.

BOWRAVILLE
About 30 minutes' drive west of Nambucca is the small township of Bowraville, home to an Aboriginal community.

Shopping
The Bawrrung Culture Centre (☎ 6564 7151) at 64b High St sells paintings, arts and crafts such as printed sarongs and scarves, greeting cards and elaborately decorated animal head puppets for kids. Ring for opening times.

Ngurrala Arts and Crafts (☎ 6568 4400) is another outlet for local artists, selling T-shirts, backpacks, teapots and jewellery, as well as canvas paintings and boomerangs. You can also buy 'dream catcher' mobiles in the Aboriginal colours of black, red and yellow. The shop is set in landscaped gardens (it was a former palm nursery) at 7 Wirrimbi Rd (between Bowraville and Macksville via Newee Creek).

COFFS HARBOUR
Organised Tours
Wiruungga Dunggiirr of Gambaarri Tours (☎ 6655 4195) has taught people in Europe and South America about Aboriginal dance and culture. In Australia his cultural and historical trips visit nearby rainforests and a number of Aboriginal sites on the coast between Red Rock (with its ochre clay sites) and Valla, just north of Nambucca Heads. Wiruungga's walking and bus tours are conducted according to demand.

Coffs Harbour Historical Museum
Exhibits at this museum (☎ 6652 5794), 191a High St, include Aboriginal grinding stones and axes, and a list of Aboriginal names for local landmarks. Information at

the museum states that 'the local Kumbain-geri people knew the Coffs Harbour area as Womboynerahlah – the place where kangaroos camp'. Admission is $2 ($0.50 children). It's open 1.30 pm to 4 pm Tuesday to Thursday, and Sunday.

Places to Stay
The recently refurbished, Indigenous-owned Hawaiian Sands Motel (☎ 6652 2666), on the corner of Park Beach Rd and Ocean Parade, is close to the beach and features a fully licensed restaurant that sells Australian-Pacific food. If you are interested in purchasing any of the Indigenous artefacts on display at reception, ask the owner, Graham Emzin.

Shopping
Classic Koori Designs (☎ 6658 4249) is a Coffs Harbour-based company headed by Glenny Naden, a member of the Gabi Gabi clan in south Queensland. Glenny uses both traditional and contemporary designs on decorated plates, picture frames and didjeridus made from Australian woods such as cedar and mulga. You can also purchase ceramic plates, jewellery, silk and wool scarves and 'rock art' paperweights. Items are sold at a stall in the market in the shopping village car park, on the corner of Orlando and High Sts, from 8 am to noon every Sunday.

CORINDI
Yarrawarra Aboriginal Cultural Centre
The meaning of Yarrawarra is 'Meeting place', and the Yarrawarra Aboriginal Cultural Centre (☎ 6649 2669), Lot 170, Red Rock Rd, is so named because its coastal site – 40km north of Coffs Harbour – was a gathering place for different clans. Today the centre is a meeting place for Indigenous and non-Indigenous people, with an art gallery, cafe, bush tours, dormitory accommodation and conference facilities. Guides can show you how fish were caught in a rock pool when there were two tides in one night, and take you to two nearby middens, around 1000 and 4000 years old respectively. You can also visit an 'ochre trading place' where people gathered and traded ochre for tools or other prized resources; visitors can use the clays to paint themselves. Average cost for tours is from $5.50 per person.

Places to Stay
The cultural centre provides dorm accommodation, and double and single rooms, catering to school and community groups of up to 70 people. There is a commercial kitchen on the premises. Prices start at $13.75 per person, up to $25 per person, depending on group size.

GRAFTON
The Durahrwa centre (☎ 6643 4851), 76 Heber St, in South Grafton, produces ceramics decorated with stories from the local area. You can order the designs on cups, plates and whole dinner sets.

Yaegl Country
Lower Clarence River

Yaegl country encompasses the Clarence River's lower reaches, where it divides into a number of tributaries, channels and small islands before opening into the Pacific Ocean.

The best way to visit the many Aboriginal sites in the area is to take the **Lower Clarence Aboriginal Tourist Site Drive**, a self-drive trip that takes in 13 significant Aboriginal sites. The drive begins at the Maclean lookout, with the story of the giant serpent who travelled up the Clarence River shaking off barnacles that became the different tribes in the area. It ends at the Woombah Midden, reputed to be the largest midden on Australia's east coast (a 3000-year-old dingo tooth was found here). Don't remove anything, including oyster shells, from this midden.

You can pick up leaflets showing the drive route from the Grafton tourist centre (☎ 6642 4677), on the corner of Spring St and the Pacific Hwy, in South Grafton; from the Grafton NPWS office (☎ 6641 1500); or at the Maclean Visitors Centre (☎ 6645 4121), in the Ferry Park complex on the Pacific Hwy just south of Maclean.

GIBRALTAR RANGE NATIONAL PARK
The area now known as the Gibraltar Range National Park, south of the Gwydir Hwy between Glen Innes and Grafton, was used by the Ngoorabul, Bundjalung and Gumbainggir nations in seasonal cycles of hunting and food gathering. But with the expansion of European settlement in the

1840s, the tribes were pushed out of the best lands along the river banks into the less hospitable rugged mountain regions.

Five **walking trails** in the park depart from the Mulligans Hut picnic area leading to Dandahra Falls, the Barra Nula Cascades, the Atrichornis/Murrumbooee Cascades, Tree Fern Forest and The Needles. The latter are six granite outcrops which, according to one Aboriginal legend, are six sisters who were turned to stone by their pursuer's curse. The 6km return walk to The Needles is mostly flat and well paved, with the final stretch involving a few rockier climbs. Contact the NPWS office in Grafton (☎ 6641 1500) or Glen Innes (☎ 6732 5133) for more information.

Bundjalung Country

Far North Coast

INFORMATION
See the Information section under Gumbainggir Country earlier for details of *Our Land, Our Spirit: Aboriginal Sites of North Coast New South Wales*.

BUNDJALUNG NATIONAL PARK
Bundjalung National Park stretches north to Evans Head between the Pacific Hwy and the coast. The park's extensive middens and old camp sites indicate it was a popular Bundjalung spot. The turn-off to Evans Head is at Woodburn, or further along the highway at Broadwater.

The Gumma Garra walk to a **scarr tree** begins at the southern edge of the car park at the end of Bundjalung Rd. *Our Land, Our Spirit* says there are two stories attached to this tree. One is that the bark was removed by young boys being trained in canoe making (the scar is too small for a full-size canoe). The other story is related to the legend of the Three Brothers who populated the land, in which it is thought the bark was removed to repair one of the brothers' canoes.

For Discovery program information about the park, call the NPWS Lismore office (☎ 6627 0200). The Ngulingah Local Aboriginal Land Council (☎ 6621 5541), in Lismore, and Birrigan Gargle Local Aboriginal (☎ 6646 1664), 1 Rocky Laurie Ave, Yamba, might be able to put you in touch with local custodians and Elders for teaching and tours.

GURRIGAI ABORIGINAL ARTS & CRAFTS
Gurrigai (☎ 6682 2749) sells mostly local artwork, along with a significant number of pieces from the Outback and crosshatch paintings from Arnhem Land. There is a huge range of items for sale, including wooden coffee tables, tea tree and aloe vera cosmetics and coaster sets. Gurrigai is also well stocked with books, including Burnum Burnum's *Travellers Guide to Aboriginal Australia*. Gurrigai is in the New Italy Museum complex on the Pacific Hwy, about 10km south of Woodburn.

BYRON BAY
The East Coast Blues and Roots Festival, held every year in Byron Bay over Easter, traditionally has a strong Indigenous component. Past acts have included Christine Anu, Archie Roach and Ruby Hunter, Tiddas and one of the great Elder statesmen of Australian country and blues, Jimmy Little. For transport, booking, camping and program information, phone ☎ 6685 8310 or visit www.bluesfest.com.au.

LISMORE
Information
Indigenous Organisations The Ngulingah Local Aboriginal Land Council (☎ 6621 5541) is at 53 Conway St and can organise bush tours and storytelling if you ring in advance.

Tourist Offices The NPWS office (☎ 6627 0200) is in the Colonial Arcade, 75 Main St, Alstonville, east of Lismore on the road to Ballina. You can pick up Discovery tour programs and maps of Bundjalung National Park walks here.

Courses
You can enrol in single-semester units at the College of Indigenous Australian Peoples at Southern Cross University (☎ 6620 3318). Depending on class sizes, you can also negotiate with lecturers to sit in on the popular introductory course, the Bundjalung Cultural Heritage unit.

Bora Ring
A bora ring has now been incorporated into the Tucki General Cemetery, situated on a hill that overlooks the Richmond River valley.

COMMON GROUND

Janice Slater

They say life begins at 40. It began at 45 for me. Imagine a series of events so major that you decide to drastically change your lifestyle. In my case, I packed up and moved from the dry climate of WA to the lush, green, banana-growing coast of Coffs Harbour (NSW), part of the Gumbainggir nation. After two years I packed up again and moved inland to Lismore – rainforest country, or at least it *was*, until intensive logging put an end to that.

I have lived in northern NSW for about three years now – a red dirt Badimaya woman from WA, I now feel welcome in Bundjalung country. Being part of the Indigenous community means we are never alone, no matter where in Australia we live.

It doesn't take long to feel at home when you are an Indigenous person. That's the wonderful thing about my people. Indigenous Australians have a commonality, a sense of belonging that only culture and historical background can engender. Common ground. We are black, we share the same culture and we have all been affected in some way by past experiences of oppressive government policies. Since the invasion and colonisation of Australia, Indigenous people have suffered immensely under cruel policies that attempted to annihilate a culture that had successfully survived for tens of thousands of years. It is our strength, our spirituality, our sense of community and our ability to laugh in the face of great adversity that has kept our culture alive. That is our way.

Janice Slater

I am a Badimaya woman from the Yamitji nation, born and raised in Western Australia. I am 49 years old, the mother of four children and five grandchildren. After raising my family, I found that I needed to further my skills in the area that has always been of interest to me – creative writing. A series of events led me to NSW, which meant sacrificing family and has now led me to further education.

Although I am a published writer, I needed to further my skills to enable me to gain stable employment and that is why I am now undertaking a Bachelor of Arts (Double Major Writing, Minor Indigenous Studies) at Southern Cross University in Lismore, NSW. I continue to write while studying for my degree and plan to publish a collection of my short stories and poems in the future.

Initiation ceremonies were held here and it is a very significant site. Ngulingah Local Aboriginal Land Council asks that you don't enter the ring or take anything away from it. The ring is near the Tucki Tucki Nature Reserve, 16km south of Lismore on the Woodburn road (leave Lismore on Wyrallah St).

Entertainment

The Lismore-based Goobah Goobah Koori Theatre Company (☎ 6662 1533) often performs dance, storytelling, music and songs. Past works includes a Bundjalung translation of Samuel Beckett's *Waiting for Godot*.

Shopping

Bundjalung Way art and craft shop (☎ 0401 014 555), 53 Conway St, is on the ground floor of the land council building. You can buy children's clothes, T-shirts, ceramics, and baskets woven from bangalow palms and banana leaves. The shop is open 9.30 am to 4 pm Thursday and Friday.

NIMBIN ROCKS

Nimbin Rocks are three thick stalagmite-shaped peaks lying approximately 6km south of town, and clearly seen from the road to Kyogle in the west and the road from Lismore in the south. The rocks are a very sacred men's site connected to a clever spirit man called Nyimbunji (probably the source of the name Nimbin). *Our Land, Our Spirit* says that 'initiated men wanting to take tests to become 'clever' men could go to the site to train in the occult, ventriloquism, psychology, magic and hypnotism. They could become invisible, turn into their totems, heal illnesses, ward off evil spirits or magic death spells'. The land around the rocks belongs to two local Aboriginal communities, and is off limits without their permission to enter.

TWEED HEADS
Minjungbal Aboriginal Cultural Centre
The Minjungbal Aboriginal Cultural Centre (☎ 07-5524 2109), Kirkwood Rd, South Tweed Heads, is named after the Minjungbal people who lived around the lower estuaries of the Tweed River. The centre's exhibition space is a great introduction to the history and culture of the Minjungbal. Artefacts on display include shields marked with spear dents and turtle shells that were used as baby cradles. There are photos and displays of the early blackbirding days of the late 1800s and early 1900s, when native Kanaks from New Caledonia, mostly young men, were enslaved and brought to Queensland and northern NSW to work on sugar cane farms.

The Minjungbal gift shop sells Indigenous art, including coffee tables made from yellow box and blue gum, and paintings from Tobwabba (see the Forster-Tuncurry section earlier).

Minjungbal is open 9 am to 4 pm weekdays and to 3 pm Saturday. Admission to the museum is $6.60/3.30. Dance demonstrations and didjeridu players can be booked ahead for a fee.

Things to See & Do
The **bora ground** behind the exhibition and gift shop complex was a traditional ceremonial site and dance circle for men. Visitors are asked not enter the ring.

A boardwalk runs through the mangroves of the adjacent **Ukerebagh Island Nature Reserve**. Minjungbal tour guides can point out native foods such as wild ginger, passionfruit, and flax ferns used for flour ($11/6.60).

Wollumbin is the Bundjalung name for Mt Warning. This mountain, formed by a massive volcano 20 million years ago, now dominates the Tweed Valley. The name could mean 'Cloud catcher' or 'Weather-maker' (a reference to the thunder and lightning that spectacularly strikes the mountain). Many Indigenous people who live in and around Tweed Heads will not climb the mountain out of respect for the original owners, and due to the sacred nature of the site. Contact the Tweed Byron Local Aboriginal Land Council (☎ 6674 3600) for more details before you climb the mountain.

Ngoorabul Country
New England North

GLEN INNES
Aboriginal outlaw Black Tommy was tried here in 1876 and acquitted, but 18 months later he was fatally shot by local constables before a fair trial for new charges of murder and horse stealing could be held. At a time when massacres of Indigenous people in the New England area were shockingly common, Black Tommy's death was notable for the subsequent outcry from the white community. His supporters boycotted the Bald Hob Hotel, where they believed he had been drugged and betrayed.

In his book *Outlawed Bushranger: Black Tommy*, Glen Innes historian Colin Newsome compares the local population's reaction to his death with that of Americans to the death of Martin Luther King, explaining Black Tommy's popularity as being due to his many acts of humanity and bravery. He reportedly saved a little white boy from a wild sow in a sty, and he battled floods and rain to bring sulphur from Glen Innes to a farm-woman who was suffering from diphtheria.

Black Tommy was reputed to have a secret gold mine, but he always evaded those who tried to find the source of his wealth. Renowned for his many escapes, he sometimes used a water lily stem to stay under water until his pursuers had left. *Outlawed Bushranger: Black Tommy* is available from the Glen Innes Visitor Centre (☎ 6732 2397) and the Glen Innes newsagency (☎ 6732 2181).

Indigenous Organisations

The Cooramah Aboriginal Cultural Centre (☎ 6732 5960) is on the corner of MacKenzie St and the New England Hwy, south of the township. The gallery has an exhibit of artefacts dating to the early 1800s, and sells paintings, decorated emu eggs, place mats and boomerangs.

Places to Eat

The Koori Cuisine restaurant is at the same address as the cultural centre. It serves meals such as bush burgers with kangaroo and emu meat, vegetarian spinach and ricotta burgers and *witjutie* (witchetty) grub salad.

THE WILLOWS

The Willows, a 1400-hectare property on the Severn River about 35km north-west of Glen Innes, offers Murray cod fishing, bushwalking and bird-watching. It is equipped with barbecues, picnic and camping grounds and toilet facilities. Guides will take you on walks, tell you about the Aboriginal culture of the area and provide bush tucker and dance displays. Bookings for camping (from $16 per vehicle per night) and fishing (from $80/140 per day with/without own equipment) can be made at Cooramah Aboriginal Cultural Centre (see Glen Innes earlier).

TENTERFIELD
Information

The visitors information centre (☎ 6736 1082), on the New England Hwy (Rouse St) to the south of the town centre, takes bookings for Woollool Woollool tours (see Organised Tours).

Organised Tours

The award-winning Woollool Woollool Aboriginal Culture Tours (☎ 6736 3209) has been developed by the Moombahlene Local Aboriginal Land Council in Tenterfield to take visitors to nearby Bald Rock and Boonoo Boonoo National Park (pronounced bunna-b'noo).

Bald Rock, Australia's largest granite monolith, was a neutral meeting ground for three tribes: the Githabal in the north-east, the Dingghabal in the north and the Wahlebal in the south. The largely treeless, smooth appearance of Bald Rock has been likened to Uluru – but unlike Uluru, it is

appropriate (and fun) to climb to the top. Tours are $54/102.60 per single/couple.

Anaiwan Country

Armidale Area

ARMIDALE
Information

You can pick up maps and directions to Mt Yarrowyck (see the Around Armidale section later) at the NPWS office (☎ 6776 4260), 87 Faulkner St.

Organised Tours

Singer and songwriter Fay Ball runs Fable Tours of the Arts (☎ 6773 6419), a walking tour through significant buildings in Armidale, including the New England Regional Art Gallery, which currently houses both contemporary and older Aboriginal artworks from the region. The tour concludes at the Aboriginal Cultural Centre & Keeping Place building, where dancers, traditional tucker and storytellers can often be arranged with advanced notice.

Aboriginal Cultural Centre & Keeping Place

The Aboriginal Cultural Centre & Keeping Place (☎ 6771 1249), on Kentucky St, displays both touring exhibitions as well as local artwork from the Armidale region (known to Aboriginal people as Anaiwan, a tribal language group and people of this region). The main purpose of the centre is to preserve traditions and provide facilities for study. There is also a small shop that sells printed T-shirts, umbrellas and carved emu eggs.

Local guides here can take you to visit rock art at Mt Yarrowyck or tailor individual tours to the many waterfalls and art sites in the 'Gorge Country' region, ie, the eastern edge of the New England tableland. The centre is open 10 am to 4.30 pm weekdays, and on weekends when touring exhibitions are showing.

AROUND ARMIDALE

A **red ochre rock painting** was recorded at Mt Yarrowyck in the 1960s, and today a well-marked 3km loop walking track takes you to the site. Developed with Armidale's Aboriginal community, signposts along the track describe the vegetation and the possible significance of the site. The markings could be bird tracks, eggs or even human figures. To get to Mt Yarrowyck, leave Armidale westward along Bundarra Rd and travel for just over 28km until you reach the Uralla–Bundarra Rd. Turn right and continue for 1km to the Mt Yarrowyck Nature Reserve.

Kamilaroi Country

Central North

TAMWORTH

Aboriginal artists such as Jimmy Little and Troy Cassar-Daly are among the major stars of Australia's country music scene, and the Tamworth Country Music Festival, held in January, invariably features a large contingent of Indigenous musicians and singers. For programs, tickets and accommodation details and bookings, contact Tamworth Tourism (☎ 6755 4300).

GUNNEDAH

The Red Chief Local Aboriginal Land Council (☎ 6742 3602) runs full- or half-day tours to significant rock paintings, tree carvings and bora grounds. Routes and prices are tailored to visitors' interests.

Burial Site

At Gunnedah Visitors Centre (☎ 6742 4300), about 120km north-east of Coonabarabran on the Oxley Hwy, you can see the grave-site of Cumbo Gunnerah, an 18th-century Aborigine known as 'Red Kangaroo'. His burial place is marked by a bronze cast of the scarr tree that once stood at the site. Further details of his life are outlined in *The Red Chief* by Ion Idress.

MYALL CREEK

On 10 June 1838, some 28 Wirrayaraay women, children and old men were brutally hacked to death at Myall Creek station (see the Myall Creek entry in the History section at the beginning of this chapter). Exactly 162 years later, a **granite memorial** and walking trail dedicated to their memory was opened. The memorial is on the Bingara-Delungra road on a small hill overlooking the Myall Creek valley. To reach it, leave Bingara town on the north-east road and look for the turn-off to Inverell. Take this road for about 17km

until you reach Whitlow Rd, then turn right – the memorial car park is just a few metres from the turn-off. You can bring a stone from your own area as a pilgrimage to the place.

NARRABRI

Wahn Designs (☎ 6792 4146), 50 Mooloobar St, sells all original screen-printed designs on kids' clothes (two years and up), bags, pillowcases and patchwork quilts, as well as women's jewellery.

MOREE

In 1965 Aboriginal rights activist and university student Dr Kumantjayi Perkins and a group of Freedom Riders broke into the Moree Baths, which excluded Aboriginal children. The protesters, inspired by similar actions in the USA, travelled throughout north-western NSW towns highlighting discrimination, segregation and often appalling living standards: in some shops Aboriginal women were even made to buy dresses before trying them on. These days the Moree Hot Mineral Baths and Swimming Pool (☎ 6752 7480), on the corner of Gosport and Anne Sts, welcomes everyone.

Moree Plains Gallery

The Moree Plains Gallery (☎ 6757 3320), on the corner of Frome and Heber Sts, specialises in Aboriginal art, particularly work from local Kamilaroi people, who are long recognised as expert woodcarvers who traditionally have decorated trees with ceremonial and symbolic designs. Just inside the main entrance is the striking Myall Tree, carved by well-known artist Lawrence White. The gallery is housed in a former bank built in 1910, and the old vault contains some of the best preserved examples of the heavy brass breastplates that many Indigenous people were cruelly forced to wear. The gallery is open 10 am to 5 pm Tuesday to Friday, and to 2 pm on Saturday. Visitors are encouraged to make a $2 donation.

Shopping

The Yurundiali Aboriginal Co-op (☎ 6752 7581) at 3 Endeavour Lane produces clothing using ancient and contemporary designs, and sells artworks.

The Nindethana Aboriginal Corporation (☎ 6752 1816) at 19 Greenbah Rd also sells Aboriginal artworks and clothing.

AROUND MOREE

The Wiawa Aboriginal Corporation (☎ 6795 3288) at Lot 301 Rose St, Wee Waa, sells artworks, carved emu eggs and produces clothing in Indigenous designs. A branch of the corporation (☎ 6792 4146) at 52 Mooloobar St, Narrabri West, concentrates on screen-printing and artefact production.

Wailwan Country

Macquarie River Area

COONABARABRAN

Coonabarabran, whose name means 'An inquisitive person', is the base town for access to Warrumbungle National Park (see Around Coonabarabran later).

Information

Indigenous Organisations The Coonabarabran Local Aboriginal Land Council (☎ 6842 3137) in the Strand Arcade, Shop 8, 86–90 John St, has an after-hours number for didjeridu sales (☎ 6842 3130).

Tourist Offices The information centre (☎ 6842 1441) on the Newell Hwy has an Aboriginal history display, including Dreaming stories and examples of stone tools. There are a couple of leaflets available outlining the Aboriginal history of the area and the meanings of place names.

The NPWS office (☎ 6842 1311) on Cassilis St can provide information about Warrumbungle National Park.

Organised Tours

Warrumbungle Light (☎ 6843 4446) is run by Milton Judd, who shares his knowledge of the Warrumbungles and the Aboriginal culture, history and ecology of the Coonabarabran area. All-day tours are available to small groups, with advance booking required. Prices for adults are $75, including lunch (minimum two people).

During some school holidays, NPWS (☎ 6842 1311) provides a Discovery program of Warrumbungle that includes Aboriginal culture walks.

WARRUMBUNGLE NATIONAL PARK

'Warrumbungle' is a local Aboriginal word for 'crooked mountains'. The Visitor Centre (☎ 6825 4364) is 33km west of Coonabarabran. Park use and camping site fees apply. See the Coonabarabran section earlier for details on Aboriginal culture tours into the park.

COONAMBLE

Coonamble, comes from 'gunambil', meaning, among other things, 'full of shit'; the town was probably named after the introduction of cattle to the area.

Information

The North West Regional Land Council (☎ 6822 1333), on the corner of Maule and Namoi Sts, services a number of communities in the area and provides information to visitors.

Shopping

The Ellimata Centre (☎ 6822 1544) at 16 Castlereagh St sells arts and crafts. It's open 8 am to 5 pm weekdays.

WALGETT

Walgett translates variously as 'Plenty of water' and 'Meeting of the waters'. The town hosts an annual multicultural carnival in September. Contact the Walgett information centre (☎ 6828 1399) for details.

Shopping

At Gamilaroi CDEP (☎ 6828 1968), 107 Wee Waa St, artists produce innovative glass-topped coffee tables inlaid with spears and boomerangs, as well as pottery, painted tiles and carved emu eggs. Orders can be taken (prices on application). The CDEP is open 9 am to 4.30 pm Monday to Thursday.

BREWARRINA

Brewarrina, meaning 'Fisheries', borders Wangaypuwan, Wailwan, Kamilaroi and Barranbinya country, and many families from these and more remote areas were forcefully relocated to the Brewarrina Mission. Members from 16 language groups were made to share cramped quarters, with no sensitivity given to their cultural needs.

Brewarrina was also the home of Lloyd Boney, a local Aboriginal football hero who, at the age of 28, was found hanging by a sock in his jail cell an hour after he was incarcerated in 1987. The ensuing riots by outraged locals resulted in the Royal Commission into Aboriginal Deaths in Custody, the final report of which was released in 1991 (see Politics in the Facts about Aboriginal Australia & Torres Strait Islands chapter).

Organised Tours
The Brewarrina museum (see later) runs Walkabout Tours for groups. You can camp under the stars, visit ancient sites in the area and listen to Dreaming stories around the campfire, while preparing and eating bush tucker. Prices are $165 per adult for a full overnight tour.

Brewarrina Aboriginal Cultural Museum
This museum (☎ 6839 2421) on Bathurst St is an excellent experience. There's an audio-visual theatrette, historical photographic collection and replicas of bush and mission life, and hunting equipment. Tours, included in the entry fee, are conducted on arrival and are very informative. The museum also stocks an extensive range of paintings, books, tapes, postcards and other items relating to Aboriginal culture. It is open 9 am to 1 pm and 2 to 5 pm on weekdays, and 9 am to 1 pm on Saturday, plus advance group bookings can be made to open on Sunday (admission $6.60).

Brewarrina Fisheries
After a tour, you can amble along the banks of the Barwon River, where you can see Brewarrina fisheries (Ngunnhu), a series of stone traps where for countless generations the Ngiyampaa people have caught fish to feed the huge annual inter-group gatherings that they hosted.

Despite industrial quarrying, these traps are still in use today. In summer, you may be able to buy fresh catch from a local.

Wangaypuwan Country

Riverine Area

BOURKE
Information
Indigenous Organisations The Nulla Nulla Local Aboriginal Land Council (☎ 6872 2056) at 4–6 Oxley St provides information to tourists about local events and activities.

The Muda Aboriginal Corporation (☎ 6872 1233) is establishing a cultural centre on Sydney Rd, including a museum, which should be fully operational by the time of this publication.

Tourist Offices The information centre (☎ 6872 2280) on Anson St has the *Back O' Bourke Mud Map Tours* leaflet, which details drives to places of Indigenous interest, including Mt Gundabooka (see Around Bourke later) and Brewarrina.

Radio While in and around Bourke, tune into 2CUZ FM (106.5) for informative and entertaining listening. This Aboriginal radio station is run by the Muda Aboriginal Corporation.

Things to See & Do
Be sure to see Dr Fred Hollows' **grave** in the Bourke cemetery. A non-Indigenous Australian, Hollows did much to improve the health of Indigenous peoples in Australia.

Centacare (☎ 6872 1551) at 28 Oxley St has an Indigenous dance troupe, which can be booked for festivals around the country.

Shopping
Beautiful works by young artists are available from Centacare (see Things to See & Do). Another good place to buy artworks and see artists in residence is the Gundabooka Aboriginal Corporation (☎ 6872 1007) at 23 Anson St.

AROUND BOURKE
Mt Gundabooka, between Bourke and Cobar, is of spiritual significance to local Aborigines and features exquisite **cave paintings**, including depictions of the Brewarrina fisheries (see the entry earlier) and Biame. Before heading out, book entry at the tourist office in Bourke and pay at Mt Gundabooka; site camping fees apply. NPWS Bourke (☎ 6872 2744) at 21 Mitchell St can provide guided tours. It is essential to check road conditions before driving out, as this rough road is open only in dry conditions.

At Byrock, 78km south of Bourke on the Mitchell Hwy, you can see an **ancient waterhole** that Biame made by digging the rock hole with his stone axe.

WARREN
The turn-off to Warren from the Oxley Hwy/Mitchell Hwy corner is marked by an

Cracking a smile: the Centacare Dance Troupe

Indigenous carved pole and a road sign – perhaps a true symbol of Reconciliation!

Shopping

Warrana Aboriginal Corporation (☎ 6847 3092) at Lot 3 Maple St offers visitors the chance to meet artists in residence and to buy works directly from them.

COBAR
Information

The information centre (☎ 6836 2448), on the Barrier Hwy, houses a heritage centre with Indigenous content. You can collect the *Cobar Mudmaps* brochure here, with details of a drive to Mt Grenfell (see Mt Grenfell Historic Site later).

Great Cobar Outback Heritage Centre

This museum (☎ 6836 2448) has interesting displays on local Aboriginal life. You can see bush medicine specimens and photographs, as well as play a fascinating ironstone xylophone, which is based on ancient local usage of ironstone chunks as musical instruments. There is also a facsimile of the Mt Grenfell rock caves. The museum is open 8 am to 5 pm daily (from 10 am on Sunday); admission is $5.50 ($3.50 concession/children, those under five free).

MT GRENFELL HISTORIC SITE

Eighty kilometres north-west of Cobar, including 33km of gravel road, is Mt Grenfell Historic Site. This site protects Aboriginal cave art depicting over 1300 images of human figures, mammals, reptiles and linear designs in three caves along a well-watered gully. Archaeological evidence shows the site was still in use less than 200 years ago. No camping is allowed. At the time of writing this site was in the process of being handed back to the traditional owners. The Cobar Local Aboriginal Land Council (☎ 6836 1144) can provide up-to-date information.

The 5km three-hour **Ngiyampaa Walk** takes you to the top of the ridge for a fabulous view of the Cobar pediplain, where local Aborigines would have lived, hunted and foraged for centuries. Contact Cobar NPWS (☎ 6836 2692) for details of the walk.

Wiradjuri Country

Central West

INFORMATION

Wiradjuri Places by Peter Rimas Kabaila provides an interesting Indigenous history of the region.

ORANGE
Indigenous Organisations
The Orange Land Council (☎ 6393 8600), 42 Dalton St, and the Orange Reconciliation Group (☎ 6360 7975), 138 Sale St, are both good contact points for information on activities of Indigenous interest.

Museum
The local museum collection includes a 300-year-old tree carved with Aboriginal designs. Closed at the time of writing, it should be open again by the time of this publication. Check with the visitors centre (☎ 6361 5226, e ovc@ix.net.au) on Byng St.

Shopping
Boree Aboriginal Corporation (☎ 6362 7187) at 7 Colliers Ave sells beautiful locally made artworks.

AROUND ORANGE
About 30km north-west of Orange, then 2km off the Mitchell Hwy, is the **grave of Yuranigh**, an Aboriginal man who acted as a guide on many of Thomas Mitchell's exploratory expeditions. There are scarr trees within the site. It's best to drive along the 2km gravel road then walk in from the gate, as the site is surrounded by a boggy cow paddock.

THE DRIP
There are ancient **Aboriginal rock paintings**, depicting hand stencils by Indigenous visitors over the millennia, at The Drip (also known as Hands on Rock), about 40km north-west of Gulgong. You can camp at this waterhole, which is west of the Goulburn River National Park.

DUBBO
Organised Tours
The Wirrimbah Direct Descendants (☎ 6882 2175) can provide specialist tours giving a local Indigenous cultural history of the area, including visits to sites of significance, bush tucker and Dreaming stories. It is preferred you provide your own transport, though hire vehicles can be arranged. Prices are on application.

Dubbo Museum & History Centre
This museum (☎ 6882 5359) at 24 Macquarie St has an interesting Aboriginal display. The Aboriginal room has carved trees and material culture items such as spear points, grind stones and hunting and fighting implements. *A Treatise on the Aborigines of Dubbo and District*, an unpublished manuscript by EJ Garnsey, is available for purchase. Written around 1944, it is an excellent and informative read. Admission is $5.50 adults, $3.90 concession, $1.10 children and families at $12.10. Carers for people with disabilities receive free entry. It is open noon to 4.30 pm daily (closed Good Friday, Christmas Day and New Year's Day).

Shopping
The Red Earth Gallery (☎ 6884 7031, e lewis@crt.net.au) is at 12 Victoria St, with a variety of Aboriginal art, craft, artefacts and souvenirs on sale. Its speciality is paintings and didjeridus. It's open 10 am to 5 pm daily.

GILGANDRA
Pulkurru Aboriginal Corporation (☎ 6829 6273) at 6 Warraween St can provide information on current Indigenous events and activities.

At the time of writing, the Gilgandra Cultural Centre was being planned, and should include a gallery devoted to the Aboriginal culture of the area.

COWRA
Information
Indigenous Organisations The Wiradjuri Land Council (☎ 6342 4808) is in the Gumbuya Office Complex on Young Rd. It can provide information on current Indigenous events and activities.

Books *Wiradjuri Spirit Man* by Cowra-born HJ Wedge features images and interpretative stories of his delightful and evocative artworks.

Murals
The **Lachlan River Bridge Pylons** in Olympic Park feature a number of beautifully executed murals with Indigenous themes. The project was coordinated by local Indigenous artist Kym Freeman and painted with the assistance of local high school students. Olympic Park is next to the Visitor Information Centre on the Mid-Western Hwy.

WEST WYALONG AREA
Information
The Murrin Bridge Local Aboriginal Land Council (☎ 6898 1119) at 39 Foster St and the Murrin Bridge Aboriginal Advancement Corporation (☎ 6898 1644), both in Lake Cargellico, are good points of contact for visitors. The corporation was moving at the time of writing, so phone for its address.

Shopping
The West Wyalong Local Aboriginal Land Council (☎ 6972 3493) has a shop at 76–78 Main St, which sells artefacts, souvenirs and books. The building was officially opened in 1988 by Wiradjuri Elder, Agnes Coe.

Kejole Korri Studio (☎ 6898 1708) sells Aboriginal products from 98 Grace St, Lake Cargellico, about 100km north-west of West Wyalong. Condoblin Local Aboriginal Land Council (☎ 6895 4194) at 112 Bathurst St, Condoblin, 100km north of west Wyalong, can put you in touch with local artists.

WAGGA WAGGA
Information
The Wiradjuri Regional Land Council (☎ 6921 6544) on Docker St can put you in touch with local artists; one artist can even etch your portrait on an emu egg.

Walking Trail
The **Wiradjuri Walking Track** begins and ends at the Visitor Information Centre (☎ 6926 9621) on Tarcutta St, after a 30km tour. Although this is not actually an Indigenous interpretative walk, it does provide some spectacular views of local Wiradjuri country.

NARRANDERA
Information
The visitor centre (☎ 6959 1766) on Cadell St sells books, maps and locally produced Aboriginal merchandise.

Organised Tours
Sandhills Artefacts (☎ 6959 2593) on Flood St can tailor a tour to meet your interests and available time. You can experience an interpretative guide to local sites and feast on fresh bush tucker. Tours range from two hours to one week. A trip along the Murrumbidgee River can also be organised.

Prices (on application) depend on numbers and the extent of the tour.

Shopping
A must visit is Sandhills Artefacts, where didjeridus, boomerangs and carved emu eggs are made on site and you can meet with the artists.

GRIFFITH
Information
The visitors centre (☎ 6962 4145) on the corner of Banna Ave and Jondaryan St sells Indigenous products. The NPWS office (☎ 6966 8111) at 200 Yambal St has an Indigenous cultural officer.

Things to See
The Western Riverina Community Library (☎ 6962 2515) on Banna Ave has a Local History Resources Room, featuring a worthwhile collection of Indigenous photos and oral histories of the area. It is open 10 am to 4.30 pm weekdays.

The Pioneer Village Museum (☎ 6962 4196) is just out of town (follow the road signs) and features Aboriginal scarr trees. It's open 8.30 am to 4.30 pm daily. Admission is $6.60 for adults.

GOOLGOWI
The tiny township of Goolgowi, 50km north of Griffith, is the base for the Carrathool Shire Council (☎ 6965 1306, e touristofficer@carrathool.nsw.gov.au). At the time of writing, the Tourism & Promotions Officer was in the process of compiling a study of Indigenous tourism activities in the region.

ALBURY
For information on the Albury area, see the Wiradjuri/Duduroa/Yiatmathang Country section in the Victoria chapter.

Yuin Country
South Coast

The Yuin people are made up of 13 different groups, which include the Wodi Wodi, Dharumba and Wandandian peoples. Kinship, country and Dreaming stories form a strong interrelationship between these groups.

MY WONDERFUL GRANDPARENTS

Barry Cooper

At night I used to stand just inside the doorway of my grandparents' tin shack and look out into the dark to where they slept in their old rusted van. Through its side window I could see flickering candlelight. I would shout, 'Nan – Pop, can I come and sleep with you?'...'Oh, all right then,' they'd shout back.

My Pop always had stories to tell me. It was his stories that kept me wavering inside the door. What if a Bagiinj (an evil spirit) should grab me? What if a Dulagal (an ape-like creature) tripped me as I scampered over the black dirt, and took me away to do nasty things to me? My sister and I would pester my wonderful grandparents day and night for something to do – whatever sex life they had would have been whittled away to a distant memory.

My grandparents lived on an Aboriginal Reserve by the name of Wallaga Lake, just south of Tilba Tilba (NSW), underneath the shadow of Gulaga (Dromedary) Mountain. This is my Mother's Country – the land of the Yuin People – although my sister and I were raised in the small seaside town of Tathra, further to the south of Wallaga Lake.

Tathra Primary School was a world away from Wallaga. On Monday morning I would stand, upright and cold, wearing long grey shorts and socks discretely displaying the requisite amount of flesh and knee bone. I would often think of Nan and Pop and my cousins back at Wallaga Lake. I'd wonder whether Nan had cooked some damper. Was she spreading jam on it and drinking sweet black billy tea as well? To this day when I pass a yard or a field where someone is burning leaves I remember my Nan's fireplace and how the smoke used to follow me whenever I shifted out of its way. I'd gaze into the orange embers looking for the face of the devil that Nan said appeared only to naughty little boys. She impaled slices of bread with a small pitchfork made of wire. The bread would darken on one side and then be turned over. All the time I'd be shifting away from the smoke as the fire crackled and the sparks flew. We were stubborn children, Nan said, that's why the sparks flew.

The sparks flew at school too when teachers discovered I didn't attempt any homework due to my occasional walkabouts to Wallaga Lake. But because I lived in an all-white town, I needed that cultural contact. I needed to see other Kooris that looked, acted and felt like me. I needed to be with my people.

Today I tell my sons, Joshua and Macon, the same stories my Pop and Nan told me. Whenever I tell these stories, my boys are enchanted and transformed – as am I. That is the legacy my grandparents left me. That is their gift, and I feel privileged.

Barry Cooper

I was born in Nowra, on the south coast of NSW. My sister and I were raised in Tathra, a small and beautiful seaside town. We lived for a time at other places and we constantly mixed with other Kooris. I left Tathra when I was 18, when I fell in love with a beautiful Koori girl from up the coast.

In 1997 I enrolled in the Indigenous pre-law program at the University of NSW. I have been studying Arts Law ever since and have two lively, intelligent sons who keep me on my toes. As well as cultivating my cynicism, I enjoy walking, fishing, drawing, writing and watching the footy.

INFORMATION

As well as the Indigenous organisations listed later in this section, visitors can con-

tact Merrimans Local Aboriginal Land Council (☎ 4473 7288) in Wallaga Lake, Wagona Land Council (☎ 4476 1144) in

Narooma and Bega Local Aboriginal Land Council (☎ 6492 3950) in Bega.

SHOPPING

South coast outlets for Aboriginal art and crafts include Great Warrior Aboriginal Art (☎ 4464 2320), Shop 9, The Berry Stores, 97 Queen St, Berry. Laddie Timberys Aboriginal Arts & Crafts (☎ 4441 5999), 1 Dent St, Huskisson, makes boomerangs and other material culture items. It also handles the Bidjigal Dancers, which perform on a commission basis for large groups (book well in advance). It also provides boomerang-throwing lessons and other cultural activities. Laddie also sells his work at the La Perouse Markets, in Sydney, each Saturday.

The South Coast Aboriginal Culture Centre (☎ 4421 4433, e scacc@shoalhaven.net.au) on Junction St, Nowra is planning to establish a shop and can provide information on retail outlets in the area. Umbarra Aboriginal Cultural Centre (☎ 4473 7232) at 246 Bermagui Rd, Akolele has a retail outlet and a museum display.

BOODEREE NATIONAL PARK
Information

Booderee means 'Plentiful Bay'. The Booderee National Park, on Jervis Bay, is jointly managed by the Wreck Bay Aboriginal community and Environment Australia. The park entry is $5 per car. For information on camping in the area, contact Booderee Visitor Centre (☎ 4443 0977), at the entrance to the park and including a small museum with Aboriginal artefacts. Entrance to the Wreck Bay Aboriginal community is not permitted.

Organised Tours

Barry's Bush Tucker Tours (☎ 4442 1168, 0410 744 744), 14 Bottom St, Booderee, will teach you about the seasons and how the flora and fauna heralds their arrival. You can collect medicinal plants and yarn with Barry around the campfire. As a special treat you can explore the bush by spotlight, witnessing the habits of nocturnal creatures. Special two- and three-day 'discovery camps' are also available. Short tours start at $12 per adult.

ULLADULLA
Information

The Ulladulla Local Aboriginal Land Council (☎ 4455 5883, e budamurra@fas

SOUTH COAST

trac.net.au) is at 66 Deering St. It handles Giriwa Garuwanga Arts & Crafts and takes bookings for the Bunan Dancers (which perform on a commission basis for large groups, especially tour and school groups – book well in advance), as well as Coomee Nulunga Cultural Tours.

Walking Trail
The **Coomee Nulunga Cultural Trail** was established by the Ulladulla Local Aboriginal Land Council. It begins near the Lighthouse oval car park on Deering St. A large sculpture of **Bulan Yuin** (the Corroboree man), a local creator ancestral being, welcomes you to the land. A main feature of the track is following the path of the Rainbow Serpent down to a secluded beach. Walkers are expected to stick to the track. While it's self-paced, for an organised and informative tour, contact the Ulladulla land council.

WALLAGA LAKE NATIONAL PARK
This small park takes in most of the western shore of Wallaga Lake, a beautiful tidal lake at the mouth of several creeks. Shell middens and artefacts such as cutting stones can be seen. Merriman Island, in the lake off Regatta Point, is off limits because of its significance to the Aboriginal community. Camping is not permitted and there are no picnic or toilet facilities.

UMBARRA CULTURAL TOURS
Umbarra Cultural Tours (☎ 4473 7232), run by the Yuin people from Wallaga Lake Koori community, has tours of Wallaga Lake and other places of historical and cultural importance such as Gulaga (Mt Dromedary) and Biamanga (Mumbulla Mountain). Other activities, which must be organised in advance, include spear throwing, bark hut construction, ochre painting, boomerang throwing and sampling bush tucker. Opening hours are 9 am to 5 pm weekdays. Prices are around $50 per adult for a four-

hour tour, eg, to Gulaga. Admission to the cultural centre here is free.

MURRAMARANG ABORIGINAL AREA
The Murramarang Aboriginal Area, 2km south of Bawley Point, features an excellent coastal walk where you can see shell middens and ochre sites. The Bomaderry Tourist Centre (☎ 1800 024 261 toll free) has details.

EDEN
Information
The Eden Local Aboriginal Land Council (☎ 6496 1922) is at 11 Chandos St.

Jigamy Farm
Just out of Eden is Jigamy Farm (☎ 6496 1922), the local cultural centre. Just getting under way at the time of writing, ring to see if it's open. It will probably operate mainly in the summer tourist season and will feature local Indigenous information and artefacts.

Ngunnawal Country
Australian Capital Territory & Around

CANBERRA
Information
Indigenous Organisations The Australian Institute for Aboriginal and Torres Strait Islander Studies (AIATSIS; ☎ 6246 1111) is relocating to the Acton Peninsula, next to the National Museum of Australia, in 2001. AIATSIS is an independent Commonwealth statutory authority and houses a vast library of resources relating to Indigenous peoples (open to the public; closed Tuesday). Ring to make an appointment.

The Australian Heritage Commission (☎ 6217 2111) has a Register of the National Estate detailing sites of significance

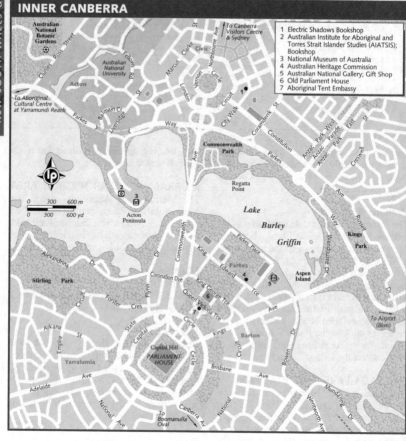

INNER CANBERRA

1 Electric Shadows Bookshop
2 Australian Institute for Aboriginal and
  Torres Strait Islander Studies (AIATSIS);
  Bookshop
3 National Museum of Australia
4 Australian Heritage Commission
5 Australian National Gallery; Gift Shop
6 Old Parliament House
7 Aboriginal Tent Embassy

across the country (Web site: www.ahc.gov. au). Sites include the Tent Embassy (see Politics in the Facts about Aboriginal Australia & the Torres Strait Islands chapter), on King Victoria Terrace opposite Old Parliament House.

The Ngunnawal Aboriginal Land Council (☎ 6297 4152) plans to set up an Aboriginal Cultural Centre at Yarramundi Reach, on the western shore of Lake Burley Griffin, in 2001. It will focus on the culture and history of Indigenous peoples of the Canberra region.

Tourist Offices The Canberra Visitors Centre (☎ 6205 0044, 1800 026 166 toll free, fax 6205 0776), 330 Northbourne Ave, is a useful stopping-off point for visitors interested

in Indigenous sites and activities around Canberra. Web site: www.canberratourism .com.au.

Books *Wiradjuri places* (vol 1) by Peter Rimas Kabaila includes information on Ngunnawal country. *Belconnen's Aboriginal Past*, also by Kabaila, provides a glimpse into the archaeology and Aboriginal occupation of Belconnen, a suburb of Canberra.

Parliament House

Michael Nelson Tjakamarra's **Meeting Place** mosaic is in the forecourt of Parliament House (☎ 6277 5399). It represents a gathering of Aboriginal groups. Parliament House also has a permanent display of Aboriginal art, including the **Yirrkala Bark**

CANBERRA GALLERIES, MUSEUMS & SHOPS

Readers should be aware that the names of deceased members of the Aboriginal community may be cited in this section. Mentioning the personal name of someone who has died recently can cause offence, anguish and grief in some Aboriginal cultures.

The following venues are all within easy reach around Canberra. Compared to Sydney and Melbourne, the number of recommended places, including bookshops with Aboriginal books, is very small. Still, it is not possible to list them all here. See the Shopping section in the Facts for the Visitor chapter for further information.

Australian Institute of Aboriginal and Torres Strait Islander Studies Bookshop (☎ 6246 1191). This bookshop has an excellent and interesting range of books on Indigenous Australia. However, at the time of writing it was about to close in preparation for a permanent move to the new National Museum of Australia (see earlier); phone for opening hours. The library here is one of the most comprehensive in Australia on Indigenous issues. Web site: www.aiatsis.gov.au

Australian National Gallery (☎ 6240 6502) Parkes Place. Many of Australia's most distinguished and prominent Aboriginal and Torres Strait Islander artists can be seen here, with some of the finest examples of their art. The gallery emphasises the importance of Indigenous art by giving it prominence in Gallery One (to the left of the reception area). Directly in front at the entrance is a striking painting by Jack Wunuwun (1930–90), *Banumbirr the Morning Star*. There's a beautiful rare sculpture on display (circa 1943), attributed to Pankalyirri, of a Djidjgargal spirit child from Lake Disappointment carved and engraved out of mulga wood. Also on show are three works by the famous bark painter Yirawala (1903-76), who is sometimes referred to as the 'Picasso of Arnhem Land'. The centrepiece is the Australian art masterwork, *Yanjilypiri Jukurrpa* (Star Dreaming), from 1985. This magnificent painting was one of the first large-scale collaborative canvases to emerge from the Yuendumu community north-west of Alice Springs and was painted by Paddy Jupurrurla Nelson, Paddy Japaljarri Sims and Larry Jungarrayi Spencer.

As well as the treasures in Gallery One, the gallery has led the way in terms of incorporating Aboriginal and Torres Strait Islander and non-Indigenous art together in the Gallery of Australian Art on level one. Three fine historical items here include an incised wooden spear thrower (circa 1860) from New South Wales, a South Australia fighting club from 1845 and a stunning broad shield (circa 1860) from south-eastern Australia. Admission is free to the permanent collection. The gallery is open 10 am to 5 pm daily. Web site: www.nga.gov.au

Australian National Gallery Gift Shop (☎ 6240 6420). The gallery shop sells a limited range of Indigenous products, including books, posters ($13) and stationery sets ($9). There are Desert Design silk ties ($66), and scarves ($80); pottery and ceramics (from $50); and a few sculptures and some weaving. Jigsaw puzzles (500 pieces) by Aboriginal artist Robert Campbell Junior are $24. Probably the best buy is the attractive gallery T-shirt, featuring a painting by Gudthaykudthay ($21.50). The bookshop opposite has no Aboriginal books worth mentioning, which is disappointing considering the magnificent Aboriginal art collection just around the corner. The shop is open the same hours as the gallery.

Electric Shadows Bookshop (☎ 6248 8352) City Walk (near the cinema of the same name). This bookshop has a small range of Aboriginal and Torres Strait Islander books, including biographies, histories and a few on art. It's open 9 am to 9 pm weekdays, 12.30 pm to 6.30 pm on Sunday and usual shop hours during Christmas.

National Museum of Australia (☎ 6208 5000). Currently under construction and opening in 2001 on the Acton Peninsula, by the shores of Lake Burley Griffin. The museum will be based around three thematic galleries: Australian society and history since 1788, the interaction of people with the Australian environment, and Aboriginal and Torres Strait Islander cultures and histories. Phone ahead for admission details or visit the museum online. Web site: www.nma.gov.au

Petition (see the History section in the Northern Territory chapter) and the **Barunga Statement**. This document, written on bark, calls for civil rights, self-determination, land rights and other political and economic changes. It was presented to former prime minister Bob Hawke in June 1988 at the Barunga community in the Northern Territory. Parliament House is open to the public 9 am to 5 pm daily. Free guided tours begin at 9 am and follow every half-hour.

Australian National Botanic Gardens

On the lower slopes of Black Mountain, these botanical gardens feature the **Aboriginal Plant Use Walk**, with a range of native plants used by Aborigines across the country. There are utilitarian plants for weaving baskets, medicinal herbs, sweet treats and others. Pick up a pamphlet from the gardens' information centre. There are free guided walks at 11 am weekdays and at 11 am and 2 pm on weekends.

The information centre (☎ 6250 9540) on Clunies Ross St is open 9.30 am to 4.30 pm daily.

Special Events

Organised by the Australian Heritage Commission (☎ 6217 2111), The Art of Place: The National Aboriginal and Torres Strait Islander Heritage Art Award is held in even-numbered years around August. Indigenous artists from across the country are invited to submit entries depicting a place they nominate for listing on the National Estate.

NAIDOC week is celebrated annually in July. For details on the Canberra festivals' activities, contact the ACT NAIDOC committee (☎ 0411 020 027).

The Aboriginal Corporation for Sporting and Recreational Activities (☎ 6295 8557, e koori_sport@tpg.com.au), at Boomanulla Oval in Narrabundah, organises regular sporting, recreational and cultural activities. Their interesting programme includes traditional Aboriginal games presented by the ACT Traditional Games Program (☎ 0408 228732), boomerang throwing and storytelling by Uncle Ben Blakeney (☎ 6284 3946), and a community store in which local Aboriginal artists sell their wares.

Another highlight on the Canberra calendar is the Harold 'Crow' Williams Annual Memorial Rugby League Knockout, which is held in September. Born in Cowra, Harold Williams (1946–94) was an Indigenous football hero who played mainly in the Canberra region.

NAMADGI NATIONAL PARK

In Namadgi National Park, south of Canberra, Aboriginal depictions of kangaroos, dingos, large birds and humans, painted in ochre thousands of years ago, can be seen at **Yankee Hat Rock** (for a description of the walk see the boxed text 'Yankee Hat Walk'). Visitors should be well prepared and record details of their trip in the bushwalking register at the park visitor centre (☎ 6207 2900). Permits are required for camping in the park.

QUEANBEYAN
Information

The Ngunnawal Land Council (☎ 6297 4152) is at 28 Rutledge St, Queanbeyan, which is also the address of the Ngunnawal Elders Council.

The ATSIC Queanbeyan Regional Council (☎ 6297 7144) and the land council can provide information on Indigenous activities in Queanbeyan.

YASS

Ngunnawal Community Care (☎ 6226 3799), opposite the hospital on Cliff St, is establishing the **Ngunnawal Walk** around Riverbank Park on the Yass River. It will highlight old camp sites, mission houses and include an Elders Memorial Garden, and already includes a painted mural under Hume Bridge.

Special Events

Each October Yass holds the Cooma Cottage Festival, which includes Indigenous participation.

Gundungurra Country

Goulburn Area

GOULBURN
Information

The Pejar Aboriginal Land Council (☎ 4822 3552), at 81 Bourke St, has an interesting

YANKEE HAT WALK

Distance: 6km
Duration: 2 hours
Standard: Easy
Start & Finish: Car park by Old Boboyan Rd
Nearest Town: Tharwa

YANKEE HAT WALK

The main Indigenous rock art sites in Australia's sub-alpine country are protected in the ACT's mountainous Namadgi National Park. These ranges have been profoundly important to the Ngunnawal people for thousands of years; the name Namadgi is the Aboriginal word for the mountains south-west of Canberra. There is evidence of people camping in the area near the Gudgenby River, in the park, from 3700 years ago and until at least 800 years ago; the area is a rich source of food – snakes, platypuses, waterbirds, and Bogong moths, which are found among the highest peaks during summer.

The Yankee Hat paintings, the largest collection in Namadgi, are grouped together low down on a big rounded granite boulder, one of several in a cluster overlooked by Yankee Hat mountain (the name of a nearby peak which looks like an American colonial hat). Faint red-brown figures are the oldest, and the lighter-coloured ones are the most recent. Ochre was used to make red paint, and clay for the white; they were turned into a paste by adding water, sap, animal oils or blood. Most of the figures are either abstract images or representations of humans; others resemble dingos and possibly kangaroos, wombats or koalas, echidnas or turtles, and emus or brolgas. The figures look very much like those found in southern and central western NSW; they are of enormous cultural significance.

To reach the start of the walk to the rock art site, first of all drive to Namadgi National Park visitor centre on Naas Rd, 37km south of Canberra via Tharwa Drive. Then drive south along Naas Rd (bitumen surface) for 29km to the turn-off for Old Boboyan Rd and follow this gravel road for 3.7km to a car park.

The visitor centre (☎ 02-6207 2900) is open daily and well worth some time – there are good displays about the park's cultural and natural features. Pick up a copy of the excellent leaflet about the Yankee Hat walk and the handy *Namadgi Guide* ($4).

The walk starts at the car park and is clearly signposted with waymarkers; there is a bridge over Bogong Creek and boardwalks across the swampy bits. Good strong shoes are OK for this walk; the weather up there can be decidedly chilly, so make sure you pack a fleece jacket and a waterproof. In the small town of Tharwa, 2km on the Canberra side of the visitor centre, the shop (open daily) sells takeaway food, drinks and petrol.

The Yankee Hat paintings are very precious *and* very fragile. Please don't touch the art or the rock surface, because your oily skin will damage the paint, and little pieces of paint and rock can come off. All Aboriginal sites and artefacts in the ACT are protected by law, so it is an offence to damage them.

cultural display room and can also undertake local historical research for you, however you will need to enquire in advance about this service, (prices are available on application).

Shopping

Koori Kullas (☎ 0418 411 215) sells paintings and other small Indigenous artworks, including computer graphics. Ring for further details; prices on application.

Wiljali Country

BROKEN HILL

Information
The NPWS office (☎ 8088 5933, fax 8088 4448), 183 Argent St, has information about Mutawintji and Kinchega National Parks (see those sections later in this chapter), and offers tours of both parks. The office is open 8.30 am to 4.30 pm weekdays.

Organised Tours
All tour operators based in Broken Hill run day trips (and longer ones on demand) to Mutawintji and Kinchega National Parks from about $90 per person. However, none are owned or operated by Aborigines. See the Mutawintji and Kinchega National Parks sections later for details on more authentic tours to these parks.

Three reliable and budget-priced agencies are Broken Hill's Outback Tours (☎ 8087 7800), Silver City Tours & Travel (☎ 8087 3144) and Tristate Safaris (☎ 8088 2389).

Broken Hill City Art Gallery
This art gallery (☎ 8088 5491), on Chloride St, features a permanent display of Aboriginal art, and frequently holds temporary exhibitions of Indigenous paintings. It is open 10 am to 5 pm weekdays, and 1 to 5 pm on weekends. Admission is $3.30 per person.

The adjoining entertainment centre (☎ 8088 5490) has occasional performances of Aboriginal music and dance.

Broken Hill Sculptures
This collection of huge rock carvings is most attractive at sunset. One carving was created by Badger Bates, a local Aborigine, and two others by Tiwi Islanders. Most tour operators run sunset tours from about $20 per person. Informative brochures ($1) – and keys to the gate ($5.50, plus $10 deposit) for full vehicle access – are available from Broken Hill Visitor Information Centre (☎ 087 6077).

Shopping
The Thankakali Aboriginal Cultural Centre (☎ 8087 6111), on the corner of Beryl and Buck Sts, houses an impressive number of reasonably priced paintings, carvings and crafts, mostly accessible along an underground boardwalk. Near the cafe inside is a display of compact discs of Indigenous music, which you can listen to before buying. The centre is open 9 am to 4 pm weekdays, and 10 am to 3 pm on weekends. Web site: www.thankakali.com.au.

Wandjiwalgu Country

MUTAWINTJI (MOOTWINGEE) NATIONAL PARK
Mutawintji (often erroneously labelled as Mootwingee) is a comparative oasis, rich in Aboriginal history. The hundreds of rock carvings, cave art and remains of hearths and other artefacts indicate that for over 8000 years the area was populated by various Aboriginal tribes, all attracted by rock holes permanently full of water. The park was returned to the traditional owners in 1998, and is now jointly operated by the Mutawintji Local Aboriginal Land Council and the NPWS.

Inside the park, the **Mutawintji Historic Site** was, and still is, the setting for numerous important ceremonies, and is a treasure trove of rock art. Independent travellers are *not* permitted to enter this site (but they can enjoy the rest of the park): access is only possible on an organised tour (see Organised Tours later).

The signs at the start of the access roads off Silver City Hwy indicate current road conditions to and around the park, or check with the NPWS office in Broken Hill (see that section).

Information
The Mutawintji Visitor Centre inside the park usually has 'visitor guide' pamphlets, but it may be prudent to pick one up at the NPWS office beforehand. This pamphlet details a number of walks (up to 5.5km) and drives (some are barely passable in a 2WD in dry weather) – but *not* in the Mutawintji Historic Site. The many useful notice boards along the way explain local Aboriginal culture and history, but it's still far better to visit on an organised tour.

The faded outdoor display at the visitor centre explains some Aboriginal culture and history, but the information boards at the entrance to the Homestead Creek camping ground are considerably more enlightening.

B U S H   M E D I C I N E   BUSH MEDICINE BUSH MEDICINE BUSH MEDICINE BUSH

A detailed knowledge of the environment, centuries of experimentation (trial and presumably error), and an abundance of plant and animal species has created a wealth of traditional Aboriginal bush medicine. For many ailments there are several remedies, depending on location and season, and many plants have several uses.

One of the most highly regarded medicines of the central desert, the sap of the ghost gum (1) is soaked in water or boiled to make a strong disinfectant. As a liniment it also helps aches, cramps and muscular pain. Skin infections are washed with the soapy pods of Acacia holosericea, known as mandull, and an infusion of its roots treats laryngitis (3). Mangol (cocky apple or Planchonia careya) (4) is used for soothing prickly heat and as an antiseptic for packing deep wounds. Good health includes a sense of wellbeing, and so bush products also have their cosmetic uses. Goanna oil (2) keeps the skin glossy and prevents it from drying, while the abrasive leaves of the sandpaper fig (Ficus opposita) (5) are useful for sanding back warts. Even the droppings of the zebra finch (6) have their use: mashed up with water they have a cooling, soothing effect for sore or swollen eyes.

An amazing variety of bush food can be collected in Australia, as long as you know what to look for. See the Food – Bush Tucker section (page 93) for details.

The nectar of grevillea species, like the inland flame tree (1) of the central desert can be sucked for their sweet nectar. Hunting out native fruits and berries (2) is a favourite pursuit with children. Collecting tubers is harder work; here Esther Managku unearths some yams (3). The large nuts of the boab tree (4) are harvested in the Kimberley for their pith, which tastes like sherbert. The roots can also be tapped for water. Large animals are generally hunted by men, while women usually hunt the smaller ones. Tracks, like this emu footprint (5) can be used to help locate them. Cooking techniques include steaming food in pit ovens, roasting on hot coals or the bar-becue – such as these magpie geese ready to feed the crowds at the Oenpelli Open Day in Arnhem Land (6) – and baking smaller game, like goannas, in the ashes (8). Kangaroo berries (7), found in the southern states, are yellow when ripe (Jan/Feb), but highly poisonous if eaten when green. Out of sea-son they can be crushed and tossed into a lake to stun the fish so they are easier to catch.

Organised Tours

The Mutawintji Local Aboriginal Land Council (☎ 8088 7000), based in Broken Hill, runs Mutawintji Heritage Tours of the park, including the Mutawintji Historic Site. Tours leave every Wednesday and Saturday between April and November at 10.30 am from the Homestead Creek camping ground. Get there about 15 minutes beforehand. Costs are $16.50/5.50/27.50 for adults/children/families.

The NPWS runs a Discovery program with Aboriginal guides most days during the Easter, July and September (but not Christmas) school holidays. Tours include the Historic Site and leave from the Homestead Creek camping ground. The cost is $11/5.50/27.50 for adults/children/families; contact the NPWS in Broken Hill (see that section) for more details.

The tour operators listed in the Broken Hill section earlier also offer trips to Mutawintji, including to Mutawintji Historic Site.

Barkindji & Danggali Countries

Darling River Area

WENTWORTH

At the junction of the Murray and Darling Rivers, Wentworth has been a popular meeting point for various Aboriginal tribes for over 40,000 years.

Information

The tourist office (☎ 5027 3624, e tourism @wentworth.nsw.gov.au), on Darling St, is a gold mine of information about local Aboriginal history and culture.

Organised Tours

The best tour operator in the Mildura/ Wentworth area is Harry Nanya Tours (☎ 5027 2076, e carnma@ruralnet. net.au), on Sandwych St. This Aboriginal-owned and -operated company offers a range of one-day and overnight tours to Mungo National Park (see later) and half-/full-day trips ($28/55 per person) around Wentworth which concentrate on local Aboriginal heritage. Other tours are listed on its Web site (www.harrynanyatours .com.au).

Scarr Tree

Alongside the western car park in the delightful 2 Rivers Ski Reserve is a huge dead scarr tree, with a helpful explanation nailed to it. To get there, follow Silver City Hwy southeast over Tucker's Creek and then head towards the Wentworth District Hospital.

Shopping

Harry Mitchell Arts & Crafts (☎ 5027 2076), on the corner of Silver City Hwy and Sandwych St, offers a vast range of authentic, locally made goods.

MUNGO NATIONAL PARK

Discoveries at this remote and spectacular park revealed that about 40,000 years ago (and possibly up to 60,000 years), Aborigines settled on the banks of the fertile lakes here. The lakes dried up about 15,000 years ago, so the Aborigines had to adapt to a harsh semi-desert environment.

These days, local Aboriginal communities are strongly involved in the preservation of the park and act as tour operators and guides.

Information

The park visitor centre has outstanding displays about local Aboriginal history and culture, including explanations about catching and cooking fish, and several Dreaming stories.

Information about road conditions to and around the park is available on signs at the start of Arumpo Rd (from Mildura), the park visitor centre, and the NPWS office in Buronga (see the Mildura section in the Victoria chapter).

The excellent book *Mungo National Park* ($11), published by the NPWS, is available from the NPWS office in Buronga, Mungo Lodge (near the visitor centre) and, usually, the tourist offices in Mildura and Broken Hill.

Organised Tours

The Discovery programs organised by the NPWS include plenty of information about Aboriginal history and culture, and usually involve Indigenous tour guides. Tours are held most days during the Easter, July and September (but not Christmas) school holidays, and they usually leave from the visitor centre. The cost is $5.50/2.20/13.20 for

NEW SOUTH WALES & ACT

LAKE MUNGO – MY GRANDMOTHER'S COUNTRY

Raeleen Berriman

The ancient Mungo National Park is the country of the Barkindji, Muthi Muthi and Ngiyaampa peoples – the traditional custodians. We are born of this land; we are part of this land in affinity with our Mother Earth. Rich in Aboriginal history, this is the country of our ancestors and whenever we visit, we 'feel' their presence. Our spiritual connection is strong and we know we are protected.

Many thousands of years ago, when Lake Mungo was full of water, it was a meeting place for the tribes of the area. They would gather here for ceremonies and rituals, to trade, hunt and generally socialise. The gatherings still take place today, but in a more contemporary sense. Our complex kinship system is still very much intact and we are proud of our cultural heritage.

Lake Mungo is part of the Willandra Lakes system and is World Heritage-listed, partly because of archaeological finds, which confirm Aboriginal culture as the world's oldest continuing culture. Today the park has some of the oldest Aboriginal sites in Australia – there are the remains of cooking hearths, campfires, artefacts and middens, some of which have been carbon-dated to 60,000 years. Emus and kangaroos roam Mungo, along with many other species of animal and bird life. These creatures are the tribal totem for some, and also a traditional food source. Wedge-tailed eagles can often be seen, along with the willy wagtail and the small black and white bird called the peewee. According to the Dreamtime, the peewee is an Aboriginal woman named Cleistene, who was banished from her camp for breaking traditional law.

The Aboriginal people who belong to Mungo all have a deep relationship with the land, plants, animals and each other. These relationships were set down in the Dreamtime and today we still acknowledge them very strongly. I feel proud and privileged to have this connection to my Grandmother's country.

Raeleen Berriman

Raeleen was born and grew up at Menindee, NSW, on the banks of the Paaka (Darling River). She is a member of the Barkindji Aboriginal community, the Darling River people. Her tribal totem is Kalti the Emu and her moiety is Kilparra. Raeleen is a descendant of the Nanya tribe.

A personal and spiritual affinity with the Lake Mungo area means that Raeleen is able to be in touch with her grandmother's country.

A deep commitment to her Aboriginal culture and the Reconciliation process has resulted in Raeleen presenting cultural awareness sessions to a variety of non-Indigenous participants in various states.

Raeleen is an avid reader and keen traveller, loves new places and meeting people, including friends she's never met before. Raeleen manages Ngangana Aboriginal Multi-Service Outlet in Gol Gol for the Dareton Home Care Service of NSW. She is a member of the NSW State Committee on Ageing and the Ageing & Disability Department Regional Advisory Group.

adults/children/families; more details are available from the NPWS office in Buronga (see Information).

There are three Aboriginal-owned and/or -operated companies that also offer tours of Mungo:

Harry Nanya Tours (see the Wentworth section earlier in this chapter) runs day trips ($55 per person), sunset trips ($60) and overnight trips ($170)

Jumbunna (☎ mobile 0412 581 699, @ jumbunna @hotmail.com) in Mildura offers day ($46) and overnight trips ($190)

Ponde Tours (☎ 5023 2488, @ ponde@vic .ozland.net.au) 162 7th Ave, Mildura, mainly caters to large groups, but also runs trips for individual tourists

Things to See

The shimmering white cliffs known as the Walls of China are where you're most likely to see remains of Aboriginal **hearths**, **campfires** and **burial sites**. A display board located between Lakes Mungo and Leaghur contains some limited explanations about Aboriginal history and culture. While it is possible to drive around the park on a self-guided tour, if you have any interest whatsoever in Aboriginal history and culture (which is, after all, the main attraction of Mungo), go on an organised tour.

KINCHEGA NATIONAL PARK

Although less publicised and less popular than Mutawintji, Kinchega is an integral part of the heritage of the Danggali and Barkindji people. The **scarr trees** along the Darling River can be seen on the self-guided 'River Drive' tour (20km), but it's better to join a NPWS Discovery program. These are held most days during the Easter, July and September (but not Christmas) school holidays and cost $5.50/2.20/13.20 for adults/children/ families; more details and bookings (advisable) are available from the NPWS office in Broken Hill (see that section).

The tour operators listed in the Broken Hill section also run tours to Kinchega.

Menindee, the town closest to the park, has a shop (☎ 8091 4274) selling Aboriginal art and serving as a park information centre.

Northern Territory

Aborigines make up nearly one-third of the Northern Territory (NT) population. The non-Aboriginal population is largely found in the cities. The entire eastern half of the Top End comprises the Arnhem Land Aboriginal Reserve, a vast, virtually untouched area with spectacular scenery, few people and some superb rock art sites. Major settlements are at Gove, on the peninsula at the north-eastern corner, Oenpelli – also known as Gunbalanya – just across the East Alligator River from Ubirr in Kakadu National Park, and Maningrida on the Liverpool River estuary.

The NT's terrain ranges from monsoon forest to desert. Important tribal groups include the Tiwi people who live on Bathurst and Melville Islands – rising seas cut off these islands from the mainland 4000 years ago – the Warlpiri in the south-east and the Arrernte in the south.

History

Philip Morrissey

EARLY HISTORY

Firestick farming was practised and involved the selective burning of undergrowth in forests and dead grass on the plains. This encouraged new growth, which in turn attracted game animals to the area. It also prevented the build-up of combustible material in the forests, making hunting easier and reducing the possibility of major bushfires.

Contact with the Macassan trepangers (sea-cucumber fishermen from Sulawesi in modern-day Indonesia) goes back to the 18th century. Relations were generally harmonious and reciprocal – largely because the Macassans were not interested in Aboriginal land and respected the cultural integrity of the Aborigines. In fact some Aborigines travelled with the Macassans back to Sulawesi, and in 1988 as part of the Bicentennial program, a *prahu* was sailed once more from Sulawesi and contact was re-established between Macassans and Aborigines.

EUROPEAN INVASION

Early European attempts at settlement all failed until Palmerston – its name was later

HIGHLIGHTS

Telephone code: ☎ 08
Indigenous population: 51,876
Overall population: 189,990
Area: 1.35 million sq km

- Absorbing the timeless grandeur and Anangu history of Uluru (Ayers Rock)

- Attending a cultural-awareness workshop at Alice Springs or Tennant Creek

- Discovering the legacy of Albert Namatjira at the old Hermannsburg Lutheran Mission

- Sampling bush tucker on a guided tour at Alice Springs or Wallace Rockhole

- Taking in the superb art at Buku-Larrngay Mulka Art Centre & Museum, deep in far-east Arnhem Land at Yirrkala

- Marvelling at the ancient rock art and the rich traditions preserved at Kakadu National Park

- Learning traditional bush crafts and cooking on a tour at Manyallaluk or Daly River

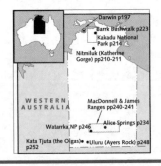

changed to Darwin – was established in 1869. The completion of the Overland Telegraph Line in 1872 made life in the NT easier, and the discovery of gold and copper attracted miners. Settlers with cattle entered the NT from South Australia (SA) and north Queensland. In 1877 the first Christian mission was established at Hermannsburg by Lutherans, and Catholic and Methodist missions followed elsewhere.

RESISTANCE

Conflict marked the arrival of Europeans. The Tiwi repulsed an attempted British settlement on Melville Island in the 1820s. An attack on the Barrow Creek Telegraph Station, in which two settlers were killed, led to massacres in which up to 50 Aborigines were killed. A similar attack on a Daly River copper mine in which four miners were killed led to another massacre. The last officially recorded massacre of Aborigines in the NT occurred at Coniston Station, north-west of Alice Springs, in 1928. The murders went on over a fortnight but a Board of Inquiry found they were justified and the police responsible were exonerated.

ABORIGINALS ORDINANCE

The Aboriginals Ordinance of 1918 imposed restrictions on Aboriginal rights to own property and seek employment, and allowed the state to remove children from Aboriginal mothers if it was suspected the father was non-Aboriginal. The aim was to stop the development of a so-called 'half-caste' population and to forcibly assimilate its members. Evidence was heard from many of these 'stolen children' as part of the Stolen Generations Inquiry but none has been successful in claiming any form of compensation from the government (see History in the Facts about Aboriginal Australia & the Torres Strait Islands chapter). Arnhem Land was declared an Aboriginal reserve in 1931 and the policy of segregation gave some protection to the traditional communities living there.

SOCIAL CHANGE

In general, Aborigines in the NT lived with the lack of freedom normally associated with slavery. The involvement of Aborigines in the war effort during WWII gave many of them the chance to experience fair working conditions and better treatment and proved to be an empowering experience. Though there were no major advances in the treatment of Aborigines by the government – for instance, NT Aborigines worked outside any industrial award system until 1968 – there was increasing self-assertion by Aborigines.

In 1966 Gurindji stockmen walked off Wave Hill Station in the NT's south-west, and returned to their homeland. The walk-off was prompted by the sexual abuse of Aboriginal women by settlers, but evolved into a dispute over wages and working conditions and finally into a dispute over land. After a long-running battle, the federal government gave some of the Gurindji lands back in 1975. It was a noteworthy victory because Wave Hill was first settled in the 1880s and pastoral interests had always taken precedence over Aboriginal rights in the NT. (See also the boxed text 'The Wave Hill Stockmen's Strike' later in this chapter.)

In 1963 Yirrkala Elders protesting the taking of their land for bauxite mining sent a bark petition to the Australian parliament. This was followed by legal action against the federal government and bauxite mining. Though the action was unsuccessful, it brought the issue of land rights into national consciousness and the government came under increasing pressure to legislate for Aboriginal land rights. In 1976 it eventually passed the Aboriginal Land Rights (NT) Act (usually referred to as the NT Land Rights Act).

ABORIGINAL LAND RIGHTS (NT) ACT

This act remains Australia's most powerful and comprehensive land rights legislation. It established three Aboriginal Land Councils, which are empowered to claim land on behalf of traditional Aboriginal owners. The act gave Aborigines in the NT indisputable title to all Aboriginal reserves (about 20% of the territory) and a means for claiming other Crown land. It also provided for mineral royalties to be paid to Aboriginal communities.

Under the act the only land claimable is unalienated land outside town boundaries, ie, land that no-one else owns or leases, which is usually semidesert or desert. Thus, when the Anangu owners of Uluru (Ayers Rock) claimed traditional ownership of Uluru and Kata Tjuta (the Olgas), their claim was disallowed because the land was within a national park. It was only by amending two acts of parliament that Uluru-Kata Tjuta National Park was handed back to the traditional Anangu owners, on

NORTHERN TERRITORY

NORTHERN TERRITORY

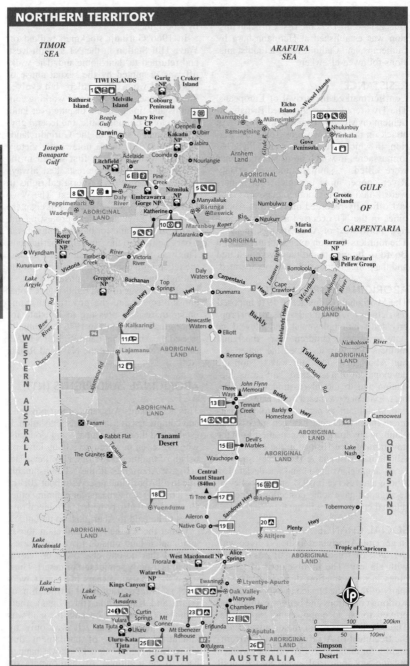

NORTHERN TERRITORY

1 Tiwi Tours; Patakijiyali Museum; Ngaruwanajurri Crafts; Tiwi Designs; Pottery
2 Injalak Arts & Crafts Centre
3 Dhimurru Land Management Aboriginal Corporation; Northern Land Council; East Arnhem Land Tourist Association; Birds, Bees, Trees & Things Tours; Nambara Arts & Crafts
4 Buku-Larrngay Mulka Art Centre & Museum
5 Day Tours; Willis' Walkabouts; Cultural Centre; Camping Area
6 Sacred Site; Rock Art; Walking Trail
7 Nauiya Nambiyu Aboriginal Community; Merrepen Arts Gallery & Festival; Leadership Accommodation Centre
8 Camping Tours (from Darwin)
9 Jankanginya Tours; Lightning Brothers Site
10 Jawoyn Association; Northern Land Council; Mimi Aboriginal Art & Craft; Banyan Art Gallery; Coco's Katherine Didjeridoos
11 Caravan Park
12 Lajamanu Warnayaka Arts
13 Sacred Site
14 Central Land Council; ATSIC; Kraut Downs Station Tours; Devil's Marbles Tours; Anyinginyi Congress Cultural
Centre; Papulu Apparr-Kari Language Centre; Anyinginyi Arts
15 Cultural Site
16 Urapuntja Artists
17 Aaki Gallery; Red Sand
18 Warlukurlangu Artists Art Centre
19 Sacred Site
20 Camping Ground
21 Rock Art & Fossil Sites Tours; Camping Ground
22 Itirkawara Sacred Site; Organised Tours
23 Arts & Crafts Shop; Camping Area
24 Visitor Centre; Organised Tours
25 Sacred Site; Uluru Experience Tours
26 Community Store Crafts

the condition that it was immediately leased back to the Australian Nature Conservation Agency (now Parks Australia).

At present almost half of the NT has either been claimed, or is being claimed, by its traditional Aboriginal owners. The claim process is extremely tedious and can take many years to complete, largely because the NT government has opposed almost all claims. Elderly claimants may well die before a claim is resolved. Claimants are required to prove that under Aboriginal *law* they are responsible for the sacred sites on the land being claimed. Once a claim is successful, Aboriginal people have the right to negotiate with mining companies and ultimately accept or reject exploration and mining proposals. This right is strongly opposed by the mining lobby, despite the fact that traditional Aboriginal owners in the NT only reject about one-third of these proposals outright.

SELF-DETERMINATION
The assimilation policy was replaced in 1972 by a policy of self-determination, which in theory allowed Aboriginal communities to identify their own priorities and manage policy implementation. A 'back to homelands' movement began in the 1970s as people left the settlements for their own land. In the north many family groups returned to their traditional land and established 'outstations'. In some areas there are Aboriginal commu-

nity schools, where Aboriginal pupils are taught in both English and their tribal language. The larger towns also have residential colleges for Aboriginal students.

Today, many Aboriginal people in the NT still live in appalling conditions, and alcohol and drug abuse remain widespread problems, particularly among young and middle-aged men. Aboriginal communities have taken up the challenge to eradicate these problems – many communities are now 'dry', and there are a number of rehabilitation programs for alcoholics and other drug users. The problem of petrol sniffing is slowly being addressed.

TRADITIONAL SOCIETY
The use of vehicles has helped communities to organise ceremonies and to gather food. Food gathering is connected to seasonal patterns – in Arnhem Land six seasons are recognised, each connected to the appearance of certain foods. There is a great diversity of food – in fact some communities might eat 90 different animal foods and 80 different plant foods in the course of a year. These could range from native seeds to freshwater turtles, goannas, kangaroos, birds, fish and bush vegetables, bush honey from the hives of native bees and honey ants. The availability of cattle and buffalo mean that some communities now eat more meat than in the past.

The Northern Territory is one of the most important centres for the 'Aboriginal arts

NORTHERN TERRITORY

industry' and many communities employ community arts advisers. As well as paintings featuring dot and *rarrk* (cross-hatching) designs, superb pottery, fibrecraft, carvings and fabric prints are produced. Tiwi people are famed for their *pukumani* poles – tall carved and painted tree trunks used to mark grave sites. These are now in demand as art objects.

Language

TOP END

The Top End is a local term for the northern half of the NT. The region encompasses a variety of different environments, each with distinct plants and animals, as well as a great diversity in indigenous lifestyles, cultures and languages.

Kriol

One of the most widespread Aboriginal languages in Australia today is Kriol. It has more than 20,000 speakers throughout most of the Katherine region and the neighbouring Kimberley region in Western Australia (WA), and has become the first language of many young Aboriginal people.

Kriol first arose early last century, when surviving members of eight language groups took refuge at a church mission based at Roper River to escape the killings being carried out by cattle-station companies. Many adults who came to the Roper River Mission from surrounding areas were multilingual, but not in exactly the same languages. Moreover, children hadn't yet developed full competence in as many languages as their parents.

The only language understood by everyone was a fairly widespread, English-based pidgin that had been brought north from New South Wales (NSW) with the cattle trade a few decades before. Children at the mission heard more of this pidgin than of any other language, not least because the missionaries housed them in dormitories away from their Elders. The children acquired the pidgin as their first language from which they created a full language to fulfil their everyday communication needs.

While based on English, Kriol has been heavily influenced by traditional Aboriginal languages in the sounds it uses, in its vocabulary and in its structure. For example, many Aboriginal languages have two pronouns for 'we' – one that includes the person you're speaking with and one that doesn't. The Kriol pronoun *yunmi* means 'we' (you and I), while *mintupala* means 'we two' (not including you).

Kriol speakers use large numbers of words from their traditional languages, especially for place names, traditional culture, names for local flora and fauna, and for Aboriginal personal names, relationship terms and body parts. As Kriol speakers living in different areas draw on different traditional Aboriginal languages for vocabulary, Kriol has a great deal of regional variation.

Many words taken from English have changed in meaning to embody traditional concepts and distinctions. So if a Kriol speaker talks about his or her *mami* (mother), mami can mean biological mother, that woman's sisters, her husband's brothers' wives, as well as the women who carry the same *skin name* as those female blood relations the speaker calls mami.

Useful Contacts Additional language-related information can be found through:

Booklets in Kriol can be obtained from Barunga Press, PMB 117, via Katherine, NT 0852
Centre for Australian Languages & Linguistics (☎ 8939 7111) Batchelor College, Batchelor, NT 0845
Summer Institute of Linguistics (SIL) (Australian Aborigines and Islanders Branch; ☎ 8984 4488) Post Office, Berrimah, NT 0828

In & Around Darwin

The traditional language of Darwin, Larrakia, is today spoken only by a few Aboriginal Elders. The languages you'll hear in Darwin are indigenous to other areas, spoken by people who are immigrants or visitors to the city. However, members of the local Larrakia community are currently working to record and revive their ancestral language.

In Kakadu, Litchfield and Nitmiluk (Katherine Gorge) National Parks, only older members of Aboriginal communities are fluent in their ancestral languages. Younger people mostly speak Kriol.

Off the coast immediately to the north of Darwin, Tiwi is spoken on Bathurst and Melville Islands. It appears to be unrelated to any other language of the region.

Katherine Region

In the township of Katherine it's possible to find members of all the language groups of the Katherine region such as the Jawoyn traditional owners, as well as others from further afield. Many of the traditional languages of Katherine are known only to some older people, and most Aboriginal communities in the area speak a variety of Kriol as their first or main language.

Aboriginal people in this region use the terms 'sun-go-down' to refer to the people, lands and languages in the western Katherine region, and 'sun-rise' to refer to the east, a distinction that reflects cultural and linguistic differences between the two regions.

Sun-Go-Down The traditional country of the Wardaman is west of Katherine, although most Wardaman people now live in and around Katherine. Wardaman is still spoken and/or understood by some young people.

Lajamanu is now a Warlpiri-speaking community because authorities moved large numbers of Warlpiri people away from their traditional homelands further south and onto lands traditionally owned by Kartangarrurru and Gurindji people. Gurindji is still spoken in communities to the north of Lajamanu, although the main language of children and young adults is a variety of Kriol that is influenced by Gurindji.

Ngarinyman is the main traditional language represented at Yarralin and it's spoken over a large area to the north-west as far as Kununurra in WA and northward to Timber Creek.

In and around Timber Creek, the local language has few remaining speakers. Jaminjung is spoken to the west as far as Kununurra and to the north in some Daly region communities.

Sun-Rise East of Katherine, major centres of Aboriginal populations include Borroloola on the McArthur River (several language groups), Ngukurr on the Roper River (numerous language groups which have few speakers living in the area), Minyerri (formerly Hodgson Downs), Jilkminggan at the headwaters of the Roper River, and several communities on the Central Arnhem Hwy.

In communities further east of the Roper Valley, Mangarrayi is spoken fully only by some older people.

Around Bulman, traditional languages are spoken fully by some older adults, while younger adults tend to be able to understand their traditional languages but don't usually speak them fully.

Useful Contacts More language-related information can be found at:

Diwurruwurru-jaru Aboriginal Corporation (☎ 8971 1233) PO Box 89, Katherine, NT 0851
Katherine Regional Aboriginal Language Centre (☎ 8971 1233) Pearce St, Katherine, NT 0850; PO Box 89, Katherine, NT 0851

NORTHERN CENTRAL REGION

Most languages of northern central Australia are part of the Kunwinjkuan language group. An important regional centre is Maningrida, which is between east and west Arnhem Land. There are significant cultural differences between Arnhem Landers who affiliate with the 'west side' and those who affiliate with the 'east side'. Burarra people affiliate with the 'east side', while a variety of Bininj Kunwok is the language spoken by inhabitants of Maningrida affiliated with the 'west side'.

Travelling through the northern central region of the NT, you may come across speakers of these languages:

Area	Languages Spoken
Arnhem Land escarpment	Kunwinjkuan languages
Pine Creek area	Warray
Katherine, Pine Creek, Barunga, Beswick and the south-western edge of the escarpment	Jawoyn
Western and northern rim of the Arnhem Land escarpment	dialects of Bininj Kunwok
Northern and southern rim of the escarpment	Dalabon and Rembarrnga

NORTH-EAST ARNHEM LAND

There are eight main Aboriginal communities in north-east Arnhem Land. Their languages are commonly known outside the region as the Yolngu (sometimes spelled Yuulngu) languages. In this area, each clan claims to have a distinct language variety, and there are some 50 clans. A network of lands belonging to different clans is linked

NORTHERN TERRITORY

by song, ceremony and language created by ancestral beings.

In all communities, the population is still linguistically diverse. Only one language of the region has become extinct. All communities are still multilingual, although the population of speakers of several varieties is ageing.

The most widely spoken Yolngu varieties are Kijnan (around Ramingining), Djambarrpuynu (from Milingimbi to Gapuwiyak) and Dhuwaya (Yirrkala).

At Numbulwar, Kriol is the first language of most young people, but a major effort is being undertaken in the community to maintain traditional languages, particularly Nunggubuyu. Anindilyakwa is still the first language of Indigenous people on Groote Eylandt, off Arnhem Land's east coast.

Useful Contacts
More language-related information can be found at:

East Arnhem Language Centre (☎ 8978 2477) via Yirrkala School, PO Box 936, Nhulunbuy, NT 0881

THE DALY REGION
Languages from several language groups are spoken in the Daly region, south-west of Darwin. Missionaries encouraged the use of Murrinh-patha, the language of the traditional owners of the country in which the mission was located, and a Bible and dictionary were produced in the language. It has now become the standard language of the whole community, although the community is working on documenting other local languages.

Useful Contacts
More language-related information can be found at:

Nauiyu Nanbiya Language Centre (☎ 8978 2427) PMB 28, Daly River, NT 0822

CENTRAL AUSTRALIA
At the time of the European invasion of central Australia, around 38 main languages and dialects were thought to be spoken in the region. Today, many language groups have moved from their traditional country and of the original 38 about seven are now endangered, and four are extinct or nearly extinct.

The main surviving language groups in central Australia are the group of Arandic languages, dialects of Warlpiri and Warumungu, and dialects of the Western Desert language.

Arrernte
The Arandic language group has around 4500 speakers. The territory of Arrernte-speakers extends very roughly over the south-eastern quarter of the NT (encompassing the Simpson Desert), and also into SA. Arrernte, the major language of the Arandic group, has a number of dialects.

Warlpiri
Warlpiri is part of the Ngarrkic language group. Warlpiri has five major dialects, which differ mainly in vocabulary and pronunciation to reflect the influence of neighbouring languages. An estimated 3000 people speak Warlpiri, most as their first language.

Warlpiri speakers live in a number of quite large communities around the edge of traditional Warlpiri country – the heart of which is the Tanami Desert. Many Warlpiri spend at least part of the year in the many small outstations in Warlpiri country.

Warlpiri is a very vigorous language that's spreading well outside its traditional country. It's spoken by 1000 or more people as a second language as far north as Darwin, west to Fitzroy Crossing in WA, east to Tennant Creek and other Barkly Tableland communities, and south to Alice Springs and the northern Western Desert communities. Most young and middle-aged Warlpiri can read and write their language.

Western Desert
The Western Desert language is Aboriginal Australia's largest traditional language group, with an estimated 4000 to 5000 speakers of Western Desert dialects, including Pitjantjatjara, Yankunytjatjara, Pintupi and Luritja. Western Desert dialects are spoken widely throughout central Australia in the south of the NT, north-west SA, southeast WA and east almost to Queensland.

Pitjantjatjara (also known as Pitjantjara) is one of the better-known Western Desert dialects. While not one of its traditional languages, Pitjantjatjara is often heard in Alice Springs and in some communities west of

Alice. Visitors to central Australia are likely to meet Pitjantjatjara and Yankunytjatjara speakers at Uluru and Kata Tjuta, and Pitjantjatjara and Luritja speakers at Watarrka (Kings Canyon). Speakers of Western Desert dialects call themselves Anangu.

Useful Contacts

More language-related information can be found at:

Institute for Aboriginal Development (IAD; ☎ 8951 1311, fax 8953 1884, ⓔ general.info @iad.edu.au) 3 South Terrace, Alice Springs, NT 0871; PO Box 2531, Alice Springs, NT 0871

Information

INDIGENOUS ORGANISATIONS

The Northern Land Council (NLC; ☎ 8920 5100, fax 8945 2633), 9 Rowling St, Casuarina, in Darwin, is the place to go for permits to visit or cross Aboriginal land anywhere in the Top End. Write to the Permits Officer, PO Box 42921, Casuarina, NT 0811. There are also regional offices in Katherine, Jabiru (see those sections for details) and Nhulunbuy. The NLC also maintains a fairly comprehensive Web site at www.nlc.org.au with information and media releases about Aboriginal issues.

The Aboriginal & Torres Strait Islander Commission (ATSIC; ☎ 8944 5566, fax 8944 5599) is at 38 Scaturchio St, Casuarina.

NATIONAL PARKS

The Northern Territory Parks & Wildlife Service (☎ 8999 5511) has an excellent range of free leaflets covering all the main national parks and reserves (except Kakadu) of the Top End, plus maps and a limited range of publications. These are available at the Darwin Regional Tourism Association (DRTA) office (see the Darwin section for contact details).

NEWSPAPERS & MAGAZINES

There are two free, quarterly newspapers covering Aboriginal news and issues territory-wide: *Land Rights News* (☎ 8920 5100), PO Box 42921, Casuarina, NT 0811, a joint publication of the Central and Northern Land Councils; and *ATSIC NT News* (☎ 8944 5566), PO Box 40670, Casuarina,

NT 0811, which is published by Darwin's ATSIC office. Both papers contain plenty of interesting reading for non-Indigenous people, too. They're not usually available at news agencies, but you can generally pick up copies at the front office of any major Aboriginal organisation in the NT.

RADIO & TV

Based in Alice Springs, the Central Australian Aboriginal Media Association (CAAMA) operates a radio station (call sign 8KIN) that broadcasts through AM, FM and shortwave networks throughout the NT, most of SA, and parts of NSW, Victoria and WA. The focus of the station is to provide a service to Aboriginal people, particularly in remote areas. However, its varied programs and different style to mainstream commercial radio have also made it popular with many non-Indigenous listeners.

You can pick up a program and a map showing broadcast centres from CAAMA (☎ 8952 9202), 101 Todd St, Alice Springs, or check its Web site (www.caama.com.au).

Imparja (☎ 8950 1411), 14 Leichhardt Terrace, Alice Springs, is an Aboriginal-owned and -run commercial TV station. It has a 'footprint' which covers one-third of the country (mainly the NT, SA and western NSW). The station broadcasts a variety of programs – you'll find these advertised in local newspapers – ranging from current affairs and soap operas to pieces made by and for Aboriginal people.

Web site: www.imparja.com.au

Permits

For permits to visit Aboriginal land in the Top End, contact the NLC in Darwin (see Indigenous Organisations under Information earlier).

Permits to visit Aboriginal land in the southern half of the NT are issued by the Central Land Council (☎ 8951 6320, fax 8953 4345), in Alice Springs (see the Alice Springs section in this chapter for more details on the council), which will fax you an application form.

There are two kinds of permit. For straightforward travel along an established route you need a transit permit, which can usually be processed within 48 hours. But if you want to visit a community, or in fact conduct any activity other than through-travel, then you require an entry permit. These take from two weeks to one month to process.

A transit permit is required for the Yulara-Kaltukatjara (Docker River) road, but not for either the Tanami Rd or the Sandover Hwy where these cross Aboriginal land. Travellers may camp overnight without a permit within 50m of the latter two routes. On the Tanami Rd, you can call in to Yuendumu and fuel up without a permit (see Yuendumu later in this chapter for information).

Organised Tours

There are a number of tours with significant Aboriginal content available to parts of the NT from Darwin. They involve driving or flying to regions covered in detail elsewhere in this chapter (see those sections for full details).

Tiwi Tours (☎ 1800 183 630, fax 8924 1122, e aussieadventure@attglobal.net) has excellent one- and two-day tours to the Tiwi Islands, a short flight off the coast from Darwin. The tours are owned by the Tiwi people and are run by Aussie Adventure Holidays. One-/two-day tours cost $279/548 per person.

Aussie Adventure Holidays (☎ 1800 811 633, fax 8924 1122, e aussieadventure @attglobal.net) also runs Peppi Tours. These are two-day, 4WD camping tours to a small Aboriginal community in the Daly River region (see that section for tour details) south-west of Darwin.

Davidson's Arnhemland Safaris (☎ 8927 5240, e dassafaris@onaustralia.com.au) runs extended tours to west Arnhem Land for $385 per person per day including flights from Darwin.

Larrakia Country

Darwin Area

DARWIN
History
The Darwin peninsula had been the preserve of the Larrakia Aboriginal people for thousands of years before the arrival of whites in the 1860s. (The word *larakia* is actually trade-Malay for 'lead-in', used in reference to vessels turning into the wind as they anchor.)

With the arrival of whites, the 700 or so Larrakia people were forced to vacate their traditional lands and inevitably came into violent conflict with the new arrivals, despite attempts by the first administration, under Surveyor-General George Goyder, to avoid conflict. Goyder, unusual among early administrators in that he refused to retaliate when one of his staff was murdered by the local Aboriginal people, was still very much a government man. His mistrust of the local people ran deep, despite the fact that the Larrakia had generally been friendly to the European invaders.

As Darwin (or Palmerston as it was then known) developed, the Larrakia people were pushed to one side. Many started living on Lameroo Beach right below the city centre. In 1912 they were moved to a new camp at Kahlin Beach with people from a number of other groups. It was felt at the time that there was no need to keep the groups separated as their culture had largely broken down. While this was true to a large extent, there was considerable intertribal conflict within the camp.

In recent years members of the Larrakia community have made a number of native title claims over land in and around the Darwin area, mostly the claims have been on Crown Land that is vacant. Some of these have been successful, with the result that the local Larrakia community must now be consulted over many development issues in and around Darwin.

Information
Indigenous Organisations See the Information section, at the beginning of this chapter, for contact details for the NLC and ATSIC offices in Darwin.

Tourist Offices The DRTA Information Centre (☎ 8981 4300, fax 8981 0653, e info@drta.com.au) is on the corner of Knuckey and Mitchell Sts. It's open 8.30 am to 5.30 pm weekdays, 9 am to 2.45 pm Saturday and 10 am to 1.45 pm on Sunday. It stocks hundreds of brochures and can book just about any tour or accommodation in the NT.

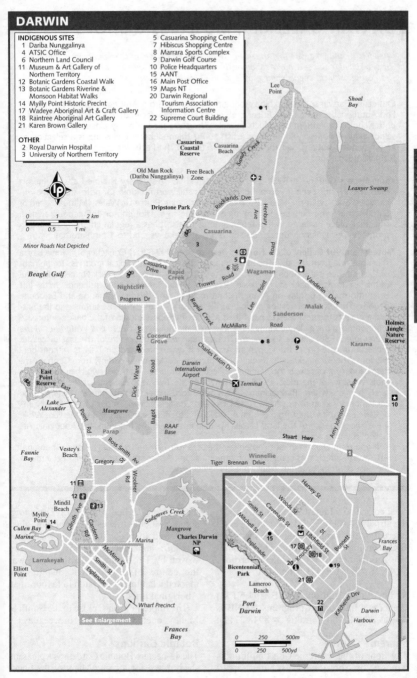

DARWIN

INDIGENOUS SITES
1 Dariba Nunggalinya
4 ATSIC Office
6 Northern Land Council
11 Museum & Art Gallery of
   Northern Territory
12 Botanic Gardens Coastal Walk
13 Botanic Gardens Riverine &
   Monsoon Habitat Walks
14 Myilly Point Historic Precinct
17 Wadeye Aboriginal Art & Craft Gallery
18 Raintree Aboriginal Art Gallery
21 Karen Brown Gallery

5 Casuarina Shopping Centre
7 Hibiscus Shopping Centre
8 Marrara Sports Complex
9 Darwin Golf Course
10 Police Headquarters
15 AANT
16 Main Post Office
19 Maps NT
20 Darwin Regional
   Tourism Association
   Information Centre
22 Supreme Court Building

OTHER
2 Royal Darwin Hospital
3 University of Northern Territory

Lee
Point

Shoal
Bay

Casuarina
Coastal
Reserve

Casuarina
Beach

Sandy Creek

Old Man Rock
(Dariba Nunggalinya)

Free Beach
Zone

Leanyer Swamp

Dripstone Park

Rocklands Dve

Henbury
Ave

0 1 2 km
0 0.5 1 mi

Minor Roads Not Depicted

Casuarina

Casuarina
Drive

Rapid
Creek

4
5
6

7

Wagaman

Trower Road

Lee Point Road

Vanderlin Drive

Beagle Gulf

Nightcliff

Progress Dr

Coconut
Grove

Rapid Creek

McMillans Road

Malak

Sanderson

8

9

Karama

Holmes
Jungle
Nature
Reserve

East
Point
Reserve

East

Point

Rd

Lake
Alexander

Mangrove

Dick Ward Drive

Bagot Road

Charles Eaton Dr

Darwin
International
Airport

Terminal

10

Ludmilla

Parap

RAAF
Base

Fannie
Bay

Vestey's
Beach

Ross Smith Av

Gregory St

Woolner
Rd

Stuart Hwy

Winnellie
Tiger Brennan Drive

Amy Johnson Ave

11
12 13

Mindil
Beach

Myilly
Point 14

Cullen Bay
Marina

Gilruth Ave

Gardens Rd

Larrakeyah

Elliott
Point

McMinn St

Smith St

Esplanade

Sadgroves Creek

Mangrove

Marina

Charles Darwin
NP

See Enlargement

Wharf Precinct

Frances
Bay

Frances
Bay

Harvey St

Woods St

Smith St

Cavenagh St

Mitchell St

Litchfield St

Bennett St

Esplanade

16

15

17
20
21

18

19

22

Knuckey

Bicentennial
Park

Lameroo
Beach

Port
Darwin

Frances
Bay

Kitchener Drv

Darwin
Harbour

0 250 500m
0 250 500yd

DARWIN GALLERIES, MUSEUMS & SHOPS

Readers should be aware that the names of deceased members of the Aboriginal community may be cited in this section. Mentioning the personal name of someone who has died recently can cause offence, anguish and grief in some Aboriginal cultures.

Outlets in Darwin sell and exhibit Aboriginal art mainly from Arnhem Land and other Top End Aboriginal communities. Prices are generally a bit lower than in Sydney and there's a better choice of authentic products for sale. There are far too many places in Darwin that sell or exhibit works by Indigenous artists to list them all here. Following is a selection of recommended outlets. See the Shopping section in the Facts for the Visitor chapter for further information.

Karen Brown Gallery (☎ 8981 9985) 22 Mitchell St. This gallery is aimed at the fine art market only, but even if you're not buying it's still worth a look. Of note are acrylic-on-canvas works by Gertie Huddleston and, in particular, Prince of Wales (Mitbul), a senior Larrakia man who only began painting a few years ago. Though non-Indigenous-owned, this small place has a good reputation among artists. It has a regular changing exhibition program. The gallery is open 9.30 am to 5 pm weekdays, and to 1 pm Saturday.

Museum and Art Gallery of the Northern Territory (☎ 8999 8201) Conacher St, Fannie Bay, a short bus ride from the city. The museum is by the sea, set in tropical grounds. To the right of the entrance is the Aboriginal Art Gallery, with a rock art panel by Dick Nguleingulei, one of the last artists to paint in the classic x-ray rock art style of West Arnhem Land. On the left is an informative display on Arnhem Land rock art, and the Pre-Estuarine and Estuarine periods. There's an interesting exhibit on the preparation of bark for painting and the natural pigments (ochres) used to paint them. Some of the best known of the bark painters are represented in the gallery. Johnny Bulun Bulun's famous *Magpie Geese and Waterlilies at the Waterhole* (1988) can be seen here. (This painting was at the centre of the first successful prosecution case under the Copyright Act after it was reproduced on T-shirts without permission.) There's an excellent display of Dupun (hollow log bone coffins) from Central Arnhem Land. Also of note is the S Holmes collection of *tutini* (burial poles), which in six sections form the story of the major Purukuparli myth of the Tiwi people. Some of these tutini are rarely seen elsewhere. Bark paintings are a major focus here, with magnificent historical and contemporary examples by Mawalan Marika and Charlie Matjuwi, among others. Equally impressive examples of art from central Australia and the Kimberley can also be viewed. While there's no evidence of the local Larrakia people profiled in the museum, the Aboriginal Art Gallery is worth a visit.

If you're in Darwin in late September, be sure to catch the annual National Aboriginal Art Award, which was inaugurated by the museum. At the museum you will see some of the best contemporary art from around the country.

There's also a tourist information desk at the airport (☎ 8945 3386) opens to meet all international and major domestic incoming flights during the Dry season. The Automobile Association of the Northern Territory (AANT; ☎ 8981 3837) is on Smith St.

Radio Radio station 8KNB (94.5 FM) broadcasts Indigenous programs. 8KNB is operated by Radio Larrakia (☎ 8948 2711).

Supreme Court
The floor of the Supreme Court building is a mosaic by Aboriginal artist Nora Napalt-jari Nelson. Called *Milky Way Dreaming*, some 700,000 pieces of Venetian glass were used to make it. Also on display is *Kooralia and the Seven Sisters*, a rug woven by Tim Leura Tjapaltjarri that was the centre of a copyright dispute and marked a landmark decision in favour of an Aboriginal artist.

The Supreme Court, close to the Smith St Mall, is open 8 am to 5.30 pm weekdays.

Botanic Gardens
The 42-hectare Botanic Gardens is a pleasant, shady place for a walk. Many of the plants

continued...   Gary Lee

Museum hours are 9 am to 5 pm weekdays, and from 10 am weekends (closed Christmas Day and Good Friday). Admission is free.
Web site: www.nt.gov.au/dam

Museum Shop Conacher St, Fannie Bay. This small shop has a fair selection of Aboriginal books. The art books are mainly related to NT Aboriginal art, but there are some good titles on history, politics and bush foods. There aren't a lot of Aboriginal products here, though there are some nice postcards and the Mini Heath tea towels are a bargain at $15 each. Hours are the same as for the museum.

Raintree Aboriginal Art Gallery (☎ 8981 2732) 20 Knuckey St. This is the only Aboriginal-owned and -operated place in the city. Established for over 16 years, the Indigenous proprietor has 30 years experience in the field. There's an excellent range of work from investment pieces to fine-quality souvenir arts and crafts. Limited-edition watercolour prints by Harold Thomas, the designer of the Aboriginal flag, cost around $250. Attractive *dilly* bags woven with bush string from Elcho Island and Maningrida are from $50 to $72. The Dunilli Arts marbled fabric lengths are $20 a metre, while the Tiwi armbands are $36 and delightful, small carved and painted wooden birds by Tiwi artist Francella Tungatalum are $48. There's a large range of beautiful paintings by Lofty Nadjemerrek, Peter Nabarlambarl, Djardi Ashley and Bobby Nganjmirra, to mention a few. Works on bark, canvas and paper in this gallery are of the highest quality, with some beautiful pieces on offer. Small acrylic paintings on board are $48 to $132. The authentic *yidakis* (didjeridus) by Yothu Yindi Balanydja are very attractive and reasonably priced from $137. Special freight and insurance rates are available to anywhere in the world. The gallery is open 9 am to 5 pm weekdays, and to 3 pm Saturday. From May to October it's also open 10 am to 2 pm Sunday, or by appointment.

Wadeye Aboriginal Art and Craft Gallery (☎ 8981 9362) 31 Knuckey St. This is a community-controlled gallery and shop with some of the most reasonable prices in town. All the art and crafts come from the Wadeye (Port Keats) community south of Darwin, and there's a nice range on offer. Attractive woven dilly bags are $66 to $176, unstretched canvases are a reasonable $220 to $550 and framed acrylics on paper cost up to $800 – look out for William Parmbuk's works. Attractive Wadeye didjeridus are well priced ($99 to $176) and printed-cotton didj bags are only $27. There are some eye-catching T-shirts by Palngun Creations, which are a steal at $16.50, as are its cute children's T-shirts for $20. Shell, grass-stem, seed and gum-nut necklaces are $35, with woven baskets $165 (large) and $55 (small). Painted baobab nuts by the Parmbuk women are $44. There are also some unusual *nulla-nullas* (war clubs) by the Mudi Dudi tribe for $88 and a small selection of postcards. Operating hours are 9 am to 4.30 pm weekdays, and 10 am to 3 pm weekends.
Web site: www.wadeyeart.com.au.

NORTHERN TERRITORY

were traditionally used by local Aborigines, and three self-guiding Aboriginal Plant Use Trails have been set up – pick up brochures for each at the garden information centre.

The three walks take in three major habitats – Riverine & Open Forest, Monsoon Vine Forest and Coastal Plants. The walks are all signposted and the plants of interest are marked with poles bearing Aboriginal designs. The riverine and monsoon habitat walks are both in the main part of the gardens and start close to the visitor centre, while the coastal walk is in the coastal section of the park at the northern end of Mindil Beach.

Casuarina Coastal Reserve

Sites of Aboriginal and historical significance are preserved in this stretch of fine, sandy beaches between Rapid Creek and Lee Point, although none of these are marked. A rock offshore, known to the Larrakia as Dariba Nunggalinya (Old Man Rock), is a registered sacred site. It is said that interference with the rock led to Cyclone Tracy.

Special Events

The small, four-day Barddiy'wanga String Festival, held in August at the Myilly Point

PANDANUS WEAVING

Esther Managku, with the assistance of Lawungkurr Maralngurra

First you go into the bush to get that *manbelk* (pandanus). The best ones have long, long leaves. They can't have (insect) holes in them. They high up, so you get hook stick (inverted fork of a branch) and you bring those leaves down, wrap them in your hand and then pull them out of the tree. Then those leaves are broken (split in sections with the thumb) and the little prickles are taken off. Then you boil him with colour.

There are many colours and they come from many plants. Yellow is from the root of two trees – *mandjundum (Pogonobolus reticulatum)* and *mangukmayin* (cheesefruit; *Morinda citrifolia*). You dig him up with crowbar and digging stick. Sometimes those roots go straight down. Hard work that one. We put that colour in a billy can with the pandanus. First of all we make him yellow, that pandanus. And after that if we take the ashes from where you make your fire, you can make him turn to red. I tell you straight (I tell you the truth)! To make green I put dry pandanus in the fire. Then I take those ashes and put them in the billy can and make him little bit green (pale green) in colour. Other colours come from grass roots. *Wirdilwirdil (Haemodorum coccineum)* is that small grass. *Wirndilk* is a bigger grass *(Haemodorum)*. I wash those roots, take the skin off with a knife, then smash the roots with a stone and put it in the billy can. But this one I don't put ashes. It turn to pink, light purple, dark purple. If I have lots I can cook it in a drum. February is purple time. We call that time *gudjewg* (Wet season). But March/April is good too. That time we call *banggereng*. Those *gundalk* (grasses) start getting seed then.

Each billy can and each colour separate together (colours are made in separate containers). Then you hang that pandanus out to dry. I leave it there in the hot sun. Then you thread him (put a pandanus strand through the eye of a large needle). Then you hold that bunch of pandanus – make him straight. You stitch (blanket stitch) and then you pull them stitches tight. I make him bend (fold the sewn pandanus over). I make a hole here tight. Then go (stitch) in same hole. I learned this weaving from my teacher when I was in the school. Her country was at Gunbalanya (north-west Arnhem Land). She the same skin colour as me. I don't know the number how old I was when I learn, maybe six year old; that's the time I been start, maybe even seven or eight. That's a long time to make baskets – more than 60 years. My mother she didn't know how to make this type of basket, only *gundjabarrk* (shoulder bag), *djerret* (string bag), *balabala* (floor mat), *walabi* (net for catching fish) and *mandjabo* (big net for catching fish). They use that medicine tree – *mangolk*, and also *manbudbud*, *manwonge* and *manbonde* – all got string.

When we make big mats we sit on them, on the floor. Miriam my *dada* (little sister) she can make them, but she got bad eye now. I now want to teach my other dada, Lawungkurr...If I feel good I can make basket with handle, or without. Tablemats too. I can make two baskets in one sun. I start morning time. By afternoon I finished.

Historic Precinct, brings together women from seven different Top End communities. The women are all artists, designers and string-makers, and the festival features live music, workshops and exhibitions. For more details, phone the coordinator on ☎ 8941 3150.

Held every year in September, the Festival of Darwin features a broad range entertainment and art events, many with an Aboriginal focus.

Kunwinjku Country

Western Arnhem Land

The Arnhem Land escarpment and its outliers is like a huge gallery for literally thousands of Aboriginal rock art sites of incredible variety, age and interest. Access to Arnhem Land is by permit only (see the Oenpelli section later in this chapter for details).

Access to Oenpelli (Gunbalanya) is across the East Alligator River from Ubirr in Kakadu.

INFORMATION
Books
Catherine & Ronald Berndt recorded children's stories from western Arnhem Land in their book *The Land of the Rainbow Snake* (1979).

ORGANISED TOURS
Day Trips from Kakadu
Three companies operate out of Jabiru concentrating on the area immediately across the East Alligator River, and each goes to different places according to their arrangements with the local people.

Lord's Arnhemland Safaris (☎ 8979-2970, ℮ lords@topend.com.au), a partly Aboriginal-owned company, offers day trips into the Mikinj Valley, east of Oenpelli from Jabiru. The tour takes in Injalak Arts & Crafts Centre and a walk up Injalak Hill at Oenpelli, as well as some excellent rock art sites and the superbly picturesque Mikinj Valley itself. An Aboriginal guide accompanies each trip. The cost is $160 per person ($120 for children under 14).

Kakadu Parklink (☎ 8979 2411, 1800 089 113, ℮ kakair@kakair.com.au) has weekday Arnhemlander tours from Jabiru into the Mikinj Valley for $145 ($116 children), and the trips are usually accompanied by a local Aboriginal guide. During the day you are taken to the Injalak Arts & Crafts Centre, and visit some extraordinary rock art sites, a burial site and a men's initiation site. Lunch is taken by a spectacular wetland, with views of the Arnhem Land escarpment.

Magela Tours (☎ 8979-2114, ℮ magela @topend.com.au) is a joint-venture company part Aboriginal-owned. It offers day tours into Arnhem Land from Jabiru, although some of the trip is at Canon Hill in Kakadu. The highlight of the day is a boat cruise on the Magela River system. Group sizes are small (maximum 10), so tours remain personal, although no Aboriginal guides are used. Tours cost $150 ($100 for children under 15).

Extended Tours
Davidson's Arnhemland Safaris (☎ 8927 5240, ℮ dassafaris@onaustralia.com.au) has been taking people into Arnhem Land for years to its concession at Mt Borradaile, on Umorrduk land north of Oenpelli, where there is a comfortable safari camp. While the main focus of the camp is as a superbly secluded place to relax and fish, the Aboriginal rock art and burial sites in the vicinity are excellent. Staying at the camp costs $385 per person per day, which includes meals, guided tours and fishing, and air charters to and from Darwin or Jabiru.

OENPELLI (GUNBALANYA)
Oenpelli (Kunbarllanjanja; more commonly spelt Gunbalanya) is a small Aboriginal town 17km into Arnhem Land across the East Alligator River from the Border Store in Kakadu.

The town started as Paddy Cahill's station early in the 20th century. Cahill was a white settler involved in NT's largely unsuccessful foray into dairy farming. He later turned to buffalo as a more secure form of income. In 1925 the station passed to the Church Missionary Society, and it stayed a mission until self-determination in the 1970s.

The town is generally only accessible to visitors with a permit and the main reason to come here is to visit the Injalak Arts & Crafts Centre.

Permits
Before you can visit you must obtain a permit from the NLC in Jabiru (☎ 8979 2410), which collects a fee of $13.20 per person aged over 18. Permits are issued on the spot; see the Jabiru section for NLC office hours.

Check the East Alligator River tide times at the Bowali Visitor Centre or NLC office in Jabiru, as the crossing (Cahill's Crossing) can be flooded for a few hours around high tide at the beginning of the Dry.

Injalak Arts & Crafts Centre
Injalak (☎ 8979 0190) is both a workplace and shopfront for artists and craftspeople who produce traditional paintings on bark and paper, plus didjeridus, pandanus weavings and baskets, and screen-printed fabrics. Although the range is not huge, prices are very competitive with other outlets in the region. All sales benefit the artists and therefore the community. Injalak offers discounts to YHA members. Credit cards are accepted

NORTHERN TERRITORY

NORTHERN TERRITORY

IS THIS THE DEATH OF OUR ANCIENT FISHING TRADITION?

I will always remember as a young boy, when I first saw my cousin Dookie and his grandfather Gurio clearing the fish trap at low tide. I would be curious and excited when I saw the amazing variety of fish, crabs, stingrays, and even the odd deadly box jellyfish. A good catch meant a good feed for many locals of Darwin.

You only had to look at old Gurio and knew that he had worked hard all his life. He was known as the 'Master of Fish Traps' and everything he knew had been passed down many generations. I wasn't going to miss out on the opportunity of working alongside my cousin and being taught by the 'Grandmaster' (Gurio), so I became a part of this treasured family tradition. I began learning the skilled art of constructing and managing fishtraps. The work was hot and tough, sometimes frustrating and demanding – particularly if the crocodiles beat us to the catch; or when other fishermen disrespectfully dropped their lines into the trap for an easy catch. But the rewards from a good catch always outweighed the obstacles.

COURTESY OF GEOFFREY ANGELES

Geoff Angeles displays a barracuda caught using Grandmaster Gurio's fish trap design – a ring of poles strung with mesh to form a freestanding net. The catch is gathered at low tide. Fish trap designs vary across Australia, including woven baskets used in conjunction with stone arrangements to trap fish in rivers.

Aborigines and Torres Strait Islanders have many different methods and structures to catch fish. However, the design used by Gurio was the most effective I have ever seen. Made of sticks and mesh to form a freestanding-style net, this trap could be strategically altered by varying the height and angle. The trap was highly adaptable and could be set up in diverse locations, ranging from shady mangrove estuaries to windswept beaches. The trap could even be tailor-made to specifically catch certain fish species such as my favourite, golden snapper. Although simple, our fish traps are far more cost-effective and less detrimental to the environment than today's fishing technology.

The best time to visit Injalak is in the morning, which is when most of the artists are at work. Tours can be arranged to the small hill north of Oenpelli known as Long Tom Dreaming (or Injalak Hill). There are some fine rock art galleries here and a knowledgeable local guide can explain their significance to you. The guide's services cost $60 per group for a two-hour tour – it's a hot climb – and you must be at Oenpelli by 10 am. Injalak is closed on Sunday.

Special Events
On the first Saturday in August an open day is held, with local artefacts for sale and sports and dancing events. Permits are not required to visit Gunbalanya on this day.

Yolngu Country

Eastern Arnhem Land

The eastern part of Arnhem Land that is of interest to visitors is the remote Gove

continued...

Geoffrey Angeles

On top of that, modern fishing operations have never been able to match the quality of our catch.

The fish traps were not just about catching fish. They were also about bringing our people together. There was always a buzz of excitement when family and friends gathered after a good day's catch to select their choice of fish, crabs and prawns. Prices were cheap, everything was fresh, and there was always the opportunity for a friendly barter. Plus, you didn't have to put up with the hustle and bustle of a shopping centre.

I grew up with fishing and was taught well by my father, uncles and grandfathers. I am now a father myself and wish to pass on this time-honoured custom to my own young sons. But when I recently inquired about a fish trap licence in Darwin, I was brusquely informed by the Fisheries Department that they were 'no longer allowed', as they were 'deemed to be an unsuitable fishing operation'. For us, this is not simply a 'fishing operation'. It is a culturally significant and ancient family practice that not only generated a healthy sense of wellbeing, but also strengthened community ties.

Fish traps have been a part of our people's lives for thousands of years. All we ask is for the lawmakers to talk with us first, instead of just telling us we can no longer follow our forefathers' footsteps.

Geoffrey Angeles

Born and bred in Darwin. I am a Kungarakan man from my grandfather's side and Gurindji from my grandmother's side.

My country on the Kungarakan side covers the areas surrounding Batchelor and Adelaide River. We identify ourselves as the Paperbark people. The Gurindji would be best remembered by the historic walk-off, led by the famous Vincent Lingiari, in protest against unequal pay.

I grew up with fishing and hunting and played Aussie Rules, rugby and basketball, carrying on the tradition of my grandfather, parents, aunties and uncles.

I graduated in Perth in 1997 with a BApp Sc in Aboriginal Community Management and Development.

Before moving to the Menzies School of Health Research, I worked for the Northern Land Council for five years in north-east Arnhem Land. I have been at Menzies for six years as a health researcher and play an advocacy-type role between the organisation and Aboriginal people on all health matters.

Peninsula in the far north-east. This is the home of the Yolngu people, who are arguably the most high-profile of all Aboriginal nations in the country. This is thanks in large part to the success of the band Yothu Yindi, which had a string of hits in the 1980s and '90s. The band's lead singer and songwriter and a former Australian of the Year, Mandawuy Yunupingu, and other members of the band hail from the Gove Peninsula. Other prominent Yolngu include Galurrwuy Yunupingu, brother of Mandawuy and another Australian of the Year and former head of the NLC; Gatjil Djekurra, a former head of ATSIC; the actor David Gulpilil; and David Malangi, who painted the Aboriginal images which appeared on Australia's first one dollar note in the 1960s.

The Gove Peninsula is also the site of the Nabalco bauxite mine, which produces a large percentage of Australia's bauxite ore for export. It was the establishment of the mine in the 1960s which

MAINTAINING CULTURE

In north-east Arnhem Land we refer to ourselves as Yolngu people. My clan is the Gumatj. As Gumatj people we are born into the Yirridja *moiety* (skin classification), marrying people only of the opposite moiety, Duwa. Our wives or husbands come from half a dozen different clans, each with its own distinctive dialect in the language group known as Yolngu matha. In our formative years we grow up speaking our mother's language. As a young child I can remember walking down the coast with my mothers (my father had 12 wives). My father and the other men would travel ahead of us in their dugout canoes, hunting for fish and turtle for the evening meal. As we walked down the coast to Dhaniya and other places of importance to my family, my mother would tell me how the country we were crossing was formed and where to find water. In her language, Galpu, she'd name the animals and the birds and the plants and describe their creation. She and the women of our extended family would show us which fruits and berries and tubers were good for eating and how to prepare them. Working together, the women – our mothers, our sisters – would show us how to get wild honey from the trees and shellfish from the rocks. They'd dig for sweet potato, gather fruits and berries in season and hunt for file snakes in the swamps. And they'd show us which creatures and plants to avoid. In the evening, at a designated site down the coast, the men and older boys would come ashore in their dugout canoes, bringing the day's catch of reef fish, dugong, turtle or stingray. The women would have cooking fires going by then. They'd produce woven baskets of fruit and vegetables collected during the walk and we'd all tuck in for a feed. That traditional education began when I was a toddler.

ANTHONY GEERNAERT – PHOTO COURTESY OF MUSHROOM RECORDS

When I was older my father took over my education. He taught me his language, Gumatj, and started introducing me to aspects of men's business, teaching me how to hunt and to fish, to sing and to dance. It was a traditional Yolngu education, learning to read the land and the sea and the rivers, an education passed down as it has been through every generation for thousands of years.

Like the name of the band I later formed with my nephew, the system of relationships which Yolngu people practice is known as Yothu Yindi. Yothu Yindi translates as Child and Mother. It's the belief system our culture is driven by, the ultimate source from which we draw our power as a society. In our society, the opposite moiety always inherits responsibility for education at a deeper level, maintaining balance between the clans.

Through their music, Yothu Yindi bring an insight into traditional Yolngu culture to the urban world

led to the first attempt by Aboriginal people to attain land rights through the legal system (see History later).

The main settlement on the Gove Peninsula is Nhulunbuy, which was established as the service town for the mine. It still fulfils that role, but with a population of 4000 it is now the fourth-biggest town in the NT and has become the major administrative centre for eastern Arnhem Land. The other major settlement here is the Aboriginal community of Yirrkala, 20km south of Nhulunbuy.

There are many other Aboriginal communities in eastern Arnhem Land, including Ramingining, Galiwinku (Elcho Island),

continued...   Mandawuy Yunupingu

In the activities in the men's camps when the various clans gathered for extended funeral, initiation or other ceremonial business, an uncle of the opposite moiety was always there, paying special attention to the strength of my learning and my understanding in song and dance and painting.

Sometimes ceremonies can last for weeks. Specialist songmen will preside over the proceedings, people who've been rigorously trained in their field. The *yidaki* (didjeridu) players chosen for such engagements will have a deep knowledge of their instrument and the secret, sacred aspects associated with it. Through music, song and dance, representatives of each clan – men and women – enact stories handed down since time immemorial, each song a link in the chains of the songlines that cover our country.

The ceremonies recall the journeys taken by our ancestors when they came ashore in the east and crossed the land, creating rivers and mountains and lagoons, naming the country, populating it with fauna and flora – each species being either Yirridja or Duwa – creating the different clans of opposite moieties, giving each clan its own language, its own *stories*, its own distinctive art, its own songs. In this way we maintain the strength of our culture.

To share this experience, my clan is planning to start a Yolngu-owned ecotourism operation that will be centred on the Yothu Yindi Foundation's annual Garma Festival. For further details see the Web site at www.yothuyindi.com.

Mandawuy Yunupingu

Mandawuy Yunupingu was born in September 1956. His surname, Yunupingu, means 'Rock that will stand against anything'. Originally known as Bakamana, he took the name Mandawuy (Clay) in 1989, following the death of a man who shared his name. (Under Yolngu law the name of a dead person cannot be uttered until that person's spirit has passed on to its rightful place.) Mandawuy's skin name is Gudjuk (Hawk). His formal Yolngu name and spiritual identity is Maralitja. His ancestral totem is Baru (Saltwater Crocodile).

The first Arnhem Land Aborigine to earn a university degree, Mandawuy was principal at Yirrkala School in 1991–92. Since then he's devoted his energies to his band, Yothu Yindi, who have toured internationally and released six albums yielding hit singles like 'Treaty' and 'Djapana'.

Mandawuy was named Australian of the Year for 1992. In 1998 Mandawuy was awarded the honorary degree of Doctor of the University by the Queensland University of Technology 'in recognition of his significant contribution to the education of Aboriginal children, and to greater understanding between Aboriginal and non-Aboriginal Australians'.

NORTHERN TERRITORY

Gapuwiyak, Milingimbi and Maningrida, however these are all inaccessible to casual visitors and you must have permission from the community and the NLC to visit.

HISTORY

The Miwatj ('Morning Side') region (as the north-eastern part of Arnhem Land is called) was one of the first to be settled by Aboriginal people. The people here ally themselves very strongly with the ocean and salt water, and from it much of their law is derived. According to the Yolngu, the world was created during Wangarr, the time before the first morning. Their early history is recorded in the paintings, dances and ceremonies which relate how the creation ancestors brought the world into being, and defined the law which outlines ownership and management of the land.

The earliest contact with foreigners is related in some of the traditional songs, which tell of a visit by light-skinned people called Bayini. It is thought these may have been the Bugis people from Indonesia.

More is known about the Aboriginal relationship with Macassan trepang (sea cucumber) fishermen, who visited the Arnhem Land coast during the Dry from as early as the 16th century right up until early in the 20th century. They recognised and acknowledged Yolngu ownership of the land and water, and developed a strong relationship with the Yolngu. Even today there are songs, ceremonies and dances which have Macassan elements, and Macassan words such as *rupiyah* (money) and *bilina* (to finish) are still part of the Yolngu language.

European contact in the area began in 1623 with the visit of the Dutch explorer Willem van Colster in the *Arnhem*, which gives its name to Cape Arnhem. Matthew Flinders charted the area on his circumnavigation of the continent in 1803.

In 1907 the SA government (which administered the territory at the time) stopped issuing licences to Macassan trepangers, after pressure from European and Japanese pearlers and trepangers. But the newcomers did not have the same respect for the Yolngu people and culture, and consequently there were many problems. In 1932, 30 Japanese and European seamen were killed on the coast. Calls by the Administrator of the NT for a 'punitive expedition' were opposed by the church, the Australian Labor Party and the unions; the government was forced to instead send a peace mission. Up until this time, such punitive expeditions usually resulted in brutal massacres of Aboriginal people, and had been the standard government response to murders of whites by Aboriginal people in the NT.

In 1931 a 96,000 sq km area was proclaimed as the Arnhem Land Aboriginal Reserve. The Yolngu gave permission for a Methodist mission to be established at Yirrkala in 1934.

During WWII, two air squadrons were based on the Gove Peninsula, and around 40 Yolngu played an active role in the Special Reconnaissance Unit that was established to monitor the Arnhem Land coast for Japanese activity. The men were trained to attack invading forces but never saw any action. They were also not paid anything for their services.

In 1963 the Aboriginal people of Yirrkala made an important step in the land rights movement when they protested against plans for a bauxite mine on their land. The mine had been given the go-ahead without any Yolngu consultation. They sent a petition to the federal government, written in both Yolngu and English, pasted to two sheets of stringy-bark and surrounded with traditional motifs. This became known as the Bark Petition, and is still on display in Parliament House, Canberra (a photocopy is displayed at the museum in Yirrkala – see later). While the Yolngu failed to stop the mine, their protest led to the formation of a government committee to investigate the matter and the Yolngu received some compensation.

After a further protest to the NT government in 1968, a Supreme Court judge presiding over the case declared: 'If ever a system could be called "a government of laws and not of men", it is that shown in the evidence before me...I hold that I must recognise the system revealed by the evidence as a system of law'. Despite this acknowledgment of ownership, the land was declared *terra nullius* ('empty land') at the time of British annexation and the mine was allowed to proceed. Although the case was lost, it did lay the groundwork for the powerful Aboriginal Land Rights (NT) Act 1976. Under this, Arnhem Land was returned to its original owners.

While the act did provide for management of Aboriginal land by Indigenous people, it only recognised ownership over land, and not the sea, which for the saltwater Yolngu was a major shortcoming. It was only in 1998 that the Federal Court ruled in favour of a native title claim to offshore areas (an area of 2000 sq km around Croker Island off the coast of western Arnhem Land).

One feature of Yolngu life in the Miwatj region was the establishment of the Homeland movement in the 1960s. Similar to the Outstation movement in central Australia, it saw the establishment of 25 self-contained communities in the region.

INFORMATION

Indigenous Organisations

The Dhimurru Land Management Aboriginal Corporation (☎ 8987 3992, ⓔ dhimurru @octa4.net.au), an independent, community-based organisation, has its office next to the Captain Cook Shopping Centre, about 1.5km from the centre of Nhulunbuy. This is the place to come for Recreation Permits (see Permits later).

The NLC (☎ 8987 2602) has its office in Endeavour Square, the main shopping centre in Nhulunbuy.

Tourist Offices

For information on the area contact the helpful East Arnhem Land Tourist Association (☎ 8987 2255), which has an office attached to the bottle shop of the Walkabout Lodge on Westall St, Nhulunbuy.

CD-ROMs

The Dhimurru Land Management Aboriginal Corporation has produced a CD-ROM with a range of information on the Manydjarrarrnga-Nanydjaka (Cape Arnhem) area, one of the recreation areas accessible (with a permit) from Nhulunbuy.

Senior Ranger, Nanikiya Munungurritj, said the CD-ROM brings together two knowledge systems:

Producing the CD was a new way of recording old knowledge – our knowledge of the cultural and natural landscape of Nanydjaka, but also including non-Indigenous information about the area. We hope it will be a useful resource for maintaining Yolngu knowledge about Nanydjaka in our community and also for educating visitors to the areas about Indigenous associations with the country.

The CD costs $25 and is available from the Dhimurru office in Nhulunbuy.

PERMITS

If you are flying in to Gove, no permit is needed, but to venture outside Nhulunbuy to any of the designated recreation areas – mainly beaches close by – you need to get a Recreation Permit ($20) from the traditional owners through the Dhimurru Land Management Aboriginal Corporation (see Indigenous Organisations earlier). These are issued on the spot. A permit is not necessary to visit the highly recommended

Buku-Larrngay Mulka Art Centre & Museum in Yirrkala (see later).

If you want to drive to Nhulunbuy along the Central Arnhem Rd from Katherine, a permit from the NLC (☎ 8972 2650) in Katherine is required. These permits are only issued to people who have confirmed accommodation bookings in Nhulunbuy or are visiting friends or relatives there. Allow at least two weeks for the issue of a permit.

ORGANISED TOURS

Birds, Bees, Trees & Things (☎ 8987 1814, ⓔ bbtt@octa4.net.au) is a one-man outfit based in Nhulunbuy. Day tours are run out to Daliwuy, a designated recreation area near Cape Arnhem, a couple of hours' drive from Nhulunbuy. Visitors spend the day with the local Yolngu community, and get involved with everyday activities such as fishing and weaving. There is no set schedule, and costs vary depending on numbers ($295 to $500 per person).

VOLUNTEER WORK

There are some opportunities for volunteer work with Dhimurru Land Management, which is involved with projects such as turtle rescue, fauna surveys and upgrading facilities (eg, walking trails) in the recreation areas. During the turtle nesting season from April to July, a helicopter heads out most days (weather permitting), flying along the coast in search of stranded turtles. There is usually one seat available for a paying passenger ($200), and the trip lasts from one to three hours, depending on the number of turtles (if any) found. This is a fantastic opportunity to view the spectacular coastline, but it's a bit hit and miss as far as getting on the flights is concerned.

BUKU-LARRNGAY MULKA ART CENTRE & MUSEUM

Visitors should not miss the Buku-Larrngay Mulka Art Centre & Museum at Yirrkala (☎ 8987 1701, ⓔ yirrkala-arts@octa4.net.au); Web site: www.aboriginalart.com.au. This centre is considered to be one of the major repositories of bark painting, carved totems and other artefacts in the country. Pride of place goes to the superb Yirrkala Church Panels (see the boxed text). Also on display is a fascinating collection of historical photographs, mostly dating to the time of the

THE YIRRKALA CHURCH PANELS

Hugh Finlay

In 1962 the Yolngu Waruki Cooperative proposed that two panels of paintings which depicted the descent of Yolngu from ancestral beings be made. There was to be one from each of the two *moieties* (or groupings) which underpin the Yolngu kinship system: Duwa, the Larva of the Horned Beetle; and Yirridja, the Maggot. Everything in Yolngu life – people, places, animals, the elements – has a value in this system. They were to be of sacred designs (or *miny'tji*) and be a visible illustration of Yolngu connections and claims to the land and the sea – basically their native title claim.

It was proposed that these panels be hung either side of the cross in the Methodist Mission Church at Yirrkala. The intention was to show that Yolngu belief and Christianity could coexist and were not incompatible.

When completed, the superb panels were hung in the church. It is somewhat ironic that very shortly after the panels were installed that Aboriginal land was excised for the Nabalco bauxite mine without any consultation. The panels remained in the church until the 1970s when the new minister at the time had them removed, as he found them 'dangerously heathen'.

The two masonite panels, each measuring 1.2m x 3.6m, are now on display in a separate room at the Buku-Larrngay Mulka Art Centre & Museum at Yirrkala and should not be missed.

Special Reconnaissance Unit during WWII (see History earlier), and a copy of the Bark Petition of 1963.

The art centre also has an extensive range of pieces for sale – probably the largest selection in the NT. Bark paintings range from about $30 to $3000, *yidaki* (didjeridus) are from $100 to $350, and there are also unusual *larrakitj* (mortuary containers). These are not the sort of thing you tuck under your arm and take on the plane, but the centre can arrange for shipping of any items.

Attached to the centre is a print workshop producing limited-edition works on paper, and here too are fine pieces for sale.

The centre is open 8 am to 4.30 pm weekdays, and 9 am to noon Saturday. Admission to the museum is $2. Permits are not required to visit the art centre, but visitors are not allowed to go anywhere else in Yirrkala.

SPECIAL EVENTS

The week-long Garma Festival, held annually in August or September, is a local cultural festival organised by the Yothu Yindi Foundation as a celebration of Yolngu culture. It is held at Gulkula on the Gove Peninsula, the place where, according to Yolngu Law, the ancestor Ganbulabula brought the yidaki into being.

Currently attendance is by invitation only, but this may change so it's worth making inquiries. Contact the Yothu Yindi Foundation (e yyf@bigpond.com) or visit the Web site at www.yothuyindi.com.

SHOPPING

About 5km from Nhulunbuy near the deepwater port, Nambara Arts & Crafts (☎ 8987 2811) is a small gallery and craft outlet. One of the highlights here are the woven pandanus fibre mats made by Yolngu women. The centre also sells artworks by artists from all over eastern Arnhem Land, and although the selection is small the quality is high.

The gallery is signposted in the Yirrkala Business Enterprises compound. It is open 8.30 am to 4.30 pm weekdays, and 9 am to noon Saturday.

Jawoyn Country

Katherine Area

Despite being one of the largest and most active groups in the Top End, there are surprisingly few opportunities for visitors to make contact with the Jawoyn people. The visitor centre at Nitmiluk (Katherine Gorge) is about the limit of it.

However, there are excellent Aboriginal tours at Manyallaluk, north-east of Katherine. While this is on what is traditionally Jawoyn land, the people who actually own the land now and are running the tours come from a number of Top End Aboriginal groups.

HISTORY

The area to the north and east of Katherine (including the town itself) is the traditional home of the Jawoyn people, one of the major nations of the Top End. Following land claims in recent years they have received the title to large parcels of land, including Nitmiluk (Katherine Gorge) National Park and the southern part of Kakadu National Park. More recently the Jawoyn have made a claim of parts of Katherine itself.

European contact in the area started with the establishment of pastoral leases in the second half of the 19th century. The Jawoyn were seen by whites as wild, and in many cases were systematically hunted. The discovery of gold at Pine Creek in 1871 meant still more traditional land was taken over for use by whites.

A tin mine was established in the district at Maranboy, and a government battery established there in 1915. It acted as something of a magnet for Jawoyn people, as it was not only a source of employment and white-man's goods such as flour and tobacco, but it was also a safe place where they could avoid being killed on the cattle stations. In 1923 a small Aboriginal reserve was established here. From the 1920s, Jawoyn people gained limited employment in local farming enterprises and also at the tungsten mine that operated on Eva Valley Station (present-day Manyallaluk).

During WWII Aboriginal people were confined to 'native control camps', and there was one such camp at Maranboy. The camps saw the bringing together of Aboriginal people from a number of different cultures, including the Jawoyn. In 1951, as part of the federal government's assimilation program, a new welfare settlement was established at Barunga, 50km east of Katherine.

Within Katherine, the Jawoyn continued to camp at various places, usually associated with employment, and these camps are to some extent still in use today. The Jawoyn lifestyle is still partly one of mobility, though most people have a permanent base, such as Katherine, Barunga or Beswick, and make longer but less frequent trips into the bush.

KATHERINE
Information
Indigenous Organisations The Jawoyn Association (☎ 8971 1100) has its office in the Pandanus Plaza on First St and, while not a visitors centre as such, may be useful if you have a specific inquiry.

The NLC's Katherine office (☎ 8972 2650) is on Katherine Terrace. Inquire here about permits to travel on the Central Arnhem Rd to the Gove Peninsula.

Tourist Offices The Parks & Wildlife office (☎ 8973 8888) is on Giles St.

Shopping
Mimi Aboriginal Art & Craft, on Pearce St across the old railway line, is an Aboriginal-owned and -run shop selling products made over a wide area. Opening hours are extremely erratic.

Banyan Art Gallery, in the arcade off First St, has a small range of bark paintings and other crafts.

You are free to inspect the workshop at Coco's Katherine Didjeridoos at 21 First St, opposite the cinema, and works are on sale. A plain or decorated didj will set you back $100 to $300.

NITMILUK (KATHERINE GORGE) NATIONAL PARK
Nitmiluk (Katherine Gorge) National Park is one of the Northern Territory's major attractions. Title to the land was handed back to the Jawoyn people in 1989 following a land claim over a wider area, and the park is leased to the NT Conservation Land Corporation (a government body) and managed as a national park by the Parks & Wildlife Commission.

The 99-year lease guarantees Jawoyn people traditional rights over the area, allowing for activities such as hunting, food gathering and ceremonies, and the Jawoyn people have a majority on the park's management board. The lease also guarantees some Aboriginal employment in the park – there are a number of Jawoyn rangers and trainees.

While the park is on Aboriginal land, there are no real opportunities to meet Aboriginal people. There are a number of

NORTHERN TERRITORY

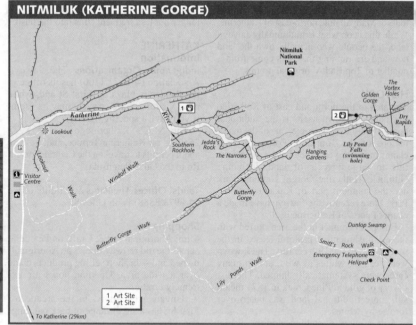

NITMILUK (KATHERINE GORGE)

1 Art Site
2 Art Site

To Katherine (29km)

small rock art sites in the park itself, but very few are accessible.

The gorge and the country around is of significance to the Jawoyn, and there are a number of important sites. For instance, Bolung, the Rainbow Serpent, is said to reside in the pools of the second gorge, so there are certain rules attached to swimming, fishing and drinking the water there.

Information

The best place to find out more about Jawoyn Law and culture is at the park visitor centre (☎ 8972 1886), which has excellent displays and information on Aboriginal lore, as well as the park's geology, wildlife and white history. It's open 7 am to 7 pm daily. In line with the desires of the traditional owners, there's no entry fee to the park, although this is to some degree built into the price you pay for boat cruises up the gorge.

Information sheets detail the wide range of marked walking tracks that start at the centre and traverse the picturesque country south of the gorge. Some of the tracks pass Aboriginal rock paintings up to 7000 years old. The *Guide to Nitmiluk (Katherine Gorge)*

National Park has more detail on these walks and is available from the visitor centre.

Organised Tours

Extended bushwalks with overnight camping are led by Willis' Walkabouts (☎ 8985 2134), which offers a nine-day walk through remote country from Manyallaluk to Nitmiluk with an Aboriginal guide. The first day of the walk includes a day tour at Manyallaluk. Advance bookings are essential.

MANYALLALUK

Manyallaluk is the former 3000 sq km Eva Valley Station abutting the eastern edge of Nitmiluk National Park, the southern edge of Kakadu and the south-western edge of Arnhem Land. It is in Jawoyn country but the business is owned by Mayali and Ngalkbun Aboriginal people from further east in Arnhem Land, with whom the Jawoyn share some traditions. The name Manyallaluk comes from a Frog Dreaming site found to the east of the community.

The Manyallaluk community operates one of the most successful and highly regarded Indigenous tourism operations in

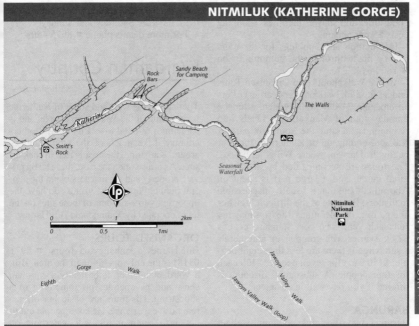

NITMILUK (KATHERINE GORGE)

the Top End (see Organised Tours). While it's possible to just turn up to the community and camp, the real reward comes in taking one of these tours.

The community store has a limited range of locally made crafts for sale – bark paintings, didjeridus and baskets. Prices are very reasonable.

Please note that Manyallaluk is a dry community, so alcohol is prohibited.

Organised Tours

The Manyallaluk day tours are very informal and are based at the community. The focus is on meeting with the local people and spending a day with them in various activities.

The day starts at around 9.45 am with billy tea and damper, where visitors are introduced to the guides and given some background to the community. This is followed by a plant-use walk, and then an excellent lunch, cooked over the fire by the spring-fed swimming hole – damper, barramundi and kangaroo livened up with some locally gathered bush-tucker herbs.

The afternoon is spent learning some of the women's crafts, and trying your hand at

painting with ochres, fire lighting, didjeridu playing and spear throwing.

The one-day trip includes transport to and from Katherine, and operates on weekdays from mid-March to mid-October, and Monday, Wednesday and Friday from mid-October to mid-December. The cost is $132/71.50 for adults/children and is well worth the money. If you are driving, you can get yourself to Manyallaluk (about 100km from Katherine, 35km of which is gravel), and the tour is then $99/60.50.

Two-day trips are also offered. Day one is the same as the day tour, but in the late afternoon visitors are taken by 4WD out to a bush camp by a scenic waterhole. On the second day visitors travel by vehicle through the stone country to a number of rock art sites on the community. Lunch is taken by a superb plunge pool – great for a refreshing swim – before heading back to the community in the late afternoon. The cost of these trips is $450/200 for adults/children.

If you camp at the community without taking the tour, you are restricted to the grassy camping area. It's a very pretty site by a spring-fed pool, and there's power and good toilet and shower facilities. Camping costs $5 per person.

Information and bookings for the tours can be made through the community on ☎ 1800 644 727.

Willis' Walkabouts (see Organised Tours under Nitmiluk National Park earlier) offers an amazing 21-day walk, which, after the one-day tour of Manyallaluk, heads into Arnhem Land and the southern part of Kakadu, ending up at Katherine (the tour begins in Darwin, where Willis' is based). The tours are accompanied by an Aboriginal guide, and a large part is spent on Aboriginal land that is usually inaccessible to visitors. Because of the difficult logistics and permit considerations, the trips may not run each year. The cost standard cost is $2795 (varies with group size), and there's a surcharge if there are less than eight people: $150 each for seven people, $400 each for four people. A substantial discount is offered if you pay well in advance.

BARUNGA

Barunga is an Aboriginal community about 80km east of Katherine on the Central Arnhem Rd. There are no visitors facilities and permits are required for any visit – see the NLC in Katherine (see that section earlier). The community is of interest to visitors for its festival held over the Queen's Birthday long weekend in June. During the festival permits are not required and visitors can camp within the community.

Barunga is a dry community, so alcohol is prohibited.

Barunga Wugularr Sports & Cultural Festival

In June the Barunga Wugularr Sports & Cultural Festival draws Aboriginal people from all over the Top End and from as far away as Kununurra in WA. While it is mainly a sporting festival, there are also traditional arts and crafts, as well as dancing and spear-throwing competitions. Throughout the weekend there are a number of live bands playing, and on the Saturday night a Battle of the Bands competition is held.

For non-Indigenous visitors the festival offers the rare chance to stay in a community for a few days. Although the festival goes from Friday through to Monday, the main days are Saturday and Sunday.

For more details phone ☎ 8975 4505.

Wardaman Country
Wider Katherine Area

The land to the west and south of Katherine is the home of the Wardaman people, and is sometimes referred to as Lightning Brothers country. Like much of the stone country around Katherine, the area is rich in rock art sites. As is also often the case, these lie on private property and are inaccessible to the general public. Fortunately, visitors do have the opportunity to visit some of these sites on the tours operated by Yidumduma Bill Harney.

ORGANISED TOURS

Bill Harney's Jankangyina Tours (☎ 8971 0318) is the only operation in the area. Bill, a Wardaman Elder, is basically a one-man show and he operates on something of a shoestring. His tours are basic but offer a real bush experience. He takes people out to his bush camp at Ingaladi waterhole on Willeroo Station, from where the superb Lightning Brothers rock art site is just a short drive. While the rock art is undeniably impressive, a large part of the experience on these tours is just talking with Bill Harney. He is one of the NT's characters and has quite a few fascinating stories to tell of the 'assimilation' days. Bill's life has been documented in the book *Born under the Paperbark Tree*, as told by Bill Harney to Jan Wositzky.

The tours don't run to any set schedule, so it's a matter of contacting Bill as far in advance as possible and trying to set something up.

Kakadu National Park

Kakadu National Park is one of the natural marvels of the NT. The longer you stay, the more rewarding it is, and it offers probably the greatest opportunity in the territory to delve into Aboriginal culture. It boasts significant rock art sites and encompasses a variety of habitats, including some stunning wetlands and a mass of wildlife. All these combine to make it one of the top tourist destinations in the country, and have gained it World Heritage listing as an area of both cultural and ecological importance.

The name Kakadu comes from the language of the Gagadju people, one of the three major groups of traditional owners of the area – the others being the Gundjehmi and the Jawoyn. The park also encompasses the land of a number of smaller clans, including the Mirrar, whose land has been in the spotlight, as it is the site of the controversial Jabiluka uranium mine.

Much of Kakadu is Aboriginal land, leased to the federal government for use as a national park. The entire park is jointly managed by Parks Australia and the traditional Aboriginal owners, 10 of whom sit on the 14-member board of management. There are around 300 Aboriginal people living in several Aboriginal settlements in the park and in the township of Jabiru, and about one-third of the park staff are Aboriginal people. In addition, a number of Aboriginal Elders are employed to advise Parks Australia on management issues.

The traditional owners are also represented through five associations, which own a number of the park's material assets – for example, the hotels at Jabiru and Cooinda, the Border Store and the Yellow Water cruise operation, plus the Ranger Uranium Mine Lease.

HISTORY

Aboriginal people have lived in the Kakadu area for at least 23,000 years, and possibly even 50,000 years, as indicated by artefacts such as stone tools, ochre and grindstones found at a number of sites. The rocky nature of the rugged countryside that typifies much of the park offered excellent shelter to the Aboriginal people, and many of these shelters bear art sites of world importance.

In the 1890s a few Europeans started to make a living from shooting buffalo for hides in the Alligator rivers region. Foremost among these was Paddy Cahill (see the Oenpelli section earlier).

In 1969 and 1972 the precursors to Kakadu National Park, the Woolwonga and Alligator Rivers Wildlife Sanctuaries, were declared. Under the Aboriginal Land Rights (NT) Act of 1976, some land titles were granted to the traditional Aboriginal owners in 1978, and the proclamation of Stage One of the Kakadu National Park was made the following year.

In 1997 the Jawoyn people of the Katherine region were granted title to two former cattle stations in the southern section of the park. The land was immediately leased back to the government to remain in use as national park.

Today the park is occupied by a number of different groups (or clans), each with a different language and often different traditional practices. Although many of these traditional practices have been modified or lost altogether in the years since contact with whites, the traditional owners still have strong personal and spiritual links with the land.

The languages still spoken by Aboriginal people in the park are Gundjehmi and Kunwinjku, spoken by the people living in the vicinity of the Arnhem Land escarpment; and Jawoyn, which is spoken by the people in the southern reaches of the park. Gagadju was the dominant language in the park area early last century, but it is no longer in widespread use.

National Park Status

At nearly 22,000 sq km, Kakadu is the largest national park in Australia. It was proclaimed a national park in three stages. Stage One, the eastern and central part of the park including Ubirr, Nourlangie, Jim Jim and Twin Falls and Yellow Water Billabong, was declared in 1979. Stage Two, in the north, was declared in 1984 and gained World Heritage listing for its natural importance. Stage Three, in the south, was finally listed in 1991, bringing virtually the whole of the South Alligator River system within the park.

In the late 1990s Kakadu was receiving some 220,000 visitors per year, mostly in the Dry. The park's annual budget is about $10 million, of which about $3 million comes from entry fees, the balance being provided by the federal government.

MINING

In 1953 uranium was found in the region. Twelve small deposits in the southern reaches of the park were worked in the 1960s but were abandoned following the declaration of the Woolwonga Wildlife Sanctuary.

In 1970 three huge deposits, Ranger, Nabarlek and Koongarra, were found,

NORTHERN TERRITORY

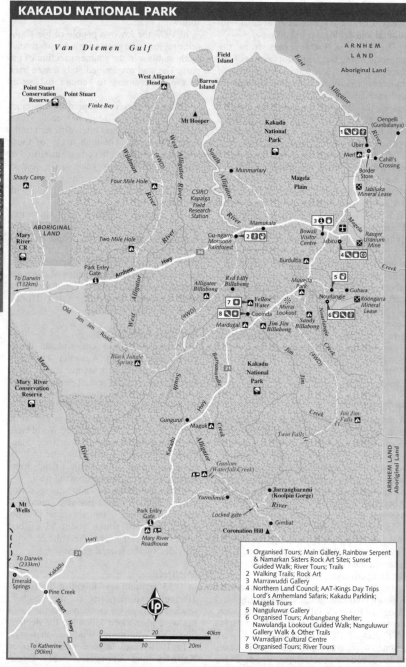

KAKADU NATIONAL PARK

1 Organised Tours; Main Gallery, Rainbow Serpent & Namarkan Sisters Rock Art Sites; Sunset Guided Walk; River Tours; Trails
2 Walking Trails; Rock Art
3 Marrawuddi Gallery
4 Northern Land Council; AAT-Kings Day Trips Lord's Arnhemland Safaris; Kakadu Parklink; Magela Tours
5 Nanguluwur Gallery
6 Organised Tours; Anbangbang Shelter; Nawulandja Lookout Guided Walk; Nanguluwur Gallery Walk & Other Trails
7 Warradjan Cultural Centre
8 Organised Tours; River Tours

followed by Jabiluka in 1973. The Nabarlek deposit (in Arnhem Land) was mined in the late 1970s, and the Ranger Uranium Mine started producing ore in 1981. Most of the Aboriginal people of the area were against the mining of uranium on traditional land, but were enticed with the double lure of land title and royalties.

The royalty agreements struck with Energy Resources of Australia Ltd (ERA, the company which operates Ranger) provide for an annual lease payment of $200,000, plus a royalty fee of 4.25% of the gross sales revenue from the mine. Some of this money is paid to the NLC, which then distributes it to Aboriginal associations across the NT, while some is paid direct to the associations, which then distribute it among the traditional owners.

The proposed Jabiluka mine site was the scene of widespread protest and sit-in demonstrations during the 1998 Dry season. Things came to a head when a UN delegation inspected the mine site to assess whether the damage it was causing would endanger Kakadu's World Heritage listing. The delegation found that Jabiluka could degrade Kakadu's pristine environment.

Despite these findings, and the objections of the Mirrar clan, the mine was given the go-ahead. It is currently under development, although further development has been stalled while negotiations continue as to how best deal with the ore which is mined.

GEOGRAPHY, FLORA & FAUNA

In all, there are six major topographical landforms within the park: the sandstone Arnhem Land escarpment, the riverine floodplains, the coastal estuaries and tidal flats, monsoon rainforests, lowlands and the southern hills.

Each of the landforms has its own distinctive type of vegetation, and this in turn dictates the birds and animals that are found in each. Over 1600 plant species have been recorded in the park, and a number of them are still used by the local Aboriginal people for food, bush medicine and other practical purposes.

Arnhem Land Escarpment & Plateau

A straight line on the map separates Kakadu from the Arnhem Land Aboriginal Land to its east, which you cannot enter without a permit. The meandering sandstone Arnhem Land escarpment, a dramatic 100m- to 200m-high sandstone cliff line that provides the natural boundary of the rugged Arnhem Land plateau, winds some 500km through east and south-east Kakadu. The plateau itself is surprisingly dry, mainly because the water drains away quickly into the deep gorges and tumbles off the escarpment as thundering waterfalls in the Wet season down onto the plains.

The soil on the plateau is also relatively shallow and low in nutrient, and so the vegetation is confined to species which can tolerate the generally poor conditions, such as spinifex grass and sandstone pandanus – both plants have been used extensively by Aboriginal people.

Mammals most commonly encountered are wallaroos (black and common), which are found on the lower slopes. A number of birds, such as white-lined honeyeaters and chestnut-quilled rock pigeons, are also endemic.

One of the most famous sandstone country inhabitants is Leichhardt's grasshopper, a beautiful blue and orange insect that was not seen by science until 130 years after its 'discovery' in 1845. The Aborigines knew it, though, and called the grasshoppers Aljurr, the children of Namarrgon (Lightning Man), because they are said to call their father to start the storms before the Wet.

The escarpment country offers some of the most spectacular scenery in Kakadu, and also has the greatest concentration of art sites – Ubirr and Nourlangie are both outliers of the escarpment.

Floodplains

In the Wet the vast floodplains of Kakadu's four north-flowing rivers turn the north of the park into a kind of huge, vegetated lake. From west to east the rivers are the Wildman, the West Alligator, the South Alligator and the East Alligator. The wetlands offer some of the most spectacular sights of the park, and have been considered sufficiently important to be placed on the List of Wetlands of International Importance. Some of the more accessible wetland areas include Yellow Water, Mamukala, Ubirr and Bubba.

The river floodplains were a major source of food for local Aboriginal people – turtles, fish and crocodiles are all found in abundance. Areas that are perfectly dry underfoot in September will be under 3m of water a few months later. As the waters recede in the Dry, some loops of Wet-season watercourses become cut off, but don't dry up. These are *billabongs* – and they're often carpeted with water lilies and are a magnet for water birds, particularly magpie geese, jabirus, cormorants and herons.

Many of the wetlands and permanent waterholes are fringed by stands of tall trees, predominantly broadleafed and weeping paperbarks. Freshwater mangroves and water pandanus are other plants suited to the floodplain environment.

Coastal Estuaries & Tidal Flats

The coastal zone has long stretches of mangroves, important for halting erosion and as a breeding ground for marine and bird life. There are 29 mangrove species known to exist in Australia; 21 of these grow in Kakadu.

Birds of the coast include mangrove kingfishers, mangrove robins, mangrove warblers and chestnut rails.

Animal life includes turtles (green and flatback), saltwater crocodiles and mangrove monitors.

The tidal flats behind the mangroves are quite rich from the sediment deposited by the rivers, but due to occasional inundation caused when the tidal waters break through natural levees, plant life is restricted to those that can tolerate salt water.

Monsoon Rainforest

Isolated pockets of monsoon rainforest appear throughout the park, and are of two types: coastal and sandstone.

Coastal monsoon rainforest is dominated by banyan, kapok and milkwood trees, and generally appears along river banks or other places where there is permanent water, either above or below ground.

Sandstone monsoon rainforest occurs along the gorges of the escarpment, such as at Jim Jim Falls.

Lowlands

About half the park, predominantly the southern section, is dry lowlands with open grassland or woodland. The main tree of the woodland, and one which dominates much of the Top End, is the Darwin woollybutt

eucalypt. Other eucalypts include Cooktown ironwoods and Darwin stringybarks. Below the canopy provided by these trees, pandanus palms and other small trees grow, while the ground is covered by annual grasses. Naturally enough, these grasses are the dominant form of vegetation in the grasslands, and after the Wet can shoot up to 2m high, making the most of the moisture before the ground dries up during the Dry.

While probably the least spectacular country in the park, the lowlands are the richest in bird and animal life. Parrots, rosellas and cockatoos are abundant, while on the ground wallaroos, dingoes, bandicoots, possums and tree-rats are all common.

Southern Hills

The hills in the southern part of the park are different from those elsewhere, such as the Arnhem Land plateau, in that the rocks are of volcanic origin. Erosion of this material has led to different soil types to elsewhere in the park, this in turn giving rise to distinctive flora and fauna types.

This area of the park is in Jawoyn country, and is known by the Jawoyn as 'Sickness Country', where the Creation Ancestor Bula went underground. The area is considered dangerous by the Jawoyn, and it is believed that if Bula is disturbed, devastating earthquakes and fire will destroy the world.

One of the most noticeable and widespread eucalypts found here, especially in the Gunlom vicinity, are the instantly recognisable northern salmon gums, with their smooth, pink trunks. Other common trees include scarlet gums, variable-barked bloodwoods and the Darwin box.

Common birds of the hills include various rosellas, pigeons, kites, honeyeaters and whistlers. Wallabies, wallaroos and goannas are all residents here, as are freshwater crocodiles.

Rivers and creeks of the southern hills are lined with paperbarks; also found here are pandanus, wattles and native bamboo. This is important habitat for a variety of owls, goshawks and pigeons, and the beautiful rainbow pittas, which can occasionally be observed on the forest floor.

CLIMATE

The great change between the Dry and the Wet makes a big difference to visitors to

It can take less than a day to weave a basket but it takes much longer to prepare the materials, especially when they are dyed. Here Kunwinjku weavers Esther Managku and Miriam Nganjmirra demonstrate all the stages.

Esther and Miriam head out to find manbelk (pandanus) for weaving (1). They use hooked sticks to pull the pandanus from the tree (2). The materials for natural bush dyes are then gathered, including tree bark (3) and the roots of special plants (4). Esther splits the pandanus into workable strands and strips it of its spikes (5). It is then dyed in batches and hung out to dry (6). The dried pandanus takes on a wide variety of colours (7). These are used to create patterned basket designs (8).

WEAVING

Indigenous weaving techniques vary across Australia and range from the construction of hardy fish traps to fine (but tough) string *dilly* bags. Included here is a shade wall made of woven coconut-leaf mats in the Torres Strait (1). In Arnhem Land and the Top End, weavers make use of natural dyes to add colour to their materials (2, 4). Meanwhile, the famous Ngarrindjeri weavers from the Coorong region in South Australia favour natural tones. Among the many traditional designs are the 'two-sister baskets'. These are made of two identical round pieces ('sisters') stitched together to make neat baskets used for gathering herbs (3). Other Ngarrindjeri designs include freestanding baskets (6) and small mats (5). See also the boxed text 'Ngarrindjeri Weaving' on page 309 for more information.

Kakadu, the largest national park in the country, is jointly owned and managed by Parks Australia and its traditional owners, who lease much of the park's area to the Federal government for use as a national park. They include the Gagadju people who lend the park its name.

Kakadu's lush coastline features mangrove wetlands (1) and wetlands filled with water lillies (2). In the drier areas a traditional technique called 'firestick farming' (3) is used to burn off undergrowth and so prevent large-scale bushfires in the Dry season, as well as to encourage tender regrowth, which attracts game. Kakadu's rock art galleries, such as the one at Ubirr (4), are among the finest in Australia. The art documents thousands of years of history, including the time of European contact (5). Freshwater crocodiles (6) share the park with their more lethal cousins – the salt-water crocs. The South Alligator River winds its way straight through Kakadu in the Dry (7), while in the Wet it bursts its banks and floods the northern regions of the park.

Kakadu is famous for its diversity. It features six major ecosystems and passes through six seasons in the annual cycle, providing the local communities with a rich supply of bush tucker. See the Kakadu National Park section on page 212 for more information.

The desert oak in its early life (1) looks nothing like the adult version and is often mistaken for a different species. Spiral pandanus trees (2) can be harvested for their nuts, although it's very hard work. Meanwhile the seeds, bulbs and stems of waterlillies (3) can all be eaten. The many waterholes (4) in the park are a rich source of food and are excellent sites for birdwatching. The jabiru (5), with its long red legs, and sulphur-crested cockatoo (6) are easy to spot. Termites build their enormous mounds (7) among the spear grass – which grows up to 2m during the Wet season.

Kakadu. Not only is the landscape transformed as the wetlands and waterfalls grow, but Kakadu's unsealed roads become impassable in the Wet, cutting off some highlights, such as Jim Jim Falls. The local Aboriginal people recognise six seasons in the annual cycle.

Gunumeleng This is the 'build-up' to the Wet, which starts in mid-October. Humidity and temperatures rise (to 35°C or more) – and the number of mosquitoes rises to near plague proportions. By November the thunderstorms have started, billabongs are replenished and the water birds and fish disperse. Traditionally this is when the Aboriginal people made the seasonal move from the floodplains to the shelter of the escarpment.

Gudjewg The Wet proper continues through January, February and March, with violent thunderstorms and an abundance of plant and animal life thriving in the hot, moist conditions. Most of Kakadu's rain falls during this period.

Banggereng April is the season when storms (known as 'knock 'em down' storms) flatten the spear grass, which during the course of the Wet has shot up to 2m in height.

Yekke From May to mid-June is the season of mists, when the air starts to dry out. It is quite a good time to visit – there aren't too many other visitors, the wetlands and waterfalls still have a lot of water and most of the tracks are open.

Wurrgeng & Gurrung This is the late Dry (July and August), and the most comfortable time to visit Kakadu. It is when wildlife, especially birds, congregates en masse around the shrinking billabongs, but it's also when most tourists come to the park.

ORIENTATION

Kakadu National Park is huge. It's 170km from Darwin at its nearest boundary, and stretches another 130km from there across to the western edge of Arnhem Land. It is roughly rectangular and measures about 210km from north to south.

Only two main roads traverse the park, both sealed and accessible year-round, and most points of interest and places to stay are reached off these highways (the Stuart and Kakadu Hwys).

Access from the west (Darwin and the Stuart Hwy) is via the Arnhem Hwy, which stretches from the Stuart Hwy to the township of Jabiru (90km from the boundary).

Mamukala is a wetland 7km past the South Alligator bridge on the Arnhem Hwy. From there it's 29km to the turn-off to one of the major rock art sites in the park, Ubirr, 36km to the north-east near the East Alligator River. This road also gives access to Oenpelli and Arnhem Land, but note that a permit is needed to enter Arnhem Land (inquire at the NLC in Jabiru).

The Kakadu Hwy turns south off the Arnhem Hwy shortly before Jabiru. It runs past the Park Headquarters and Bowali Visitor Centre (2.5km), the Nourlangie turn-off (21km), Muirella turn-off (28km), Jim Jim Falls turn-off (41km), Cooinda turn-off (47km) and on to the Gunlom turn-off (88.5km), the southern entrance to the park (137km) and Pine Creek on the Stuart Hwy (202km).

The road is bitumen all the way to the southern park gate, as well as beyond to the Stuart Hwy.

Maps

The *Kakadu National Park Visitor Guide* booklet, which includes good maps, is included with your entrance fee. It's an excellent publication and will get you around the park safely.

The Hema *Kakadu National Park* 1:390,000 map is updated regularly and is widely available. Bowali Visitor Centre sells 1:100,000 topographic maps covering most parts of the park; they can also be studied at the centre. These are essential for bushwalking in some areas of Kakadu.

INFORMATION

Kakadu National Park is open year-round. Access roads to Jim Jim and Twin Falls and to West Alligator Head are closed during the Wet, and attractions in the southern part of the park, such as Gunlom, are accessible only to 4WDs in the Wet.

Bowali Visitor Centre

The excellent Bowali Visitor Centre (☎ 8938 1121) is itself a highlight of the park. The building sits on Mirrar clan land, and Bowali is the local name for the main creek in the area.

The centrepiece of this award-winning building is a walk-through, state-of-the-art display which explains Kakadu's habitats from both the Gukburlerri (Aboriginal) and Guhbele (non-Aboriginal) perspectives. It's informative and interesting, and a few features should keep the kids happy.

The building also houses an information desk with plenty of leaflets on various aspects of the park, cafe, gift shop as well as toilets (including disabled).

The Marrawuddi Gallery sells a good range of souvenirs, T-shirts and books on Kakadu.

Bowali is open 8 am to 5 pm daily; allow a couple of hours to get the most out of a visit. It's on the Kakadu Hwy about 2.5km south of the Arnhem Hwy, and a walking track connects it to Jabiru, about 2km away (30 minutes).

Entry Fees

An entry fee of $16.25 (children under 16 free) is paid at the park gates as you enter. This entitles you to stay in the park for 14 days. You may be approached by someone trying to sell you their ticket once they've finished with it, as most people stay far less than 14 days. Avoid the temptation to buy a used ticket – they are checked by park staff and recycled tickets are easily detected. If you're caught with an unofficial one you'll be obliged to fork out for a new ticket. Ticket sales account for a substantial portion of park revenue and you're not doing anyone a favour by trying to avoid the cost.

A 'Territorian Ticket' ($65) covers one vehicle and all its occupants, as well as camping fees at the Mardugal, Muirella Park, Merl and Gunlom camping grounds. It's a good option if you plan to visit the park several times – and will get you into Uluru-Kata Tjuta as well (see later in this chapter) – but it is available only to Australian residents and can't be used for a rented vehicle.

Disabled Access

There is wheelchair access to the main gallery and Rainbow Serpent art sites at Ubirr, Anbangbang rock shelter (the main gallery at Nourlangie), the plunge pool at Gunlom, Bowali Visitor Centre and Warradjan Aboriginal Cultural Centre near Cooinda.

Wheelchairs can also be accommodated on the Yellow Water cruise – advise staff when booking.

PERMITS

If you want to camp outside designated camping grounds in Kakadu, a permit is required from the Bowali Visitor Centre.

ORGANISED TOURS

There are a bewildering number of tour operators who can take you into Kakadu, so shop around. Tours suit every taste from comfortable 'soft adventure' to 4WD trips that get right into the wrinkles of the escarpment. Ask about student/YHA discounts, stand-by rates and Wet-season specials. The park entry fee of $16.25 is generally not included in tour prices.

Most tours start from Darwin, although a few start inside the park itself.

From Darwin

Two-day tours typically take in Nourlangie, Ubirr and the Yellow Water cruise, and cost from around $170. A three-day tour could include the art sites, Yellow Water cruise and access to 4WD areas such as Jim Jim Falls; expect to pay $330 and up. Four days should cover the above sights, but give longer time at each for about $430. Longer trips, for $550 or so onwards, will give you time to really appreciate the park and maybe get into somewhere remote.

Some companies also offer extensions into Arnhem Land and packages that combine Litchfield and Nitmiluk (Katherine Gorge) National Parks.

From Jabiru

For day trips to Ubirr, which include the Guluyambi river cruise (see River Trips in the Ubirr section), tours are run by AAT-Kings (☎ 1800 334 009, ⓔ austours @aatkings.com.au) for $75/38 adults/children from Jabiru.

Into Arnhem Land

A couple of outfits offer trips into Arnhem Land from Kakadu, although they only nip across the East Alligator River to Oenpelli and the Mikinj Valley. For details see the Organised Tours at the beginning of the Kunwinjku Country section earlier.

ROCK ART SITES

Kakadu National Park's rock art sites were critical to the park's World Heritage listing. More than 5000 sites are known, the oldest dating from more than 20,000 years ago; two of the finest (and most accessible) collections are the galleries at Ubirr and Nourlangie (see the Ubirr and Nourlangie sections later and Rock Art in the Visual Art

KUNWINJKU PAINTING

Peterson Nganjmirra, with the assistance of Lawungkurr Maralngurra

I am of the Djalama clan of the Kunwinjku (freshwater people of north-west Arnhem Land). We call ourselves Bininj (the people). Painting has always been very important to Bininj. Old men like my *mowa* (father) and my mowa's mowa (grandfather) painted on rocks to teach their children and grandchildren about their country and the animals, like kangaroos and snakes. They were guided in what to paint by the land's ancient spirits, which grew from generations of Bininj living and dying there. Some *stories* were good, showing people gathering food; others were bad, showing people as food for crocodiles! Bininj also paint on tree bark for initiation ceremonies. *Balanda* (white people) who came to Gunbalanya were interested in the painting, and together Bininj and Balanda decided we should paint for exhibitions down south.

The bark is cut from *manborrogorr* (Darwin stringybark), at Gunumeleng (the time of the first storms) to Bangerreng (the end of the Wet season). At this time the bark is easily removed because the sap is flowing. Otherwise, it sticks really hard to the tree and can't be removed. The bark is now called *dolobo*. While wet, it is laid flat and weighed down with stones until it dries. This takes about a month, depending on how much sun there is. Then it is sanded. The traditional way is to use the leaves of *manlarr* (sandpaper fig). Cross-sticks are made from young manbohdogorr saplings to keep the bark from twisting. The cross-sticks are tied together with *kunyarl* (bush string) made from *manbornde* (banyan tree).

Our paints come from special white and yellow clay found in fresh water. Red, brown and orange comes from rocks, which are on the top of hills or near creeks. It is hard to find good rocks. These rocks are ground on a hard stone and water is added to make the colour bright. Gum is taken from *manmolak* (bil-lygoat/Kakadu plum tree) and mixed in to make the finished paint. Big brushes made from the bark of manborrogorr are used to paint the background. The stems of *many-ilk* (sedge) are split and chewed to make small brushes for *rarrk* (cross-hatching) – the fine lines are drawn at angles to each other and used to fill in the figure. The rarrk is different for each clan. Even the thickness of the line depends on your *moiety* (skin classification). People belonging to the Duwa moiety paint thick lines, while Yirridja people paint thin ones. If a Yirridja artist wants to paint thick lines, he must ask a Duwa person either for permission, or to do it for him. This person can be a father or their father's brothers or sisters (children and mothers share one moiety; fathers have the other). If the artist wants to paint another's Dreaming, then again he must ask permission. For instance, if a man with Water Python Dreaming wanted to paint Crocodile Dreaming, then he would have to ask permission of a person who had that Dreaming. When there is a ceremony, men paint Dreaming animals on their bodies. Red is mainly worn by men who want to scare people; white and yellow are worn by older, wiser men who are highly respected.

Peterson Nganjmirra

Peterson was born in 1954 in Gunbalunya; his cord was cut by the Aboriginal nurse. He had four brothers, two of whom are dead, and one sister.

From a very early age Peterson watched his male relatives paint and learned the ancient techniques from them. He got to do little sections of their pictures. But when he was sent to school, painting was nearly forgotten.

In the '70s Peterson began drinking, after the death of his wife. He sometimes reminisces on what life was like before there was alcohol. Then he met Stephanie, and stopped drinking 'for her'.

He was ordained an Anglican minister in the mid-1980s, a service which received Australia-wide media coverage. Presently Peterson, Stephanie and their two children live in Darwin, but intend to return to Arnhem Land and a more traditional lifestyle in a couple of years.

RICHARD I'ANSON

The rarely visited Nanguluwur Gallery in Kakadu National Park is a long overhang featuring rock art up to 30,000 years old

special section for more information on techniques).

For the local Aboriginal people the rock art sites are a major source of traditional knowledge – their historical archives, if you like, because they have no written language. The most recent paintings, some executed as recently as the 1980s, connect the local community with the artists. Older paintings are believed by many Aboriginal people to have been painted by Spirit People, and depict stories which connect the people with creation legends and the development of Aboriginal Law.

The majority of rock art sites open to the public are relatively recent, and some visitors feel somewhat cheated when they learn that the paintings were only done in the 1960s. Many people are also surprised to learn that the old paintings they are seeing have actually been touched up by other Aboriginal people quite recently. In fact this was not uncommon, although the repainting could only be done by a specific person who knew the story that was being depicted. What also comes as a surprise is the way the

paintings in a particular site are often layered, with newer paintings being placed right over the top of older ones.

The conservation of the Kakadu rock art sites is a major part of the park management task. As the paintings are all done with natural, water-soluble ochres, they are very susceptible to water damage from drip lines running across the rock. To prevent this sort of damage, small ridges of clear silicon rubber have been made on the rocks above the paintings, so the water flowing down the rock is diverted to either side, or actually drips right off. Dust also affects the paintings; most of the accessible sites – which may receive up to 3000 visitors a week – have boardwalks that keep the dust down and keep people at a suitable distance from the paintings.

GUIDED WALKS & TALKS

In the Dry a variety of free activities are put on by the park staff. It's well worth going along to some of these informal talks – in fact it's vital if you really want to learn about the park and its traditional owners. The talks and slide shows generally last about 45 minutes, while the walks can be up to a couple of hours. The staff are generally dedicated people who are well informed and keen to share that knowledge with visitors. While the staff are careful to be seen as apolitical, they are usually quite open and forthright when asked about difficult or sensitive issues.

Full details are given on a leaflet that you will be given on entering the park. The main tours with an Aboriginal focus are as follows.

Art-Site Talks

These are held at the various rock art sites at Ubirr and Nourlangie. At Ubirr the talks focus on the impressive Main Gallery and on the women's Rainbow Serpent site. At Nourlangie the talks take in Anbangbang rock shelter.

Guided Walks

Guided walks held at Ubirr (Sunset Walk) and at Nourlangie (Nawulandja Lookout) give excellent views over the Magela Creek wetlands and the Arnhem Land escarpment, respectively.

Walking Tracks

There are plenty of other marked walking tracks within the park. The main one of interest is to the Nanguluwur rock art gallery near Nourlangie.

SHOPPING
Outlets for the sale of Aboriginal artefacts include Injalak Arts & Crafts (☎ 8979 0190), PMB 131 Oenpelli, NT 822, in Oenpelli (see the Kunwinjku Country section).

Marrawuddi Gallery (☎ 8979 2777), PO Box 206 Jabiru, NT 886, in the Bowali Visitor Centre, is a general gift shop with some genuine Aboriginal crafts and all the usual tacky pseudo-Aboriginal crafts – tea towels, place mats and playing cards (virtually all bearing Made in Taiwan or similar labels).

Warradjan Gallery, at the Warradjan Aboriginal Cultural Centre near Cooinda, offers the best opportunity for buying Aboriginal crafts in the park. See the Warradjan Aboriginal Cultural Centre section later.

SOUTH ALLIGATOR
This area, 2.5km west of where the Arnhem Hwy crosses the South Alligator River, is not quite as heavily used as other areas, such as the rock art sites. There's a camping ground, bar, well-stocked shop and some easy walks in the vicinity.

At the river itself there's a boat ramp and picnic area near the bridge.

Gu-ngarre Monsoon Rainforest
This easy 3.5km flat walk (about 90 minutes) skirts the South Alligator resort through monsoon forest and woodlands, then passes Anggardabal billabong. It's an excellent walk for learning about Aboriginal plant use.

UBIRR
Ubirr is an outlying outcrop of the Arnhem Land escarpment, some 39km north of the Arnhem Hwy, famous for its spectacular Aboriginal rock art site.

The Ubirr paintings are in many different styles. They were painted during the period from over 20,000 years ago right up to the 20th century, although most are from the freshwater period, which began about 2000 years ago. Allow plenty of time to seek out and study them.

The rock art site is open 8.30 am to sunset daily from 1 May to 30 November, and 2 pm to sunset between 1 December and 30 April.

The view across the floodplain from the top is stunning, especially at sunset.

Main Gallery
An easily followed path from the Ubirr car park takes you through the main galleries and up to a lookout with superb views. There are paintings on numerous rocks along the path, but the highlight is the main gallery with a large array of well-executed and preserved x-ray-style wallabies, possums, goannas, tortoises and fish, plus a couple of *balanda* (white men) with hands on hips. There are also a few Mimi spirit figures (depicted as distorted human figures) painted high up on the rock in a seemingly inaccessible spot. It's said that the Mimi spirits were able to lift the rock down, paint the figures and then place the rocks back in place.

Rainbow Serpent
Also of major interest here is the Rainbow Serpent painting, a women's business site which even today is not visited by Aboriginal men. The Rainbow Serpent is a powerful creation figure, and it makes appearances at important sites across northern Australia.

In Kakadu the serpent is a woman, Kuringali, who painted her image on the rock wall at Ubirr while on a journey through this area. This journey forms a creation path that links the places she visited: Ubirr, Manngarre, the East Alligator River and various places in Arnhem Land.

To the traditional owners of the park, Kuringali is the most powerful spirit. Although she spends most of her time resting in billabongs, if disturbed she can be very destructive, causing floods and earthquakes, and one local story has it that she even eats people.

Namarkan Sisters
The Namarkan Sisters are shown with string pulled taut between their hands. It seems they live in the stars, and can travel down pieces of string into people's bodies and make them ill.

The story of the Namarkan Sisters is told to warn young children about the dangers of crocodiles. The sisters were sitting together by a billabong one day when one dived into the water, changed into a crocodile, then paddled back and frightened the life out of her sister. She then changed herself back and returned to her sister, who related how she had been terrified by a crocodile.

NORTHERN TERRITORY

The first sister got such a kick out of this that she repeated it over and over. Finally the other sister realised what was going on, and retaliated in the same way. The sisters then realised that if they were to turn themselves into crocodiles permanently, they could scare and eat anyone they pleased.

Today the Namarkan Sisters are present in all crocodiles, evident in the lumps behind the eyes and in their great skill and cunning as hunters.

River Tours

Aboriginal-guided Guluyambi river trips are held on the East Alligator River near the Border Store in the north of the park. These are excellent, highly recommended trips with the emphasis on Aboriginal culture and their relationship with the land. The tour operation is a joint venture between white-owned Kakadu Parklink and the Aboriginal Jabiru Association, which provides the guides.

The tours take their name from the *guluyambi* (paperbark rafts), which were used on the river by the traditional owners. The trip involves a slow cruise up the East Alligator River, with guides pointing out the uses for the various trees and plants found along the water's edge. Crocodiles (freshwater and saltwater) are often seen sunning themselves on the bank. Passengers are also given some insight into traditional lore, hunting and handicraft making.

Dry-season trips leave from the upstream boat ramp at East Alligator and cost $29/14 per adult/child. Book at the Border Store (☎ 8979 2474) or with Kakadu Parklink (☎ 1800 089 113). The cruise (1¾ hours) is marketed as an Aboriginal cultural tour. Aboriginal guides are usually on board. Tours leave at 9 and 11 am, and 1 and 3 pm. A free shuttle bus runs between the boat ramp and the Border Store and Merl camping ground.

During the Wet, Guluyambi operates a half-day tour leaving from Jabiru at 8 am and noon daily. This tour includes a boat transfer across the picturesque Magela Creek and a bus drive on to Ubirr. This tour provides the only means by which visitors can get to Ubirr when it is at its best.

Walking Tracks

There are four tracks in the Ubirr area:

Ubirr Art Site Walk (1km return; one hour; easy) An informative track around the rock art galleries, and there's a short but steep side-track to a lookout with great views over the East Alligator River floodplain – it's popular at sunset.

Manngarre Monsoon Rainforest Walk (1.2km return; 20 minutes; easy) This walk starts by the downstream boat ramp near the Border Store, and for much of the way is along a raised boardwalk.

Bardedjilidji Sandstone Walk (2.5km; 90 minutes; easy) This is a slightly longer walk starting from the upstream picnic area car park. It takes in wetland areas of the East Alligator River and some interesting eroded sandstone outliers of the Arnhem Land escarpment.

Rock Holes Sandstone Walk (8km; three hours; moderate) This is an extension of the Bardedjilidji Walk, taking in more of the same country.

JABIRU

The township of Jabiru was built to accommodate workers from the nearby uranium mines and was completed in 1982. It was originally intended as a temporary settlement, but has developed into the major service centre for Kakadu.

The main reason to visit Jabiru is for a permit to visit Oenpelli (Gunbalanya), to take a tour of the mine or to buy supplies.

Permits

For permits to visit Oenpelli, across the East Alligator River, contact the NLC (☎ 8979 2410) on Flinders St near the shopping centre. The office is open 8 am to 4.21 pm (!) weekdays. Permits cost $13.20 per person and are issued in about half an hour.

NOURLANGIE

The sight of this looming, mysterious, isolated outlier of the Arnhem Land escarpment makes it easy to understand why it has been important to Aboriginal people for so long. Its long, red, sandstone bulk, striped in places with orange, white and black, slopes up from surrounding woodland to fall away at one end in sheer, stepped cliffs, at the foot of which is Kakadu's best-known collection of rock art.

The name Nourlangie is a corruption of *nawulandja*, an Aboriginal word that refers to an area bigger than the rock itself. The Aboriginal name for part of the rock is Burrunggui. You reach it at the end of a 12km sealed road which turns east off the Kakadu Hwy, 21km south of the Arnhem Hwy. Other interesting spots nearby make it worth spending a whole day in this corner of Kakadu National Park. The last few kilometres of the road are closed from around 5 pm daily.

BARRK BUSHWALK

Matt Fletcher

Duration: 4½ to 5½ hours
Distance: 12km
Standard: Medium
Start/Finish: Nourlangie Rock car park
Closest Town: Jabiru
Public Transport: No

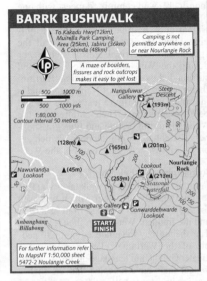

BARRK BUSHWALK

To Kakadu Hwy(12km), Muirella Park Camping Area (25km), Jabiru (36km) & Cooinda (48km)

Camping is not permitted anywhere on or near Nourlangie Rock

A maze of boulders, fissures and rock outcrops makes it easy to get lost

Nanguluwur Gallery

Steep Descent
▲(193m)

0   500   1000 m
0   500   1000 yds
1:80,000
Contour Interval 50 metres

▲(128m)

▲(165m)   ▲(201m)

Nawurlandja Lookout   ▲(45m)

Lookout   Nourlangie Rock
▲(213m)

(259m)   Seasonal waterfall

Anbangbang Gallery

Anbangbang Billabong

START/FINISH

Gunwarddehwarde Lookout

For further information refer to MapsNT 1:50,000 sheet 5472-2 Noulangie Creek

This spectacular walk links Anbangbang and Nanguluwur, two of the most important Aboriginal rock art sites in Kakadu. These sites offer a visual record of a constantly changing world and Dreaming *stories*. Paintings show extinct animals (such as the thylacine, or Tasmanian tiger), seasonal food sources and the arrival of Indonesian and European sailors. Styles have also evolved. One of the earliest was the 'naturalistic' style, which depicted people and animals in colour, while the more recent 'x-ray' style shows creatures' bones and organs. Some paintings are contemporary, others 30,000 years old.

In order to protect Kakadu's cultural heritage (and environment), walking is carefully regulated (permits are required for all overnight walks) – many sacred sites are not open to uninitiated Aboriginal people, let alone tourists. However, the Barrk Sandstone Walk is one of many purpose-built trails that day visitors can enjoy.

This challenging circuit over Nourlangie Rock is steep at times. Keep an eye out for black wallaroo (males are barrks) and chestnut-quilled rock pigeons. Both are endemic to Kakadu and Arnhem Land. Frilled lizards often display on the road during the 'Build Up' and Wet.

The 12km tarmac access road (open 7 am to sunset) begins 19km south of Jabiru. There's a car park and toilet close to the Anbangbang rock shelter, the start of the trail. Start walking early in the morning and carry at least 3L of water per person. Route descriptions are found in *Kakadu by Foot* ($3) and the Park Notes available from Bowali Visitor Centre (see Information earlier in this section). Ranger-led guided walks take place at Anbangbang (which has some wheelchair access) during the Dry season (see Guided Walks & Talks).

Two of Anbangbang's highlights are the depictions of Namarrgon the Lightning Man and Nabulwinjbulwinj, a dangerous spirit who eats females after striking them with a yam.

Namarrgon wears his lightning as a band connecting his arms, legs and head, while the stone axes on his knees and elbows make the thunder.

From the **Anbangbang rock shelter,** orange triangle waymarks lead steeply north-east past **Gunwarddehwarde Lookout** up onto Nourlangie Rock and across a rugged, boulder-strewn plateau before descending a narrow gully to open eucalyptus woodland on the northern side.

The trail then bends west to the **Nanguluwur Gallery** (also accessible by foot and 4WD), a long overhanging cliff which displays 30,000 years of Aboriginal rock art. Huge barramundi, once often caught in the East Alligator River, are displayed in x-ray style along with paintings of European ships. Stencilled hand-prints (a form of artist signature) are also found here.

Continue south-west along the trail that slowly swings west then south, cutting up and over a spur of boulders then south-east back to the car park.

Nourlangie Art

The major character in the main gallery at Nourlangie is Namondjok (pronounced na-mon-jock), who committed incest with one of his clan sisters. Next to Namondjok is Namarrgon (na-mad-gon), or the Lightning Man. He is responsible for all the spectacular electrical storms that occur during the Wet, and here he is depicted surrounded by an arc of lightning. Barrginj (bar-geen) is the wife of Namarrgon, and is the small female figure just to the left and below Namondjok. Their children are the Aljurr, beautiful orange and blue grasshoppers (Leichhardt's grasshopper), which are only seen just before the onset of the Wet.

Anbangbang Rock Shelter

From the main car park a walk takes you first to the Anbangbang shelter, which was used for 20,000 years as a refuge from heat, rain and the frequent Wet-season thunderstorms. The shelter may have housed up to 30 people of the Warramal clan, people of the greater Gundjehmi language group. Archaeological finds have revealed that the shelter was in almost constant use from about 6000 years ago to the time of white contact.

Walking Tracks

Nourlangie is probably the most visited part of the park. There are five walking tracks at points along the access road, but the two main ones which take in the art sites are listed below. See also the boxed text 'Barrk Bushwalk'.

Nourlangie Art Site The best way to view the excellent rock art sites around the base of Nourlangie is on this 1.5km, one-hour walk (easy to moderate). The Anbangbang rock shelter is the main gallery, and is accessible by wheelchair. Elsewhere the track is steep in parts; to have a good look at the paintings, allow at least one hour. The gallery here was repainted in the 1960s by Nayambolmi (also known as Barramundi Charlie), a respected artist, fisherman and hunter whose country was actually further to the east in Arnhem Land.

From the gallery you can walk on to Gunwarrdehwarrde Lookout, where you can see the distant Arnhem Land escarpment, which also includes Namarrgon Djadjam, the home of Namarrgon.

Nanguluwur Gallery This outstanding rock art gallery sees far fewer visitors than Anbangbang simply because it's further to walk and has a gravel access road. The 3.5km walk is easy, taking two hours. Here the paintings cover most of the styles found in the park, including a good example of 'contact art', a painting of a two-masted sailing ship towing a dinghy.

WARRADJAN ABORIGINAL CULTURAL CENTRE

This centre (☎ 8979 0051) near Cooinda gives an excellent insight into the culture of the park's traditional owners, the Bininj. Put aside a good couple of hours. The building itself is circular, which symbolises the way the Aboriginal people sit in a circle when having a meeting; the shape is also reminiscent of the *warradjan* (pig-nosed turtle), hence the name of the centre.

Inside, the displays depict Creation stories when the Nayuhyunggi (First People) laid out the land and the law, and the winding path you follow through the display symbolises the way the Rainbow Serpent moves through the country.

It's an excellent display, offering insights into Bininj Law, crafts, hunting, fishing, kinship system, contact and employment in early European ventures.

There's a small auditorium where visitors can view a variety of topical documentaries (on request), and a craft shop that sells locally made items, such as didjeridus and T-shirts, and other less authentic souvenirs such as stubby holders featuring Aboriginal designs.

The centre is open from 7.30 am to 6 pm daily. During the Dry, tours of the centre are given from 10 to 11 am and 1 to 2 pm Friday to Sunday.

Malak Malak Country

Daly River Area

DALY RIVER

The town of Daly River (Nauiya Nambiyu), about 240km and three hours' drive southwest of Darwin, is an idyllic spot on the river of the same name. The **Nauiya Nambiyu Aboriginal community** is about 6km away from the Daly River township, the main reason for a visit being the excellent Merrepen

Arts gallery here. It's also one of the only communities which has accommodation for casual visitors.

Daly River town centres around the colourful Daly River Pub, owned by the Nauiya Nambiyu Aboriginal community and rebuilt after the 1998 floods.

History
Early contact with Europeans had been relatively friendly, from the time John Mac-Douall Stuart came through here in 1862. This all changed in the 1880s when five Europeans who had established a copper mine were attacked by local Aboriginal people. Four of the miners died, and the attack sparked a vicious response from the Resident in Palmerston. A punitive party was dispatched, and men, women and children were massacred at will. When the incident became public there was a major outcry. The leader of the party, Corporal George Montagu, and other members were questioned by a board of inquiry established by the SA government, but amazingly they were all cleared of any wrongdoing.

The late 1880s saw Jesuit missionaries move into the area, and they soon established four missions. Three of these folded fairly quickly, and the last was finally closed in 1899, bringing to an end nearly two decades of relative peace between the European and Aboriginal communities. Christianity failed to supplant Aboriginal beliefs.

Information
Visitors are welcome at Nauiya Nambiyu without a permit. Note that this is a dry community.

Merrepen Arts
The excellent Merrepen Arts gallery (☎ 8978 2533, ⓔ merrepen@topend.com.au) is the major outlet for artists from the surrounding area as far away as Wadeye (Port Keats) on the coast to the west. The elevated building was constructed in 1998 following the floods that devastated the Daly River area that Wet season, and so the artwork is safe from any future floods. Like most other buildings in the town, the old single-storey gallery building (now used as a craft space) was about 1.5m under water – the high-water mark is still clearly visible on the walls.

Most of the work for sale here is produced by women of the area – paintings, batiks, screen-prints, T-shirts. There is also a small range of men's work, such as highly decorated spears, woomeras (throwing sticks for spears) and didjeridus.

The gallery is open 8 am to 5 pm weekdays, and 10 am to 2 pm every second Saturday. If your visit is on an 'off' Saturday, you can phone a day or two in advance and the staff can usually arrange to open the gallery for you.

Merrepen Arts Festival
The one-day Merrepen Arts Festival is held on a Saturday in early June at Nauiya. Several Aboriginal communities from around the district, such as Wadeye, Nauiya and Peppimenarti, display their arts and crafts. Music, dancing and bush tucker are also featured. Phone Merrepen Arts for more details (see earlier).

Places to Stay
The Leadership Accommodation Centre (☎ 8978 2460) is set in a beautiful grassy spot in the Nauiya Nambiyu community, right on the banks of the Daly River. It is open to all visitors, and consists of a number of interconnected transportable buildings. All rooms have air-con and fan, with singles at $35 with common facilities, and there are a couple of self-contained family units (five beds), complete with kitchen, bathroom and TV for $45 for a double or $75 for a family. Common facilities include a kitchen and a lounge/TV room. For directions to the centre, ask at the general store.

ORGANISED TOURS
The Peppimenarti Aboriginal community, west of Daly River, hosts two-day camping tours, although the tours themselves are run by Aussie Adventure Holidays (☎ 1800 811 633, fax 8924 1122, ⓔ aussieadventure @attglobal.net).

Peppi Tours start in Darwin, and on the way to Peppimenarti call in at Nauiya Nambiyu and Merrepen Arts. They then head west to a bush camp site on the Peppimenarti community. A day is spent with the Peppimenarti. Visitors are shown the methods involved in making various crafts, such as woven baskets, mats and *dilly* bags. There is also the opportunity to purchase these items from the community. Lunch on day two is taken at Merrum Lagoon, and following a visit to beautiful Pandela Falls, the tour returns to Darwin.

The tours leave Darwin on Monday and Wednesday from May to October. The cost is $486 for adults and $437 for children.

UMBRAWARRA GORGE NATURE PARK

About 3km along the Stuart Hwy south of Pine Creek is the turn-off to Umbrawarra Gorge Nature Park, 22km south-west along a dirt road (often impassable in the Wet). It's a quiet, little visited spot with some Aboriginal rock art sites and safe swimming.

The gorge is the Dreaming site of Kunangarrk-ngarrk, the white-bellied sea-eagle. Here he caught and ate a barramundi; the white flakes in the granite rock are said to be the scales of the barra, the quartz outcrops are the eagle's droppings. Rock art can be seen – with some difficulty – high along the gorge walls, on the right-hand side about 300m from the car park as you walk into the gorge. There are other even less obvious ones further in. A Parks & Wildlife sign at the car park gives a rough indication of their location.

A marked walking track leads from the car park to swimming holes in the gorge and you can swim and scramble the rest of its 5km length. There's a spartan camping ground close by with pit toilets and fireplaces.

Tiwi Islands

Bathurst & Melville Islands

Bathurst and Melville Islands are two large, flat islands about 80km north of Darwin. Owned by the Tiwi Aboriginal people, they are commonly known as the Tiwi Islands. The Tiwis have a distinct culture and although the islands have little in the way of tourist facilities, they can be visited on organised tours.

The Tiwi peoples' island homes kept them fairly isolated from mainland developments until the 20th century, and their culture has retained several unique features. Perhaps the best known are the pukumani (burial poles), carved and painted with symbolic and mythological figures, which are erected around graves. More recently the

Tiwi have turned their hand to art for sale – bark painting, textile screen-printing, batik and pottery, using traditional designs and motifs. The Bima Wear textile factory was set up in 1969 to employ Tiwi women, and today makes curtains, towels and other fabrics in distinctive designs. (Bima designed and printed the vestments worn by Pope John Paul II on his visit to the NT in 1987.) See also the Visual Art special section.

The main settlement on the islands is Nguiu (pronounced roughly noo-you) in the south-east of Bathurst Island, which was founded in 1911 as a Catholic mission. On Melville Island the main settlements are Pularumpi and Milikapiti.

Around 2500 of the 4000 Tiwi Islanders live on Bathurst Island and follow a non-traditional lifestyle. Some go back to their traditional lands on Melville Island for a few weeks each year. Descendants of the Japanese pearl divers who regularly visited here early last century also live on Melville Island.

The Tiwi Islanders are generally considered to be quite independent: they decided to set up the Tiwi Land Council, separate from the NLC.

The only practical way to visit the islands is by organised tour (see Organised Tours later), as there is no public accommodation or transport on the islands, and permits are only issued if you have a reason to visit.

HISTORY

The Tiwi had generally poor relations with the Macassans who came from the island of Celebes (now Sulawesi) in search of trepang from the 17th century. This earned them a reputation for hostility which stayed with them right through the colonial era. There is some evidence that the Portuguese raided the islands for slaves in the 17th century, which may go some way to explaining the origins of this hostility.

Known European contact began with the Dutch in the 18th century. Initial contact was friendly, but the Dutch were attacked on departure.

In their efforts to colonise the north of Australia, in 1824 the British established a settlement at Fort Dundas, near Pularumpi, but it lasted less than 18 months.

In the late 19th century two SA buffalo shooters spent a couple of years on Melville

Island and, with the help of the Tiwi, reputedly shot 6000 buffaloes. The Tiwi speared one of the shooters; the other, Joe Cooper, fled to Cape Don on the Cobourg Peninsula, but returned in 1900 and spent the next 16 years with the Tiwi.

Efforts by the Catholic church to establish a mission on Melville in 1911 met with resistance from Cooper, so the mission was set up on Bathurst Island. The Tiwi were initially extremely suspicious, as the missionaries had no wives, but the situation improved in 1916 when a number of French nuns joined the mission. Cooper moved back to the mainland, also in 1916. Mission activity ceased in 1972 with self-determination (see History at the beginning of this chapter).

PERMITS

You need a permit to visit the islands, for which you must apply in writing to the Chairman, Tiwi Land Council, Nguiu, Bathurst Island, PO Box 38545, Winnellie, NT 0821. The Tiwi Land Council can also be contacted on ☎ 8981 4898, fax 8981 4282. Permits are included on the organised tours.

The only time that it's possible to visit the islands without a permit is the day of the football Grand Final in March (see Special Events later).

ORGANISED TOURS

Tiwi Tours (☎ 1800 183 630) is owned by the Tiwi Islanders, although they contract out the actual running of the tours to Aussie Adventure Holidays in Darwin (☎ 1800 811 633, fax 8924 1122, ℮ aussieadventure @attglobal.net). The relaxed day tours are highly recommended. They include return flights, visits to the early Catholic mission buildings and craft workshops, a trip to a pukumani burial site, a walk along the beach and a picnic lunch by a swimming hole (bring swimming gear). Visitors are escorted around the various sites, accompanied by a Tiwi guide and a driver. Morning tea (billy tea and damper) is taken with the local women, who explain some of their crafts, experiences of the mission days and also put on a short dance. There's also the opportunity to buy crafts at a couple of outlets (see Shopping later). At $279 (no discount for children) the tours are not cheap, but this is largely because a flight is involved,

even though it's only 12 minutes each way. The tours operate weekdays from March to November.

Tiwi Tours also operates two-day tours, which include all of the one-day tour itinerary, plus an overnight bush camp on Melville Island, the opportunity to try your hand at spearfishing and a visit to the Tomorrupi Waterfall. The cost is $548 all inclusive, and departures are on Tuesday and Thursday from May to October.

PATAKIJIYALI MUSEUM

This small museum in Nguiu is well laid-out and informative. It consists of three parts: Apupwankijimi (Tiwi Dreaming), Arrakili (Tiwi culture) and the Mission Heritage Room.

Apupwankijimi gives some interesting detail on the Tiwi people and kinship structure, including a Creation story about Murtankala (the Creator) and details of the Kurlama ceremony, a men's ceremony held annually to help heal the past year's sorrow and ensure good fortune and plentiful food for the coming year.

Arrakili is mostly a display of artefacts, such as throwing sticks, spears, baskets and adornments, and also shows the Tiwi seasonal calendar.

The Mission Heritage Room consists largely of photographs documenting life on the mission early last century.

Pitakijiyali Museum is also visited as part of the organised tours.

SPECIAL EVENTS

Tiwi Islanders are footy mad, Australian Rules being the code in question. One of the first questions visitors are asked is what Australian Rules football team they support. There are eight teams in the local league, all named after sides in the Australian Football League (AFL) competition. Grand Final day is a major event in the NT sporting calendar, and crowds as big as 12,000 have attended in the past! Permits are not required to visit Nguiu on this day, but flights are heavily booked so it pays to plan well in advance. For details phone ☎ 8945 2224.

SHOPPING

Visitors to Bathurst have the opportunity to buy crafts at three outlets in Nguiu, and these are all visited on organised tours.

NORTHERN TERRITORY

Ngaruwanajurri is a craft workshop for Aboriginal people with disabilities. The artists work on site and are usually keen to talk with visitors and discuss their work. Items for sale are mainly paintings, silk screen T-shirts and silks. Prices are reasonable (credit cards not accepted).

The other major craft outlet on Bathurst Island is Tiwi Designs (☎ 8978 3982), also in Nguiu. Artists from this workshop turn out high-quality art, and this is reflected in the high prices. It's usually possible to meet at least some of the artists who work here. The main products available are paintings (bark and canvas), printed fabrics, woven pandanus articles, didjeridus and woodcarvings.

Right next door to Tiwi Designs is a pottery. It's interesting to see the sort of work artists produce when working with a non-traditional medium such as clay. There are pieces of all sizes, and many of these are for sale.

Gurindji Country

North Barkly Region

KALKARINGI

This Aboriginal community, on the Buntine Hwy 456km south-west of Katherine, provides services to **Daguragu**, 8km north. Daguragu was formerly known as Wattie Creek and grew out of the Aboriginal stockmen's strike of 1966, which ultimately led to the granting of land to Aboriginal people (see the boxed text 'The Wave Hill Stockmen's Strike').

Tourists are not permitted at Daguragu, but you can call in to Kalkaringi and make use of its commercial facilities.

The community store operates a caravan park, which has lawn and good shade. Sites cost $11/16.50 unpowered/powered for two people; extra people are $3 each.

LAJAMANU

The Aboriginal community of Lajamanu is about 110km south of Kalkaringi on the track down to the Tanami Rd.

Shopping

Lajamanu Warnayaka Arts (☎ 8975 0330) has mainly acrylic paintings on canvas, but does not open regular hours.

Warumungu Country

Tennant Creek Area

TENNANT CREEK

Known as Jurnkurakurr to the Warumungu people, the town of Tennant Creek, 506km north of Alice Springs, has grown up around a sacred site associated with a Spiky-Tailed Lizard Ancestor. The Dreaming stories of Jurnkurakurr are depicted in a large mural on the wall of the Central Land Council office, in the centre of town.

About 40% of the town's population of 3900 is of Aboriginal descent.

Information

Indigenous Organisations The Central Land Council's regional office (☎ 8962 2343) is at 63 Paterson St, on the corner of Windley St. Note that this office does not issue travel permits. ATSIC's regional office (☎ 8962 1999) is at 1–9 Paterson St. Both are open weekdays during normal business hours.

Tourist Offices The helpful visitor information centre (☎ 8962 3388, fax 8962 2509, e info@tennantcreektourism.com.au) is 2km east of town on Peko Rd at the historic gold stamp battery. Staff will point you in the direction of Aboriginal heritage attractions in town. It's open 9 am to 5 pm daily from May to September; at other times 9 am to 5 pm weekdays, and to noon Saturday.

Books The Papulu Apparr-Kari Language Centre publishes *Aboriginal (Wumpurani) Ways of Life*. This booklet has a lot of useful cross-cultural information for non-Aboriginal visitors.

Radio & TV CAAMA Radio broadcasts 18 hours a day on 102.9 FM, while Imparja provides a TV service to the town.

Organised Tours

About 3km south of town, Kraut Downs Station (☎ 8962 2820, 0417 828 959) runs informative half-day tours where you can learn about bush tucker and medicine, try whip-cracking and boomerang-throwing and enjoy billy tea and damper for $27.50. Transport can be arranged.

Norm's Gold & Scenic Tours (☎ 0418 891 711, e norm@fwcth.com.au) offers

THE WAVE HILL STOCKMEN'S STRIKE

Aboriginal stockmen played a major role in the early days of the pastoral industry in the NT. Because they were paid such paltry wages (which often never materialised) a pastoralist could afford to employ many of them, and run his station at a much lower cost. White stockmen received regular and relatively high wages, were given decent food and accommodation, and were able to return to the station homestead every week. By contrast Aboriginal stockmen received poor food and accommodation and would often spend months in the bush with the cattle.

In the 1960s Vincent Lingiari was a stockman on the huge Wave Hill Station, owned by Vesteys, a British company. His concern with the way Aboriginal workers were treated led to an appeal to the North Australian Workers Union (NAWU), which had already applied to the Federal Court for equal wages for Aboriginal workers. The Federal Court approved the granting of equal wages in March 1966, but it was not to take effect until December 1968.

Lingiari asked the Wave Hill management direct for equal wages but the request was refused and, on 23 August 1966, the Aboriginal stockmen walked off the station and camped in nearby Wattie Creek. They were soon joined by others. Before long, only stations which gave their Aboriginal workers not only good conditions, but also respect, were provided with workers by Lingiari and the other Gurindji Elders.

The Wattie Creek camp gained a lot of local support, from both Aboriginal and non-Aboriginal people, and it soon developed into a sizable community with housing and a degree of organisation.

Having gained the right to be paid equally, Lingiari and the Gurindji people felt, perhaps for the first time since the arrival of the pastoralists, that they had some say in the way they were able to live. This victory led to the hope that perhaps they could achieve something even more important: title to their own land. To this end Lingiari travelled widely in the eastern states campaigning for land rights, and finally made some progress with the Whitlam Government in Canberra. On 16 August 1975, Prime Minister Gough Whitlam attended a ceremony at Wattie Creek which saw the handing over of 3200 sq km of land, now known as Daguragu.

Lingiari was awarded the Order of Australia Medal for service to the Aboriginal people, and died at Daguragu in 1988.

The story has a short postscript: late in December 1998 secret government documents on the Wave Hill Strike were made public for the first time. They revealed that the government feared the strikers were being infiltrated by communists.

NORTHERN TERRITORY

afternoon trips to the Devil's Marbles for $55.50, including a barbecue dinner.

The Tourist's Rest Tennant Creek Hostel (☎ 8962 2719, e trest@topend.com.au) runs trips out to the Devil's Marbles for $60 including a night's dorm accommodation. These operate from June to October.

Cultural Centres

Anyinginyi Congress, a local Aboriginal health organisation, runs a cultural centre (☎ 8962 2593, e artgallery@swtch.com .au) at 1 Irvine St where you can watch local craftsmen making boomerangs and other wooden objects. The centre also hosts

changing exhibitions of work by Aboriginal artists from all over the NT. It's open 10 am to 5 pm Tuesday to Friday.

At the time of writing, the Julalikari Council (☎ 8962 2699) was about to start the construction of a meeting place in Paterson St, just north of the ATSIC office. Stage 1, to be open by July 2001, is to include an arid zone ethno-botanical garden, two traditional dance rings (performance areas), an arts and crafts shop, and a cafe. It's proposed that men's and women's dance troupes will hold public performances there. Stage 2 will have displays on the history and culture of the Warumungu people.

WHY DOTS?

Ever since Aboriginal 'dot style' painting became flavour of the month in the early 1970s, the most asked question has been, 'Why dots?' Many scientific and arty reasons have been put forward by learned scholars who all believe passionately in their respective theories. But to get a practical answer you have to look at the actual art practice.

The dot painting movement began with the association of a young school teacher named Geoffrey Bardon and senior Aborigines of the Papunya community in central Australia. From what was essentially a learning tool to teach the community's children about their magnificent cultural heritage, dot painting became a world-famous modern art movement. But why dots? This is where it really gets interesting! One of the most impressive aspects of central Australian Aboriginal art is the little known practice of 'ground painting' or technically, art *construction* of ochre-coloured vegetable matter, which is used to create elaborate designs upon the earth that also appear as the imagery on dot paintings. This rarely practised cultural activity is created for teaching and other social purposes, and when Bardon asked senior Aboriginal people in the community to create images for teaching on the Papunya school walls, little did they know that within their lifetimes, most of these artists would be

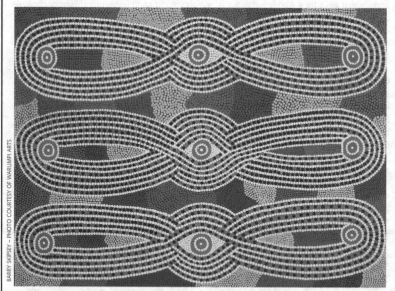

BARRY SKIPSEY – PHOTO COURTESY OF WARUMPI ARTS

Men's Ceremony by Paddy Carroll Tjungerai. Dot painting is one of the most recognisable forms of contemporary Indigenous art.

Courses

The Papulu Apparr-Kari Language Centre (☎ 8962 3270, fax 8962 1380, e papak @tennant-creek-high.nt.edu.au) at 17 Windley St runs one-day workshops in cultural awareness. Visitors are welcome to attend, and the cost is $50 including lunch. It also has a course that includes an overnight camping trip and a visit to a sacred site with Warumungu Elders, who teach about local culture – there may even be a *corroboree* (ceremonial gathering). This costs $80 and includes meals, but you must provide your own swag.

continued...

Peter Yanada McKenzie

as collectible as any of the old masters of European art. The creation of ground paintings begins with the gathering of raw materials, ochres from the earth and plant material from a local bush known as *womalu*. The leaves have a soft fleshy texture which, when chopped up with a tomahawk, resembles the soft material used in futon mattresses. The womalu is coloured with ochre and the ground is prepared by sweeping up loose dirt with a 'bush broom'. Water is spread all over the required area to obtain a smooth surface when dry. The *kurdu* (design's 'owner') directs the *kurdu-langus* (helpers) in the way the design should be created.

Now for the logical answer to the famous question, 'Why dots?' When workers actually put the material on the surface of the earth, they very delicately place a small section held between their fingers in position and gently pat it down. To assist the material sticking to the earth, water or human blood may be used. The ceremony is accompanied by a cultural performance from the person who is responsible for the *story*. Placing the plant material with fingers on a ground painting is replaced by acrylic paint being gently dropped onto prepared canvas by such devices as the end of a paintbrush, a cotton bud or simply a brush with the hairs almost cut off. The mystery of 'Why dots?' is answered simply by the observation that cultural transfer of imagery from traditional earth-borne art materials to modern acrylic and canvas is practised with the same delicate manner as the original ground paintings!

See also the Visual Art special section.

Peter Yanada McKenzie

Peter Yanada McKenzie is an Aboriginal man from the historic La Perouse Aboriginal community in Sydney. He is a former university lecturer in Australian Aboriginal art, culture and history. His other callings have included commercial and fine artist, photographer, jewellery designer, songwriter and musician.

Peter has worked as an exhibition developer on a social history project about his community, La Perouse, for the Powerhouse Museum in Sydney and has curated an international Aboriginal art presentation at the Centre Georges Pompadour in Paris for the major exhibition *Magiciens de la Terre* in 1989.

Peter was awarded an Aboriginal overseas study award in 1982 and attended Clark University in Worcester, Massachusetts, USA. He has a Master of Fine Art degree from the University of New South Wales and was a Fulbright scholar to the USA in 1994. Peter is the designer of the national label of authenticity which was set up by the Australia Council to protect Aboriginal artists' copyright matters.

He has recently curated an exhibition of urban Aboriginal art at the Boomalli Aboriginal Artists Gallery in Sydney, prior to taking up PhD study in Aboriginal history and music at Macquarie University.

Special Events

The Desert Harmony Festival of Arts & Culture, held every year over eight days in late September, has Aboriginal participation in such diverse areas as poetry reading, traditional dance and rock-band performances. Contact the Tennant Creek Town Council (☎ 8962 2401) for a program and festival dates.

Shopping

Anyinginyi Congress also owns and operates Anyinginyi Arts (☎ 8962 2593), a good arts and crafts shop on Paterson St near the transit centre. The works on display – and there is some great art at very reasonable prices – are produced by artists from the surrounding Barkly region, which stretches from the Barkly Tableland to Barrow Creek. As well as paintings on canvas there are also items such as didjeridus, weapons, T-shirts, Aboriginal music (CDs and tapes) and much more. The shop is open weekdays and Saturday mornings during normal business hours.

THE PEBBLES
Twelve kilometres north of Tennant Creek is the turn-off west to The Pebbles (known to Aboriginal people as Kundjarra), a formation of granite boulders like a miniaturised version of the better-known Devil's Marbles. This is a women's sacred site but it's OK to go there; Anyinginyi Congress in Tennant Creek has received a government grant to provide information signs.

DEVIL'S MARBLES
The Devil's Marbles Conservation Reserve, 110km south of Tennant Creek, features numerous outcrops of large red boulders scattered over the floor of a shallow valley – its Aboriginal name, Karlwe Karlwe, means 'Round Objects'. This striking area is rich in the Creation stories of the Alyawarre, Anmatyerre, Kaytej and Warumungu people. There are many caves under the rocks that form the homes of ancestral beings.

Organised tours to Karlwe Karlwe leave from Tennant Creek – see the Organised Tours entry earlier for details.

Anmatyerre Country
North of Alice Springs

TI TREE
The small town of Ti Tree, 193km north of Alice Springs, is a service centre for surrounding Aboriginal communities as well as for travellers on the Stuart Hwy.

Skull Creek, 15km north of town, was the scene of a massacre of Aborigines by a police-led 'punitive' expedition in 1874. This and other killings – mainly of innocent people – were in reprisal for the fatal spearing of two white men by Kaytej warriors at the Barrow Creek Telegraph Station.

Shopping
Along from the roadhouse, the friendly Aaki Gallery has some beautiful work by local Anmatyerre people. On display are dot paintings, weapons, decorated objects (tapping sticks, wooden dishes and the like) and seed necklaces, all at very competitive prices. The shop is open 8.30 am to 5 pm daily except Wednesday.

Over the road, Red Sand has a large selection of good-quality arts and crafts produced by Anmatyerre people, as well as artists from the Utopia area. The shop has many dot paintings (from $35), decorated didjeridus (from $80) and carved wooden objects. It also has souvenir lines such as T-shirts, sarongs, postcards and place mats – these all feature Aboriginal motifs. It's open 8 am to 7 pm daily, and you can often watch artists at work.

NATIVE GAP
On the boundary between Anmatyerre and Northern Arrernte country, the Native Gap Conservation Reserve is a rest stop on the Stuart Hwy 110km north of Alice Springs. Arulte Artwatye – the name means 'Back of the shoulder gap' referring to the shape of nearby hills – is a registered sacred site associated with the deeds of a Carpet Snake Ancestor. A sign near the picnic area gives more information. Camping is not permitted here.

Alyawarre Country
North-East of Alice Springs

As elsewhere in the Outback, the loss of food resources and the fouling of precious water supplies by cattle caused bloody conflicts between pastoralists and Aborigines. The so-called Sandover Massacre of the 1920s resulted in the deaths of about 100 Alyawarre, either shot or poisoned for cattle-spearing.

ARLPARRA
Arlparra is an Aboriginal community on the Sandover Hwy about 250km north-east of Alice Springs. It's the administrative and service centre for the communities on Utopia station, which is now owned by local Aboriginal people.

Art Gallery
Near the community store, Urapuntja Artists (☎ 8956 9506) represents 130 local

artists, including a number of national and international repute. The work on display generally includes paintings on linen, pastels on paper, limited-edition prints, batik and wooden sculptures – you can see examples in the Desart shop in Alice Springs. You need an entry permit to visit and this can best be arranged through the art centre.

Warlpiri Country

Tanami Desert

YUENDUMU

The Aboriginal community of Yuendumu, with a population of around 850, is just off the Tanami Rd about 300km north-west of Alice Springs. It's by far the largest settlement between Alice and Halls Creek in WA.

You don't need a permit to travel on the Tanami Rd or visit the town's commercial facilities, but as elsewhere it is forbidden to go sightseeing around the community.

Yuendumu Festival

Every year on the long weekend in August, the town hosts the three-day Yuendumu Festival, a major sporting carnival for Aboriginal people from all over the Western Desert region. While the emphasis is on team sports – mainly Australian Rules football and softball – other activities such as spear-throwing and a 'battle of the bands' also take place.

Visitors are welcome and no permits are required to visit the town over this weekend. However, there is no accommodation, so you'll need to bring camping gear and be prepared to rough it. Note that alcohol is prohibited.

Shopping

Yuendumu has a thriving art community, and the work put out by the Warlukurlangu Artists art centre (☎ 8956 4031, ℮ warlu @oze.com.au) is highly regarded both nationally and internationally. The centre, which represents around 160 artists, specialises in large collaborative paintings on canvas – these cost upwards of $10,000 a piece – and fine art acrylics; all major works come with a certificate of authentication. Also on display are limited-edition prints and traditional carved objects. Warlukurlangu Artists has a unique painting style, with bold patterns and vivid colours.

You don't need a permit to visit the art centre (get directions at the community store), but it would be wise to ring ahead before making a special trip. It is open most weekdays and you can usually watch artists at work. It has a Web site at www.warlu.com.

Arrernte Country

Alice Springs Area

The Arrernte people are divided into five subgroups (Central, Northern, Southern, Eastern and Western) based on dialect. The traditional country of the Central Arrernte (the smallest subgroup) is centred on Alice Springs.

ALICE SPRINGS

To the Central Arrernte people, most of the landforms in and around Mparntwe (the site of Alice Springs) were created by three distinctive groups of Caterpillar Ancestors that met and held ceremonies there. One group (the Utnerrengetye) had travelled from Mt Zeil, far to the west, while the others (the Ntyarlke and Yeperenye) had come from Emily Gap in the east. Many local Arrernte consider themselves to be direct descendants of these Caterpillar beings.

About 20% of the town's population of 27,000 is of Aboriginal descent.

Information

Indigenous Organisations The Central Land Council's head office (☎ 8951 6320, fax 8953 4345) is at 31–33 Stuart Hwy, about 1km north of the town centre. ATSIC's regional office (☎ 8959 4211) is in the Commonwealth Building at 54 Hartley St. Both are open weekdays during normal business hours.

Tourist Offices The Central Australian Tourism Industry Association (CATIA; ☎ 1800 645 199, 8952 5800, fax 8953 0295, ℮ visinfo@catia.asn.au) is on Gregory Terrace in the centre of town. The helpful staff can direct you to most Aboriginal tours and attractions in and around town. It also issues permits to travel on the Mereenie Loop Rd to Watarrka (Kings Canyon). The office is open 8.30 am to 5.30 pm weekdays, and 9 am to 4 pm on weekends and public holidays.

CATIA's information desk at the airport is open for most major incoming flights.

NORTHERN TERRITORY

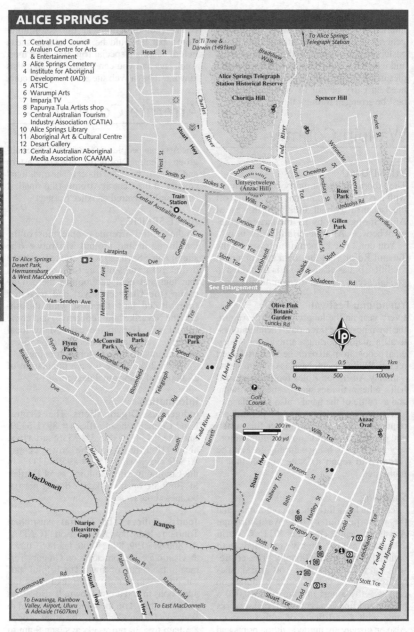

ALICE SPRINGS

1 Central Land Council
2 Araluen Centre for Arts & Entertainment
3 Alice Springs Cemetery
4 Institute for Aboriginal Development (IAD)
5 ATSIC
6 Warumpi Arts
7 Imparja TV
8 Papunya Tula Artists shop
9 Central Australian Tourism Industry Association (CATIA)
10 Alice Springs Library
11 Aboriginal Art & Cultural Centre
12 Desart Gallery
13 Central Australian Aboriginal Media Association (CAAMA)

The Northern Territory Parks & Wildlife Service (☎ 8951 8211), which maintains a desk inside the CATIA office, produces a comprehensive range of brochures and leaflets on all the parks and reserves in the Centre.

Libraries The Alice Springs Library (☎ 8952 2303), on Gregory Terrace next to the tourist office, has a good selection of Indigenous-related books, including a special central Australia collection. The library is open 10 am to 6 pm weekdays (to 5 pm Wednesday and Friday), 9 am to 1 pm on Saturday, and 1 to 5 pm on Sunday.

ATSIC's regional office has a small library; you can browse through its periodicals and reports between 8 am and 4.30 pm weekdays.

Books & Maps *The Arrernte Landscape* by David Brooks is an illustrated guide with maps to the Creation stories and sites of Mparntwe. *Bush Foods – Arrernte Foods from Central Australia* by Margaret-Mary Turner shows how Aboriginal people obtain sustenance in an arid environment.

IAD Press publishes the language guides *A Learner's Wordlist of Eastern & Central Arrernte*, *A Learner's Guide to Eastern & Central Arrernte* and the comprehensive *Eastern & Central Arrernte to English Dictionary*. Eastern and Central Arrernte, which have over 1500 speakers, are both spoken in and around Alice Springs. IAD's *Introductory Dictionary of Western Arrernte* includes quite a bit of cultural information.

Also from IAD Press is the *Central Australian Languages Colour Map*, which covers the immediate area around Alice Springs.

Radio & TV CAAMA Radio broadcasts 18 hours a day on 8KIN 100.5 FM, while Imparja provides a TV service to the town.

Organised Tours

A large number of tours operate out of Alice Springs and the tourist office can provide details. The following are tours that relate directly to Aboriginal people.

Oak Valley Tours (☎ 8956 0959) is an Aboriginal-owned and -run organisation based in Alice Springs that does a day trip to Ewaninga, Mpwellare, Oak Valley and Rainbow Valley, all of cultural significance to Arrernte people. The cost is $121 including a barbecue lunch. It also does extended tours for small groups (maximum nine passengers) to places as far afield as Uluru.

The Aboriginal Art & Culture Centre (☎ 8952 3408, e aborart@oze.com.au), 86–88 Todd St, has a four-hour morning tour for $82.50 (children $44) which makes an excellent introduction to Aboriginal culture and contemporary issues. Non-Indigenous Australians will find some of the topics discussed – such as the sorry history of race relations in Australia, and what it's like to be forced to live in two worlds – to be thought-provoking, if not confronting. The tour includes a 1½-hour bushwalk to find bush tucker and medicine, an explanation of Aboriginal religion and a performance of traditional dancing – you might even learn to sing a song in Pitjantjatjara. Minimum numbers may apply on the bushwalk.

The culture centre also runs a day tour for groups (minimum five people) which incorporates the morning tour and a visit to the Alice Springs Desert Park. As well, it offers an evening performance and three-course dinner for $79 (children $45), including transport. Check its Web site at www.aboriginalart.com.au.

Central Arrernte Elder Oopy Campbell runs a morning culture tour at his Angateyepe homeland 17km west of Alice Springs. The tour, which is highly recommended, includes a scenic 1.6km bushwalk on which Oopy shows you traditional shelters and talks about his Dreaming. During morning tea of billy tea and damper you learn about such topics as Central Arrernte history, the kinship system and what Reconciliation means to local Aboriginal people. The tour finishes with lessons in spear- and boomerang-throwing. You can make a booking by contacting Oopy on ☎ 8955 1197 or ring his agent Linda in Alice Springs on ☎ 8953 4015, the price of $60 (children $30) includes return transport from town.

Visual Arts & Specialist Tours (VAST; ☎ 8952 8233, e pyates@vast.com.au) takes small groups to remote Aboriginal communities and rock art sites that are otherwise off-limits. The cost is $1500 per group per day (maximum seven passengers), including permits, camping equipment and meals. Check out its Web site at www.vast.com.au.

Air Tours Among its offerings, which include charters to Uluru and Watarrka, Personalised Scenic Flights (☎ 8952 4625, e australianoutbackflights@aopa.com.au) does a day or overnight trip to Patjarr in the Western Desert country. This is a great opportunity to learn something of the

NORTHERN TERRITORY

ALICE SPRINGS GALLERIES, MUSEUMS & SHOPS

Readers should be aware that the names of deceased members of the Aboriginal community may be cited in this section. Mentioning the personal name of someone who has died recently can cause offence, anguish and grief in some Aboriginal cultures.

Alice Springs has many shops and galleries selling Aboriginal art and crafts, all mostly concentrated in and around the Todd Mall in the centre of town. Following is a selection.

Aboriginal Art & Cultural Centre (☎ 8952 3408) 86 Todd St. This should be the first place you visit in Alice Springs. This multi-award-winning centre is a fully Aboriginal-owned and -operated enterprise, established by the Southern Arrernte people's Pwert Marnte Marnte Aboriginal Corporation. This is also one of the very few places where an Aboriginal person will be behind the counter. The friendly and knowledgeable Arrernte staff here are very helpful. The shop and gallery have a good range of items available and prices are reasonable. Didjeridus are from $60 for a small one to $400 for a large one. The music sticks (clapsticks) are a good buy at $20 for small, $25 for medium and $30 for large, from a variety of attractive plain and painted ones. Beautiful unstretched canvases by Warlpiri, Arrernte and Ali Curung artists are from $250 to $750. Attractive framed watercolour landscapes by Peter Taylor, a Southern Arrernte artist, are $1250 (ask if discounts are available). There are intricately painted, carved wood *coolamons* from $175 and Walkatjara T-shirts are $40. Check out the B Kngwarreye hand-painted ceramic oil burners and candle pots for $40. His leaf bowls are also eye-catching and a good buy at $70. If ceramics are too fragile to carry, consider the very nice mounted mini-prints on cards by some prominent painters such as Warlpiri artist Michael Nelson Jagamara and Alyawarre artist Freddie Jones Kngwarreye; at only $20 these would make ideal gifts. There is a popular didj 'school' here ($11 for one hour) where everyone 'graduates'. Inquire for times. There is also an interesting living history museum display, which includes historical artefacts recently returned by the South Australian Museum – look for the fascinating emu-feather Kadaitja shoes. The centre is open 8 am to 5 pm weekdays, and to 2 pm weekends.
Web site: www.aboriginalart.com.au

Araluen Arts Centre (☎ 8951 1120) Larapinta Drive. This is also the town's performing arts centre and has some interesting Aboriginal elements incorporated into the building. Outside on the eastern wall is a huge mural designed by noted artist Clifford Possum Tjapaltjari. In five sections, the painting depicts ground- and body-painting designs used for various ceremonies such as the important Yerrampe Jukurrpa (Honey Ant Dreaming) and men's and women's Jukurrpa (Dreaming). Although it's looking a bit faded these days and could do with a touch-up, it's still worth a look.

In the centre's foyer is a large stained-glass window designed by another noted artist, Wenten Rubuntja. In three *stories* are depicted the Mparntwe Dreamings of the Arrernte people and their country around Alice Springs. The smallest stained-glass windows were designed and made by Aboriginal students from Yirara College, a local secondary school for Aboriginal students. Inside, the permanent Albert Namatjira Gallery highlights the life of this eminent artist, and that of his mentor Rex Battarbee. There are some interesting historical paintings (1925–1972) and displays that will give you a good background to the Hermannsburg school of painting. The centre's main gallery has a changing exhibition program, often with major Aboriginal art shows. The centre is open 10 am to 5 pm daily (closed Christmas Day and Good Friday); admission is $7.
Web site: www.nt.gov.au/dam

CAAMA Shop (☎ 8952 9207) 101 Todd St. This shop is in the Central Australian Aboriginal Media Association (CAAMA) building. CAAMA and the shop are Aboriginal-owned and -operated enterprises. You'll find a small but good range of authentic products at reasonable prices. There are nice hand-painted T-shirts ($38.50), beautifully painted wooden tissue-box holders ($250) and smaller boxes (from $42.95). The Mutijulu Warka painted

continued...   Gary Lee

ceramics are very attractive with small bowls ($22) and plates ($18.50). Woven Ininti seed place mats ($260) catch the eye, though the Ininti jewellery might better suit your budget, with necklaces for $17.60 and bracelets $16, some with gum nuts. The range of traditional and contemporary Aboriginal CDs and cassettes is probably the best in town; many are produced and recorded by CAAMA. There is also a very good selection of books on central Australian Aboriginal art, Indigenous social and cultural issues, history and politics. The CAAMA shop is open 9 am to 5 pm weekdays, and to 2 pm on Saturday.
Web site: www.caama.com.au

Desart Gallery (☎ 8953 4736) corner of Stott Terrace and Bath St. This is another Aboriginal-owned and -controlled place that's well worth visiting. Desart is the Association of Central Australian Aboriginal Arts and Crafts Centres, selling and exhibiting beautiful works by its member artists and art centres. The quality products are well priced for all budgets. Keringke Arts, part of the Ltyentye Apurte (Santa Teresa) community, is well represented here. Their desert-oak-framed acrylics on paper start at $440, ceramic fruit bowls are $180 and beautiful silk scarves are just $45. The woven spinifex baskets from Ernabella are from $66 to $210 and there is a good selection of striking Desart T-shirts by Michael Nelson Jagamara, Freddie Jones Kngwarreye and Thawinyti Williamson, Ilyipi Terone and Evelyn Nungurrayi for a reasonable $30. Ask to see the magnificent, individually hand-painted desert gum-nut hanging screen by Pantjiti Tjiangu of Ernabella, a steal at $1320. Artists work at the large studio attached to the gallery, and you can visit and talk or watch them at work. The gallery has regular monthly exhibitions always worth checking; phone for details. Opening hours are 10 am to 4 pm Monday to Saturday.
Web site: www.desart.com.au

Janganpa Artists (☎ 8953 6111). This group of male Warlpiri and Anmatyerre artists, traditional dancers and singers is represented by Desart, where they utilise the attached studio. Visitors are very welcome to visit and watch the artists who are working here, so it's worth phoning Desart to find out which artists are working. Hours are the same as Desart's.
Web site: www.desart.com.au

Jukurrpa Studio and Gallery (☎ 8953 1052). This is a collective of women artists from a diversity of language groups. Also represented through Desart, they work out of the studio at specific times, which you can find out by phoning ahead or just dropping in at Desart. You can buy directly from the artists here and talk about your purchases. Hours are the same as Desart's.
Web site: www.desart.com.au

Papunya Tula Artists (☎ 8952 4731) 78 Todd St. This long-established shop deals with the fine-art end of the market. It represents artists from Papunya. Prices reflect the high quality of paintings on offer and all the well-known and emerging artists are represented. If you're looking for an investment piece or a big-budget item, this is the place to come. Even if you're not buying, it's worth a visit to see some fine examples of central Australian art. Gallery hours are 9 am to 5 pm weekdays, and 10 am to 2 pm Saturday.
Web site: www.papunyatula.com

Warumpi Arts (☎ 8952 9066) Shop 7, 105 Gregory Terrace. This small shop and gallery sells mainly paintings by artists from Papunya and those from there living in Alice Springs. It is Aboriginal-owned and -controlled, although no Aboriginal people work here. Papunya is visited regularly and the shop works directly with the artists there. Mostly unstretched canvases are on offer, but the variety is good and there are some prominent artists' works available – Dinny Nolan, Long Jack Phillipus, Don Tjungarai, Topsy Napaltjara, Emma Nungarai and Eurawi Nungala, to mention a few. Small acrylics on canvas are $22, larger ones $800 to $1400, with linen ones from $100 to $200. First-edition prints cost around $200. The shop is open 10 am to 5 pm weekdays, and to 2 pm Saturday.
Web site: www.warumpi.com.au

NORTHERN TERRITORY

lifestyle and culture of a small, isolated Aboriginal community.

Another interesting option is to join a mail run to remote communities west of Alice with the Aboriginal-owned airline Ngurratjuta Air (☎ 8953 5000). Half-day flights ($242) depart Tuesday and Thursday and full-day flights ($352 including lunch) leave on Wednesday and Friday.

Cultural Centre

The IAD (☎ 8951 1311), Web site: www.iad.edu.au/iad, at 3 South Terrace has a Language & Cultural Centre, one of whose main roles is to promote the Aboriginal cultures of central Australia to Indigenous and non-Indigenous peoples. It does this through its language and cultural-awareness courses; visitors unable to take the courses are welcome to drop in and meet the staff, who will be happy to answer questions.

IAD Press – the publishing arm of IAD – and its trade imprint Jukurrpa Books mainly publish works by Indigenous writers and artists. Its numerous titles include such fields as language, culture, oral history, natural history, art, fiction, autobiographies, Aboriginal issues and cross-cultural information. IAD Press (☎ 8951 1334, e iadpress@ozemail .com.au), also at 3 South Terrace, has a bookshop (see Books & Maps earlier for details of some of its publications).

Parks & Gardens

Untyeyetweleye (Anzac Hill) This is a good spot to orientate yourself as the lookout on top of the hill gives a great view of the town centre and surrounding hills and ranges. To Arrernte people the hill is linked with several ancestors including a Corkwood-Woman whose spirit lives in the ground here. Signs at the lookout give the totemic associations of 13 cultural sites, including **Alhekulyele** (Mt Gillen), which dominates the view westward. This striking feature is the nose of a Dingo Ancestor that travelled to Alice Springs from the Simpson Desert.

Alice Springs Desert Park

About 3km out of town along Larapinta Drive, the Alice Springs Desert Park (☎ 8951 8788) is a superb wildlife park at the foot of the MacDonnell Ranges. The 1300-hectare park features the major ecosystems of central Australia and how Aboriginal people relate to them. This is reinforced by the free short talks (around 20 to 30 minutes) and demonstrations given by Aboriginal guides at various venues throughout the day.

The park is open 7.30 am to 6 pm daily (closed Christmas Day), with the last entries at 5.30 pm – you'll need around three hours for a good look. Entry costs $18 (children $9).

Olive Pink Botanic Garden

On Tuncks Rd about 1km south-east of the town centre, this 16-hectare garden features the native plants that grow within a 500km radius of Alice Springs. It honours Olive Pink, who was the garden's first curator and a great advocate for Aboriginal rights.

There is a lot of information on the Aboriginal use of plants on displays in the visitor centre and scattered through the garden. A sign on top of **Thararletneme** (Meyers Hill), where there's a good view, gives the totemic associations between local Arrernte people and several landmarks in and around town. The lookout point is on the head of a Ntyarlke caterpillar.

The garden is open 10 am to 6 pm daily (closed Christmas Day and Good Friday).

Albert Namatjira's Grave

You'll find the final resting place of the great Western Arrernte watercolourist on the southern side of the Alice Springs Cemetery, off Memorial Drive. The headstone – of red sandstone – features a terracotta tile mural of three of Namatjira's ancestral Dreaming sites in the MacDonnell Ranges. The tiles forming the mural were moulded and glazed by his granddaughter, Elaine, a member of the Hermannsburg Potters (see the Ntaria entry later in this chapter).

Courses

The Institute for Aboriginal Development (see Cultural Centre earlier) has been running courses in local Indigenous languages for about 20 years. The languages taught include Arrernte, Pitjantjatjara and Warlpiri, and all courses involve traditional language speakers of the area – this is a great way to learn about culture as well. Introductory courses run for 30 hours and are offered either as a one-week block, or over weekends or evenings. The courses cost $330 and are run according to demand.

Special Events

Desert Mob Art Show Held each year in September/October, the critically acclaimed Desert Mob Art Show at the Araluen Centre for Arts & Entertainment on Larapinta Drive displays the recent work of over 30 central Australian Aboriginal art centres. The works of new as well as internationally recognised artists are shown, and you can purchase these direct from the centres. Featured are exhibits from well-known organisations such as the Hermannsburg Potters, Papunya Tula Artists, Keringke Arts and Utopia Awely Batik.

Beanie Festival While the Desert Mob Art Show is serious stuff, the Beanie Festival at the Araluen Centre is a hands-on fun event featuring beanies (woven hats designed for warmth) and anything else made from fibre and fabric. You can watch Aboriginal women using traditional spinning techniques to make yarn from just about anything that's spinnable: unwashed sheep's wool, kangaroo fur, camel hair, human hair, emu feathers, budgie feathers! Then they crochet the beanies – emu-feather beanies are popular with visitors, but if you're from overseas, check that you'll be allowed to take them home. Other activities include demonstrations of basket-weaving using spinifex (a spiky desert grass), and a fashion parade featuring Aboriginal-made fabrics and batik.

The festival takes place each year over four days on the first weekend in July. It has a Web site (www.beaniefest.calliejo.com).

NAIDOC Week Held in the first week of July, NAIDOC kicks off on Monday with a street march and flag-raising ceremony. The format changes every year, but you can generally count on enjoying Indigenous bands, cultural activities and art exhibitions, as well as sports carnivals. Contact ATSIC on ☎ 8959 4211 for a program.

Sports Events Aboriginal athleticism and football skills are on display at the Easter Lightning Carnival, which is contested by 25 Aussie Rules teams (20 of them Aboriginal) from communities from as far away as the Top End and WA. It's held annually over the Easter long weekend at Traeger Park.

There's also a winter Aussie Rules competition involving eight teams from Aboriginal communities outside Alice Springs. You can watch the action at Traeger Park every Saturday between mid-April and mid-September.

HARTS RANGE

On the Plenty Hwy about 220km north-east of Alice Springs, the Atitjere Aboriginal community is close to Mt Palmer, one of the most popular gem-fossicking areas in the Harts Range.

The Atitjere Community Store (☎ 8956 9773) operates a basic but attractive bush camping ground where sites cost $5 per person.

EMILY GAP

Following the Ross Hwy east of the Stuart Hwy for 10km, you arrive at Emily Gap (Anthwerrke to Central Arrernte people), the first of two scenic gaps in Emily & Jesse Gaps Nature Park. A registered sacred site, this is one of the most important Creation sites in the Alice Springs area – it was from here that many of the Caterpillar ancestral beings of Mparntwe originated. Low down on the cliff-face inside the gorge are some faded red-and-white paintings depicting the Caterpillar story.

CORROBOREE ROCK

Known to the Eastern Arrernte people as Antanangantana, Corroboree Rock is the main feature of Corroboree Rock Conservation Reserve, 43km from Alice Springs. A registered sacred site, this unusual dog-toothed outcrop is associated with a Perentie (large, dark-coloured monitor lizard) Ancestor of the Eastern Arrernte people; a small cave in the rock was once used as a storehouse for sacred objects. Despite the name, it is doubtful if the rock was ever used as a corroboree area, as there is no surface water in the vicinity.

A short walking track leads from the car park around the base of the rock.

N'DHALA GORGE

The N'Dhala Gorge Nature Park, 90km east of Alice Springs, is another important religious site for the Eastern Arrernte people.

NORTHERN TERRITORY

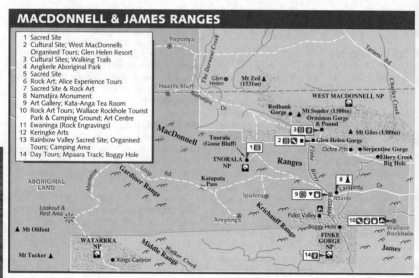

MACDONNELL & JAMES RANGES

1 Sacred Site
2 Cultural Site; West MacDonnells
   Organised Tours; Glen Helen Resort
3 Cultural Sites; Walking Trails
4 Angkerle Aboriginal Park
5 Sacred Site
6 Rock Art; Alice Experience Tours
7 Sacred Site & Rock Art
8 Namatjira Monument
9 Art Gallery; Kata-Anga Tea Room
10 Rock Art Tours; Wallace Rockhole Tourist
   Park & Camping Ground; Art Centre
11 Ewaninga (Rock Engravings)
12 Keringke Arts
13 Rainbow Valley Sacred Site; Organised
   Tours; Camping Area
14 Day Tours; Mpaara Track; Boggy Hole

This deep, rugged gorge, known as Irlwentye to Eastern Arrernte people, contains thousands of rock engravings, as well as painting sites and rock shelters. The engravings, most of which probably date from within the past 2000 years, are of two styles: pounded and finely pecked. Designs include concentric circles, animal tracks and human figures.

You'll see some engravings along the 1km walking track that leads from the car park and camping area into the main gorge. The final 10km of the access road is 4WD only.

Organised Tours
Road conditions permitting, Alice Experience Tours (☎ 1800 803 174) includes N'Dhala Gorge on its 4WD trips into the East MacDonnell Ranges. The tour costs $89 (children $62).

LTYENTYE APURTE
About 80km south-east of Alice Springs, the Eastern Arrernte community of Ltyentye Apurte (Santa Teresa; population 500) had its beginnings when the Catholic mission of Santa Teresa was established here in the 1950s. Prior to that, the present town area was a sacred rainmaking site.

Shopping
Ltyentye Apurte has a busy art community, and Keringke Arts – an association of local women – has a very good reputation for its unique contemporary designs and vibrantly colourful style. The art centre (☎ 8956 0956, ⓔ keringke_arts@yahoo. com) normally displays a range of high-quality arts and crafts, including acrylics on canvas, hand-painted silks and ceramics, and decorated wooden objects, all available at discount prices. Most times you can watch artists at work.

It's possible to visit (weekdays only), but first you need to arrange a permit with the art centre. Examples of the centre's work can be seen at the Desart shop in Alice Springs, or you can check out its Web site at www.aboriginalaustralia.com.au.

EWANINGA ROCK CARVINGS
The Ewaninga Conservation Reserve, 39km out of Alice on the rough and dusty Old South Rd, protects Aboriginal rock engravings on a small outcrop of sandstone. Senior Eastern Arrernte custodians of the site say that the meaning of the symbols is sacred and too dangerous to reveal to the uninitiated.

The Aboriginal-owned Oak Valley Tours visits Ewaninga on its day trip to Rainbow Valley (see Organised Tours in the Alice Springs section).

OAK VALLEY
The small Oak Valley Aboriginal community is between the old and new Ghan railway

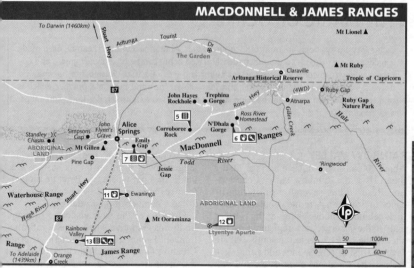

MACDONNELL & JAMES RANGES

crossings on the Hugh River Stock Route, about 100km from Alice Springs. It operates day tours out of Alice Springs, but there's also a 2½-hour local tour taking in rock art and fossil sites and delving into bush tucker ($17; children $8.50). Phone ☎ 8956 0959 for more information.

There's a pleasant camping ground with hot showers, toilets, shade shelters and barbecues (firewood supplied). The cost is $7 per person.

CHAMBERS PILLAR

Chambers Pillar Historical Reserve is 160km from Alice Springs via the Old South Rd and Maryvale Station. Itirkawara, the main attraction, is a red-and-yellow sandstone column that rises 50m above the sand plain. This striking feature is an important Dreaming site for the Southern Arrernte people, and was a landmark for early non-Aboriginal travellers.

Itirkawara was a Knob-Tailed Gecko Ancestor with great strength and a violent temper. In one incident he killed a number of other ancestors with his stone knife, then flouted the law by taking a girl of the wrong skin group to be his bride. The pair were banished to the desert where both turned to stone – Itirkawara became the pillar and the girl became **Castle Rock**, about 500m away.

There's a basic camping ground with toilet and fireplaces, but you need to bring water and firewood. A 4WD is required for the last 44km from the turn-off at Maryvale Station homestead.

NT Luxury Day Tours (☎ 8952 7751, ℮ info@ntluxurydaytours.com.au) and The Outback Experience (☎ 8953 2666, ℮ 4wdtours@outbackexperience.com.au) visit Itirkawara for $155.

APUTULA

Back on the Old South Road, you eventually arrive at Aputula (Finke), an isolated Southern Arrernte community by the Finke River 230km south of Alice Springs. The township started life as a railway siding on the old Ghan line and grew to have a white population of about 60 people. With the opening of the new Ghan line further west in 1982, administration of the town was taken over by Aboriginal people. These days the population is around 400, almost all of them Indigenous.

You do not need a permit if you just wish to pass through Aputula or make use of its commercial facilities.

The Aputula Store (☎ 8956 0968) has a selection of locally produced wooden crafts in stock. It's open 8.30 to 11.30 am and 1.30 to 4.30 pm weekdays, and Saturday morning.

THE MAGIC OF OCHRE

Ochre has always been an important commodity in Aboriginal culture. It can be used medicinally and is a valuable traditional trade item. Red ochre can be mixed with grease and eucalyptus leaves to form a decongestant balm; and it is said that white ochre has magical powers – it can be mixed with water and then blown from the mouth, a practice which is said to cool the sun and calm the wind. Ochre is also used extensively for body decoration and in painting.

RAINBOW VALLEY

About 100km south of Alice Springs via the Stuart Hwy, the Rainbow Valley Conservation Reserve has several sites of significance to Southern Arrernte people – a large rock behind Rainbow Valley, at the western end of the reserve, is a registered sacred site. In the rocky hills to the south-east are several art sites (engravings and paintings), rock shelters and old camp sites, and you may stumble across them while you're bushwalking in the area. Please remember not to disturb any artefacts.

Most of the time the area around Rainbow Valley looks harsh and lifeless, but after good rains filled the nearby claypan this became an important place for hunting and gathering. It gave the people a chance to 'rest' the country around the longer-lasting waterholes, and they would stay here until the claypan dried up again.

There is an exposed camping area near the claypan with pit toilets and gas barbecues.

Organised Tours

Tour companies visiting Rainbow Valley include Oak Valley Tours, which does a day trip for $121 (see Organised Tours in the Alice Springs section).

NT Luxury Day Tours and The Outback Experience visit Rainbow Valley for $135. See the earlier Chambers Pillar section for contact details.

Extended camel safaris from Camel Outback Safaris (☎ 8956 0925) at Stuart's Well also visit Rainbow Valley.

SIMPSONS GAP

Off Larapinta Drive about 23km from Alice Springs, Simpsons Gap (Tyunpe to Central Arrernte people) is the main attraction in Simpsons Gap National Park. The gap is linked to Perentie and Eagle Ancestors of the Central Arrernte people; a cluster of jagged rocks high up on its eastern side marks the spot where two Perentie brothers took revenge on some devil men who had killed a number of their relatives.

Displays at the park visitors centre and Simpsons Gap give some general information on Tnengkare (the Western Arrernte Creation Time), rock engravings, ochre and the Creation stories of Simpsons Gap. The park is open 5 am to 8 pm daily.

STANDLEY CHASM

Continuing west on Larapinta Drive, you cross Aboriginal land for the entire 29km between the Simpson Gap and Standley Chasm (Angkerle) turn-offs. The chasm, where there's an Aboriginal-run refreshment kiosk (☎ 8956 7440), is close to the boundary between Central and Western Arrernte country. The chasm's English name honours Ida Standley, who was the first schoolteacher in Alice Springs – her school for Aboriginal children was relocated to Jay Creek (Iwupataka), near the Standley Chasm turn-off on Larapinta Drive, in 1925.

Standley Chasm is open 8 am to 5 pm daily, and entry costs $5.

SERPENTINE GORGE

Off Namatjira Drive 93km from Alice Springs, Serpentine Gorge is watched over by Wedge-Tailed Eagle and Water Serpent Ancestors of the Western Arrernte people. This is a traditional sanctuary area for wildlife and plants – hunting and gathering is strictly prohibited here, as is swimming. Indeed, traditionally it is not even permitted to drink from the waterhole without first observing a strict ritual laid down by the Serpent Ancestor during the Creation Time.

OCHRE PITS

Continuing west along Namatjira Drive you come to the Ochre Pits, which has some interesting information signs relating to ochre (*ulpa* to the Western Arrernte) and its importance to Aboriginal people. Except for a small deposit of yellow ochre, which is still used today, the material at this minor quarry site is of poor quality.

ORMISTON GORGE

From the Ochre Pits it's a further 26km to Ormiston Gorge (Kwartetweme to Western Arrernte people), where the main waterhole is a registered sacred site associated with an Emu Ancestor. The area around the waterhole was once an important ceremonial ground. An interesting display in the visitors centre, which includes a dot painting and taped song, both by the site's traditional custodian, tells the story of the Emu's travels.

Most visitors congregate at the gorge entrance. For those who want to explore further afield, several walks that start and finish at the visitors centre are recommended. There's a small camping area nearby.

GLEN HELEN GORGE

Like other permanent waters in the West MacDonnell Ranges, the waterhole at the entrance to Glen Helen Gorge (Yapulpa) was a major drought refuge for the Western Arrernte. Glen Helen Gorge is linked to Itye, the Moon Man, who visited here while looking for a bride – he found one at the nearby Organ Pipes. An information sign on the walk down to the waterhole tells more about this story.

A **lookout** on Namatjira Drive on the western side of the Finke River (Lhere Pirnte) gives a fine view of **Mt Sonder** (Rwetyepme) to the north-west. This striking feature is linked to several totemic beings, the main one being a euro (a large species of wallaby) from the Western Desert. You can walk up to the summit from **Redbank Gorge**, but the traditional custodians ask that you don't camp on top or light fires there. Displays at the Redbank Gorge car park talk about the Euro Ancestor, and Albert Namatjira.

Organised Tours

Centremen Tours (☎ 8952 6708) visits Glen Helen Gorge and other attractions in the West MacDonnell Ranges on its day tours ($76) from Alice Springs. Sahara Outback Tours (☎ 1800 806 240, e sahara @saharatours.com.au) includes Glen Helen Gorge on its five-day camping tour to Uluru, Watarrka, Wallace Rockhole and the West MacDonnell Ranges.

Places to Stay

The Aboriginal-owned Glen Helen Resort (☎ 8956 7489, bookings ☎ 1800 896 110) is in a spectacular setting by the Finke River 500m from the gorge. It has basic rooms with shared facilities sleeping up to four people for $76 ($66 summer low-season), or more upmarket motel-style units costing $143 ($121 summer low-season). Alternatively, you can camp ($18/22 unpowered/ powered for doubles); the camping ground was being upgraded at the time of writing.

GOSSE BLUFF

From the Tyler Pass lookout you get a nice view south to the prominent circular ridge, Gosse Bluff, that the Western Arrernte call Tnorala. This striking, crater-like feature originated during the Creation Time when a baby-carrying dish, complete with baby, toppled off the edge of a celestial dancing ground and crashed to Earth – the baby had been left there by some Milky Way women while they danced.

Some of the rocks thrown up by the impact have the power to make certain bush foods, so by performing the correct rituals the people could ensure there was always plenty to eat. Signs at the car park and a nearby lookout in the centre of Gosse Bluff give more information.

Gosse Bluff is enclosed within a conservation reserve which is jointly managed by the traditional Western Arrernte custodians and the rangers at Ormiston Gorge; check with the rangers about access (usually 4WD only). Much of the reserve is covered by a registered sacred site and is off-limits to visitors.

WALLACE ROCKHOLE

The Western Arrernte community of Wallace Rockhole, off Larapinta Drive about 115km from Alice Springs, was established in 1974 as an outstation of Hermannsburg Mission (see the Ntaria section later). Now around 110 people live here on their ancestral land. Visitors are welcome and do not need a permit for tours or to stay in the camping ground.

Organised Tours

You can learn about local history and culture on a very interesting and entertaining one-hour rock art tour ($8.50; children $4.50); it covers a short bushwalk, the traditional uses of many plants, and a visit to an art site where you'll see hand stencils and engravings. This tour also forms part of a four-hour tour featuring bush tucker in season, as well as kangaroo tail cooked in the ground ($30; children $15). The usual guide, while not an Aboriginal person, is extremely knowledgeable about local customs and lore. Bookings are essential for all tours (☎ 8956 7993).

Three Alice Springs-based companies include the rock art tour in their itineraries: Alice Springs Holidays (☎ 8953 1411, e res@alicespringsholidays.com.au) does a three-day accommodated tour via Wallace Rockhole to Watarrka and Uluru; Sahara Outback Tours (☎1800 806 240, e sahara @saharatours.com.au) does a five-day camping tour to Uluru, Watarrka, Palm Valley and the West MacDonnell Ranges; and The Alice Wanderer (☎ 8952 2111, e alicewand @ozemail.com.au) visits Wallace Rockhole as part of its day tour to Palm Valley and the old Hermannsburg mission ($120 all inclusive).

Places to Stay

Wallace Rockhole Tourist Park & Camping Ground (☎ 8956 7993) has a pleasant camping area with grassed sites and good facilities. Sites cost $17/20 unpowered/ powered for two people, and there are also on-site vans ($45) and en suite cabins ($80), both sleeping four persons.

Shopping

The art centre next to the camping ground has a range of good-quality, reasonably priced arts and crafts, all produced locally. These include acrylics on canvas, hand-painted ceramics, carved animals and silk-screened T-shirts.

NAMATJIRA MONUMENT

Back on Larapinta Drive, 8km east of Hermannsburg, is a roadside monument to Albert Namatjira. Today the artistic skills of central Australian Aboriginal people are widely recognised. This certainly wasn't the case in 1934 when Namatjira started painting his landscapes (see the boxed text 'Albert Namatjira' in the Visual Art special section).

NTARIA (HERMANNSBURG)

The Western Arrernte town of Ntaria (Hermannsburg), which includes the old Hermannsburg Lutheran Mission, is just off Larapinta Drive 125km from Alice Springs. Permits are not required to visit the mission or commercial facilities.

The Mereenie Tour Pass can be bought at the service station (☎ 8956 7480) near the main entrance to town. Locally produced arts and crafts can be purchased at the mission.

Hermannsburg Mission

Founded in 1876, Hermannsburg was named after the Hermannsburg Mission Institute in Germany, where its first two pastors studied. At one time it had a population of 700 Western Arrernte people. The mission also supported a herd of 5000 cattle and various cottage industries, including a tannery.

In 1982 the title was handed back to the Arrernte people under the Aboriginal Land Rights (NT) Act of 1976. Since that time most of the town's residents have left and established small outstation communities on traditional clan territories over the old mission lease – there are now 35 such outstations. Although about 200 Aborigines still live at Ntaria, its main function these days is to provide support and resources for the outlying population.

Today the old mission is a tourist attraction. Among the **whitewashed stone buildings** there's a church, a school and various houses and outbuildings, restored with a federal government grant in 1988. One building houses an **art gallery** which provides an insight into the life and times of Albert Namatjira. It contains examples of the work of numerous Hermannsburg artists, including two Namatjira originals.

The best place to start a visit to the historic precinct is **Kata-Anga Tea Room** (☎ 8956 7402) in the missionary's house. This, like most other buildings in the precinct, is constructed in traditional German farmhouse style; it has a marvellous old-world atmosphere and its walls are adorned with interesting photos by eminent anthropologist Baldwin Spencer.

Here you can relax with a light lunch, or a bottomless cup of tea or coffee and a large slice of home-baked cake – naturally, apple strudel is a speciality. As well, the tearoom sells a good range of reasonably priced paintings (including watercolour landscapes), Namatjira prints, decorated wooden crafts and ceramics produced by the highly regarded Hermannsburg Potters – their brightly glazed pots make terrific mementoes, and you can pick one up here for as little as $60.

Admission to Hermannsburg costs $4.50 (children $3); a leaflet for a self-guided walk explains the various buildings and their history. For an extra $3.50 you can take a guided tour which includes the Namatjira private collection (minimum four people). The precinct is open 9 am to 4 pm daily (from 10 am December to February), but closes Easter Friday and from Christmas Day to 2 January).

Organised Tours See Organised Tours in the Palm Valley section later for details of tours that visit Hermannsburg.

FINKE GORGE
History
For thousands of years the Finke River formed part of an Aboriginal trade route that crossed Australia, bringing goods such as sacred red ochre from the south and pearl-shell from the north to the central Australian region. Far from being desert, the area around Ntaria (Hermannsburg) had an abundance of game animals and food plants. It was a major drought refuge for the Western Arrernte people, who obtained water from soaks, or shallow wells, which they dug in the sandy riverbed. An upside-down river (like all others in central Australia), the Finke flows beneath its dry bed most of the time. As it becomes saline during drought, the Western Arrernte call it Lhere Pirnte (hence Larapinta), which means 'Salty River'. It was their comprehensive knowledge of its freshwater soaks that enabled them to survive the harshest droughts.

Palm Valley
The main attraction in Finke Gorge National Park, Palm Valley (Mpulungkinya) is steeped in Western Arrernte culture. The palms and cycads you see in this lush oasis are young Fire Ancestors who, having been burned in a huge bushfire to the north, were picked up by strong winds and dropped in the Palm Valley area. Today, their traditional headdresses are seen as the palms' shaggy fronds and their fire-blackened bodies as the dark trunks.

There are several walks in the area, including the 5km **Mpaara Track**. This interesting walk, which offers good views, has information signs relating to a Western Arrernte adventure story from the Creation Time. The moral of the tale – it involves murder, maggots and bloody revenge – is not to go walking in the hills alone. This is sound advice for modern visitors too.

Organised Tours Day tours from Alice Springs to Palm Valley and the old Hermannsburg mission are run by AAT Kings Tours ($99; ☎ 8952 1700), NT Luxury Day Tours ($155 including Simpsons Gap and Angkerle; ☎ 8952 7751), Palm Valley Tours ($85; ☎ 1800 000 629, e tours @palmvalleytours.com.au) and The Alice Wanderer ($120 including Wallace Rockhole; ☎ 8952 2111, e alicewand@ozemail .com.au).

Sahara Outback Tours (☎ 1800 806 240, e sahara@saharatours.com.au) visits Palm Valley as part of a five-day camping tour to Uluru, Watarrka, Wallace Rockhole and the West MacDonnell Ranges.

Boggy Hole
Boggy Hole is a large permanent waterhole in Lhere Pirnte, about 25km downstream from Mpulungkinya. The 4WD access track crosses Aboriginal land for the 16km from Ntaria (Hermannsburg) to the national park boundary. Although there is no requirement for a permit to use the road, camping is not allowed in the area and visitors must stay on the main route.

In the 1880s Boggy Hole was a police camp from which Mounted Constable William Willshire and his Aboriginal troopers rode the ranges, quelling black resistance to white settlement. It seems their method of doing this was to shoot as many Aborigines as possible, prompting a Hermannsburg missionary to write in 1885: 'In 10 years time there will not be many blacks left in this area and this is just what the white man wants.'

NORTHERN TERRITORY

A year later the missionaries were protesting vigorously at the alarming decrease in the Aboriginal male population. It was thanks largely to their efforts that the police were moved in 1893 and Willshire brought to trial for his excesses. He wasn't convicted, but the trial ended his bloody career in the NT. The stone remains of the police camp (not to be confused with those of a more recent safari camp) are on the waterhole's eastern bank.

Luritja Country

South-West of Alice Springs

WATARRKA (KINGS CANYON)
History
Watarrka is the Luritja name for a strip of country along the path taken by a large group of Kuningka (Native-Cat Men) during the Creation Time. These ancestors had travelled up Kings Creek to the Kings Canyon Waterhole, where they held ceremonies before continuing their journey north.

In 1872 the white explorer Ernest Giles travelled through this area and found numerous Aboriginal people living here. But by the 1920s the country had been abandoned due to conflicts with pastoralists and loss of resources.

Today, however, much of the land in this area has been handed back to its traditional owners. There are a number of registered sacred sites, as well as three Aboriginal communities within the park boundaries, and local Luritja people play a decision-making role in the management of the national park.

Permits
You need a permit from the Central Land Council (☎ 8951 6320, fax 8953 4345) in Alice Springs to travel to Watarrka along the Mereenie Loop Rd, which passes through Aboriginal land west of Ntaria (Hermannsburg). The permit includes the informative *Mereenie Tour Pass* booklet ($2), which has a route map. Permits are issued on the spot by CATIA in Alice Springs, the Glen Helen Resort, the Hermannsburg service station and the Kings Canyon Resort.

Organised Tours
Lilla Aboriginal Tours, an Aboriginal-owned and -operated tour company based at Lilla community, has a couple of good offerings. You can book on ☎ 8956 7909, or inquire at reception at Kings Canyon Resort (see Places to Stay).

Depending on demand, the four-hour Guided Canyon Walk features a walk around the canyon rim with an Aboriginal guide. It's a unique opportunity to see this stunning landscape from a more ancient

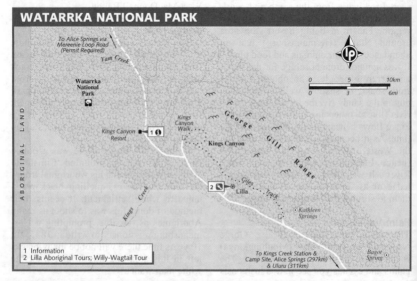

WATARRKA NATIONAL PARK

To Alice Springs via Mereenie Loop Road (Permit Required)

Yam Creek

Watarrka National Park

ABORIGINAL LAND

Kings Canyon Resort ■ 1

Kings Canyon Walk

Kings Canyon

George Gill Range

Giles Track

Kings Creek

2 Lilla

Kathleen Springs

0   5   10km
0   3   6mi

1 Information
2 Lilla Aboriginal Tours; Willy-Wagtail Tour

To Kings Creek Station & Camp Site, Alice Springs (297km) & Uluru (311km)

Bagot Spring

perspective. The rate is $33 per person and a minimum of 20 applies.

The Willy-Wagtail Tour is a two-hour walk and talk at Lilla which makes an excellent introduction to the local culture, both traditional and contemporary. On the tour, you visit art sites and a scenic rockhole, learn about bush tucker and bush medicine, and hear the Aboriginal point of view on many different issues. The tour costs $38.50 (children $27.50).

Outback Scenic Adventure Tours (☎ 8953 5292), Sahara Outback Tours (☎ 1800 806 240, e sahara@saharatours .com.au) and Wayoutback Desert Safaris (☎ 1800 224 324, e info@wayoutback .com.au) include Watarrka on their camping tours from Alice Springs.

Walks

The park has several walking tracks, including the strenuous **Kings Canyon Walk** (6km) around the canyon rim. It offers views down to the waterhole where the Kuningka danced, and the route winds through large sandstone domes that represent the bodies of young Kuningka. You can learn more about these ancestors on the Aboriginal-guided tour.

There's also the sealed **Kathleen Springs Walk**, which is 2.5km return and is suitable for wheelchairs. The track takes you to a deep plunge pool inhabited by a giant Water Serpent, the guardian of all waterholes in the park. Information signs en route explain various aspects of the area's Aboriginal heritage.

Places to Stay

Kings Canyon Resort (☎ 8956 7442, bookings ☎ 1800 817 622), which is 50% owned by Aboriginal shareholders, provides a range of commercial facilities to park users. These include a small store and service station (open 7 am to 7 pm daily), cafe, restaurant and bar. The reception desk has park information.

There are also comfortable guesthouse rooms with shared facilities sleeping up to four people for $40 per person (double or twin rooms cost $92). The resort's upmarket motel units cost from $305 (from $256 summer low-season). Alternatively, you can camp on the grounds of the resort ($26/29 unpowered/powered for doubles).

MT EBENEZER ROADHOUSE

Mt Ebenezer Roadhouse (☎ 8956 2904), on the Lasseter Hwy 56km from the Stuart Hwy, is owned by the nearby Imanpa Aboriginal community. It's a good place to stop for morning or afternoon tea, and there are some very competitively priced Aboriginal arts and crafts in the gallery. You can pick up a good souvenir in the form of a small bush-tucker painting by a local artist for as little as $45, or pay over $1000 for something grander.

The roadhouse has a basic, dusty camping area where sites cost from $10/11 unpowered/powered for two people. There's also a motel (closed at the time of writing).

The opening hours are 7 am to 8 pm daily.

MT CONNER

From the Luritja Rd intersection 58km beyond Mt Ebenezer, the Lasseter Hwy swings towards the south. It's along this stretch that you get the first glimpses of Mt Conner (Artula), a large mesa (table-top mountain) which looms 350m above the sandy plain about 20km south of the road. To local Aboriginal people this is the home of the Ice-Men, who venture forth on winter nights and leave frost as a sign of their passing.

On first sighting many people mistake the mesa for Uluru, but on closer inspection it bears no resemblance. A rest area on the highway 26km beyond the Luritja Rd turn-off is a good vantage point to take in the scene.

Uluru Experience (☎ 1800 803 174, e bookings@ecotours.com.au) does a good afternoon tour to Mt Conner from Yulara for $180 (children $125).

Pitjantjatjara & Yankunytjatjara Country

Around Uluru

ULURU (AYERS ROCK)

Please be aware that alcohol (grog) is a problem among Anangu living at Mutitjulu, near Uluru. This is a 'dry' community and, at the request of the Mutitjulu community leaders, the liquor outlets have agreed not to sell it to Anangu people. You may be approached in the car park at the shopping centre by Anangu who want you to buy alcohol on their behalf. The community leaders appeal to you not to do so.

The world-famous Uluru, which towers 348m above the surrounding sandplain, is like nothing else on Earth. For most visitors to Australia Uluru is a 'must see', as it undoubtedly ranks among the world's greatest natural attractions. Uluru-Kata Tjuta National Park is included on the UN World Heritage list.

This entire area is of deep cultural significance to the local Pitjantjatjara and Yankunytjatjara people, who refer to themselves as Anangu. They officially own the national park and have leased it to Parks Australia until 2084. Decisions related to managing the park are made by the 10 members of the Board of Management, six of whom are Anangu.

There are plenty of walks and other activities at Uluru, Kata Tjuta and the nearby township of Yulara, and it is not at all difficult to spend several days here. Unfortunately, though, most group tours are very rushed; they squeeze in a quick afternoon tour at Uluru, photos at sunset, a morning at Kata Tjuta next day and then off – 24 hours in total if you're lucky.

History

Tjukurpa Non-Aboriginal archaeologists suggest that Aboriginal people have inhabited this part of Australia for at least 22,000 years, but in traditional belief Anangu have been here since time began. According to the law laid down during the Creation Time (Tjukurpa, pronounced chook-oor-pa), all landscape features were made by ancestral beings; the Anangu are the descendants of these beings and it is their responsibility to look after their ancestral lands. Tjukurpa is a philosophy providing answers to fundamental questions about existence and in fact is the very cornerstone of Anangu culture.

A number of totemic ancestors are associated with Uluru, and their deeds are told in the marks and other natural features on and around the rock. These ancestors include Kuniya (the Woma Python), Kurpany (an evil dog-like creature), Liru (the Brown Snake), Lungkarta (the Blue-Tongued Lizard) and Mala (the Rufous Hare Wallaby). Their Tjukurpa stories are introduced at the park's cultural centre and on Aboriginal-guided walks in the area.

The informative leaflet *Welcome to Uluru-Kata Tjuta National Park* contains a detailed explanation of Tjukurpa. It also discusses some important cross-cultural issues you should be aware of.

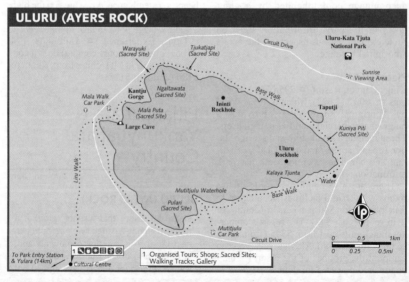

ULURU (AYERS ROCK)

Warayuki (Sacred Site)
Tjukatjapi (Sacred Site)
Circuit Drive
Uluru-Kata Tjuta National Park
Sunrise Viewing Area
Kantju Gorge
Ngaltawata (Sacred Site)
Base Walk
Mala Walk Car Park
Ininti Rockhole
Taputji
Mala Puta (Sacred Site)
Large Cave
Kuniya Piti (Sacred Site)
Uluru Rockhole
Liru Walk
Kalaya Tjunta
Water
Mutitjulu Waterhole
Base Walk
Pulari (Sacred Site)
Mutitjulu Car Park
Circuit Drive
To Park Entry Station & Yulara (14km)
Cultural Centre
1 Organised Tours; Shops; Sacred Sites; Walking Tracks; Gallery

0   0.5   1km
0   0.25   0.5mi

Uluru belongs to the Pitjantjatjara and Yankunytjatjara people, who call themselves Anangu. During the Tjukurpa (Creation time) powerful beings, the ancestors of the Anangu, created Uluru. These ancestors include Kuniya (the Woma Python), Kurpany (an evil dog-like creature) and Mala (the Rufous Hare Wallaby). Their biographies are written on the landscape and etched into the features of the rock itself.

The sacred red soils around Uluru are home to calandrines (1) and other hardy wild-flowers. Images of the Mala Ancestors adorn the rock (2). Uluru is famous for its changing colours, which vary from bright orange to deep purple. At sunset the rock glows red (3, 4). Each crevice and texture in the rock face (5, 6) is woven into Anangu stories, which you can learn on guided tours. It rarely rains at Uluru, but when it does the desert springs to life (7).

This spectacular collection of 36 giant red domes rising out of the flat desert was named Kata Tjuta, meaning 'Many Heads', by the Anangu people. Geologically linked to Uluru and of similar spiritual significance, its weathered formations were mapped by events of Tjukurpa (the Creation time), which are an inextricable part of the cultural landscape. See also the Uluru (Ayers Rock) section on page 247.

The distinctive rust red colour of the domes and the soil surrounding Kata Tjuta is caused by the oxidation of iron in the rock (1). Surrounding vegetation includes desert casuarina trees and mulga bush (2), black-barked desert oak (3), and tiny but brilliant wildflowers (6). Shallow pools of water lie in the shadowed canyons of Walpa (Mt Olga Gorge) (4). The rocks can appear strikingly different depending on the time of day (5, 7), and at sunset Kata Tjuta holds its own light show to rival Uluru's (8).

RICHARD I'ANSON

CHRIS MELLOR

ROBYN COVENTRY

RICHARD I'ANSON

RICHARD I'ANSON

RICHARD I'ANSON

RICHARD I'ANSON

PAUL SINCLAIR

CLIMBING ULURU

It's important to realise that it goes against Anangu spiritual beliefs to climb Uluru, and they would prefer that you didn't. This is because the climb to the top follows in the footsteps of Mala ancestors of the Tjukurpa (see History in this section). As well, Anangu feel responsible for the safety of all visitors to their land, and are greatly saddened when someone is injured or dies on the Rock. So far 35 have died there, mostly from falls and heart attacks.

Although the number of visitors to Uluru has risen steadily over the years, the number of people actually climbing it is declining. Meanwhile, sales of ideologically sound 'I Didn't Climb Ayers Rock' T-shirts are on the rise.

The Anangu call the people climbing up the 'Minga Mob'. You just have to look at the rock from a distance to get the joke – *minga* means 'ant'.

Recent History The white explorers who first visited Pitjantjatjara and Yankunytjatjara country during the early 1870s were later followed by pastoralists, missionaries, doggers (dingo hunters) and welfare patrol officers.

As non-Aboriginal activity in the area increased, so to did the contact and conflict between Aboriginal and white culture. With the combined effects of stock grazing and drought, many Anangu found their hunting and gathering options being increasingly threatened. This in turn led to a growing dependence on the white economy.

In the 1920s the NT, WA and SA governments set aside the Great Central Aboriginal Reserve for Aboriginal people. Reserves were seen, according to the *NT Annual Report* of 1938, as '...refuges or sanctuaries of a temporary nature. The Aboriginal may here continue his normal existence until the time is ripe for his further development'.

'Development' referred to the assimilation aim of providing Aboriginal people with skills and knowledge that would enable them to fit into white society. The policy failed across the country.

By 1950 a road had been pushed through to Uluru from the east, and tourism was beginning to develop. As early as 1951 the fledgling Connellan Airways applied for permission to build an airstrip near Uluru. In order to facilitate this, the area of Uluru and Kata Tjuta was excised from the reserve in 1958 for use as a national park. Soon after motel leases were granted and the airstrip constructed.

The first official ranger and Keeper of Ayers Rock at the Ayers Rock & Mt Olga National Park was Bill Harney. This famous Territorian spent many years working with Aboriginal people and contributed greatly towards non-Aboriginal understanding of their culture.

With the revoking of pastoral subsidies in 1964, which until that time had compensated pastoralists for food and supplies distributed to passing Aboriginal people, many Anangu were forced off the stations. They gravitated to Uluru, but could no longer sustain themselves completely by traditional ways. Needing money to participate in the white economy, they were able to earn some cash by selling artefacts to tourists.

By the 1970s it was clear that planning was required for the development of the area. Between 1931 and 1946 only 22 people were known to have climbed Uluru. In 1969 about 23,000 people visited the area. Ten years later the figure was 65,000 and now the annual visitor figures are approaching the 400,000 mark.

The 1970s saw the construction of the new Yulara Resort some distance from Uluru – the original facilities, which were too close, were having a negative impact on the environment. Many of these were bulldozed, while others were taken over by the Mutitjulu Aboriginal community.

Increased tourism activity over the years led to Aboriginal anxiety about the desecration of important sites. The federal government was approached for assistance and by 1973 Aboriginal people had become involved with the management of the park. Although title to many parcels of land in the NT had been handed back to Aboriginal people, national parks were excluded from the Aboriginal Land Rights (NT) Act of 1976.

It was not until 1979 that traditional ownership of Uluru-Kata Tjuta was recognised by the government. In 1983, following renewed calls from traditional owners for title to the land, the federal government announced that freehold title to the national park would be granted and the park leased back to what is now Parks Australia for a period of 99 years. The transfer of ownership took place on 26 October 1985.

Information

Park Entry The entry station on the Yulara-Uluru road is open daily, with times changing monthly between winter (6.30 am to 7.30 pm) and summer (5 am to 9 pm).

Entry to the national park costs $16.25 (free for children under 16), and this is good for a three-day visit. A $65 'Territorian Pass' is valid for a year and includes access to Kakadu.

A significant proportion of the funds generated by the entry fee system is paid to the traditional owners as part of the lease agreement. They ask that you keep your unexpired ticket as a souvenir, not resell it to another visitor.

Books *Punu – Yankunytjatjara Plant Use*, compiled and edited by Cliff Goddard & Arpad Kalotis, will interest anyone who wants an insight into how Aboriginal people survive in an arid environment.

The Anangu share their knowledge of the landscape, seasons, plants, animals and Tjukurpa of the Uluru area in *Mingkiri*, by the Mutitjulu community and Lynn Baker.

Anangu Way by Nganampa Health is a high-quality hardback featuring over 50 paintings by Pitjantjatjara, Yankunytjatjara and Ngatatjara people. The images are accompanied by stories relating to Aboriginal health issues.

IAD Press of Alice Springs publishes the *Pitjantjatjara/Yankunytjatjara to English Dictionary*, *Pitjantjatjara/Yankunytjatjara Pocket Dictionary*, *A Learner's Guide to Pitjantjatjara/Yankunytjatjara* and the *Pitjantjatjara/Yankunytjatjara Picture Vocabulary*.

Organised Tours

Ranger-Guided Tours The free, ranger-guided Mala Walk is a good way to learn about the Mala Tjukurpa and how Anangu and rangers work together to manage the park. You also visit an art site and see the tracks of a Marsupial Mole Ancestor; the tour ends at Kantju Gorge, one of the prettiest spots in the national park. Tours depart daily from The Climb car park at 8 am (10 am May to September) and take about 1½ hours; you don't have to book. From Kantju Gorge you can either return to the car park or continue around the base of Uluru.

Anangu-Guided Tours Owned and operated by the Mutitjulu community, Anangu Tours (☎ 8956 2123, ℮ LBANANGU @anangutours.com.au) has a tour desk in the park's cultural centre, as well as at the Tour & Information Centre in Yulara. Its tours are led by an Anangu guide and are a great opportunity to get a new perspective on the land. Bookings are essential for all tours. Web site: www.anangutours.com.au

The two-hour Liru Walk takes you on a pleasant bushwalk from the cultural centre to The Climb car park. It focuses on traditional skills such as how to make bush glue, light a fire using dried kangaroo dung, make a *piti* (wooden dish) and carry the dish on your head. You'll also hear the Tjukurpa stories associated with the battle between Liru and Kuniya, the Mala men and their fight with the evil Dog-Man, and how Lungkarta's greed brought him undone. The tour departs daily at 8.30 am (earlier from October to March); it costs $47 (children $24) if you're driving yourself to the start point.

The two-hour Kuniya Walk starts at the cultural centre, where your Anangu guide introduces some of the Tjukurpa stories of Uluru. Then it's off to Mutitjulu waterhole to hear more about the clash between Kuniya and Liru (see History earlier). You'll also hear about daily life, learn about the food and medicine plants found along the way, and visit an art site where some of the symbols are explained. The tour departs daily at 3.30 pm (4.30 pm in summer) and the self-drive option costs $47 (children $24).

Anangu Tours has several other offerings. One is the Aboriginal Uluru Tour, which lasts around five hours and includes sunrise viewing, breakfast at the cultural centre, a short base tour and the Liru Walk;

it costs $98 (children $69), or $79 ($54) without breakfast.

Another tour is the Uluru Cultural Centre Tour. This features a tour of the cultural centre with an Anangu guide, a short base tour and an evening tour back at Yulara for $72 (children $50). There are also three 24-hour passes which include morning and afternoon tours; these start from $143 (children $97).

Non-Aboriginal Tours Operating out of Yulara, Uluru Experience Tours (☎ 1800 803 174, e bookings@ecotours.com.au) is highly recommended for its guides' knowledge and understanding of, and sensitivity to, Anangu culture and issues. It runs several trips into the park, including walking- and vehicle-based tours around Uluru (both $83 including breakfast; children $65), and a tour of Kata Tjuta and the surrounding dunes ($59/49).

If you're in a hurry, Personalised Scenic Flights (☎ 8952 4625, e australianoutback flights@aopa.com.au) of Alice Springs does a one-day return charter to Uluru flying over the West MacDonnell Ranges, Watarrka and Kata Tjuta. The tour costs $512 per person (minimum two passengers), including the entry fee, a base tour and lunch.

A number of bus tours visit Uluru from Alice Springs; inquire at the tourist office there. Be aware that not all operators inform passengers of Anangu concerns about climbing Uluru (see the boxed text 'Climbing Uluru').

Walking Tracks

Note that there are a number of Aboriginal sacred sites around the base. These are clearly signposted, and to enter, damage or photograph these areas is a grave offence to the Anangu – as well as making you liable to a hefty fine!

There are several walking tracks at Uluru and you can explore a couple of them on the ranger- and Anangu-guided tours.

Details of the Mala and Mutitjulu walks, including the Tjukurpa associated with these areas, are given in the excellent, self-guided walks brochure *Insight into Uluru*. It's available from the cultural centre and costs $1.

Base Walk It takes a good three or four hours to walk the 9.4km around the base of Uluru, with many stops to admire the landmark features and cave paintings, or just revel in the unique atmosphere. It's a great way to explore Uluru; most visitors are in too much of a rush to do the walk, so you'll often have the path pretty much to yourself.

Note that climbing of Taputji – a rock outcrop near the north-eastern side of Uluru – is not allowed.

Mala Walk This walk, which features the Creation story of the Mala men, starts from the base of the climb and takes about 1½ hours at a very leisurely pace. You can do the walk on your own, or there are ranger-guided tours daily (see Organised Tours). The track is suitable for wheelchairs.

Mutitjulu Walk Mutitjulu, a permanent waterhole on the southern side of Uluru, is the home of Wanampi, a Water-Snake Ancestor. It's just a short walk from the car park, and you can either do it by yourself or go with an Anangu guide on the Kuniya Walk (see Organised Tours). The walk features the Creation story of the clash between Kuniya and Liru; this track is suitable for wheelchairs.

Liru Walk This 2km track wanders through mulga scrub from the cultural centre to the base of Uluru. It takes about 45 minutes one-way, and is another one you can do with an Anangu guide (see Organised Tours).

Cultural Centre

The Uluru-Kata Tjuta National Park Cultural Centre (☎ 8956 2299) is inside the national park, just 1km before Uluru on the road from Yulara. This excellent facility, which includes two arts and crafts outlets, a souvenir and coffee shop, and a park information desk, is open 7 am to 5.30 pm daily (to 6 pm from November to March inclusive). It's worth putting aside at least one hour, preferably more, to have a good look around the centre before visiting Uluru itself.

There are two main display areas, both with multilingual information: the Tjukurpa display features wall murals of Anangu art

NORTHERN TERRITORY

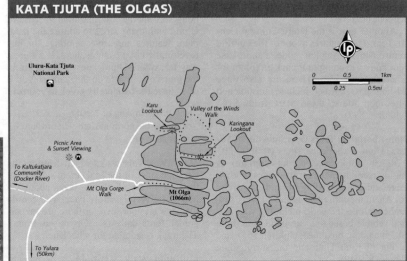

KATA TJUTA (THE OLGAS)

Uluru-Kata Tjuta
National Park

Karu
Lookout

Valley of the Winds
Walk

Karingana
Lookout

Picnic Area
& Sunset Viewing

To Kaltukatjara
Community
(Docker River)

Mt Olga Gorge
Walk

Mt Olga
(1066m)

To Yulara
(50km)

and Tjukurpa stories; and the Nintiringku-pai display focuses on the history and management of the national park. Ask at the information desk for the colourful and informative leaflet *Art of Uluru-Kata Tjuta National Park* – it's one of a set of four 'park notes' ($1).

The centre has a picnic area with free gas barbecues. You can book Aboriginal-led tours around Uluru at the Anangu Tours desk (☎ 8956 2123).

Shopping

The following places, which are in the cultural centre, are all owned by Anangu.

Maruku Arts & Crafts Maruku Arts & Crafts provides an opportunity to see artists and craftspeople at work. The shop has a large quantity of good-quality stock, mainly paintings and wooden crafts. Large dot paintings on canvas cost around $400 to $2000, and there are small bush-tucker paintings on boards from $15. One of the most interesting pieces on sale is a traditional 'woman's kit' (around $1000); it includes a digging stick, club, large and small carved wooden dishes, necklace and a woven head cushion (used to carry the large dish).

Everything here is created in the surrounding desert regions; it's one of the cheaper places in central Australia to buy arts and crafts, as you're buying direct from the artists. Certificates of authenticity are issued with most major pieces.

The shop is open 8.30 am to 5.30 pm daily.

Web site: www.users.bigpond.com/maruku

Walkatjara Art Centre You can also watch local artists at work at the Walkatjara Art Centre, which is contained within the Winkiku Exhibition Space. The speciality here is ceramics painted in a blend of traditional and contemporary styles. You can also buy a range of other arts and crafts produced by Anangu, including woven spinifex baskets, paintings on canvas and board, hand-painted silk scarves and limited-edition prints. The centre is open 9 am to 5.30 pm weekdays, and 9.30 am to 2 pm weekends.

Ininti Store The well-stocked Ininti Store & Cafe sells refreshments and snacks as well as a large range of good-quality souvenirs. You'll find hand-painted T-shirts with Aboriginal motifs, carved wooden animals, videos about Anangu, books by and about Aboriginal people and culture, decorated gum-nut necklaces, painted emu eggs and much more. The shop is open 7 am to 5.30 pm daily.

KATA TJUTA (THE OLGAS)

Kata Tjuta, a cluster of huge rounded rocks, stands about 30km west of Uluru (53km by road from Yulara).

Meaning 'Many Heads', Kata Tjuta is of great significance to Anangu and is associated with a number of Tjukurpa stories. However, as these relate to secret ceremonies involving the education and initiation of men, they are not for general consumption.

Kata Tjuta Walks

The main walking trail is a scenic 7.4km loop (2½ to four hours) via the aptly named Valley of the Winds. It's not particularly arduous, but there is some scrambling – be prepared with drinking water and sun protection. Another walk (50 minutes) takes you into Walpa (Mt Olga Gorge).

YULARA

Yulara is the service village for the Uluru-Kata Tjuta National Park and has effectively turned one of the world's least hospitable regions into an easy and comfortable place to visit. It lies just outside the national park, 21km from Uluru and 53km from Kata Tjuta.

The Yulara Visitor Centre (☎ 8957 7377) contains interesting displays on local Aboriginal lore. These include a traditional dwelling *(wiltja)* built by men from Mutitjulu. The centre is open 8.30 am to 7.30 pm daily. Unfortunately, there is no message here that Anangu would prefer that visitors don't climb Uluru (see the boxed text 'Climbing Uluru' earlier).

Organised Tours

Tours with Anangu Tours, Uluru Experience Tours and other operators can be booked at the Tour & Information Centre (☎ 8957 7324), open 8.30 am to 8.30 pm daily.

A couple of companies run camping tours into the Anangu-Pitjantjatjaraku Lands of northern SA. See the Pitjantjatjara & Yankunytjatjara Country section in the South Australia chapter.

NORTHERN TERRITORY

Queensland

The state of Queensland covers the traditional lands of two distinct Indigenous peoples, that of Australian Aborigines and Torres Strait Islanders. The Torres Strait Islands are in the area between the tip of the Cape York Peninsula and Papua New Guinea. (For details see the Torres Strait Islands chapter.) The Aboriginal people of Queensland often call themselves Murris.

You may find that some of the Indigenous tour operators listed in this chapter are not promoted by booking agents or tourist offices, so you may have to contact them directly for further information.

History

Philip Morrissey

EARLY HISTORY

It is generally believed that Aborigines reached Sahul, the Pleistocene landmass connected to New Guinea, by sea. While Cape York is the closest point on mainland Australia to another landmass contemporary archaeologists believe that entry into Australia by the first Aborigines was from the north-west of the continent. After sea levels rose 6000 years ago, Arnhem Land and New Guinea were cut off from Cape York.

Before Europeans arrived, Queensland was the most densely populated area of Australia, supporting as many as 100,000 to 120,000 people in about 200 tribal groups of between 500 and 1500 people each. The Cape York Peninsula alone may have supported up to 30,000 people.

Coastal tribes lived on an amazingly wide variety of plants and vegetables, supplementing their diet with fish, turtles and dugongs (sea cows) from the sea. Shellfish were collected and eaten on the beaches; evidence of these feasts in the form of huge shell middens has been found all along the Queensland coast, at places such as Weipa, Fraser Island and Double Island Point. Some middens are 13m high, and made up of 200,000 tonnes of shells.

Inland tribes were expert game hunters, using nets to catch kangaroos, spears to kill emus and boomerangs to bring down birds. Stone dams were built in rivers to trap fish.

Telephone code: ☎ 07
Indigenous population: 104,817
Overall population: 3.46 million
Area: 1.727 million sq km

- Exploring one of the world's largest collections of prehistoric art at the Quinkan rock art galleries

- Taking a guided tour to learn about the bounties of wet tropics rainforests with a Kuku-Yalanji Elder

- Tuning in to the Woodford Folk Festival, a major annual event for Indigenous performers, musicians, storytellers and artists from around the country

- Camping at the tip of mainland Australia and learning about the cultural heritage of Injinoo Country

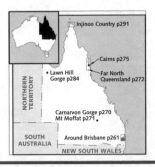

Injinoo Country p291
Cairns p275
• Lawn Hill Gorge p284
Far North Queensland p272
NORTHERN TERRITORY
Carnarvon Gorge p270
Mt Moffat p271
SOUTH AUSTRALIA
Around Brisbane p261
NEW SOUTH WALES

In the arid north-west, the Kalkadoon people in the Mt Isa area dug wells up to 10m deep to supply themselves with water. In rainforest areas, people ate wild berries and other plants, and the coastal mangroves provided water-lily tubers and seeds, mangrove pods, crabs and shellfish.

As well, inter-tribal barter systems and well-developed trading routes followed the major river systems. Cape York tribes were in regular contact with Torres Strait Islanders, in terms of both warfare and trade. In some cases cultural beliefs were modified as a result of the contact. The bunya nut – the large seeds of a pine cone – was an important item of seasonal food in the south-east. The annual harvest was controlled by the Waka Waka people, and tribes would meet to trade during the harvest.

EUROPEAN INVASION

Dutch mariners visited Cape York in the 17th century, and in 1770 Captain James Cook spent time there repairing the *Endeavour*. Aborigines were seen when Moreton Bay was surveyed in the 1820s, and their fine physiques were taken as indicating that the country was fertile. Subsequently, in 1824 Brisbane was set up as a military outpost and a penal settlement established at Moreton Bay for convict recidivists.

The first private land sales were held in 1842. By 1870 large areas of arable land had been occupied and settlers forged into ever more remote areas. In the 1880s gold was discovered and a new wave of migration began, with 50,000 Chinese and European miners arriving for the Palmer River gold rush alone. Timber cutting also attracted new settlers.

RESISTANCE

Tribal boundaries, hunting rights and sacred grounds were all ignored in the land grab. Many Europeans and Chinese were killed in the resulting war, but the Aborigines ultimately lost every battle. For instance, the Wargamayab people were trapped on Hinchinbrook Island and systematically killed. In another incident, in 1873 the Guugu-Yimidhirr made a desperate attack on a convoy of miners, soldiers and Native Police headed for the goldfields. They attempted to pull the muskets from the hands of the invaders, but were defeated at the site on the Normanby River since known as Battle Camp.

In 1884, in the last major battle of the 19th century, the Kalkadoon were conclusively defeated at Battle Mountain near Cloncurry. The battle had been fought on even terms until the Kalkadoon warriors formed themselves into battle ranks and marched into the musket fire of settlers and Native Police. No satisfactory explanation for this tactic has ever been given (see History in the Kalkadoon Country section for more details).

In 1859 Queensland became a separate colony. Many of its parliamentarians were pastoralists and the Native Police and their officers were directed to 'disperse' any large party of Aborigines – it was understood that 'dispersion' could be conducted with unrestrained violence. The Native Police were responsible for some of the bloodiest massacres in Australian history. This paramilitary force was made up of Aborigines from conquered tribes from other regions. With their skills in tracking and bushcraft, combined with the use of European weaponry, Native Police troopers negated any advantages the Aboriginal resistance might have had. The force was abolished in 1900.

Southerners and visitors from England were often shocked at the brutality of Queensland practices. One society lady from New South Wales (NSW) was surprised to

HORNET BANK

Philip Morrissey

As with other parts of Australia, settlers justified their own atrocities by accusing Aborigines of treachery – though they routinely killed Aboriginal women and children and distributed poisoned flour. The Hornet Bank Massacre in 1857, in which the Jiman tribe attacked a remote station on the Dawson River, was typical of the time. The Jiman killed a widow, seven of her children and three shepherds, after having suffered years of brutal treatment at the hands of settlers; in 1856 pastoralists had given Aborigines strychnine-laced Christmas pudding, and rape of Jiman women was commonplace.

The men of the homestead attacked were known rapists, and the punishment meted out to the settlers, in accordance with Aboriginal law, was made to fit the crime. Following the attack on the homestead, a revenge 'posse' was made up of squatters and members of the Native Police. The reprisals continued for six weeks, at the end of which not one Jiman was left in the Dawson Valley.

QUEENSLAND

1   Mapoon Council; Bush Camping
2   Bush Camping
3   Snappy Tours; Uningan Nature Reserve
4   Bush Camping
5   Napranum Aboriginal Community Council
6   Lockhart River Aboriginal Council; Lockhart River
    Arts & Culture Centre
7   Bush Camping
8   Coen Regional Aboriginal Corporation
9   Bush Camping
10 Pormpuraaw Aboriginal Community Council; Crocodile
    Farm; Bush Camping
11 KLANRO; Bush Camping
12 Rock Art Site; Tours; Kalkadoon Tribal Culture
    Keeping Place; Frank Aston Underground Museum; Mt Isa
    Aboriginal Media Association; Trading Arts & Crafts
13 Museum of Tropical Queensland; Perc Tucker Regional
    Gallery; Jubinbara Gallery
14 Coral Beach Track
15 Rock Art; Bora Rings; Organised Tour
16 Outback Aussie Tours; Stockman's Hall of Fame
    & Outback Heritage Centre
17 Aramac Station (Rock Art)
18 Artesian Country Tours
19 Blacks Palace
20 Rock Art Site; Mimosa Culture Circuit
21 Dreamtime Cultural Centre & Lodge Motel
22 Korrawinga Community Farm
23 Scarr Trees
24 Barambah Emu Farm
25 Miles Historic Village
26 Fabulous Outback Escapes; CDEP Aboriginal Workshop
27 Axe-Grinding Grooves; Bora Ring
28 David Fleay Wildlife Park (Heritage Talk & Dance)

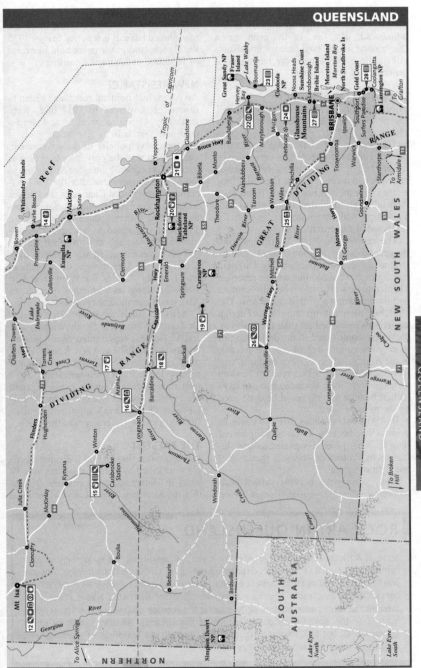

find that her host kept the ears of Aboriginal massacre victims nailed as trophies to his homestead. By the 1870s even some Queensland settlers could see the brutalising effects these massacres were having on a generation of settler youth.

CREATION OF RESERVES

The battles having been won, there was still the problem of what to do with the survivors. In 1897 the Aboriginal Protection and Restriction of the Sale of Opium Act was passed. This forced Aborigines onto reserves where their lives were minutely regulated and they had no civil rights. The Chief Protector under the Act had greater rights over Aboriginal children than their parents had. This Act, with amendments, essentially remained in force until 1984.

The reserves isolated Aborigines from the general community and ensured that their treatment escaped public scrutiny. Different tribal groups were combined in the reserves. This led to new affiliations but also conflict and the breakdown of traditional *law*. The churches also set up missions. Though sometimes more benign than the reserves, these also contributed to the destruction of Aboriginal culture and offered no security to the Aboriginal people. For example, residents of Mapoon, a Presbyterian mission on Cape York, were forced to move in 1891 so that bauxite mining could be conducted on the mission site.

In 1901 Palm Island, off the coast of Townsville, became a feared punishment reserve. Aborigines designated as troublemakers by Protectors were sent there, without right of appeal.

Many Aborigines became skilled bush workers, although Aboriginal men living under the Act had their wages paid directly to Protectors, who decided how much the men should have. It is reported that by 1935 the Queensland government held in excess of £290,000 of Aboriginal earnings.

NEW RESISTANCE

An Aboriginal political resistance began to re-emerge, however. In 1957 there were strikes by Aboriginal workers at Palm Island and Yarrabah, as resentment grew at the oppressive policies of the government. Queensland was the only state to refuse to transfer its responsibilities for Aborigines to the federal government after the 1967 referendum (see Social Change in the History section of the Facts about Aboriginal Australia & the Torres Strait Islands chapter). The state continued to administer Aboriginal affairs through its own department.

The government finally handed over title from the Department of Aboriginal and Islander Affairs for Palm Island in 1985–86, along with its other reserves, to Aboriginal community councils.

Activists such as Pastor Don Brady, Oodgeroo Noonuccal (Kath Walker) and Joe McGuiness represented Aboriginal interests in the 1950s and 60s. Young Aboriginal activists linked with Aboriginal protests in Australia's southern states, and a long slow process of social change began in the 1970s. This was speeded up by the collapse of Queensland's ultra-conservative Bjelke Peterson government in the 1990s.

THE PRESENT

It is estimated that 20,000 Indigenous people were killed by European settlers over 50 years in 19th-century Queensland. Despite this, the Aboriginal community has survived

▌ROCK ART IN QUEENSLAND
Philip Morrissey

Some of Australia's largest rock art sites are found in Queensland. The escarpment country surrounding Laura is famed for its distinctive paintings of Quinkans (spirit beings). The area was first discovered by Europeans in the 19th century, with further discoveries in 1959. Post-contact art is also featured, including representations of the hated Native Police – it's thought the artists were attempting to counter the menace of European settlement with magic (see the Kokowarra Country section of this chapter). Another significant site is Carnarvon Gorge in Carnarvon National Park, which has hundreds of paintings and engravings (see the Garingbal Country section).

and their heritage is rich, alive and well. The population has also continued to grow.

Large areas of Cape York are designated Aboriginal land and many Aboriginal organisations and communities have established land resource management strategies to promote bio-diversity conservation. In 1996 pastoralists, the Cape York Land Council and environmentalists signed an agreement to work together to protect and maintain wilderness areas and to develop ecologically sustainable pastoral industry.

In 1996 the High Court of Australia ruled that traditional Aboriginal rights to land could coexist with leasehold rights to land held by pastoralists. This became known as the 'Wik decision', after the Wik and Thaayorre peoples of western Cape York, who were the claimants. Further agreements between pastoralists and Aboriginal communities have been ratified since then. For more information, see the boxed text 'Wik, Four Judicial Elders & Sammy Davis Junior' in the Facts about Aboriginal Australia & the Torres Strait Islands chapter.

Language

BRISBANE AREA

The Yuggera language was one of the languages spoken in what is now called Brisbane. By the 1930s the language had become extinct, but records remain of several Yuggera place-names for the Brisbane area:

Place Name	Yuggera Word
Ballina	Baluna
Brisbane	Miangin
Coomera	Kumar/Kamir-Kamir
Long Pocket	Tuwong
Mt Coot-tha	Kuta
Mt Gravatt	Kaggar-Mabul
New Farm	Binkinba
Toowong	Banera
White's Hill	Bulimba

THE NORTH

Guugu-Yimidhirr is spoken north-west of Cooktown, in northern Queensland. It was once spoken along the coast from the Annon River in the south to the Jeannie River in the north, and west to Battle Camp. Around 100 speakers of Guugu-Yimidhirr now live in Hopevale, around 50km north of Cooktown. English is slowly replacing Guugu-Yimidhirr as the community's main language, with younger people speaking a mixture of Guugu-Yimidhirr and English.

Two distinct dialects – Thalun-thirr, meaning 'Coastal' and Warrgurgaar, meaning 'Inland' – have now combined to form one dialect. Some Guugu-Yimidhirr names for local areas include:

Place Name	Guugu-Yimidhirr Word
Battle Camp	Balnggarr
Cooktown	Waymbuurr
Hopevale	Dyuubi
Jeannie River	Yalmba

Jirrbal (Dyirbal) is an almost extinct Australian Aboriginal language of north-east Queensland. The Jirrbal language was spoken in northern Queensland, south of Cairns, in rainforest areas. By the early 1980s only 40 to 50 speakers of the central Jirrbal dialect remained, along with around 30 speakers of other dialects.

Place Name	Jirrbal Word
Hinchinbrook Channel	Balan Milbirmi
Lake Eacham	Yidyam
Lake Barrine	Barany
Lake Euramoo	Ngimun
Tully Falls	Balan Gariya
Tully River	Balan Dabun

CAPE YORK PENINSULA

Wik-Mungkan is one of the Wik dialects, once spoken to the south, inland of, and on the west coast of Cape York Peninsula. Early last century, a community was established at Aurukun, north of where the Archer and Watson Rivers meet, which became a gathering place for threatened clans in the region. Wik-Mungkan, originally spoken along the Archer River, became the dominant language of this community.

Today, around 1000 people speak Wik-Mungkan as either their first or second language, and at Aurukun it forms part of a bilingual education program at the community school.

Hey you!	Aayang!
Goodbye. (general)	Appow.
Goodbye.	Paanthanow. (literally, 'Camp well.')
Yes.	E'e'.
No.	Ya'a.

USEFUL CONTACTS

Guugu Yimidhirr Language Centre (☎ 4060 9260) CPO, Hopevale, Qld 4871

Yugambeh Museum, Language & Heritage Centre (☎ 3807 6155) Plantation Rd (corner of Martens St), Beenleigh, Qld 4207

Information

PERMITS

A permit is needed to visit Palm Island and Wujal Wujal, to pass through Hopevale and the cross the Dulhunty River in Cape York. Permits are not needed for Yarrabah or Cherbourg. For more information, see the relevant sections in this chapter, and the Travel Permits section in the Facts for the Visitor chapter.

NATIONAL PARKS

Entry to all Queensland national parks is free, but camping is permitted only with a permit. Permits cost $3.85/15.40 per person/family (ie, two adults and two children aged 5 to 18) per night. Camping sites at popular parks, such as Carnarvon Gorge, must be booked months ahead. Camping permits can be obtained from the relevant park offices or paid at honesty boxes in parks without a permanent office. See the Queensland Parks & Wildlife Service (QPWS) Web site: www.env.qld.gov.au.

BOOKS

If you're interested in the Indigenous communities of Cape York, try Nonie Sharp's *Footprints along the Cape York Sandbeaches*, which examines the history and culture of the communities at the tip. *The Australian Geographic Book of Cape York* by Hector Holthouse is another excellent read. There are a number of guidebooks available with important information on travelling in Cape York – see the boxed text 'Travelling in Cape York' later in this chapter for details.

SPECIAL EVENTS

Sports fans should keep an eye on local papers and the *Koori Mail* for news of the Queensland Aboriginal Rugby League Association (QARLA), which at the time of writing was planning to start an 'all-blacks' competition, to be up and running by the winter of 2001.

Yuggera Country

Around Brisbane

BRISBANE AREA

History

Traditionally, Indigenous people of the Brisbane River region and North Stradbroke Island travelled around their country to attend initiations and fighting ceremonies, and joined their neighbours at bunya feasts. It is thought that the rich resources of Moreton Bay enabled the locals to create a comparatively sedentary society that co-operated to build substantial huts, and in fishing and hunting dugongs.

In 1824 a British penal colony was established at Humpybong ('Dead houses'), which was named Redcliffe Point by the invaders. However, the first site was abandoned, partly because of Indigenous resistance, and the penal colony was moved inland to the banks of the Brisbane River.

The mangrove-fringed peninsula on which Brisbane's City Botanic Gardens now sit was a traditional hunting and fishing area known as Min-an-jin, and it formed part of a regular pathway across the river to Wooloon-cappem (Woolloongabba). This all changed after 1828, when the area became a vegetable farm for the Moreton Bay penal colony, and then in 1855 a botanical reserve. The Jagera, Yuggera, Ugarapul and Turrbal peoples are among the traditional owners in Brisbane.

Information

Indigenous Organisations The Brisbane Aboriginal Council of Elders (☎ 3846 5257) is at 121 Cordelia St, South Brisbane 4101.

Tourist Offices The Queen St Mall information kiosk (☎ 3229 5918) is open 9 am to 5 pm Monday to Thursday, to 8 pm Friday, to 4 pm Saturday, and 10 am to 4 pm Sunday.

Naturally Queensland Information Centre (☎ 3227 8187), 160 Ann St, is the main information centre for the QPWS, and handles bookings for Fraser Island and Carnarvon National Park. It is open 8.30 am to 5 pm weekdays.

Radio The Brisbane Indigenous Media Association (☎ 3892 0100, [e] info@4aaa.org.au) operates 4AAA (98.9 FM) broadcasting Murri music. Website: www.4aaa.org.au.

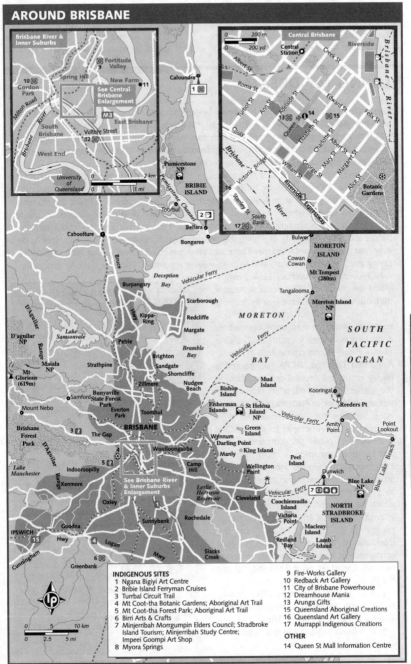

AROUND BRISBANE

Brisbane River & Inner Suburbs

Fortitude Valley
Spring Hill
10 Gordon Park
Milton Road
New Farm 11
See Central Brisbane Enlargement
M3
East Brisbane
South Brisbane
Vulture Street 12
West End
University of Queensland
Caloundra 1

Central Brisbane

Riverside
Central Station
Albert St
Roma St
Creek St
Turbot St
Ann St
Edward St
Adelaide St 13 14 15
Felix St
Queen St
Elizabeth St
Charlotte St Albert St
Mary St
Margaret St
George St
William St
Botanic Gardens
Alice St
Brisbane River
Victoria Bridge
Quay
Riverside Expressway
16
Stanley St
South Bank
17

Pumicestone NP
BRIBIE ISLAND
Pumicestone Channel
Toorbul
Bellara 2
Bongaree
Caboolture
Bulwer
MORETON ISLAND
Cowan Cowan
Mt Tempest (280m)
Bruce Hwy
Deception Bay
Vehicular Ferry
Burpengary
Tangalooma
Scarborough
Moreton Island NP
Kippa-Ring
Redcliffe
MORETON
Margate
SOUTH PACIFIC OCEAN
D'Aguilar Range
Lake Samsonvale
Petrie
Bramble Bay
BAY
D'aguilar NP
Maiala NP
Mt Glorious (619m)
Strathpine
Brighton
Sandgate
Shorncliffe
Vehicular Ferry
Samford
Zillmere
Nudgee Beach
Mud Island
Kooringal
Reeders Pt
Bunyaville State Forest Park
Everton Park
Bishop Island
St Helena Island NP
Point Lookout
Mount Nebo
Toombul
Fisherman Islands
Vehicular Ferry
Amity Point
Brisbane Forest Park
The Gap
BRISBANE
Green Island
Peel Island
3
Woolloongabba
Wynnum
Darling Point
King Island
Dunwich
8
Lake Manchester
5
See Brisbane River & Inner Suburbs Enlargement
Camp Hill
Manly
Wellington Point
Blue Lake NP
Blue Lake Beach
Indooroopilly
Kenmore
Leslie Harrison Reservoir
Cleveland
Vehicular Ferry
7
NORTH STRADBROKE ISLAND
Oxley
Sunnybank
Rochedale
Coochiemudlo Island
Victoria Point
Macleay Island
IPSWICH
15
Goodna
Logan Mwy
Slacks Creek
Redland Bay
Lamb Island
Cunningham Hwy
Greenbank
6

N

0   5   10 km
0   2.5   5 mi

QUEENSLAND

INDIGENOUS SITES
1 Ngana Bigiyi Art Centre
2 Bribie Island Ferryman Cruises
3 Turrbal Circuit Trail
4 Mt Coot-tha Botanic Gardens; Aboriginal Art Trail
5 Mt Coot-tha Forest Park; Aboriginal Art Trail
6 Birri Arts & Crafts
7 Minjerribah Morrgumpin Elders Council; Stradbroke Island Tourism; Minjerribah Study Centre; Impeei Goompi Art Shop
8 Myora Springs

9 Fire-Works Gallery
10 Redback Art Gallery
11 City of Brisbane Powerhouse
12 Dreamhouse Mania
13 Arunga Gifts
15 Queensland Aboriginal Creations
16 Queensland Art Gallery
17 Murrappi Indigenous Creations

OTHER
14 Queen St Mall Information Centre

Mt Coot-tha Forest Park

The Turrbal people gathered on the slopes to the west of modern-day Brisbane in order to collect *ku-ta*, the honey produced by native bees in tree hollows found in the majestic towering eucalyptus trees.

A 600m **Aboriginal Art Trail** takes you past seven art sites with the work of local

---

LIVING MY DREAM
Janzey McDonald

Cancer. How did this happen? I had never been seriously ill in my life. The only time I had been hospitalised was to give birth to my daughter, Cassidy. That day at the doctor's surgery was a huge turning point in my life. From that day, I decided I was going to follow my dreams. I resigned from my job in real estate and decided to take some time off not only to focus on my health, but also to focus on my soul.

Then one day, it was as if God sent me a sign. I was invited along to the official year 2000 launch at the Aboriginal Centre for the Performing Arts (ACPA), along with other people I had been working with at an Indigenous theatre company. As soon as I heard the students sing, I knew exactly where I belonged. Something grabbed hold of me deep down inside and I felt so alive, so happy. After the performance, I spoke to one of the school administrators about the possibility of joining the performing arts course. As fate would have it, the very next day they contacted me! There was an unexpected opening. One spot only. As the saying goes, the rest is history and I am now living my dream – singing, dancing and acting.

ACPA's director, Michael Leslie, established the school in 1993 because he saw that Australia was lacking quality training for aspiring Indigenous artists. The school, based in Brisbane, has since opened its doors to non-Indigenous students. Growing from a three-month course to a two-year Advanced Diploma, ACPA has earned a highly respected reputation, maintaining the highest student retention rate of any tertiary institution in Australia, with all graduates securing consistent employment in the arts industry. Among its activities, ACPA is involved in public performances – local and national productions – many involving Indigenous communities around Australia. Students and graduates also travel overseas to perform in festivals and conferences, which has resulted in a rapidly increasing interest in international student exchange programs. In 2004, ACPA will host the International Association of Blacks in Dance conference in Brisbane. For more information, call the school on ☎ 3211 9600 or see the Web site at www.acpa.com.au.

Just a couple of months after joining ACPA, I was admitted to hospital again... There was no more cancer. These days, my motto in life is to do it today and listen to your heart.

Janzey McDonald

From a mixed heritage of Aboriginal and South Sea Islander from her mother and Scottish from her Australian father, Janzey McDonald was born in Mackay in north Queensland in 1969. Before being accepted into the Aboriginal Centre for the Performing Arts in Brisbane at the age of 31, she'd already tried a few jobs – journalist, policewoman, real estate consultant and firefighter.

Now with a daughter Cassidy, aged four, and married to a Scotsman named John (or Jock!), her return to the arts was no surprise, although a health scare with cancer hurried the decision along. The family is full of talent. Mum Anne is a singer, sister Nadine an artistic director and Dad Noel (or Nudge) comes from a large family of natural performers.

These days Janzey is aiming for brighter stars like Broadway and Hollywood. No dream is impossible.

Aboriginal artists commissioned to commemorate the International Year of the World's Indigenous People in 1993. Natural ochres, acrylics and charcoal were used to create stencilled and free-hand rock paintings inspired by symbols and beings from the *stories* of different communities.

Mt Coot-tha Botanic Gardens

At Mt Coot-tha Botanic Gardens (☎ 3403 2535, fax 3403 2552, e vsomg@bit.net.au) there's a self-guiding **Aboriginal Plant Trail**. Interpretative signs along the paved track (suitable for wheelchairs) explain traditional and contemporary uses of local rainforest plants for food, medicine, shelter, utensils and tools. Pick up a brochure at the gardens information kiosk and allow a leisurely hour to enjoy the trail. The trail is in the south-east corner of the gardens, near the main entrance.

The gardens are open 9.30 am to 4 pm daily.

Brisbane Forest Park

The **Turrbal Circuit Trail** is a 1.7km walk at Bellbird Grove west of Brisbane, which explains the interaction of Turrbal people with their rainforest environment. There are interpretative signs along the way and a replica of a rainforest encampment with bark huts, fireplaces and artefacts. The walk takes about 50 minutes to complete.

North Stradbroke Island

The Nunukul, Nughie and Goenpul tribes inhabited North Stradbroke for thousands of years and at Wallen Wallen Creek, just south of Dunwich, artefacts have been found that date back more than 21,000 years. Just north of Dunwich, Myora Springs was a favoured camping site and parts of a large midden can be seen on the banks of the spring. Unfortunately, many more middens have been destroyed by sand-mining operations.

Probably Australia's best-known Aboriginal poet and writer, Oodgeroo Noonuccal (or Kath Walker), was born on North Stradbroke Island in 1920 and buried there in September 1993. Her book *We Are Going*, published in 1964, was the first published work by an Aboriginal woman; her other works include *Father Sky and Mother Water*, which she also illustrated, and *My People*.

Information

Indigenous Organisations Members of Minjerribah Moorgumpin Elders Council (☎ 3409 9723, 3821 0057), PO Box 106, Dunwich, Qld 4183, are available for cultural talks to schools and community groups.

Books Oodgeroo Noonuccal (Kath Walker) relates Dreaming stories and reminisces about growing up on Stradbroke in *Stradbroke Dreamtime*. *Mindjerribah – An Indigenous Story of North Stradbroke Island* tells the Aboriginal story of the island, and is available at Impeei Goompi (see the Shopping section, later).

Minjerribah Study Centre Minjerribah Study Centre (☎ 3409 9445, fax 3409 9566), Oxley Parade, Dunwich, caters for school, university and club groups, and can organise guided walks and talks with Elders from Minjerribah Moorgumpin. Activities on offer include workshops in fire-lighting, spear-making, dancing, bush tucker and art. Check out their Web site: www.stradbroke.com.

Shopping

Impeei Goompi (☎ 3409 9926), on Ballow Rd, Dunwich, sells locally made products, including crafts, art, jewellery, pottery and souvenirs. It's open from 9 am to 4 pm daily.

Special Events

The DAR Festival, held annually in Brisbane from 29 May to 5 June, is a festival of dance, music, storytelling, new media, art and theatre. DAR means 'Earth, ground and country'; check the Web site at www.darfestival.com.

Entertainment

The site of the City of Brisbane Powerhouse (☎ 3254 4518, fax 3254 4153, e info @brisbanepowerhouse.org), at 119 Lamington St, New Farm, was once a fishing and hunting spot for local clans. A power station was built here in 1928 and today it has been refurbished as a performing arts centre. Its jam-packed program occasionally features Aboriginal and Islander dance troupes. Check out the calendar of events on its Web site (www.brisbanepowerhouse.org) or events listings in the *Courier-Mail* and *This Week in Brisbane*.

QUEENSLAND

BRISBANE GALLERIES & SHOPS

Readers should be aware that the names of deceased members of the Aboriginal community may be cited in this section. Mentioning the personal name of someone who has died recently can cause offence, anguish and grief in some Aboriginal cultures.

There are far too many places in Brisbane that sell or exhibit works by Indigenous artists to list them all here. Following is a selection of recommended outlets. See the Shopping section in the Facts for the Visitor chapter for further information.

Arunga Gifts (☎ 3221 0982) Shop 15, Brisbane Arcade, 156 Queen St. This quaint shop has a variety of Indigenous souvenir products – painted turtle shells, gift-wrapping paper, mouse pads, tea-towels, painted picture frames, T-shirts, trinket boxes, jewellery boxes, hats, bags, playing cards, animal magnets, and Aboriginal flag badges and painted designs on polished agate. Don't miss the painted kangaroo skins, carved and painted emu eggs and the magnificent selection of canvas paintings by local Aboriginal artists. It's open 9 am to 5 pm Monday to Thursday, to 7 pm Friday, 10 am to 3 pm Saturday and 11 am to 3 pm Sunday.

Birri Arts and Crafts (☎ 3200 1111) 53–65 Cheviot St, Greenbank. Birri provides the opportunity to buy direct from an Aboriginal artefact manufacturer. The owner, Ian Skeen, learned his craft from his father and maintains the continuity of these local Indigenous cultural traditions. He makes and sells killer, hunting and returning boomerangs; *clapsticks*; didjeridus; spears and many other artefacts. Visit by appointment only.

Dreamhouse Mania (☎ 3844 9994) 602 Stanley St, South Brisbane. Owned and operated by Aboriginal artist Marrisa Spencer, Dreamhouse Mania offers an opportunity for both up-and-coming and established Aboriginal artists to showcase and sell their work. The shop purchases artwork from local and interstate artists creating a diverse range of options for shoppers. Each year, the shop releases a calender of printed painting ($8). The Aboriginal artefacts and souvenir products on sale include emu eggs (carved and painted), left-handed, common and come-back boomerangs and didjeridus; didjeridu lessons are also available. Select from the range of clothing including sarongs, shirts, T-shirts, blouses, caps, and hats (made from leather and material). For something unique, check out the jewellery made from porcupine quills and wood as well as the Australian icon charms for charm bracelets. Don't miss the painted turtle shells, hand-painted terracotta pots and the excellent range of bark paintings on sale. Make sure you visit this treasure house of Aboriginal cultural products. It's open 10 am to 4.30 pm Tuesday to Saturday. Web site: www.dreamhousemania.com.au

Fire-Works Gallery (☎ 3216 1250) 678 Ann St, Fortitude Valley. In an informal and community-orientated atmosphere, this gallery provides a fine blend of art and social conscience, with a definite political agenda and an ethical approach to Indigenous art. You can meet and talk with the artists in residence about their work. Fire-works deals mainly with contemporary artwork, and also sometimes in historic works. Showcasing the work of both emerging and established artists, it conducts about six exhibitions a year. It's open 11 am to 6 pm Tuesday to Friday, and to 5 pm on Saturday.

Impeei Goompi (☎ 3409 8127) on Ballow Rd, Dunwich, North Stradbroke Island. Impeei Goompi translates as 'Going into Dunwich'. Run by the Quandamooka Community Development Employment Program, part of the Quandamooka Land Council, this shop is an Aboriginal community enterprise set up as an alternative employment program for local artists to retail their work. Explore the great variety of local Aboriginal arts and crafts ranging from cards, bags, paintings, shell picture frames and calenders to artefacts such as boomerangs, spears, clapsticks, returning boomerangs, didjeridus and jewellery. Check out the fine selection of books by local Indigenous authors. For something special, you can't go past the ceramic turtle- and clam-shell bowls. It's open 9 am to 4 pm daily.

Murruppi Indigenous Creations (☎ 3844 0255) Shop PO 1, South Bank House, Little Stanley St. In the beautiful South Bank precinct of inner Brisbane, the owner of Murruppi,

continued...   Elizabeth McNiven

Dan Murphy, named his shop in honour of his father Murruppi, an Aboriginal man from the Jirrbal language group of the Atherton Tablelands. This shop offers an opportunity to purchase Indigenous cultural items in an informed and friendly atmosphere. There is an exceptional variety of souvenir products, including the paint-your-own boomerang kit, Aboriginal flags, mouse pads, coasters, posters, jewellery, T-shirts, hats, bags, painted stones, printed writing paper, gift-wrapping paper, hats and hat bands, and the superbly painted wooden covered photograph albums. The range of artefacts includes come-back boomerangs, *coolamons*, *dilly* bags, shields, didjeridus, clapsticks and spear throwers. With a fine collection of canvas paintings, framed pictures, pottery and a great variety of CDs, along with an excellent range of books on Aboriginal art, heritage, culture and children's stories, you can't go past this shop. It's open 9.30 am to 5 pm Monday to Thursday, 10.30 am to 9.30 pm Friday, 10 am to 5 pm Saturday and 1 pm to 5 pm Sunday.

Ngana Bigiyi Art Centre (☎ 5491 8596) Shop 2, 60 Bulcock St, Caloundra. On the Sunshine Coast, this is an Aboriginal community corporation enterprise formed by four Aboriginal Community Development Employment Programs (CDEPs), designed to improve the socio-economic position of Aboriginal people in the area. (Ngana Bigiyi means 'Our Dream'.) The centre trains Aboriginal people in the retail industry and conducts courses in screen-printing and ceramics. You can buy a fine selection of souvenir products, including locally produced boomerangs, *bullroarers*, spears, clapsticks, emu eggs, painted kangaroo skins, ceramic items, screen-prints, lino prints and canvas paintings. All products are reasonably priced. It's open 9 am to 5 pm daily.

Queensland Aboriginal Creations (☎ 3224 5730) 119 Elizabeth St. This shop offers a fine collection of Indigenous arts and crafts from across Queensland, along with a selection of superb artwork from interstate artists. It was established in 1959 by the Department of Aboriginal and Torres Strait Islander Policy, to support the development of Aboriginal and Torres Strait Islander communities towards self-sufficiency by providing a retail outlet for their artists and craftspeople. The shop now supports emerging artists through major exhibitions (October to December).

Items for sale include a fantastic range of clothing by Balarinji, Desert Designs, Jamin and Outstation. Check out the range of T-shirts, dresses, bathing suits, silk ties, scarves and dress shirts. There is an excellent choice of Aboriginal music, including audio tapes, CDs, CD-ROMs, and videos by artists such as Yothu Yindi, Warumpi Band and Christine Anu, plus a great range of *didjeridu* recordings. If you're suffering from aches or pains, try the Barambah Emu oil products. Artefacts

Elizabeth McNiven

I am a Budjiti woman from the Paroo River country of NSW and Queensland. In 1993 I graduated from the University of Canberra with a Bachelor of Arts degree in Communication, and completed a six-year Skills Development Program in Cultural Resource Management in the Film Archive of the Australian Institute of Aboriginal and Torres Strait Islander Studies.

I created and sold *Spirit Dreaming*, a neon sculpture, to the National Gallery of Australia. My graphic artwork is printed on calendars, posters, postcards, diaries, certificates and annual reports.

I have conducted Aboriginal culture and art workshops across the Australian Capital Territory and NSW. My poetry was published by Penguin in the book *Inside Black Australia*, which was edited by Kevin Gilbert and won the 1988 Human Rights Award.

I have worked as an arts consultant, a native title researcher, a program director, a creative producer, a senior land rights officer and a publicity officer.

QUEENSLAND

BRISBANE GALLERIES & SHOPS

continued...

on sale include fighting sticks from central Australia, and didjeridus from the NT and Western Australia. There is also a fine array of souvenir products, including ceramic trinket boxes, coasters and carved wooden animals. If you're in the market for innovative Indigenous creations, you can't go past the Wathaurong Glass products, which include platters, bowls and other handmade items. If you only have time to visit one shop in Brisbane, this is the place. It's open 9 am to 5 pm Monday to Thursday, to 6 pm Friday, to 4 pm Saturday, and 10 am to 4 pm Sunday.

Queensland Art Gallery (☎ 3840 7303) corner of Melbourne and Grey St, South Brisbane. This gallery is part of the Queensland Cultural Centre at South Bank. Aboriginal art is displayed throughout the gallery. Gallery 2 displays a permanent collection of contemporary Indigenous Australian art, gallery 11 shows Australian art from the 1920s to 1955 (including works by Albert Namatjira), and gallery 13 shows Australian art post-1975 (including works by Ron Hurley). Wander through this relaxed and spacious environment and take in the work of Indigenous Australia's finest artists. The staff are friendly and helpful. Free guided tours of the gallery are held daily at 11 am, and 1 and 2 pm (at 11 am, and 2 and 3 pm on weekends). Free, short, focus talks begin at 1.30 pm daily. Entry to the gallery and the guided tours is free. The gallery also houses a research library, open 10 am

Bundjalung Country

The Gold Coast

DAVID FLEAY WILDLIFE PARK

David Fleay Wildlife Park (☎ 5576 2411, fax 5535 6623, e fleays@env.qld.gov.au) runs a Heritage Talk with an Aboriginal ranger on Monday, Tuesday and Wednesday at 11.30 am. The talk touches on stories, culture and customs of the Kombumerri and Bundjalung peoples. Dance performances are combined with the talks on Monday and Tuesday (this might be extended in future).

The park is open 9 am to 5 pm daily (except Christmas Day); admission costs $13/8.50/6.50 for adults/pensioners/children; it's $33 for families.

Gubbi Gubbi Country

The Sunshine Coast

A local story relates how the distinctive volcanic formations that tower above the coastal plain came to be formed. One day Tibrogargan noticed that the sea was rising and gathered his children to flee to safety. He ordered his son Coonowrin to help Beerwah, the mother, who was heavily pregnant, but Coonowrin fled. Angered, Tibrogargan struck him with his club and

dislodged his neck. When the floods subsided Coonowrin begged his father's forgiveness, but Tibrogargan could only weep tears of shame at his son's cowardice; likewise, his brothers and sisters wept copious tears and this explains the many streams running off the mountains today.

Tibrogargan turned his back on his son and today gazes far out to sea, while Coonowrin hangs his head and cries. Several well-preserved archaeological sites can be seen against this scenic backdrop (see the Glasshouse Mountains section later).

ORGANISED TOURS

Ferryman (☎/fax 3408 7124, e ferryman @ferryman.com.au), 7 Sylvan Beach Esplanade, Bribie Island, runs cruises through Pumicestone Passage and can show you an extensive midden at Mission Point. The commentary relates the wildlife and ecology of this outstanding area to the traditional inhabitants.

The three-hour cruise leaves at 9.30 am on Thursday and costs $22/13 for adults/children under 14; families (two adults and two children) cost $58. A two-hour cruise runs at 2 pm on Sunday during school holidays and long weekends; it costs $16.50/9; families are $44. A six-hour cruise departing 9 am costs $54/20, and includes lunch and refreshments (this cruise is dictated by the tides). Web site: www.ferryman.com.au.

QUEENSLAND

continued... Elizabeth McNiven

to 5 pm daily. Also browse the gallery shop's comprehensive range of books on Aboriginal art, culture and politics, plus the superb collection of T-shirts on sale that are printed with the artwork of prominent Aboriginal artists. The gallery is open 10 am to 5 pm daily.
Web site: www.qag.qld.gov.au

Redback Art Gallery (☎ 3357 6064) 60 Kartoum Street, Gordon Park. Redback provides great inspiration to explore both ceremonial and contemporary expressions of Indigenous Australian culture. The gallery showcases a diverse range of innovative artwork by Indigenous Australians, including superb prints from the Kimberley and the Tiwi Islands; beautiful canvas painting from Utopia (NT); rainforest swords, shields and fire-maker sets from far north Queensland; and a fabulous selection of earthenware from Hermannsburg, Northern Territory (NT). Don't miss the traditionally designed ceremonial dance costumes for men and women, made from contemporary fibres. The range of jewellery on display includes magnificent iridescent shell necklaces from Tasmania, Ernabella hand-painted eucalyptus and quandong seed necklaces, and Kimberley necklaces made from baobab nut seeds. Redback is open noon to 5 pm Tuesday to Saturday. Make an appointment to visit outside these hours.
Web site: www.redbackart.com.au

GLASSHOUSE MOUNTAINS

Numerous **axe-grinding grooves** can be seen on the sandstone pavements along Little Rocky Creek, 2km south of Landsborough on the Old Gympie Rd. The grooves were made where hard volcanic stone axes were sharpened on the soft sandstone.

There's a well-preserved **bora ring** a few kilometres away at Glass House. Now hemmed in by housing, the bora ring (a circular ground used for ceremonies) measures about 22m across, but erosion and time have worn down the once 5m-wide embankment considerably. The best way to find it is to turn west off the Bruce Hwy onto Johnston Rd (signposted) and follow it for about 2km; the bora ring is 600m north of Johnston Rd behind a pine plantation.

Barunggam Country

Darling Downs

MILES HISTORIC VILLAGE

A room in this museum (☎/fax 4627 1492) of mainly white-Australian history displays a mixed bag of artefacts, including grindstones, shields, didjeridus and boomerangs, and illustrates various Aboriginal stories.

The village is open 8 am to 5 pm daily (except Christmas day). Entry is $10/8/3/2 for adults/pensioners/secondary students/primary students; or $20 for a family ticket.

Waka Waka Country

Sunshine Coast Hinterland

CHERBOURG ABORIGINAL COMMUNITY

Set up by the Queensland government as an Aboriginal settlement in 1904, Cherbourg was originally called Barambah. The first occupants came from about 13 tribes and walked there from near Woodford in 1906. People from some 40 groups from all over Queensland were forcibly moved to Cherbourg, where many were subjected to some particularly harsh treatment.

Cherbourg is now controlled under a Deed of Grant in Trust (DOGIT, a special form of title established by the Queensland government in 1984 that allows community-level land trusts to own and administer former reserve lands), and Cherbourg Community Council (☎ 4168 1866, fax 4168 2727) manages ventures such as beef and stud cattle, dairy and woodwork.

The modern Cherbourg belies its past and you're welcome to look around the town. Murals produced by local people adorn the walls of various buildings, such as the cultural centre and supermarket. A new botanic gardens is soon due to open next to Barambah Emu Farm (see later). Cherbourg recently came into national focus as the only Queensland Aboriginal community through

QUEENSLAND

which the 2000 Olympic Torch Relay passed. A number of community members were involved in the relay.

Cherbourg News, the official newsletter of the Cherbourg Community Council, tells what's on around Cherbourg and periodically publishes snippets of local history. The community's radio station, 4UM Us Mob Radio (87.8 FM) is on the main street.

Barambah Emu Farm

Cherbourg boasts Queensland's first commercial emu farm (☎ 4168 2655), which now supplies breeding stock to other emu farms and supplies emu meat to restaurants. The farm is open to the public and there are displays of hand-carved emu eggs and fine emu leather.

A 30-minute tour of the farm costs $5 and leaves at 9.30 and 11 am, and at noon. It's open 8 am to 3 pm daily (except Friday).

Shopping

Paintings from Cherbourg artists can be bought through Gondwana Creations Fine Arts (☎ 4168 1144, 0401 523 779), Web site: www.gondwana.cx, which takes only a modest commission.

SPECIAL EVENTS

The very popular Woodford Folk Festival (☎ 5496 1066), Web site: www.woodford folkfestival.com, is held annually from 27 December to 1 January. It is a major focus for Indigenous performers, musicians, storytellers, artists and craftspeople from around the country. The packed schedule is spread over three Murri venues within the festival grounds (Corroboree Ground, Talking Circle and Murri Stage). Expect to see a wide variety of live music and participate in lively debates or workshops on traditional crafts, eg, basket-, string- and fire-making. Intimate, open-air encounters with Elders are encouraged, and informal contact and communication between Indigenous and non-Indigenous people is an important part of the festival experience. Organisers make great efforts to respect tradition, eg, didjeridu-playing is restricted to men and various forums are held in which men, women or youths only may participate. Each year the festival is opened by Dungidau Elders and it is traditional for each dawn to be

ushered in by some of the country's best didjeridu players. And with Aboriginal storytellers relating fireside Dreaming stories at night, it's no wonder that advance bookings are essential for this festival.

Badtjala Country

Fraser Coast

KORRAWINGA COMMUNITY FARM

The Korrawinga Aboriginal community (☎ 4124 6908, fax 4124 6935) runs this former cattle ranch as an organic farm that aims to become self-sufficient. Visitors to Korrawinga are conducted around the community and market gardens, nursery, and a bush tucker and medicine trail, and farm enterprises such as tea-tree and protea plantations. Locally made arts and crafts, and handmade jewellery are also for sale.

Guided tours are conducted every Wednesday at 9.30 am. The cost is $15/10/5 for adults/pensioners/children ($30 for a family pass), which includes morning tea and transfers to and from Hervey Bay. Bookings are essential.

FRASER ISLAND

The original name for Fraser Island is K'gari which means 'Paradise' and is named after a spirit who helped the Great Spirit, Beeral, create the earth and other worlds. K'gari loved earth so much she asked Beeral to let her live there and so he changed her into a beautiful island, with trees and animals for company, and limpid lakes for eyes through which she could gaze up at the heavens, her former home.

Originally numbering about 2000, by 1867 disease and genocide had reduced the Badtjala people to 300 to 400. In 1897 most survivors were rounded up and taken to Bogimbah mission on the island; after Bogimbah closed in 1904 the detainees were taken to Yarrabah in north Queensland. A few Badtjala remain on K'gari today.

The island takes its non-Aboriginal name from the captain of a ship that was wrecked further north in 1836. Making their way south to look for help, a group of men from the ship fell in with the Badtjala. Some of the group died during their two-month wait for rescue, but others survived with the assistance of the Badtjala people.

Apart from many **middens** and ancient fireplaces along the east coast, little trace of the Badtjala remains: there are **scarr trees** at Boomanjin and the sandblow east of Lake Wabby periodically uncovers small flakes of chert where stone blades were made.

Organised Tours

Sunrover Expeditions (☎/fax 3203 4241, ⓔ howard@powerup.com.au) runs two-, four- and five-day 4WD tours from Brisbane to Fraser Island that can include some of the island's Badtjala sites.

Darumbal Country

Rockhampton Area

ROCKHAMPTON
Information

Radio station 4US (100.7 FM) broadcasts Indigenous programmes seven days a week. For information contact the Central Queensland Aboriginal Corporation for Media (☎ 4772 5466).

Dreamtime Cultural Centre

Set in about 12 hectares of bushland with shady paths and signposted food and medicine plants, Dreamtime Cultural Centre (☎ 4936 1655, fax 4936 1671) features displays on Aboriginal and Torres Straits Islander heritage, such as artefacts, art and weapons, as well as a sports Hall of Fame.

The main reason to visit, however, is to take a tour. You'll be given an entertaining talk on Torres Strait Islanders, and can walk through a giant replica dugong with more photos and artefacts. There are demonstrations of boomerang-throwing and didjeridu-playing, and the Ted Mitchell Gallery introduces the stencil art, lifestyle and culture of Queensland's central sandstone area with a short film, reproductions of rock art and various artefacts including a bark hut.

The centre is open 10 am to 3.30 pm daily, and 1½-hour tours are run daily at 10.30 am and 1 pm. Admission is $12/8.25/5.50 for adults/pensioners/school children; backpackers and tertiary students pay $9.90 and family tickets start at $26.40.

Places to Stay

Right next door to, and run by, the cultural centre is Dreamtime Lodge Motel (☎ 4936 4600, fax 4936 4611), a modern resort-style accommodation complex that boasts 31 air-conditioned motel-style rooms, a saltwater pool, and indoor and outdoor meal areas. Rooms are $66/68 a single/double.

Gangulu Country

Capricorn Hinterland

BLACKDOWN TABLELAND NATIONAL PARK

The Blackdown Tableland (QPWS; ☎ 4986 1964) is a spectacular sandstone plateau which rises suddenly out of the surrounding plains to a height of 600m. The Gangulu people visited the tableland for thousands of years, although little remains of their presence: by the 1900s all but a few hundred were killed, dispersed or had succumbed to smallpox and influenza.

The 2.8km **Mimosa Culture Circuit** leads to a rock overhang where stencils of hands and stone axes can be seen in the red and orange pigments that occur naturally in the area. Interpretations along the trail surmise aspects of the Gangulu lifestyle from the topography, vegetation and fauna of the tableland.

Garingbal Country

Carnarvon Area

CARNARVON NATIONAL PARK

Much of Carnarvon Gorge remains as it probably was thousands of years ago, when the cabbage palms and cycads growing along the wooded gorge floor were an important food source for the Garingbal people, as demonstrated by large quantities of cooked cycad nuts found in Cathedral Cave (see later). Aboriginal art can be viewed at three main sites, all with interpretations and boardwalks.

Information

The park office and information centre (☎ 4984 4505, fax 4984 4519) is open 8 am to 5 pm daily.

Books *The Riches of Ancient Australia* by Josephine Flood gives sober descriptions of the main archaeological and art sites at Carnarvon Gorge.

QUEENSLAND

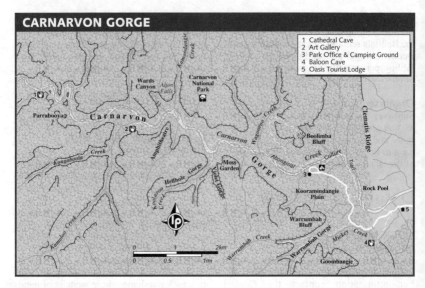

CARNARVON GORGE

1 Cathedral Cave
2 Art Gallery
3 Park Office & Camping Ground
4 Baloon Cave
5 Oasis Tourist Lodge

Organised Tours

Sunrover Expeditions (☎/fax 3203 4241) runs a six-day 4WD tour from Brisbane to Carnarvon Gorge, including a full-day walk to the Art Gallery and Cathedral Cave (see later). Tours depart once a month from March to October, but special trips can be arranged for groups of five or more. The cost is $840/600 adults/children ($1400/1100 if you stay at nearby Oasis Tourist Lodge).

Carnarvon Gorge

The 500m **Aboriginal Culture Trail** leads to Baloon Cave, an overhang that catches the morning sun in winter. The cave features hand and axe stencils (*baloon* is a local word for axe – rock from the cave was possibly used to make stone axes), and the track is signposted at intervals with information about various plants useful to the Garingbal.

Art Gallery The turn-off to the Art Gallery is passed after 5.6km along the track to Cathedral Cave. This 750m detour leads to a spectacular assemblage of stencils, engravings and free-hand paintings – best viewed between late morning and mid-afternoon. Among the stencils of adults' and children's hands, stone axes, boomerangs and nets is a composite stencil of a humanoid with outstretched arms. Other obvious motifs are red and white nets and three free-hand drawings of white goannas, although they may be difficult to see against the sandstone in certain light. At the far end of the gallery are hundreds of engravings, including kangaroo footprints, human feet, a nest of emu eggs, a 10m serpent and the paw-print of an unknown, five-toed animal. However, most obvious and in spectacular abundance are the engravings of vulvas – nowhere else in Australia are they engraved with such regularity.

Cathedral Cave This massive overhang 9.3km along the gorge is extensively decorated with stencils and free-hand paintings in red and yellow ochre. It was occupied more than 3500 years ago and excavations show that more art is buried up to 90cm beneath the surface. A free-hand humanoid spirit figure unique in the area holds a significant position high on the rock face. Other interesting motifs include a double-handed forearm stencil; panels of repeated boomerang stencils indicating that a group of hunters used the site; and stencils of oval *che-ka-ra* (melo shell pendants) that originated in Cape York Peninsula and were traded with other tribes in the area.

Mt Moffatt

The many sandstone rock shelters of the lower southern and high northern areas are now the Mt Moffatt section of the national park (QPWS; ☎ 4626 3581). Moondungera, the Rainbow Serpent, is said to have created the Maranoa River, and in severe droughts created a big spring flowing out of the range to carve out the winding, sandy river bed.

Among the strange sandstone formations along the entrance road are **The Tombs**, a network of natural tunnels that was once a burial ground. Skeletons wrapped in decorated bark cylinders were discovered by Europeans here in the 19th century and excavations have shown this site was in use at least 9400 years ago. The burial sites have all been vandalised, but you can still see rock art, including stencils of che-ka-ra, the shell pendants traded from the Cape York area.

Numerous stencils are preserved at **Kenniff Cave**, the first archaeological site to be excavated in Queensland and one of the most important sites in central Queensland. Excavations in the 1960s uncovered traces of habitation 3.28m below the surface, indicating the cave's use 19,500 years ago. A boardwalk equipped with push-button solar lighting allows you to examine the red and dark ochre stencils, including weapons known only from stencil art, and a few free-hand motifs. A rare human-like figure painted free-hand in red ochre, over red hand stencils, is located low down on the south-western wall. Flash photography is permitted. Kenniff Cave is about 250m from the car park.

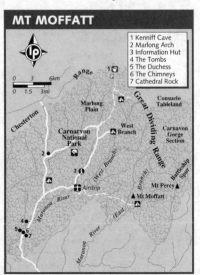

MT MOFFATT

1 Kenniff Cave
2 Marlong Arch
3 Information Hut
4 The Tombs
5 The Duchess
6 The Chimneys
7 Cathedral Rock

0   3   6km
0   1.5   3mi

Range

Marlong Plain

Consuelo Tableland

Chesterton

Great Dividing Range

Carnarvon National Park

West Branch

Carnarvon Gorge Section

(West Branch)

Airstrip

Battleship Spur

Mt Percy ▲

▲ Mt Moffatt

Maranoa River

(East)

River

Giya Country

Whitsundays

AIRLIE BEACH
Information
The QPWS office (☎ 4946 7022) is on the corner of Shute Harbour and Mandalay Rds. Opening hours are 9 am to 5 pm weekdays, to 1 pm on Saturday.

Coral Beach Track
A self-guided 1km walking track, which explains the traditional uses of some of the region's rainforest and mangrove plants, has been created by the QPWS with the help of the Giru Dala Council of Elders, the traditional custodians of the Whitsunday homeland region.

Leaflets are available at the trailhead. To get there, turn left at Whitsunday Drive, just past the Shell service station as you come into Shute Harbour. The trail begins at a car park on your left about 1km along.

Nyawaygi, Gugu-Badhun & Bindil Country

Townsville Area

Townsville borders three traditional country areas: Nyawaygi country, Gugu-Badhun country and Bindul country. In the 1870s local Aborigines were often kidnapped for work on pearling and fishing vessels and after 1918 many were forcibly moved to Palm Island, which became the focus of the area's Aboriginal community life for several decades. After WWII, Torres Strait Islanders began arriving to work on the railway, and in the cane and pearling industries; as restrictions on Aboriginal movements decreased, more came to town in the 1960s. Townsville now hosts many Aboriginal health, welfare and cultural agencies and is a major centre for Islander culture.

TOWNSVILLE
Radio
The Townsville Aboriginal & Islander Media Association Inc (☎ 4772 5466) broadcasts 4KIG (107 FM).

QUEENSLAND

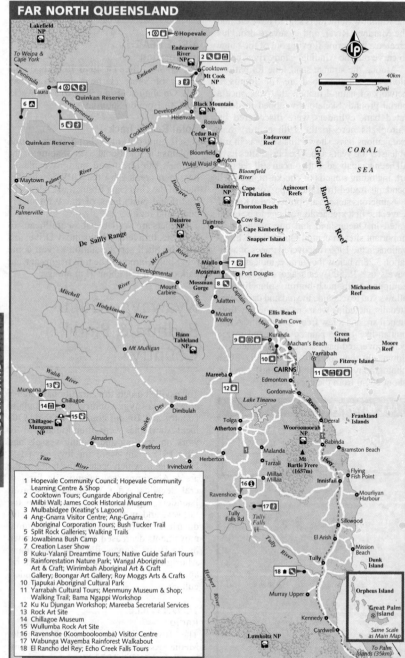

FAR NORTH QUEENSLAND

1 Hopevale Community Council; Hopevale Community Learning Centre & Shop
2 Cooktown Tours; Gungarde Aboriginal Centre; Milbi Wall; James Cook Historical Museum
3 Mulbabidgee (Keating's Lagoon)
4 Ang-Gnarra Visitor Centre; Ang-Gnarra Aboriginal Corporation Tours; Bush Tucker Trail
5 Split Rock Galleries; Walking Trails
6 Jowalbinna Bush Camp
7 Creation Laser Show
8 Kuku-Yalanji Dreamtime Tours; Native Guide Safari Tours
9 Rainforestation Nature Park; Wangal Aboriginal Art & Craft; Wirrimbah Aboriginal Art & Craft Gallery; Boongar Art Gallery; Roy Moggs Arts & Crafts
10 Tjapukai Aboriginal Cultural Park
11 Yarrabah Cultural Tours; Menmuny Museum & Shop; Walking Trail; Bama Ngappi Workshop
12 Ku Ku Djungan Workshop; Mareeba Secretarial Services
13 Rock Art Site
14 Chillagoe Museum
15 Wullumba Rock Art Site
16 Ravenshoe (Koombooloomba) Visitor Centre
17 Wabunga Wayemba Rainforest Walkabout
18 El Rancho del Rey; Echo Creek Falls Tours

Museum of Tropical Queensland

This fabulous new museum (☎ 4726 0606, fax 4721 2093, ⓔ info@mtq.qld.gov.au), 78–102 Flinders St East, with a Web site at www.mtq.qld.gov.au, features two permanent displays reflecting the region's rich Aboriginal culture and its more recent but strong associations with the Torres Strait Islands.

The absorbing Aboriginal Artefact Exhibition features a great collection of 400 artefacts and artwork collected in the Townsville region over the past 100 years. Set up as a record of culture and history, the artefacts are displayed in glass cabinets with no attempt at interpretation – deliberately so. More unusual items on display include a snakeskin lighter cover and a woven grass fly swat.

The Ailan Kastom Bilong Torres Strait features traditional toys, tools, weapons, costumes and headdresses, as well as a display on the Coming of the Light which includes videos and photos (see the boxed text 'The Coming of the Light' in the Torres Strait Islands chapter for more information on the annual festival). There are unusual items woven from coconut leaves in the shape of animals; fantastic carved headdresses in the shape of sharks and birds; shooting star and comet 'dance machines' (dancing accessories); and musical instruments. Other displays describe the life and times of Eddie Koiki Mabo, and the efforts of Islander men and women during World War II.

The museum is open from 9 am to 5 pm daily, except Good Friday and Christmas Day (1 to 5 pm on ANZAC Day). Admission costs $9/5/6.50 for adults/children aged four to 16/concession; a family ticket costs $24. There's a good gift shop in the foyer with a range of books, videos and artefacts for sale.

Perc Tucker Regional Gallery

The Perc Tucker Regional Gallery (☎ 4727 9011, fax 4772 3656, ⓔ ptrg@townsville .gov.au), at the Denham St end of Flinders St Mall, sometimes has complementary displays to the Museum of Tropical Queensland. A calendar of forthcoming events is published annually. It's open 10 am to 5 pm weekdays, to 2 pm on weekends. Admission is free.

Shopping

Jubinbara Gallery (☎ 4771 3771, fax 4771 5486, ⓔ rjb@jubinbara.com.au), Web site: www.jubinbara.com.au, in Flinders St Mall, is not Indigenous-owned of quality crafts, paintings, and souvenirs made by loc other communities around Aus.

PALM ISLANDS

The Palm Island group is made up of 10 main islands. All of the islands are Aboriginal reserves, apart from Orpheus, which is predominantly national park, and nearby Pelorus, which is crown land.

The Aboriginal (and non-Aboriginal) names of the main islands are Goolboddi (Orpheus), Yanooa (Pelorus), Culgarool (Brisk), Inoogoo (Cura-cao), Garoogubbee (Eclipse), Soopun (Esk), Carbooroo (Falcon), Eumilli (Fantome), Havannah and Bukaman (Great Palm).

No tourist facilities are up and running yet, but there are plans to start reef cruises in the future. The only accommodation is Palm Island Motel (☎ 4770 1047), Mango Ave, Palm Island, where rooms cost $65. It's also possible to camp on some of the islands, book through QPWS.

Permits

Unless you're part of an extended family from the Palm Islands, you must obtain written permission from the Palm Island Aboriginal Council (☎ 4770 1177), Main St, Palm Island, Qld 4816, or the Department of Aboriginal and Torres Strait Islander Policy and Development office (☎ 4799 7470) at 187–209 Stanley St, Townsville, Qld 4810, before you can land on any of them. You'll need to declare the purpose of your visit, the number of people in your party, and when and how long you plan to stay.

Jirrbal Country

Atherton Tableland & Tully Area

INFORMATION

Displays at the Ravenshoe (Koombooloomba) Visitor Centre (☎ 4097 7700) explain the rainforest lifestyle of the Jirrbal (Dyirbal) people. There's a palm leaf shelter, the process of preparing poisonous black bean seeds for eating is shown and there's a fibreglass cast of a *jidu* tree – a carved totemic rainforest tree. Opening hours are 9 am to 4 pm daily (except Christmas Day).

QUEENSLAND

RANCHO DEL REY

El Rancho del Rey (☎ 4066 7770, fax 4066 7824, ℮ elrancho@znet.au) is a working cattle ranch with accommodation. Although not Indigenous-owned, a Jirrbal guide can take you on a half-day walk to Echo Creek Falls, explaining bush tucker and medicine on the way.

To get to El Rancho del Rey, turn off Bruce Hwy 8km south of Tully and follow Davidson Rd for 24km.

WABUNGA WAYEMBA RAINFOREST WALKABOUT

This 3km walking track, taking about 45 minutes return, has information signs explaining the cultural significance of the rainforest to the local Aboriginal people. The track starts 7km east of Ravenshoe along the Tully Falls Rd. Tours by Jiddabul Community Rangers may start up in future – inquire at Ravenshoe Visitor Centre (see Information earlier).

Yidinjdiji Country

Cairns Area

YARRABAH ABORIGINAL COMMUNITY

The Yarrabah Aboriginal community started as an Anglican mission in 1892. Most of the original inhabitants were local Yidinjdiji and Gungganjdiji tribes dispossessed by the wholesale clearance of forest for sugar cane and cattle. But in subsequent decades, the state government forcibly relocated Indigenous people to Yarrabah from many parts of Queensland; up to 80% of residents were removed from their traditional lifestyles to live on the mission between 1896 and the late 1940s. In 1957 a strike was held to protest conditions, but to no avail; and various other protests since then have achieved only a DOGIT.

The name (originally Yarraburra) refers to the white-bellied sea-eagle, or fish-hawk, and its flight as it hunts; a model of one sits inside the entrance to the Menmuny Museum (see later).

You don't need a permit to visit Yarrabah.

Information

Books & Videos Reminiscences of Yarrabah include *Visiting Yarrabah* by Maree Four-mile; *Reaching Back: Queensland Aboriginal People Recall Early Days at Yarrabah Mission*, edited by Judy Thomson; and *Green Meat and Oily Butter – Memories of Yarrabah* by Mollie Coleman (available at Menmuny Museum).

A locally made documentary, *Like Rubies in the King's Crown*, made by a Cairns-based Indigenous film crew, has interviews with Elders and looks at the removals to Yarrabah, the human rights issue and the 1957 labour strike, and discusses the history of Yarrabah mission within the wider context of the Stolen Generations.

Organised Tours

Yarrabah Cultural Tours (☎ 4031 7661, ℮ yarrabah@hotshop.com.au), Web site: www.hotshop.com.au, operates a one-day tour from Cairns that combines the attractions at Yarrabah with a visit to a nearby crocodile farm. The itinerary includes a guided tour through the Menmuny Museum, dancing performed by the Yarrabah dancers, boomerang- and spear-throwing with didjeridu accompaniment, a visit to Yarrabah's organic tea-tree farm and distillery, and demonstrations of arts and crafts.

The tour is a joint venture of an operator in Cairns and the Yarrabah community, with part of the proceeds going back to the community. The full-day itinerary costs $89 including lunch and refreshments. Tours depart Cairns at 9.30 am on Monday, Wednesday and Friday.

Menmuny Museum

Owned and run by the Yarrabah Community Council, Menmuny Museum (☎ 4056 9154) is named after a warrior with whom Yarrabah's first missionaries established a trusting relationship. Photos and panels explain the history of the community and the Stolen Generations; and among the artefacts on display are some nifty flower arrangements made from feathers. Traditional dances are performed daily at 10.45 am and 2 pm.

Behind the museum there's a 1200m **boardwalk** through the rainforest with signboards explaining the traditional uses of various native plants for food, medicine and raw materials for implements. Allow at least 30 minutes to enjoy the walk.

To get to the museum, turn right (along Back Beach Rd) at the police station, 33km after leaving Bruce Hwy; from there follow the yellow signs another 1km. The museum is open 8.30 am to 4.30 pm weekdays. Museum entry costs $3/2 for adults/children, students and pensioners, plus $3/2 for the boardwalk.

Shopping

The souvenirs, arts and crafts on sale at Menmuny Museum, include locally printed T-shirts, traditional and contemporary paintings, spears, pottery and tea-tree oil.

Bama Ngappi (☎ 4056 9146) is a workshop down Back Beach Rd past the museum, where you can drop in to buy arts and crafts made and painted on site. It's usually open 8 am to 4 pm Monday to Thursday.

CAIRNS
Information

Indigenous Organisations Cairns is a regional centre, and many organisations that operate in the Cape are headquartered here. The Cape York Land Council (☎ 4053 9222, fax 4051 0097, e adm@cylc.org.au), 32 Florence St, is an excellent contact point for communities on the Cape. Its Web site is www.cylc.org.au.

The Balkanu Cape York Development Corporation has an informative Web site featuring all the Cape York Aboriginal communities at www.balkanu.com.au.

National Parks There are a number of national parks in the Cape that are jointly managed with their traditional owners. Contact the Indigenous Joint Management Unit of the QPWS (☎ 4046 6600, fax 4046 6751) at 10–12 McLeod St for more information.

Books *Djabugay Country* by Timothy Bottoms is subtitled *An Aboriginal History of Tropical North Queensland* and is well-illustrated with historic photos. *Daintree* by Lloyd Nielsen is a beautifully-illustrated guide to the region's ecology, with an interesting section on rainforest Aborigines.

Radio Bumma Bippera Media Aboriginal & Torres Strait Islander Corporation (☎ 4052 1155) broadcasts 4C1M (98.7 FM).

Organised Tours of Cape York

A host of companies operate 4WD tours, fly/drive tours and cruises from Cairns to Cape York. None of these tours focus primarily on Aboriginal culture, but they are a popular way to travel on the Cape. Most offer a trip to Thursday and Horn Islands as an optional extra. The Cairns Regional Tourist Information Centre (☎ 4051 4066) can help to arrange most tours in the Cape York region.

Billy Tea Bush Safaris (☎ 4032 0077, fax 4032 0055, e info@billytea.com.au), Web site: www.billytea.com.au, runs tours to the tip of Cape York, which take in Split Rock Galleries at Laura and pass through Wujal Wujal. Optional excursions to Thursday Island are available. Costs for nine-/14-day tours are $1870/1980 per person.

Oz Tours Safaris (☎ 1800 079 006 toll free, fax 4055 9918, e oztours@internet north.com.au), Web site www.oztours. com.au, runs seven- and 16-day 4WD camping safaris to Cape York, visiting the Split Rock Galleries and the Bamaga Aboriginal community, with optional excursions to Thursday Island. They also offer fly/drive tours from Cairns to the Tip (as it's often called), incorporating a cultural tour of Coconut Island. This is the only organised tour of an outer island in the Torres Strait. All-inclusive tours start from $1695 for a seven-day trip, or $2050 for 12 days.

Jowalbinna Bush Camp (☎ 4051 4777, fax 4051 4888, e jowalbinna@adventures .com.au), Web site: www.adventures.com.au,

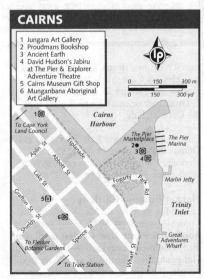

CAIRNS

1 Jungara Art Gallery
2 Proudmans Bookshop
3 Ancient Earth
4 David Hudson's Jabiru at The Pier & Explorer Adventure Theatre
5 Cairns Museum Gift Shop
6 Munganbana Aboriginal Art Gallery

0   150   300 m
0   150   300 yd

Cairns Harbour

To Cape York Land Council

Aplin St
Esplanade
Abbott St
Lake St
Grafton St
Shields St
5
6
Spence St
To Flecker Botanic Gardens
To Train Station

The Pier Marketplace
2
3
4
Fogarty Park Rd

The Pier Marina

Marlin Jetty

Trinity Inlet

Wharf St

Great Adventures Wharf

QUEENSLAND

CAIRNS GALLERIES, MUSEUMS & SHOPS

Readers should be aware that the names of deceased members of the Aboriginal community may be cited in this section. Mentioning the personal name of someone who has died recently can cause offence, anguish and grief in some Aboriginal cultures.

There are far too many places in Cairns that sell or exhibit works by Indigenous artists to list them all here. Following is a selection of recommended outlets. See the Shopping section in the Facts for the Visitor chapter for further information.

Ancient Earth (☎ 4051 0211) Shop A13, The Pier Marketplace, Pier Point Rd. Ancient Earth displays a treasure house of Indigenous cultural objects and artworks. The fabulous selection includes hunting, payback and ceremonial spears, spear-throwers, shields, morning-star poles, burial poles, baskets woven with natural fibres and coloured with natural pigments, *dilly* bags, rain-sticks, digging sticks, carved emu eggs, seed and shell necklaces, fired and glazed ceramic works and hand-carved sculptures. There is a fine range of Aboriginal art books. This gallery sells the work of some of Aboriginal Australia's leading and emerging artists. It's open 8 am to 10 pm daily.

Cairns Museum Gift Shop (☎ 4051 5582), corner of Lake and Shields Sts. This gift shop is in the picturesque Cairns School of Arts building, and is operated by the local historical society, with an impressive array of books by contemporary Aboriginal and non-Aboriginal writers on topics such as Aboriginal art, culture, history and politics. There is also a fine collection of Aboriginal children's stories, and a series on Aboriginal legends. The gift shop is open 10 am to 4 pm daily (to 3 pm on Saturday).
Web site: www.cairnsmuseum.org.au/museum.html

David Hudson's Jabiru at the Pier (☎ 4031 5964) Shop 63, The Pier Marketplace, Pier Point Rd. A local Indigenous musician and artist, David Hudson provides a rounded cultural experience for visitors to his shop. The walls display his canvas paintings, which are a vibrant blend of native flora and fauna infused with symbolic Aboriginal designs. There is a fine array of Aboriginal souvenirs including boomerangs, didjeridus, carved emu eggs and T-shirts. Check out the range of Indigenous music, particularly David's didjeridu recordings. All are very reasonably priced. You can even attend one of David's personal painting workshops, which gives you the opportunity to paint your own didjeridu, boomerang or art piece with David's creative guidance. Or you could just chat with David over a cup of tea while he produces your very own piece of customised art. This is a golden

runs 4WD tours from Cairns to the Quinkan galleries on Cape York Peninsula (see the Kokowarra Country section later for details).

Other tour operators which offer trips on the Cape include:

Cape York Adventure Safaris (☎ 4093 8347)
Guides to Adventure (☎ 4091 1978)
Heritage Kamp-Out Safaris (☎ 4038 2628)
Wild Track Adventures (☎ 4055 2247)

Flecker Botanic Gardens
Under the shadow of Mt Whitfield, these tropical gardens (☎ 4044 3398) feature an **Aboriginal Plant Use Garden** displaying many rainforest plants used by Djabuganjdiji, Gungganjdiji, Yidinjdiji and Yirrganjdiji people. Pick up a leaflet from the gardens

information office. There's also a self-guiding walk ($2) that points out and explains a few other useful plants.

Guided walks are held at about 1 pm weekdays (except on public holidays); the content varies, depending on the interest of the group each day, but you could ring ahead and request an Aboriginal theme. Guided walks cost $5 per person (minimum of two) and last approximately 1½ hours.

The botanic gardens are open 7.30 am to 5.30 pm weekdays, and 8.30 to 5.30 pm on weekends and public holidays. Entry is free.

Entertainment
Internationally acclaimed Tjapukai musician David Hudson puts on a 45-minute didjeridu show on Monday, Wednesday and Friday

continued...   Elizabeth McNiven

opportunity for informal interaction with Aboriginal art and culture in a relaxed and tranquil atmosphere. Contact David for bookings and prices. Jabiru is open 9.30 am to 10.30 pm daily. Web site: www.davidhudson.com.au

Jungara Art Gallery (☎ 4051 5355) The Esplanade. Jungara means 'Pelican' in the Bundjalung language. An awe-inspiring fully painted didjeridu 3.25m long (reputedly the biggest of its kind in the world) graces the entrance. Huge desert paintings by famous Aboriginal artists such as Clifford Possum hang high on the gallery walls. Don't miss the magnificent range of artwork produced by local and interstate Indigenous artists. Also view the tasteful array of crafts, artefacts and souvenirs showcased in an open and spacious environment. With a fantastic range of books on Aboriginal art and cultural traditions including children's stories, there is something at Jungara for everyone. It's open noon to 10 pm weekdays and from 2 pm on weekends.

Munganbana Aboriginal Art Gallery (☎ 4051 3080) Andrejic Arcade, 55 Lake St. Munganbana translates as 'Mountain water' in the Jirrbal language of the Atherton Tablelands and Upper Tully region. The entrance boasts a traditional rainforest shelter made of paperbark. Primarily showcasing the works of gallery owner Munganbana, the shop also sells a small but exceptional collection of artworks by other local Aboriginal artists and features the spectacular Bama Ngappi pottery from the Yarrabah Aboriginal Community, south of Cairns. Although Munganbana specialises in limited-edition lino prints, he also sells a diverse range of canvas paintings, clapsticks, didjeridus, batik silk wall-hangings, hand-painted shields, polished wood boomerangs, and a fantastic range of printed designs on clothing. Don't miss the woven hats and bags inspired by the colours of the Aboriginal and Torres Strait Islander flags. Every Saturday morning from 9 am to noon, Munganbana conducts a lino-printing workshop (book one month in advance). Munganbana is open 10 am to 5 pm weekdays, to 1 pm on Saturday. Entry is free. Web site: www.munganbana.tnq.com

Proudmans Bookshop (☎ 4051 4993) Shop G11, The Pier Marketplace, Pier Point Rd. Proudmans specialises in a fine range of quality books on Aboriginal art, culture, politics, heritage and children's stories. The selection includes educational books, novels and poetry by noted Indigenous authors, through which you can enrich your understanding of Aboriginal languages, bush foods, paintings, archaeology, social justice and law. Browse the Web site database to access available titles. Proudmans is open 9 am to 9 pm daily. Web site: www.proudmans.com.au

QUEENSLAND

night at the Explorer Adventure Theatre (☎ 4041 7772) upstairs at The Pier, starting at 7 pm. Admission is $15 per adult ($7.50 for children). Tickets can also be bought at David Hudson's Jabiru at The Pier (☎ 4031 5964) – see the Cairns 'Shopping' boxed text.

AROUND CAIRNS
Tjapukai Aboriginal Cultural Park
This cultural park (☎ 4042 9900, fax 4042 9988, e tjapukai@tjapukai.com.au), Web site: www.tjapukai.com.au, north-west of Cairns, features theatres, a museum, art gallery and traditional camp site to give visitors an insight into the original inhabitants of the Tjapukai tribal area. Tjapukai communities and Elders own the land and have a substantial share in the venture.

The Magic Space museum here displays Tjapukai artefacts once held in Brisbane's Queensland Museum, with murals and ambient lighting. Creation Theatre explains the spiritual beliefs of Tjapukai people in their own language (now rarely spoken), translated through headphones. Performers interact with holograms and animation to tell their stories. The History Theatre – subtitled 'A Survival Story' – presents an audiovisual treatment of Aboriginal history, the impact of white people and where things may go in future.

The Tjapukai Dance Theatre is a covered outdoor auditorium where songs, dances and culture are explained. At the Traditional Camp you learn about bush food and medicine, try boomerang- and spear-throwing, and play a didjeridu.

Tjapukai is open 9 am to 5 pm daily (except Christmas Day and New Year's Day). Each segment is shown at regular intervals; allow at least two to three hours to experience everything. The History, Creation and Tjapukai Dance Theatres have shows/performances regularly throughout the day (phone for times).

There are also regular demonstrations in the Cultural Village (again, phone for times), plus demonstrations of spear- and boomerang-throwing continuously from 9.30 am to 5 pm.

Various packages are available for visitors: basic entry, which includes all the features mentioned here, costs $27/13.50/67.50 for adults/children/family (two adults and two children), plus $15/7.50 per adult/child for return shuttle to Cairns.

Djabuganjdiji Country

Kuranda Area

KURANDA
Rainforestation Nature Park

Rainforestation (☎ 4093 9033, fax 4093 7578, ⓔ res@rainforest.com.au), Web site: www.rainforest.com.au, hosts the Pamagirri Dancers, who perform a selection of dances and songs illustrating Dreaming legends from various parts of north Queensland. There are two performances daily of eight dances, including the Mosquito Dance, the Silent Snake and the Cassowary Dance. Included in the price of admission are demonstrations of boomerang- and spear-throwing and didjeridu-playing; a walk-through Aboriginal village; and a chance to talk to musicians, artists and weapon makers demonstrating their skills in the Pamagirri Cultural Centre.

Rainforestation is on the Kennedy Hwy just east of the Kuranda turn-off. It is open daily (except Christmas Day) and admission to the Pamagirri Dancers costs $15.50/8.75/43.75 per adult/child/family. The dancers perform at 11.30 am and 2 pm, and Dreamtime Walks and Pamagirri Cultural Centre talks are held at 11 am, noon and 1.30 and 2.30 pm.

Entertainment

The Mayi-Wunba Dancers (☎ 0412 574 475) are a local dance troupe that perform

at the back of Kuranda Heritage Markets. There are four 30-minute shows on Wednesday, Thursday, Friday and Sunday at 11 am, and noon, and 1 and 2 pm. Admission is $10/5 for adults/children and students, and $25 for families. Videos and cameras are permitted.

Kuku-Yalanji Country

Greater Daintree Area

ORGANISED TOURS

Native Guide Safari Tours (☎ 4098 2206, fax 4098 1008) at 58 Pringle St, Mossman, Web site: www.nativeguidesafaritours.com.au, is an award-winning company that offers an authentic introduction to Kuku-Yalanji culture and the ecology of the Daintree region. Kuku-Yalanji Elder Hazel (Nalba) Douglas, and partner Thomas, run an excellent and fun one-day 4WD culture/adventure tour of the area from Port Douglas north to Cape Tribulation. Included on the itinerary are a walk through Mossman Gorge, the Daintree River crossing, and either Marrdja or Dubuji Mangrove Boardwalk for discussions on wildlife, bush tucker and medicine. Kuku-Yalanji stories about various landmarks are told with a running commentary on the Greater Daintree's history and ecology.

Tours run from Monday to Saturday and include a picnic lunch. The price for a full-day tour is $130/90 for adults/children (three to 14 years) from Cairns (including transfer to Port Douglas by Quicksilver catamaran); and $120/80 from Port Douglas. Half-day and private charter tours are available.

MOSSMAN GORGE
Organised Tours

Kuku-Yalanji Dreamtime Tours (☎ 4098 2595, fax 4098 2607, ⓔ yalanji@internet north.com.au), Web site: www.internetnorth.com.au/yalanji, runs two-hour walks in Mossman Gorge with traditional custodians. At a gentle pace and easy gradient you'll visit cave paintings and other sites along part of a network of story places, sacred sites and Dreaming legends. Along the way explanations are given of the uses the Kuku-Yalanji put to various plants, and you'll see a traditional dwelling and a demonstration of paint-making. Tea and

KURANDA GALLERIES & SHOPS

Elizabeth McNiven

Readers should be aware that the names of deceased members of the Aboriginal community may be cited in this section. Mentioning the personal name of someone who has died recently can cause offence, anguish and grief in some Aboriginal cultures.

There are far too many places in Kuranda that sell or exhibit works by Indigenous artists to list them all here. Following is a selection of recommended outlets. See the Shopping section in the Facts for the Visitor chapter for further information.

Boongar Art Gallery (☎ 4093 8906) 5 Therwine St, the Original Market. Boongar is a Waka Waka man, and in his language his name means 'Small dingo'. For a dynamic cultural interaction visit the gallery and talk to Boongar about his work, including his use of traditional flora and fauna images in his bark and canvas paintings. The shop houses a superb display of traditional artefacts made from polished wood, including nulla-nullas, didjeridus and boomerangs. There is a range of printed designs on clothing. Other products by Boongar include instructional booklets about the didjeridu and audio tapes on learning to play the instrument. The gallery is open 9 am to 9 pm Wednesday to Friday and on Sunday.

Roy Moggs (☎ 4093 0413) Heritage Markets, Rob Veivers Drive. This Aboriginal craftsperson and artist makes and sells traditionally handcrafted didjeridus. With the aid of the termites that eat the hollow in the log and using the techniques of his ancestors, Roy creates magnificent and captivating instruments. Also take a look at the beautiful miniature didjeridus with stands and the superbly crafted boomerangs and *coolamons* (basinshaped wooden dishes). Other artefacts include beautifully fashioned vases, jewellery and serviette rings. Artefacts are produced from Australian blue box and black wattle and all items are reasonably priced. It's open 9 am to 3 pm daily.

Wangal Aboriginal Art & Craft (☎ 4093 9296) 40 Coondoo St. Wangal. This shop is a subsidiary of the KMKM (Kuranda, Mantaka, Koah and Mona Mona) Aboriginal Corporation, and showcases the work of local Aboriginal artists and crafts people from the Kuranda, Mantaka, Koah and Mona Mona communities. Wangal means 'Boomerang' in the local Djabuganjdji language. Request a boomerang-throwing demonstration and witness the amazing aerodynamics. This is definitely the place to buy boomerangs, with an extensive range of Y, U, cross, hunting, common, left-handed and kangaroo-shaped boomerangs (prices start from $25). The shop also sells beautifully handcrafted and reasonably priced shields, plaques, didjeridus and clapsticks, designed, produced and sold by the local Indigenous people.

While you're in Kuranda, take time to visit the other KMKM subsidiaries: Mantaka Furniture for handmade wooden furniture, Kuranda Hardware for technical solutions and the Strangled Mango Cafe for a taste of traditional bush foods. Wangal is open 8 am to 4 pm weekdays, and 9 am to 3 pm on weekends.

Wirrimbah Aboriginal Art & Craft Gallery (☎ 4093 3265) Lot 11 Kay Rd, Emerald Creek via Mareeba, 24km west of Kuranda on the Mareeba Rd. Wirrimbah means 'To preserve' in the Dubba-Ga language of the gallery's Aboriginal owner and operator, Wayne 'Turrong' Peckham. Explore the superb range of Aboriginal souvenirs, from didjeridus, *nulla-nullas* (club), boomerangs and clapsticks to postcards, tea-towels, bags and bookmarks. Listen to and select from a great collection of traditional and contemporary Indigenous music on the interactive CD machine. For something completely different, check out Wayne's award-winning foot didjeridus, made from the roots and shafts of trees. Don't miss the beautiful landscape paintings of the Dubba-Ga tribal area produced by Wayne and members of his family, using natural pigments and acrylic on canvas. All products carry the National Indigenous Arts Advocacy Association (NIAAA) label of authenticity. Wirrimbah is open 9 am to 3.30 pm daily. Make an appointment or just drop in. Web site: www.wirrimbah.com.au

QUEENSLAND

damper are served under bark shelters after the walk, while the guide describes the rainforest flora and fauna of Mossman Gorge. There's also a community shop, open 9 am to 4 pm, which sells artefacts and locally made art.

Walks depart at 10 am, noon and 2 pm weekdays; weekend walks can be organised ahead of schedule. Bookings are essential. The walk costs $16.50/8.25 for adults/children. A minibus can pick you up and drop you at accommodation in Port Douglas and Mossman for $40.70/19.80 (including the walk), for the 10 am tour.

MAREEBA
Shopping
You're welcome to drop into Ku Ku Djungan (☎ 4092 4908), 28 Costin St, where there's a painting workshop. Locally made goods are on sale here and at Kuranda Noctarium (☎ 4093 7344) on Coondoo St, Kuranda. The workshop is normally open 9 am to 4 pm Monday to Thursday.

Mareeba Secretarial Services (☎ 4092 5366), 107 Byrnes St, is the main outlet for an award-winning Chillagoe artist, Georgina Lee Cheu (see the Chillagoe section later).

MIALLO
Creation Laser Show
A regular attraction at the Karnak Playhouse (☎ 4098 8144, fax 4098 8191, ℮ karnak @internetnorth.com.au), is the hi-tech Creation laser show, in which fibre optics and 3D effects accompany a performance by the Karnak Bama Dance Troupe.

The show is held at 8 pm on Wednesday and Saturday; entry costs $27.50 (children half-price). A combination of dinner at Karnak's Kubirri Restaurant plus the show costs $55. Bookings are essential.

CAPE TRIBULATION
The coast road follows the broad Bloomfield River, before crossing it 30km north of Cape Tribulation. The Wujal Wujal Aboriginal community is on the northern bank of the river. Students from Wujal Wujal recently created and erected 24 signs along the route which inform the visitor of the Kuku-Yalanji names for landmarks, such as Kija (Roaring Meg) and Jukar (Bloomfield Beach).

Permits
Entry to Wujal Wujal is by permit only – write to the Wujal Wujal Aboriginal Council (☎ 4060 8155, fax 4060 8250), Post Office, Wujal Wujal, Qld 4871. State your intended dates of travel, reason for visit, number in your party and proposed length of stay.

CHILLAGOE
Chillagoe-Mungana National Park
There are a number of significant rock art sites around Chillagoe, two of which are accessible in the Chillagoe-Mungana National Park (QPWS; ☎ 4094 7163, fax 4094 7213).

Also known as Balancing Rock, the ancient **Wullumba** art site is a shelter where incisions in the rock face have been deepened by successive occupants. Naturally occurring red ochre and white clay have been used to daub symbols, which were probably last repainted 100 years ago and are now weathered.

The art at **Mungana** is in a beautiful site among the extraordinary karst limestone formations of the park. Motifs include freehand drawings of lizard-like creatures in white ochre. Take the dirt road west of Chillagoe towards Mungana for 15km, then turn off for Royal Arch Caves. The site is right next to the road about 2km along.

Chillagoe Museum
Among the wonderfully cluttered and eclectic collection at Chillagoe Museum (☎ 4094 7109) is a selection of artefacts from the Chillagoe area, as well as north Queensland and the Northern Territory.

The museum is open 8.30 am to 5 pm daily, and entry costs $5/4/1.50/12 per adult/pensioner/child/family.

Shopping
Local Aboriginal painter Georgina Lee Cheu incorporates the stories of the region's older people into her tapestries and paintings on marble. Georgina was the first Australian to receive an International Women's Creativity in Rural Life award from the Women's World Summit Foundation. Although she works in Chillagoe, most of her work is sold through Mareeba Secretarial Services (see the Mareeba section earlier).

Guugu-Yimidhirr Country

Cooktown area

HISTORY

The Guugu-Yimidhirr were well established in the region 34,000 years ago, living off the abundant fish and game in the area's reefs, rivers and rainforested ranges. But when gold was found at Palmer River, Cooktown became a rowdy port for the rush of 50,000 prospectors between 1873 and 1876. The Guugu-Yimidhirr resisted the invasion, and Hell's Gate, a narrow pass on the track between Cooktown and the Palmer River, was the scene of frequent ambushes. It is estimated that 17 Europeans and Chinese were killed, but in the end the Guugu-Yimidhirr were unable to repel the invaders. At least 13 warriors were killed at Battle Camp in 1873 when they tried to storm a miners' camp; and at Cape Bedford in 1879 at least 28 were killed in retaliation for the nonfatal spearing of two whites. Guugu-Yimidhirr people in town fared little better, and declined in numbers from 1000 in the early 1870s to 100 or so by 1897. Many survived only by seeking sanctuary in the Lutheran mission at Cape Bedford, which later moved to Hopevale.

INFORMATION
Books

Life and legends of local people are covered in *Milbi: Aboriginal Tales from Queensland's Endeavour River* by Tulo Gordon & John B Haviland. Tulo Gordon, a Hopevale man, also illustrated *Old Man Fog and the Last Aborigines of Barrow Point* by Roger Hart (the last surviving Barrow Point man) and John B Haviland.

COOKTOWN
Information

Cooktown Travel Centre (☎ 4069 5446, fax 4069 6023, e cooktowntravel@bigpond .com), in the Charlotte St Centre, opposite Cape York Tyres and Auto Centre, is open 8 am to 6 pm weekdays, to noon on Saturday, and 3 to 5 pm on Sunday. It is a helpful stop for local knowledge and stocks a small selection of artefacts and art made at Hopevale Aboriginal community (see later). A 4WD vehicle can be hired here for $50 an hour (plus fuel).

Organised Tours

Cooktown Tours (☎/fax 4069 5125, e cktn tour@tpg.com.au), Web site www.cook townau.com, runs a full-day tour to Laura, the Split Rock Galleries and Lakefield National Park for $100/70 per adult/child (minimum charge $250).

Gungarde Aboriginal Centre

Founded in 1982, Gungarde Community Centre Aboriginal Corporation represents Cooktown's Aboriginal residents, provides housing at Hopevale Aboriginal community and runs a school bus.

The Gungarde Aboriginal Centre (☎ 4069 5412), south of the Cooktown Hotel on Charlotte St, sells a selection of arts and crafts by local and Cape York Aboriginal artists and a good selection of books. Gungarde is open 8 am to 5 pm Monday to Thursday, to noon on Friday.

Milbi Wall

On the Cooktown foreshore, about 100m past the statue of Captain James Cook, the Milbi (ie, Story) Wall is a colourful symbol of Reconciliation erected in 1998 by the Gungarde Aboriginal community. This community-based project depicts Guugu-Yimidhirr history, lifestyle and stories in hundreds of colourful ceramic tiles.

Also along the foreshore, interpretative boards show Guugu-Yimidhirr and European historical associations with the area.

James Cook Historical Museum

The James Cook Historical Museum (☎ 4069 5386) has a room devoted to exhibits of Aboriginal artefacts from the Cooktown region and other parts of northern Australia, including Mornington Island. Among the *gulkas* (spears), *milbayarrs* (spear-throwers) and other items are a nautilus-shell necklace, 'king' plates worn by respected Elders, a stone oyster pick from Mornington Island in the Gulf of Carpentaria and some huge stone axe-heads from the Cairns area. A hall devoted to the exploits of Captain Cook includes a panel describing the first white contact with the Guugu-Yimidhirr, plus reproductions of Sydney Parkinson's drawings from 1770 of Indigenous people. Upstairs there's a dugout canoe from Marina Plains on Cape York Peninsula.

QUEENSLAND

The museum is open from 9.30 am to 4 pm daily between April and January; Monday, Wednesday and Friday in February; and closed in March. Admission costs $5.50/1.65 for adults/children.

Mulbabidgee (Keatings Lagoon)
This small conservation park protects wetlands and surrounding vegetation and has been used for thousands of years by the Gungarde people as a source of food and bush remedies. There's a walking trail with signposts describing traditional uses of some of the plants.

HOPEVALE ABORIGINAL COMMUNITY
Hopevale (originally called Elim and located at Cape Bedford) was established in 1886 by a Lutheran missionary to aid the decimated and dispossessed remnants of the Guugu-Yimidhirr people in the wake of the Palmer River gold rush. His successor was interred at the start of WWII and the inhabitants forcibly moved to Woorabinda near Rockhampton, where many died. In 1949 the remaining Guugu-Yimidhirr returned to Hopevale's current site and in 1986 the community became the first in Queensland to receive land under the DOGIT scheme.

Permits
A permit is not needed to visit Hopevale, but note that to pass through en route to other local attractions, a permit is required and costs $10 per vehicle per day. Permits are available at the Hopevale Aboriginal Community Council (☎ 4060 9133, fax 4060 9131), Muni St, Hopevale, Qld 4871.

Special Events
The Hopevale Show & Rodeo is staged in July or August each year. For further information, contact the Hopevale Community Council.

Shopping
Community-made artefacts, including firesticks, stone axes, spears, boomerangs, didjeridus and art are available at Hopevale Community Learning Centre – the green house beside the airstrip (behind the red-brick building that houses Guugu Yimithirr Warra Ltd).

Kokowarra Country
Laura Area

Hundreds of rock art galleries dot the sandstone escarpments straddling the base of Cape York Peninsula, many featuring a distinctive style of paintings that feature spirit figures known as Quinkans. Justifiably famous, together they represent one of the biggest and most important collections of prehistoric art in the world. Hundreds of sites are protected by the Quinkan Reserve.

ORGANISED TOURS
The Ang-Gnarra Aboriginal Corporation (☎ 4060 3200) at Laura offers guided tours of the Split Rock Galleries in the area by prior arrangement.

From Cairns, you can fly or drive to Quinkan country with Jowalbinna Bush Camp (☎ 4051 4777) – see that section later. See also under Organised Tours in the Cairns and Cooktown sections.

SPLIT ROCK GALLERIES
These fine rock art galleries are the most accessible of the 1200 famous Quinkan galleries found in the area. Split Rock gives a taste of the larger sites in the region and features paintings, engravings and stencils of people, animals and plants. From the car park, a walking trail leads up to the escarpment then loops across the plateau to the various galleries.

Most visitors do the short (15-minute) walk which, after a steep climb, reaches a breezy overhang decorated with ochre paintings and engravings. Motifs include human and animal figures in red, orange, purple and white; a spiteful spirit figure with a knobbed appendage and bent limbs; and kangaroo tracks followed by human footprints, thought to represent a hunt. The site's engravings are thought to be at least 13,000 years old.

Those with more energy can do a full three-hour circuit that takes in the Turtle Rock and Guguyalangi galleries. The short walk costs $5 and the long walk $10 (children under 16 free); there is an honesty box at the car park for payment.

LAURA
Information
Indigenous Organisations Opened in 1999, Ang-Gnarra Visitor Centre (☎ 4060 3200), is

run by the Ang-Gnarra Aboriginal Corporation, can provide information on the Quinkan galleries. It's open 8 am to 4 pm Monday to Thursday. A small selection of books, music, postcards and T-shirts are also on sale.

Books The Ang-Gnarra Aboriginal Corporation produces two colourful introductions to Quinkan art: *Quinkan Rock Art* and *Our Country, Our Art, Our Quinkans*.

It's worth trawling through the works of Percy Trezise, the first white man to see and catalogue many of the Quinkan sites in the 1950s. Recommended reading includes *Quinkan Country, Dream Road – A Journey of Discovery* and *Last Days of a Wilderness*. In 1971 he produced *Rock Art of South-East Cape York* for the former Australian Institute of Aboriginal Studies (now AIATSIS).

Bush Tucker Trail
A bush tucker trail out the back of the Ang-Gnarra Visitor Centre has signs explaining some local bush foods.

Special Events
The Laura Aboriginal Dance Festival is Cape York's major festival, held near Laura on the banks of the Laura River. It brings together Aborigines from all over Cape York for three excellent days of dancing, music, crafts and other activities such as spear- and boomerang-throwing. The festival is held in June of odd-numbered years.

Contact the visitor centre (see Information) for up-to-date information on festival dates and programs.

Places to Stay
If you're staying for the festival, Ang-Gnarra Visitor Centre (see Information earlier) has a caravan park with BBQs, a pool, children's playground and laundry facilities.

JOWALBINNA BUSH CAMP
A dusty 36km west of the Peninsula Development Rd, Jowalbinna Bush Camp (☎ 4051 4777, fax 4051 4888, **e** jowalbinna @adventures.com.au), Web site: www .adventures.com.au, was established by Steve Trezise, son of Percy Trezise. There are many walks, of which the main ones are Brady Creek Circuit, an easy day-walk which includes Death Adder, Honeymoon, Red Lady, Garfish Sorcery and Tent Shelter;

Emu Dreaming and Giant Wallaroo, which include old engravings and some large paintings; and Yam Camp and Yam Dreaming on Shepherd Creek, a short half-day walk to a yam fertility ceremonial site.

Visitors can stay in comfortable cabins or camp, and participate in half- and full-day guided walks to view many of the significant Quinkan sites on the property. These sites include camp sites and ceremonial grounds, figurative paintings and abstract engravings. A couple of sites (Emu Dreaming and Death Adder) can be reached by wheelchair.

You can visit Jowalbinna with your own 4WD or as part of a tour from Cairns. To self-drive and camp costs $7 per person per day; self-drivers can also stay in the huts for $60 a double (bookings are essential). Meals are extra and range from $15 to $25. Guided tours range from $55 to $90 per person.

The 4WD tours from Cairns start at $535 per person for a three-day/two-night trip including all meals, transport, accommodation and guiding services. The four-day trip ($745) includes a night in Cooktown. Flying visits can also be arranged, starting at $800 per day for two people, from either Cairns or Cooktown.

Waanyi Country
Lawn Hill Area

LAWN HILL NATIONAL PARK
To the Waanyi people, who have enjoyed this spot for perhaps 30,000 years, Lawn Hill (QPWS; ☎ 4748 5572, fax 4748 5549) is Boodjamulla, Rainbow Serpent country. The idyllic waterholes here were created during the Dreaming travels of the Rainbow Serpent, to provide permanent water to keep his skin wet. It is said that if Boodjamulla ever leaves the area, the waterholes will dry up.

Two rock shelters featuring Waanyi rock art are easily accessible to visitors from the camping ground.

Rainbow Dreaming
This rock shelter in Lawn Hill Gorge has an ochre painting thought to represent Boodjamulla, said to live in Duwadarri waterhole nearby. At the foot of the shelter are a grindstone and a midden showing where Waanyi

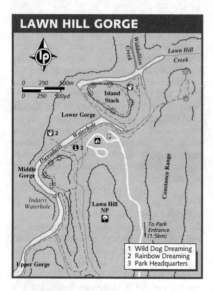

LAWN HILL GORGE

Waddadilla Creek

Lawn Hill Creek

0 250 500m
0 250 900yd

Island Stack

Lower Gorge

Dawadarri

Waterhole

Constance Range

Middle Gorge

Indarri Waterhole

Lawn Hill NP

To Park Entrance (1.5km)

Upper Gorge

1 Wild Dog Dreaming
2 Rainbow Dreaming
3 Park Headquarters

people have feasted on *malumalu*, the freshwater mussels once so abundant that they were known as 'water beef'.

Wild Dog Dreaming

This shelter was formed during the Dreaming wanderings of the Ancestral Dingo, who on his journey from the south followed the Constance Range to the site, then journeyed further north to Doomadgee. The yellow ochre 'rainbow' shapes depicted at Wild Dog Dreaming are thought to represent arch-shaped objects held by performers during the wild dog or dingo dance. The Waanyi people occupied the site for perhaps 17,000 years and possibly as long as 30,000 years. Scattered at the foot of this beautiful sandstone bluff are thousands of fragments of malumalu shells, a grindstone and rusted tin goods from more recent occupation of the site. There are also many engravings, thought to be of great age, most obvious of which are 'cup and ring' motifs.

Kalkadoon Country

Mt Isa Area

HISTORY

Also known as Kalkatungu, the Kalkadoon are probably one of the few tribes that could

readily be named by white Australians. Not surprisingly, the reasons for this stem from their fierce resistance to invasion that culminated in a desperate last stand in 1884.

As pastoralism and mining concerns pushed into their country during the 1860s, some Kalkadoons initially worked for the settlers. But conflict inevitably arose after 1878 and the Kalkadoon waged guerrilla-style raids on pastoralists – even killing five Native Police one night in 1883. For several years they fought and harassed their opponents to a standstill, but when one Frederick Urquhart took charge of the demoralised Native Police, the Kalkadoon suffered a reversal of fortune.

In September 1884, 600 Kalkadoon warriors occupied a rocky hill – now known as Battle Mountain – some 22km south-west of Kajabbi, where they fought a last battle against Native Police and armed settlers. Despite valiant resistance, during which they nearly killed Urquhart, the Kalkadoon spears and clubs were no match for firearms. After scattering a cavalry charge from their rocky positions, the cream of the Kalkadoon warriors were cut down mercilessly as they charged downhill into the guns. Their bodies were left to the dingoes and carrion birds, and for years afterwards their bones littered the hillside. An estimated 900 Kalkadoons were killed between 1878 and 1884.

MT ISA
Information

Tourist Offices The information desk at the Riversleigh Fossil Centre (☎ 4749 1555), next door to the Kalkadoon Tribal Culture Keeping Place (see later), is staffed 8.30 am to 4.30 pm weekdays, and 9 am to 2 pm weekends and public holidays.

Books *This Land Australia We All One People* by Ken Isaacson, a Kalkadoon man, describes his people's heritage and some of the art sites around Mt Isa. *Six Australian Battlefields* by Al Grassby & Marji Hill eloquently describes the last stand of the Kalkadoon.

Organised Tours

A half-day tour with a Kalkadoon guide takes in three rock-art sites close to Mt Isa – Sun Rock, Porcupine Dreaming (where you can see hundreds of pecked engravings) and Warrigal Dreaming (Painted Rock). You'll also have a chance to sample witchetty grubs and wild honey, and learn about bush medicine.

The four-hour tour leaves from the Kalkadoon Tribal Culture Keeping Place at 8 am and 1 pm daily, and costs $50 per person (minimum of four people), which includes billy tea and entry to the *keeping place* (a special site where Aboriginal culture is retained and strengthened). Bookings are essential and can be made on ☎ 4749 3838.

If the keeping place is shut, tours can also be booked next door at the Riversleigh Fossil Centre (see Information earlier).

Kalkadoon Tribal Culture Keeping Place

The Kalkadoon Tribal Culture Keeping Place (☎ 4749 3838) on Marian St was set up to preserve, promote and increase public awareness of Kalkadoon culture, artefacts and spirituality. The centre offers talks to schools, tourists and the public; advises on rock art protection, bush tucker, culture and history; provides learning materials and displays of artefacts; and sells locally produced crafts and art. Inside the keeping place there is a small museum, with displays on bush tucker, art, wooden implements and routes of trade. The opening hours are 9 am to 5 pm weekdays, or you can make an appointment. Admission is $2.

Organised tours to local rock art sites are run from here (see Organised Tours earlier).

Frank Aston Underground Museum

An empty cylindrical storage tank at the Frank Aston Underground Museum (☎ 4743 0610) houses the Kalkadoon Cultural Learning Centre, a display created by people indigenous to the Mt Isa area; and photos, artefacts and dioramas on the Lardil people of Mornington Island.

The Kalkadoon camp-setting diorama features spear-making, *coolamons* (basin-shaped wooden dishes), grinding stones, a termite mound used as shelter, ochres and a hut made from spinifex. Display cabinets describe aspects of Kalkadoon and Lardil ceremonies, food and medicines.

The museum is open 9 am to 4 pm daily; entry costs $5/3/1 per adult/pensioner/child.

Mt Isa Aboriginal Media Association

This thriving media organisation (☎ 4749 1338, e mobfm@mtisa.topend.com.au), 71 Miles St, comprises Mob TV (producing local news and ads) and Mob Radio (tune to 100.9FM for Hot Country in Stereo!). Next to the radio studio there's the Mob Shop, which sells CDs, tapes, books, clothing and locally made handicrafts. It's open 8.30 am to 5 pm weekdays.

Open days are held during NAIDOC Week in July. If you ring ahead, a free studio tour can be arranged.

Underground Hospital

Due to open by the time you read this, two walkways leading into Mt Isa's Underground Hospital have been planted with more than 50 plant species traditionally used by the Kalkadoon as bush medicine. Small plaques describe their names and uses.

Shopping

Trading Arts & Crafts Aboriginal Corporation (☎ 4749 0611, fax 4749 0311, e artcraft @one.net.au), 25A Miles St, stocks a wide range of locally produced artefacts, jewellery, traditional and contemporary paintings, and art supplies.

Guwa Country

Winton Area

CARISBROOKE STATION

Carisbrooke Station (☎/fax 4657 3984, e densmith@bit.net.au) is a working sheep and cattle station, in the stark mesas of the Cory's Range 87km south-west of Winton. A gorge on the property features two overhangs with **rock art**, including hand stencils and some unique ochre crosses; three **bora rings** (ceremonial grounds) made of rocks; and an initiation site littered with stone chips.

Full-day tours take in all the sites plus various other historical features on the property. The cost, which includes lunch and 'smoko', is $110 per person (minimum of four); pensioners and concession pay $105 and children under 12 are free. Between April and November, tours run from Carisbrooke (where there's accommodation) from Monday to Saturday; and from Winton on Tuesday, Wednesday and Thursday. Advance bookings are essential.

QUEENSLAND

Iningai Country

LONGREACH
Stockman's Hall of Fame & Outback Heritage Centre

Pastoralism owed much of its success to thousands of Aboriginal men and women, whose roles are acknowledged in a lamentably small corner of this otherwise fine museum (☎ 4658 2166, fax 4658 2495, e museum@outbackheritage.com.au), Web site: www.outbackheritage.com.au. Words and old photos commemorate their achievements, and other sections of the museum give an all-too-brief explanation of Indigenous lifestyles, trade and contact with Macassans, from Ujung Pandang in southwestern Sulawesi.

A large painting near the museum entrance depicts Witchetty Grub Dreaming by Colin Dixon Tjapanunga, a Warlpiri man, at a site west of Yuendumu (NT).

The Hall of Fame is open 9 am to 5 pm daily (except Christmas Day); admission costs $17/14/8 for adults/concession/children. The museum bookshop has a good range of works by Aboriginal writers, such as Queenslander Herb Wharton (see Herb's piece 'Cultural Tourism – Can It Help Create Paradise on Earth?' in the Facts for the Visitor chapter).

BLACKS PALACE

About 130km south-east of Blackall is Blacks Palace (sometimes known as Marsden Cave), the most extensive rock art site known in Queensland's Central Highlands and Australia's largest stencil art site. Overhangs at the base of a 150m-long sandstone cliff contain spectacular galleries with numerous engravings, stencils and colourful free-hand paintings. Parts of the site have been badly vandalised, and originally contained burial sites; axe-grinding grooves can still be seen and there are numerous other rock art sites in the surrounding area.

Blacks Palace is on private property and access is only possible as part of a guided tour. Outback Aussie Tours (☎ 1300 787 890, fax 4658 3350, e info@outbackaussie tours.com.au), Web site: www.outback aussietours.com.au, based in Longreach, is scheduled to commence trips to Blacks Palace in 2001.

ARAMAC STATION

Aramac station features a stunning rock-art site, estimated to be 10,000 to 12,000 years old, on a 120m-long overhang. Among the thousands of pecked engravings are animal, bird and human footprints, giant tracks possibly representing extinct megafauna, and a 20m-long carved serpent. Repeated boomerang images are thought by some to represent moons, which may give credence to a theory that the site was once a great meeting place.

Access to the site is only by an organised tour with Artesian Country Tours (☎ 4651 2211, fax 4651 2499), which runs a day trip from Barcaldine, departing at 7.30 am on Wednesday and Saturday. The cost is $110/ 55 per adult/child, and includes lunch and refreshments.

Gunggari Country

CHARLEVILLE
Information

Radio Radio station 4RR (105.7 FM) broadcasts a local mixture of Murri and country music from 5 am to 5 pm five days a week switching to the national Indigenous radio satellite at other times (see the Radio & TV section in the Facts for the Visitor chapter). 4RR-FM is operated by Bidjara Media & Broadcasting (☎ 4654 1112, fax 4654 3604, e bidjleg1@esprov.com.au).

Organised Tours

During a Charleville sightseeing tour with Fabulous Outback Escapes (☎ 4654 1114, fax 4654 1116, e fabulousescapes@ozemail) you can follow the creation of a didjeridu from cutting and debarking, to seeing it being painted back in the CDEP Aboriginal Workshop (see later), then played after a beeswax mouthpiece is added. A minimum of six people is required for this tour – inquire for prices.

CDEP Aboriginal Workshop

Run by the Bidjara Aboriginal Housing and Land Co Ltd, the Community Development Employment Program (CDEP) Aboriginal Workshop (☎ 4654 3016, fax 4654 3601, e bidjara@esprov.com.au) sells a good range of quality art and handicrafts, including hand-painted jewellery from echidna spines and hand-carved emu eggs. Visitors can do a tour of the workshop, parts of which are painted with traditional motifs, with an enthusiastic guide who explains the art and artefacts, and may give an impromptu didjeridu demonstration.

The workshop is opposite the visitor information centre on the Mitchell Hwy. Admission is a gold coin donation and opening hours are 8 am to 4 pm weekdays (and on Saturday by request). Large groups can make appointments.

Kowanyama DOGIT

Mitchell River Area

KOWANYAMA

Kowanyama, which means 'Place of many waters', is home to Aboriginal people from three main tribal groups – Kokobera, Kokokmnjen and Kunjen.

Information & Permits

Call into the Kowanyama Land and Natural Resource Management Office (KLANRO; ☎ 4060 5187, fax 4060 5250), behind the supermarket, when you arrive to advise of your presence and arrange camping permits.

Special Events

The biggest sporting event on the Cape is the Kowanyama Rugby League and Softball Carnival, held annually on the Queen's Birthday long weekend in June, unless it's delayed by a late Wet season. Teams (and their enthusiastic supporters) come from as far away as Lockhart River and Mornington Island, often travelling for a couple of days to get there.

Kowanyama also hosts a rodeo in late August or early September.

Kowanyama DOGIT Camping Areas

The community runs four camp sites that are popular fishing and bird-watching spots. You must first get a permit from KLANRO (see the Information section earlier) as sites may be closed for cultural and seasonal reasons.

Kowanyama Guest House (☎ 4060 5195, fax 40060 5124) offers rooms with bath for $25/50 for singles/doubles.

Pormpuraaw DOGIT

Edward River Area

PORMPURAAW

The community of Pormpuraaw is home to people from the Mungkan and Thaayorre language groups. It's cut off by floods for eight months of the year.

At the time of writing, the community was planning to develop a visitors centre selling local arts and crafts.

Information & Permits

All visitors must report to Pormpuraaw Aboriginal Community Council (☎ 4060 4175, fax 4060 4130) on arrival in town and arrange camping permits. You'll find it on the western side of town.

Crocodile Farm

The Pormpuraaw crocodile farm raises hatchlings up to 60cm long. You can watch the hatchlings being fed (chickens) at 3.30 pm on Thursday – go to the office, which is in a *donga* (makeshift shelter) behind the Edward River Hotel, and let them know you'd like to see feeding time.

QUEENSLAND

TRAVELLING IN CAPE YORK

Monique Choy

Cape York is an intrepid destination and you should not attempt a trip unprepared. Large sections of the cape are cut off completely in the Wet season (January to March) and cannot be accessed by road. In the Dry, you'll need all the usual gear for travelling in a remote area, and you must carry water. There are also saltwater crocodiles in this region. For essential safety information, check one of the dedicated guidebooks, such as Ron & Viv Moon's excellent *Cape York – An Adventurer's Guide*, which includes a chapter on the Aboriginal communities in the area. *Cape York – A 4WD Experience* by Lynn & Yvonne Fraser is another good guide. The area is extensively covered in Lonely Planet's *Outback Australia*.

Special Events

Locals claim that Pormpuraaw's annual Croc Races is the only such event in the world. It's held annually at the end of July to raise money for the Royal Flying Doctor Service.

Pormpuraaw DOGIT Camping Areas

There are two camping grounds on the Pormpuraaw DOGIT with drinking water and toilet facilities. You need a permit from Pormpuraaw Aboriginal Community Council (see Information & Permits earlier). The cost is $25 per vehicle per night.

The council also runs a guesthouse (☎ 4060 4131) in town, which has spotless dorm rooms for $75 per night including all meals. Bookings are essential.

Lakefield National Park

Lama Lama, Guugu-Yimidhirr, Kuku Yalanji and Kuku Thaypan people have camped by the waterholes in the Lakefield National Park for thousands of years. You too can camp here for $3.85 per night, and it's wise to book in advance. Contact the ranger for more information on ☎ 4060 3271.

Kaanju Country

Central Cape York

COEN

Coen is a traditional meeting ground for Ayapathu and Northern Kaanju people, and there are six major community groups living in the town:

Lama Lama	Princess Charlotte Bay region
Northern Kaanju	Wenlock River area
Southern Kaanju	Archer River and Coen region
Ayapathu	Ebagoola and Yarraden region
Olkolo	Coleman and Alice rivers
Wik Mungkan	North-west of Coen – Mid-Archer, upper Kendall and Holroyd Rivers

Information

Indigenous Organisations The Coen Regional Aboriginal Corporation (☎ 4060

1192, fax 4060 1179) is on Taylor St. The office sells some locally made products such as T-shirts ($20). It can also organise tours of significant sites in the area if you make arrangements a couple of weeks in advance.

At the time of writing, the corporation was about to open the Coen Cultural Centre in a mud-brick building on the southern side of town. The centre will include information on the Indigenous history of the region and will offer bush tucker and local arts and crafts.

MUNGKAN KANDJU NATIONAL PARK

Bush camping is allowed in the Rokeby (or Kandju) section of this national park, named after its two traditional owner groups, who jointly manage the park. A camping permit costs $3.85 per night at Rokeby ranger station. For more information contact the ranger on ☎ 4060 1137.

The area between the eastern and western sections of Mungkan Kandju National Park, surrounding Merapah Station, contains the area of land that was handed back with the Wik decision (see the main History section at the start of this chapter).

Aurukun Shire Lands

Mid-Western Cape York

AURUKUN
Information & Permits

You must get written permission in advance to visit Aurukun lands. Most people visit to use the camping ground at False Pera Head. Contact the Aurukun Shire Council (☎ 4060 6800, fax 4060 6191) at 39 Kang Kang Rd, Aurukun, Qld 4871, for more information. There are tight restrictions on bringing alcohol into the community.

FALSE PERA HEAD

This beach camping ground is a popular fishing spot about 100km north of Aurukun, with showers and toilets provided. You must pay for your camping permit in advance, either at the Aurukun Shire Council (see Aurukun earlier), or the Pax Haven Caravan & Camping Ground at Weipa (see the Weipa section). It costs $33 per vehicle per week plus $5.50/2.75 per person per night for adult/children.

Alngith & Thaynakwith Country

Weipa Peninsula Area

The Weipa Peninsula is rich in shellfish, and there are around 500 midden mounds, up to 13m high and consisting mainly of cockle shells, along the Hey, Mission, Embley and Pine Rivers. All of these middens are protected under the Queensland Cultural Record Act.

NAPRANUM

The Aboriginal community of Napranum, just a few kilometres south-east of Weipa, is home to people from around 15 different tribal groups from around Cape York. Many people have come to the area for jobs in the mining industry.

Information & Permits

You must get a permit to visit Napranum DOGIT land from the Napranum Aboriginal Community Council (☎ 4069 7855, fax 4069 7445), PO Box 538, Weipa, Qld 4874, on Moun-ding St. It's open 9.30 am to 4 pm Monday to Thursday, to 3.15 pm Friday.

Special Events

The Ruchook Festival, held in June or July in even-numbered years, showcases Indigenous culture. There's a focus on dance with Aboriginal, Torres Strait and visiting Pacific Islander dancers all performing. There are also displays of arts and crafts from around the area. The event is held at the Ruchook Festival Grounds and there's a cover charge of $5.

WEIPA
Information & Permits

The popular Pax Haven Caravan & Camping Ground (☎ 4069 7871, fax 4069 8211) is a good source of information on the area and can also provide permits for the camping and fishing areas on Napranum, Mapoon and Aurukun DOGIT lands. For Indigenous information on the Weipa area, check with the Napranum Aboriginal Community Council (see the Napranum section, earlier).

At the time of writing, there were plans to build a visitors centre at Evan's Landing, which would also include an Aboriginal keeping place.

Organised Tours

Snappy Tours (☎ 4069 7572) has permission from local Elders to cover Aboriginal heritage in its boat tours of the region. Tours last for 2½ hours and cost $35/20 (plus GST) for adults/children. You can book at the Pax Haven Caravan & Camping Ground (see earlier).

Uningan Nature Reserve

This pleasant reserve protects mangrove wetlands, large middens and significant Indigenous plants. There are a number of short walks through the reserve, as well as picnic areas.

The **Mangrove Walk**, which passes traditional food plants, is described in *An Explorer's Guide to Weipa and Napranum*, written by members of the local Indigenous community and published by Rams Skull Press (☎ 4093 7474). The *Uningan Nature Reserve Handbook* also contains a chapter on Aboriginal environment and culture. It's out of print but a copy is available for reference at the Pax Haven Caravan & Camping Ground.

Uningan is on the eastern side of town. To get there, turn right at the junction of the road to Marpuna and follow it south to cross over the railway, and then back north. The start of the Mangrove Walk is 100m to the left of the Pistol Club.

Special Events

The Croc Eisteddfod is a cross-cultural festival, held at the Weipa North State School around mid-July, which draws together communities from around the Cape. Check with the Napranum Aboriginal Community Council for details (see the Napranum section, earlier).

PENNEFATHER RIVER

There's a camping ground in the Napranum DOGIT on the beautiful Pennefather River, north of Weipa.

Permits are available from Napranum Aboriginal Community Council (see the Napranum section) or the Pax Haven Caravan & Camping Ground (see Weipa), and cost $33 per vehicle plus $5.50 per person per night.

Mapoon DOGIT

Red Beach Area

MARPUNA (MAPOON)

The township of Marpuna, or Old Mapoon, is home to a number of tribal groups:

Tjungundji	Red and Cullen Beaches
Yupangati	Flinders Camp
Warrangu	Skardon/Namalletta
Taepathigi	Batavia
Thaynakwith	Pine River Region

In 1963 people from Marpuna were removed at gunpoint to New Mapoon at the tip of Cape York (see the New Mapoon section later) to make way for mining. The homes and church in the community were burnt down to prevent their return. In defiance, parts of the New Mapoon community have since made their way back to Old Mapoon to rebuild their community.

Information & Permits

The Mapoon Council (☎ 4090 9124, fax 4090 9128), PO Box 213, Weipa, Qld 4874 is open 8 am to 4.30 pm Monday to Thursday, to noon on Friday, and to noon on Friday. Turn right at the T-intersection in town and you'll see the council on your left. You can get a permit to camp here, but you don't need a permit if you're just making a day trip. The community rangers that patrol the area are a great source of local information.

Mapoon DOGIT Camping Grounds

The Mapoon Council runs six camping areas on the beaches and rivers of the region, some with water, showers and composting toilets. Permits are available from the council, the Pax Haven Caravan & Camping Ground (see the Weipa section), or from the ranger's residence (contact the ranger through the council). The cost is $33 per vehicle for up to a week, plus $5.50 per person per day.

Lockhart River DOGIT

Mid-Eastern Cape York

LOCKHART RIVER

Lockhart River Mission was established in 1922 and the Lockhart River Aboriginal Council became a local government in 1987. People from six tribal groups live in the town:

Wuthathi	Shelbourne Bay
Kuku-Yau	Pascoe River area
Kanthanumplo	Lockhart River Community area
Uutaalnganu	Night Island
Umpila	Nesbet River
Kaanju	Central Cape York

Information & Permits

A permit is not required to enter the community, but visitors are asked to respect the community's privacy. Use of cameras and videos is not permitted. For more information, contact the Lockhart River Aboriginal Council (☎ 4060 7144, fax 40607139, ⓔ lrcc@bigpond.com), Lockhart River, Qld 4871. The office is open 8 am to 5 pm weekdays.

At the time of research, the community was planning to establish a bird-watching camp near the airstrip, and also a community-run radio station to broadcast throughout the Lockhart River DOGIT on 96 FM.

Rams Skull Press (☎ 4093 7474) has published *An Explorer's Guide to Lockhart River* in collaboration with the Lockhart River Art Gang, which includes local sights and interviews with artists.

Lockhart River Arts & Culture Centre

The community-run Lockhart River Arts & Culture Centre (☎/fax 4060 7341) developed from a successful art program at the local high school in 1995. Today artists from the Lockhart River Art Gang are well known throughout Australia. You can meet the artists at work in a wide variety of media such as screen-printing, lithographs, batik, painting, woodwork, jewellery and weaving, from 9 am to 6 pm daily. Paintings sell for up to $800 and tea-towels for $5.

IRON RANGE NATIONAL PARK

The traditional owners of this national park are the Kuku-Yau people, who were forcibly removed from the area into missions in the 1920s. Today the park is jointly managed with its traditional owners. There are a number of beautiful camping areas. National park fees ($3.85 per night) apply. Contact the ranger for more information on ☎ 4060 7170.

Injinoo Country

Northern Peninsula Area

This multicultural area bordering the Torres Strait is the goal of most travellers in Cape York, who are lured by the chance to stand on the northernmost tip of mainland Australia, traditionally known as Pajinka.

HISTORY

Like the rest of the Cape, the Tip has always been densely populated. Traditionally, people lived a seminomadic lifestyle, relying heavily on the sea and their double-outrigger canoes. They were great warriors and there's a long history of tensions with the European invaders, as well as between local tribal groups.

In 1606, Aboriginal warriors killed members of the Dutch crew of the *Duyfken* and in 1770, after initial friendly contact, locals drove Captain Cook away from the Endeavour River with fire for refusing to share a catch of turtles. Despite this rather too warm reception, Cook sailed north and stepped ashore at Possession Island, originally called Thunadha, to claim the entire east coast of Australia – encompassing hundreds of Aboriginal nations – for Britain.

The first European settlement was established at Somerset (Pulu) in 1864. In the same year Frank Jardine, son of the first magistrate, led an expedition to Somerset with 250 head of cattle. He was the second European to attempt the overland journey, the first – Edmund Kennedy – was speared

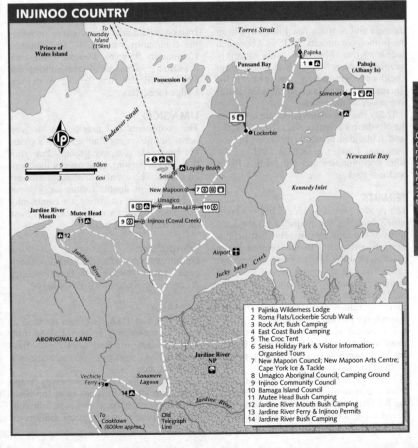

INJINOO COUNTRY

QUEENSLAND

1 Pajinka Wilderness Lodge
2 Roma Flats/Lockerbie Scrub Walk
3 Rock Art; Bush Camping
4 East Coast Bush Camping
5 The Croc Tent
6 Seisia Holiday Park & Visitor Information;
   Organised Tours
7 New Mapoon Council; New Mapoon Arts Centre;
   Cape York Ice & Tackle
8 Umagico Aboriginal Council; Camping Ground
9 Injinoo Community Council
10 Bamaga Island Council
11 Mutee Head Bush Camping
12 Jardine River Mouth Bush Camping
13 Jardine River Ferry & Injinoo Permits
14 Jardine River Bush Camping

to death at Escape River in 1848. Jardine was resisted all the way by local warriors and his party shot at least 30 Aborigines at the Battle of Mitchell River, before making it to the top. Jardine gained a reputation as a ruthless murderer among local tribes until his death in 1919, but he also opened up the cattle industry on the Cape, in which many Indigenous people were to find employment.

At the start of the 20th century, Aboriginal people from the various communities in the region established and ran their own settlement at Injinoo (Cowal Creek), which was not officially recorded by the government until 1916. The community managed its own affairs until WWII brought an influx of thousands of soldiers to the area and the Department of Native Affairs took over administration.

In the late 1940s Torres Strait Islanders from Saibai established the townships of Bamaga and Seisia a few kilometres from the Injinoo community. In 1963 Aboriginal people from Marpuna were forcibly removed to New Mapoon and people from Lockhart River set up the township of Umagico. Bamaga became the administrative centre of the region.

Today the five communities are known as the Northern Peninsula Area (NPA) and the land is divided primarily between Injinoo Custodial Land, the DOGIT lands of the other communities and the Jardine River National Park.

PERMITS

You need a permit to access Injinoo land, which includes the majority of the land north of the Dulhunty River. Most people pay when they get to the Jardine River crossing (☎ 4069 1369), open 8 am to 5 pm daily. You can also get a permit from the Injinoo Community Council (☎ 4069 3252). It costs $88 for private vehicles, covering return ferry crossing and the informative *Injinoo Handbook*.

The permit also allows you to camp in areas north of the Jardine (see Bush Camping Areas later), to fish and to camp at sites south of the Jardine.

The Department of Environment and the Injinoo community ask that all travellers use the ferry crossing at Jardine River and do not drive across the river at the vehicle ford, which damages the banks.

ORGANISED TOURS

Organised tours are offered through Pajinka Wilderness Lodge (see that section later) and Seisia Holiday Park (see the Seisia section).

INJINOO

There are five major groups, identified by the Injinoo Community Council, living in the community today. Their traditional lands cover the whole NPA area.

Anaggamuthi	Seven Rivers – western
Atambaya	Macdonell – central
Wuthathi	south-eastern
Yadhaykenu	Cairn Cross – eastern
Gudang	Red Island, Somerset – northern

Information

The Injinoo Community Council (☎ 4069 3252, fax 4069 3253), together with the Injinoo Apudhama Association, manages the community's custodial lands. Injinoo Community Rangers, who patrol the area, are also a good source of local information. The council also runs Pajinka Wilderness Lodge (see later).

UMAGICO

The community of Umagico, on the road between Injinoo and Bamaga, runs a pleasant beachside camping ground. Pay your fees ($6 per person) at the store or the council office. There's also a basic guesthouse with single or double rooms for $35 per night. At the time of writing, the community had plans to open a nature walk and bush tucker trail near the beach.

Information

For information contact the Umagico Aboriginal Council (☎ 4069 3148, fax 4069 3115, e umagico@iig.com.au), 6 Woosup St.

BAMAGA

In 1947 Chief Bamaga Ginau decided to move his community to the mainland from Saibai Island, just 8km from Papua New Guinea (PNG) to escape flooding and a lack of fresh water.

Bamaga is the largest community in the NPA, with all the facilities most travellers need. There is a hospital, police station, supermarket, bakery, news agency and service station.

Information

The Bamaga Island Council (☎ 4069 3211, fax 4069 3264) is on Adidi St. At the time of writing, the council was building a four-star hotel.

Special Events

The Bamaga Annual Show is held in August or September each year and features rodeo events, horse races, carnival stalls and an amusement fair.

Entertainment

The community canteen, in the unmarked building across the road from the supermarket, is a good place to meet the locals. They hold discos on Friday night.

You can also check out the footy on Friday night during the season (April to September), or basketball matches on Tuesday and Thursday night from around May to June.

NEW MAPOON

The community of New Mapoon was established in 1963. See the Marpuna section earlier for a history of this community.

Information

For information, contact the New Mapoon Council (☎ 4069 3277, fax 4069 3107) on Brown St. Web site: www.iig.com.au/new mapooncouncil.

Special Events

In September the community hosts a sports festival with races, dancing, traditional food and art stalls.

Shopping

A number of local artists sell their work through the New Mapoon Arts Centre, including T-shirts and paintings (ranging from $30 to $250). Contact the council for details, or you can purchase art through the council Web site (see the Information section earlier).

On the northern side of town, Cape York Ice & Tackle also sells some arts and crafts made by the New Mapoon community, including paintings (from $120), beaded jewellery ($5 to $30), drums and *whaps* (turtle-hunting spears). This place is also a good source of local information and you can book charter tours here.

LOYALTY BEACH

The New Mapoon community owns the beachfront Loyalty Beach Campground and Fishing Lodge (☎ 4069 3372, fax 5069 3770, ℮ FishCapeYork@c130.aone.net.au), 2km north of Seisia.

There are basic air-con dongas with shared kitchen facilities for $60/90 for singles/doubles, as well as camping sites for $6 per person. The New Mapoon Dancers sometimes perform here during the peak season.

SEISIA

The Islander town of Seisia was established at Red Island Point around the same time as their fellow Saibai Islanders set up at Bamaga. The name is derived from the first initials of the founder, Mugai Elu's father and his brothers: Sagaukaz, Elu, Isua, Sunai, Ibuai and Aken.

Seisia is an idyllic spot for the weary traveller to relax after the long journey to the Tip.

Information

The Seisia Holiday Park (☎ 4069 3243, fax 4069 3307, ℮ seisiaresort@bigpond.com), run by Seisia Island Council, is a mine of information. You should approach the holiday park rather than going directly to the council. Souvenirs such as baskets, mats and spears are on sale.

During the tourist season, the Seisia Island Dancers sometimes give performances.

Organised Tours

Seisia Holiday Park is the booking agent for all tours, the ferry service to Thursday Island, taxis and anything else available.

Tours include guided fishing trips, pearl farm tours, croc-spotting, half- or full-day 4WD tours of the Tip ($60/95) and scenic flights. Indigenous heritage is covered by many of these tours, which are usually based on chartering a boat or plane, and costs vary according to numbers.

You can also book tours of the Torres Strait Islands here. A day trip to Thursday Island and Ngurapai (Horn Island) with Peddells Ferry & Tour Bus Service, including lunch and guided tours, costs $138; it leaves at 8 am and returns at 3.30 pm. The ferry can also pick you up from Punsand Bay or Pajinka Wilderness Lodge. Torres

Strait Tours also offers tours of Thursday and Horn islands, including lunch, for $156 (plus GST).

Charter flights to outer islands are available, although you must get permission from the Island councils to visit (see the Outer Islands section of the Torres Strait Islands chapter for details). Charter flights to Saibai Island for the market in which Papua New Guinea villagers come to sell their wares can be arranged for around $185, depending on dates and numbers.

Places to Stay
Camping is available at Seisia Holiday Park ($8 per person). Also here is the Seisia Seaview Lodge, with units for $85/96 for singles/doubles, and a kiosk and BYO restaurant.

JARDINE RIVER NATIONAL PARK
The eastern side of the NPA is dominated by the Jardine River National Park, on the traditional lands of the Anaggamuthi, Atambaya, Yadhaykenu and Gudang people. There are many sites of significance such as Story (known in other parts of Australia as Dreaming) places and Story beings. The park is jointly managed with its traditional owners and you can camp ($3.85 per night) at some magical sites within the park, such as Eliot and Fruit Bat Falls, Captain Billy Landing and on the Jardine River itself. Contact the ranger (☎ 4060 3314) for more information.

THE CROC TENT
Souvenirs and tourist information are available at the Croc Tent (☎/fax 4069 2052) at Lockerbie. Artefacts for sale include PNG spears ($15 to $25), such as those traded through the Torres Strait, inlaid masks ($16 to $75) and jewellery. It's open 8 am to 6 pm daily.

ROMA FLATS/LOCKERBIE SCRUB WALK
Signposted off the road to Pajinka, this pleasant rainforest walk has numbered stops corresponding to the guide in the *Injinoo Handbook* of features significant to Aboriginal people. Allow one to two hours.

SOMERSET ART SITE
A difficult 4WD road leads to Somerset (Pulu), where there is a beachfront cave

with Aboriginal paintings. Let the Injinoo-owned Pajinka Wilderness Lodge know if you want to visit the cave, as it is sacred to the community, or take one of the lodge's guided tours (see Pajinka Wilderness Lodge later). The cave is only accessible at low tide; to get there, head north along the shore from the camping ground, past the graves of Frank and Sana Jardine.

BUSH CAMPING AREAS
The permit to enter Injinoo lands (see Permits earlier) allows you to camp at designated areas around the Tip. The camping areas have basic facilities, such as pit toilets, and are at Somerset (Pulu), East Coast, Mutee Head (Ukumba), the Jardine River Mouth (Thayanhaku) and on the north bank of the Jardine River between the ferry and the Old Telegraph Line.

PAJINKA WILDERNESS LODGE
The Pajinka Wilderness Lodge (☎/fax 4069 2100, 1800 802 968 toll free) is a top-end resort run by the Injinoo Aboriginal community and is only 400m from the northernmost tip of mainland Australia (traditionally known as pajinka). There is a resident naturalist and fishing guide, and 4WD tours with Aboriginal guides can be organised (see Organised Tours later). The lodge is a great source of information on the traditional owners of the area. Its Web site at www.pajinka.com includes Indigenous history and cultural information about the tip of Cape York. Cabin-style rooms with bath cost $297/275 per person for singles/doubles in the peak season, including all meals, or $220/198 in the Wet (or 'green') season. The lodge also has its own camping ground, with unpowered sites for $8 per person. A licensed kiosk sells limited supplies in the peak season.

There is a regular ferry service from Pajinka to Thursday Island.

Organised Tours
Pajinka offers a range of field trips for its guests, including half-/full-day trips to Somerset ($35/60) taking in the art site and middens. Bush tucker tours with Injinoo Elder Rusty Williams are available to guests and nonguests for $35. The 2½-hour tours look at the practical and spiritual side of food and medicinal plants in the region.

South Australia

At the time of European settlement, South Australia (SA) is thought to have been home to between 10,000 and 15,000 Aboriginal people living in 43 tribal groups. About half of these people lived in the temperate, well-watered area between Gulf St Vincent (near Adelaide) and the Victorian border. While the arid inland was sparsely populated, few parts of SA were permanently uninhabited. Even the hostile Simpson Desert in the far north-east was occupied on a year-round basis.

The 1996 census pegged the Aboriginal population of SA at just over 22,000, which is probably a little higher than it was at the time of European settlement. Many of the state's Aborigines (41%) live in Adelaide. Nunga, a term used by many Adelaide-area Aborigines to refer to themselves, means 'The people'. The three main Aboriginal cultural-linguistic groups in SA are the Ngarrindjeri, whose traditional lands take in the lower Murray lakes, in the south-east; the Pitjantjatjara, whose lands are in the north-west of the state, and the Kaurna, whose country includes the Adelaide Plains area.

History

Philip Morrissey

The earliest known relics of the Aboriginal occupation of SA are rock carvings near Olary, in the state's east, dated at 43,000 years old. Another important archaeological site is Koonalda Cave, near the border with Western Australia (WA). Chalcedony (a type of quartz) was mined there 14,000 to 24,000 years ago. Deep within the cave, the soft walls feature mysterious incised patterns made by hand. Similar markings are found in Prung Kart Cave near Mt Gambier in the south-east. Owalinja, on the western border with the Northern Territory, has an important gallery of desert art representing the Yankunytjatjara Dreaming. Rock paintings are also found in Yourambulla Caves in the southern Flinders Ranges (see Yourambulla Caves under Adnyamathanha Country later).

TRADITIONAL LIFE
Various hunting techniques have been employed in SA. On the Coorong wetlands,

HIGHLIGHTS

Telephone code: ☎ 08
Indigenous population: 22,052
Overall population: 1,480,000
Area: 984,277 sq km

■ Exploring the Aboriginal Cultures Gallery at the South Australian Museum, an outstanding display on the heritage of the Kaurna and other Aboriginal peoples

■ Visiting Yourambulla Caves and their rock art detailing several Adnyamathanha Dreaming stories

■ Touring Ngaut Ngaut Conservation Park, a significant gallery of stunning rock art along the cliffs of the Murray River

■ Introducing yourself to the heritage of the Adnyamathanha and Arabunna people at the Wadlata Outback Centre

■ Visiting Tandanya, SA's foremost cultural centre has art galleries and a souvenir shop, and offers didjeridu performances

■ Viewing Chambers Gorge, galleries of rock carvings containing the sort of symbols found near Uluru (Ayers Rock)

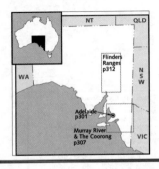

long crescent-shaped lines of rock were built along the shore to catch fish as the water level receded. On Eyre Peninsula men went spear

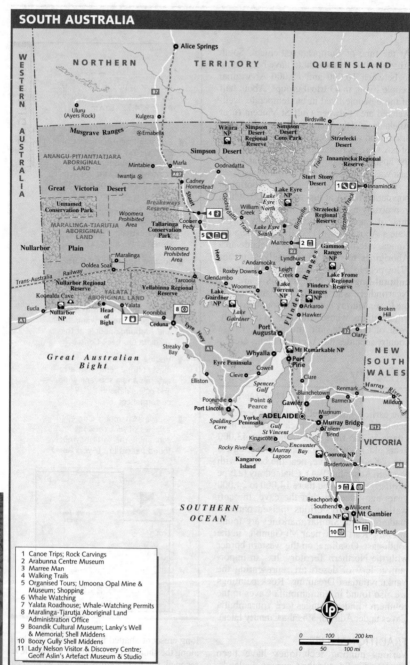

SOUTH AUSTRALIA

1 Canoe Trips; Rock Carvings
2 Arabunna Centre Museum
3 Marree Man
4 Walking Trails
5 Organised Tours; Umoona Opal Mine & Museum; Shopping
6 Whale Watching
7 Yalata Roadhouse; Whale-Watching Permits
8 Maralinga-Tjarutja Aboriginal Land Administration Office
9 Boandik Cultural Museum; Lanky's Well & Memorial; Shell Middens
10 Boozy Gully Shell Middens
11 Lady Nelson Visitor & Discovery Centre; Geoff Aslin's Artefact Museum & Studio

fishing at night in shallow water using burning brands as torches. In the south-east, bird snaring was carried out from wickerwork hides. The Ngarrindjeri built semipermanent weatherproof huts and their women were famed for their weaving and basket making (see the boxed text 'Ngarrindjeri Weaving' in the Ngarrindjeri Country section later). They also used unique spears, called the *kaike* and *yarnde*, which could kill at a distance of 90m. On the Murray River and associated wetlands, food sources were harvested with the aid of canoes made from the bark of river red-gums. Consequently scarr trees, which can be identified by the huge scars of bark removal, are still common in these areas.

Trade routes extended throughout SA to the far reaches of the continent. One trade route ran from Lake Alexandrina through the Flinders Ranges and south-west Queensland to the Gulf of Carpentaria. Some of the items traded had spiritual significance, while others were practical commodities, such as *pituri* (a highly sought-after narcotic which required careful preparation) and certain types of stone and wood for making tools or weapons.

COLONISATION

South Australian Aborigines suffered the first impact of European settlement long before the colony's establishment in 1836. Soon after the arrival of the First Fleet in 1788 epidemics of European diseases, originating in Sydney, swept westwards along the Murray. The most serious of these was smallpox. In 1830 the explorer Charles Sturt noticed great gaps in the ages of the Aborigines he met, remarking how obvious it was that death was among them. Similar reports were made by George Angas, one of SA's founders.

Kangaroo Island, though once connected to the mainland, had been uninhabited for thousands of years when Matthew Flinders landed in 1802. It then became a base for sealers who brought Aboriginal women from Tasmania and also began raiding the Encounter Bay area for women. Whaling was carried out at Encounter Bay and Spalding Cove prior to official settlement.

By the time SA was colonised by free settlers in 1836, a humanitarian movement was under way in England. In 1835 Lord Glenelg, the secretary of state for the colonies, had made it clear that the proper treatment of Aborigines was of 'first importance'; Governor Hindmarsh's proclamation of 1836 (which declared SA a British province) threatened punishment for the mistreatment of Aborigines and promised to promote their advance in civilisation and conversion to the Christian faith. Notwithstanding these ideals, the preamble to the South Australian Constitution Act, which established the province, defined the lands of South Australian Aborigines as 'waste and unoccupied' and suitable for colonisation.

RESISTANCE

In 1838 clashes took place with overlanders bringing stock from New South Wales (NSW). The overlanders initiated attacks on Aborigines, who were punished by massacres when they retaliated. There were frequent bloody clashes around the Murray River and Eyre Peninsula. Conflict among Aborigines also occurred, when weaker tribes were pushed out of their own lands by white settlement and forced to forage on the lands of larger tribes. Aboriginal women were always vulnerable to attacks and exploitation. In the late 19th century there were reports of Aboriginal girls between the ages of 11 and 14 suffering from venereal disease: some white bushmen believed they could ease the symptoms of gonorrhoea by giving the disease to a woman.

Humanitarian ideals combined with colonisation produced contradictory outcomes. For instance, when the brig *Maria* ran aground on the Coorong in 1840, the Ngarrindjeri saved the survivors, but then killed them when they molested Ngarrindjeri women. An on-the-spot trial and execution of two Ngarrindjeri men was carried out by a military detachment. As a consequence Governor Gawler was in danger of being tried for murder, having let the execution go ahead.

PROTECTION

Under pressure from the Colonial Office in London, a 'Protector of Aborigines' was appointed to ensure the welfare of Aboriginal people, though in practise it was the rights of settlers that were given pre-eminence. In the early 1840s Governor Gawler opened ration distribution depots in an attempt to pacify Aborigines and compensate them for the loss of land and food sources. Police administered the depots and their strategic locations were used to control the movements of Aborigines. In 1842 the Waste Lands Act reserved land for Aborigines with a view to encouraging them to take up agriculture, but within 20 years most of this land had been leased to settler farmers.

By 1860 it was a case of 'sweet water, stolen land' and the emphasis of most ration depots shifted from appeasement to saving a people devastated by colonisation. The Aboriginal population, particularly in settled areas, declined dramatically: 40 years after settlement it was estimated that the colony's Aboriginal population had fallen by 50%.

MISSIONS

As happened elsewhere during the 19th century, Australian mission stations were established by the churches with the aim of segregating and protecting Aborigines. Missions were established at Poonindie, Koonibba, Point Pearce and Point McLeay (Raukkan). The most significant figure among the churchmen was George Taplin. Taplin worked with the Ngarrindjeri and left a detailed record of many of their traditional customs and beliefs. A gifted linguist, he also translated parts of the Bible into Ngarrindjeri. In a later and more bizarre version of this humanitarianism, Daisy Bates settled among Aborigines at Ooldea Soak. Bates, who had sadistic fantasies and a neurotic hatred of 'half-castes', needed the Aborigines more than they needed her, yet established a reputation in the eyes of the Australian public as a great benefactor and expert on Aborigines. In the 20th century Pitjantjaraku (Pitjantjatjara people) were evicted from Ooldea Soak and nearby Maralinga so that rockets and atomic weapons could be tested (see the boxed text 'British Nuclear Tests at Maralinga' later in this chapter). The American-controlled Nurrungar military intelligence base built on Kokatha lands was closed in 1999.

LAND RIGHTS

In 1966 the South Australian government made the first move of any Australian state to give Aboriginal people title to their land. This involved the creation of the Aboriginal Lands Trust, in which title was vested to the missions and reserves still operating in SA. These lands are leased back to their Aboriginal occupants, who have repeated rights of renewal. At the same time the South Australian parliament passed the Prohibition of Discrimination Act. The Aboriginal Affairs Act gave South Australian Aborigines the right to run their own communities.

In 1981 the Pitjantjatjara Land Rights Act came into effect, giving freehold title over a vast area in the far north-west to the Anangu-Pitjantjatjara. A further 76,000 sq km, which had been taken over by the federal government as part of the Maralinga project, was returned to its traditional owners in 1984. Land held under Aboriginal freehold title cannot be sold or resumed and no development of any kind can take place without the permission of the traditional owners. Outsiders need a permit from the appropriate council to enter (for details see Pitjantjatjara & Yankunytjatjara Country in this chapter).

EMPOWERMENT

There was always a progressive, humanitarian element in South Australian colonisation and this led to developments in advance of the rest of Australia. Walkerville Aboriginal School was set up in 1844 and was ahead of its time in that it made some concessions to the local Kaurna culture. David Unaipon, a Ngarrindjeri man, is credited as the inventor of the stump-jump plough (a plough that can negotiate tree stumps) and wrote a number of fine short stories that connect Ngarrindjeri traditional beliefs and Christianity. A Faculty of Aboriginal and Islander Studies was established at the University of South Australia, and the Centre for Aboriginal Studies in Music (CASM) was opened at the University of Adelaide. Tandanya, an Aboriginal-controlled art gallery and cultural centre, has operated in Adelaide since the 1980s and features regular exhibitions of Aboriginal art and culture (see Cultural Centres under Adelaide).

Other aspects of South Australian life have been less progressive. The appointment of Aboriginal pastor Sir Doug Nicholls as Governor by the Dunstan government in the 1970s became the subject of mean-spirited controversy which in part contributed to Sir Doug retiring from the position after five months. In many rural areas and provincial centres racism is rife, but positive developments have taken place as part of the process of Reconciliation. In 1996 Aborigines and settlers walked 80km from Adelaide to Hindmarsh Island, originally called Kumarangk, to protest against the building of a bridge over the island and as a gesture of Reconciliation (see Goolwa in the Ngarrindjeri Country section). Coloured Stone, one of Australia's most respected Aboriginal bands, is led by Bunna Lawrie, who comes from Koonibba Aboriginal community near Ceduna (see the Music section in the Facts about Aboriginal Australia & the Torres Strait Islands chapter, written by Bunna Lawrie). One of Australia's most acclaimed Indigenous artists, Ian Abdulla, depicts scenes from his boyhood on the Murray. SA's Aboriginal footballers have distinguished themselves in Australian Rules football and one of them, Gavin Wanganeen, is a winner of the prestigious Brownlow Medal.

Language

Probably the best known Aboriginal language of SA is Pitjantjatjara (also known as Pitjantjara), spoken throughout the Anangu-Pitjantjatjara Aboriginal Lands of northern SA, down almost to the Great Australian Bight. (See the Language section of the Northern Territory chapter for information on Pitjantjatjara.) Many speakers of Yankunytjatjara also live on these freehold lands.

KAURNA

The traditional language of Adelaide and the surrounding plains is Kaurna. It had several dialects, spoken from Crystal Brook (near Port Pirie) in the north to Cape Jervis (near Kangaroo Island) in the south.

Many place-names derived from Kaurna words have survived in and around Adelaide:

Place Name	Kaurna Word
Aldinga	Ngultingga
Onkaparinga	Ngangkiparringga
Noarlunga	Nurlungga
Uraidla	Yurreidla

After the European colonisation of Adelaide, speakers of Kaurna dwindled, and the last

fluent speaker died early last century. However, Kaurna is undergoing a revival, with speakers drawing on records to create language programs at the primary and secondary level and produce literature in the Kaurna language (see Courses in the Adelaide section for details about language courses).

Information

TOURIST OFFICES

The South Australian Tourism Commission (SATC) Travel Centre (☎ 655 276, fax 8303 2249) at 19 King William St, Adelaide, is open 8.30 am to 5 pm weekdays, and 9 am to 2 pm on weekends. It also has a useful Web site (www.visit-southaustralia.com.au).

NATIONAL PARKS

A Desert Parks Pass is required to enter and camp at Innamincka Regional Reserve, as well as Simpson Desert Conservation Park, Simpson Desert Regional Reserve and Witjira and Lake Eyre National Parks. A pass costs $80 for the first year (then $50 per year) and is available in Adelaide from The Environment Shop (☎ 8204 1910), 77 Grenfell St, and the Royal Automobile Association (RAA; ☎ 8202 4540) in Hindmarsh Square. It is also available from relevant National Parks & Wildlife South Australia (NPWSA) offices, and tourist centres, eg, Hawker Motors (Hawker), Underground Books (Coober Pedy), Innamincka Trading Post, Wadlata Outback Centre (Port Augusta), Oasis Cafe (Marree) and the Pink Roadhouse (Oodnadatta). For more details call the Desert Parks hotline (☎ 1800 816 078 toll free).

To enter Flinders Ranges National Park, you need a Flinders Park Pass, which costs $6 per visit and is available from self-registration booths along the main roads into the park, or from the Wilpena Pound Visitor Centre and the NPWSA office in Hawker.

Kaurna Country

Adelaide Plains Area

ADELAIDE

For over 40,000 years the comparatively prosperous and peaceful Kaurna people lived in the hills and along the sea (mostly in summer) in an area now occupied by the city of

Adelaide. The Kaurna called the area Tandanya, meaning 'Place of the red kangaroo'.

More information about the Kaurna can be found in *Aboriginal Adelaide*, published by the Anthropological Society of SA, and available from the South Australian Museum Shop in Adelaide.

Organised Tours

Following is a list of Adelaide-based tour operators that run trips around SA and western NSW focusing on Aboriginal culture. Only Parakeelya and Tauondi are Aboriginal-owned and/or -operated but all use local Aboriginal guides. The Cultural Centres section, later, has details about tours run by Tandanya, the National Aboriginal Cultural Institute.

By Jingo
(☎ 8390 2355, ⒠ byjingo@cobweb.com.au, PO Box 518 Montacute 5134) runs a three-day 4WD 'Aboriginal Cultural Adventure' around the Flinders Ranges for $525 per person.

Community Aid Abroad
(☎ 8232 2727, ⒠ bwitty@ozemail.com.au, 1st Floor, Da Costa Bldg, 68 Grenfell St) is a non-profit organisation which offers seven-day trips ($1070 per person) to experience Arabunna culture (near Marree); more details are available on its Web site at www.caa.org.au/travel.

Ecotrek & Bogong Jack Adventures
(☎ 8383 7198, ⒠ ecotrek@ozemail.com.au, PO Box 4 Kangarilla 5157) offers an excellent range of hiking tours around Mutawintji (New South Wales), Flinders Ranges and Gammon Ranges National Parks, and to the region around Innamincka; more details are on its Web site: www.ecotrek.com.au.

Mulpa
(☎/fax 8520 2808, ⒠ francis@chariot.net.au, PO Box 815 Virginia, SA 5120) has a range of detailed and imaginative trips, including tag-along 4WD tours of the northern Flinders Ranges.

Parakeelya Cultural Centre
(see Cultural Centres later in this section) offers tailored, all-inclusive camping tours, mainly to the Flinders Ranges and Outback SA for about $100 per person per day; a minimum of four people is required.

Tauondi Cultural Agency
(☎ 8240 0300, fax 8240 0786) at 1 Lipson St, Port Adelaide, is part of the renowned Tauondi Aboriginal College, one of only five independent Aboriginal-operated colleges in Australia. It offers detailed three-hour tours of the South Australian Museum, Tandanya and the Adelaide Botanic Garden combined, as well as individual tours of Cleland Conservation Park and Adelaide Zoo (see the Walking Trails section, following).

The college has plans to open an Aboriginal art gallery, plant trail and souvenir shop at its centre in Port Adelaide.

Walking Trails

Cleland Conservation Park Tauondi (see Organised Tours earlier) operates guided tours along the **Yurridla Trail** in Cleland Conservation Park (☎ 8339 2444) at 11 am and 1.30 pm on Wednesday and Sunday. The tour includes Kaurna Dreaming *stories* about the Mt Lofty Ranges, east of Adelaide, and costs $3 per person, plus entry fee to the park ($9.50/5.50/23.50 for adults/children/families). Bookings (essential) should be made with the park.

Morialta Conservation Park Morialta comes from the Kaurna word for 'always flowing', a reference to the spectacular Morialta waterfalls. Three-hour cultural tours of the park are offered by Kaurna guide Norman Brusnahan (☎ 8364 3408) for about $17.50 per person, excluding transport, though he currently caters mainly to school groups. In the future the park itself intends to implement self-guided walking trails with an Aboriginal cultural component.

Adelaide Botanic Garden Tauondi and Tandanya (see respectively Organised Tours earlier and Cultural Centres later) run guided tours along the **Aboriginal Plant Trail** in the Adelaide Botanic Garden, which focus on the Indigenous use of plants for food and medicines. Free guided tours of the trail incorporating some limited information (but more, if requested) about Aboriginal plant use are also offered by non-Indigenous guides through the Friends of the Botanic Gardens of Adelaide (☎ 8226 8803). A minimum of five people is required.

Adelaide Zoo The **Kanggarlta Trail** at the zoo (☎ 8267 2434) explores the relationship between Aboriginal people and Australian wildlife. Guided tours (mainly for school groups) are run by Tauondi (see earlier).

Tjibulki Trail There are plans (perhaps a long way from fruition) to mark with plaques and cairns a trail around Adelaide and the Fleurieu Peninsula following the Dreaming Path of Tjibulki (see Parks, Squares & Gardens later).

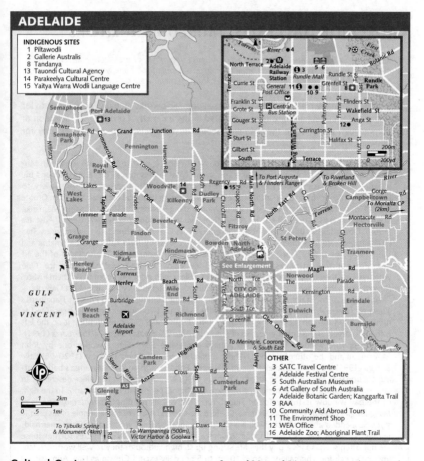

ADELAIDE

INDIGENOUS SITES
1 Piltawodli
2 Gallerie Australis
8 Tandanya
13 Tauondi Cultural Agency
14 Parakeelya Cultural Centre
15 Yaitya Warra Wodli Language Centre

OTHER
3 SATC Travel Centre
4 Adelaide Festival Centre
5 South Australian Museum
6 Art Gallery of South Australia
7 Adelaide Botanic Garden; Kanggarlta Trail
9 RAA
10 Community Aid Abroad Tours
11 The Environment Shop
12 WEA Office
16 Adelaide Zoo; Aboriginal Plant Trail

Cultural Centres

Tandanya Tandanya, the National Aboriginal Cultural Institute (☎ 8224 3200, e tandanya@tandanya.on.net), is an Aboriginal-owned and -operated cultural institute which boasts extensive art galleries and craft workshops, and a comprehensive gift and bookshop. The cafe is excellent and serves traditional bush tucker.

Inside, the performance centre features didjeridu shows every day at midday. Admission to the art galleries (including *didjeridu* show if you're there at midday) costs $4.50 per person. A guided tour ($11) includes a look at the facilities, galleries, the didjeridu shop and a souvenir pack. Other tours, which include the Adelaide Botanic Garden and South Australian Museum, cost

from $20 to $54 per person but require seven days' notice and a minimum of eight people.

Tandanya is at 253 Grenfell St (at the far eastern end) and is open 10 am to 5 pm daily. Check out its Web site at www.tandanya.on .net/info.htm. See also the boxed text 'Adelaide Museums, Galleries & Shops'.

Parakeelya Cultural Centre Parakeelya (☎ 8244 5744, e guranda@camtech.net.au) at 356 Torrens Rd, Kilkenny, offers a small collection of authentic crafts for sale, and can arrange tours (see the Organised Tours section, earlier). In the future Parakeelya plans to hold regular performances of Aboriginal dance and music for visitors to the site.

ADELAIDE GALLERIES, MUSEUMS & SHOPS

Readers should be aware that the names of deceased members of the Aboriginal community may be cited in this section. Mentioning the personal name of someone who has died recently can cause offence, anguish and grief in some Aboriginal cultures.

There are too many places in Adelaide that sell or exhibit works by Indigenous artists to list them all here, outlets are mostly concentrated in the inner city. Following is a selection of recommended outlets. See the Shopping section in the Facts for the Visitor chapter for further information.

Art Gallery of South Australia (☎ 8207 7000) on North Terrace, next to the South Australian Museum, doesn't have a lot of Aboriginal art on show. What it does display is scattered around the galleries, so you have to seek it out. There are only seven works in the Australian Art Gallery, to the right of the reception desk. Included here is an interesting historical bark painting from Groote Eylandt in the Northern Territory (NT), titled *Orion and the Pleiades* (1948) by Minimini Mamarika (1904–72). There's also a well-known Albert Namatjira watercolour, *Ghost Gum, Central Australia* (1956). Downstairs in the basement the Decorative Arts Gallery features two contemporary Tiwi (NT) earthenware sculptures. One is the painted *Dingo Vase* by John Patrick Kalantumama and the other is the quirky *Turtle Boat* by Mark Puatjimi, both from 1999. The majority of the art gallery's Aboriginal art works are hung around the stairwell at the west wing entrance. One wonders why they haven't been hung in a proper gallery with sufficient room to do them justice. Nevertheless, this space is called the Santos Atrium, or Contemporary Aboriginal Art Gallery.

At the top of the stairs you are greeted by an amazing painting: Clifford Possum Tjapaltjarri's *Yuelamu Honey Ant Dreaming* (1980). On either side are two large sculptural pieces. On the right is a 1994 *lorrkon* (hollow log coffin) by Terry Ngamandara. Complementing it on the left is the tall carved and painted wood *Spirit Figure* by Alec Wurrmala called *Galabarrbarra* (1991). In the opposite window bay are two equally impressive *Spirit Figure* works, one by John Mowandjul and the other by Jackie Nabulaya. Kimberley artist Rover Thomas' (1926–98) *Lake Baragu* (1991) is a fine example of this artist's work. Paddy Fordham Wainburranga's bark painting *Missionaries Coming to the Artist's Country* (1990) is a striking narrative piece describing an important historical event experienced by many Aboriginal peoples in Arnhem Land. To the right of the bay window is Turkey Tolson Tjupurrula's marvellous painting *Straightening Spears at Ilyingaungau* (1990). This work shimmers before the eye and is a very fine example of his unique style. Suspended above the stairwell are three magnificent carved wood *yawk yawk* (mermaid) figures (1994) by Owen Yalandja from Mumeka, near Maningrida (NT). Figures such as these are not often seen, so it's a pity they are strung up so high, although they're well worth stretching one's neck for. The gallery is open 10 am to 5 pm daily except Christmas Day. Admission is free, except for special exhibitions.
Web site: www.artgallery.sa.gov.au

Art Gallery of South Australia Bookshop (☎ 8224 3220) on North Terrace, has only a small selection of Indigenous books for sale. As expected, the books on art are quite good and there are a couple of Pitjantjatjara seed necklaces and a few attractive postcards for sale, but that's about it. Strange, since this place touts itself as 'the most comprehensive arts bookshop' in Adelaide. Hours are 10 am to 4.45 pm daily except Christmas Day and Good Friday.

Gallerie Australis (☎ 8231 4111) on North Terrace is in the forecourt of the Hyatt Regency. Aimed more at the fine-art investment end of the market, the gallery prices reflect this. Even if you can't afford to buy, you'll see some fine examples of Aboriginal art here. Of note are the attractive acrylics on canvas by Kathleen, Violet and Emily Petyarre, and those by Dorothy Napangardi. Out front is a beautiful Aboriginal-designed forecourt and wall mural by well-known local artist Darryl Pfitzner (Milika). Aboriginal imagery is portrayed in ceramic tiles and a long sculpted curving wall which pays tribute to the Kaurna people of Adelaide. Titled *Yerrakartarta* and commissioned in 1995, the forecourt is certainly impressive and worth a look. Gallery hours are 10 am to 6 pm Monday to Friday and noon to 4 pm Saturday; it's closed Sunday, public holidays and all of January.

continued...   Gary Lee

South Australian Museum (☎ 8207 7500) on North Terrace features the Aboriginal Cultures Gallery. This new gallery is housed over two levels and is well worth the effort to visit, as it is one of the most well-designed and culturally sensitive museum displays on Aboriginal cultures in the country. A visit here will give you one of the best introductions to the vast complexity and diversity of Aboriginal cultures in Australia today and in the past. There is an abundance of fascinating information to take in here and a second visit is probably not a bad idea. Inside and surrounding the entrance on the immediate right is a historical collection of striking tin dance masks, found discarded at Port Hedland in Western Australia in 1953. They had been abandoned there several years before, after a large public ceremony that brought people together from the surrounding desert. You won't see masks like these anywhere else. On the immediate left as you enter is a large and fascinating photo-portrait montage of Aboriginal people, both historical and contemporary from around the country, interspersed with filmed 'living' portraits.

There is far too much of interest to mention in detail in this remarkable gallery. The displays are highly informative and very well planned. Much of the material on show is historical with most of it unique and never exhibited before. The visitor will be given detailed insights into Aboriginal life in all its manifestations, such in the arts, religion, hunting, *law*, bush medicine, material culture, politics, music, dance, aesthetics and spirituality, to mention just a few of the diverse subjects not usually offered to the general public. There are excellent individual touch-screen computers loaded with all manner of information to complement the displays. These are placed throughout the two floors of exhibits and are very popular, judging from the lack of empty chairs in front of them.

If you want to find out more information on the displays, pop into the Indigenous Information Centre on level two. The Aboriginal staff are helpful and there are free computer terminals to access. There's a small research library too. The gallery is open 10 am to 5 pm daily except Good Friday and Christmas Day. There's a free daily 40-minute guided tour with one of the Aboriginal guides; book at the Museum Shop. Entry is adults $10, children under-14 free. Web site: www.samuseum.sa.gov.au

South Australian Museum Shop (☎ 8207 7500) on North Terrace is to the right at the museum entrance. It has a very good selection of SA Aboriginal books on art, politics, law, culture and history. The posters at $16 are a good buy, featuring Aboriginal paintings from the Museum's extensive Aboriginal collections. The children's Aboriginal storybooks are always worth a look and there's a fairly good variety available. There's only a small selection of arts and crafts on offer, so you'd be better off looking elsewhere for those; the books are your best buy here. There is an excellent catalogue on the Aboriginal Cultures Gallery available for $14.25. This comprehensive and informative publication is worth buying, especially after visiting the gallery itself. Shop hours are 10 am to 4.45 pm daily except Christmas Day and Good Friday. Web site: www.samuseum.sa.gov.au

Tandanya Shop (☎ 8224 3220) at 253 Grenfell St is a national Aboriginal cultural institute housed in its own impressive building. The Tandanya shop is to the left at the entrance and has a fairly good variety of Indigenous products on offer. The range of books in particular is excellent, with an interesting selection available. There are titles on South Australian Aboriginal arts, history, myths and some autobiographies of people from the Aboriginal community as well. The seed-pod and nut-case necklaces come from north, central and south-eastern Australia, and are well priced from $20 to $50. Nicely painted boomerangs from the central desert area range from $33 to $60. Bullurru Designs hankies are $6.50, painted cloth panels are $18.20 and attractive T-shirts go for $36.20 to $40.95. The didjeridus start at $99 and go up to $300. Ernabella Arts hand-painted silk scarves sell for $66 to $88. In the small attached Tjilbruke Gallery, paintings start at $100, with limited edition prints from $300. There's a changing exhibition program, so check to see what's on in the main gallery. The Aboriginal staff are very helpful and shop is open from 10 am to 5 pm daily. Web site: www.tandanya.on.net

SOUTH AUSTRALIA

Living Kaurna Cultural Centre In recognition of the importance of Warriparinga (see Parks, Squares & Gardens) to the Kaurna people, the Living Kaurna Cultural Centre is currently being built (and due for completion by late 2001) at Warriparinga. The centre will include an indoor and outdoor interpretative centre (predominantly about the Kaurna) and an Aboriginal art gallery. It will be open 9 am to 5 pm daily, and a small fee may be payable. The entrance will be along Sturt Rd.

Parks, Squares & Gardens

The Dreaming story of Tjibulki, who roamed the Fleurieu Peninsula and created the freshwater springs along the coastline, is fundamental to Kaurna culture.

Warriparinga Sturt River (Warri Parri) is where Tjibulki's nephew, Kulultuwi, was killed, and **Warriparinga**, a park on the corner of Sturt, Marion and South Rds, is recognised as a traditional meeting place of the Kaurna.

Inside the park, the **Tjibulki Trail Gateway** symbolically commemorates the Tjibulki Trail (see Walking Trails earlier). The tree trunks represent, among other things, deforestation through colonisation and urbanisation; the circles symbolise freshwater springs created by Tjibulki's tears; and the thin paths indicate the flow of the Sturt River and the renowned gully winds of the area. A nearby **scarr tree** was most probably cut to make a shield or dish.

Tjibulki Spring & Monument Tjibulki initially took Kulultuwi's body to the Tjibulki Spring site, **Tulukudank**, created by Tjibulki's tears, and then to Cape Jervis. Near the spring site (next to the Kingston Park Caravan Park kiosk), steps lead up to a cliff-top **granite monument,** which recognises the Kaurna and the legend of Tjibulki. The monument is along Strickland Rd in Kingston Park (16km south of central Adelaide), opposite Kingston House.

Piltawodli Piltawodli (Kaurna for 'Possum Home') is a small but delightful memorial to the establishment in the 1830s of a Kaurna settlement, which included the first Aboriginal school in the state. It's here that German missionaries first helped to record the Kaurna culture and language. The memorial is opposite the Red Ochre Restaurant, off War Memorial Drive, in Adelaide.

Courses

The Workers Educational Association (WEA) Adult Education (☎ 8223 1979, ℮ wea@ao11.aone.net.au) at 223 Angas St runs 'Introduction to Aboriginal Art' courses through the Internet for $17 – they're available to anyone at any time. It also offers one-day 'Aboriginal Art Tours' ($42 per person) several times a year, which explore rock art and campsite remains in the Adelaide Hills with Kaurna guides. More details are available from the WEA Web site (www.wea-sa.com.au).

Yaitya Warra Wodli Language Centre (☎ 8269 3601, ℮ yaityawarra@camtech .net.au) at 301 Churchill Rd, Prospect, is a new Aboriginal-run centre which intends to offer short-term language courses (eg, in Pitjantjatjara and Kaurna) to the public. Contact the centre for more details.

Special Events

Adelaide's renowned Festival of Arts (☎ 8226 8111), held in March in even-numbered years, includes some Indigenous art and cultural performances. Its Web site is at www.adelaidefestival.org.au. The supplementary Fringe Festival (☎ 8231 7760), however, offers more Aboriginal music and dance. Its Web site is at www.adelaide fringe.com.au. For both festivals, some performances are held, and information and bookings are available, at the Adelaide Festival Centre on King William St. Aboriginal music and dance are also a popular feature of Womadelaide (☎ 8271 1488), held in February in odd-numbered years.

Tandanya often holds exhibitions of Aboriginal art, and regularly features special performances of Indigenous music and dance. The notice board inside the centre is always a great source of information about upcoming events.

Tauondi Aboriginal College has an open day on the second Thursday of September (in Youth Cultural Week). Several other special events are held in and around Adelaide during National Reconciliation Week (late May) and National Aboriginal and Islander Day of Celebration (NAIDOC) Week (mid-July) – check the local Aboriginal press or the Tandanya notice board for details.

MY BLUE WATER DREAMING

Tony Wallace

Not only have Aboriginal people always had a close bond with the land, they have also had an affinity with the ocean. Back in 1993, the inaugural Billabong Indigenous Surfing Invitational was held at Wreck Bay, an Aboriginal community near Booderee National Park (see the NSW chapter), on the south coast of NSW. This surf event brought together Aboriginal surfers from all over the country. I can still remember the wonderful stories we shared and the great waves we surfed together. Since those early years of the Billabong Indigenous events, I have been competitively involved with surf coaching and surfing longboards. I have also been involved in surf camps, some of which involved Aboriginal communities. These camps are designed to encourage young people to become involved in surfing not only by providing the necessary equipment, but also by offering quality coaching. One camp involved young Aboriginal people from Ceduna and Koonibba Aboriginal community, both in SA. Another surf camp, also in SA, involved young Aboriginal students from Port Lincoln High School. These camps motivated me to pursue my dream of establishing an Indigenous surf club in Australia.

Today I am the President of South Australia's first Indigenous Boardriders Surf Club, the Tarni-Burkama Indigenous Boardriders Surf Club Association (☎/fax 8386 3442, e wwallace@ekno.com), which I helped to set up in July 2000. In the Kaurna language, *tarni-burkama* translates as 'people of the surf'. Our unique club is near the sand dunes of the popular Moana Beach Conservation Park, about 35km south of Adelaide. This is a very auspicious location – not only were the sand dunes in this area traditionally used by the Kaurna people as a summer camp – they were also traditionally considered to be a fertility site. Another organisation which was established to foster the development of surfing within Indigenous communities and to nurture elite Indigenous surfing talent is the Indigenous Surfing Association (☎ 07-5520 1150).

The surfing bug bit me at an early age. I have always lived by the sea and it was the lure of the water that led me to surf. I never thought that doing something I love so much would bring me so many rewards. In 1997 I was South Australia's NAIDOC Aboriginal Sportsperson of the Year (for excellence in surfing). I had always thought of surfing as an alternative to mainstream sport, so it was a great feeling to see it in the limelight.

Tony Wallace

My mother's parents are members of the Stolen Generations. My Dad's mother's mother was a Wuthathi person of Cape York Peninsula, born at sea, and his father was from the Wallis Islands in the Pacific. Mother grew up on Old Mapoon Mission and Dad spent his childhood on Keriri (Hammond Island). I was born into a family of five and grew up in Cairns, where the surf bug got me.

In 1976 I headed for SA. I remember weekends playing football on Saturday and Mum taking me surfing on Sunday. I found employment in the advertising industry as a junior commercial artist and left the industry 10 years later as a studio manager.

I'm now completing a TAFE course in Aboriginal Community Management and Administration. I have represented SA at five national longboard titles.

I grew up in suburbia and have been an urban dweller all my life. I'm lucky to have had parents with close family ties and strong cultural beliefs and values.

I am a single parent now with three children of my own. I want to enjoy my family and share my surf culture with anyone who has an interest in this lifestyle.

SOUTH AUSTRALIA

The South Australian Museum (see the boxed text 'Adelaide Museums, Galleries, & Shops') organises activities (mainly for children) during school holidays to link with its excellent Aboriginal Cultures Gallery. Tickets for events and performances (mostly free) and details are available from the museum.

International Environment Day (early June), held in Belair National Park (☎ 8278 5477) in the Adelaide Hills, boasts a strong Aboriginal component.

More information about the special events mentioned in this section is detailed in the booklet *Arts SA*, available from the SATC Travel Centre (see Information at the start of this chapter).

Meru Country

Lower Murray

For over 40,000 years the Murray River has been a major source of fresh water, fish, plants and bark (for canoes) for the Meru people, who often settled along its banks in comparatively large numbers. Some of the cliffs between Mannum, east of Adelaide, and Berri, near the Victorian border, are treasure troves of rock art (most of which is off-limits), and hundreds of scarred gum trees dot the river banks, especially along the eastern side of the Murray, opposite Blanchetown.

BERRI

About 500m north-east of Vaughan St (the end of the main street) is A Special Place for Jimmy James. James was a Pitjantjatjara man who lived and worked in the Riverland as a tracker for 30 years, and helped the police to arrest about 40 criminals and to rescue about 10 lost people. The place is serene, but there isn't much to see other than a monument made from black granite by James' nephew, Bluey Roberts, a renowned Aboriginal artist. More information about James can be found in *Lost & Found: Life of Jimmy James, Black Tracker* by Robert Holmes, available at the SA Museum bookshop in Adelaide.

Under the western (Berri) side of the main bridge is the **Bridge Mural**, which depicts Ngurundjeri Dreaming stories about the Murray and the Coorong (see The Coorong under Ngarrindjeri Country later).

WINMANTE ARTS & CULTURAL TOURISM CENTRE

This centre (☎ 8583 2027), owned and operated by the local Aboriginal community, is currently a modest concern, with a small but varied number of crafts for sale (mostly made by Pitjantjatjara people in far-north SA), and a tea room. The management has ambitious plans to expand the centre, and to offer visitors cultural tours, musical and dance performances, an arts and crafts workshop and a nature trail.

The centre, open from around 9 am to 5 pm daily, is in Glossop, along the Sturt Hwy between Berri and Barmera.

NGAUT NGAUT CONSERVATION PARK

Often still referred to as Devon Downs, this park is home to one of Australia's most significant archaeological sites. As the centre of Wumbulgal Purka Bidni (Black Duck Dreaming), it is sacred to the Meru and Ngarrindjeri people: remains of **campfires** and **burial sites**, as well as stunning **rock art**, clearly indicate several temporary settlements, perhaps over 8000 years old. Of major interest are **carvings** of dolphins, which may have once swum this far inland.

The park is just off the road along the eastern bank of the Murray River, between Purnong and Nildottie. It is not signposted, and individual entry is not permitted – *all* visitors must be part of a guided tour.

Guided tours of Ngaut Ngaut are operated by Aboriginal Elder Richard Hunter (☎ 8570 1202, fax 8570 1203), and are included in the expensive but delightful two- to five-day boat cruises on PS *Murray Princess* (☎ 8569 2511) and MV *Proud Mary* (☎ 8231 9472). Both of these boat companies offer two-night weekend packages departing from along the Murray (ie, Murray Bridge, Blanchetown or Mannum), which cost from $270 per person; or considerably more if you want a cabin with views and transport to/from Adelaide. Alternatively, if you contact Hunter and time a visit to the park to coincide with a tour by boat passengers (currently Thursday and Saturday), a tour will cost only $5 per person. If you arrange a separate tour (with a minimum of 10 people), the cost is around $10 per person.

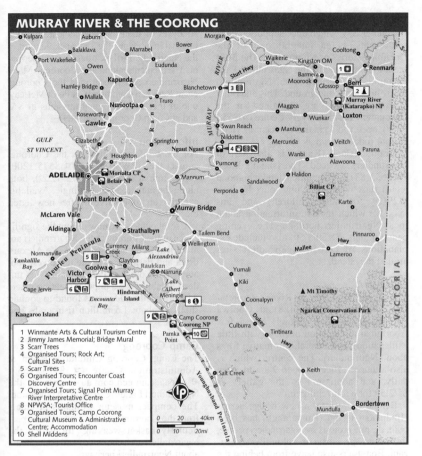

MURRAY RIVER & THE COORONG

1 Winmante Arts & Cultural Tourism Centre
2 Jimmy James Memorial; Bridge Mural
3 Scarr Trees
4 Organised Tours; Rock Art;
   Cultural Sites
5 Scarr Trees
6 Organised Tours; Encounter Coast
   Discovery Centre
7 Organised Tours; Signal Point Murray
   River Interpretative Centre
8 NPWSA; Tourist Office
9 Organised Tours; Camp Coorong
   Cultural Museum & Administrative
   Centre; Accommodation
10 Shell Middens

Ngarrindjeri Country

Lake Alexandrina & the Coorong

The rich resources of Lake Alexandrina and the Coorong supported a number of semi-permanent settlements of Ngarrindjeri people for over 6000 years. The Ngarrindjeri – in fact, a collective term for about 18 different tribes – are united by a complex and distinct language, and a belief in their Dreaming Ancestor, Ngurundjeri, who created the Murray and the Coorong. (Coorong comes from the Ngarrindjeri word *kurangh*, meaning 'long neck' and referring to the very thin Younghusband Peninsula.)

More information about the Ngarrindjeri can be found in the excellent booklet, *Ngurunderi: An Aboriginal Dreaming*, available at the SA Museum bookshop in Adelaide (see the boxed text 'Adelaide Museums, Galleries & Shops' earlier).

ORGANISED TOURS

Two companies offer boat tours of the Coorong that include sites of Ngarrindjeri significance: *Coorong Experience* (☎ 8555 1133) and *Spirit of Coorong* (☎ 8555 2203). Both leave from behind the interpretative centre in Goolwa (see later). One-day Coorong cruises by both companies, departing from Goolwa, cost from $64/32 for adults/children. A range of more budget-priced, authentic and ecofriendly tours are offered by Coorong Nature Tours (☎ 8574 0037, e coorongnat @lm.net.au). None of these tours is Aboriginal run or uses Aboriginal guides, however.

VICTOR HARBOR

Encounter Bay, which once supported large settlements, is an integral part of the Dreaming stories of Ngurundjeri. **The Bluff** (called Longkuwar by the Ngarrindjeri), for example, was formed when Ngurundjeri threw his club to the ground. This and other Dreaming stories are explained in the Encounter Coast Discovery Centre (☎ 8552 5388), open 1 to 4 pm daily, in central Victor Harbor (once known as Pultung).

Granite Island (Kaike) is also part of Ngurundjeri's legend. The island's kiosk (☎ 8552 8311, e granite.island@bigpond .com) runs whale-watching tours by boat ($29/19 for adults/children) and bus ($14/12) which include information about local Ngarrindjeri heritage. The evening penguin tours ($8.50/5.50) also include explanations of certain Ngarrindjeri sites around the island.

GOOLWA

The Signal Point Murray River Interpretative Centre (☎ 8555 3488) at Goolwa (which means 'The elbow') has a few Aboriginal artefacts on display (with little explanation), and several informative films about Ngurundjeri. The centre (which is also a tourist office) is open 9 am to 5 pm daily, and admission to the gallery is $5/2.50 for adults/children.

Behind the centre, a new bridge across Hindmarsh Island (Kumarangk) has been built, despite protests by Ngarrindjeri people, for whom the island is culturally significant. Boat tours also leave from behind the centre (see Organised Tours earlier).

SCARR TREES

For thousands of years, the Ngarrindjeri have used canoes for fishing, transport and ceremonies (according to Dreaming stories, Ngurundjeri travelled down the Murray on a bark canoe).

Along the many rivers flowing into Lake Alexandrina are many superb examples of scarr trees, huge river red-gums where a chunk has been carved out in the obvious shape of a canoe. One signposted example is along Winery Rd, near the River Finniss about 6.5km north-east of Currency Creek village; another is about 650m along a marked trail starting from the Lions Picnic Park in Currency Creek.

THE COORONG

Analyses of shell middens indicate that the original inhabitants, the Tanganekald (part of the Ngarrindjeri tribe), often created permanent settlements along the Coorong. Many Ngarrindjeri still live around the Coorong, eg, at Raukkan Community at Point McLeay, one of the first Aboriginal missions in SA, and at Camp Coorong (see later).

Information

For more information about the Coorong, contact the NPWSA office (☎ 8575 1200) or the tourist office (☎ 8575 1259), both along the main road in Meningie. Available at both is an informative and free newsletter, the *Tattler*.

Useful outdoor displays about the significance of the Coorong to the Ngarrindjeri are at Tailem Bend north-east of Lake Alexandrina and Parnka Point, the narrowest spot along the Coorong. Parnka Point was understandably once a popular meeting place, where a shell midden was found to contain shells of about 1.5 million fish, crabs and cockles.

Camp Coorong

The Camp Coorong Cultural Museum & Administration Centre (☎ 8575 1557, e nlpa@camtech.com.au) is run by the Ngarrindjeri Lands & Progress Association. The compact museum contains artefacts from the Coorong, locally made crafts (particularly basket weaving, for which the Ngarrindjeri are renowned) and some items about Ngarrindjeri heritage.

Accommodation is available on site, and includes campsites with facilities ($8.80 per person), dorm beds ($16.50) and cabins ($49.50 per double).

Ngarrindjeri cultural tours are available around local sites and further afield in the Coorong, and basket-weaving lessons are also possible. Contact the centre for current details and costs.

The centre is open 9 am to 5 pm daily. It's about 11km south of Meningie, on the corner of Princes Highway and Seven Mile Rd.

Special Events

In October 1999 the inaugural Ngarrindjeri Ngrikilun Corroboree was held at Raukkan, along the shores of Lake Alexandrina, and was open to the public. The organisers of

NGARRINDJERI WEAVING

Jared Thomas

Ellen Trevorrow is one of many Ngarrindjeri people who dedicate their life to the legacy of Ngarrindjeri culture and weaving. Ellen lives with her family at Camp Coorong, the Race Relations, Cultural Education and Recreation Centre of the Ngarrindjeri Lands & Progress Association. Ellen began weaving 19 years ago and was taught by her Elder, Aunty Dorothy Kartinyeri, one of the many people responsible for passing on the basket-making tradition.

Weaving has always been of significance to the Ngarrindjeri people of the Coorong. Before European contact, the wetlands in this part of Australia were prolific, but they are now gradually depleting with rising salinity levels and drainage. The cold winds from the lagoons and the Southern Ocean, and the many foods that were gathered along the Coorong, made weaving integral to the life and culture of the Ngarrindjeri. In traditional times, men and women wove items such as baskets, mats and fish-traps for everyday use. Today Ngarrindjeri people continue to weave items that were used by their predecessors for hunting, gathering, storage and warmth. Positives that have flowed from the new generation of weavers include the increased care and growth of rushes and the protection of the Coorong's fresh water, which is integral to all life in the area.

Highly respected in her field and teaching Ngarrindjeri weaving workshops at Camp Coorong, Ellen has seen the way that weaving has assisted in race relations and the passing on of cultural knowledge. Ngarrindgeri weavers and non-Indigenous weavers from the region gather at Camp Coorong for weaving sessions. International Indigenous weavers visit Camp Coorong to share weaving techniques and aspects of their culture.

Today, younger Ngarrindjeri generations embrace weaving and it plays a major role in their development. Weaving to the Ngarrindjeri provides much more than the final product of a mat, basket or other item. The collecting of rushes (used by Ngarrindjeri weavers) that grow by fresh water, the soaking of the rushes in preparation for work, and the time it takes to complete a weaving, gives Ellen time to discuss Ngarrindjeri culture and history with her children, friends, relatives, and tourists. Ellen explains:

When I began weaving, my children were little but they always came with me to help collect rushes and supported me, as did my nieces, nephews, brothers, sisters and my husband, Tom. Now that my children are older they go out by themselves and collect rushes for weaving. This is important because it gives them time alone together doing something that gives them a sense of responsibility and pride in their culture.

Jared Thomas

Jared is a young Nukunu man from Port Augusta, SA. Jared is a graduate of a Bachelor of Arts degree and Graduate Diploma in Creative Writing from Adelaide University.

Jared's first play, *Flash Red Ford*, was staged in Uganda and Kenya in 1998, and two of his short fiction works are published by ABC Books and Wakefield Press. He is currently developing a new play and working in varying capacities on film script development and within the film industry. He is a regular correspondent for the *Koori Mail*, the national Aboriginal and Torres Strait Islander newspaper.

Jared was the recipient of the 2000 South Australian Colin Thiele Scholarship for Literature and was a finalist in the South Australian Young Australian of the Year in the arts category.

SOUTH AUSTRALIA

this weekend of dancing, music and art hope that it becomes an annual event. More information is available from the organisers (☎ 8215 0088, e thinc@ozemail.com.au).

KANGAROO ISLAND

Kangaroo Island, called Karta (apparently from the Ngarrindjeri words for 'Island of the Dead'), was uninhabited when Europeans first arrived in 1802. However, stone implements found in Murray Lagoon (in the south) indicate that the island was inhabited over 16,000 years ago, ie, *after* it broke away from the mainland.

According to the Ngarrindjeri Dreaming story, Ngurundjeri dived into the sea off the western end of the island, and then entered the spiritual world. This is explained in more detail at an information shelter at the Flinders Chase National Park headquarters at Rocky River. The island boasts several sacred sites, but almost all have been deliberately kept secret.

Rainbow Walkabouts (☎ 8553 5350, e kiecology@kin.on.net, PO Box 290 Kingscote, SA 5223) is an ecofriendly company that offers a range of tours focusing significantly on the heritage of Kangaroo Island. One-day all-inclusive tours starting in Kingscote cost from $215 per person. More details are available from its Web site (www.rainbowwalkabouts.com.au).

Boandik Country

South-East Coast

Rock art found inside dozens of caves in the south-east has been dated back about 28,000 years, while remains of boomerangs more than 10,000 years old – probably the world's oldest-known wooden artefacts – have been found near Millicent. (None of the rock art sites is open to the public, however.)

The Boandik ('People of the Reeds') are renowned for their woodcarving and basket-weaving skills, and examples are displayed at the outstanding Aboriginal Cultures Gallery at the South Australian Museum (see the boxed text 'Adelaide Museums, Galleries & Shops' earlier).

More information about the Boandik (and the Ngarrindjeri people) is included in a small but informative booklet, *The Aboriginal People of the South East* by Pam

O'Connor, available at the tourist offices in Millicent and Mt Gambier.

BEACHPORT

The Boandik Cultural Museum (☎ 8735 8208) contains an extensive display of artefacts, photographs and memorabilia from the Boandik and other Aboriginal people (privately collected by a non-Indigenous person). It's on McCourt St and open 10 am to 3 pm daily. Admission is $4/1 for adults/children.

A short walk from North Railway Terrace or North West Terrace is **Lanky's Well**, built for horses tended by Lanky, a tracker and an important survivor of the Boandik people. He died in 1904, and was buried under a small but emotive **memorial** that remembers him as the last of his people. The memorial is in the far right-hand corner of the Beachport Cemetery, about 5km from Beachport along the road to Millicent.

Beachport Conservation Park, 2km north-west of town, has numerous collections of **shell middens**. The largest heaps are at Three Miles Rock and Big Midden, but these places are only accessible by 4WD or on foot, 3km from the end of a track that is often impassable in winter by a conventional vehicle.

CANUNDA NATIONAL PARK

The most outstanding (and most accessible) collection of **shell middens** in the area is adjacent to the two lookouts at Boozy Gully, at the end of the road through Canunda National Park.

There are information displays about middens at the Boozy Gully car park, and opposite the NPWSA office (☎ 8735 6053). The office, which is also responsible for Beachport Conservation Park, is 500m west of Southend (from where there is a road to Canunda).

MT GAMBIER
The Lady Nelson Visitor & Discovery Centre

This tourist office-cum-museum (☎ 8724 9750, e theladynelson@mountgambiertourism.com.au) boasts, among other things, a reconstructed midden; an explanation about the Dreaming ancestor Craitbul (who created the nearby volcanoes); a marvellous audiovisual display about Christina Smith (a 19th-century Scottish woman who worked with the Boandik); and information about, and replicas of, cave rock art. The Discovery Centre, on Jubilee Hwy East, is open 9 am to 4.15 pm daily (the tourist office closes at 5 pm) and admission is $7.70/3.30 for adults/children, and $18.70 for families.

Geoff Aslin's Artefact Museum & Studio

This private collection of artefacts (owned by a non-Indigenous local with a speciality in Aboriginal cave rock art) is worth visiting for anyone with a specific interest in Boandik heritage. The museum (☎ 8725 0005) is in a private home on the corner of Wireless Rd West and Perriam St, but visits are only possible after 4 pm weekdays and only by appointment. Entrance is free, but a small donation for upkeep is appreciated.

Nukunu Country

Upper Spencer Gulf

PORT AUGUSTA

This large town is home to a permanent settlement of displaced Indigenous people, including Adnyamathanha people from the northern Flinders Ranges (see Adnyamathanha Country later).

Information

The NPWSA office (☎ 8648 5310, fax 8648 5311) for the southern Flinders Ranges is at 9 Mackay St.

Radio Umeewarra Aboriginal Media Association broadcasts 5UMA (89.1 FM).

Wadlata Outback Centre & Tourist Office

This centre (☎ 8642 4511, e wadlata @wadarid.mtx.net), on Flinders Terrace, has outstanding displays on making spears and cooking kangaroos, and features some Dreaming stories from the Adnyamathanha and Arabunna people about the formation of Lake Eyre and the Flinders Ranges. It's open 9 am to 5.30 pm weekdays, and 10 am to 4 pm on weekends. Admission is $8.25/4.95 for adults/children, and $19.80 for families.

Inside, the tourist office (☎ 8641 0793) is a major source of information about the Flinders and the Outback. It has the same opening hours as the Wadlata Outback Centre.

WAUKERIE CREEK TRAIL

The Waukerie Creek Trail is a three-hour (one-way) walk which provides a scenic snapshot of the Nukunu people, with several **scarr trees** and **hollow trees** (used for shelter) along the way. The trail runs between Woolshed Flat (16km south-west of Quorn on the road to Port Augusta) and the Waukerie Falls, south-east of Quorn.

A pamphlet, with a poor map and some limited explanations, is available from the tourist office (☎/fax 8648 6419, e tourism @flindersrangescouncil.sa.gov.au) on Seventh St, Quorn. The trail is closed from November to April.

Adnyamathanha Country

Northern Flinders Ranges

Adnyamathanha, which means 'Hills People', is a collective term used for the Indigenous people of the northern Flinders Ranges (including the Kuyani to the west). The original inhabitants of this area – who have lived here for over 15,000 years – were comparatively prosperous because they had access to valuable sources of high-quality red ochre, used for artistic, ceremonial and medicinal purposes. When the Europeans settled here, many Adnyamathanha men proved adept as farm hands.

An excellent series of display boards halfway along the road between Parachilna and Blinman, west of Lake Torrens, explains Aboriginal trade routes with an emphasis on red ochre.

INFORMATION

There are tourist offices at Hawker Motors (☎ 8648 4014, e hawkmts@dove.mtx .net.au) in Hawker, and in Quorn (see Waukerie Creek Trail earlier), but the offices at Port Augusta (see earlier) and Wilpena Pound are far better. The NPWSA office (☎ 8648 4244, fax 8648 4242) for the central and northern Flinders Ranges is on Elder Terrace, Hawker.

Books & Pamphlets

Flinders Ranges Dreaming by Dorothy Tunbridge is a collection of 50 Adnyamathanha Dreaming stories with many maps and

FLINDERS RANGES

1 Leigh Creek Station Cultural Tours; Accommodation
2 Iga Warta Cultural Tours; Camping Ground
3 Nepabunna Organised Tours; Accommodation
4 Ranger's Office
5 Wadna Yaldha Vambata Rock Engravings
6 Wilpena Pound Visitor Centre
7 Adnyamathanha Monument
8 Arkaroo Shelter Rock Paintings
9 Rock Engravings
10 Arkaba Trail Rides
11 Fray Cultural Tours; NPWSA; Tourist Office
12 Yuralypila Rock Art
13 Kanyaka Waterhole; Death Rock
14 Tourist Office
15 Wadlata Outback Centre; Tourist Office; NPWSA

To Marree &
Alice Springs   Lyndhurst

Mt Harris
(743m)

Mt Curtis
(516m)

Mt Clive
(610m)

Gammon Ranges
National Park   Mt Painter

Arkaroola

Yankaninna Range

Weetootla
Gorge

NEPABUNNA
ABORIGINAL
LAND

Leigh Creek   Copley

Nepabunna
Community

Balcanoona
Homestead

1   Iga Warta   Italowie
Gorge   4

Mt Jeffery
(729m)   2   3   Wertaloona

NANTAWARRINA
ABORIGINAL
LAND

Mt Goddard
(698m)

Mt Hack
(1086m)

Lake
Frome

Mt Tilley
(1018m)

Mt Roebuck
(706m)   5   Mt Chambers Ck

Mt Hemming
(799m)

Lake
Torrens

Parachilna

Patawarta Hill
(1015m)

Mt Chambers
(409m)

Blinman

NORTH FLINDERS
RANGES

Balcoracana

Mt Hayward
(865m)

Flinders Ranges
National Park

Mt Mantell
(295m)

Reaphook Hill
(390m)

Woodforde Creek

Wilpena Pound
Visitor Centre

6   Stokes Hill
Lookout   7

St Mary Peak

Wilpena
Pound

Sacred
Canyon

Mt Josephine
(375m)

Moralana
Creek

8   9

Arkaroo
Rock

SOUTH FLINDERS
RANGES

Wilyerpa Hill
(882m)

Salt
Creek

Beare
Creek

10   Arkaba
Woolshed

Scott Hill
(523m)

Willochra
Creek

To Coober Pedy
& Alice Springs

Hawker   11

Fleet Hill
(201m)

Yourambulla
Caves

12

Kanyaka
Homestead   13

Mt Dick
(485m)

Uroonda
Hill
(639m)

Belton

47

Minburra
Plain

The
Dutchmans
Stern Con.
Park   Quorn

14

Willochra
Plain

To Broken
Hill

Stuart Hwy

Waukerie
Creek Trail

Carrieton   Johnburgh

87

PORT
AUGUSTA   Stirling
North

15

Eyre Hwy

To
Perth

Wilmington

56   Orroroo

Yunta

Lincoln Hwy

Blanche
Harbor

Mt
Remarkable
Nat. Park

32

0   20   40km
0   10   20mi

beautiful photographs. The book was an initiative of young Adnyamathanha who were afraid of losing their heritage.

The Flinders Ranges: An Aboriginal View ($2.20) is a slim but useful introduction to Adnyamathanha Dreaming stories, and explains the uses of various plants found in the Flinders. It's available from The Environment Shop in Adelaide (see National Parks under Information at the start of this chapter).

Interpreting Rock Art of the Flinders Ranges ($1.20) is a very useful pamphlet which explains the meanings of many of the symbols used in Adnyamathanha artwork. It's available from most information outlets around the Flinders.

Adnyamathanha Art & Dreaming ($7.50) is a series of individual pages which explain Adnyamathanha art symbols, and Dreaming stories about the Flinders and Gammon ranges. It's available from Iga Warta and the Gammon Ranges National Park Headquarters at Balcanoona Homestead (see later in this chapter).

ORGANISED TOURS

Fray Cultural Tours (☎ 8648 4303, PO Box 187 Hawker, SA 5434), based in Hawker, is Aboriginal-owned and -operated, and offers a range of tours from one to six days to most places of Aboriginal cultural interest between Hawker and Arkaroola (in the Gammon Ranges National Park). Rates are available on application.

Arkaba Trail Rides, run by an Adnyamathanha Elder, offers tours on horseback to important burial and art sites (among other places) in and around Arkaba Station. Tours cost $20 per person per hour (minimum of two people); contact the Wilpena Pound Visitor Centre (see Flinders Ranges National Park later) for bookings (essential).

They leave from Arkaba Woolshed, 16km north-east of Hawker on the road to Wilpena Pound.

The NPWSA organises various tours and walks during the Easter and September school holidays using Adnyamathanha guides, which focus on places like Sacred Canyon (see later). Aboriginal art lessons and campfires with Dreaming stories are also available. Contact the Wilpena Pound Visitor Centre for details and bookings.

Leigh Creek Station (about 6km east of Leigh Creek) runs various cultural tours with Adnyamathanha guides, eg to Red Gorge ($30 per person), which is on private property. It also offers horse riding and budget-priced accommodation. Contact the Leigh Creek Tourist Office (☎ 8675 2723) for more details and bookings.

Iga Warta and the Nepabunna Community also offer tours around the Gammon Ranges National Park – see these sections later for details. Most of the Adelaide-based operators mentioned in the earlier Adelaide section also run tours of the Flinders.

YOURAMBULLA CAVES

Although probably never inhabited, these marvellous caves boast a collection of detailed **rock art**, such as emu tracks, that explains several Dreaming stories. Surprisingly, most of the art is painted with black dyes rather than the red ochre commonly found in the region. The Adnyamathanha name for the caves, Yuralypila, means 'Two Men', and refers to the twin peaks to the east. More information is included on a display at the car park.

Three sites are currently open to visitors; allow at least one hour to visit all three. The turn-off is 11km south-west of Hawker on the road to Quorn.

REMOTE ROUTES IN SOUTH AUSTRALIA

Much of Outback SA is in remote country.

These areas are sparsely populated by small communities with limited supplies of fuel, water or other necessities. There are vast distances between medical services or telephones and in many areas, flooding during the Wet season can make travel impossible. Conversely, it's not wise to tackle the tougher routes in arid areas during the hottest part of the year.

Don't attempt a trip unprepared. For essential safety information, check out Lonely Planet's *Outback Australia*, or another reliable guide.

FLINDERS RANGES DREAMING

The 'spirit of place', almost palpable in the Flinders Ranges, has inspired a rich heritage of Dreaming stories. Many of these are secret, but others related by Adnyamathanha Elders explain the creation of the landscape and the native birds and animals that inhabit it.

Arkaroola comes from Arkaroo, the name of the Dreaming Serpent Ancestor. Suffering from a powerful thirst, Arkaroo drank Lake Frome dry, then carved out the sinuous Arkaroola Creek as he dragged his bloated body back into the ranges. Arkaroo went underground to sleep it off, but all that salty water had given him a belly ache. Now he constantly moves about to relieve the pain, which explains the 30 to 40 small earth tremors that occur in the area each year.

Another story relates that the walls of Ikara (Wilpena Pound) are the bodies of two Akurra (giant snakes), who coiled around Ikara during an initiation ceremony, creating a whirlwind during which they devoured most of the participants.

In another story, the bossy eagle Wildu sought revenge on his nephews, who had tried to kill him by building a great fire. All the birds were caught in the flames, and, originally white, they emerged blackened and burnt. The magpies and willy wagtails were partially scorched, but the crows were entirely blackened, and have remained so to this day.

KANYAKA WATERHOLE & DEATH ROCK

Overlooking the pretty Kanyaka Waterhole is a 7m-high quartzite boulder called Death Rock. According to one story, local Adnyamathanha people would place their dying kinsfolk here to see out their last hours.

There are two ways to reach the waterhole and rock: either walk 20 minutes along the slightly confusing trail from the woolshed, 400m from the Kanyaka Homestead ruins (signposted 25km south of Hawker along the Quorn road); or walk 10 minutes from the car park at the turn-off to Death Rock, 1.5km south of the turn-off to the ruins.

FLINDERS RANGES NATIONAL PARK
Information

The Wilpena Pound Visitor Centre (☎ 8648 0048, fax 8648 0092), on the road to the Wilpena Pound Resort, is *the* place for any information about the Flinders. Inside there's a small display of Adnyamathanha implements, and pamphlets detailing some Dreaming stories are also available. The centre is open 8 am to 6 pm daily. For information on entry fees, see the National Parks section under Information at the start of this chapter.

Wilpena Pound

The best-known feature in the Flinders is Wilpena Pound, the natural basin known to the Adnyamathanha as Ikara. One theory about the name 'Wilpena' is that it means 'Bent Fingers', because the shape of Wilpena resembles a cupped hand. The most famous landmark is Ngarri Mudlanha (St Mary Peak).

Arkaroo Rock

This site was first occupied over 6000 years ago, and initiation ceremonies were still being held here in the 1940s. The rock shelter boasts numerous paintings of reptiles, leaves and human figures, using yellow and red ochre, charcoal and bird lime, which explain, among other things, the formation of Wilpena Pound. The display boards at the start of the trail provide full explanations about the history and artwork.

The rock shelter is a moderate 30- to 45-minute walk (one-way) from the car park. The turn-off is 15km south of Wilpena Pound on the road to Hawker.

Sacred Canyon

Sacred Canyon is home to more than 100 Adnyamathanha **rock engravings** featuring abstract designs and animal tracks, many with unusually large circles. The engravings are dotted along the rocks, just a serene 250m walk from the car park. There is an information board at the car park, but nothing else is signposted.

The track to Sacred Canyon starts 1km north of the turn-off to Wilpena Pound along the Hawker–Blinman Rd. The 14km track to the canyon is potentially impassable to 2WD vehicles after heavy rain.

Stokes Hill Lookout

This scenic lookout is an unlikely place for several very informative display boards about Adnyamathanha art and Dreaming stories which explain, for example, the abundance of coal at Leigh Creek and the creation of Wilpena Pound. Nearby is a monument to the Adnyamathanha people. The steep but generally passable track starts along the Blinman–Hawker Rd.

CHAMBERS GORGE

Mt Chambers – known to the Adnyamathanha as Wadna Yaldha Vambata (Boomerang Crack Hill) – features galleries of **rock carvings**, often produced by 'pecking' at the surface with a hard rock. Interestingly, many of the carvings feature the sorts of circles and lines found near Uluru (Ayers Rock), and relate creation legends – that of Wilpena Pound, for example. Particularly impressive are the engravings in a small gorge before the main Chambers Gorge.

Explanations about the carvings and engravings are detailed in the display boards at the car park, and in *A Field Guide to Chambers Gorge* by Graham C Medlin, available at the Wilpena Pound Visitor Centre.

The turn-off to Chambers Gorge is along the Balcanoona–Blinman Rd; the access road (10km) is rough and only accessible in a 4WD or a sturdy 2WD with a high clearance. To reach the carvings, walk up from the car park along the small gorge on the left; the first major gallery is 350m upstream and on the left, just before a small waterfall.

GAMMON RANGES NATIONAL PARK

The Gammon Ranges are known to the Adnyamathanha as Arrkunha ('Place of Red Ochre'), due to the importance of red ochre to them. The national park which surrounds the ranges is now under the custodianship of the traditional owners.

The ranger's office (☎ 8648 4829), at Balcanoona Homestead, sells maps and books about the Flinders and Gammon National Parks. Outside, a display board explains Adnyamathanha Dreaming stories,

and other similarly informative boards can be found at Italowie Gorge, the start of the trail to Weetootla Gorge and the southern end of the road to Arkaroola.

IGA WARTA

Iga Warta (☎ 8648 3737, e enquiries @igawarta.mtx.net) is an impressive outfit, owned and operated by ambitious Adnyamathanha people. It offers a number of cultural tours and walks to local sites (from $22 to $44 per person), overnight tours to Red Gorge (from $160 per person) and campfire evenings with Dreaming stories, Indigenous music and bush tucker ($11 per person). Also available are courses in Aboriginal art and horse riding ($22 per person per hour). Its Web site (www.igawarta.mtx.net) has more information.

Pre-set tents (including a swag) on the extensive campgrounds cost $10 per person, meals are available on request.

Iga Warta is about 50km east of Copley along the road to Arkaroola. It's worth a stop if only to buy a (soft) drink and have a chat with the friendly staff.

NEPABUNNA COMMUNITY

About 5km further east along the Copley–Arkaroola Rd, tiny, neat Nepabunna Community is on a mission established in 1931. In 2000 the United Nations gave the community an award for creating the world's first Indigenous Protected Area, 58,000 hectares of traditional land allocated for the conservation of the fragile environment.

Nepabunna is not as well organised as Iga Warta (see earlier) for tourism. Details about horse riding and tag-along 4WD trips to Aboriginal sites in the Gammon Ranges and Red and Chambers Gorges are available from the community centre (☎ 8648 3730, 8648 3764). The school offers bunk beds to the public for about $20 per person.

Wirangu Country

Nullarbor Plain

The Nullarbor (which is actually Latin for 'No trees') has a rich Aboriginal history. However, most of the cultural sites west of Ceduna are inaccessible, require permits and/or need an accompanying ranger from the NPWSA office.

BRITISH NUCLEAR TESTS AT MARALINGA   Denis O'Byrne

Maralinga is an Aboriginal word for thunder. On the northern edge of the Nullarbor Plain, the British exploded atom bombs at Emu in 1953 and Maralinga in 1956 and 1957. The largest explosion, equivalent to a 26.6 kilotonne conventional bomb, was detonated on a balloon about 300m above ground level.

Between 1960 and 1963 the British conducted a number of 'safety tests' with simulated bombs containing plutonium at Maralinga. These were detonated with conventional explosives to discover whether or not nuclear weapons would release nuclear energy in the event of an accident.

Prior to the tests, most of the nomadic Aborigines who lived in the area were moved to Yalata, west of Ceduna. Concerns about the effects of the tests on local Aboriginal people prompted a Commission of Enquiry in the mid-1980s. It found that they had suffered greatly because of the tests and that the bomb sites were still contaminated. The commission also suggested that it was Britain's responsibility to clean up the mess. Finally, in 1998, after years of argument and stalling, a $104 million operation (40% funded by the British government) cleaned up much of the contaminated area.

CEDUNA

Ceduna, from the Wirangu word for 'resting place', is home to several Aboriginal organisations. Contact the administration office (☎ 8625 2946, fax 8625 3076) on McKenzie St for permits to visit Maralinga-Tjarutja Aboriginal land.

The tourist office (☎ 8625 2780) is on Poynton St (the main shopping street).

YALATA

Yalata Aboriginal community is predominantly made up of southern Pitjantjatjara and Kokatha people, resettled from around Maralinga following British atomic testing (see the boxed text 'British Nuclear Tests at Maralinga'). The Yalata Roadhouse (☎/fax 8625 6807), which is owned by the local community, has a small shop with some locally made arts and crafts for sale.

Whale-Watching

Whales feature in several Dreaming stories, and the occasional beached whale was used by the Wirangu and other Aboriginal tribes for food and implements (see also the Music section).

Between June and October each year, dozens of southern right whales pass through the Great Australian Bight Marine Park to breed or give birth. The best spot (on land) to watch these magnificent creatures is the Head of Bight, which is on Yalata Aboriginal land, so permits are required ($7.70 per adult per day, children free). It's best to get the permits at the unmissable White Well Ranger Station (during whale season ☎/fax 8625 6201) at the turn-off to the Head of Bight. Otherwise, try the Yalata Roadhouse or the tourist office in Ceduna.

Money from permits for whale-watching (and fishing) helps maintain and improve the fragile local environment and provides much-needed income to the Yalata community.

More information about whale-watching is available on the Web site (www.webmedia.com.au/whales) run by the South Australian Whale Centre.

Outback

This section covers Kuyani, Arabunna, Antakarinja and Yawarawarka country.

MARREE

Almost opposite the Oasis Cafe, the Arabunna Centre (☎ 8675 8351) has a small, haphazard museum with some artefacts and early photographs of Arabunna people, and some carvings for sale. It's open around 9 am to 4 pm weekdays; entry is by donation.

About 70km north-west of Marree is the Marree Man, a 4km long outline of an Aboriginal warrior and possibly the largest work of art in the world. Its origin is unknown (some say it was put there by personnel from one of the US bases), but it appeared in the desert sands in 1998. It can only be seen from the air, so Central Air Services (☎ 8675 8352, fax 8675 8399), based at the Oasis Cafe, offers flights from $140/110 (80 minutes) for adults/children to $240/160 (two hours) over the Marree Man and parts of Lake Eyre.

COOBER PEDY
The name of this town comes from the words *kupaka* ('white man') and *piti* ('hole'), in reference to the large number of locals who live in dugouts to shelter from the extreme summer heat. The helpful tourist office (☎ 8672 5298, e dccp@cpcouncil.sa.gov.au) is along the southern end of Hutchinson St (the main road through town).

Organised Tours
Most operators offer tours that include the Breakaways and the Aboriginal Interpretative Centre (see later in this section). Try Radeka Breakaway Tours (☎ 8672 5223), Explorer Tours (☎ 1800 196 500 toll free) or Oasis Tours (☎ 8672 5169), which has extended evening tours of the Breakaways ($22 per person). The tours ($35) offered by Desert Cave Tours (☎ 8672 5688) include the Breakaways and a visit to the camp of Kuru Tjilipi Tjutaku Elders. (None of the operators is, however, Aboriginal-owned or -run.)

Umoona Opal Mine & Museum
This museum has several informative (and free) displays about local Aboriginal heritage. Further inside, the Aboriginal Interpretative Centre features a typical *wiltja* (a shelter made from a mulga tree) and audio-video displays about Dreaming stories. The interpretative centre is only accessible by guided tour ($6.60), offered at 10 am, noon, and 2 and 4 pm daily.

Shopping
Very little of the Indigenous art on sale is made locally. Underground Cafe has a reasonable selection of hand-painted crafts, and Umoona Opal Mine & Museum has an array of Indigenous souvenirs. Underground Books (☎ 8672 5558), Post Office Hill Rd (west of the main road), has an outstanding selection of books about Aboriginal culture and history.

BREAKAWAYS RESERVE
This stony desert was once an inland sea and home to various Aboriginal tribes for thousands of years. The informative interpretative shelter at the first lookout outlines the significance of the three major landmarks: *papa* ('two dogs'), also called the Castle; *kalaya* ('emu'); and *ungkata* ('dragon lizard'). These can be admired from the three lookouts, or from along short walking trails (detailed at the interpretative shelter).

The reserve is jointly managed by the Antakarinja Land Council. One-day permits ($2.20) can be obtained (for the current day, or in advance) from the tourist office in Coober Pedy on weekdays, or Underground Books on any day (see Coober Pedy).

The turn-off is about 22km north-west of Coober Pedy, along the Stuart Highway.

INNAMINCKA
Cooper Creek has always been an important meeting place for Ngamini, Yawarawarka and Dieri people, particularly because of the area's permanent source of fresh water.

The creek can be explored by canoe, past Cullyamurra Waterhole (28m deep and permanently full), to **rock carvings**. An interpretative display at the headquarters of the Innamincka Regional Reserve explains the local Aboriginal heritage.

The canoe trips of Cooper Creek, and Coongie Lakes nearby, offered by Ecotrek & Bogong Jack Adventures (see Organised Tours in the Adelaide section earlier) go past numerous Indigenous sites. Canoes can also be hired at the Innamincka Hotel (☎ 8675 9901).

Pitjantjatjara & Yankunytjatjara Country

Far North-West

INFORMATION
Independent tourism is not encouraged on Aboriginal land in the state's north-west. If you have a valid reason for going there, you can contact the AP (Anangu Pitjantjatjaraku) office at Umuwa, near Ernabella (☎ 8950 1511, fax 8950 1510) and ask staff to send a permit application form.

FIRST CONTACT IN THE WESTERN DESERT

The people of the Western Desert were the last Aborigines to have contact with non-Aboriginal people. The last to abandon their autonomous hunter-gatherer lifestyle were a small group of Pintupi, who in 1984 walked into Kintore, a community 350km north-west of Uluru (Ayers Rock).

First contact in other parts of the Western Desert is also relatively recent, even in the Uluru region where today nearly 400,000 tourists visit annually. Although Ernest Giles passed through the Western Desert region in the 1870s, during the following 50 years visits by outsiders were so infrequent that many desert people didn't see a non-Aboriginal person until the 1930s or 40s, or even later.

Until the 1960s, government patrol officers searched out people who still lived in the traditional way and trucked them from remote parts of the Western Desert to various settlements. This was part of a government policy stating that Aborigines should be encouraged to abandon their traditions and become assimilated into mainstream white society.

In other areas, Aboriginal people were forcibly removed to make way for the testing of military hardware. In 1946 a guided-missile range was established at Woomera (SA), within what was then the Central Desert Aboriginal Reserve. Until at least 1966, groups of Aborigines were brought in from areas where testing had taken place. In some cases these people had been traumatised by rockets but had not experienced face-to-face contact with whites.

As well as testing conventional weapons, in the 1950s the Australian government permitted the British to detonate atomic devices at Emu Junction 500km south-west of Uluru, and at Maralinga a little further south. The authorities claimed that prior to detonation two patrol officers combed thousands of square kilometres, ensuring that no Aborigines were harmed by the tests. However, the Aborigines have another story: They say that as a result of these tests many people became sick and died.

Yami Lester is a Yankunytjatjara man who was a child when one of the British nuclear devices was detonated 180km from his home. As a result of radioactive fallout, Yami saw many of his relatives sicken and die; some years later, he went blind. *Yami – The Autobiography of Yami Lester* (IAD Press, Alice Springs) provides an excellent insight into many aspects of early Western Desert contact, as well as the struggle for land rights which took place some decades later.

Radio

PY Media Association broadcasts 5NPY (106.1 FM) from Umuwa.

ORGANISED TOURS

You can visit this region with a couple of tour companies operating from the Northern Territory – few other tours in central Australia can offer such a deep insight into traditional Aboriginal culture. Costs include payment to Anangu people as guides and teachers, as well as permit fees and all meals.

Desert Tracks (☎ 8956 3120) is an Anangu-owned organisation that runs one-to eight-day tours from $280 per person per day. All tours visit Cave Hill in the Musgrave Ranges, in SA's far north-west – one of the most extensive rock-art galleries in central Australia. Tours depart from Yulara (see the Northern Territory chapter).

Uncharted Journeys (☎ 8952 6206, e snowice@oze.com.au) offers a seven-day tour from Alice Springs which places an emphasis on the discovery of Anangu and personal spirituality. The tour costs $1815 per person and swag hire is extra; there's another seven-day tour without Anangu involvement for $1090.

Tasmania

Tasmania was known to European settlers as Van Diemen's Land until 1856 when its name was changed to Tasmania. It is estimated that there were between 5000 and 10,000 Aborigines in Tasmania when Europeans arrived. The word Palawa, 'the first man', is used today by some Tasmanian Aborigines as a collective noun for their people.

History

Philip Morrissey

For the Tasmanian Aborigines, history since European arrival is a story of dispossession and genocide, in which they were virtually annihilated. There are few historical parallels for the thoroughness of their destruction. In its repercussions, this genocide continues to affect the contemporary Australian nation. Common attitudes for Australians range from a state of denial to, even in recent years, a sentimental cult of mourning the 'last Tasmanian'. Tasmanian Aborigines and their culture, however, have survived changes in government policy and settler attitudes, to maintain their cultural identity and reassert their sovereignty.

EARLY HISTORY

Aborigines have lived in Tasmania for 35,000 years, and possibly longer – the sea now covers many areas of early occupation and this makes precise archaeological dating impossible. Up to about 10,000 years ago, land bridges joined Tasmania to the rest of Australia. The sea level was much lower, and the Tasmanian climate much drier and colder. Aborigines at that stage settled the western side of Tasmania, where extensive grasslands supported the animals, in particular wallabies, that they hunted. The eastern part of the state was probably too barren for settlement.

When the last ice age ended between 18,000 and 12,000 years ago, sea levels rose and Tasmania was separated from mainland Australia. From that time on, the culture of Tasmanian Aborigines diverged from that of their mainland counterparts. While on the mainland people developed more specialised tools for hunting, like boomerangs, pronged spears, woomeras and hafted stone tools, the

HIGHLIGHTS

Telephone code: ☎ 03
Indigenous population: 15,322
Overall population: 474,400
Area: 67,800 sq km

▮ Watching top Indigenous acts from around Australia creating a ruckus in January at the Oyster Cove Festival

▮ Catching the mutton-birding season in April, a continuing tradition that goes back tens of thousands of years

▮ Arranging for an Aboriginal guide to tell you the story behind Tasmania's fascinating heritage

Tasmanian people continued to use simpler tools and plain wooden spears. However, the Tasmanian Aborigines developed specialised boat designs that were sometimes more sophisticated than those used on the mainland. Rolls of bark or reeds were bound together to form canoes capable of carrying families.

Aborigines made perilous trips in bark canoes to offshore islands and hunted seals and mutton birds. The simplicity of Tasmanian material culture and the culture-blind attitudes of many Europeans has led many to overlook the adaptability and intelligence of the Tasmanian Aborigines. But their simple technologies were well adapted to the harsh Tasmanian climate, and they gave continual proof of their adaptability

TASMANIA

TASMANIA

1 Museum
2 Wybalenna Historic Site
3 Flinders Island Aboriginal Association Inc
4 Wombat Point
5 Steep Island
6 Preminghana
7 West Point
8 Cave Shelters; Banksia Grove/
Caves Circuit
9 Tiagarra; Rock Marking Trail
10 Musselroe Point
11 Bay of Fires
12 Blue Tier
13 Binalong Bay
14 St Helens Point
15 St Helens History Room
16 Rock Shelter

17 Aboriginal Elders Council of Tasmania;
Reconciliation Walking Trail;
Queen Victoria Museum & Art Gallery; TACWAC
18 Deloraine Aboriginal Cultural Association;
Jahadi Outdoor Adventures
19 Trowunna Wildlife Park; Tengenowa Dreaming
20 Cradle Mountain Visitors Centre
21 West Coast Pioneers Memorial Museum
22 Trial Harbour
23 Henty Dunes
24 Strahan Visitors Centre; History Exhibition;
Risby Cove Complex
25 Sarah Island
26 Franklin River Nature Trail
27 Lake St Clair Park Centre
28 Kutikina Cave
29 Ballawinne Cave
30 Waubedebar's Grave
31 Waterloo Point
32 Richardsons Beach Middens; Walking Tours/Trails
33 Wielangta State Forest; Sandspit River Reserve
34 Risdon Cove
35 Oyster Cove
36 South East Tasmanian Aboriginal Corporation
37 Wargata Mina
38 Bligh Museum of Pacific Exploration; Adventure Bay

through thousands of years of occupation in all sorts of climactic extremes. As the guerilla war with the Tasmanians took its toll on settlers (see Resistance later), some Europeans conceived a grudging respect for the adversaries they had once despised.

As the climate changed after the last ice age, the vegetation in the western half of the state altered, enabling tall forests to become established, while in the east rainfall increased and extensive grasslands developed. Most of the Aborigines abandoned their caves and shelters and followed the animals they hunted to the more open eastern side. Those who remained in the west lived primarily on the coast. Tasmania produced abundant food including swans, ducks, the eggs of sea birds, seals, mutton birds, wallabies, wombats, possums and emus. Shellfish, including abalone, were an important part of the Tasmanian Aborigines' diet, although archaeological evidence shows that about 4000 years ago they stopped eating bony fish. No adequate scientific explanation has been given for this.

Tasmanian Aborigines were organised in 'bands' of 40 to 50 people who had rights to specific areas of land. Each band was part of one of the nine main language groups. Ochre was mined at Mt Vandyke, Mt Housetop and St Valentine's Peak in Tasmania's north and was an important ceremonial and social commodity. Women played an important role in its distribution and care. Tasmanian Aborigines protected themselves from the cold by rubbing a mixture of fat, ochre and charcoal on their bodies. There is no evidence of the dingo ever having been in Tasmania, suggesting that it arrived in Australia after Tasmania had been cut off from the mainland. When Europeans arrived however, the Tasmanian Aborigines quickly saw the advantages in using dogs in hunting and showed an uncanny skill in taming and training them. As on mainland Australia, fire was extremely important in managing the land and early European explorers such as Abel Tasman saw the smoke of distant fires and observed that the land had been burned.

EUROPEAN INVASION

In 1642, Tasman landed at Fluted Cape on Bruny Island; in the 1770s British mariners stopped at Adventure Bay on Bruny Island, home of the Nuennone people, to take on water. It was on one of these visits that Captain James Cook was struck by the vivacity and good humour of an Aboriginal man who had a hunched back. William Bligh was a member of that expedition and when he returned in 1788 as commander of his own expedition he saw the same man again.

The human quality in these encounters did not survive the European invasion of Tasmania in 1803, when a settler base was established at Risdon. Shortly after arrival, British soldiers fired on peaceable Aborigines and massacred an undisclosed number of men, women and children. Forcing out the Indigenous people, the settlers usurped their traditional hunting grounds and sacred places. Over time more settlers were brought in and given grants of the most arable land.

Governor Thomas Davey produced a 'Proclamation to the Aborigines' in 1816, which showed Aborigines and settlers living

This document reads: 'Why Massa Gubernor' said Black Jack – 'You Proflamation all gammon' 'How blackfellow read him em? He no learn him read book' 'Read that then' said the Governor, pointing to a picture.

COURTESY NATIONAL LIBRARY OF AUSTRALIA

TASMANIA

TASMANIA

together amicably with equal rights under settler law. Though the assumption was that Aborigines had no option but to adopt European modes of life, the proclamation represented for the time a spirit of idealism – but the background to this was a brutal colonial society, plagued by social problems and on the brink of starvation.

RESISTANCE
By the 1820s, the period known as the Black War had well and truly begun. Regarding the Aborigines as subhumans, settlers perpetrated shameless atrocities. Tasmanian Aborigines responded with fierce guerilla warfare. Despite their simple weapons they inflicted heavy casualties on the settlers, who responded with increased brutality. Europeans abducted Aboriginal children to use as forced labour, raped and tortured Aboriginal women (especially on the north coast), gave poisoned flour to friendly tribes, and laid steel traps in the bush. There was a growing realisation by colonists that they were engaged in a war with the Indigenous people over land. For the Tasmanian Aborigines, it was a hopeless fight – for every settler they killed, a hundred more arrived.

MARTIAL LAW
In 1828, martial law was proclaimed by Lieutenant-Governor George Arthur in Tasmania's central districts, giving soldiers the right to arrest or shoot on sight any Aboriginal person found in an area of European settlement. This was an extreme measure even within the precedents of English Common Law and showed the extent to which the settlers had been cowed by the Tasmanian Aborigines. Martial law was intended to break the Aboriginal resistance by striking terror into the Aboriginal community.

THE BLACK LINE
In 1830, in an attempt to flush out all Aborigines and corner them on the Tasman Peninsula, a human chain of about 2200 men, known as the Black Line, was formed by settlers and soldiers. In spite of the military precision with which it was executed, the line was a farce; the Aborigines heard the settlers and soldiers coming from miles away and they succeeded in capturing only an old man and a boy. The failure of the Black Line confirmed the fears of settlers

that they could not defeat the Aborigines by force of arms.

In the following three years, George Augustus Robinson travelled over most of the state and persuaded virtually all the Aborigines in mainland Tasmania to lay down their arms. He used encouragement where it worked. Where persuasion didn't work, especially in the west where the Aboriginal communities were still relatively intact, he used force. As Robinson was mounting his final expeditions, Europeans were virtually abandoning the west coast, and historian Lyndall Ryan argues in *The Aboriginal Tasmanians* that 'the western Aborigines would probably have survived if Robinson had not captured them'. Contemporary perceptions of Robinson and his so-called 'friendly mission' are well illustrated in Benjamin Duttereau's 1840 oil painting, *The Conciliation*, showing Robinson surrounded by the Tasmanian tribes. This painting can be seen in the Tasmanian Museum & Art Gallery in Hobart.

Strong historical evidence suggests that the Aborigines who followed Robinson were enticed by a verbal treaty that promised them sanctuary and the trusteeship of land. Instead, they were subjected to European attempts to 'civilise' and 'Christianise' them and made to work for the government. After enduring a number of moves to places such as Sarah Island on the west coast, they were finally settled at Wybalenna (Black Man's Houses), on Flinders Island. One by one they died from a combination of despair, poor food and respiratory disease.

OYSTER COVE COMMUNITY
In 1847 the surviving residents of Wybalenna petitioned Queen Victoria, complaining of their treatment. The petition makes clear that the Wybalenna Aborigines did not regard themselves as prisoners, but had freely given up their country as a result of an agreement made on their behalf by Robinson with Lieutenant-Governor Arthur, and that they had kept their part of the agreement.

Wybalenna was eventually abandoned and the survivors transferred to mainland Tasmania. Of the 135 who had been sent to Flinders Island, only 47 survived to make the journey to Oyster Cove, 15km south of Hobart. The new accommodation was substandard – it had previously been assessed as not fit for convicts and conditions were

PEOPLE OF THE COMMUNITIES

Philip Morrissey

Some remarkable people passed through Wybalenna and Oyster Cove. Fanny Cochrane Smith was a child of Wybalenna. She was born there in 1834 and reared by settlers, who trained her as a domestic servant. Fanny lived at Oyster Cove before marrying William Smith, a former convict. The couple had a large family and many Tasmanian Aborigines from the mainland of Tasmania trace their descent from her.

William Lanney was a member of the last Tasmanian Aboriginal family to be rounded up and taken to Wybalenna. Within five years his family, with the exception of William and a brother, were dead. William became a whale-spotter on whaling ships. He returned to Oyster Cove seriously ill from cholera. When he died at the age of 34 in 1869 his body was plundered by the representatives of medical science. The morgue was broken into and William Lanney's head skinned, his skull removed, and another substituted. Annoyed at missing out on the head, the Royal Society of Tasmania took his hands and feet.

It didn't end there – his grave was robbed within 24 hours of his burial. Lanney's employers and associates from the whaling industry tried to protect his body, but they were competing with unscrupulous men. Some of the Tasmanian medical establishment had lost all sense of human decency – Dr George Stokell of the Royal Society of Tasmania had a tobacco pouch made from William Lanney's skin.

worse than at Wybalenna. The whole venture seems to have been a clear instance of criminal negligence by the authorities and the demoralised Tasmanian Aborigines fell deeper into despair. Within 10 years half of them were dead.

Truganini, the last of the Oyster Cove community, died in 1876, prematurely celebrated by settler Australians as the 'last of her tribe'. She had lived in fear that the indignities suffered by William Lanney would be inflicted on her own body after death (see the boxed text 'People of the Communities'). Her fears were well founded – with state government consent her body was exhumed and the skeleton exhibited at the Museum of the Royal Society of Tasmania from 1904 to 1947. Her remains were finally returned to the Tasmanian Aboriginal community and cremated in 1976.

FURNEAUX ISLANDS COMMUNITY

While the official attempts to 'save' the Tasmanian Aborigines foundered because of neglect, cruelty and bad faith, an unlikely group of men provided another avenue for community survival. European sealers had been working in Bass Strait since 1798. They raided tribes along the coast, kidnapping Aboriginal women as sexual partners and workers.

The sealers, however, were distinguished from other settlers in that they were not interested in Aboriginal land and by the early 19th century something of a reciprocal relationship with coastal tribes had developed. Sealers journeyed to the coast in summer, where they met Tasmanian Aborigines making seasonal journeys to harvest mutton birds. Sealers traded dogs and other items with these people and Aboriginal women accompanied them to the Bass Strait islands. Aboriginal men occasionally went with them.

The Tasmanian establishment, and people like George Augustus Robinson, disapproved of the sealers and their women. Robinson tried to have them evicted from Flinders Island and made use of the term 'half-caste' to describe the descendants of sealers and Aboriginal women. This contemptuous term became the standard Tasmanian term for the Furneaux Group Aborigines (though a disproportionately high number of Islanders have served in Australia's defence forces during wars).

Cape Barren Island was designated an Aboriginal reserve in the 1880s. The Cape Barren Reserve Act of 1912 tried to make this conditional on the Islanders becoming farmers. There was also continual inducement and coercion of Islanders to move to the Tasmanian mainland and assimilate. In

1995, the state government returned 12 sites, including Oyster Cove, Kutikina Cave and Steep Island, to the Tasmanian Aboriginal community. Wybalenna followed in 1999.

Language

At least nine, and perhaps as many as 16, languages were spoken in what's now known as Tasmania. There appears to be no clear connection between the languages of Tasmania and those of the mainland; nor between the languages of Tasmania and any language spoken elsewhere. Around 15,000 people of Aboriginal descent live in Tasmania, although no Indigenous languages remain.

Some Aboriginal language was still being used in the early years of the 20th century among family groups on the Furneaux Islands, and on mainland Tasmania. Today, some language is still remembered by Elders of Aboriginal communities, and a handful of words have remained in use. The Palawa Kani language of Tasmania is currently undergoing a revival, with words being reconstructed and incorporated into school curricula for Aboriginal children.

USEFUL CONTACTS
Tasmanian Aboriginal Centre (TAC) Palawa Kani Program (☎ 6234 8311) 198 Elizabeth St, Hobart, Tas 7001

Information

INDIGENOUS ORGANISATIONS
The Tasmanian Aboriginal Land Council (TALC; ☎ 6231 0288, fax 6231 0298, ✉ talcorp@netspace.net.au), 4 Lefroy St, North Hobart, manages many of the sites which have been given back to the Aboriginal community, including Preminghana on the north-west coast and Kutikina Cave.

The Tasmanian Aboriginal Centre (TAC; ☎ 6234 8311), 198 Elizabeth St, Hobart, manages the Oyster Cove and Risdon Cove sites, and organises the Oyster Cove Festival.

Other regional bodies operate throughout the state – see the regional sections in this chapter for details.

National Parks
A day pass into any national park in Tasmania costs $9.90 per vehicle (up to eight

people) or $3.30 per person. Two-month holiday passes for entry into all parks are $33 per vehicle or $13.20 per person. These are available from park entry booths and visitors centres throughout the state. The Parks & Wildlife Service (PWS; ☎ 6233 6191) has an excellent Web site: www.parks.tas.gov.au.

BOOKS
Aboriginal Elder Ida West's *Pride Against Prejudice – Reminiscences of a Tasmanian Aborigine* is available at bookshops in Hobart and Launceston. There's also the *Tunapi* series which features Palawa stories, essays and photographs.

There are many books on the history of Tasmania's Aborigines by non-Indigenous people: *The Aboriginal Tasmanians* (1996) by Lyndall Ryan is very popular. It contains descriptions of traditional land uses and follows the community's history up to the 1990s. In *Fate of a Free People* (1995), Henry Reynolds re-examines the Black War from an Aboriginal perspective and puts a case for Tasmanian Aboriginal land rights. The *Aboriginal People of Tasmania* by Julia Clark is a good brief overview, while at the other end of the spectrum Brian Plomley's lengthy tomes examine the history of Wybalenna and George Robinson's 'friendly mission'.

FILMS
One of the best films about Tasmania's Indigenous community is *Black Man's Houses* (1992), made by Steve Thomas in association with the Flinders Island Aboriginal Association. It documents racial tensions on Flinders Island.

Organised Tours

TALC (☎ 6231 0288) keeps a list of Aboriginal heritage officers who can take you on interpretative tours of significant sites around Tasmania for around $250 to $300 per group per day (plus GST).

TAC (☎ 6234 8311) can arrange interpretative tours of important sites that it manages around the state.

Indigenous-owned commercial operators include Tengenowa Dreaming (☎ 6363 6162, fax 6367 6213), based at Trowunna

Wildlife Park, and Jahadi Outdoor Adventures (☎ 6363 6172, ✉ jahadi@microtech.com.au), based in Deloraine, which both offer tailored cultural tours throughout Tasmania.

Aboriginal cultural guides can provide tours to significant places all over the state, so check with operators listed in the Organised Tours sections of this chapter. These people are generally Aboriginal speakers who provide cultural talks to school groups and other organisations, and are not commercial tour operators. They run tours on an informal basis and you'll usually need your own transport. It's more economical to arrange a group.

South East Tribe Country

Hobart and South-East Tasmania

The South East Tribe were excellent mariners, building bark catamarans to cross Storm Bay from Bruny Island to the Tasman Peninsula.

HOBART

Tasmania's capital stands on the traditional land of the Mouheneenner band of the South East Tribe and the area was known to them as Nibberloonne. The land east of the Derwent River was the territory of the Oyster Bay Tribe, some sites on their traditional land are included in this section.

Information

Indigenous Organisations See the Information section earlier for details on TAC and TALC. TALC was planning to establish a display centre at its North Hobart office by the end of 2001, so you may be able to make an appointment to view the collection.

University Association The Centre for Aboriginal Education (☎ 6226 2772, 6324 3491) at the University of Tasmania, Riawunna, often runs exhibitions and workshops.

Walking Trail

The Aboriginal Heritage Trail at Bedlam Walls, near Risdon Cove, takes you along the waterfront to a cave shelter, a midden site and a stone quarry. Interpretative boards explain the history of the area, which was a winter camp of the Moumairremener band

of the Oyster Bay Tribe. The walk takes 45 minutes (return) and starts at the end of Geilston Bay Rd. To drive to it head north from the city, cross the Tasman bridge and take the first left towards Lindisfarne. Geilston Bay Rd is about 4km along, the second left after Geilston Bay High School.

Tasmanian Museum & Art Gallery

One of the best displays of Aboriginal history and culture in the state is at the Tasmanian Museum & Art Gallery (☎ 6235 0777), 40 Macquarie St. The Aboriginal galleries are on the 1st floor – one room features Indigenous artefacts from around Australia and another room is dedicated to Tasmanian Aborigines. Here there is a fine collection of *maireeners* (shell necklaces) from Cape Barren Island as well as displays on traditional culture, the Black War and the modern Aboriginal community. This is also a rare chance to see some Tasmanian Aboriginal rock engraving – a segment of carved rock removed from Preminghana on the north-west coast is on display. The bookshop beside the entrance sells a wide range of books, many of which are not available elsewhere.

The museum is open 10 am to 5 pm daily (admission free). Free guided tours taking in the Aboriginal galleries are offered from Wednesday to Sunday at 2.30 pm.

Risdon Cove Historic Site

Risdon Cove, across the Bowen Bridge, is the site of the first massacre of Aboriginal people in Tasmania and also the site of the first European settlement in 1803. Risdon Cove is on Aboriginal land and is managed by TAC. The pyramid-shaped information buildings were closed at the time of writing, but you can use the picnic and barbecue facilities and ponder the history.

Organised Tours TAC can arrange interpretative tours of significant places on the site, including a rock shelter and an important meeting ground. Rates are negotiable.

Special Events

On 6 December 1995, 12 parcels of land were handed back to the Aboriginal community. Each year, close to this date, a celebration is held at Risdon Cove, which is one of the sites. It features free cultural performances; check with TAC for details.

TASMANIA

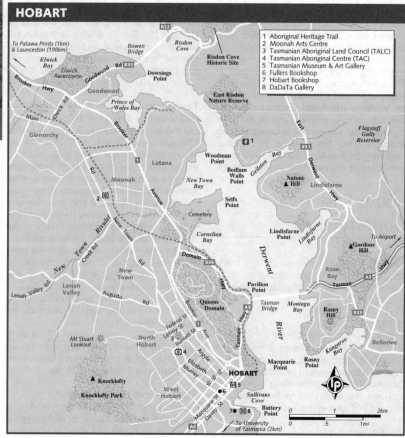

HOBART

To Palawa Prints (1km)
& Launceston (198km)

	Aboriginal Heritage Trail
1	
2	Moonah Arts Centre
3	Tasmanian Aboriginal Land Council (TALC)
4	Tasmanian Aboriginal Centre (TAC)
5	Tasmanian Museum & Art Gallery
6	Fullers Bookshop
7	Hobart Bookshop
8	DaDaTa Gallery

The Moonah Arts Centre (☎ 6228 1192), 65 Hopkins St, Moonah, holds an annual NAIDOC week exhibition of Indigenous artists in July (see also Special Events in the Facts for the Visitor chapter for more on NAIDOC week).

Shopping

Palawa Prints (☎ 6249 5122, fax 6249 3418), 1 Berriedale Rd, Berriedale (about 10km north-west from the city centre), Indigenous-owned and run by the Womens Karadi Aboriginal Corporation, sells a range of products made by Tasmanian Aboriginal artists. Products include T-shirts ($25 to $30, or $40 for long sleeves), painted emu eggs ($100 to $150), shell necklaces ($250 to $300), jewellery, and modern and

traditional basket designs (starting at around $15). These prices do not include GST.

Items can be made to order and Palawa Prints has a register of Aboriginal artists who can be commissioned. It also runs workshops, such as using natural dyes from the bush and basket weaving, for around $30 plus materials (phone for details and dates). Palawa Prints is open 9 am to 5 pm weekdays, but ring ahead to make sure. Turn off the Booker Hwy at the Berriedale (East) exit, turn right and follow the road under the highway, then take a left onto Berriedale Rd. The shop is in the old train station.

In the city centre, DaDaTa Gallery (☎ 6224 8988, fax 6224 8989), shop 3, 77 Salamanca Place, displays work by local Aboriginal and Torres Strait Islander artists, such as Verna Nichols and Nigooli Newley. Prices range from around $25 for a small painting or painted river stone to $1780 for a large canvas. The gallery is open 10 am to 5 pm daily and some of the works can be viewed on its Web site: www.geocities.com/dadatagallery.

Bookshops The Hobart Bookshop (☎ 6223 1803, fax 6223 1804, ℮ hobooks@ozemail .com.au), 22 Salamanca Square, is open daily and has a good range of books on Tasmanian Aborigines, as well as Indigenous mainlanders. Fullers Bookshop (☎ 6224 2488, fax 6223 8217), 140 Collins St, also has a good selection.

OYSTER COVE AREA
Information
The South East Tasmanian Aboriginal Corporation (SETAC; ☎ 6295 0004, fax 6295 0535, ℮ setac@trump.net.au), 92 Mary St, Cygnet, is a contact point for the Aboriginal community living in the region.

Oyster Cove
After petitioning Queen Victoria to allow them to return to mainland Tasmania, the 47 survivors of the Wybalenna settlement on Flinders Island were taken to Oyster Cove (also known as Mena Loongana, Mannina), an important traditional camp, in 1847.

This historic site became the base of a land rights protest when Aboriginal activists occupied it on 16 January 1984 and lobbied for its return to the Indigenous community. They erected a sign at the entrance quoting Xavier Herbert, a white Australian novelist:

Until we give back to the black man just a bit of the land that was his, and give it back without provisos, without strings to snatch it back, without anything but complete generosity in concession for the evil we have done to him – until we do that, we shall remain what we have always been so far: a community of thieves.

Their campaign was successful and today Oyster Cove is on Aboriginal land.

You can visit Oyster Cove independently, but it is worthwhile contacting TAC for information on interpretation.

Oyster Cove is off the Channel Hwy, around 5km south of Snug. Turn left into Manuka Rd and continue straight ahead

onto the gravel road when the sealed road bends to the right.

Oyster Cove Festival The best time to visit Oyster Cove is during the Oyster Cove Festival, held annually on the Saturday closest to 16 January, the date when Aboriginal activists occupied the site. This is the largest Indigenous festival in the state and attracts a big crowd to see local artists and musicians as well as some of the top Indigenous acts from around the country. The festival is free and you can bring your own food to cook. There's also food for sale, as well as Palawa arts and crafts.

Nuennone Country
Bruny Island Area

BRUNY ISLAND
Truganini was born on Bruny Island, and it was here that she met George Augustus Robinson who lived at Missionary Bay. Mt Mangana on the South Island is named after Truganini's father, who was a leader of the Nuennone Band of the South East Tribe.

Organised Tours
Aboriginal guide Buck Brown (☎ 6257 1611), 232 Rheban Rd, Spring Beach (near Orford), offers tours of the area for $250 (plus GST) per day for up to 12 people.

During summer you can take a tour with the South West Passage Cruising Company (☎ 6298 1062) in Dover, which incorporates Indigenous heritage into tours on the *Olive May*, a 100-year-old Huon pine vessel. Cruises start from $180 for four hours (two people).

Bligh Museum of Pacific Exploration
This tiny museum (☎ 6293 1117) has a display on Tasmanian Aborigines. It's in Adventure Bay and is open 10 am to 3 pm daily. Entry is $4/2 for adults/children.

Oyster Bay Tribe Country
East Coast

The estate of the Oyster Bay Tribe, the largest tribe in Tasmania with an estimated

700 to 800 people, was Tasmania's beautiful east coast. They wintered by the shore and moved inland for the summer.

ORGANISED TOURS

Buck Brown offers cultural tours of the region. He focuses on low-impact ecotourism, covering the Aboriginal landscape and heritage, native plants and bush tucker. For contact details and prices, see Organised Tours under Nuennone Country earlier.

WIELANGTA STATE FOREST

Wielangta is believed to be a word meaning tall trees. About halfway between Copping and Orford, the Sandspit River Reserve has a 20-minute rainforest walk that passes rock formations once used as shelters.

SWANSEA
Walking Trail

On Waterloo Point, wrapping around the headland behind the golf course, is the Loontitetermairrelehoiner Aboriginal Heritage Walk. It passes middens and mutton bird rookeries, and interpretative boards explain a little about Aboriginal history. The walk is named after the band of the Oyster Bay Tribe that once lived in the area.

FREYCINET NATIONAL PARK

In this national park, you can pitch your tent in the same area that was used as a winter camp by members of the Oyster Bay Tribe for thousands of years. The area is rich in shellfish and the large middens along Richardsons Beach, just 1.5km into the park, are one of the signs of Aboriginal occupation.

At the time of writing, information on Aboriginal culture in the area was being planned for the new visitors centre, expected to open late 2001. Phone ☎ 6257 0107 for details. National park entrance fees apply (see Information at the beginning of this chapter).

Walking Tours

Freycinet Lodge (☎ 6257 0101, ⓔ info@frey cinetlodge.com.au) incorporates Aboriginal heritage into its **History Stroll** along Richardsons Beach and also offers a **Bush Tucker Stroll**. Walks are free to guests of the lodge and others can join them for free if there are places left.

BICHENO

This town began as a sealers port and was called Waubs Bay Harbour after an Aboriginal woman, Waubedebar, who was enslaved by sealers as a wife and servant in the early 19th century. A strong swimmer, she later became famous for rescuing two sealers when their boat was wrecked 1km offshore. Years after her death, the town erected a grave, which you can still visit, in the park at the end of Burgess St.

North East Tribe Country

The North-East

The North East people didn't travel as much as the other tribes of Tasmania. They kept the plains in their territory clear with firestick farming. The snowy country of Ben Lomond National Park belonged to the Ben Lomond Tribe.

Many significant places have been identified in the north-east, but are difficult to find or recognise unless you have a guide. These include rock shelters at Mt Victoria, rock engravings on the Blue Tier and middens at Musselroe Point, Binalong Bay and Round Hill Point. St Helens Point is an important area for gathering bush tucker. Information boards are planned for some of these places.

ORGANISED TOURS

Local Aboriginal historian Gloria Andrews can take you on an informal tour of the sites in the region, which are in her traditional country and are not easily accessible if you visit independently. Tours run for one or two hours and cost $25 per hour; you must provide your own transport. Gloria can be contacted through the St Helens History Room (see later in this section).

ST HELENS

A midden found at Kings Park in St Helens (known as Kunnara Kunna to Indigenous people) suggests that the town is built on a traditional camp.

St Helens History Room

This small but excellent museum (☎ 6376 1744, ⓔ historyroom@vision.net.au), at 61

TASMANIA

Cecilia St, has displays on the North East Tribe with artefacts that you can handle, including ochre stones, grinding stones, flint blades (such as those used for scarification) and a good collection of reference material. You can also inquire here about Indigenous arts and crafts for sale, such as maireeners and kelp water carriers and Aboriginal guided tours. The history room is open 9 am to 4 pm weekdays, plus on weekend mornings during summer. Entry is $2/1 for adults/children (plus GST).

BAY OF FIRES
As well as being a traditional camp, the Bay of Fires is a favourite spot for today's tourists. It was named by Tobias Furneaux in 1773 to describe the number of Aboriginal fires he saw along the shore. The foreshore, lagoons and heathlands are all part of a coastal reserve which contains high middens and pit cairns, possibly used to trap food.

From St Helens a minor road heads north-east to meet the coast at the start of the Bay of Fires and continues up as far as The Gardens. The northern end of the bay can be reached on the C843 road to the settlement of Ansons Bay.

North Midlands Tribe Country
Tamar & Macquarie Rivers Area

The country of the North Midlands people included the largest kangaroo hunting grounds in Tasmania, but this land also attracted European sheep farmers, who fought the local people for the plains that had been already cleared through traditional fire management.

LAUNCESTON
The original name of the Tamar River was Ponrabbel, and Indigenous people still know this area as Ponrabbel. Tribal groups once met together at appointed times of the year in an area of common ground near Launceston.

Information
The Aboriginal Elders Council of Tasmania (☎ 6334 3138) is at 163 St John St.

Walking Trail
At the time of writing the Launceston City Council had plans to open a Reconciliation Walking Trail at Royal Park, on the boardwalk area near Home Point. The theme of the walk is the 13 parcels of land returned in 1995 and 1999 to the Tasmanian Aboriginal community, and features the work of local artists.

Queen Victoria Museum & Art Gallery
The Queen Victoria Museum & Art Gallery (☎ 6331 6777), on Wellington St, has a display on Aboriginal Tasmanians, and it includes maireeners, bull kelp water carriers and throwing sticks. There are also a number of portraits in the Art of the Colony gallery. The museum is open Monday to Saturday 10 am to 5 pm and 2 to 5 pm on Sunday, entry is free. The Aboriginal collection will be moved to the Inveresk Railyards in Invermay Rd where a new section of the museum is opening in late 2001.

Shopping
The Tasmanian Aboriginal Corporation for Women's Arts and Crafts (TACWAC; ☎ 6334 9378, fax 6334 1399, e ykopper @tas.kwik.com.au), 163 St John St, is in the same building as the Elders Council and sells traditional arts including shell necklaces and bull kelp water carriers.

Bookshops Birchalls (☎ 6331 3011), 118–120 Brisbane St, has a good collection of books on Indigenous Australia, as does Petrarch's Book Shop (☎ 631 8088), 89 Brisbane St.

DELORAINE
Information
The Deloraine Aboriginal Cultural Association (DACA; ☎ 6362 3168), 34 Parsonage St, has links with Aboriginal artists in the region.

Organised Tours
Hank Horton runs Jahadi Outdoor Adventures (☎/fax 6363 6172, e jahadi@microtech .com.au), 900 Mile Creek Rd, offering tailored tours to significant sites throughout the state such as Rocky Cape and Freycinet National Parks. Bush tucker meals can be included and you can learn how to erect a

humpy to sleep in. The tours were developed from Hank's program of teaching culture to Aboriginal kids at risk and they are used to raise money for this work. Phone for current tour prices.

North Tribe Country

Central North Area

The North Tribe's traditional area incorporates three important ochre mines at Mt Vandyke, Mt Housetop and St Valentines Peak, which formed the basis of trade with neighbouring tribes.

DEVONPORT

Tiagarra

The Tasmanian Aboriginal Cultural Centre (☎ 6424 8250, fax 6427 0506) is at Mersey Bluff in Devonport, on the road to the lighthouse. It's known as Tiagarra, which means 'keep'.

Control of the centre was handed over to the Mersey Leven Aboriginal Corporation in 1995 and they are progressively updating the displays. The museum has exhibits on bush tucker, traditional dwellings and the history of European invasion. Guided tours are offered if you book in advance and information is available in English, German and Japanese.

The centre includes a shop selling Indigenous products from Tasmania and the mainland, and a coffee shop. It's open 9 am to 5 pm daily; admission is $3/2 for adult/concession (plus GST).

Walking Trail

There is some debate over whether the 250 rock marking sites on Mersey Bluff are traditional Aboriginal engravings or were formed naturally. Regardless of the scientific debate, the area around Tiagarra was, and continues to be, a highly significant place for Palawa people. You can see for yourself by following the walking trail past seven rock engravings, including two believed to be a seal and an emu. A map of the sites is available from Tiagarra.

TENGENOWA DREAMING

Based at Trowunna Wildlife Park, south of Devonport, Tengenowa Dreaming (☎ 6363 6162, fax 6367 6213) is owned by Darlene Mansell, a local Aboriginal woman with an intimate knowledge of Kooparoona Niara (Koopa Country), which means 'mountains of the spirit'. This area is also known as the Great Western Tiers. It is rich in Indigenous heritage.

Tengenowa offers one-hour wildlife tours for $8 per person (plus GST), relating the traditional *stories* of animals at the wildlife park, and 40-minute cultural walks for $4 per person (plus GST). Tailor-made guided tours to significant Aboriginal sites throughout Tasmania can also be arranged.

Trowunna Wildlife Park is named after an Aboriginal word for Tasmania, and is 2km from Chudleigh, east of Mole Creek on the way in from Deloraine. It's open 9 am to 5 pm daily year-round.

North West Tribe Country

North-West Coast

In this area the bands of the North West Tribe built villages of bark huts. The coast south of Macquarie Harbour was the land of the South West Tribe.

When the British invaded, the conflict with the North West Tribe was brutal. There was a massacre at Cape Grim on the north-west tip in 1827 when an estimated 30 Aborigines were shot in reprisal for driving a flock of sheep over a cliff.

Steep Island, north of Cape Grim, has been returned to the Aboriginal community.

ROCKY CAPE NATIONAL PARK

There are a number of significant caves in this park (an area known as Tang Dim Mer to Indigenous people). South Cave was excavated in 1965 and it was found that it was first used 8000 years ago, and then until it was completely filled with midden material. Interpretative signs providing cultural information are currently being updated and a new viewing platform is being constructed after a recent fire in the park.

Four important caves can be accessed. From the eastern end, starting at the Sisters Beach boat ramp, you can take the **Banksia Grove/Caves Circuit** walk which passes Lee Archer Cave and Wet Cave (one hour return).

From the western end at Rocky Cape Rd (turn right at Rocky Cape Roadhouse) you can visit the North and South Caves; both are a 20-minute return walk. There are interpretative signs at **South Cave**, which is reached by a trail up the hill from the car park at Burgess Cove. **North Cave** is sign-posted off the road to the lighthouse. National park fees apply.

Organised Tours

Rocky Sainty (☎ 6435 0442, 6452 4997) is an Aboriginal Parks & Wildlife Service ranger based at Smithton. He privately runs tours of the area looking at Indigenous culture and the ways it is being revived. Tours cost $220/ $33 (plus GST) per day/hour for a group.

ARTHUR PIEMAN PROTECTED AREA & NORTH-WEST COAST

The north-west of Tasmania has seen minimal disturbance from non-Aboriginal development. As a result, many cultural sites have been preserved, including some of the state's most important rock engravings, large middens, artefact scatters and hut depressions where settlements once stood.

There are significant sites all along the coast north and south of Marrawah and at the time of writing TALC had plans to put up interpretative signs along the Arthur River-Temma Rd about the heritage values in the area. Sites of particular significance include Preminghana, West Point, Sundown Point and Trial Harbour. There are also mid-dens and artefact scatters in the 30m-high sand dunes at Henty Dunes.

The area beyond the town of Temma can only be accessed by experienced drivers with 4WD vehicles. The roads are danger-ous and vehicles are lost each year on beaches and river crossings.

Organised Tours

If you want to visit these sites, it's advisable to arrange a trip with an Aboriginal guide or heritage officer who can explain their sig-nificance to you. TALC (☎ 6231 0288) keeps a list of heritage officers who can take you to the sites for around $250 to $300 per day for a group. Rocky Sainty can also pro-vide tours of these sites (for contact details and prices, see Organised Tours under Rocky Cape National Park earlier). Most Aboriginal guides have a good knowledge

of this area; see Organised Tours sections throughout this chapter for other options.

Preminghana

Preminghana (formerly Mt Cameron West) was returned to the Aboriginal community in 1995 and is managed by TALC. The area contains significant rock carvings and other important sites, but there is no general access for the public. If you want to visit independently, you can drive to the car park (take the gravel road north of Marrawah, then the first road on the left) and ask the resident caretaker (☎ 6457 1247) for permission to have a look around.

ZEEHAN

There is an interesting display at the **West Coast Pioneers Memorial Museum** (☎ 6471 6225) in gallery 4A, focusing on the rich culture and near genocide of the North West and South West Tribes. It also has a cast of rock engravings at Premin-ghana. The museum is on Main St, and is open 8.30 am to 5 pm daily. Admission is $5/3 (plus GST) adult/concession.

STRAHAN
History Exhibition

The West Coast Reflections exhibition at the Strahan Visitors Centre (☎ 6471 7622, fax 6471 7533), on The Esplanade, has an excellent display on the Aboriginal history of the area, put together by members of the Indigenous community. It includes infor-mation on the Aboriginal campaign to pre-vent the Franklin River being flooded.

Also included is an ironic take on the kind of display featuring tagged archaeo-logical finds often seen in museums throughout Australia – a telephone is ex-hibited, which is apparently an implement used by Aborigines in the 1990s for the pur-poses of communication, such as chatting or organising protest actions.

The visitors centre is open 10 am to 6 pm daily. Entry to the exhibition is $3/2 (plus GST) adult/concession, children free.

Shopping

The gallery at the Risby Cove Complex (☎ 6471 7572), on The Esplanade, exhibits the work of local Aboriginal artist Mick Quil-liam, or Mick Q. He also sells items direct (☎ 6471 7775, @ mickq@tpg.com.au) and can make pieces to order. Mick paints canvases (from $150) and emu eggs (from $85) and creates painted wooden jewellery (from $14), wall hangings, *nulla nullas* (traditional clubs) and *clapsticks* (music sticks that are struck together). Prices do not include GST. Check out his Web site at www.southcom. com.au/~vern/Webdesign/MickQ.

SARAH ISLAND
Members of the South West Tribe were imprisoned at the penal colony on Sarah Island before being removed to Flinders Island. At the time of writing there were plans to set up sculptures featuring Aboriginal voices on Sarah Island. The island is in Macquarie Harbour and is incorporated in daily tour cruises from Strahan. Gordon River Cruises (☎ 6471 7187) offers full-day trips for $62 in summer (including lunch) and World Heritage Cruises (☎ 6471 7174) charges $44 for a full day, plus $8 for lunch.

Central West

FRANKLIN-GORDON WILD RIVERS NATIONAL PARK
There are a series of major cave sites in the Franklin River valley, and these played a significant part in the region being listed as a World Heritage Area. Ballawinne Cave and Kutikina Cave are now on Aboriginal land, as is Wargata Mina cave further south.

Much of the park consists of deep river gorges and thick rainforest, but the Lyell Hwy traverses its northern end, where there are a number of signposted features of note, including a few short walks. Early European explorers encountered Aboriginal huts near the place where the highway crosses the Franklin River. You can walk the short (20-minute) **Franklin River Nature Trail** here to take a closer look at the river. National park fees apply.

Kutikina Cave
The most significant cave in the park is Kutikina Cave, which is on Aboriginal land. The cave was occupied for more than 5000 years during the last ice age.

The cave is in remote forest and the only way to reach it is by rafting down the Franklin River during summer. Information boards and a walkway have been set up

inside the cave to provide cultural interpretation and protect the site. The Franklin is truly a wild river and rafting it can be hazardous. Rafting Tasmania (☎ 6239 1080 in Hobart) offers 10-day ($1800) and four-day ($1045) trips, stopping at Kutikina. World Expeditions (☎ 02-9264 3366 in Sydney) does a nine-day trip ex-Hobart for $1639 and Peregrine (☎ 03-9662 2700 in Melbourne) offers trips starting at $1265 for five days.

Big River Tribe Country
Lake Country

The Big River Tribe, sometimes called the Laimairrener people, lived in this area in central west Tasmania, making trips to the coast during the winter to share seasonal foods with neighbouring tribes.

CRADLE MOUNTAIN-LAKE ST CLAIR NATIONAL PARK
The Cradle Mountain region was used as an avenue on the yearly round to collect resources and there are rock shelters and artefact scatters in the park. Cider gum trees, found only in this area of Tasmania, were used to collect alcohol.

According to Lyndall Ryan in her book *The Aboriginal Tasmanians*, one of the Big River Tribe's seasonal roads linked Lake St Clair to Cradle Mountain, just as the famous Overland Track does today.

The Cradle Mountain Visitors Centre (☎ 6492 1133) is open daily and has four display boards detailing Aboriginal uses of the area and some Indigenous reference material. At the Park Centre (☎ 6289 1172) at Lake St Clair, originally known as Leeawuleena, you can buy Indigenous resources and there are plans to set up an Indigenous display featuring contemporary fibre sculptures and an Indigenous forest and grassland walk.

Furneaux Islands

FLINDERS ISLAND
Between 1829 and 1834, the Aboriginal people who had survived Tasmania's martial law (which gave soldiers the right to arrest or shoot any Aboriginal person found in a

settled area) were brought to Flinders Island to be resettled, civilised and Christianised.

A number of islands have been returned to the Aboriginal community in the Furneaux group: Babel Island, Mt Chappell Island, Badger Island, Big Dog Island and part of Cape Barren Island.

If you want a taste of modern Aboriginal culture, the best times to visit are during the mutton-birding season (late March to late April) or during the Wybalenna Festival (January).

Information
The Flinders Island Aboriginal Association Inc (FIAAI; ☎ 6359 3532, fax 6359 3622, ⓔ fiaai@bigbond.com) is the place to go for all information about the Indigenous community on Flinders Island. Its office is on West St, Lady Barron. At the time of writing FIAAI planned to set up an arts centre to display traditional arts. During and just after the birding season they sell mutton birds – around $2.50 for a skinned bird and $2.70 for a cleaned one.

Organised Tours
FIAAI can sometimes arrange informal interpretative tours of sites in the area, for around $100 to $150 per day.

Wybalenna
The Wybalenna Historic Site, which was returned to the Aboriginal community in 1999, is a memorial to a tragic phase of Aboriginal history and many of the survivors of the Black War on the mainland died here. The chapel, cemetery and a homestead remain on the site. Other sites of interest here are Lillies Beach, where the stumps of the original wharf still stand, and Port Davies.

If you want to visit Wybalenna independently, other than during the festival, you need to check with FIAAI first.

The Chapel The restored chapel contains a display case with maps of the original settlement and photos of an excavation of the site in 1970.

Cemetery The Aboriginal graves in the cemetery are at the eastern end, but only the European graves are marked with headstones. Mannalargenna, the great leader of the North East Tribe, is buried here. In 1991, the Aboriginal community identified and marked the graves and set up a memorial cairn which read:

'Repossession of Wybalenna
15.7.91
For all those Aboriginal people that walked and still walk this land'

The graves and memorial were vandalised shortly after they were erected. The story of this incident is told in the film *Black Man's Houses*.

Homestead The homestead is on the spot where George Robinson's cottage once stood. It is the site of the Wybalenna Festival.

Museum
The Furneaux Historical Research Association Inc runs the museum at Emita, on the way to Wybalenna at 8 Fowlers Rd. It has a good collection of archival material, relating to the Aboriginal history of Flinders Island. There is also a replica mutton-birding shed that gives you a feel for the industry as it was in the early days.

The museum is open on weekends and public holidays from 1 to 5 pm; weekdays in summer from 1 to 5 pm and at other times by arrangement; phone ☎ 6359 2010. The museum is staffed by volunteers and entry is $2 (children under 14 free).

Wybalenna Festival
In January each year the Aboriginal community kicks up its heels at the Wybalenna Festival. A stage is set up for musicians, traditional foods are cooked, and artists sell their work. It's a casual event and non-Indigenous people are welcome to take part – don't forget to bring your guitar.

You can camp for free at the site, toilets are provided, and you don't need to inform FIAAI if you visit Wybalenna during the festival. Check with FIAAI to confirm festival dates.

BIG DOG ISLAND
Big Dog, or more officially Great Dog Island, is owned by the Aboriginal community. This is where the mutton-birding industry is based (see the boxed text 'Birding on Big Dog'). The mutton-birding season usually lasts from the end of March to the end of April.

BIRDING ON BIG DOG

Monique Choy

The short-tailed shearwater has many names. Known to zoologists as the *Puffinus tenuirostris* and to Aborigines as the *yolla* or moon bird, it is probably most commonly known as the mutton bird.

Each September, around 23 million mutton birds return to south-eastern Australia from their tour of the Pacific which takes them as far north as the Arctic Circle. Their first task is to clean out and repair their burrows from the previous year. They then head out to sea again before returning in November for the breeding season, which lasts until April. A single egg is laid in the burrow and the parents take turns to incubate it.

Once the chick has hatched, both parents feed the fledgling until mid-April, when all the adult birds depart, leaving the young to fend for themselves until they can follow their parents north.

The chicks produce *gurry* oil in their stomachs; this oil is high in nutrients and keeps them alive while their parents are away. It is these untended chicks which are the target of the birders, who plunge their hands into frosty burrows, risking tiger snake bites, to bring the chicks out.

Working six days a week, using a technique they have perfected over thousands of years, the birders pull the young birds from their rookeries, break their necks and hang them on spits across their shoulders to carry them to the sheds. The birds are first gurried, when their oil is squeezed into a bucket. They are then scalded in boiling pots, which makes it easier to remove their downy feathers. The feathers are rubbed off the bird, their legs, head and wings are chopped and they are thrown into the steam room. Here they are opened, gutted, racked and packed into a freezer unit. They are then shipped to Lady Barron and on to the wider market.

The birds make good eating and the gurry oil derived is prized for its medicinal benefits. The birding season is also a time of cultural renewal when many people from the community who have moved to the mainland return (like the mutton birds) for the season. Families come together, children are shown the ropes and stories are shared at the end of a hard day's work.

You can go over to Big Dog Island (a short trip from Lady Barron) to see the birders at work in the shed run by FIAAI, but you must get permission from the shed boss first by contacting FIAAI.

A group of six to 10 people can charter the *Strait Lady* (☎ 6359 4507, fax 6359 4533) for three to four hours, for $50 per person (plus GST). You can't visit Big Dog outside the birding season.

CAPE BARREN ISLAND

There is a thriving Aboriginal community on Cape Barren which traces its heritage, like most Tasmanian Aborigines, to the sealing community of Aboriginal women and European men – sometimes called the 'Straitspeople' – who were based here in the early 19th century.

Part of the island (Wombat Point) has been returned to the Aboriginal community and many of the Elders continue traditional art and craftwork. Of particular note are the maireeners made by the women, which can be purchased through TACWAC (see the Launceston section). There are few facilities for visitors on Cape Barren, just some walks around the island.

Torres Strait Islands

The Torres Strait Islands are scattered across the reef-strewn waters of Torres Strait, running like stepping stones from the top of Cape York to the south coast of Papua New Guinea, about 150km north of the Australian mainland. The islands, politically part of Australia, have a population of about 8500. The people are Melanesians, racially related to the peoples of Papua New Guinea.

While Waiben (Thursday Island; or TI as it's usually known) is the 'capital', there are 17 inhabited islands, the northernmost being Saibai and Boigu. Boigu is only 6km from New Guinea. After Thursday Island, the largest group of people live on Badu, where the population numbers around 800. Most of the inhabited islands have populations of between 100 and 200 people.

History

Philip Morrissey

EARLY HISTORY

The islands of the Torres Strait have been inhabited for at least 4000 years. The islands are geographically diverse, with three main types: the rocky, mountain-top extension of the Great Dividing Range makes up the western group that includes Thursday Island and Muralag (Prince of Wales Island); the central group of islands, dotting the waters east of the Great Barrier Reef, is little more than a collection of coral cays; while the third group is volcanic in origin and is in the far east of the strait, at the very northern end of the Great Barrier Reef.

The Torres Strait Islanders are a unique and culturally distinct group of people who have absorbed and transformed influences from their neighbours. They traded commodities and implements with Cape York Aborigines in the south and Papuans in the north. The traditional diet varied from island to island but included dugong (a large herbivorous tropical sea mammal), fish and shellfish, turtle, yam and taro.

Religious practices were also exchanged. Kuiam, a hero-cult figure, originated in Cape York and travelled to the coast of New Guinea. The most powerful cult however

was the Malo-Bomai cult, which was administered by priests known as Zogo le. Malo and Bomai were heroic beings and it has been suggested that aspects of the cult still survive in Torres Strait Island Christianity.

Islanders conduct a unique ceremony known as a 'tombstone opening'. It marks the end of mourning a deceased person. A tombstone is unveiled and after a religious service there is a celebration with dancing and feasting. Many mainland Torres Strait

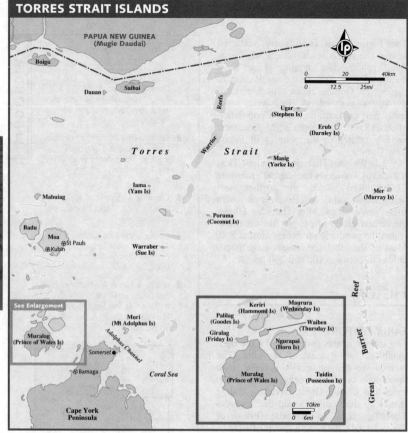

TORRES STRAIT ISLANDS

Islanders return to the islands for these events; see the boxed text 'Tombstone Unveiling Ceremony'.

Torres Strait languages show traces of Papuan and mainland Aboriginal languages. A melodious creole is also widely spoken in the strait (see the Language section, later).

EUROPEAN ARRIVAL

European contact began in the 17th century with Dutch and Spanish mariners. In 1606, the Spaniard Luis Vaez Torres sailed through the strait and in 1770 Captain James Cook sailed up the east coast of Australia and stopped at Possession Island to claim the whole east coast of Australia for King George III. The Islanders have a fierce culture and may have discouraged prolonged visits.

On 1 July 1871 missionaries from the London Missionary Society landed on Erub (Darnley Island). The annual Coming of the Light Festival celebrates the arrival of Christianity on Erub (see the boxed text 'The Coming of the Light') in the Thursday Island section. Unlike many Indigenous peoples in Australia, the Islanders saw Christianity as a liberating force, in particular from inter-island warfare and sorcery, but also from the depredations of the pearlers and trepangers.

The Queensland government established an administrative centre on Thursday Island in 1877 and formally annexed the islands in 1879. As the centre of the pearling industry (see the boxed text 'The World's Your Oyster'), this settlement grew rapidly; despite the industry's decline, it is still the most densely populated island. The government's policy was one of separate and isolated development for the Islanders. It attempted to impose segregation, bar Islanders from hotels, and make sexual relations between Islanders and other races an offence. As an adjunct to this policy people of 'mixed race' were relocated to Moa and Keriri (Hammond Island).

POLITICAL CHANGE

The government also appointed its own chiefs as representatives for the Islanders. These men, known as *mamooses*, were ineffective and were replaced with elected councils. In 1936 Torres Strait Islanders working on government-owned *trochus* (tropical crustaceans) boats went on strike in protest against the paternalistic attitudes of the government. The strike continued for nine months, until concessions were made allowing Island Councils more say in the management of boats. When WWII began, over 800 Islanders served in the Torres Strait. When it ended many Islanders travelled to the mainland to work as cane-cutters and railway fettlers. There are now Torres Strait Islander communities all over Australia, with most concentrated in Brisbane and the coastal cities and towns of Queensland.

The specific needs and identity of the Torres Strait has usually been ignored by Australian governments – born out by the fact that Torres Strait Islanders were first counted in the census as Polynesians and later as Pacific Islanders. As part of a recognition of the specific needs of the Torres Strait a Torres Strait Regional Authority was established in 1994.

MABO

Mer (Murray Island), a fertile island in the eastern group, became famous when Koiki (Eddie) Mabo and three other Murray Islanders commenced legal action to have traditional title to their land recognised in Australian common law. After 10 years of hearings the High Court of Australia found in 1992 that the Mer people owned the land prior to annexation. This simple decision put paid to the fiction of *terra nullius* which had underpinned the European occupation of Australia, and paved the way for the Commonwealth Native Title Act. Tragically, Koiki died only months before the judgment was handed down. See also the boxed text entries 'The Battle of Mabo' and 'Terra Nullius' in the History section of the Facts about Aboriginal Australia & the Torres Strait Islander chapter.

Language

Three main languages are spoken in the group of small islands scattered across the Torres Strait. Kala Lagaw Ya and Meriam Mir are the original Indigenous languages of the strait, and are still spoken in some areas. However, the English-based creole Yumpla Tok (formerly known as Torres Strait Broken) serves as the region's lingua franca.

Yumpla Tok is spoken on a daily basis on the central and eastern islands of the Torres Strait, as well as on Waiben (Thursday Island), Ngurapai (Horn Island) and Keriri (Hammond Island), although most adults maintain their traditional Indigenous languages.

KALA LAGAW YA

Kala Lagaw Ya, believed to be related to mainland Aboriginal languages, has four dialects and is spoken by around 3000 people in the Torres Strait. It's spoken on the western islands of Saibai, Dauan, Boigu, Mabuiag, Badu and Moa (Kubin), and the central islands of Ngurapai, Masig, Poruma, Iama and Warraber, as well as in Seisia and Bamaga on the Cape York Peninsula.

Welcome	Sew ngapa
Goodbye	Yawa
How are you?	Ngi midh?
Fine	Balabayginga
Yes/No	Wa/Lawnga

MERIAM MIR

Meriam Mir is spoken by close to 2000 people from the eastern islands of Erub, Ugar and Mer, where it's mainly spoken by adults. It belongs to the Trans Fly family of languages, spoken along the Papuan coast. Meriam Mir once had two dialects, which differed in some vocabulary and sounds, but only the Mer dialect now survives.

Welcome	Maiem
Goodbye	Yawo
How are you?	Nako manali?
Fine	Sikakanali
Thank you	Eswau
Yes/No	Baru/Nole

TORRES STRAIT ISLANDS

TOMBSTONE UNVEILING CEREMONY

The most significant celebration in the Torres Strait is the unveiling of the tombstone of a loved one.

This ceremony is the culmination of burial rituals that usually span three years. They start with the funeral (a time of sorrow), which is followed by the first anniversary of the death, the arrival of the headstone, the laying of the foundation for the headstone, and finally the tombstone unveiling itself (a time of celebration).

Immediately following a death and the funeral, the family of the deceased begin amassing money to buy the headstone. This was the case with the passing of my uncle. Our family contributions to the ceremony included gifts of colourful and fine fabrics, household linen and bedding, traditional artefacts, as well as traditional and modern jewellery.

On the first anniversary of his death, my uncle's material possessions were sorted and shared among his male friends and relatives.

It is two years before the third stage of the ritual takes place. Great care was taken in picking the gravestone for my uncle, a photograph and brief biography of the deceased, along with verses from the Bible were supplied to the masons. When the custom-designed gravestone arrived, a special place was set aside for it in the family home and our extended family gathered for a preview and a small celebratory dinner.

A few weeks later, work started in the cemetery, clearing the *surum yalgamai* (grave site) and laying the foundations for the gravestone. When the tombstone was installed and covered with a tarpaulin, another small celebratory feast with prayers was held by the extended family. A date was set for the *kulau gudpudai* (tombstone opening ceremony) and preparations got under way.

Marigeth (in-laws) of the deceased play an important role in the ritual. The organisation of the celebratory feast is their responsibility, as well as performing special tasks during the ceremony. The tombstone unveiling is a public event, an open invitation is extended to everyone in the community, including visitors and tourists.

YUMPLA TOK

Yumpla Tok is an English-based creole which developed mainly from the Pacific Island pidgin, Bislama, which was brought from Vanuatu to the Torres Strait by Pacific Islander labourers.

A variety of languages were spoken by labourers living in the Torres Strait Islands during the 20th century, including Japanese, Malay, some dialects of Chinese, and Indigenous Torres Strait languages. Bislama became established as the first language of children born after WWII and subsequently developed into the creole language Yumpla Tok.

Differences have arisen in the varieties of Yumpla Tok spoken on the eastern islands and those spoken on the central and western islands, with examples of vocabulary being borrowed into Yumpla Tok from the different Indigenous languages spoken in the two regions.

Welcome	Maiem
Goodbye	Siyu/Yawo
How are you?	Wis wei (yu)?
Fine	Orait
Thank you	Eso po yu
Yes/No	Wa/No

USEFUL CONTACTS

James Cook University Language Centre (☎ 07-4781 5517) Townsville, Qld 4811

Magani Malyu Kes (Torres Strait Islander Resource Unit; ☎ 07-4771 5740) 458 Flinders St, Townsville, Qld 4810

Information

INDIGENOUS ORGANISATIONS

For information on the island communities, go directly to the island councils (see the Information sections in this chapter). The two Islander communities on the mainland, Bamaga and Seisia, are covered in the Queensland chapter.

continued...   Leonora Adidi

The day finally arrived and I was among the hand-picked nieces and female cousins of the deceased chosen to decorate and wrap the tombstone with garish floral cloths, silk, taffeta, satin and lace. Other fabrics were neatly folded and laid out to display along with the bed linen, crocheted *lava lavas* (lap-laps), crystal vases filled with silk roses and intricately carved wooden artefacts such as spears, harpoons, bows, arrows and *warup* (drums). The centrepiece was a totemic object of a carved wooden shark. Beaded and shell jewellery and coloured scarves adorned the brightly veiled monument. The fence enclosing the gravesite was strung with coconut leaves and freshly picked purple and orange bougainvillea blossoms. A ribbon was then hung across the narrow garlanded entry to the enclosure. The completed grave was a beautiful, celebratory sight which displayed the creativity of the whole community.

Around mid-afternoon, people assembled at the gateway of the cemetery and the ceremony commenced. An Anglican priest and his laymen lead the solemn procession to the gravesite, to the accompaniment of hymns sung in our language Kalau Kawau Ya (a dialect of Kala Lagaw Ya), and the beating of warup. Upon reaching the site, a long prayer was intoned to bless the tombstone, and totemic songs were sung and chanted. Then the master of ceremonies (MC) called a special guest, an elderly uncle, to cut the ribbon. He then invited the family to enter the enclosure and encircle the decorated tombstone. The marigeth filed in and unveiled the tombstone. When the unveiling was complete, the MC announced a special guest, a well-respected friend of the deceased, to read the inscription on the tombstone. There was a closing prayer and a song and with that the ceremony was over. The family and gathered guests proceeded to the hall to begin the feast and dancing.

Travellers are often welcome at tombstone unveilings. When one is planned, a public notice of general invitation is published in the local paper and on community noticeboards. Dress is neat and casual for visitors and tourists. Photography is usually permitted.

TORRES STRAIT ISLANDS

The Torres Shire Council (☎ 4069 1336, fax 4069 1845), PO Box 171, Thursday Island, is the local government body for the Torres Strait region, but only administers services in the inner-island group.

The Island Co-ordinating Council (☎ 4069 1446, fax 4069 1868), PO Box 501, Thursday Island, is the peak state government body responsible for the Torres Strait.

The Torres Strait Regional Authority (☎ 4069 1247, fax 4069 1879), PO Box 261 Thursday Island, funded by the federal government, handles land claims and funds Torres Strait policies and programs. It has the same powers as the Aboriginal and Torres Strait Islander Commission (ATSIC) in the Torres Strait. Its Web site (www.tsra.gov.au) has information on each populated island.

BOOKS

The beautifully illustrated *Thathilgaw Emeret Lu – A Handbook of Traditional Torres Strait Islands Material Culture* by Lindsay Wilson is a good introduction to the culture through its arts and artefacts. John Singe's *Torres Strait: People and History* and *Among Islands* are brief histories of the region. *Edward Koiki Mabo – His Life and Struggle* by Noel Loos & Koiki Mabo looks at the man behind the historic Mabo claim. For more information about the Mabo claim see the History section earlier and in the Facts about Aboriginal Australia & the Torres Strait Island chapter. Ron Edward's *Traditional Torres Strait Island Cooking* explains how to cook up an island feast in a *kup mari* (pit oven).

NEWSPAPER & MAGAZINES

The local newspaper, the *Torres News* (☎ 4069 1531), sells for $1.55. Another useful reference is the *Thursday Island Business and Community Directory* ($3.30). This is essentially a telephone directory covering the Torres Strait and the Northern Peninsula

TORRES STRAIT ISLANDS

THE WORLD'S YOUR OYSTER

Torres Strait Islanders traditionally used pearlshell for making breastplates and decorating masks, but the discovery of pearlshell in the waters of the Torres Strait by Europeans during the 1860s led to an invasion of boats and crews in search of this new form of wealth. They were also joined by trepangers, who collected trepang (also known as bêche-de-mer), a sea slug considered a delicacy in Chinese cuisine. It was a wild and savage time with murder and blackbirding (a form of kidnapping for sale into slavery) common. Pearlers and trepangers kidnapped Islander men for labour and Islander women as sexual partners. Largely beyond the reaches of the law, they plundered the people and resources of the Torres Strait with impunity. Diseases introduced by the pearlers and trepangers were also responsible for a drastic reduction in the Islander population.

The pearling industry became the lifeblood of the Torres Strait until WWII. There were two ways of gathering pearlshell: 'swimmer divers' who collected shells in shallow water and 'helmet divers' who worked in deep water. Both methods were dangerous. 'Swimmer divers' could be attacked by sharks, while 'helmet divers' often used poor equipment and had minimal knowledge of the physiological aspects of deep diving. Death from the 'bends', or decompression sickness, was common – 700 Japanese divers lost their lives prior to WWII. The 'Darnley Deeps' were particularly dangerous because of the depth at which divers worked. Cyclones were a seasonal menace and the worst of these, in March 1899, destroyed the Torres Strait pearling fleet, killing hundreds of men.

After WWII, the pearling industry declined though many Islanders continued to work in the industry. An attempt to develop a cultural pearl industry was set back when an oil tanker hit a rock in the 1970s, spilling tonnes of oil into the strait.

See also 'Grandad's Memories of Pearlshells & Japanese Bombs' later in this chapter.

Area (NPA) of Cape York. It also contains maps of Thursday Island and Ngurapai (Horn Island).

RADIO
Listening to 4MW (☎ 4069 1524) talkback will keep you informed on all the local debates. It broadcasts 'straight from the strait', in the Torres Strait and the NPA on 1260 AM.

SPECIAL EVENTS
The Coming of the Light is celebrated throughout the islands each year on 1 July to commemorate the day in 1871 when the London Missionary Society landed on Erub (Darnley Island), bringing Christianity to the Torres Strait. Today, Islanders remain overwhelmingly Christian.

Shopping

Art and artefacts from the Torres Strait are widely available at shops on Thursday Island,

including wonderful cassowary feather headdresses (from $15), intricately carved spears (around $10 to $35) and drums (from around $55).

QUARANTINE
There is a strict quarantine between the Torres Strait and mainland Australia. You must not carry live animals (including cats and dogs), live plants or plant parts, meat, soil, milk, feathers, skins or egg products from the Torres Strait onto mainland Australia. For more information, contact the Australian Quarantine and Inspection Service (☎ 4069 1185).

Inner Island Group

The inner islands, including Thursday Island, are the traditional lands of the Kaurareg people, who are Aboriginal rather than Islander and have strong links to the traditional owners of the NPA region. The Kaurareg lived primarily on Muralag (Prince of Wales Island) until they were removed to Keriri (Hammond Island) early in the 20th century. At the time of writing there were no facilities for visitors on Muralag, although a recreation and camping area was planned. Contact the Torres Shire Council (☎ 4069 1336) for information on the current Kaurareg authority.

The airport for the inner islands is on Ngurapai, a 15-minute ferry trip ($6 one way) from Thursday Island.

WAIBEN (THURSDAY ISLAND)

Thursday Island (often referred to as TI), is little more than 4.5 sq km in area, with the main town of Port Kennedy on its southern shore. The Tamwoy, Rose Hill, Aplin, Waiben and Quarantine (TRAWQ) community lives on the north-western side of the island.

History

Waiben means 'dry place' and it was due to the lack of fresh water that the Kaurareg did not live on the island permanently, but rather visited it periodically from Muralag.

The Torres Strait pearling boom began in 1869 and in 1877 the administrative centre of the area was moved to Thursday Island from Somerset on the tip of Cape York. By the 1890s the industry was dominated by Japanese pearlers, but Thursday Island had become a multicultural mix of Indigenous people, white administrators and missionaries, pearlers and trepang fishermen from Japan, China, Malaya, the Philippines, Sri Lanka and the Pacific Islands.

The island was evacuated during WWII and became the headquarters for the forces stationed in the strait.

Information

The helpful Peddells Ferry & Tour Bus Service (☎ 4069 1551), at Engineers Wharf, offers boat and bus tours (see Organised Tours later) as well as general information.

The Torres Shire Council (☎ 4069 1336), 68 Douglas St, has limited tourist information. It houses a library, with a collection of books on the Torres Strait, open 9 am to 4 pm weekdays and 10 am to noon on Saturday. Special borrowing arrangements can be made for visitors. Visit the library Web

TORRES STRAIT ISLANDS

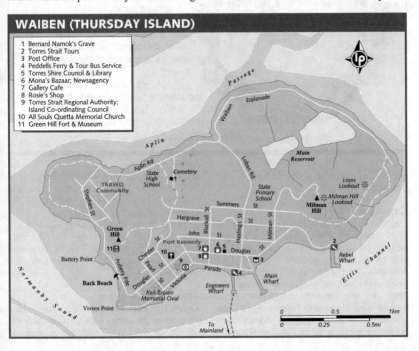

WAIBEN (THURSDAY ISLAND)

1 Bernard Namok's Grave
2 Torres Strait Tours
3 Post Office
4 Peddells Ferry & Tour Bus Service
5 Torres Shire Council & Library
6 Mona's Bazaar; Newsagency
7 Gallery Cafe
8 Rosie's Shop
9 Torres Strait Regional Authority;
   Island Co-ordinating Council
10 All Souls Quetta Memorial Church
11 Green Hill Fort & Museum

GRANDAD'S MEMORIES OF PEARLSHELLS & JAPANESE BOMBS

My Grandad, Ali Drummond, is one of the last pearlshell divers from the pearlshell industry boom days of the Torres Strait. A kind, witty and wise man, he is a much-loved personality of Thursday Island.

The Torres Strait pearlshell industry was experiencing a second boom when Grandad began his pearling career in 1932 at the age of 15. Pearlshell was used to make various items including buttons, buckles, knife handles and even the decoration on jewellery boxes. However, after WWII the demand for pearlshell declined with the introduction of plastic, which was easier and cheaper to produce. During the heyday of the pearlshell industry, my Grandad worked on several pearling luggers with Japanese, Malay, Polynesian and Papua New Guinean crews, and started on three pounds, five shillings a month – a good wage at that time. A hard worker, he earned as much as £1000 in a season. His record total for a season was 22 tons of pearlshell.

During his pearling career, Grandad worked in various positions including crew member, cook, chief diver (number one) and skipper. He was the number one diver for about eight years. The dangers of pearlshell diving were many but the rewards were good. The 'Darnley Deeps' (near Erub) was one of the most dangerous places to dive and many divers died from the bends (nitrogen bubbles in the bloodstream caused by rising to the surface too quickly).

'The bends was like ants crawling all over you then it would hit you – boom all of a sudden,' explains my Grandad, who had experienced the bends several times.

My Grandad also lived to tell the tale of the Japanese bombing raids in 1942, during WWII. 'It was a thrill to watch a dogfight in the air, and the echo of machine guns firing at each other,' he says.

---

site at cwpp.slq.qld.gov.au/tilibrary which has tourist information.

Organised Tours

Peddells Ferry & Tour Bus Service (☎ 4069 1551, fax 4069 1365), Web site www.ped dellsferry.com.au, offers bus tours of Thursday Island, taking in the Green Hill Fort Museum and the cemetery (see Things to See), and touching on the Indigenous heritage of the region. The tour costs $14.50/6.50 for adults/children or you can combine it with the Gateway Torres Strait Resort tour of Ngurapai (see the Ngurapai section later) for $68.60, including lunch. You can also take these tours from the mainland (see the Seisia section of the Queensland chapter for details).

Torres Strait Tours (☎ 1800 420 666 toll free, fax 4069 1408) books the Gateway resort's Garrison Town Tour of Thursday Island, focusing on WWII history, for $17.60 (plus GST).

Things to See

Green Hill Fort Museum is run by volunteers from the Torres Strait Historical Society (☎ 4069 1551). There are displays of

continued...

Samantha Faulkner

Grandad worked as a Civilian Construction Worker. His work team, known as the 'flying gang', worked at various jobs on Palilag (Goodes Island) in the Torres Strait, such as building roads, ammunition dumps and army huts. During WWII, both my Nana (grandmother) and Aunt, along with other residents of Thursday Island, were evacuated to the Australian mainland. 'Thursday Island was like a deserted town, …it was so quiet and gloomy,' my Grandad recalls.

Grandad recently received the Civilian Service Medal Award 1939–45, in recognition for his work during WWII. Other awards he has received include the Senior Australian of the Year Award, the Australia Day Award for Sportsperson of the Year (lawn bowls), and the National NAIDOC (National Aboriginal and Islander Day Observance Committee) Award for Sportsperson of the Year (lawn bowls). Today, my Grandad is an active octogenarian who loves to fish and play lawn bowls. He says, 'It's no good to sit down and watch TV, it won't get you nowhere. I fish and when I get sick of it, I go play bowls.'

It is this optimistic approach and get-up-and-go attitude to life that makes me proud to call him my Grandad.

See also the boxed text entry 'The World's Your Oyster'.

Samantha Faulkner

Samantha is a descendant of the people of Moa in the Torres Strait and Yadhaigana on Cape York Peninsula.

Born on Thursday Island, she developed a taste for travelling at a young age, when her parents travelled to England several times. She has since been moving progressively down the east coast of Australia. In 1992 she completed a Bachelor of Arts degree in Brisbane and began a career in the Australian public service. She has worked in a number of government departments based in Canberra. Samantha is involved in the Australian Capital Territory (ACT) Aboriginal and Torres Strait Islander community through her representation on a number of committees. She was recently appointed to the ACT Aboriginal and Torres Strait Islander Consultative Council to advise the chief minister on Indigenous issues.

Samantha has satisfied the desire for travel through business and personal life, embarking on interstate and overseas travel, but enjoys coming home to Warren (husband) and Arnie (cat).

traditional artefacts and the more recent history of Thursday Island. It is open by appointment and is $3 for adults, children free.

There are a number of historic **churches** on Thursday Island, including the All Souls Quetta Memorial Church, built in memory of the 133 people who lost their lives when the SS *Quetta* sank in the Adolphus Channel in 1890. The church remains an important place of worship for local Islanders.

The **cemetery**, on the northern side of the island, is worth a visit. The grave of Bernard Namok is marked with the Torres Strait Islands flag, which he designed.

At the time of writing the Torres Shire Council had plans to develop a cultural village, which would include historical information, traditional food and souvenirs. It will also become the venue for the Torres Strait Cultural Festival (see the Special Events section, later).

Shopping

Islanders seem to make up a commemorative T-shirt for every occasion and you'll find a selection of these and other souvenirs at Mona's Bazaar (☎ 4069 1860), on Douglas St.

TORRES STRAIT ISLANDS

TORRES STRAIT ISLANDS

THE COMING OF THE LIGHT

Rhianna Patrick

'The Coming of the Light' on 1 July is one of the most important days for Torres Strait Islanders, as it signifies the arrival of the London Missionary Society (LMS) in 1871, and the birth of Christianity in the Torres Strait Islands. Held annually, the festival celebrates the very first landing of the LMS at Erub (Darnley Island).

The Coming of the Light is celebrated in different ways and in different places throughout the Torres Strait Islands and mainland Australia, but there are three common factors. Firstly, there is always a Mass or service to mark the significance of the day and, like Christmas, the story is retold. A re-enactment is always part of the celebrations, and this shows the missionaries landing at Kemus, on Erub. (When flying into Erub, you can get a bird's-eye view of a concrete version of *Surprise*, the boat which first brought the missionaries to the Torres Strait Islands. It's an amazing sight, with this boat memorial set against a backdrop of golden sands, crystal-clear blue sea and the lush tropical greenness of surrounding coconut palms.)

During the evening, there is usually a feast that includes traditional Torres Strait Islander food such as *sop sop* (various vegetables cooked in coconut milk) and authentic traditional damper (usually wrapped and cooked in banana leaves). Other traditional dishes such as pork and vegetables – which often include sweet potato, potato, cassava, onions and carrots – are cooked in a *kup mari* (pit oven). On Erub, this is a huge event attracting people from the island and beyond. Then, keeping with tradition, the women of the island help to prepare and lay out the food. As Christianity is the predominant religion of the Torres Strait Islands, grace is said before eating. Guests are usually invited to eat first, along with the Elders and men. Women and children are traditionally the last to eat (if in doubt wait until you are asked to come to the table).

Following the feast, there is traditional Torres Strait Islander dancing, which is quite unique and different to traditional Aboriginal dance. Many of the men wear brightly coloured traditional *lava lavas* (lap-laps). Festivities usually go well on into the night and visitors are often invited to join in the dancing.

For further information about the Coming of the Light celebrations, contact the Darnley Island Council on ☎ 4069 4001, fax 4069 4000.

Rhianna Patrick

I'm a Torres Strait Islander (my family is from Mer and Erub) who was born in Brisbane, but I spent the early part of my life growing up in the bauxite-mining town of Weipa.

I completed a Bachelor of Arts (in Journalism) at the University of Queensland and have worked as a breakfast announcer for Brisbane's Indigenous radio station. I love working in the media and hope to be a well-rounded journalist one day. I enjoy working in Indigenous media, as it's very satisfying to be contributing to a community that I am proud to be a part of, but I do hope to get out into the mainstream, which is the reason I studied journalism.

I also have a passion for ancient history (particularly the Romans), Brit music (any kind – if it's from the UK, I like it) and Rugby Union (I love playing it).

Rosie's Shop (☎ 4069 1297), on Douglas St, sells souvenirs like spears and headdresses, and a selection of books and music.

Another good place for books on the Torres Strait is the newsagency, CR&P Jones (☎ 4069 1118), on Douglas St.

MONIQUE CHOY

TODD CONDIE, KOORI MAIL

D LEVITT

A MARSHAL/L WALKER

RICHARD I'ANSON

TOD CONDIE, KOORI MAIL

DANCE & CEREMONY

Dance and ceremony are essential parts of Aboriginal and Torres Strait Islander heritage and remain a key form of cultural, spiritual and political expression. More than pure entertainment, traditional forms are a method of communication, of passing on stories and the law. While many ceremonies are sacred and private, there are plenty of opportunities to witness Indigenous dance today. See also the Dance section on page 53.

Naroo Dance Company (pictured here at Sydney's Matsuri Festival) are well-known for both traditional and contemporary dance (1). 'Naroo', meaning 'shake-a-leg', is a dance style from north Queensland. Arts festivals such as the high-profile Stompem Ground of Broome, WA, celebrate the diversity of Indigenous dance, as well as music, song and art (2). Here a child from the Kimberley performs at Stompem Ground (5). Ceremonies imbue events such as the hunt and fire-making with spiritual significance (3, 4). The Torres Strait Cultural Festival is a vivid display of Melanesian costumes and music (6).

In modern-day Aboriginal Australia, ancient and traditional styles are often combined with contemporary Western dance to create an exciting new art form. This melding of past and present reflects living ancestral traditions and also the lives and attitudes of Indigenous people today.

Internationally acclaimed, Sydney-based Bangarra Dance Theatre (1-4) is at the forefront of Australian contemporary dance. Its members are all Indigenous, and its choreography is a vibrant blend of ancient spirituality and body-language, urban Aboriginal perspective and modern international dance styles. Music, and particularly percussion instruments, are an integral part of Torres Strait Island dances (5). A dancer in traditional dari headdress performs at the Stompem Ground festival in Broome, WA (6). The dari is a symbol of the Islanders' cultural heritage and is represented on the Torres Strait Islands flag. See 'The Dari - Our Symbol of Peace & Unity' on page 346.

The Gallery Cafe (☎ 4069 2617), on the corner of Douglas and Blackall Sts, has an excellent selection of local paintings and prints for sale. It's open 10 am to 1 pm Thursday to Saturday, but the artwork, by both Indigenous and non-Indigenous local artists, is on display daily.

Local artist Stanley Laifoo, of Yanna Art & Craft (☎ 4069 2724), sells his paintings of traditional subjects and *stories* privately, as does Andrew Warrior (☎ 4069 1250) who produces intricate lino prints and paintings.

Special Events
The Torres Strait Cultural Festival is held in July of even-numbered years at the Ken Brown Memorial Oval. It includes sporting events, cultural performances and craft and food stalls. For information contact the Torres Shire Council (see Information earlier). Many Islanders return to the Torres Strait for this festival, and you must book accommodation months in advance if you want to visit at this time.

In odd-numbered years the Torres Strait Music Festival is held around the same time – check with the shire council for details.

The All Souls Quetta Memorial Church holds a special service and procession during the annual Coming of the Light festival (see Special Events and the boxed text 'The Coming of the Light' at the beginning of this chapter).

NGURAPAI (HORN ISLAND)
History
Ngurapai is the traditional land of the Kaurareg people, who were forcibly removed from the inner islands to Moa Island in 1922.

During WWII, Ngurapai became a battle zone, suffering eight Japanese air raids. Among the 5000 troops stationed on the island was the 830-strong Torres Strait Light Infantry Battalion (TSLIB). Almost every able-bodied Islander man in the Torres Strait – over 700 volunteers – joined the TSLIB, with only around 10 men staying behind to protect their families.

After the war, some members of the Kaurareg community returned from Moa Island to Ngurapai, where they established a community at Wasaga on the north-western side. They survived by fishing and selling firewood on Thursday Island, while protesting all attempts to remove them. In 1969 the community achieved recognition when the Horn Island Village Council was elected.

Information
The Gateway Torres Strait Resort (☎ 4069 2222, fax 4069 2211) is a good source of tourist information.

At the time of writing, a native title land claim on Ngurapai was being determined and if successful the Kaurareg may limit access to some areas. Contact the Torres Shire Council (☎ 4069 1336) for up-to-date information on the relevant local authority.

Organised Tours
The Gateway Torres Strait Resort (☎ 4069 2222) runs tours of Ngurapai, including a visit to the museum. The tour focuses on the WWII history of the island, including the TSLIB. It costs $39.60 with lunch ($23.20 without) and you can combine this with a tour of Thursday Island (see earlier).

Torres Strait Heritage Museum & Art Gallery
This excellent museum (☎ 4069 2222) at the Gateway Torres Strait Resort has detailed information on WWII, including photographs, records and a list of every member of the TSLIB. Islander carvings, art and artefacts are also on display, and there is a gallery of paintings illustrating traditional stories. Entry is $5.50/2.75 for adults/concession, or free to guests of the Gateway Torres Strait Resort or Elikiam Holiday Park (☎ 4069 2222).

Art and artefacts are on sale at the Gateway, including spears, carvings, jewellery, headdresses and T-shirts.

KERIRI (HAMMOND ISLAND)
History
The Kaurareg traditional owners were removed at gunpoint to Moa Island in 1922, to separate them from the developing administrative centre of Thursday Island.

In 1927 the Sacred Heart Fathers established a Catholic mission on Keriri for the pearl-diving community. The pearl-diving community were evacuated during WWII but returned to rebuild there and construct St Joseph's Church, consisting of 60,000 manually crushed and transported granite rocks.

TORRES STRAIT ISLANDS

THE DARI – OUR SYMBOL OF PEACE & UNITY

Adam Lees

The Torres Strait Islanders are renowned for their vibrant and unique costumes, especially the spectacular *dari* (traditional feathered headdress). The dari is prominently featured on the Torres Strait Islands flag. Consisting of a row of white feathers attached to an arched cane border, the dari sits on the forehead, tied around the head with plaited coconut-leaf twine or thin rope. The white feathers are clipped to represent fishtails. On top of the dari is a single black feather usually taken from a frigate bird. The vertical cane lines running across the centre of the dari symbolise the forehead crease lines – the lines of wisdom.

Although the dari is believed to have its origins on Mer (Murray Island, in the eastern Torres Strait), 19th-century literature suggests it was made in a similar pattern by other clan groups throughout the Torres Strait. It is ironic that the dari is often referred to as the 'headdress of peace', as it was traditionally donned by Torres Strait Island warriors during interclan warfare. The Melanesian custom known as 'payback' (revenge killings or attacks against other island clans) was the cause of much interisland warfare prior to the arrival of foreigners.

In the late 1800s, with the arrival of missionaries and other foreigners to the Torres Strait, the dari underwent a functional change from warrior attire to dance apparel. Access to new durable materials sparked a wave of creativity that saw the traditional cane frames replaced with plywood, tin plates, vinyl sheeting and even cardboard. Beads and other synthetic substances are also used as decorations.

Although the purpose and design of the dari has changed considerably over the years, the 'headdress of peace' remains the most powerful and sacred cultural symbol of the Torres Strait Islands. You can still see the traditional dari and its modern variations during certain celebrations such as the annual Coming of the Light festival in July.

Adam Lees

Mount Isa is home to the former Australian diplomat and Queensland University of Technology Business graduate, Adam Lees. Adam spent three years on a diplomatic posting in Samoa and has also travelled to other far-flung places in the Pacific.

He is active in Indigenous issues in his community and is currently employed as senior Indigenous affairs adviser with Mount Isa Mines. He is a descendant of the Meriam people of Mer in the Torres Strait and also has family connections with the Aboriginal people of Cape York Peninsula.

Adam is an avid collector of original Aboriginal and Torres Strait Islander art. His other consuming passions include surfing the Net, gardening and travelling.

Permits & Information

For information contact the Hammond Island Community Council (☎ 4069 1301, fax 4069 1692), PO Box 191, Thursday Island. If you wish to visit independently, contact the council one week in advance for a permit. At the time of writing you could only visit Keriri on a day trip; however the community was planning to develop a camping ground.

Organised Tours

A guided tour of Hammond Island visits the church and cemetery and includes a display of local arts and crafts and island dancing, although the latter is cut out if the tour runs out of time. The tour costs $39.50; contact Torres Strait Tours (☎ 1800 420 666 toll free, fax 4069 1408) at the Rebel Wharf on Thursday Island, or the Hammond Island Community Council.

Outer Islands

The inhabited outer islands are not too difficult to visit, but you must plan well in advance. These tropical islands, some of them sitting on their own coral reefs, have virtually no tourist infrastructure and very few people make the effort to see this gorgeous part of the world. But the chance to catch a glimpse of life in an isolated island community is exactly what makes the islands so appealing. The other main attractions are fishing and the beaches (watch out for sharks!).

Islanders are usually incredibly hospitable and proud of their culture. You could even find yourself learning how to weave a basket or invited along on a fishing trip. In some cases the relevant island council can arrange these sorts of activities for you. Many of the councils have plans in place to develop tourism, so the information provided here may change as the outer islands become easier to visit.

PERMITS & RESTRICTIONS

You must get permission from the relevant island council to visit any of the outer islands. The councils vary in their approach to travellers, eg, you can only make a day trip to certain islands and some councils don't allow visitors at all. At the time of writing, Poruma, Warraber and Masig were among the most open to visitors – see the individual island entries for contact details, plus the Travel Permits section in the Facts for the Visitor chapter.

Most islands have guesthouses run by the council with modern kitchen and bathroom facilities, but you must be self-catering. There is an IBIS supermarket on every inhabited island with limited supplies and EFTPOS facilities for purchases. Otherwise, you must bring everything with you, bearing in mind that there's usually a luggage limit of 16kg on the light planes operating in the strait.

Respect the privacy of Islanders during your visit. Ask permission before taking photographs and try to stay in public areas (sometimes people don't have fences around their yards).

GETTING THERE & AWAY

Most of the inhabited islands have an airstrip and there are quite a few airlines operating light aircraft in the strait. Many have scheduled services or you can charter a plane (expensive), or a boat or helicopter (also costly). Most airlines won't allow you to book a ticket before you have obtained permission from the relevant council to visit the island. For scheduled flights, you can expect to pay around (return flight) $530 for Ngurapai-Erub, $374 for Ngurapai-Poruma and $462 for Ngurapai-Masig. Sunstate (☎ 4069 1264) is linked to Qantas and operates daily flights between Cairns and Ngurapai. Skytrans runs a direct flight between Cairns and Masig.

The following airlines operate in the Torres Strait:

Aero-Tropics	☎ 4035 9138
Cape York Air	☎ 4069 2973
Northern Air Services	☎ 4069 2777
Skytrans Airlines	☎ 4069 2033
Torres Strait Airlines	☎ 4069 2121

Note that you cannot travel to Papua New Guinea from the northern islands of the Torres Strait, you must go back to Cairns and pass through normal quarantine and customs processes.

MOA

Moa is one of the largest islands in the Torres Strait and has two separate communities – Kubin and St Pauls.

Kubin

The Kubin Community Council does not currently allow travellers to visit. For information contact the Kubin Community Council (☎ 4069 4295, fax 4069 4272) via Post Office, Thursday Island.

St Pauls

The community celebrates St Paul's Day with a church service, feasting and dancing on 25 January, which visitors are welcome to attend. St Paul's Church was built by local villagers using mangrove wood for the roof trusses and mortar made by burning coral.

TORRES STRAIT ISLANDS

POPULATION

Population figures* for the Torres Strait Islands are:

Inner Islands

Waiben (Thursday Island)	2300
Ngurapai (Horn Island)	600
Keriri (Hammond Island)	225

Outer Islands

Moa	560
Badu	825
Mabuiag	210
Boigu	340
Dauan	164
Saibai	379
Warraber (Sue Island)	237
Iama (Yam Island)	400
Poruma (Coconut Island)	188
Masig (Yorke Island)	288
Mer (Murray Island)	450
Erub (Darnley Island)	375
Ugar (Stephen Island)	50

* Torres Strait Regional Authority

The airstrip on Moa is near Kubin, a 30-minute drive from St Pauls. Advise the council that you need to be picked up by the bus ($44 one way).

The council may also be able to arrange a tour of the island.

Permits & Information Contact the St Pauls Island Council (☎ 4069 4124, fax 4069 4100) via Post Office, Thursday Island, at least three weeks in advance to request permission to visit the community.
Web site: www.stpaulscouncil.com

BADU

Badu, a large island in the western group of islands, has a motel where you can stay in a room with an attached bathroom and a shared kitchen for $66/88/110 for singles/doubles/family.

Japanese B encephalitis has occurred on Badu Island in recent years, so if you plan to travel here contact your doctor for up-to-date information on this infectious disease.

Permits & Information

For permission to visit the island, contact the Badu Island Council (☎ 4069 4214, fax 4069 4121) via Post Office, Thursday Island, four weeks in advance.

MABUIAG

Stone arrangements were traditionally used to mark clan territory on Mabuiag and a stone crocodile (at the top of the hill beside the airstrip) and stone shark (at Point Naeman) are still maintained. There is limited accommodation in the guesthouse for $25 per night.

The Rams Skull Press (☎ 4093 7474) has published *An Explorer's Guide to Mabuiag Island* in collaboration with Mabuiag State School.

Permits & Information

Write to the Mabuiag Island Council (☎ 4069 4184, fax 4069 4111) via Post Office, Thursday Island, at least four weeks in advance if you want to visit.

BOIGU

Dominated by mangrove wetlands, Boigu is subject to widespread flooding in the Wet season. The island is only a few kilometres from the Papua New Guinea coast and there are strong cultural ties with the communities across the border.

Permits & Information

Contact the Boigu Island Council (☎ 4069 4093, fax 4069 4079) via Post Office, Thursday Island, for permission to make a day trip. Your application should be in writing, at least four weeks in advance.

DAUAN

Dauan is the northernmost tip of Australia's Great Dividing Range, According to Torres Strait stories, it was formed from the head of the giant man-eating snake Norinori when he was dropped into the sea by two eagles.

There is no airstrip on Dauan and at the time of writing the council was not allowing travellers to visit, but this may change as it plans to develop a resort. For details, contact Dauan Island Council (☎ 4069 4266, fax 4069 4257) via Post Office, Thursday Island.

SAIBAI

Saibai is just 3km from the Papua New Guinea coast. The island regularly hosts markets where Islanders and people from Papua New Guinea sell artwork, drums and mud crabs. Limited accommodation is available in a *donga* (temporary or portable building; $30) or guesthouse ($40).

Permits & Information
If you want to visit the island you should contact the Saibai Island Council (☎ 4069 4270, fax 4069 3180) via Post Office, Thursday Island, at least two weeks in advance.

WARRABER (SUE ISLAND)
Warraber sits in an extensive coral reef in the central islands. Visitors can stay at the guesthouse, which costs $60 per night with all meals included, or $40 without meals. The council may be able to arrange for a tour of the island including a visit to a sacred site and an arts and crafts demonstration. Enquire in advance.

Permits & Information
Call the Warraber Community Council (☎ 4069 4177, fax 4069 4183) via Post Office, Thursday Island, to arrange for permission and accommodation. If you have a large group you need to call one week in advance; with a small group you can call one or two days ahead.

IAMA (YAM ISLAND)
Surrounded by its own coral reef, Iama does not currently have facilities for visitors, although the council has plans for a hotel and arts and craft centre. Contact the Yam Island Community Council (☎ 4069 4195, fax 4069 4224) via Post Office, Thursday Island, for more information.

PORUMA (COCONUT ISLAND)
Just 1.4km long and 400m wide, the Poruma Island community has strong links with the Warraber community, who moved from Poruma due to a water shortage in the 1920s. Today an upgraded water supply has solved the problem and the council is actively encouraging visitors.

There's a guesthouse on the island ($44) and at the time of writing the council was developing top-end beachfront accommodation, due to open in 2001. The cost will be around $600 to $800 per night and there will be a strong focus on Islander culture.

Visitors will be invited to learn traditional cooking techniques with members of the local community. There are also plans for a camping ground (check with the council for details).

Permits & Information
Contact the Coconut Island Council (☎ 4069 4277, fax 4069 4280) via Post Office, Thursday Island, two weeks in advance for information and permission to visit.

Organised Tours
OzTours (☎ 1800 079 006 toll free, fax 4055 9918) includes a day trip to Coconut Island as part of its seven- and 12-day fly/drive tours of Cape York. See Organised Tours in the Cairns section of the Queensland chapter for more information, or check its Web site at www.oztours.com.au.

MASIG (YORKE ISLAND)
In 1936 this coral cay was the venue for an all-island maritime strike, with workers in the fishing, trochus and pearling industries demanding better conditions. It was one of the first moves towards autonomy in the Torres Strait and is commemorated every year on 23 August (see History section, earlier).

Today, the island is the base for fish and prawn trawlers. There are two guesthouses, which cost $25 per night, and with prior notice the council can arrange carving and weaving demonstrations.

Skytrans (4090 2033) operates direct flights between Cairns and Masig six days a week for $726 return.

Permits & Information
Write to the Yorke Island Community Council (☎ 4069 4128, fax 4069 4135, ℮ yorkecouncil@bigpond.com) via Post Office, Thursday Island, four weeks in advance if you want to visit.

MER (MURRAY ISLAND)
The home of Eddie Mabo, this island was the subject of the landmark Mabo decision in 1992. At this stage there are no facilities for tourists on Mer and the council does not allow travellers to visit.

ERUB (DARNLEY ISLAND)
Erub, in the eastern group, is of volcanic origin. It was here that members of the

London Missionary Society landed in 1871. See Special Events and the boxed text 'The Coming of the Light' at the beginning of this chapter for details of the island-wide festival that celebrates this event.

Norah's Ark (☎ 4069 4032) offers twin rooms for $75 per person, including three meals. There is no council accommodation for travellers.

Permits & Information
Contact the Darnley Island Council (☎ 4069 4001, fax 4069 4000) via Post Office, Thursday Island, four weeks in advance for more information and permission to visit. It may be able to arrange a cultural tour of the island for around $50.

UGAR (STEPHEN ISLAND)
This island is volcanic in origin and surrounded by a coral reef. Limited beachfront accommodation is available for $25 to $30 and the council may be able to organise a traditional arts and crafts demonstration.

There is no airstrip on Ugar, so you must arrange a boat from Masig or Erub. The trip from Masig takes up to an hour, and the Stephen Island Community Council can help you to arrange it (costs are negotiable).

Permits & Information
Call the Stephen Island Community Council (☎ 4069 4023, fax 4069 4029) via Post Office, Thursday Island, at least two weeks in advance if you'd like to visit Ugar.

Victoria

There are over 20,000 Koories (Aborigines from south-eastern Australia) as well as Torres Strait Islanders and Aborigines from other parts of Australia living in Victoria. More than half live in Melbourne. Significant Koorie populations are also found in Mildura, Robinvale, Swan Hill, Echuca, Shepparton, Bairnsdale, Orbost and Warrnambool. There are also several independent Koorie communities around the state, including those at Lake Condah, Lake Tyers and Framlingham.

History

Philip Morrissey

Victoria's Aboriginal population before 1788 is thought to have been around 60,000 people and possibly as high as 100,000. Ten distinct languages were spoken and there were 38 dialect groups (see the Language section in this chapter).

As with other mainland tribes, Victorian Aborigines ate a wide variety of foodstuffs. Diet varied according to region; in south-west Victoria coastal people added seals and beached whales to their diet while Aborigines living inland supplemented their diet with lerp – an insect secretion found in large quantities in mallee scrub. On the Murray River near Swan Hill, Aborigines dug channels and built wooden weirs to trap fish, and at Lake Condah in the Western District the Gunditjmara built stone channels to harvest migrating eels and other fish. Stone dwellings were also used in this area and possum-skin cloaks were worn in many parts of Victoria.

Local clans would often meet to coincide with the cyclical occurrence of natural foods such as the appearance of Bogong moths in the High Country. An important stone quarry, at Mt William near Lancefield, provided greenstone which the Kulin people used to make axe-heads and trade with neighbouring tribes.

Smallpox transmitted by European settlers at the time of the first settlement in the Sydney region had ravaged the Victorian Aborigines even before the arrival of Batman and Fawkner (see European Invasion, and the boxed text 'Batman Went a'Robbin': the Tale

NEW SOUTH WALES

Melbourne pp360-1

of a Failed Private Adventurer', later). Once Europeans settled permanently in Victoria, whooping cough, measles and influenza wreaked havoc and venereal disease played a major role in curbing Koorie population growth. By the 1880s Victoria's Aboriginal population was just over 800 people – a testimony to the toxic effect of Europeans.

VICTORIA

VICTORIA

1 Organised Tours; Mildura Arts
    Centre; Tulklana Kumbi Aboriginal Gallery
2 Organised Tours; Manatunga Artefacts
3 Tyntynder Homestead
4 Murray Outback Aboriginal Cultural Trail
5 Pirrewil Kurruk CDEP Artefact Shop
6 Kevin Williams Gallery
7 Barmah State Park; Dharnya Centre;
    Loatbaty Yarwul Tours;
    Seven Sisters Dreaming
8 Bangerang Keeping Place
9 Wiradjuri Walkabout Trail;
    Gateway Information
    Centre; Organised Tours
10 Mt Pilot; Yeddonba Aboriginal
    Rock Art Walking Trail
11 The Burke Museum
12 Baranjuk Organised Tours; Artefacts
    & Crafts Shop

NEW SOUTH WALES

MURRAY RIVER

Wentworth   Dareton
             Buronga
    Mildura **1**

To Adelaide

A20   Calder

A79   Sturt Hwy

Sunset Country

Hattah-
Kulkyne
NP

Murray-Sunset
NP

Hattah

Ouyen   Hwy

Mallee

B12

Big Desert

Wyperfeld
NP

Big
Desert
Wilderness
Park

Lake
Albacutya

B220

Lake
Tyrrell

Sea
Lake

Samarpia

Calder

Robinvale **2**

Balranald

B400

Murray

Tyntynder **3**

Swan Hill **4**

MURRAY RIVER

Deniliquin

75

5

Kerang   Cohuna
          Hwy

Loddon   Valley

Kow
Swamp

7

Barmah

B400

Echuca   **6**   Goulburn

SOUTH AUSTRALIA

To Adelaide;

Hopetoun

Rainbow

Lake
Hindmarsh

B200

Warracknabeal

Antwerp   Boung   Henty

Nhill

A8

Dimboola **14**

Little Desert
NP

Mt Arapiles
(369m)

Mt Arapiles
- Tooan Park   C240

Naracoorte

Edenhope **16**

Harrow

Horsham **15**

Wycheproof

Lake
Buloke

Charlton

Wedderburn

Inglewood
St Arnaud

B240

Avoca

17   Mt Gar
         (810m)   Stawell

18   Halls
         Gap

Grampians NP
(Gariwerd)

19

Ararat

20

21   Langi
         Ghiran SP

Pyrenees

Avoca   B180

Maryborough

Maldon

Hwy

Castlemaine

Elmore

Whipstick
State Park

Bendigo   **13**

Heathcote

Waranga
Reservoir

Murchison

Nagambie

A39

Lake
Eppalock

Seymour

River

Hume

To Adelaide   A1

Mt
Gambier   B160

Nelson

Discovery
Bay

Glenelg   Henty

Casterton

Glenelg   Hwy

23 Dunkeld

Hamilton

Lower
Glenelg
NP

Heywood

Portland

Cape
Bridgewater   Cape
               Nelson

Mt Napier
(440m)

Lake
Condah

Mt Eccles
NP

B120

Yambuk   Port
          Fairy   **26**

24

25

27

Princes

Rocklands
Reservoir

17

Lake Bolac

Lake
Bolac

Beaufort   A8

Western

B160

22

Daylesford

GREAT

Kyneton

Wallan

Kinglake
NP

M79   M31

Hume

Ballarat

A300   Western   M8   Brisbane
                         Ranges
                         NP

Fwy

Midland

MELBOURNE

Yarra   M1

Port
Phillip

Dandenong

B140

Lismore

Mortlake

Hwy

Lake
Corangamite

Colac

Framlingham   **28**

Warrnambool

Great

Peterborough

Port Campbell

Port
Campbell
NP

Otway
NP

Cape Otway

Apollo
Bay

B100

Ocean   Rd

29

Anglesea
Aireys Inlet

Angahook-
Lorne SP

30   Lorne

33   Geelong

Queenscliff

31   Torquay

32

A1

34

M1

Mornington

Rosebud   Cowes

Cape
Schanck   Phillip
           Island

BASS   STRAIT

SOUTHERN   OCEAN

VICTORIA

VICTORIA

13 Bendigo Art Gallery; Local Artwork
14 Organised Tours; Ebenezer Mission
15 Goolum Goolum Aboriginal
   Co-operative; Werrimul Arts & Crafts
16 Johnny Mullagh Memorial Cairn
17 Rock Art Sites (Gariwerd)
18 Brambuk Aboriginal Cultural
   Centre; Organised Tours
19 Bunjil's Shelter
20 Langi Morgala Museum
21 Rock Art; Scarr Trees
22 Aboriginal Dreamtime Trails
23 Historical Museum
24 Eumeralla Backpackers
25 Maleen; Deen Maar
26 Tower Hill Natural History Centre
27 Gunditjmara Aboriginal
   Co-operative; Organised Tours;
   Thunder Point Coastal Reserve

28 Framlingham Aboriginal Trust
29 Rock Art; Middens;
   Organised Tours
30 Point Addis Koorie Cultural Walk
31 Bells Beach; Glenn Romanis Mural
32 Sundial of Human Involvement
33 Wathaurong Aboriginal
   Co-operative; Organised Tours;
   Yollinko Park Aboriginal Garden
34 You Yangs Regional Park
35 Coranderrk Cemetery
36 Nature Bound Tours; Flamin' Bull
   Restaurant
37 Ninde Dana Quarenook
   Aboriginal Co-operative;
   Latrobe Regional Gallery;
   Yandina Earth
38 Ramahyuck District Aboriginal
   Corporation; Gippsland Art Gallery;

   Bataluk Cultural Trail
39 The Knob Reserve
40 Den of Nargun Walking Trail
41 Gippsland & East Gippsland
   Aboriginal Co-operative;
   Boran Glaat Cultural
   Tours; Krowathunkoolong
   Keeping Place; Gruannunnerrang
   Aboriginal Art Gallery & Arts
   Workshop; Howitt Park Scarr Trees
42 Legend Rock
43 The Lakes Entrance Aboriginal
   Arts Group
44 Burnt Bridge Reserve
45 Moogji Aboriginal Council;
   Croajingolong Wilderness
   Tours; Koorie Plant Use Trail
46 Shell Midden; Self-Guided Walk

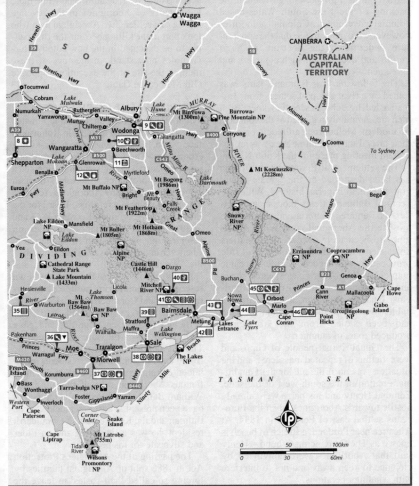

EUROPEAN INVASION

Port Phillip Bay was first surveyed in 1802 but permanent European settlement did not occur until 1835, when John Batman, in exchange for items such as knives, blankets and flour, claimed to have 'purchased' 202,430 hectares of land from the Boon wurrung and Woi wurrung chiefs of the Kulin Nation, a confederation of related tribal groups. If the event actually took place, the chiefs were actually engaging in the practice of *tanderrum*, a ceremony granting strangers the right to travel through Kulin country. Batman's venture was carried out as a private citizen without the backing of the New South Wales-based colonial government. Colonial authorities however were quick to see that the apparent sale undermined the doctrine of *terra nullius* and declared all such contracts and agreements void.

The following year Batman's party was joined by a rival group of settlers from Tasmania led by John Pascoe Fawkner. Both men are commonly regarded as the founders of modern Melbourne, although prior to their arrival the Melbourne area was an important meeting place for the Kulin Nation.

The settlement of Europeans in Victoria has been described as the 'greatest land grab in British imperial history'. Within 10 years of Batman's treaty thousands of settlers had entered Victoria and claimed the most fertile Aboriginal land. When Aborigines resisted their displacement, settlers unleashed frightening violence. Little provocation was needed – settlers became homicidal when Aborigines speared sheep and were convinced of their right to Aboriginal land. At Hamilton, a statement at a public meeting in the 1860s that the land had been stolen from the Aborigines produced roars of laughter.

The Gunai/Kurnai people of Gippsland were victims of repeated massacres, and the situation was no different for the Gunditjmara nation in the south-west of the state. Edmund Henty and his party were already hostile towards Aborigines when the Europeans settled east of Portland in 1834. At Allestree near Portland, a stretch of beach is known as The Convincing Ground – Henty said that Aborigines were convinced by violence to keep away and not to interfere with whaling operations.

Concerned by the colony's treatment of Aborigines, the English House of Commons directed that a protectorate be established to look after Aboriginal interests. The Protectors were to ingratiate themselves with Aborigines, encourage Indigenous people in building permanent homes and agriculture, and instruct in Christianity. George Augustus Robinson, who had persuaded Tasmanian Aborigines to follow him to Wybalenna (see History in the Tasmania chapter), was rewarded for his successes with the position of Chief Protector of the Port Phillip Protectorate in 1838. He was accompanied by Truganini, who while there led a party of Aborigines in the revenge killing of a settler. Two Aboriginal men who took part in the killing became the first people to be executed in the new colony. Burial poles now stand, in memory of these men, at the site of the executions opposite Old Melbourne Gaol.

ESTABLISHMENT OF RESERVES

The ineffectual Protectorate was terminated in 1849 – settlers had laughed in Robinson's face when he reproached them for killing Aborigines. The Central Board for Aborigines replaced it in 1860, and implemented a strategy of 'protecting' Aborigines through segregation. The 1869 Aborigines Act gave coercive powers to a reformed Board for the Protection of Aborigines. Between 1861 and 1880 it placed Victorian Aborigines on reserves run by Christian missionaries at Ebenezer in the north-west, Lake Condah in the Western District, Lake Tyers and Ramahyuck in Gippsland and its own reserves at Framlingham, north-east of Warrnambool, and Coranderrk near Healesville.

These reserves developed into self-sufficient farming communities and gave their residents a measure of protection. Though they were under the control of the Board and missionaries, the residents maintained cultural continuity. One of the most famous Aboriginal men of this time was William Barak. As a boy he was reputed to have been present at the agreement between Batman and the Kulin chiefs. A Coranderrk resident, he was a fine artist and an Elder and advocate for his people.

The passing of the Aborigines Protection Act in 1886 split up Aboriginal families by forcing so-called 'half-castes' to leave the

Philip Morrissey

KOORIE CULTURE

Recent years have seen the development of important Indigenous cultural initiatives in Victoria. In Melbourne the Koorie Heritage Trust, established in 1985, has collected many examples of Victorian Aboriginal art and culture. Melbourne Museum's Bunjilaka Indigenous centre features a comprehensive exhibition on all aspects of Victorian Aboriginal life and history (see the boxed text 'Bunjilaka' in this chapter). In the north of the state, the Yorta Yorta community maintains the Dharnya Centre, in the Barmah State Park. The Brambuk Aboriginal Cultural Centre in the Grampians provides tours of rock art sites and maintains a permanent exhibition (see the relevant sections in this chapter for more details on all these places).

reserves. These people were not allowed to return to visit their families without official permission. Under the Aborigines Protection Act of 1910 the Board was given further powers over Aborigines, including the right to remove Aboriginal children from their families.

In 1939 some of the residents of Cummeragunja Reserve on the New South Wales border staged a 'walk-off' in protest at the administration of the reserve. They settled on the Victorian side of the border at a site which became known as The Flat. Similarly, families left Lake Tyers and settled at a place near Drouin, in the Gippsland region, known as Jackson's Track, which was later to achieve prominence as the home of Australia's first Aboriginal world boxing champion, Lionel Rose.

KOORIE DEMANDS FOR JUSTICE & LAND

At the same time, organisations were formed. The Australian Aborigines League (AAL) was at the forefront of Aboriginal activism when it was created in 1932. It advocated for the rights of Aborigines in Victoria and nationally, and as a protest against Aboriginal exclusion from the Jubilee celebrations of 1951, the AAL produced a theatre production, *An Aboriginal Moomba*. The production showcased the best Aboriginal talent of the day. In 1958 the Victorian Aboriginal Advancement League was formed by Indigenous and non-Indigenous people to represent Victorian Koories and provide social services.

Victorian Aborigines have made repeated demands for compensation and numerous attempts to claim back their land, but only a minuscule portion of land has ever been

returned by the state. Under the terms of existing native title legislation, possibilities for successful land claims are limited and the failure of the Yorta Yorta people's native title bid – which was seen as a strong claim – was a severe setback. In future, Indigenous land use agreements may offer a more flexible alternative for practical recognition of Aboriginal sovereignty.

Language

The language spoken in the area covering Melbourne north almost to Echuca on the Murray River is Woi wurrung (for the dialect south of the Great Dividing Range) or Thagungwurrung (for the dialect north of the range). Other important languages of Victoria included Wathawurrung, spoken near Geelong; Wemba-Wemba in the Mallee region; Bunganditj in the south-west corner of Victoria; and Muk Thang, the language of the Gunai (also spelled Kurnai) of Gippsland.

Victoria's Aboriginal population was largely decimated within a few years of European settlement in 1835. Today there are no fluent speakers of an Aboriginal language, and no language from this area is used as the main means of communication within a community. However, words and expressions from traditional languages are still in use, especially in country areas. In many communities there's an increasing interest in traditional languages and culture, and efforts are under way to preserve and maintain any remaining knowledge.

Visitors to Victoria will encounter traces of traditional Aboriginal languages in three areas: in the continuing use of Aboriginal language words and expressions, in names for places and features of the landscape, and in Aboriginal words that have entered the English language and are in common use by all Australians.

Some place names borrowed into English from Victorian Aboriginal languages include:

Allambee	mishearing of **ngalambi** ('to remain/dwell'); town near Yarragon, Gippsland
Boort	('smoke'); town in Mallee, north-western Victoria
Koorumburra	('march fly'); town in Gippsland
Lara	('stone'); town north of Geelong
Leongatha	('our teeth'); town in Gippsland
Mirboo	('kidney'); town in Gippsland
Narre Warren	('red'); suburb south-east of Melbourne
Wollert	('possum'); place north of Melbourne
Wonthaggi	('Fetch!'); town on the Gippsland coast

Other words from Victorian languages that have entered Standard Australian English include:

bunyip	a mythical swamp-dwelling creature
cumbungi	bulrush
dillon bush	a plant
lerp	a form of scale or insect secretion
lowan	mallee fowl
tuan	gliding possum
yabby	a crustacean

USEFUL CONTACTS

Victorian State Language Committee (☎ 9663 9294) Level 3, 210 Lonsdale St, Melbourne, Vic 3000

Information

INDIGENOUS ORGANISATIONS

VICNET's Web network, a state government-run information site, has an Indigenous page at www.vicnet.net.au/aboriginal. It provides links to Indigenous Victorian, national and international Web pages, and is well worth a click.

Defenders of Native Title is the Victorian arm of Australians for Native Title and Reconciliation (ANTaR) and can be contacted on ☎ 9419 3613 – see Information in the Facts for the Visitor chapter for full details.

See also the Facts for the Visitor chapter for other relevant nationwide Indigenous organisations.

NATIONAL PARKS

Most national parks in Victoria (including those covered in this chapter) are free to enter. For more information, contact Parks Victoria on ☎ 131 963, Web site www.parkweb .vic.gov.au.

BOOKS

The highly recommended *Koorie Plants – Koorie People* by Beth Gott & Nelly Zola details traditional plants, their uses and some traditional non-plant foods. It's published by the Koorie Heritage Trust (see Indigenous Organisations in the Kulin Nation section later).

Fraynework Multimedia produces the impressive *Lore of the Land* CD-ROM, a lavish, encyclopedic resource that explores Australians' connection to the land. It investigates legal, cultural, social and historical issues with ingenious Web links to the latest updated information. For an extremely worthwhile $90, it can be ordered at www.loreoftheland.com.au.

Organised Tours

The Aboriginal-owned and -operated Aboriginal Dreamtime Trails in Ballarat can arrange tours from Melbourne to all parts of Victoria with local Aboriginal guides. Tours range from one-day walks around Melbourne to longer excursions around Victoria. Informal discussions about traditional and contemporary Aboriginal issues are encouraged. Tours can be tailor-made and advance bookings are essential. For details and prices, ring Steve Johnson (☎ 5342 8788, fax 5342 8719) or visit the Web site at www.ballarat.com/dreamtime.htm.

Kulin Nation

Melbourne Region

MELBOURNE

The Kulin (meaning The People or Man) nation is made up of language clans that include the Woi wurrung and Boon wurrung. The 'wurrung' in these names means 'language', and it is this language that binds the peoples of the Kulin nation together. This distinguishes them from, for example, the neighbouring Kurnai (Gunai), who occupy the Gippsland region east of the Kulin nation. Within these language groupings smaller clusters of peoples, including the Wurundjeri, occupied certain areas of land in the Kulin nation.

Information

Indigenous Organisations The Koorie Heritage Trust (☎ 9639 6555), 234–236 Flinders Lane, is a highly recommended cultural centre in the central city. It boasts an impressive collection of historical artefacts, relics and contemporary pieces from Victoria. Its shop sells an excellent range of Indigenous items from around the state. Call ahead for a tour of the collection ($4.40 per person) or drop in to view its impressive exhibitions. It's open 9.30 am to 4.30 pm weekdays (from 10 am on Monday); entry is by donation.

Lumbu Indigenous Community Foundation (☎ 9639 6272, fax 9639 8236, ⓔ lumbu @connect.net.au), 165 Flinders Lane in the city centre, is a wonderful, newly established nongovernment organisation that supports Indigenous community development. It doesn't offer unequivocal tourist information, but is happy to talk about its projects, and could offer you a link into what's going on at a grass-roots level. Lumbu is a trust fund and relies on donations (tax-deductible for Australians).

University Associations Students for Land Justice and Reconciliation (known more commonly by its acronym, SLJR – pronounced 'sledger') is the University of Melbourne's impressive student action group. Throughout the university year (from around March to October) it conducts a great range of informative forums and film festivals, and facilitates involvement in local protests. Details can be found on its excellent Web site: www.sljr.org.

Tourist Offices The Victorian Visitors Information Centre (☎ 9658 9658), in the Melbourne Town Hall building on the corner of Swanston and Little Collins Sts, provides some information (brochures, maps etc) on Indigenous attractions around Melbourne and Victoria. It's open 9 am to 6 pm weekdays and to 5 pm on weekends. However, the Koorie Heritage Trust (see earlier), just a five-minute walk south on Swanston St, provides a better, more specific service.

Libraries Aboriginal Affairs Victoria (☎ 9616 2903, fax 9616 2954), 7th floor, 589 Collins St, has the Alick Jackomos Library, with a good range of publications. Library hours are 9.30 am to 12.30 pm and 1.30 to 4.30 pm Monday to Thursday, or by appointment. Its Web page at www.nre.vic.gov.au/aav has a catalogue search engine and a list of its Victorian-specific publications.

South-east of the city centre, Monash University's Centre for Australian Indigenous Studies has the fantastic Elizabeth Eggleston Memorial Library (☎ 9905 5234), 2nd floor, Gallery Building, Clayton Campus, with a great range of Indigenous Australian resources (journals, texts, newspapers). It's open 9 am to 4.30 pm weekdays (closed 1 to 2 pm). You can't borrow resources, but material can be photocopied.

Books Meyer Eidelson's *The Melbourne Dreaming* guide is concise and insightful, detailing more than 50 of Melbourne's Indigenous places. This well-researched guide is available from major bookshops in and around Melbourne.

Radio 3CR Radio is a public radio station (855 AM; ☎ 9419 8377) with an exciting, ever-changing mob of Indigenous radio hosts and programs that deal with everything from football to politics. Programs include *Not Another Koori Show* (2 pm Monday), *Ilbijerri Chat* (9 am Tuesday), the *Koori Survival Show* (noon Wednesday), *Stone Free* (1 pm Thursday), *Songlines* (2 pm Thursday) and *Marngrook* (5.30 pm Friday).

At the time of writing Indigenous Melburnians were applying to get a full-time broadcasting license for their aspirant community station 3 Kool N Deadly (3KND; 90.7 FM). Try tuning in or call Michelle Evans at Songlines Music (☎ 9696 2022) for an update.

Organised Tours

Koonarang Tours provides extensive site tours around the south-east of Melbourne,

BATMAN WENT A'ROBBIN': THE TALE OF A FAILED PRIVATE ADVENTURER

Graham Fricke

The name Batman has been immortalized in a number of European titles and place names. There is an array of streets, parks and suburbs named after one of Melbourne's early founders. Whether John Batman deserves this tribute is open to debate.

The son of a convict, he left New South Wales at the age of 20, and lived in Tasmania for the next 18 years, apart from visits to Victoria. He distinguished himself by taking part in the infamous 'Black Line', conceived by Governor Arthur. This line was designed to drive Tasmania's Aborigines into the neck of the Tasman Peninsula and take them into custody, although it was a ridiculous failure. About four years later, Batman sailed from Launceston to Port Phillip, taking with him two Illawarra Aborigines.

In 1835 at Port Philip, he claimed to have entered into a treaty with local chiefs for the transfer of a huge parcel of land – running from present-day Port Melbourne to Mt Macedon and Flowerdale and totaling 202,430 hectares – in exchange for a number of items:

20 pairs of blankets	30 mirrors
30 tomahawks	200 handkerchiefs
100 knives	100 lb of flour
50 pairs of scissors	6 shirts

Batman maintained that he solemnised this transaction, and another involving land near Geelong, by conducting a ceremony in which soil and twigs were handed over and by having the chiefs insert their marks on two deeds.

Whether or not such a ceremony did take place – and a number of historians have charged Batman with fraud in this respect – the claim is interesting in that it reflects the reality of the Aborigines' prior occupation of the land. It negates the factual basis of the prevailing British theory that the land was *terra nullius* (no-one's land) and was thus capable of being acquired by peaceful settlement rather than conquest.

Batman returned to Tasmania where he wrote to Lord Glenelg, the Secretary of State for the Colonies. In that letter, he conceded this reality when he wrote that he had 'obtained from the chiefs of the tribe who are in fact the owners of the soil a title based on equity principles, the constructive right to the land in question'.

The authorities were neither impressed nor amused. In August 1835, Governor Bourke issued a proclamation declaring void 'every such treaty, bargain and contract with the Aboriginal Natives...for the possession, title or claim to any Lands'. Lord Glenelg supported Bourke's response, stating that the government should not recognise that the Aborigines had 'any right to alienate to private adventurers the Land of the Colony'.

Batman suffered an ignominious end. He became so incapacitated – probably from cerebrovascular syphilis – that he had to be wheeled around in a specially designed perambulator by two Sydney Aborigines. He died in 1839, not yet 39 years of age.

For more information on the Black Line, see the History section in the Tasmania chapter.

including shell middens near Beaumaris, Black Rock and Half-Moon Bay; the 'famous' Batman treaty signing site along the Merri Creek in Northcote; and bush plants and foods in Churchill National Park near Dandenong. Indigenous guide Gene Blow provides half-/full-day tours from $385/550 for groups of around 20. Call ☎ 0412 190 428 for a specially tailored tour. Dance performances can be also arranged. You'll need your own transport (prices on application).

Author Meyer Eidelson (☎ 9690 9584, e meyereidelson@yahoo.com), who wrote

The Melbourne Dreaming (see the Books section earlier under Information), offers historical group tours (half- or full-day) in and around Melbourne. Tours include information on archaeological and cultural places, plant food and wildlife uses and stone tool technology.

Art & About (☎ 0417 589 987) offers walking tours, often with Indigenous guides, which highlight the Indigenous art that can be viewed in Melbourne's galleries. Tours are conducted on demand (with a minimum group of 10) and are $25 per person, including refreshments. Meeting places for tours are arranged by phone, and wheelchair-accessible tours can be arranged.

The Eltham Living & Learning Centre (☎ 9349 3463), 739 Main Rd, Eltham, offers historical tours that cover a substantial amount of local Aboriginal heritage in the itinerary. Sites visited include a kangaroo ground, a *corroboree* (ceremonial festival) site and a visit to the important Coranderrk cemetery near Healesville. The seven-hour tours are run by an informative non-Indigenous guide, and include both transport and lunch for $30.80/26.40 adult/concession. Bookings are essential (maximum of 10 per tour).

Nature Bound Tours and the Flamin' Bull restaurant (see Places to Eat in this section) in Warragul, in the south-eastern part of the Kulin Nation, about 95km south-east of Melbourne, jointly offer a full-day tour (minimum four people) with Indigenous insights and a *didjeridu* (cylindrical wooden instrument traditionally played by Aboriginal men) performance provided by an Aboriginal guide. A highlight of the tour is exploring the Labertouche granite cave (moderate fitness required) in the lush Bunyip State Forest. Tours cost $120/65 for adults/children, which includes guides, entry to the cave, breakfast, gourmet bush tucker lunch and transfers from the Flamin' Bull restaurant. For tour bookings, contact ☎/fax 9786 6236, @ natbound@alphalink.com.au or @ rod@mrw.com.au.

See also the Organised Tours section at the beginning of this chapter for information on Aboriginal Dreamtime Trails, which runs tours around Melbourne and the surrounding area.

Walking Tours & Trails

The Aboriginal Heritage Walk through the Royal Botanic Gardens is a highly recommended stroll. The Indigenous-guided trail includes medicinal plants and plant foods as used by the area's traditional owners. The 1½-hour walks are conducted at 11 am Thursday and Friday, and on the occasional Sunday at 10.30 am and by appointment for groups. Costs are $15.40/6.60 per adult/child. Bookings are essential and can be made on ☎ 9252 2429.

The self-guided 'Another View' Walking Trail provides some excellent insights into Melbourne's living Indigenous heritage. A pamphlet (available at Melbourne's visitor information booths or from the Victorian Visitors Information Centre – see Tourist Offices earlier in this section) maps out the five-hour trail. Features include sites in the Queen Victoria Gardens and the often-laughable language of the historical Anglo-centric plaques. Also worth checking out are the tram control boxes around the city (on most street corners), many of which display the works of Indigenous artists.

Parks, Gardens & Scarr Trees

Fitzroy Gardens, east of the city centre on the corner of Wellington Parade and Clarendon St, has the stump of a beautiful **scarr tree** near the toilet block in its south-east. Ironically, a much younger testament to history (the cottage of Britain's Captain James Cook) is also in this park.

Yarra Park, near the Melbourne Cricket Ground (MCG) in East Melbourne, also houses two **scarr trees**, one near the top end of Vale St and the other uphill between Gates 6 and 7 of the MCG.

CERES (☎ 9387 2609), 8–10 Lee St, East Brunswick, has a range of indigenous plants throughout its grounds and a **Permaculture & Bushfood Nursery** (☎ 9387 4403) that sells indigenous plants (from $3), many of which are edible and have medicinal properties. The grounds are open daily during daylight hours (entry by donation) and the nursery is open 10 am to 5 pm daily. Guided tours and activities with Indigenous components can be organised (these are mainly for groups). See also the Special Events section later in this section for details of CERES' festivals.

Bundoora Park, north of the city on Plenty Rd in Bundoora, offers a good range

VICTORIA

MELBOURNE

INDIGENOUS SITES
1 CERES
2 Batman Treaty Site
3 Ilbijerri Aboriginal & Torres Strait
   Islander Theatre
4 Museum of Victoria
5 Fitzroy Stars Gymnasium
6 Scarr Tree
7 Scarr Trees
8 Wurundjeri Garden
9 Aboriginal Heritage Walks
10 Songlines Music
11 Corroboree Tree
12 The Flamin' Bull Australian Indigenous
   Restaurant-Carlton
13 National Gallery of Victoria on Russell
14 Alcaston House Gallery
15 Aboriginal Handcrafts
16 Victorian Visitors Information Centre
18 Gallery Gabrielle Pizzi
19 Lumbu Indigenous Community Foundation
20 The Koorie Heritage Trust
21 Aboriginal Affairs Victoria & Library

OTHER
17 Melbourne Town Hall

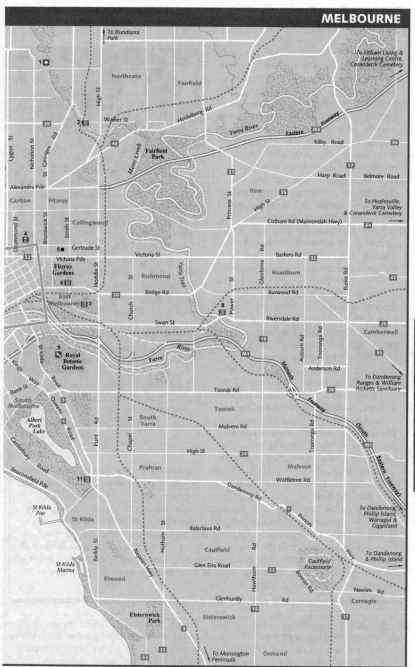

MELBOURNE

BUNJILAKA

Joseph Kennedy

Bunjilaka, Melbourne Museum's outstanding Indigenous centre, derives its name from two words of the Woi wurrung language meaning 'The land of Bunjil', the Creator Spirit of the region. Opened in October 2000, it is one of the best Indigenous spaces in any Australian museum.

Bunjilaka represents a radical reworking of the way in which Australia's Indigenous people are presented to the visiting public. As recently as the 1970s, Indigenous people had to suffer being portrayed by the old Museum of Victoria as historical phenomena – anthropological curiosities, rendered in plaster and housed in glass cases in the kinds of *in situ* poses still seen on tacky tea-towel and apron souvenirs. It was as if Indigenous people were no more relevant to contemporary Australia than Phar Lap (a stuffed racehorse and popular longtime resident of Melbourne Museum). Thankfully, such old-fashioned thinking is well and truly consigned to the curator's dustbin. At Bunjilaka it is Baldwin Spencer, the early 20th-century anthropologist and one-time director of the museum, who is rendered in plaster and displayed under glass.

This reappraisal of the museum's purpose is central to Bunjilaka. The visitor finds on Bunjilaka's threshold beautifully mounted showcases of shields and fibrecraft, displayed not simply as artefacts of material life (strictly utilitarian in nature and hence

Joseph Kennedy

I was born in a red-brick hospital in Melbourne, a descendant of the Trawlwoolway people of north-east Tasmania. Growing up in a suburban home in Essendon was hardly demanding, but life's vicissitudes soon became known to me as I embarked upon a career in the Victorian public service.

Inter-office memos were not my bag, however, and I kicked around for a while, playing in a band and generally taking it easy. Faraway lands beckoned, and a stint in Asia followed.

I returned to Australia, barely sated, and worked for a record company for a couple of years as chief box overseer. Itchy feet know no rest, to be sure, and having had enough of cardboard and CDs, I decamped again to distant climes.

Returning to pursue an adult life, I entered university and am now busy gaining a qualification in International Development that will send me once more far from Australia's golden shores, working hard, always to return.

spiritually devalued), but as works of art connecting past and present, imbued with the spirit of the land and the people. Recorded voices rise from these entrance displays: 'I am this land, this land is me'.

Bunjilaka is the culmination of the museum's understanding that it can no longer operate independently of people whose culture it once purported to preserve and now aims to celebrate. No part of Bunjilaka was initiated without Indigenous community consultation. From architectural design to the naming of galleries, all has been informed by six years of dialogue. This is a space for Indigenous Australians – their forum, their voices – and it is where non-Indigenous Australians can learn and contribute to a new understanding of this nation's past, present and future.

of informative Indigenous experiences. The park's information centre (☎ 9462 4079) is open 8.30 am to 5 pm daily, and features a terrific display about the Wurundjeri

history of the area. Behind the information centre is a **Wurundjeri garden** that contains a vast range of plants with information about their traditional Indigenous uses.

Entry to the Wurundjeri garden area is $4.40/3.30 per adult/child. The park also has a scarr tree.

A majestic **Corroboree Tree** is in St Kilda on the intersection of Fitzroy St and Queens Rd. Believed to be at least 300 years old, the tree marks an Aboriginal gathering site. There is a plaque at the base of the tree (on the road edge); take care when reading it, as cars zip by at high speed.

The **Wurundjeri Garden**, east of the city centre on Glan Avon Rd in Hawthorn, is pleasantly set on the banks of the Yarra River. The garden features a range of local indigenous plants. The excellent (free) brochure *Wurundjeri Garden Guide for Visitors*, produced by the Hawthorn Historical Society, details the garden's plants and is available on site or from Camberwell Library (☎ 9278 4655), 360 Camberwell Rd.

The serene **William Ricketts Sanctuary** (☎ 9751 1300) is on the Mt Dandenong Tourist Rd in Mt Dandenong, about 35km east of the city centre. The sanctuary and its sculptures are the work of William Ricketts, who worked here up until his death in 1993 at the age of 94. His work was inspired by the years he spent living with the Pitjantjatjara and Arrernte Aboriginal people of central Australia and by their affinity with the land. His personal philosophies permeate and shape the sanctuary, which is set in damp fern gardens with trickling waterfalls, and sculptures rising out of moss-covered rocks like spirits from the ground. The sanctuary is open 10 am to 5 pm daily (last entry 4.30 pm). Admission is $5.60/2.20 for adults/children (free for those under 10).

Gymnasium

Work up a sweat and get all buff at the Fitzroy Stars Gymnasium (☎ 9417 1145), 184–186 Gertrude St, Fitzroy. The gym has an Aboriginal board and Indigenous Australian memberships are $5.50 (for life!), and non-Indigenous memberships cost $44 per month. Membership entitles you to use all the facilities and participate in any classes, eg, kick-boxing, boxing and weight-training. One-off sessions are also available, and cost up to $5.50. The gym is open 9 am to 8 pm weekdays.

Special Events

We Iri We Homeborn is Melbourne's most lively Indigenous arts festival. Organised by the City of Port Phillip and centred around St Kilda from the first week of July (possibly changing to September), the festival showcases some of south-eastern Australia's best Indigenous theatre, art, literature, multimedia, film, dance and music. Phone ☎ 9209 6620 for program details.

National Sorry Day is held annually in Melbourne on 26 May. Thousands of participants acknowledge the pain, loss and suffering endured by Indigenous people who were separated from their parents under Australia's child removal policies. Call the Victorian Aboriginal Child Care Agency/Link-Up on ☎ 9471 1855 for details of events.

Victoria's Indigenous and non-Indigenous community celebrate NAIDOC (National Aboriginal and Islander Day of Celebration) with incomparable enthusiasm during the first week of July. Events include the NAIDOC March, the flash/formal NAIDOC Ball, the Songlines Music Festival and numerous other statewide events. Phone Aboriginal Affairs Victoria (☎ 9616 2902) for further details.

Free Indigenous music and entertainment is always incorporated into Melbourne's 10-day Moomba Festival (see the boxed text 'Up What?!'), which takes place

---

UP WHAT?!

bryan Andy

Apparently the word 'Moomba' doesn't mean 'Let's get together and have fun!', as many Melburnians may think. Local Melbourne legend has it that when suspiciously intentioned non-Indigenous people approached Aborigines to provide them with a name for their proposed festival, the word 'Moomba' was offered. 'Moomba' is said to translate as 'Up your bottom'…putting it mildly. Whatever the real origin, the title 'Moomba' has an oft-joked about, mysterious beginning – it seems that no-one can get to the bottom of it! (Yeah, that's a pun.)

GALLERIES, MUSEUMS & SHOPS

Readers should be aware that the names of deceased members of the Aboriginal community may be cited in this section. Mentioning the personal name of someone who has died recently can cause offence, anguish and grief in some Aboriginal cultures.

There are far too many places in Melbourne that sell or exhibit works by Indigenous artists to list them all here. Following is a selection of recommended outlets. See the Shopping section in the Facts for the Visitor chapter for further information.

Aboriginal Handcrafts (☎ 9650 4717) Mezzanine Level, 130 Little Collins St. This nonprofit organisation of the Uniting Church was established in the 1960s to support Aboriginal communities through sales of Indigenous works. Prices are very reasonable and there is a good selection of items. Products are from northern and central Australia, Mornington Island, the Tiwi Islands and South Australia. Small bark paintings, *coolamons* (basin-shaped wooden dishes) and boomerangs range in price from $10 to $80, bird and animal carvings are $20 to $200, and clubs, shields and spears, plus a decent range of basketry and weaving, are $100 to $300. The attractive didjeridus are well priced at $180 to $300. A *bullroarer* (long, narrow piece of wood attached to string and whirled to make a roaring sound, used in men's initiation) would make an unusual gift (from $33 to $55). There are also some good-quality carvings.

This shop is staffed by friendly non-Indigenous volunteers. You can be assured that you are buying authentic, high-quality products, with the Aboriginal artists and communities who made them benefiting directly. The shop is open 10 am to 4.30 pm Monday to Friday.

Alcaston Gallery (☎ 9654 7279) 2 Collins St (Spring St entrance). This is a fine art gallery worth visiting for the quality and workmanship of the pieces on show, including beautiful Western Desert acrylics and sculptures. Regular changing exhibitions present many of Australia's exceptional, established and emerging Aboriginal artists. Prices are in the mid-to upper range of the market. The gallery has a very good, long-established reputation for dealing with Aboriginal artists and communities.

At the time of writing, it was planning to move to new premises nearby, so phone ahead for details of current location, plus exhibitions. Opening hours are 9 am to 5.30 pm weekdays and noon to 5 pm on Saturday, and at other times by appointment.
Web site: www.alcastongallery.com.au.

Bookshops are plentiful in Melbourne, though not many have substantial amounts of Indigenous books. Some of the commercial Aboriginal art galleries have a few books, and the new Melbourne Museum has a good selection. Your best bet is to visit an Aboriginal centre, or the Koorie Heritage Trust or National Gallery of Victoria shops, where there is a good range and variety of Indigenous books on offer. Also try The Bookshelf (☎ 9428 2011), 116 Bridge Rd, Richmond, which specialises in books on Aboriginal Australia and produces a catalogue of resources available on Indigenous issues.

Gallery Gabrielle Pizzi (☎ 9654 2944) 141 Flinders Lane. This small, interesting place is aimed at the upper end of the fine-art market and is essentially an exhibiting gallery with regular changing shows. Established in 1987, it features the best work of major Aboriginal artists from northern and central Australia, the Tiwi Islands and the Kimberley region of Western Australia. Artists from urban-based centres are also to be seen, including Trevor Nicholls, Ian W Abdulla and Destiny Deacon. The gallery deals directly with Indigenous artists and communities and has a very good reputation in this regard. Paintings, sculpture, prints and photography are available with prices at the higher end, but some pieces are more affordable.

This gallery is worth a visit to view high-quality Indigenous art; phone ahead to find out what's currently on show. Opening hours are 10 am to 5.30 pm Tuesday to Friday and 11 am to 5 pm on Saturday.
Web site: www.gabriellepizzi.com.au

continued...   Gary Lee

Koorie Heritage Trust Inc (☎ 9639 6555) 234–6 Flinders Lane. This Indigenous centre should
be one of the first places you visit in Melbourne. Consisting of two small galleries and a
retail outlet, it has Victorian Koorie heritage, culture and history on show, and a number
of informative and interesting displays and exhibitions highlighting works by Indigenous
Victorian artists, both past and present. The Aunty Joyce Johnson Memorial Gallery is
named after local Gunditjmara woman, the late Joyce Johnson (1926–82), in
acknowledgment of her work in establishing the first Koorie Victorian Nindethana Theatre Company. The Lin Onus Memorial Gallery is named after the well-known and acclaimed Yorta Yorta artist, the late Lin Onus (1948–96). Phone ahead for information on
the changing exhibitions; they are usually excellent.
   The Koorie staff here are helpful and friendly. Opening hours are 10 am to 4.30 pm on
Monday and from 9.30 am Tuesday to Friday. Entry is by donation.

Koorie Heritage Trust Shop, based at the Trust on Flinders Lane. This shop sells an excellent selection of reasonably priced and well-made Koorie products. There are painted emu
eggs from $70 with special boxes to house (or post) them in ($6 each). Opaque glass
bowls and platters start at $28, and printed silk hankies are $9 and Balarinji silk scarves
$50. Clap sticks are $11, boomerangs are from $22 and didjeridus start at a very reason-
able $88. There is a good variety of Koorie postcards, stationery sets and some unusual
bead and echidna quill necklaces for $50.
   Attractive T-shirts for adults cost $24 to $27, with children's T-shirts $21 to $24. All
images printed on the T-shirts, greeting cards, postcards and posters are from the Koorie
Heritage Trust collection. The range of Indigenous books available here is very good, and
is probably the best in Melbourne. And not to be missed are the cute witchetty grub
lollies ($2 per packet).
   Fascinating historical Aboriginal artefacts on display include a beautiful dilly bag circa
1900, and a woven basket and baby carrier from around 1940. Look out also for the
beautiful contemporary possum-skin cloak by noted Koorie artist Gayle Madigan on
display (not for sale).
   All the Koorie items here are of high quality and all purchases directly support Victorian
Koorie communities, arts enterprises and artists. The shop has the same opening hours as
the Koorie Heritage Trust (see earlier in this list).
Web site: www.koorieheritage.citysearch.com.au.

Melbourne Museum (☎ 8341 7777) in Carlton Gardens beside the historic Royal Exhibition
Building was opened in October 2000 as Melbourne's flagship museum. Bunjilaka, the
impressive Indigenous centre at the museum, addresses contemporary and historical issues
and showcases art and design. Outside is an Indigenous garden with a creek and waterfall. (See the boxed text 'Bunjilaka' in this chapter.) The museum is open 10 am to 6 pm
daily and until 9 pm Wednesday to Saturday in summer. Admission is $12/6.60/9/33 for
adults/children/concession/families. Free conducted tours of the museum include a visit to
Bunjilaka, and start daily at 11 am and 2 and 3 pm – inquire at the information desk.
Web site: melbourne.museum.vic.gov.au

National Gallery of Victoria on Russell (☎ 9208 0203) 285–321 Russell St. The gallery has
temporarily relocated to Russell St and will return to St Kilda Rd (Federation Square) in
early 2003. The new gallery, to be called the Museum of Australian Art, is due to open in
March 2002, and will house a substantial part of the National Gallery's Aboriginal and Torres Strait Islander art collection. The temporary premises incorporate Aboriginal paintings
alongside non-Indigenous works. Possibly due to the cramped space here, not a lot of the
extensive contemporary Indigenous art collection is on view.
   The gallery shop has a small but interesting selection of attractive Aboriginal postcards,
posters and scarves, and quite a good selection of Aboriginal art books. The Russell St
location is open 10 am to 5 pm daily. Admission is free to the permanent collection. Phone
ahead for details of the new museum.
Web site: www.ngv.vic.gov.au

VICTORIA

in early March. Scan the Web site at www
.melbournemoombafestival.com.au for Indigenous content.

Melbourne's Fringe Festival, held annually around September/October, is a lively
source of great entertainment with Indigenous events and performances always featuring on the program. Details of dates,
times, venues and prices can be found at
www.melbournefringe.org.au.

CERES (see Parks, Gardens & Scarr
Trees earlier) holds a Bush Foods Festival
in April, featuring entertainment, activities
and (of course) Indigenous food! The Return
of the Sacred Kingfisher Festival, held in the
last week of November, is a celebration of
Wurundjeri culture and the environment.
Phone CERES on ☎ 9387 2609 for details.

The biennial Melbourne Art Fair (from
2002) is held in the first week of October.
This leading trade fair takes place in the
Royal Exhibition Building, Carlton Gardens, and features Indigenous art, with
most of it for sale. For up-to-date information phone ☎ 9482 5400 or log onto www
.artfair.com.au.

Places to Eat
The Flamin' Bull Australian Indigenous
Restaurant (☎ 9349 1174, 121 Lygon St,
Carlton) is Melbourne's newly opened version of the Warragul restaurant (see following). The restaurant is not Indigenous-owned
but it does have Aboriginal staff, and can
indulge you with what is said to be Australia's largest range of Indigenous bush
foods. The extensive a la carte menu includes
sautéed emu livers in garlic and native herb
butter ($11) and wallaby fillet with Warrigal
greens (native spinach) with roasted maca-
damia nuts ($20.20). It's at the city end of the
Lygon St restaurant strip (next door to the
post office) and is open daily for lunch
(11.30 am to 4 pm) and dinner (6 pm to late).
It's fully licensed and you can dine among
Victorian Aboriginal artworks, most of
which are for sale.

In Warragul, the Flamin' Bull (☎ 5623
2377, 9–11 Mason St) offers a similar
menu, including native eel in paperbark
($15.60), chargrilled crocodile ($24.85) and
wattleseed ice cream with Munthari berries
($7.15). Open for dinner from Thursday to
Sunday. It also conducts local tours, see
Organised Tours earlier in this section.

Entertainment
Ilbijerri Aboriginal & Torres Strait Islander
Theatre (☎ 9329 9097, ⓔ ilbjerri@vicnet
.net.au) is based in the Arts House at the
North Melbourne Town Hall, on the corner of
Errol and Queensberry Sts, North Melbourne.
Ilbijerri thrives on producing high-quality
Indigenous theatre and is no stranger to shin-
ing worldwide reviews. Memberships are
available, with donations welcomed. Its Web
site, at www.ilbijerri.org.au, has details of
current performances.

Songlines Music Aboriginal Corporation
(☎ 9696 2022), 62 Pickles St, Port Melbourne, is an Indigenous music organisation
facilitating the promotion, mentoring, training and recording of some of Melbourne's
best Indigenous performers. It usually has
huge (and ridiculously affordable) gigs
around Melbourne throughout the year – all
of which are a must! Phone for details of
upcoming events.

Wathaurong Country

GEELONG
Information
The Wathaurong Aboriginal Co-operative
(☎ 5277 0044, fax 5278 4123) at Lot 62
Morgan St in North Geelong is set in an
indigenous garden. The co-op has a small
Indigenous display and also sells some
Koorie crafts, including exquisite locally
made Indigenous-designed glassware. It's
open 9 am to 5 pm Monday to Thursday
(until 4 pm on Friday).

Organised Tours
Knowledgeable Allan Browning, one of the
Aboriginal guides on The Koorie Walkabout tour, provides an informative insight
into local Koorie history and culture. The
one-day tour visits local Indigenous sites in
Wathaurong country, including an ancient
Aboriginal meeting place. It departs from
Melbourne and costs $123 per person (min-
imum two people), including transport, a
guide and lunch. Advance bookings are
essential. For further details contact
Echidna Walkabout (☎ 9646 8249, fax 9681
9177, ⓔ ekidna@netcore.com.au).

The William Buckley Discovery Trail
runs from the You Yangs to Aireys Inlet (see

the boxed text 'Buckley's Chance'). This self-driving trail, with six significant sites including Buckley's Falls, aims to increase awareness of the unique relationship between the Wathaurong people and William Buckley. A useful brochure (free) about this trail is available from the Geelong Visitor Information Centre (☎ 5275 5797, 1800 620 888 toll free), on the corner of the Princes Hwy and St Georges Rd, about 7km north of the Geelong city centre.

Yollinko Park Aboriginal Garden

Yollinko Park Aboriginal Garden (off Barrabool Rd on the Barwon River) contains a shell midden, a traditional indigenous garden and some impressive larger-than-life sculptures of Aboriginal tools. This is a great place to picnic, and a detailed brochure is available on site or from the Geelong Visitor Information Centre (see Organised Tours earlier).

THE YOU YANGS

The You Yangs (from Wurdi Youang/Ude Youang and meaning 'Big mountain in the middle of a plain') Regional Park is about 22km north of Geelong. This park has a rock well that has been hollowed out by Aboriginal people to hold water. Entrance to the park is $3/1 per car/pedestrian. Echidna Walkabout (see Organised Tours earlier) offers Indigenous-guided tours to this park.

ANGLESEA & TORQUAY
Point Addis Koorie Cultural Walk

On the Melbourne side of Anglesea, the 1km self-interpretative Point Addis Koorie Cultural Walk features eight signs that provide an Indigenous insight into the local Aboriginal people, and the native plants and animals. Take some water and stick to the tracks, as the terrain can get very slippery.

BUCKLEY'S CHANCE
Joyce Connolly

William Buckley (1780–1856) was transported to the recently 'discovered' Port Phillip District on the HMS *Calcutta* in 1803. Shortly after arriving in Port Phillip Bay, the settlers set up camp near present-day Sorrento. Buckley and several other convicts managed to steal a gun and escape – one was shot dead in the process. The remaining three set off around the bay, thinking they were heading to Sydney, but two of them lost their nerve and turned back.

Buckley wandered for weeks, surviving on shellfish and berries, and was eventually found by two Wathaurong women. Recognising the spear Buckley was carrying (he had unwittingly plucked it from the grave of a Wathaurong warrior), they believed him to be the reincarnation of their kinsman and took him back to his 'family'. Buckley spent the next 32 years with the clan, who taught him their local customs and language as they moved across the Bellarine Peninsula (and as far afield as the Otway Ranges) in search of water, food and trade.

In 1835, another ship sailed into the bay. Not sure how he, a convict, would be received, and no longer able to speak his native tongue, Buckley tentatively approached them. The white settlers were startled by the six-foot seven-inch man emerging from the bush; they were even more surprised to discover he was an Englishman and they soon dubbed him the 'Wild White Man'.

Gradually Buckley regained his English language and a pardon was arranged to allow him to become an interpreter and intermediary. Many said that his mediation saved unnecessary bloodshed between the British and the Koories. As more settlers arrived, the task became bigger than the man and, with neither side paying much attention to his advice, he became disillusioned. Buckley subsequently left the colony for Tasmania, where he lived until his death.

So next time you hear the phrase 'you've got Buckley's', spare a thought for the real Buckley who beat the odds and not only survived, but thrived among the gracious Wathaurong people who saved his life.

There is a self-guided driving trail which provides an insight into the relationship between the Wathaurong people and Buckley – for details see Organised Tours in the Wathaurong Country section.

VICTORIA

There's a rewarding ocean view from the lookout where the walk concludes. A free pamphlet is available from most visitor information centres in the district, including the Torquay Visitor Information Centre (☎ 5261 4219).

Glenn Romanis Mural & Sundial

In the large car park at Bells Beach (about 7km south-west of Torquay) is a *jill-a-wah* (toilet) block that has a beautiful mural by Indigenous artist Glenn Romanis. Some of Glenn's work also features in the Yollinko Park Aboriginal Garden (see the Geelong section earlier).

Romanis also co-designed the Sundial of Human Involvement at Torquay. You'll find the sundial at Fisherman's Beach near Deep Creek, adjacent to the corner of The Esplanade and Darian Rd. Made from mosaic tiles, the sundial's design represents some of the Dreaming stories of the local Wathaurong people. An enlightening brochure about the sundial is available from the Torquay Visitor Information Centre (☎ 5261 4219).

Katabanut Country

Cape Otway Area

CAPE OTWAY

Information

Cape Otway – Coast of Secrets by Bruce Pascoe & Lyn Harwood is a great little text detailing the history (both Indigenous and non-Indigenous) of the Cape Otway area. It also features information on local bush tucker, plants and geography. It's available from the Great Ocean Road Visitor Information Centre (☎ 5237 6529) in Apollo Bay for $12.

Organised Tours

The best way to experience the area's many Katabanut sites is with Otway Eco-Guides (☎ 5237 7240, fax 5237 6622 [e] sue @otwayeco-guides.com.au). Its Koori Tour, with Indigenous guide Bruce Pascoe, visits the major gathering places and middens in the area and provides informative insights into traditional food, tools and medicines. A two-hour tour is $27.50 per person. You will need your own car and advance bookings are essential.

Gunditjmara Country

South-West Victoria

HISTORY

Before European invasion, this area was the territory of the Gunditjmara nation. The Gunditjmara clans who lived along the coast first saw European settlers around 1810, when whalers and sealers based themselves around Portland. The Henty family (see History at the start of this chapter) arrived in 1834, and within a few years the Hentys and other settlers had begun to extend their 'landholdings' inland, grazing their sheep on rich pastures, many of which were traditional meeting places and sacred sites of the local clans. This eventually led to bloody conflict.

During the 1840s, the Gunditjmara people fought against the invaders, attacking settlers around Port Fairy, Mt Napier and Lake Condah. The settlers replied in force, and scores of Aborigines were massacred. More insidious methods such as 'gifts' of poisoned flour were also used to kill people, and by 1846 Koorie resistance had been broken. In 1841 the Koorie population in western Victoria was estimated to be 7900; 22 years later it was around 500 or even less.

WARRNAMBOOL

Information

The Gunditjmara Aboriginal Co-operative (☎ 5562 9729) is at Harris St Reserve and is open 9 am to 5 pm weekdays. It houses a small collection of Indigenous items including a basket-weaving display and traditional weapons.

Organised Tours

Tailor-made tours of Indigenous sites in this region can be arranged with advance notice by the Framlingham Aboriginal Trust (see Framlingham in the Around Warrnambool section for details).

For tours of Maleen, see Maleen (Griffiths Island) in the Around Warrnambool section.

Thunder Point Coastal Reserve

On the outskirts of the city overlooking the sea, Thunder Point has middens (accessible by a walking track) believed to be between 3000 and 7000 years old.

LAKE CONDAH ABORIGINAL MISSION   Mark Armstrong

Lake Condah, on the western side of the Mt Eccles National Park, is the former site of the Lake Condah Aboriginal Mission. There is evidence that before European settlement, local Aborigines lived here on a semipermanent basis, rather than living the fully nomadic lifestyle often associated with hunter-gatherers. They were able to thrive here because of an abundant and constant supply of food, particularly fish from the lake, and they set up sophisticated systems to harvest fish and eels. The stone traps were designed to divert water from the lake through a series of gaps in the stones, behind which plaited baskets were placed to catch the fish.

Lake Condah was formed when Mt Eccles erupted around 19,000 years ago. The molten lava from the volcano flowed along the paths of many local streams, blocking the water and resulting in the formation of this shallow lake at the edge of the lava plains.

When the European settlers invaded the area in the 1830s and 1840s, Aborigines were driven from their traditional lands, and the majority of them were killed in subsequent years.

In 1858 a government select committee recommended that Aboriginal reserves be set up theoretically to protect the interests of the remaining Aboriginal people. In 1869, the Church of England established a mission at Lake Condah. The community maintained some traditional hunting and food-gathering practices, while at the same time the Christian missionaries were trying to 'Europeanise' and 'Christianise' them.

In 1886 the Victorian government passed the notorious Aborigines Protection Law Amendment Act, which prohibited 'part-Aborigines' under 35 years of age from living on missions. The gradual effect of this was that the community was splintered and some families were forcefully split up. By 1890, the population at the mission had fallen from 117 to 20, and the decline continued until the mission closed in 1918.

In 1984, the federal government passed land-rights legislation that led to 53 hectares of the former mission reserve being given back to the local Aboriginal community. The community now manages the site and it is no longer open to tourists.

Traditional Dance

The Kuyang Yandaa Dance Troupe performs traditional regional dances which depict local customs and beliefs. Call Jamie Commons (☎/fax 5562 5830) for details and prices. Advance bookings are essential.

Special Events

At Warrnambool, the annual Golf Day was established by a group of Aboriginal organisations to promote Reconciliation. Indigenous and non-Indigenous people gather for a friendly golf tournament, usually held in February/March. For exact dates and more details, contact Joe Chatfield at the South West and Wimmera Cultural Heritage Program (☎ 5562 3458, fax 5562 1596).

The Tarerer Festival, is held in the Warrnambool area each January (for the exact date call ☎ 5568 1528). It showcases Indigenous and non-Indigenous local musicians. Each year the concert is officially opened by local Elders and there's a focus on Reconciliation.

AROUND WARRNAMBOOL
Tower Hill Natural History Centre

There's a small Indigenous display at this centre (☎ 5565 9202), 15km north-west of Warrnambool (off the Princes Hwy en route to Port Fairy) at Tower Hill, the site of an extinct volcano. A small pictorial display briefly describes the local Aboriginal history. There is also a collection of Indigenous artefacts, including a stone-grinding dish and hand-axe. Some of the Aboriginal relics found by archaeologists in this area precede the eruption of the volcano at Tower Hill (some 30,000 years ago). The centre is open 9.30 am to 4.30 pm daily (free entry).

Griffiths Island

This island, which was named Maleen by the Maleen gunditj clan, is accessible by a short causeway from Port Fairy. The island has self-guided walks with interpretative signs about local Koorie history. The main walking track is named after Tarteel, the last Aboriginal chief of Maleen. The island also has Australia's largest mainland shear-water (mutton bird) colony, which can be seen from mid-September to late April.

Organised Tours Moonbird Tours (☎ 5568 1374, 0419 573540, e vic@myportfairy. com) operates two-hour tours of the island (usually with an Aboriginal guide), which focus on traditional lifestyles of the local Koorie people. The cost is $15 per person ($25 per family) and advance bookings are essential (minimum four people). Traditional Koorie dances can be arranged with advance notice.

Lady Julia Percy Island
About 8km offshore from Port Fairy you can see the flat-topped volcanic Lade Julia Percy Island. This sacred island, originally called Deen Maar, is the resting place of the spirits of the dead from the Gunditjmara people. The island is also where Bunjil, the Creator Spirit, departed this world.

Framlingham
Framlingham was one of several missions, or reserves, set up by the government in Victoria during the 1860s. The aim of these missions was to 'Christianise' and 'civilise' those Koories who had survived the massacres, diseases and other barbarities inflicted upon them by the European settlers.

Framlingham Aboriginal Trust The Framlingham Aboriginal Trust (☎ 5567 1003, fax 5567 1298, e fram@standard.net.au) is at Kirrae Ave, about 20km north-east of Warrnambool. It has an Indigenous display including a chronological history chart of the Aboriginal people of this area. The trust can arrange tailor-made tours of local Indigenous sites (advance bookings are essential and prices are available on application). Tours on offer include a visit to the Deen Maar Indigenous Protected Area, a deeply spiritual place at Yambuk that has walking trails and a lake. The lake attracts many birds including the rare orange-bellied parrot. The property, which is undergoing a revegetation program, has

access to a beautiful stretch of secluded beach where you can watch the wild waves. Whale-spotting is possible from around June to September. There are also brilliant views of nearby Deen Maar.

The Trust is open 9 am to 5 pm weekdays. It also operates Eumeralla Backpackers at Yambuk.

Yambuk
About 17km north-west of Port Fairy is the tiny town of Yambuk. The peaceful Eumer-alla Backpackers (☎ 5568 4204; bookings also at the Framlingham Aboriginal Trust – see Framlingham earlier) is a great place to relax. Housed in the old Yambuk school, it is named after the bloody Eumeralla Wars (Aboriginal–settler conflicts of the 1840s and 1850s). Facilities include a self-catering fully equipped kitchen, laundry and barbe-cue area. Canoes can be hired ($7 per day) to paddle along the nearby Eumeralla River. Bunk beds cost $17/12 for adults/children and a private room is $17 per person (all rooms with common bathroom).

There is also cheaper, far more basic accommodation at a nearby authentic and operational wool shed. Free lodgings at either place may be possible in exchange for help in restoring a nearby property.

Djapwurrung Country
The Wimmera

DUNKELD
If you happen to be passing through Dunkeld, a small township just off the Glenelg Hwy (B160), there's a **historical museum** in an old bluestone building on Templeton St which has a small Aboriginal display. Items include traditional wooden weapons dating back to 1897 and stone axes. The museum is open 1 to 5 pm on Sunday and public holidays, or by appointment other days – phone ☎ 5577 2558. Admission costs $2.

LANGI GHIRAN STATE PARK
This small park (free entry) is off the West-ern Hwy, 14km east of Ararat, and is a sig-nificant Aboriginal site. Langi Ghiran is derived from the Aboriginal name for the home of the black cockatoo, which is found here along with many other species of birds,

including corellas, robins, honeyeaters and finches. Spring is the best time for bird-watching. There is an Aboriginal rock art site which can be visited by tourists – for more information contact the Parks Victoria office in Beaufort (☎ 5349 2404, fax 5349 2687) or the Parks Victoria statewide information number on ☎ 131 963.

ARARAT
Ararat is known to Indigenous people as Butingitj. The atmospheric and rather ramshackle **Langi Morgala Museum**, on Queen St just off Barkly St, houses an extraordinary mishmash of items, including the Mooney collection of Aboriginal artefacts. The museum is open 1 to 4 pm on weekends, or by appointment – phone ☎ 5352 3502 or 5352 2509). Admission costs $2/0.50 for adults/children.

STAWELL
About 11km south of Stawell (known as Kobram to Indigenous people), and signposted off the road to Pomonal, is **Bunjil's Shelter**, one of the most significant Aboriginal rock art sites in southern Australia. Bunjil is the Creator Spirit of the Aboriginal people. The painting, enclosed in a protective wire grill, is enhanced by the contours of the rock and although there are interpretative signs, it is difficult to fully appreciate the significance of this subtle painting unless it is explained by Koories. The Brambuk Aboriginal Cultural Centre conducts tours to Bunjil's Shelter with an Aboriginal guide (see Organised Tours in the Grampians section later). Aboriginal Dreamtime Trails also runs tours to Bunjil's Shelter (see the Organised Tours section at the beginning of this chapter).

Jardwadjali/ Djapwurrung Country
The Grampians Area

THE GRAMPIANS
These spectacular mountains (known as Gariwerd to Indigenous people) in the Grampians National Park contain the largest collection of Aboriginal rock art sites in southern Australia. Apart from its natural rugged beauty, this region is renowned for the Brambuk Aboriginal Cultural Centre.

Information
Indigenous Organisations By far the best source of information about local Aboriginal culture, and for guided tours to the rock art sites, is Brambuk Aboriginal Cultural Centre (see later in this section).

Tourist Offices Near Brambuk is the helpful Grampians National Park Visitor Centre (☎ 5356 4381, fax 5356 4446). It has Indigenous displays and sells good maps indicating walking trails to Aboriginal rock art sites. The centre is open 9 am to 5 pm daily. Web site: www.parkweb.vic.gov.au

Books *The People of Gariwerd* by Gib Wettenhall contains interesting text and pictures pertaining to Gariwerd. This slim paperback can be purchased at various bookshops and at Brambuk Aboriginal Cultural Centre.

Organised Tours
Brambuk Aboriginal Cultural Centre offers a range of tours to local Indigenous sites with an Aboriginal guide, and this is far more rewarding than visiting them independently. Bookings must be made at least a day in advance and some tours require a minimum of three people. Tours on offer include a two-hour trip to Bunjil's Shelter near Stawell, which costs $13.20/7.70 for adults/children and includes a look at local bush foods. Tours to the other Aboriginal rock art sites in Gariwerd are also available. It is also possible to hire an Aboriginal guide for a tailor-made tour ($55 per hour; travel extra).

Brambuk Aboriginal Cultural Centre
The attractive Brambuk Aboriginal Cultural Centre (☎ 5356 4452, fax 5356 4455, e brambuk@netconnect.com.au) in Halls Gap is run collectively by five Koorie communities. It aims to maintain Koorie culture and to educate and raise visitors' awareness of local Koorie history. Its exhibitions (visual and audio) trace Koorie life from the period before European colonisation to modern times. Koorie art, clothes, weapons and tools are on display, and there is also a souvenir shop.

The award-winning building was brilliantly designed to reflect and complement the landscape and environment of the region. Many features of the interior design symbolise local Koorie communities, their

VICTORIA

beliefs and way of life: the curved seat just inside the entrance represents the caring embrace of Bunjil, the ramp upstairs is the eel Dreaming, while the theatre ceiling depicts the southern right whale (totem of the Gunditjmara people; see the Glossary for a description of 'totem').

The area around the centre has native plants traditionally used by Aboriginal people for food and medicine (a 30-minute tour costs $4.50 per person). There's also a 40-minute bush food-tasting tour and talk ($5.50) and a demonstration of boomerang-throwing ($4.40). An informative 30-minute talk about local Koorie history, which includes a didjeridu demonstration, costs $4.40 per person. During the peak holiday periods there are demonstrations of Koorie music and dance ($11 per person, including audience participation and a didjeridu lesson) on the ceremonial ground. The centre also runs special education and holiday programs, and tours with Aboriginal guides.

The centre is open 9 am to 5 pm daily (entry is free). The **Gariwerd Dreaming Theatre**, a multimedia narration of spiritual stories (tales from the Dreaming which touch on the *law*, or fundamental guiding truths) of the region, costs $4.40/2.80 for adults/children. Brambuk sometimes has touring Indigenous exhibitions – phone to see if there are any during your visit. At the time of writing, Brambuk was also planning the Tanderrum Festival, a showcase of Aboriginal Victorian culture (again, phone for details).

Rock Art
There is an extensive collection of rock art within the Grampians National Park, but not all of it is publicised or accessible. In the Northern Grampians near Mt Stapylton the main sites are **Gulgurn Manja Shelter** and **Ngamadjidj Shelter**. In the Western Grampians near the Buandik camping ground the main sites are **Billimina Shelter** and **Manja Shelter**. These rock paintings were made with either ochre or white clay, and are mostly drawings or stencils such as hand prints, animal tracks or stick figures. Brambuk Aboriginal Cultural Centre operates tours to these sites.

Places to Stay & Eat
The Brambuk Aboriginal Cultural Centre operates the nearby Brambuk Backpackers

(☎ 5356 4250, fax 5356 4609, **e** bramback @netconnect.com.au), with separate male and female dormitories ($16/19 in winter/summer per person), or private rooms with attached bathroom for $32/40 a single/double during winter or $35/45 during summer. All prices include breakfast. Facilities include a dining room with a fully equipped kitchen, a living room with TV, a barbecue area, a self-service laundry and an Internet cafe.

The Brambuk Aboriginal Cultural Centre's pleasant bush tucker cafe serves interesting fare, such as warm crocodile salad ($13.20) and *wattleccino* ($3.50). A favourite is the pumpkin soup flavoured with native lemon myrtle and served with wattleseed damper ($6).

HORSHAM
Information
Horsham is known as Wopet-Bungundilar to Indigenous people. The Goolum Goolum Aboriginal Co-operative (☎ 5382 5033, fax 5381 1563) is at 143–5 Baillie St. It's open 9 am to 5 pm weekdays.

Special Events
The Art Is... Festival in Horsham is a showcase of local art, including Aboriginal works and traditional Aboriginal dances. This festival is usually held in March/April – for details, contact the visitor information centre (☎ 5382 1832), 20 O'Callaghan Parade, open 9 am to 5 pm daily.

Shopping
Werrimul Arts & Crafts (☎ 5381 0330), 5 Firebrace St, has a fine collection of items, including exquisite hand-painted emu eggs ($80 to $120), T-shirts (adults $22 to $27, children $10 to $16), and even computer mouse pads ($4) with Aboriginal designs. Prices are very reasonable. It's open 9 am to 4.30 pm weekdays (closed noon to 1 pm).

MT ARAPILES
The Mt Arapiles-Tooan Park (known as Djurite to Indigenous people), a state park about 30km west of Horsham, has around 42 identified Aboriginal archaeological sites as well as scarr trees and rock art (not all sites are open to the public). The traditional owners of this land are the Djurid balug clan and this area is still of great significance to Aboriginal people. A tour with

a local Koorie guide is highly recommended and can be arranged by Alan Burns at the Goolum Goolum Aboriginal Cooperative (see Information under Horsham earlier).

EDENHOPE

The **Johnny Mullagh Memorial Cairn**, a simple stone obelisk standing in the grounds of the local school, commemorates the first Aboriginal cricket team to tour England. The team trained here before departing in 1868. The cairn lists the team members and their tour record: they won 14, lost 14 and drew 19 matches.

Nearby **Harrow** is Johnny Mullagh's home town, which has a memorial at the oval and his grave at the Harrow cemetery. Each Saturday at 7.30pm the town puts on a four-hour 'Harrow By Night' sound-and-light show which includes a tribute to Johnny. This costs $40 per person, which includes the show, dinner and entry to the town's museums (bookings essential – call ☎ 5588 1209). At the time of the writing, there were plans to open an interpretative discovery centre at Harrow, which will include a historic Aboriginal cricket display, insights into bush tucker and bush medicine and Koorie dance performances. For the latest information, contact Ange Newton on ☎ 5588 1209.

Wotjobaluk/ Wergaia Country

Wimmera/Mallee Area

DIMBOOLA
Organised Tours

For a tour of the Ebenezer Mission (see later in this section) with a local Koorie guide, contact the affable Alan Burns at the Goolum Goolum Aboriginal Co-operative (see the earlier Horsham section). The cooperative can also arrange guided tours with traditional Aboriginal land owners to other Indigenous sites in this region, including Djurite (see Mt Arapiles earlier). Prices are available on application and advance bookings are essential.

Ebenezer Mission

Ebenezer Mission was established in Bunyo-budnutt land (Antwerp area), about

The first Australian cricket team to tour England (1868) trained in Edenhope

COURTESY OF NATIONAL LIBRARY OF AUSTRALIA

18km north of Dimboola, by Moravian missionaries in 1859. It operated until 1904. These historic buildings are the oldest surviving mission buildings in Victoria. Once in ruins, they have been classified by the National Trust and are undergoing restoration. There's a small cemetery but the missionaries did not provide headstones for most of the Aboriginal people who lived on the reserve; make sure you stick to the walking tracks, as there are as many as 150 unmarked graves. The mission is signposted off the Dimboola–Jeparit road.

To receive the accurate Indigenous interpretation, it is highly recommended that you visit this mission with an Aboriginal guide. These tours also give you the opportunity to ask questions and visit nearby scarr trees and middens. Tours must be booked in advance – see Organised Tours earlier. If you visit the mission independently, please close the gate when you leave.

Latje Latje Country

Mildura Area

MILDURA
Information

In the foyer of the useful Mildura Visitor Information Centre (☎ 5021 4424, ⓔ tourism @mildura.vic.gov.au) are several interesting displays about Latje Latje heritage. The centre is open 9 am to 5.30 pm daily (to 5 pm on weekends), and is on the corner of Deakin Ave and Twelfth St. The Web site at www.murrayoutback.org.au covers the Mallee region.

Mungo National Park (see under Barkindji Country in the New South Wales chapter) is handled by the NSW National

Parks & Wildlife Service (NPWS) office (☎ 5021 8900), on the Sturt Hwy in Buronga (a few kilometres from central Mildura). Hattah-Kulkyne National Park is handled by the Parks Victoria office (☎ 5022 4300), on the roundabout at the junction of Langtree Mall and Ninth St in Mildura.

Organised Tours
Numerous tour operators are based in Mildura, but only two are Aboriginal-owned and/or -operated – see the Mungo National Park section in the New South Wales chapter. Also see the Wentworth section of the New South Wales chapter for details of Harry Nanya Tours, which is a good local operator.

Things to See
The **Mildura Arts Centre** (☎ 5023 3733) on Cureton Ave occasionally features exhibitions of Aboriginal art and performances of Indigenous music and dance.

Shopping
Tulklana Kumbi Aboriginal Gallery (☎ 5022 0744), at the northern end of Langtree Ave, sells high-quality crafts, mostly made at its workshop in nearby Dareton (NSW). The gallery is open 10.30 am to 5 pm weekdays, and from 11 am on Saturday.

HATTAH-KULKYNE NATIONAL PARK
The park visitor centre has displays about the park's Aboriginal history and culture, including an informative exhibit about scarr trees.

The 6km self-guided Lake Hattah Nature Drive (or walk), which starts at the visitor centre, goes past a wonderful scarr tree. There are some shell middens at the end of the Cantala Track (4WD only), and scarr trees along the Murray River, but these are fairly inaccessible.

The three tour companies listed in the Mungo National Park section in the New South Wales chapter run day trips to Hattah-Kulkyne from Mildura or Wentworth. See that section for details.

ROBINVALE
Manatunga Artefacts (☎ 5026 4799), 13 Perrin St, is an Aboriginal art and craft shop selling locally made Indigenous crafts, artefacts and clothes. It's open 9 am to 5 pm weekdays (closed noon to 1 pm).

Wemba Wemba/Wati Wati Country
Swan Hill/Kerang

SELF-GUIDED TOURS
The Murray Outback Aboriginal Cultural Trail (which includes parts of Victoria, New South Wales and South Australia) is a self-driving trail that celebrates the region's Indigenous attractions. These include *keeping places* (cultural centres), tour operators, art galleries and sacred sites. Detailed brochures are available from the Swan Hill Visitor Information Centre (☎ 5032 3033, 1800 625 373 toll free), 306 Campbell St (open daily).

TYNTYNDER HOMESTEAD
Tyntynder Homestead (☎ 5037 6380), 16km north of Swan Hill, has a small museum of rare Aboriginal artefacts dating to when the homestead was built in 1846. Guided tours of the property cost $8.15/3.85 (adult/children). There is also a shop selling locally made Indigenous crafts and artefacts. Prices range from $1 to $150. The homestead is open daily during school holidays, and by appointment only at other times.

SHOPPING
Pirrewil Kurrek CDEP has an artefact workshop (☎ 5450 4060, fax 5450 4121) on Koondrook Rd, Kerang, selling locally made boomerangs, didjeridus, emu eggs and beautiful digging sticks. Prices start at $5. The workshop is open 9 am to 5 pm weekdays.

Yorta Yorta Country
Barmah, Shepparton & Echuca

BARMAH
Information
Indigenous Organisations The Dharnya Centre (☎ 5869 3302, fax 5869 3249), on Sandridge Rd in the Barmah State Park, is a museum/information centre housing Aboriginal artefacts, a resource library, videos and some impressive displays. The centre's Yorta Yorta interpretative officers are happy to answer questions about the area and its history. They can also suggest trails (with free maps) through the magnificent Barmah

forest of wetlands and river red gums. Introductory talks and guest speakers can be arranged at cost (bookings essential; mainly for groups). Dharnya is open 10.30 am to 4 pm daily (an entrance fee applies).

Web Site Although some information is a little dated, the Yorta Yorta Web page has a great essay on the history of the Yorta Yorta by Elder Wayne Atkinson. Click on at http://users.mcmedia.com.au/~yorta/yorta.htm.

Organised Tours
Loatbaty Yarwul (meaning 'to walk and to talk') conducts tours in the Barmah State Park, 36km north-east of Echuca. Tours feature local Yorta Yorta native plants, language and scarr trees. Prices start at $10 per person (minimum of four). Tours operate from around December to August (weather permitting). Your own transport is required, although once you're in the forest, most of the tour is done on foot, so wear appropriate shoes. Bookings are essential and can be made by calling ☎ 5869 3247.

Excellent two-day Aboriginal guided tours of the Barmah region are offered by Seven Sisters Dreaming. Based around the Murray River, tours include traditional food meals, Yorta Yorta stories and visits to significant sites. You'll also visit a local Aboriginal community organisation to hear about contemporary issues. Tours depart from Melbourne (Wednesday and Saturday) at 7 am and return the following day at 6 pm. The cost is $350 (all-inclusive) and bookings are essential; for more details contact the booking agent, AUSRES (☎ 9696 0422, 1300 365 858, e res@ausres.com.au).

SHEPPARTON
Bangerang Keeping Place
Bangerang Keeping Place (☎ 5831 1020, fax 5821 0718) is on Parkside Drive. Open 9 am to 4 pm weekdays (free entry), the keeping place houses some impressive dioramas of different aspects of Aboriginal life. Its cultural officer is happy to answer any questions that you may have. Didjeridu performances and artefact presentations can be arranged (through appointment); along with traditional dance performances – costs on application. See its impressive Web site at http://saac.mcmedia.com.au.

ECHUCA
Art Gallery
Kevin Williams Gallery (☎ 5480 7604, fax 5480 7460) is on the 1st floor of the Murray Hotel Country Wares, 9 Murray Esplanade. From the Wiradjuri tribe, Kevin has had numerous exhibitions around Australia. Most pieces in the gallery are available for sale (prices from $30). The studio is open 10 am to 4 pm daily.

Jaara Jaara & Dja Dja Wrung Country
Bendigo Region

BENDIGO
Art Gallery
The Bendigo Art Gallery (☎ 5443 4991), 42 View St, houses some permanent Aboriginal artworks by Emily Kame Kngwarreye; it also has a set of Mimi (spirit) poles by various Indigenous artists. It's open 10 am to 5 pm daily (entry by donation).

Shopping
Aboriginal artwork (handmade jewellery, boomerangs, music sticks, shields and didjeridus) crafted by Brian Nelson and his family is available for sale. Brian is a Bendigo-based artist from the Yorta Yorta/Jaara Jaara clans. Call ☎ 0407 533649 to make an appointment.

Wiradjuri/Duduroa/Yiatmathang Country
Albury/Wodonga & Beechworth Regions

ALBURY/WODONGA
INFORMATION
The Gateway Information Centre (☎ 02-6041 3875, 1800 800 743 toll free) on Lincoln Causeway, Wodonga, features a small, but informative history display on the local Indigenous peoples on its back wall. The centre is open 9 am to 5 pm daily.

Tours
Organised Tours Eddie Kneebone (☎ 02-6055 6506, fax 6055 6558) operates tours that highlight Indigenous sites, including Yeddonba (see the Beechworth section later)

VICTORIA

HEAD FOR THE HILLS!

bryan Andy

Bogong moths breed in the lowlands of New South Wales (NSW), but during the warmer months (November to January) they move to the highlands to escape the heat. As adults the insects are about 5cm long and vary in colour from light brown to black. Aboriginal clans around the NSW and Victoria high plain area consider the moths a delicacy and follow them annually to these alpine areas to feast.

The moths' abdomens are over 50% fat, have a nutty flavour and are cooked in a sandy pit in which a fire has been lit. The hot coals are removed (to leave them in would singe the insect) and the moths are then stirred over the heated ashes and sand. They are then taken off the heat to cool and can be either eaten as is, or ground into a paste to make cakes.

The event that precedes the annual trek, the Mungabareena Ngan Girra Festival, has been observed for over 20,000 years. It continues to this day in Albury.

and its rock art, along with other Indigenous sites. A minimum of eight people is required ($10 each per hour), but prices are negotiable depending on numbers and times. Your own transport is required.

Self-Guided Tours Behind the Gateway Information Centre is Wiradjuri Walkabout, a free Aboriginal heritage trail that meanders along the Murray River. This self-guided 4km walk features signs detailing the local Indigenous heritage from cooking techniques through to bark canoes. Free maps for the walk can be obtained from the information centre.

Special Events

This area is famous for the Mungabareena Ngan Girra Festival (Mungabareena being the location, Ngan Girra meaning 'gathering') that takes place during the last week of November at the Mungabareena Reserve, Albury. The Mungabareena Ngan Girra precedes the journey north into the High Country to feast upon the delectable Bogong moth (see the boxed text 'Head for the Hills!'). The festival has a 20,000-year (plus!) history and continues to celebrate Aboriginal and Torres Strait Islander culture with dance, bush tucker tasting, storytelling and stalls.

Details and festival programs can be obtained from the organisers, Investment Albury Wodonga (☎ 02-6023 0100), or from the Gateway Information Centre in Wodonga (see Information earlier).

BEECHWORTH

Information

The Beechworth Visitor Information Centre (☎ 1300 366 321) is on Ford St and is open 9 am to 5 pm daily.

Organised Tours

Baranjuk (Wally Cooper) of Baranjuk Tours (☎ 5766 2360) is based in Glenrowan. Baranjuk's tours highlight Indigenous sites at Yeddonba, Mt Buffalo, Beechworth, the Ovens Valley and Rutherglen. There are no minimum numbers and you'll need your own transport. Prices start at $14 per person, with tour details on application.

Walking Trail

Just 12km north of Beechworth, Mt Pilot has the terrific Yeddonba Aboriginal Rock Art Walking Trail (on Toveys Rd, off the Chiltern–Beechworth Rd). This 45-minute, self-guided round route gives insight into the local Duduroa clan. The **rock art** at Yeddonba features faded paintings of a Tasmanian tiger, a lizard and a snake. Drop into the visitor information centre or the Burke Museum for details on how to get there.

Burke Museum

Burke Museum (☎/fax 5728 1420), on Loch St next to the Town Hall Gardens, houses an Indigenous artefacts display with shields, spears and *woomeras* (sticks used by men for throwing spears), with some dating back to the 1860s. It's open 10 am to 4.30 pm daily during school holidays, and 10.30 am

Indigenous people are often proficient athletes, and many of Australia's great sporting stars are Aborigines. By building goodwill and trust between people, sport helps break down barriers and contributes to Reconciliation.

When Cathy Freeman won gold at the Sydney Olympic Games she became an Australian icon. Her victory lap with both the Australian and Aboriginal flags in hand was a potent symbol for Reconciliation (1). Hurdler Kyle Vander-Kuyp is another Olympic hero (3). Bernard Chee comes in to land at the annual Melbourne NEC Athletics Grand Prix (2). Australian Rules Football and rugby are rich with Indigenous talent, from barefoot footy in the park on Thursday Island (4) to the annual Rugby League Knockout at Dubbo, NSW, the biggest Aboriginal sports event in Australia (5). Footballer Nicky Winmar proudly displays his black skin in defiance of racial vilification on the field (6).

SPORT SPORT SPORT SPORT SPORT SPORT SPORT SPORT SPORT SPORT SPORT

From trail-blazing Olympians to local clubs, Indigenous sport is recognised for the role it plays in personal development, life skills, health and community involvement. For more information see the Sport - Connected to Culture section on page 89.

Jenny Bedford, who plays guard for the Perth Breakers, dodges the Brisbane Blazers (1), and Baedon Choppy shoots for goal in the Australia vs India Four Nations hockey tournament (2). An up-and-coming star is the high flying Ronald Garlett (5). Halfback John Simon is an international rugby league player (3). Sports programs throughout the country are designed to encourage children, such as this Koori surf school (4). In the north, kids enjoy practising for rodeo, a very popular sport (6). Nova Peris-Kneebone, the first Aborigine to win an Olympic gold medal, began the Sydney 2000 Olympic Torch Relay starting from Uluru, NT (7)

to 3.30 pm at other times. Admission is $5.50/3 per adult/child.
Web site: www.beechworth-index.com.au/burkemus

Shopping
Baranjuk (see Organised Tours earlier) is also an artist, and he houses a collection of his own artefacts and crafts (boomerangs, paintings etc) in his shop at Gladstone St, Glenrowan (next door to the milk bar). To arrange a visit, phone ☎ 5766 2360.

Gunai/Kurnai Country
Gippsland Area

HISTORY
The Gunai/Kurnai people are estimated to have inhabited east Gippsland for at least 18,000 years. They are descendants of their Dreaming ancestors, Borun the Pelican and his wife Tuk the Musk Duck.

ORGANISED TOURS
Although the Bataluk Cultural Trail is a self-drive trail, it is far more scintillating to visit these sites on a tour with an Aboriginal guide – for details, see Organised Tours in the Bairnsdale and Orbost sections later.

MORWELL
Information
The Ninde Dana Quarenook Aboriginal Co-operative (☎ 5136 5100) is at 7–9 Buckley St and is open from 9 am to 5 pm weekdays. The organisation has plans to set up a local history/artefacts display here – phone for details.

Latrobe Regional Gallery
This gallery (☎ 5134 1364) at 138 Commercial Rd has a small permanent collection of Aboriginal art and occasionally features touring Indigenous exhibitions. The gallery is being renovated and plans to reopen August 2002.

Shopping
Owned and operated by a group of Koorie women, Yandina Earth (☎ 5133 0325) is at 41 Tarwin St and is open from 9 am to 5 pm weekdays. Yandina means 'A group of people going on a journey together'. This studio sells an assortment of handmade ceramic art with Indigenous themes, including some striking platters and urns. Prices start from $25.

SALE
Information
Indigenous Organisations The Ramahyuck District Aboriginal Corporation (☎ 5143 1644), is at 117 Foster St. It is named after an Aboriginal mission that was established on the Avon River in 1863. It has a small display of locally made arts and crafts, including screen-prints (some of which are for sale) and is open 9 am to 5 pm, Monday to Friday.

VICTORIA

BATALUK CULTURAL TRAIL
Joyce Connolly

As the Princes Hwy cuts through Gippsland, it forms the backbone of the Bataluk (Lizard) Cultural Trail, which itself follows a network of Gunai/Kurnai trails and trading routes. The trail is designed and promoted by the Gunai/Kurnai community in Gippsland to offer a greater appreciation and understanding of their traditional and contemporary lifestyles. Though it is a self-drive trail, it's far better to go on an organised tour with an Aboriginal guide – see the Organised Tours entries in the Bairnsdale and Orbost sections for details.

Places along the Bataluk Trail include the Ramahyuck District Aboriginal Corporation, the Knob Reserve, the Den of Nargun, Howitt Park, the Krowathunkoolong Keeping Place, Legend Rock, Burnt Bridge Reserve and Cape Conran. These places are further described in the Gunai/Kurnai Country section.

A brochure (free) detailing the trail is available from some of the visitor information centres en route (or try one of the organisations mentioned under Organised Tours in the Gunai/Kurnai Country section) and the sights are signposted from main roads.

Tourist Offices The Sale Visitor Information Centre (☎/fax 5144 1108) is at 8 Foster St. They can provide information about the Bataluk Cultural Trail, that starts at Sale which was originally known as Way-Put (see the boxed text 'Bataluk Cultural Trail').

Gippsland Art Gallery Sale
This gallery at 68 Foster St features touring Aboriginal exhibitions from time to time – for more information on upcoming events call ☎ 5142 3372.

STRATFORD
The Knob Reserve
Sandstone rocks here were used by the Gunai/Kurnai people as grinding stones for sharpening axe-heads. It's also likely that the river here was a popular fishing spot for eels, flathead, bream and prawns.

DEN OF NARGUN
It's believed that the legend surrounding this cave in the Mitchell River National Park resulted from the whistling sound of the wind in the cave and served the dual purpose of keeping Gunai/Kurnai children close to camp sites and scaring people away from this sacred women's site.

The den is said to be haunted by a large female creature known as the Nargun. According to the legend, the creature was able to deflect spears and boomerangs back to the thrower. A one-hour loop walk leads to a lookout, rainforest gully and the den – it contains fragile stalactites, so please don't go in. The park is signposted about 42km north-west of Bairnsdale. Access tracks lead into the park off Dargo Rd. There are three camping areas within the park and some good walking tracks.

BAIRNSDALE
Information
Indigenous Organisations Incorporating the Krowathunkoolong Keeping Place (see later in this section), the Gippsland & East Gippsland Aboriginal Co-operative (☎ 5152 1922) at 37–53 Dalmahoy St caters to the needs of the Gunai/Kurnai community throughout east Gippsland. It's open from 9 am to 5 pm weekdays, and is planning to open backpackers accommodation – phone for further information.

Tourist Offices The Bairnsdale Visitor Information Centre (☎ 5152 3444) is at 240 Main St and has brochures (free) on the Bataluk Cultural Trail. It's open 9 am to 5 pm daily.

Organised Tours
Boran Glaat Cultural Tours (☎/fax 5152 2585) can tailor-make tours to Indigenous sites in the region, including those on the Bataluk Cultural Trail. Prices vary depending on the length of the tour and minimum numbers apply (ring for details). All tours include a boomerang- or spear-throwing demonstration. Accommodation can also be arranged.

Krowathunkoolong Keeping Place
At the Gippsland & East Gippsland Aboriginal Co-operative at 37–53 Dalmahoy St, the Krowathunkoolong Keeping Place (☎ 5152 1891) is a very impressive cultural centre with some engaging and informative pictorial and artefact displays of crafts and tools used by the Gunai/Kurnai people, as well as their Dreaming and postcolonial history. It is open 9 am to 5 pm weekdays (closed noon to 1 pm); weekend visits may be possible with prior arrangement. Entry costs $3.50/2.50 for adults/children, which includes an introductory talk about the keeping place. Photography is not permitted. At the time of writing, there were plans to sell Indigenous arts/crafts and to have a Koorie artist in residence – this should be up and running by the time you read this.

Gruannunnerrang Aboriginal Art Gallery & Arts Workshop
Showcasing a fine collection of south-east Australian Aboriginal art, this gallery (☎ 5153 1002) at 2 Nicholson St is managed by the East Gippsland Aboriginal Arts Corporation. The collection includes Indigenous etchings, traditional baskets, prints and paintings. There are also occasional touring Aboriginal exhibitions (phone for details). The gallery is open 9 am to 5 pm weekdays (free entry) and many of the items are for sale.

Howitt Park
In this park is a scarr tree bearing a clearly visible 4m groove which is thought to be

more than 170 years old. This scarr is the result of bark being peeled away by Gunai/Kurnai people to build a canoe. The park is on the Princes Hwy, near the Mitchell River.

METUNG

The Aboriginal name for this town means 'Bend in the lake'. Metung is perched on a narrow spit of land and surrounded on three sides by the waters of Lake King and Bancroft Bay.

Legend Rock

In shallow water on the shore of Bancroft Bay, opposite the Metung Yacht Club, is the Legend Rock sacred site. According to Gunai/Kurnai mythology, the rock represents a hunter who was turned to stone for not sharing the food he had caught. Originally there were three rocks; unfortunately, the other two were destroyed during road construction work, but the remaining one was saved by community pressure when an injunction was issued under the Heritage Act of Victoria.

LAKES ENTRANCE

Shopping

The Lakes Entrance Aboriginal Arts Group (☎ 5155 3302), Centrepoint Arcade, The Esplanade, sells a range of Indigenous arts and crafts made by Gunai/Kurnai artists, including paintings, woodwork and jewellery. Prices start at $75. The shop is open 10 am to 4 pm daily.

BURNT BRIDGE RESERVE

Although the Gunai/Kurnai settlement at Lake Tyers, which became the focus of the country's first successful Aboriginal land rights case in 1971, is private property, Burnt Bridge Reserve (between Lakes Entrance and Nowa Nowa) has a small display board with a brief history of the community.

ORBOST

Information

There is a small Indigenous display at the Moogji Aboriginal Council (☎ 5154 2133), 52 Stanley St, which includes a locally made mural of the Snowy River Dreaming. It's advisable to ring ahead if you want to visit.

Organised Tours

Croajingolong Wilderness Tours (☎ 5154 2606/2486, fax 5154 2808) operates tailor-made tours (including the Bataluk Cultural Trail) throughout Gunai/Kurnai country with Koorie guides (prices on application). Accommodation can be arranged.

Koorie Plant Use Trail

On the compound of the Orbost Visitors Centre (☎ 5154 2424) at 13 Lochiel St is a small, verdant rainforest garden, developed by Will Cramer, which has various plants traditionally used by Koorie people for food, drink, medicine and other purposes. The centre offers informative guided tours of this short trail (possibly with an Aboriginal guide), which provide compelling Indigenous insights into the plants (these tours are only available by appointment). A free self-guided brochure about the trail is available. The centre also has a 20-minute audiovisual display about the rainforest (available on request). The centre is open 9 am to 5 pm daily.

CAPE CONRAN

The remains of a **shell midden** are visible just below the Salmon Rock viewing platform at Cape Conran. This was probably a Gunai/Kurnai venue for celebrations, feasts and ceremonies.

At East Cape Conran (often known as Sailors Grave), there is a 1.2km **self-guided walk** with signboards en route which provide insights into local Aboriginal culture. This trail was constructed by local Indigenous people in association with Parks Victoria.

VICTORIA

Western Australia

Western Australia (WA) is Australia's largest state, making up over one-third of Australia's landmass. An estimated 56,205 Aborigines live there, about 16% of the nation's total Indigenous population. Aborigines in WA use several names to refer to themselves. The Nyoongar people live in the south-west; in the south-western desert regions the people are collectively known as Wongi, and in many other parts of WA, Yamatji has become a popular generic noun.

Some of Australia's greatest Aussie Rules footballers have been WA Aborigines, as have some of its most important creative artists like playwright Jack Davis and author Sally Morgan. Jimmy Pike, the creative genius behind Desert Designs, is a Walmajarri man from the Great Sandy Desert.

History

Philip Morrissey

EARLY HISTORY
It is generally accepted that the north-west of WA was the point where Aborigines first entered Australia, and many archaeological sites emphasise the length of Aboriginal ownership of WA. At Swan Bridge, near Perth, a camp site was discovered containing stone tools and charcoal from a campfire that burned about 39,500 years ago. Fish and shellfish remains in an Aboriginal rock shelter at Mandu Mandu Creek in the Cape Range, North West Cape, have been dated to 32,000 BC – the remains of the world's oldest human necklace were also found at this site. Bone and stone tools, choppers and flakes dated to 31,000 BC were found at Devil's Lair, near Cape Leeuwin in the south-west of the state.

Huge amounts of ochre were mined over thousands of years from the Wilgie Mia site at the northern end of the Weld Range. This ochre, which symbolised the blood of a Dreaming being, was traded throughout Australia.

EUROPEAN ARRIVAL & ABORIGINAL RESISTANCE
Dutch mariners visited WA in the early 17th century and William Dampier landed on the

HIGHLIGHTS

Telephone code: ☎ 08
Indigenous population: 56,205
Overall population: 1.8 million
Area: 2.5 million sq km

■ Marvelling at the mysterious Wandjina on a guided tour of the art galleries of the Kimberley

■ Uncovering the brutal history of Fremantle and Rottnest Island

■ Camping in the desert of Wongi country around Kalgoorlie-Boulder

■ Learning how to make a spear or find bush tucker on a cultural tour of the Dampier Peninsula

■ Visiting artists at work in their studio at Balgo-Wirrimanu or Mowanjum

■ Stomping in Broome at the fantastic Stompem Ground Festival

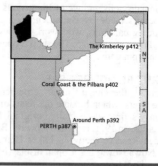

north-western coast in 1688. Macassan trepangers from the island of Sulawesi in South-East Asia had been in peaceful contact and trade with the people living on the WA coast since at least the 17th century. However, it wasn't until 1829 that a permanent European colony under the leadership of Governor Stirling was established on the Swan River, which later developed into the city of Perth.

This was Nyoongar land, and although there was an early period of peaceful accommodation, eventually the cycle of dispossession, resistance and reprisal began as the Nyoongar were robbed of their land and resources.

Nyoongar leaders such as Yagan, Weeip and Calyute led a doomed resistance. Yagan was killed by treachery and his head cut off, smoked, decorated and taken to England as an exhibit. Weeip eventually concluded a treaty with settlers – a tribute to Stirling's effective use of divide and rule tactics against the Nyoongar. Stirling's forces took Calyute's community by surprise in 1834. In spite of valiant resistance by his warriors, Stirling's soldiers carried out a general slaughter, breaking the Nyoongar resistance for good. While this is often referred to as the Battle of Pinjarra, it is more accurately described as a massacre. The following year the Murray River leaders pledged their support to Governor Stirling and the Crown.

Another famous bandit/resistance fighter of the 19th century was Jandamarra, also known as Pigeon. A Bunuba man, Jandamarra was one of the few Aboriginal resistance fighters to use firearms. He achieved mythical status among Aborigines because of his uncanny powers, and was eventually killed by an Aboriginal police tracker named Mingo Mick (who was also credited with supernatural powers). See the boxed text 'Jandamarra ('Pigeon')' later in this chapter for more information.

Settlers carried out numerous massacres. The Flying Foam Passage Massacre of 1872 is one instance, where 60 or more Aboriginal men, women and children were murdered. The Forrest River Massacre in 1926 was part of a police expedition to arrest an Elder named Lumbia, who had speared and killed a settler who had raped his wife. The incinerated remains of bodies were found and the Reverend Ernest Gribble drew the enmity of the settler community by insisting that an investigation be carried out. A royal commission found that a massacre had occurred but subsequent charges against police were dismissed through 'insufficient evidence'. Years earlier settler animosity had forced Gribble's father to leave WA when he protested at crimes against Aborigines. Children were sometimes kept after massacres as station workers and black-birding (kidnapping people to sell them into slavery) was practised on the coasts.

WA police worked in collusion with pastoral interests and, in wild west fashion, Aborigines were hanged in the main streets of some Kimberley towns. From the 1830s into the 20th century Aboriginal men were shipped from all over WA to the prison on Rottnest Island. This popular tourist spot has been described as an 'Australian gulag' and hundreds of Aborigines are buried there in anonymous graves. Aboriginal men and boys were punished by whipping long after it had been discontinued as a general punishment for settlers. Some of the most notorious of contemporary deaths in custody cases have been in WA.

Diseases also took a huge toll on Aboriginal communities. Leprosy scourged communities after it was introduced by pearlers in the 1870s – the Ngaluma people of Roebourne were almost wiped out by it.

Aborigines played major roles in the pastoral and pearling industries in the north – both Aboriginal men and women dived for pearls and Aborigines formed the bulk of stockmen.

CONFLICT & ASSIMILATION POLICIES

WA has been distinguished, even in comparison to other Australian states, by hostile and contemptuous attitudes toward Aborigines. At one point Nyoongar children were expelled from schools because of white fears of racial mixing. The Western Australian Aborigines Act of 1905 brought in wide-ranging controls over Aboriginal life. It allowed authorities to remove children, control employment, restrict movement, and deny access to alcohol. Amazingly, individuals could be assessed solely on the basis of appearance to see if they came under the act. As in other states, the Chief Protector was the legal guardian of all Aboriginal children. Sister Kate's Quarter Caste Children's Home was set up in 1933 to train 'mixed race' children for assimilation.

The Moseley Report of 1934, the outcome of a WA royal commission into the mistreatment of Aborigines, was a whitewash and ironically led to authorities being given greater powers over Aborigines.

WESTERN AUSTRALIA

WESTERN AUSTRALIA

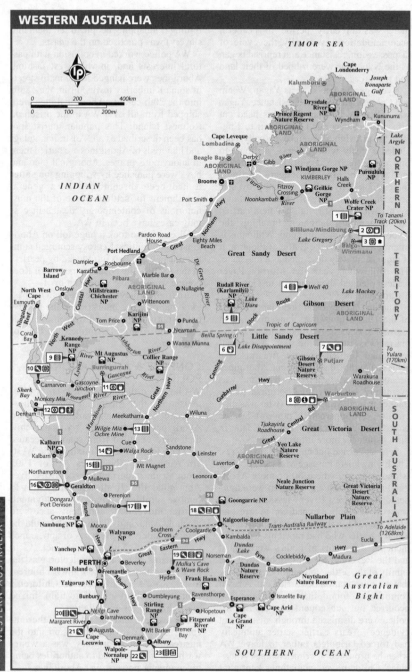

WESTERN AUSTRALIA

WESTERN AUSTRALIA

LAND ISSUES

In 1979 miners, escorted by a large contingent of police, and against the wishes of the traditional owners, entered Noonkanbah Station, south-west of Fitzroy Crossing, in a futile attempt to find oil. The Seaman Aboriginal Land Enquiry Report, commissioned by the state Labor government in 1983, produced recommendations that were too radical to be acted on and provoked a concerted, well-funded campaign to undermine Aboriginal entitlements to land. Development of the Old Swan Brewery site near Perth prompted protests and also dissension within the Aboriginal community, with many claiming it was an important Dreaming site and others denying it. There were later allegations that Aborigines had received inducements to deny the sacredness of the site.

The Indigenous Land Corporation, a Commonwealth statutory body, has purchased pastoral properties for Aboriginal communities. Although many of these properties were run down by white pastoralists, they allow Aboriginal communities to maintain traditional lifestyles as well as generate some income.

ABORIGINAL ACTIVISM

A Nyoongar man named William Harris was an early activist and in 1928 led a deputation to the state premier to protest against discrimination against 'mixed-race Aborigines'. Harris had made representations since the early part of the century on a wide range of issues affecting Aborigines

in WA. The Native (Citizen Rights) Act 1944 granted citizenship rights to Aborigines who could prove they were able to live like Europeans and were not carrying infectious diseases. The Native Welfare Act 1954 dismantled some of the controls exercised over Aborigines. The Coolbaroo League was active in the early 1960s. It held dances and social functions for Aborigines and their supporters and sympathisers and made political comment in its newspaper, the *Coolbaroo News*. In 1972, there was a full repeal of repressive legislation.

TRADITIONAL SOCIETY

Numerous middens, quarries and fish traps can be found in the southern part of WA. Flaked stone implements made in the Kimberley were traded as far as 1400km away and were highly valued items. WA has some of Australia's most significant rock art sites. The Pilbara region has major galleries of rock engravings, including images of thylacines (Tasmanian tigers), while the Kimberley has awesome galleries representing Wandjina and Rainbow Serpents. A white man named Joseph Bradshaw encountered enigmatic paintings of human figures in the Kimberley in the 1890s. Popularly known as Bradshaws, and referred to as Jungardoo by local Aborigines, the age of the paintings and their similarities with some African art has prompted wild theories about pre-Aboriginal civilisations in Australia. Recently an inscription of the date 1771, cut into a rock face in the Pilbara with a metal instrument, has prompted speculation that it was

WESTERN AUSTRALIA

inscribed by an 18th-century European, possibly marooned, and living with Aborigines.

Language

Most Aboriginal people over the age of 30 in the Kimberley, Pilbara and desert regions of WA speak one or more traditional languages, as well as varieties of Aboriginal English or Kriol. Throughout most of the state, Aboriginal people, except possibly the elderly, speak English.

THE SOUTH-WEST
At the time of colonisation, the Nyoongar language was spoken in the south-west of WA, including the Perth area. These days, few fluent speakers of this language remain, with younger Nyoongar people knowing little more than a few hundred words and a handful of phrases. Some Nyoongar words are used in place of English words in local Aboriginal English. English has in turn influenced the sound system and structure of modern Nyoongar, such as with the loss of the 'ng' sound at the start of Nyoongar words.

The legacy of the Nyoongar people includes a host of words borrowed into English for names of local plants, animals and places found in the west and south-west. Here are some placenames from the Nyoongar language you might come across: Boyanup, Burracoppin, Corrigin, Cowaramup, Cunderdin, Dandalup, Dardenup, Gnowangerup, Jerramungup, Katanning, Kellerberrin, Kirrup, Kojonup, Kondinin, Manjimup, Merredin, Mungallup, Nannup, Narrogin, Popanyinning, Porongurup, Quairading, Quinninup, Tammin, Wagerup, Wokalup, Woodanilling.

Useful Contacts
Noongar Language & Culture Centre (☎ 9202 1261) 23–25 Moore St, East Perth, WA 6004

Wangkanyi Ngurra Tjurta Aboriginal Corporation (☎ 9091 4705) 222 Boulder Rd, Kalgoorlie, WA 6430; PO Box 1470, Kalgoorlie, WA 6430

THE MURCHISON & GASCOYNE
The main surviving language of the Murchison and Gascoyne area (inland from the central-west coast), is Wadjari, originally spoken in the eastern Murchison area. Although there were a number of languages spoken in this region, the people all referred to themselves as Yamatji, and these days they call the language they speak the Yamatji language.

USEFUL CONTACTS
Yamaji Language Centre Inc (☎ 9964 3550, e yamaji@wn.com.au) 22 Sanford St, Geraldton, WA 6530

THE PILBARA
Few speakers remain of the languages of the southern and western Pilbara region, which spread from the Gascoyne to Ashburton Rivers. However, a number of languages are still spoken in the northern and eastern Pilbara. Yindjibarndi is the strongest survivor of the many languages which came together in Roebourne, and is also spoken in Onslow and other Pilbara towns. Visitors to the following areas may come across speakers of several WA Aboriginal languages: In the Karijini National Park, Bunjima, Gurrama and Innawonga are spoken; while Gurrama and Yindjibarndi are spoken in the Millstream-Chichester National Park. Below are some of the place names derived from Indigenous languages in the Pilbara.

Place name	Indigenous name
Clamina Gorge	Partiikunha
Cossak	Pajinhurrpa
Cowera Gorge	Karlayanguyinha
Crossing Pool	Murlunmunyjurna
Fortescue River	Mangkurtu
Hamersley Range (National Park)	Karijini
Manyjina Gorge	Pilirripinha
Marillana Gorge	Japurakunha
Millstream Station	Jintawirrina
Mt Nicholson	Kawuyu
Mt Alexander	Walkartatharra
Mt Brockman	Pirnayinmurru
Mt Bruce	Punurrunha
Mt Murray	Mukuriyarra
Onslow	Pirtan
Rio Tinto Gorge	Kalharramunha
Robe River	Jajiwurra
Roebourne, Jubilee Pool	Yirramakartu
Yampire Gorge	Kartirtikunha
Whim Creek	Parrkapinya
Wittenoom (Gorge)	Ngampiku

Useful Contacts

Wangka Maya Pilbara Aboriginal Language Centre (☎ 9172 2344, e alcphang@peg.pegasus .oz.au) Lot 5812, Leake St, South Hedland, WA 6722; PO Box 2736, South Hedland, WA 6722

THE KIMBERLEY

Several Aboriginal languages survive of around 15 different languages once spoken in the Kimberley region. They're spoken in the following areas:

Area	Language
Broome	Yawuru and probably also Karajarri, a Western Desert language
Cape Leveque	Bardi
Gibb River Rd	Ngarinyin
Bungle Bungle National Park, south of Turkey Creek	Kija and Djaru
Around Kununurra and Lake Argyle on the Ord River	Miriwoong
Various parts of the Kimberley, such as Fitzroy Crossing	Kriol

Useful Contacts

Kimberley Language Resource Centre (KLRC; ☎ 9168 6005, e klrchc@peg.pegasus.oz.au) Lot 158 Terrone St, Halls Creek, WA 6770; PMB 11, Halls Creek, WA 6770

Fitzroy Crossing Annexe of KLRC (☎ 9191 5124, e klrcfx@bigpond.com) Forrest Rd, Fitzroy Crossing, 6765 WA; PO Box 86, Fitzroy Crossing, 6765 WA

WESTERN DESERT

Dialects of the Western Desert language are spoken in communities across the Nullarbor Plain and in the desert; along the Canning Stock Route north across the Gibson and Great Sandy Deserts to the Kimberley; and west to the Hamersley Range and the Murchison goldfields.

Information

PERMITS

The Aboriginal Affairs Department (AAD; ☎ 9235 8000) at 197 St George's Terrace in Perth processes all applications for permits to travel on Aboriginal land trusts in WA. These include vast chunks of Aboriginal land in the state's eastern desert regions (see Information in the Perth section for more details on the AAD).

Permits are needed to visit Aboriginal communities and places in the Broome, Derby, Dampier Peninsula and Outback regions (see the relevant sections in this chapter for more information).

The Aboriginal Lands Trust (ALT), under the auspices of the AAD, manages the main Aboriginal communities, including Beagle Bay and Balgo-Wirrimanu.

Aboriginal freehold land is administered by the owners, and you must contact them direct for permission to travel across or visit their land. Request advice from the AAD if you're unsure whether a property is a land trust or freehold land.

To traverse the full length of the Great Central Rd from Laverton (WA) to Yulara (Northern Territory – NT), you need travel permits from the AAD for the WA side and from the Central Land Council in Alice Springs for the NT side (see the Alice Springs section of the Northern Territory chapter for details). You also need a permit from the AAD to drive the Gunbarrel Hwy and the northern end of the Canning Stock Route.

You can apply for a permit online at the AAD Web site (www.aad.wa.gov.au), by fax (9235 8093) or by writing to the Permits Officer at PO Box 7770, Cloisters Square, WA 6850. Note that the AAD does not issue permits for travel in South Australia (SA) or the NT.

NATIONAL PARKS

The state's national parks are administered by Conservation & Land Management (CALM). There are visitors fees charged for entering Kalbarri, Cape Range, Millstream-Chichester, Karijini, Purnululu and Mirima National Parks.

If you intend to visit more than one national park, it's worth considering a Holiday Pass ($22.50 for four weeks) or an Annual Park Pass ($51); note that camping fees are extra. Contact CALM in Perth (☎ 9334 0333, 1800 199 287 toll free) for more information, or visit the Web site at www.calm.wa.gov.au/ national_parks/park_passes.html.

WESTERN AUSTRALIA

Mooro

Perth

In Wajuk Nyoongar belief, the Swan River (Derbal Yaragan) and the landforms along its course were shaped by two Wagyl (huge Serpent Ancestors) during the Creation time. Today, the Wagyl live in an underground home beneath Kings Park.

At the time of the British invasion, the area around the river was divided among three clans. The Swan River Colony (later Perth) was established on Mooro, the homeland of Yellagonga and his people. Their territory stretched north from the Swan River to the Moore River (Maura) and they had a main camp site at Boorloo, near where the colony was founded.

Relationships between the British and the Nyoongar were friendly at first, but misunderstandings on both sides soon led to conflict and a series of murders. In 1829 Yellagonga removed his camp from Boorloo, first to Lake Mongers (Galup) then, as white settlement expanded, further north to Lake Joondalup. Finally, in the 1840s, the loss of their land reduced Yellagonga and his people to begging.

The last Nyoongar campers were expelled from Kings Park in 1915.

INFORMATION

The AAD (☎ 9235 8000) at 197 St George's Terrace provides an advocacy and support role for the state's Aboriginal people. It's a good place to start looking for contacts for Aboriginal organisations in WA, and to ask about Aboriginal tourism and cultural initiatives. It's open 9 am to 5 pm weekdays. Web site: www.aad.wa.gov.au

The Aboriginal and Torres Strait Islanders Commission (ATSIC; ☎ 9220 3211, fax 9229 3280) is at 256 Adelaide Terrace. It's open 8.30 am to 5 pm weekdays. Web site: www.atsic.gov.au

Libraries

Major Research Collections The Battye Library of Western Australian History (☎ 9427 3291) is in the Alexander Library (see Public Libraries later). It has an impressive amount of information on the state's Aboriginal people and you are welcome to browse; its archival section is open only to accredited researchers. The library is open 9 am to 9.45 pm Monday to Thursday, 9 am to 5.30 pm Friday, and 10 am to 5.30 pm on weekends.

Public Libraries Perth's major public reference library is the Alexander State Library (☎ 9427 3111) on James St, in Northbridge. It has quite a bit of material on Aboriginal history and culture, and opens the same hours as the Battye Library.

Specialised Libraries The AAD library houses a comprehensive collection of books, periodicals, reports and videos dealing with Aboriginal history and current issues in WA. You're welcome to browse weekdays between 9 am and 4 pm.

Radio Radio 6AR (Aboriginal Radio; ☎ 9325 1622, ℯ waama@iinet.net.au) is a community station broadcasting at 1170 on the AM band. Programs include lots of country and Indigenous music as well as news, current affairs, Aboriginal issues and sport. It's at 176 Wellington St in East Perth.

ORGANISED TOURS

Captain Cook Cruises (☎ 9325 3341, ℯ info@captaincookcruises.com.au) operates the Aboriginal Heritage Tour, which combines a Swan River cruise and an Aboriginal ranger-guided walk for $49/33 with/without lunch (children $35/20). The walking tour, which passes through bushland at Point Walter, lasts about 45 minutes and makes a fascinating introduction to local Nyoongar culture. Tours depart the Barrack St Jetty at 11 am weekdays from September to May.

You can contact CALM (☎ 9334 0333, 1800 199 287 toll free) to find out about any new Aboriginal-guided culture tours it may set up in and around Perth area. See also the later sections on Fremantle and Yanchep for details of CALM's culture tours in those areas.

Western Travel Bug (☎ 9204 4600, ℯ wtb@travelbug.com.au) includes a 30-minute Aboriginal-guided tour at Yanchep as part of its day trip to the Pinnacles Desert in Nambung National Park ($85).

Coate's Wildlife Tours (☎ 9455 6611) includes Aboriginal heritage sites on its tours from Perth to the Pilbara and Kimberley.

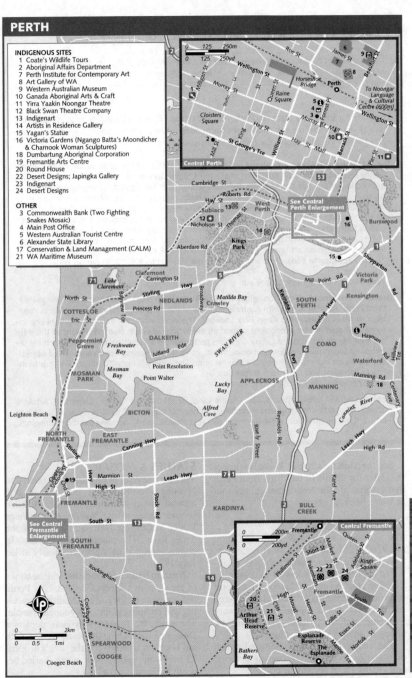

PERTH

INDIGENOUS SITES
1 Coate's Wildlife Tours
2 Aboriginal Affairs Department
7 Perth Institute for Contemporary Art
8 Art Gallery of WA
9 Western Australian Museum
10 Ganada Aboriginal Arts & Craft
11 Yirra Yaakin Noongar Theatre
12 Black Swan Theatre Company
13 Indigenart
14 Artists in Residence Gallery
15 Yagan's Statue
16 Victoria Gardens (Ngango Batta's Moondicher & Charnook Woman Sculptures)
18 Dumbartung Aboriginal Corporation
19 Fremantle Arts Centre
20 Round House
22 Desert Designs; Japingka Gallery
23 Indigenart
24 Desert Designs

OTHER
3 Commonwealth Bank (Two Fighting Snakes Mosaic)
4 Main Post Office
5 Western Australian Tourist Centre
6 Alexander State Library
17 Conservation & Land Management (CALM)
21 WA Maritime Museum

Central Perth

To Noongar Language & Cultural Centre (600m)

Roe St
James St
Wellington St
Horseshoe Bridge
Perth
Beaufort St
William St
Murray St
Raine Square
Forrest Pl
Murray St Mall
Hay St
Hay St Mall
Barrack St
Pier St
Cloisters Square
King St
St George's Tce
Mill St
Queen St

Cambridge St
Roberts Rd
Hay St
Subiaco
Nicholson St
Thomas St
West Perth
See Central Perth Enlargement
Burswood
Aberdare Rd
Kings Park
Broadway
Kwinana Fwy
Mill Point Rd
SOUTH PERTH
Victoria Park Rd
Shepparton
Clarefont
Carrington St
Stirling Hwy
NEDLANDS
Matilda Bay
Crawley
Kensington
North St
Princess Rd
Bayview Tce
COTTESLOE
Eric St
DALKEITH
Jutland Pde
SWAN RIVER
Canning Hwy
COMO
Hayman
Waterford
Peppermint Grove
Freshwater Bay
Point Resolution
Manning Rd
Mosman Bay
Point Walter
Lucky Bay
APPLECROSS
MANNING
Canning River
MOSMAN PARK
Alfred Cove
Reynolds Rd
Leach Hwy
High Rd
Leighton Beach
BICTON
Riseley Street
Karel Ave
Centenary Ave
Hilliew Tce
NORTH FREMANTLE
EAST FREMANTLE
Stirling Hwy
Marmion St
Leach Hwy
Stock Rd
BULL CREEK
Queen Victoria St
Ord St
High St
FREMANTLE
South St
KARDINYA
SOUTH FREMANTLE
Farrington
Rockingham Rd
Phoenix Rd
Cockburn Rd
SPEARWOOD
COOGEE
Coogee Beach

See Central Fremantle Enlargement

Central Fremantle
Fremantle
Queen St
Short St
Market St
Adelaide St
Kings Square
Philimore St
Pakenham St
High St
Mouat St
Henry St
Cliff St
Fremantle
South Tce
Collie St
Essex St
Norfolk St
Marine Tce
Arthur Head Reserve
Esplanade Reserve
The Esplanade
Bathers Bay

WESTERN AUSTRALIA

PERTH GALLERIES, MUSEUMS & SHOPS

Readers should be aware that the names of deceased members of the Aboriginal community may be cited in this section. Mentioning the personal name of someone who has died recently can cause offence, anguish and grief in some Aboriginal cultures.

There are far too many places in Perth that sell or exhibit works by Indigenous artists to list them all here. Below is a selection of recommended outlets. See the Shopping section in the Facts for the Visitor chapter for further information.

The Art Gallery of Western Australia (AGWA; ☎ 9492 6600), 47 James St, in the Perth Cultural Centre, Northbridge. AGWA has one of the most highly acclaimed collections of Indigenous art in the country and has permanently dedicated a large area for regularly changing displays of Indigenous works from this collection. Works by Indigenous artists from WA are a central part of the displays, with stunning artworks from a diverse range of communities including the southwest, Balgo, Warmun, Great Sandy Desert, Broome and Kimberley regions. The annual program also includes regularly changing exhibitions of contemporary works by Indigenous artists. The gallery shop has an exciting range of art publications, art reproductions, cards and a good selection of Indigenous art books. AGWA is open 10 am to 5 pm daily. There are free guided tours at 1 pm Tuesday to Friday and Sunday, with an additional tour at 12.30 pm on Friday. Admission is free.
Web site: www.artgallery.wa.gov.au

Artists in Residence Gallery/Aboriginal Western Australia (☎ 9481 7082) Fraser Ave, Kings Park, West Perth. Aboriginal Western Australia is at one of the most beautiful vantage points in Perth, high on Mt Eliza under the Kings Park Lookout. The views inside the gallery are just as impressive and should not be overlooked. Important exhibitions of works from all regions of the state are regularly shown and the gallery organises performances and cultural events. A discerning selection of biographies, children's books, music, cards, boomerangs, woven and carved objects, and books on Indigenous issues are also on offer. The gallery is open 10 am to 5.30 pm Monday to Saturday, and noon to 5.30 pm Sunday.
Web site: www.Aboriginalartworks.com

Artplace (☎ 9384 6964) Upstairs, Old Theatre Lane, 52 (1) Bayview Terrace, Claremont. Artplace actively supports emerging and established Aboriginal artists and exclusively represents WA artists. It has monthly solo exhibitions and also sells affordable art, including paintings, drawings,

---

See the Mulka's Cave & Wave Rock section later for details of day trips from Perth that incorporate the Aboriginal culture tour at Wave Rock.

CULTURAL CENTRE

The Noongar Language & Cultural Centre (☎ 9202 1261, e nlcc@iinet.net.au) at 23–25 Moore St in East Perth was established in 1986 as a means of encouraging the revival of Nyoongar language and oral histories. It's essentially a cultural resource centre for Nyoongar people, but visitors are welcome and the friendly staff will be happy to answer your questions.

The centre publishes Nyoongar/English dictionaries, books by Nyoongar authors, and videos about Nyoongar culture.

STATUES & MOSAICS

There are several public artworks related to Nyoongar culture and heritage in and around the city centre. One is a lifesize bronze statue of the Nyoongar resistance leader **Yagan**, on Heirisson Island in the Swan River. The plaque reads in part: 'In commemoration of Yagan, tragically killed July 1833'.

Ngango Batta's Moondicher, on the banks of the swan in Victoria Gardens, East Perth, is a sculpture on the site of a traditional meeting and camping place of Nyoongar people. The work, by Toogarr Morrison, depicts a Dreaming track along the water's edge, with tall boulders representing the area's original 12 freshwater lakes – now mostly buried beneath the urban sprawl.

continued... Brenda Croft

photographs, sculptures, jewellery and limited-edition prints by some of WA's most prominent and exciting Indigenous artists. Situated in a former cinema, it is a stunning three-level gallery and is only a two-minute walk from the Claremont train station and bus routes. Artplace is open 10 am to 5 pm Monday to Saturday, 2 to 5 pm Sunday.
Web site: www.artplace.com.au

Dumbartung Aboriginal Corporation/WA Aboriginal Artists' Advisory Committee (☎ 9451 4977) 295 Manning Rd, Waterford. Dumbartung is an exciting Aboriginal corporation that regularly initiates programs of Aboriginal arts education, exhibitions, performances and festivals. It also aims to raise the profile of Indigenous artists in the metropolitan market. It's open 9.30 am to 5 pm weekdays.
Web site: www.dumbartung.org.au

Ganada Aboriginal Arts and Crafts (☎ 9325 1190) 71 Barrack St. Aboriginal-owned and -managed, the Ganada outlet makes and sells a comprehensive selection of traditional and contemporary art and craft items aimed at tourists. Stocking a good selection of books on Indigenous art and culture, and selling clothing, carvings, emu eggs, art prints and music by Indigenous artists, Ganada is a worthwhile tourist stop that won't break the bank. (Its outlet in Broome is also worth visiting – see Shopping in the Broome section.) Ganada is open 9 am to 5 pm Monday to Thursday, 9 am to 8 pm Friday, 9 am to 5.30 pm Saturday, and noon to 6 pm Sunday.
Web site: www.ganada.com.au

Perth Institute for Contemporary Art (PICA; ☎ 9227 6144), 51 James St, in the Perth Cultural Centre. PICA focuses on contemporary visual art and performance and regularly includes Indigenous artists from WA and interstate in its exhibitions and events programs. It's open 11 am to 8 pm Tuesday to Sunday (7 pm in winter).
Web site: www.pica.org.au

Western Australian Museum (WAM; ☎ 9427 2700), 51 James St, in the Perth Cultural Centre, Northbridge. The First Peoples of Western Australia, Katta Djinoong ('to see and understand us') permanent display here has much to offer. The excellent display focuses not only on Indigenous societies before European invasion, but also on its devastating consequences. WAM has a fine collection of Aboriginal cultural artefacts and is a must for anyone interested in learning more about Aboriginal Australia. The WAM bookshop boasts one of the largest selections of Aboriginal studies titles in WA and offers a wide selection of books ranging from biographies and children's books, to archaeology and anthropology. WAM is open 9.30 am to 5 pm daily.
Web site: www.museum.wa.gov.au

Also in Victoria Gardens is a brightly coloured mosaic which tells the *story* of the **Charrnock Woman**. Produced by a collaboration of Aboriginal and non-Aboriginal artists, this eye-catching work is the first depiction of a Nyoongar Dreaming story to be used as public art in the city.

Two Fighting Snakes, at the entrance to the Commonwealth Bank on Forrest Place, is an impressive floor mosaic designed by Tjupuralla Matthew Gill, from Balgo Hills in the state's far north. It depicts his father's traditional country near Lake Mackay.

SPECIAL EVENTS
National Aboriginal and Islander Day of Celebration (NAIDOC) Week, held in July,

is a celebration of Aboriginal survival. It's a great chance to meet Aboriginal people and take in performances of theatre, dance, storytelling and music, as well as many other activities ranging from award-giving ceremonies to barbecues to sporting events. You can pick up a program from the AAD or Aboriginal and Torres Strait Islander Commission (ATSIC).

COURSES
The Noongar Language & Cultural Centre (NLCC; ☎ 08-9202 1261, fax 9202 1262, ✉ nlcc@opera.linet.net.au), 23–25 Moore St, East Perth, runs half- and full-day workshops in cultural awareness. These explain Nyoongar values and the balancing act that must be performed by people living in two

worlds. Workshops are run according to demand and are very reasonably priced; a minimum of five participants is required. You can write to PO Box 6060, East Perth, WA 6892.

ENTERTAINMENT
Theatre
Yirra Yaakin Noongar Theatre (65 Murray St, ☎ 9202 1966) is the state's major Indigenous theatre company. It specialises in plays by new and established Aboriginal writers and, because much of the material is taken from real life experiences, puts on some of the most powerful works on Perth's performing arts calendar. Yirra Yaakin is a regular performer during NAIDOC Week and at national events such as the Festival of Perth and the Adelaide Festival of Arts. To find out what's happening, phone or check the Web site at www.yirrayaakin.asn.au. Visitors are welcome to drop into the theatre to watch rehearsals and meet the cast.

Black Swan Theatre Company (☎ 9388 9388), Web site: www.bstc.com.au, is non-Indigenous but has a policy of supporting Aboriginal writers and actors. Each year it produces at least one Indigenous play; it held the world premiere of *Bran Neu Dae*, by Jimmy Chi. Black Swan is based in the Subiaco Theatre Centre (☎ 9325 3344) at 180 Hamersley Rd, Subiaco.

Dance
There are several Nyoongar dance troupes – such as Richard Wally's Aboriginal Dance Group, Dindima and Bindjareb Middar – based in and around the metropolitan area. However, the only place where Nyoongar dance is performed on a regular and frequent basis is Tumbulgum Farm, about 45km south of the city (see the Mundijong section later). Otherwise the best chance of catching a performance is during special events such as NAIDOC Week, the Festival of Perth and Back to Pinjarra Day.

Wajuk Country

Around Perth

FREMANTLE
History
To the Wajuk Nyoongars, Fremantle (Munjaree) was significant for the same reason that the British settled Fremantle – it was at the mouth of the Swan River, a place where tracks converged. There was a river crossing near the present-day train station, but it was destroyed during the construction of the port. This action caused such major disruption to the pattern of Nyoongar life that a powerful curse was placed on the head of CY O'Connor, the engineer-in-charge.

Nyoongar oral history tells of the sea inundating the land from the present coastline to beyond Rottnest Island. As this happened some 6500 years ago, it places these oral traditions among the world's oldest.

Walking Tour
The Aboriginal-guided tour Sharing the Dreaming offered by CALM is an eye-opening opportunity to learn the history of Fremantle from a different perspective. Among other things you: visit the Round House and try to imagine what it must have been like to be incarcerated there; hear the Nyoongar theory as to why CY O'Connor killed himself; and learn of the tragedy of Yagan. The tour, which lasts for an hour, departs from the WA Maritime Museum in Cliff St at 11.30 am on Wednesday, Friday and Sunday. The cost is $11 (children $5.50) and you book at the museum (☎ 9431 8469).

While you're waiting for the tour to start it's worth having a look at the Aboriginal **mangrove-log raft** from northern Australia. The display is near the museum's front desk.

Round House
Built in 1831, this building, at the western end of High St, was the colony's first prison – Yagan was imprisoned here in 1832 prior to being sent to Carnac Island to be 'civilised'. Later it was used to hold Aboriginal prisoners before they were taken to Rottnest Island. Conditions here were absolutely appalling, with prisoners forced to spend their nights crammed shoulder-to-shoulder in tiny cells.

The Round House is open 9 am to 5 pm daily; admission is $2.

ROTTNEST ISLAND
The Aboriginal-guided tour in Fremantle introduces the Dreaming tracks that run under the sea from the mainland to beyond Rottnest Island (Wadjemup). The island was

FREMANTLE GALLERIES, MUSEUMS & SHOPS

Brenda Croft

Readers should be aware that the names of deceased members of the Aboriginal community may be cited in this section. Mentioning the personal name of someone who has died recently can cause offence, anguish and grief in some Aboriginal cultures.

Quite a few places in Fremantle sell or exhibit works by Indigenous artists. Below is a selection of recommended outlets.

Desert Designs (☎ 9430 4101) 114 High St Mall. Paintings from Indigenous artists Jimmy Pike, Doris Gingingara and Deaggiddit are applied, with permission, to fashion fabrics under the label Desert Designs. It makes silk tops, dresses, T-shirts, knit patterns, children's wear and scarves, which are all beautifully made. As part of its commitment to the advancement and greater understanding of Indigenous culture, Desert Designs attaches the Dreamtime story behind each design to every garment sold. It's open 9 am to 5.30 pm weekdays, 10.30 am to 5.30 pm Saturday and 11 am to 5.30 pm Sunday.
Web site: www.ctl.com.au/desert/desert.htm

Fremantle Arts Centre (FAC; ☎ 9432 9555) 1 Finnerty St. Housed in a heritage building that was once a women's prison and an asylum, FAC is a dynamic arts organisation committed to Indigenous arts, which it promotes through exhibitions, projects and diverse cultural programs. The bookshop offers books covering Indigenous and political issues, biographies, children's books, posters, cards and postcards; and the craft shop has many beautifully crafted objects by WA's most accomplished artists. FAC is open 10 am to 5 pm daily.
Web site: www.fac.org.au

Japingka Gallery (☎ 9335 8265, ⓔ japingka@iinet.net.au) 47 High St. Japingka represents all major regions and styles in its fine two-level art gallery. The gallery features new exhibitions every five to six months, which give an in-depth focus on the works of specific artists. The gallery sells everything from vast dot canvases, didjeridus, art books, handmade pure wool rugs to delicate works on paper. Situated in the heart of Fremantle's west end it is open 9.30 am 5.30 pm weekdays, 10.30 am to 5.30 pm Saturday and 11 am to 5.30 pm Sunday.

Indigenart: The Mossenson Galleries (☎ Subiaco 9388 2899, Fremantle ☎ 9335 2911) 115 Hay St, Subiaco; 82 High St, Fremantle. Indigenart operates from two distinctly different premises known as the Mossenson Galleries. Exhibitions are regularly mounted that present Indigenous art from central Australia, Arnhem Land and the Kimberley. The gallery represents many contemporary Indigenous artists from other regions of Australia. It holds cultural tours, educational activities and didjeridu lessons, stocks paintings on canvas, bark and paper and sells weavings, ceramics, textiles and other artefacts. Subiaco Gallery is open 10 am to 5 pm Monday to Saturday; Fremantle Gallery is open 10 am to 5 pm Monday to Saturday, noon to 5 pm Sunday.
Web site: www.indigenart.com

cut off by rising sea levels some 6500 years ago and there appears to have been no Aboriginal occupation since that time. Indeed, to the Nyoongar people, Wadjemup is the home of spirits.

From 1838 to 1931 the island served as a prison for Aboriginal males from all over WA. About 3700 men and boys were imprisoned there in that time, often for such crimes (under British law) as cattle-spearing and petty theft, but also for being 'troublemakers'. The prisoners were poorly clothed and fed, kept in grossly overcrowded cells, and made to perform hard

labour such as quarrying and building work. Over 370 prisoners died on Rottnest, mostly from disease; 60 succumbed to an influenza epidemic in 1883.

Information
The island's visitor information office (☎ 9372 9752) is open 8.30 am to 5 pm daily. It's near the main jetty where the ferries arrive.

Museum & Old Buildings
The museum has a small display that graphically describes the hellish conditions under

AROUND PERTH

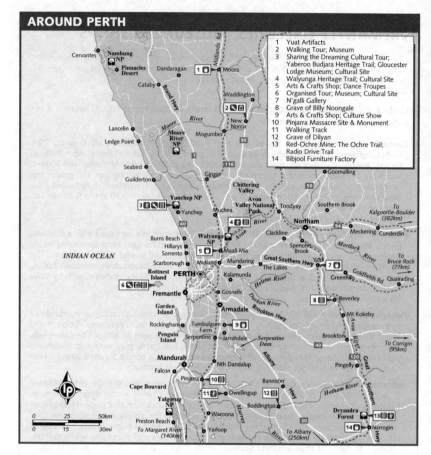

1	Yuat Artifacts
2	Walking Tour; Museum
3	Sharing the Dreaming Cultural Tour; Yaberoo Budjara Heritage Trail; Gloucester Lodge Museum; Cultural Site
4	Walyunga Heritage Trail; Cultural Site
5	Arts & Crafts Shop; Dance Troupes
6	Organised Tour; Museum; Cultural Site
7	N'galli Gallery
8	Grave of Billy Noongale
9	Arts & Crafts Shop; Culture Show
10	Pinjarra Massacre Site & Monument
11	Walking Track
12	Grave of Dilyan
13	Red-Ochre Mine; The Ochre Trail; Radio Drive Trail
14	Bibjool Furniture Factory

which Aboriginal prisoners were incarcerated – imagine being locked in a 5 sq m cell with nine other prisoners, the only waste disposal a bucket of water sloshed around the floor once a day. It's open 11 am to 4 pm daily and entry costs $2.20.

All of Rottnest's 19th-century buildings were constructed by Aboriginal prisoners. These include the museum (1857), the prison (1864) and the first lighthouse (1842), as well as the sea wall. The prison, known as 'The Quad', is now used for visitor accommodation.

You can visit the old buildings and the Aboriginal cemetery, where 364 prisoners were buried, on a free, one-hour guided tour that departs the information centre at 11.30 am and 2 pm daily.

WALYUNGA

Walyunga National Park, 40km north-east of Perth, contains the largest known Aboriginal occupation site within 80km of the metropolitan area. Thanks to its abundant food resources this area was an important ceremonial meeting place and contact point for Nyoongar clans from as far away as York and the Moore River. It also had good deposits of chert and quartz suitable for making tools. These were created by a Wagyl, which shaped the river and land in this area.

The park (ranger ☎ 9571 1371) is open 8 am to 6 pm daily. Entry costs $9 per car.

Walking Track

The 1.2km Walyunga Heritage Trail is a pretty walk along the west bank of the Avon

River between Walyunga and Boongarup Pools. A number of information signs en route introduce the traditional uses of local plants and animals, as well as a couple of the area's spirit entities. These include the evil Warrdarchi – hairy little creatures that catch swimmers and steal babies who cry in the night!

Entertainment
Maali Mia (☎ 9296 0704), an Aboriginal-owned arts and crafts gallery at 8991 West Swan Rd in Henley Brook, has Nyoongar dance troupes performing from time to time. This is usually when there's a special event being held in the Swan Valley.

Shopping
The Maali Mia gift shop's speciality is returning boomerangs, which are carved on the premises – you can watch them being made and learn how to throw them. There is a wide variety of good-quality pieces on sale, including traditional and contemporary paintings on canvas, music (CDs and tapes), decorated ceramics and glassware, *didjeridus* and weapons. All items are the work of Aboriginal people.

Maali Mia is about 9km north of Midland and 12km south of Walyunga National Park, on West Swan Rd just north of the intersection with Forest Rd. It is open 10 am to 5 pm daily.

YANCHEP
Yanchep National Park, 51km north of Perth, covers 28 sq km of native woodland. It also includes Loch McNess – home to a Wagyl and, in times past, an important ceremonial meeting place for Nyoongar people living between the Swan and Moore Rivers. The name Yanchep comes from *yanget*, the Wajuk Nyoongar word for the bulrushes that grow at the edge of the lakes in this area.

Information
The park visitor centre (☎ 9561 1004), which is open daily, has a couple of *Park Notes* leaflets dealing with the Aboriginal history of the area. Entry to the park costs $9 per car.

Organised Tours
Nyoongar rangers often conduct culture programs which include Creation time story-telling sessions, bush tucker walks and history walks. These are held daily over the summer and autumn school holidays, and at other times depending on demand; the various activities cost from $5 (children $2.50).

Sharing the Dreaming is an excellent Aboriginal-guided cultural tour that includes a short bush tucker walk around the lake. You'll learn such basics as how traditional shelters were constructed, how the family fire was sited, and the manufacture and uses of *bigo* (an araldite-like cement). This substance, which is made from dried kangaroo dung, charcoal and grass-tree *(balga)* resin, is immensely strong. In fact, it is only in the last 25 years that modern technology has been able to produce a cement that equals it for strength. The tour lasts about 1½ hours, costs $9 (children $3.50) and runs in the afternoon between Sunday and Thursday.

Yaberoo Budjara Heritage Trail
The 28km Yaberoo Budjara Heritage Trail links Loch McNess to Lake Joondalup in the south. It follows a chain of lakes which were a major source of food and water for the Nyoongars – an excellent brochure gives quite a bit of information about Aboriginal history and heritage along the way. At the time of writing the track was closed for major realignments and its future wasn't clear.

Gloucester Lodge Museum
The Gloucester Lodge Museum has several displays relating to Nyoongar history of the area. There are the usual artefacts including a kangaroo-skin cloak, and a replica of a traditional shelter. It's open 11.30 am to 4.30 pm Tuesday, Wednesday, Saturday, Sunday and public holidays; entry costs $2.

MUNDIJONG
Tumbulgum Farm (☎ 9525 5888), off the South Western Hwy between Byford and Mundijong, has a two-man 'culture show' – complete with audiovisual commentary – featuring a Nyoongar dancer and a didjeridu player. This is a rare opportunity for visitors to watch Nyoongar traditional dance. The show is held daily and lasts 25 minutes, finishing with demonstrations of spear and boomerang-throwing; admission is $10 (children $5).

Upstairs is an arts and crafts shop selling kangaroo-skin rugs, paintings, didjeridus,

WESTERN AUSTRALIA

carved emu eggs and weapons, mostly the work of local Nyoongar.

Yuat Country

North of Perth

NEW NORCIA
Australia's only monastic town, New Norcia was founded in 1846 as a Benedictine mission to the Aborigines. The monks were convinced that only 'the blessing of civilisation and religion' would save the Aboriginal people from the disastrous effects of white settlement. Accordingly, they planned to establish an independent, self-supporting community in which Yuat Nyoongars would be encouraged to settle as landholders.

By 1910 New Norcia was changing its direction from being a bush mission to an educational centre for Aboriginal and non-Aboriginal children. It still continues in this role, although on a much more modest scale than formerly.

Information
The tourist information office (☎ 9654 8056) is open daily except Christmas Day. Opening hours from November to July inclusive are between 10 am and 4.30 pm, and from August to October 9.30 am and 5 pm.

Walking Tour
The 'New Norcia Heritage Trail' brochure ($3), available from the tourist office, takes you on a self-guided tour to many of the town's historic sites. These include St Joseph's Orphanage & School for Aboriginal girls, and the cemetery, where white wooden crosses mark the numerous Nyoongar graves.

Museum
The museum, which adjoins the tourist office in St Joseph's, has a few small but interesting displays related to the mission's early Aboriginal residents. These include the Willaway family tree and historic photographs of local friends of the mission. There's also a fine collection of traditional artefacts, including some magnificent stone points, from the Kimberley region in the state's north.

The museum is open the same hours as the tourist office; admission costs $4.50 ($1 for children under 12).

MOORA
Moora, 172km north of Perth, is on the banks of the Moore River (Maura to the Nyoongar).

Shopping
At the northern end of Padbury St, Yuat Artifacts sells arts and crafts – mainly contemporary ceramics, but also landscape paintings, silk-screened T-shirts and traditional weapons – produced by local Aboriginal people. The shop is open 8.30 am to 4.30 pm weekdays.

DALWALLINU
The name 'Dalwallinu' is said to mean 'a place to rest awhile' in the Yuat dialect.

The tourist office (☎ 9661 1101) on Park Drive has a map that will take you to a **gnamma hole** (small rockhole) in a granite outcrop about 40km east of town. This is an attractive picnic spot, particularly in the wildflower season.

Places to Eat
Owned and operated by Aboriginal people, *Rails Coffee Terminal* (Park Drive) is a friendly cafe in the old train station, a stone's throw from the tourist office. It sells reasonably priced snacks and light meals, either takeaway or to enjoy in the cafe's pleasant al fresco eating area. The cafe is open from 9 am to 8 pm daily (closed Saturday afternoon). Ask here about local Aboriginal arts and crafts.

Balardung Country

Western Wheatbelt

YORK
Shopping
One of the many good things in this historic tourist town is the Nyoongar-owned and operated N'galli Gallery (☎ 9641 2529), at 105 Avon Terrace. This well-stocked arts and crafts shop has some wonderful pieces, with traditional designs a strong feature. The stock on display is reasonably priced and includes didjeridus, dot paintings, photographs, wooden carvings, ceramics, music and books. These are all the work of Aboriginal people, many of whom are local. The gallery is open most days from 9 am to 5 pm.

BEVERLEY

The grave of a Nyoongar, Billy Noongale, who accompanied Sir John Forrest on his expedition from Perth to Adelaide in 1870, is in the cemetery off Brooking St. Noongale died on 30 June 1904, aged 52 years.

Nyaki Nyaki Country

Southern Wheatbelt

MULKA'S CAVE & WAVE ROCK

Mulka's Cave, 21km north of Hyden, is the hollowed-out under section of a huge granite slab. This is an Aboriginal **art site** featuring dozens of faded **hand stencils** and several barely discernible **paintings**, the origins and meanings of which are not known, located close to the famous Wave Rock.

It's believed that the highest stencils were left by Mulka, who was the fruit of a forbidden liaison between a man and woman from the wrong skin groups. He was immensely strong but had crossed eyes, which prevented him from becoming a good hunter. Mulka, who lived in the cave, turned to eating children, and when his mother chastised him he killed her as well. Forced to flee, he made it as far as Dumbleyung, 150km to the south, where he was caught and speared to death.

About 300m from Mulka's Cave is a **gnamma hole** that would have been a valuable source of drinking water for Nyoongar people – perhaps even Mulka himself. The hole is poorly signposted and not very easy to find.

The tourist centre (☎ 9880 5182) at the Wave Rock Wildflower Shop in Hyden has a map showing how to get to Mulka's Cave.

Organised Tours

Tours led by a Nyoongar guide depart daily from the Wildflower Shop in Hyden, taking you on a 45-minute (or longer) stroll to **Hippo's Yawn** (a traditional birthing place) via Wave Rock itself. You'll hear the story of Wave Rock's association with the evil Milky Way woman, learn how fire and water were used to make gnamma holes, visit Hippo's Yawn and learn something of the traditional uses of local plants. The tours cost $12.50 per person for groups under five people ($7.50 between five and 10), and you book at the Wildflower Shop.

Day trips from Perth that include Mulka's Cave and the Aboriginal-guided tour at Wave Rock are run by Australian Pinnacle Tours ($119; ☎ 1800 999 304 toll free) and Feature Tours ($105; ☎ 9479 4131).

Pinjarup Country

South of Perth

PINJARRA

Information

The Pinjarra tourist office (☎ 9531 1438), on the corner of George and Henry Sts, is open 8.30 am to 4.30 pm weekdays and 9 am to 4 pm weekends. It has an excellent leaflet, written by Pinjarup Nyoongar people, giving an account of the Pinjarra Massacre from their perspective (see the History section at the beginning of this chapter for more information).

Monuments

At the time of writing local Nyoongar had received a grant to build a monument at the site of the Pinjarra Massacre, which took place near the cemetery on the outskirts of town. The monument is to include mosaics that tell the story of the massacre. It will also give the names of those who were killed.

Special Events

Every year on the closest Saturday to October 28 (the anniversary of the Pinjarra Massacre), Nyoongars hold the Back to Pinjarra Day festival. A celebration of Nyoongar culture as well as a commemoration of the massacre, the festivities include speeches, storytelling, dance, theatre, bands and arts and crafts stalls. Among its regular highlights is the performance of the play *Bindjareb Bindjareb*, which recounts the massacre. As well, there are usually performances by the local dance troupe Bindjareb Middar (see Entertainment in the earlier Perth section).

DWELLINGUP

Nyoongar people did not spend a lot of time hunting and gathering in the jarrah forests of Dwellingup. Rather, they travelled through in winter to late spring while en route between the major food centres of Boddington and Mandurah.

The **Forest Heritage Centre** (☎ 9538 1395) on the outskirts of Dwellingup has a

700m walking track with numerous signs giving information on the traditional uses of forest flora. One of the most useful plants was balga, which had over 25 uses including the healing of human relationships. It was also a source of food, thatching for shelters, fire-lighting materials, and an ingredient in a super-strong bush cement (see Organised Tours in Yanchep section earlier). The centre is open 10 am to 5 pm daily; admission is \$5.50 (children \$2.20).

Wiilman Country

South-East of Perth

BODDINGTON

The grave of a Nyoongar man, Dilyan, who accompanied Sir John Forrest on his expedition from Perth to the Kimberleys in the 1880s, lies in the forest about 4km from Boddington on the road to Dwellingup. The grave, which is signposted, is about 200m past the town cemetery and 100m off the road.

DRYANDRA FOREST

About 160km south-east of Perth, the Dryandra Forest is a rare haven for 13 of the mammal species that formed part of the traditional Nyoongar diet. Several of these species have disappeared elsewhere in the south-west as a result of habitat destruction and predation by introduced animals, particularly foxes.

The Nyoongars mainly lived here during the wetter months, when food and water were abundant, then retreated to coastal areas such as Mandurah to see out the hot, dry summer.

There are several cultural sites in the reserve and you can visit one of them – a small red-ochre mine – on **The Ochre Trail**. This 5km path, which is poorly marked in places, takes you on a pleasant ramble through a picturesque woodland of white-barked wandoo (a kind of eucalypt). A handful of information signs en route tell you a little of the forest's Aboriginal heritage.

There's also a 25km **radio drive trail** where, by tuning to 100FM, you can listen to broadcast commentaries as you move from site to site. These include stories of the local Nyoongars and their relationship with the forest.

Brochures are available from Narrogin's CALM office (☎ 9881 9200), on Hough St and the caretaker (☎ 9884 5231) at Lion's Dryandra Village, which is in the forest about 30km north of Narrogin.

NARROGIN

Narrogin is said to mean 'place of flood gums' or 'place of water' in the Wiilman Nyoongar dialect.

Shopping

Nyoongar craftsmen create magnificent pieces of furniture at the Aboriginal-owned Bibjool, on Graham Rd in the town's southern industrial area. A full range of fine furniture is manufactured on site using solid timber (mainly jarrah and sheoak) salvaged from local native forests.

You can visit the workshop on weekdays between 8 am and 4.30 pm (2.30 pm on Friday) and, provided a guide is available, do a free tour of the milling, drying and woodworking areas – ring the manager first on ☎ 9881 4008 (after hours ☎ 9881 5464). They'll take factory orders and build to your specification.

Wardandi Country

South-West Corner

NGILGI CAVE

Near Yallingup is the mystical Ngilgi Cave, so named for its association with a battle fought between Ngilgi and the evil Wolgine during the creation time. The full story is told by a series of information panels in the waiting area.

Organised Tours

Semi-guided tours of the cave depart daily every 30 minutes between 9.30 am and 3.30 pm (later on long weekends and school holidays). The tour lasts around an hour and costs \$13 (children \$5).

There's also a three-hour cultural awareness tour with Mitch Hutchins, the granddaughter of a Wardandi Nyoongar Elder. This tour features a bushwalk through coastal woodland from the cave up to Wardanup Hill, which has great views – it's a whale-watching spot. En route Mitch talks about a wide range of topics including totemic ancestors, Nyoongar contemporary history, *law*, spirituality and family values, and bushcraft. You also get to taste bush tucker in season and learn the Nyoongar names and uses of many local plants and animals. The tour winds down with a hilarious didj session at the cave.

Mitch does a similar bush culture tour along the Dijwarka Walking Trail, which winds through jarrah forest near Jarrahwood, on the Vasse Hwy between Busselton and Nannup. Both these tours are for larger groups – you're welcome to tag along – and cost $15 (children $8). Book with Waljin Consultancies on ☎ 9756 2075.

MARGARET RIVER
Organised Tours
Bushtucker Tours (☎ 9757 9084) at Prevelly Park combines walking and canoeing along the Margaret River. This four-hour tour, which was set up with advice from Nyoongar people, delves into the Aboriginal heritage of the river, its people and plantlife. You can try 25 kinds of bush tucker (including smoked kangaroo and emu, quandongs, and bardi grub pâté) and visit ancient rock shelters. The tour operates most days, leaving at 10 am; it costs $33 (children $16.50) and a minimum of two adults applies.

Minang Country
South Coast

DENMARK
The name for Denmark in the Minang Nyoongar dialect, Koorabup, means 'place of the black swan'. The sea yielded a rich harvest for local Nyoongar, and the remains of old fish traps have been found in **Wilson Inlet**. See the Fish Traps section under Albany.

Provided the tide is low you can see one of the fish traps with Sandpiper Cruises (☎ 0417 182 327), which does boat tours of Wilson Inlet from October to May.

ALBANY
The British military garrison that occupied Albany (Kincinnup) from 1827 to 1830 enjoyed friendly relations with the Minang Nyoongar people who lived around King George Sound. This was partly because the soldiers provided protection from woman-stealing raids by lawless white sealers and whalers, and partly because they took up only a little land (around 15 hectares). Fighting between Nyoongar people and British settlers broke out in the hinterland in 1838, with guerilla warfare continuing until the 1890s.

Information
The AAD's regional office (☎ 9842 3000) at 129 Aberdeen St is a good source of information on where to find Nyoongar tourism-based ventures in the Albany district. It opens weekdays during normal business hours.

Fish Traps
The remains of stone fish traps recorded in 1791 by Captain Vancouver can still be seen at low tide in shallows by the northern shore of **Oyster Harbour**. The traps, which were crescent-shaped and up to 100m long, were made of boughs and cross-sticks, with a low stone wall along the bottom to stop the fish escaping. Early white visitors were reportedly amazed at the large quantities of fish caught in traps like this.

To reach them, head out of town along tourist route No 6 and take the first turn right (Morilla Rd) past the King River bridge. Turn left onto Barameda Rd; there's a fish trap right in front of the information sign off the end of the road.

Museums
The Western Australian Museum – Albany (☎ 9841 4844), on Residency Rd near the waterfront, has displays relating to the Nyoongars, including the accounts of a couple of 1820s white visitors (Phillip King and Dumont D'Urville), who describe meetings they had with local Aborigines. On display is a cloak made from kangaroo skins, plus the usual wooden artefacts. There's also an introduction to the Wagyl, a serpent being who made the streams and springs, controls rainfall, and is generally responsible for the region's fresh water. This is one of the Nyoongars' main spirit ancestors.

The museum has several informative 'fact sheets' relating to the Aboriginal people of the south-west. These include 'A Noongar Geography of Albany and A Noongar History of Strawberry Hill' and 'Aboriginal Fishing in South-Western Australia'. It's open 10 am to 5 pm daily.

WESTERN AUSTRALIA

Wongi Country

South-Western Desert

KALGOORLIE-BOULDER

Information

Indigenous Organisations The AAD regional office (☎ 9021 5666) is on the corner of Brookman and Cassidy Sts. ATSIC (☎ 9021 1655) is at 14A Throssel St. Both are open weekdays during normal business hours.

Tourist Offices The helpful Kalgoorlie-Boulder Tourist Centre (☎ 9021 1966, fax 9021 2180, e kbtc@gold.net.au), on the corner of Hannan and Cassidy Sts, is a good source of information on Aboriginal tourism ventures in the district. The office is open 8.30 am to 5 pm weekdays and 9 am to 5 pm weekends.

Organised Tours

The Aboriginal-owned and -operated Kurrawang Emu Farm is in the Kurrawang community 18km west of Kalgoorlie off Route 94. The emphasis here is on egg production rather than byproducts like meat and oil. You can learn about emu management and breeding on informative tours that last from 30 minutes and cost $6 (children

---

A DREAMTIME NIGHTMARE: ABORIGINAL CULTURE & WHITEMEN MINING

The Tjukurrpa (Dreaming) is the period of creation. It is the past, the present and the future. It is our religion and our cosmology. It explains how ancestral beings created the world – both the natural and cultural landscape – and how in their interactions they gave us laws that regulate all things.

The evidence and spiritual energy of this creation is in the land, and is most powerful at sacred sites. Aboriginal people who follow the laws of the Tjukurrpa understand the land and our place in the cosmos in terms of this ancient tradition. We are part of its creative force and are responsible for its management and renewal. That is why we are obligated to protect sacred sites.

In the goldfields, many Wangkatja (or Wongutha) still follow the Tjukurrpa. Wangkatja is a general term for an Aboriginal person, it is not a tribal group. There are many different tribes/peoples in the goldfields; for example, I am a member of the Ngalia people. Today the term Wangkatja more accurately reflects a national (First Nation) identity arising from an amalgam of tribal groups or peoples.

Wangkatja still speak their languages and still teach their history. All of this occurs within, and despite, the modern mining towns with their rapacious industry of digging, drilling and destroying.

The Aboriginal history of the goldfields region is old and shrouded in the mists of time. Unfortunately little is known of the Aboriginal story of the goldfields. In the past it was convenient to deny or ignore the Aboriginal connection to the land and just exploit it for its natural resources. However this land is rich in Aboriginal culture. The entire landscape is culturally defined – each hill, creek, tree and animal has a name, a history and a place in the Tjukurrpa. Each element of the landscape has a connection between the Tjukurrpa and Wangkatja of the past and the present.

At a place north of Leonora known to local Wangkatja as Katampul, archaeologists dated Aboriginal occupation of the region back 21,000 years before the present, that is 21 millennia! The evidence of occupation was in a cave with countless stone artefacts and campfire remains buried in layers up to 2m deep. I assisted on this dig at Katampul in 1990 and while sitting in that cave, watching the rain pour, I imagined the past. What was it like 21,000 years ago? I imagined a family at the onset of the ice age sitting down to their meal beside a warm campfire on the cave floor some 2m below me. Did they follow the

$3). Tours are available on demand daily except Sunday between 9 am and 3 pm.

Yamatji Bitja Aboriginal Bush Tours (☎ 9093 3745, 0407 378 602, ℮ Geoffstokes@bigpond.com) is another Aboriginal-owned and -operated business. The friendly owner, Geoff Stokes, offers several tours – all highly recommended – that aim to teach you about the heritage of Kalgoorlie's Wongi people.

Geoff's twilight tour ($35; children $17.50) involves storytelling around a campfire with billy tea and damper. Day trips ($80; children $40) go out about 40km from Kal, introducing such topics as Wongi history, bush skills, and the plants and animals and their association with the creation time. You'll learn even more on his overnight trips ($170; children $85), which go into the heart of Geoff's traditional country about 200km from town. Swags and meals are included, and advance bookings are recommended for all tours.

Museum of the Goldfields

The Museum of the Goldfields, at 17 Hannan St, has an ethno-botanical garden featuring plants used by Western Desert Aborigines. Inside there are only a couple of Aboriginal displays: one of traditional

---

continued...   Kado Muir

Tjukurrpa beliefs too; or perhaps they are the Tjukurrpa or Dreaming ancestral beings we worship today?

Katampul is a feature in many Tjukurrpa stories that converge at an important site not far north. The Wayuta Tjukurr (path of the Dreaming Ancestral Possum Being) travels up to Katampul from Kalgoorlie way in the south. The Kaliya Tjukurr (Emu Dreaming) passes through here from the north heading south and other sacred Tjukurrpa paths crisscross the region. These Tjukurrpa paths are the 'songlines' of Bruce Chatwin fame, but they are also a system of knowledge and belief that is written in the land and read and understood through song, dance, design and narrative.

Kalgoorlie, the regional centre, is Kalkula Tjukurr (Bush Banana or Silky Pear Dreaming). There is a rockhole called Kalkula a stone's throw from a backyard in Williamstown (a dying suburb of Kalgoorlie), which in a bastardised form gave its name to the modern mining city. Not many whitefellas know it exists. Coolgardie, the region's first town, is built on a traditional Aboriginal centre. A major rockhole was dug out and turned into the town water supply, before the Perth to Kalgoorlie pipeline was built to supply the water. All around Coolgardie are important sites where cultural practices are maintained.

All of this knowledge, culture and insight are shared by Wangkatja in the Aboriginal art of the region. You can find out the real story of the goldfields through the bush tours operated by Wangkatja, through the cultural awareness courses, the books written by Wangkatja and by taking time to meet Wangkatja themselves.

For further information contact Kado Muir (☎ 0419 866 506, ℮ admin@kado.com.au), PO Box 409, Leonora, WA 6438. Web site: www.kado.com.au

Kado Muir

Kado Muir is a member of the Ngalia people and is active in the Ngalia people's fight for land rights.

As a result of progressing through western and traditional cultural education, he is a firm proponent of recording, interpreting and passing on the knowledge and culture of Aboriginal people to future generations and those with a genuine desire to understand. Kado is a researcher, artist and businessman.

WESTERN AUSTRALIA

artefacts and the other contemporary art. It is open 10 am to 4.30 pm daily.

Special Events

NAIDOC Week (held in September in Kal) kicks off on with a parade up Hannan St and finishes with a cabaret on Saturday night. In between are netball and Aussie Rules carnivals, a country and western music night, a culture day with men's and women's dancing, and many other activities. Non-Aboriginal people are welcome to attend; you'll find the program advertised in the *Kalgoorlie Miner*.

Shopping

The friendly Kurrawang Emu Farm (see Organised Tours earlier) has a shop that sells an impressive variety of creams and lotions, even shampoo and sports rub, made from emu oil. You can buy a plain, blown emu egg for $11 or splurge on a magnificent, locally carved one for $165. Also on sale are local wooden crafts such as decorated didjeridus, tapping sticks and carved animals. The shop is open 9 am to 4 pm daily except Sunday.

There are a couple of places in Kal where you can buy arts and crafts produced by Aboriginal people of the Western Desert region. The Desert Art Shop (☎ 9091 5504) at 9 Hannan St has some beautiful work in the form of dot paintings and contemporary oil portraits of Aboriginal people. There are also didjeridus and carved animals. It is open 10 am to 5.30 pm weekdays and 10 am to 1 pm Saturday.

At 222 Dugan St, the modest exterior of the Goldfields Aboriginal Art Gallery conceals an impressive horde of reasonably priced arts and crafts. Among the more unusual offerings are fire-straightened spears, emu-feather shoes and woven spinifex baskets. The shop is open 8 am to 5 pm weekdays, 8 am to 1 pm Saturday, and 11 am to 1 pm Sunday.

Yamatji Country

Geraldton Area

GERALDTON

The traditional boundary between the Nyoongar and Yamatji cultural groups is around 100km south of Geraldton. Several Geraldton suburbs, such as Karloo, Tar-

coola and Utakarra, are named after Yamatji cultural sites in those areas.

Sir George Grey passed this way in 1839 and found strongly built dwellings, cleared pathways and soakages dug out to a depth of 5m, indicating that Yamatjis were settled semipermanently along rivers in the area. Nine years later, the WA governor, Charles Fitzgerald, was attacked by Yamatji warriors about 40km north of Geraldton. At least one Yamatji man was killed and the governor was speared in the leg.

Information

Indigenous Organisations The AAD regional office (☎ 9964 5470) is at 21 Chapman Parade, while ATSIC (☎ 9964 3640) is at 17 Lester Ave.

Tourist Offices The Marra Gallery (see Shopping later) is the best place in town to find out about Yamatji tourism-based ventures in the Geraldton district.

Alternatively, try the Geraldton-Greenough tourist office (☎ 9921 3999, fax 9964 2445, **e** tourism@wn.com.au) in the town centre on the corner of Chapman Rd and Bayly St. It's open 8.30 am to 5 pm weekdays, 9 am to 4.30 pm Saturday and public holidays, and 9.30 am to 4.30 pm on Sunday.

Newspapers & Magazines The free, fortnightly newspaper *Yamaji News*, which is published at 22 Sanford St (☎ 9964 3550, **e** yamajinews@wn.com.au), covers news and issues of interest to Yamatji people. The paper is widely available throughout the Yamatji cultural area; in Geraldton you can pick up a copy at Aboriginal organisations and delis around town.

Organised Tours

The Geraldton Streetwork Aboriginal Corporation (☎ 9921 2890) has set up a two-hour culture tour at Gunnado Farm near Walkaway, 30km south-east of town off Hwy 1. The tour, available from April to September, includes an Aboriginal-guided bushwalk, storytelling, spear- and boomerang-throwing, traditional shelters and bush tucker. Group bookings are preferred.

Yamaji Language Centre

The Yamaji Language Centre (☎ 9964 3550) at 22 Sanford St publishes word lists and dictionaries for various Yamatji languages. While this is basically a cultural and language resource centre for Yamatji people, visitors who want to learn about Yamatji culture are welcome.

Museum
At the time of writing a regional branch of the **Western Australian Museum** was being constructed off Chapman Rd opposite the tourist office. The main aim of its Aboriginal heritage displays, which were being developed in consultation with the Yamatji community, is to 'enable the visitor to understand the significance of the region to Aboriginal people past and present'.

Shopping
The Marra Gallery, in the Old Railway Building on Marine Terrace, has some great arts and crafts by people from the Yamatji cultural area. On display are paintings on canvas (both traditional and contemporary styles), handmade ceramics, didjeridus, weapons and other carved wooden objects, hand-painted silks and gum-nut jewellery. The shop is open 10 am to 3 pm weekdays.

BUTTERABBY GRAVE SITE
The Butterabby Grave Site, about 18km south of Mullewa, is a grim reminder of the conflict that took place between Yamatji people and the British invaders. In 1864, following several clashes in the area, two white men (a settler and a shepherd) were fatally speared near here. Five Yamatji men were arrested and subsequently sentenced to death under British law for the killing of the shepherd; a sixth was sentenced to life imprisonment for the manslaughter of the settler. To demonstrate that continued resistance was pointless, the police rounded up a number of Yamatjis and forced them to watch their relatives being hanged at Butterabby.

A small monument was later erected at the grave site, which today is a low grassy knoll surrounded by wheat paddocks. The inscription, now mostly illegible, read:

In these graves lie James Rudd speared here at Butterabby 23 Sept 1864, also Garder, Wangayakoo, Yourmacarra, Charlacarra, Williacarra – natives sentenced in Perth and hanged here 28 Jan 1865 for the spearing of Thomas Bott at Butterabby 22 August 1864.

To get to the grave site take Mingenew Rd off the Geraldton-Mullewa road – the turnoff (west) is 15km from the road and the grave is 2km past the turn-off. The Mullewa tourist office (☎ 9961 1505), on Jose St, has a map as well as the booklet 'Wildflower Country', which includes a version of the Butterabby story.

Wadjari Country
Murchison River Area

CUE
Situated 640km north-east of Perth on the Great Northern Hwy, Cue's region was once a meeting and trading territory for Aboriginal people from all over Australia. It is now widely known as a historic gold-mining town.

There are a number of significant sites in the area. Two of the most celebrated are the Wilgie Mia Ochre Mine and Walga Rock (Walganna).

Information
The Cue shire is developing Aboriginal tourism proposals for the region. Contact the Cue Tourist Bureau (☎ 9963 1216) in Robinson St for updates. Note it is only open from April until October.

WILGIE MIA
Wilgie Mia, north-west of Cue, has been mined by Aborigines for thousands of years for its red ochre.

Due to safety concerns, the local Aboriginal people discourage tourists from visiting Wilgie Mia, so please respect their wishes. Red ochre has been mined here for possibly more than 30,000 years. Aborigines used scaffolding, stone hammers and wooden wedges to remove thousands of tonnes of rock to get to the ochre, believed to have been traded as far away as Queensland.

The mine drew people from numerous clan groups who left many notable sites to record their presence.

WALGA ROCK
Walga Rock (also known as Walganna), about 47km south-west of Cue via Austin Downs Station, is a rock monolith that juts 50m out of the surrounding scrub. It is one

CORAL COAST & THE PILBARA

1 Wangka Maya Pilbara Aboriginal Language Centre;
  Western Desert Puntukurnuparna Aboriginal Community;
  Dalgety House Museum; Two Mile Ridge Engraving Site;
  Community Arts Centre
2 Murujuga Rock Engraving Sites
3 Karratha Tourist Bureau; Jaburara Heritage Trail;
  Rock Engravings
4 Deep Reach Pool; Chinderwarriner Pool
5 ATV Tours; Cardabia Station Stays
6 Karijini NP Visitors Centre & Shop
7 Punda Rock Engraving Site
8 Pilbara Iron Country Tag-a-Long Tour
9 Wanna Munna Rock Art Site
10 Beedluboondu, Mundee & Ooramboo Rock Engraving Sites;
   Burringurrah Community Aboriginal Corporation Tours

of the largest, best-preserved painted art sites in WA.

Walga Rock is a protected site and Indigenous people (along with the government) intend to further preserve the surrounding area. Presently the corroboree area has been fenced in, and there is little interpretative information available.

The 60m rock shelter at its base houses a gallery of desert-style paintings of lizards, birds and animals, and hand stencils in red, white and yellow ochre.

At the northern end of the gallery, a ship with twin masts, a funnel and four wavy lines beneath is depicted. Many theories abound as to who painted it – including one that it was painted by shipwrecked sailors

and another that a shearer did it – but like many sites, the story was never written and is now lost. Aboriginal families still use the area as a day picnic camp; check with the Cue Tourist Bureau (see earlier) to ensure the road is open.

MT AUGUSTUS NATIONAL PARK

Mt Augustus National Park, or Burringurrah as it is known to the local Wadjari people, is about 850km north of Perth. It can be accessed from the North West Coastal Hwy via Carnarvon, then east through Gascoyne Junction or from the Great Northern Hwy via Meekatharra. Mt Augustus is the largest solid 'rock' in the world, it is twice the size of Uluru (Ayers Rock) and three times as old.

ABORIGINAL SITES IN WA
Trudi Ridge

Aboriginal spirituality is based on creation stories, describing the way the ancestors left their marks on the land. There are approximately 17,000 registered sites in WA and most of these are unmarked on maps and access is restricted. Sites are not always public knowledge.

Knowledge of sites is not equally distributed within a tribal group. Knowledge is dependent on a person's age, status, sex or personal relationship with a particular site. There are separate male and female stories of the same country or site. As Aboriginal people we expect you to behave in the same manner that you would when entering a church or other religious site.

In 1969 a site (Weebo) was desecrated and led to the WA Aboriginal Heritage Act being proclaimed in 1972, which makes it an offence to disturb any site.

Sites can be broadly separated into two categories: ethnographic sites and archaeological sites. Ethnographic sites are sites for which information is available, such as sites in current use for rituals, camping areas, or areas where resources such as food have been obtained. Archaeological sites are areas containing physical evidence of occupation, normally near existing or former water sources.

Sites can be man-made structures, ceremonial or mythological sites, massacre grounds, modified trees, paintings, burial sites, engravings, grinding patches and grooves, middens, quarries or artefact sites.

Thalu Sites

Thalu sites, also known as tribal increase sites, are places that are the focus for ceremonies that assist Aborigines to keep the traditional ways alive. The ceremonies are carried out by asking the spiritual forces to assist the people in their endeavours, mainly to enhance the natural forces, eg, in the west Pilbara there is a Murrumbari (Black Beetle) thalu site. This site consists of a large flat rock close to a river with smaller grinding stones located underneath it. As the people rub the large flat rock with the smaller grinding stone, they call out in language the names of the places where they want the beetle to breed. This helps increase the abundance of the black beetle as a food source. Sites can be deceptive – what you see is not all there is.

See also the boxed text 'Archaeological Sites'.

WESTERN AUSTRALIA

Mt Augustus has three known Aboriginal Dreaming stories, and while details differ among the three, each holds the same thread – probably the best known is that about a boy called Burringurrah, who was undergoing his initiation into manhood. The Burringurrah Community Aboriginal Corporation (see following) can show you around – being the traditional custodians of the rock they know the area well.

Free maps of Mt Augustus, that detail the location of the Aboriginal sites mentioned below, are available from the Mt Augustus Outback Tourist Resort (☎ 9943 0527), 5km north-east of the rock.

Organised Tours

The Burringurrah Community Aboriginal Corporation (☎ 9943 0979, fax 9943 0982) conducts tours (walking and 4WD tag-along tours) around its country. A Mt Augustus walking tour is $35 per person, with a minimum of five people required. It can also do bush tucker, hunting and women's business (no fellas allowed) tours. Call the office and speak to Ray Wallis, who organises these. All tours begin at the Mt Augustus Outback Tourist Resort. See also the Burringurrah Aboriginal Community section later.

Sites

The occupation of the Wadjari people is made obvious with the rock engravings at the Beedoboondu, Mundee and Ooramboo sites. In the past, numerous stone tools and evidence of their production have been found in the area; if you happen across any make sure you don't disturb them.

Beedoboondu (Flintstone) is a Dreaming site dedicated to the Bush Fly. Here you can see rock engravings of animal tracks and hunters. At **Mundee** you can see, quite clearly, engravings depicting kangaroos, emus and bustard tracks. The engravings are in a series of overhangs. **Ooramboo** features engravings of animal tracks on a rock face.

BURRINGURRAH ABORIGINAL COMMUNITY

Information

Burringurrah Community Aboriginal Corporation (☎ 9943 0979, fax 9943 0982) is a small community of artists about 40km south of Mt Augustus, on the Landor Rd. It

is worth visiting for its excellent artwork displayed in the community gallery. If visiting you'll have to seek permission to go there so phone before making the trek, and upon arrival report to the community office.

It's open 8.30 am to 4.30 pm weekdays, and weekend visits can be arranged if you call ahead. It's best to go between April and October, but watch out as temperatures have been known to climb to a whopping 47°C. The community asks that you refrain from taking photos or bringing alcohol and drugs into the community – please respect its wishes.

Malkana Country

Shark Bay Area

DENHAM

The Aboriginal community here is only tiny, but the Yadgalah Aboriginal Corporation (☎ 9948 1318) at 53 Frances Rd is hoping to develop enterprises and an organised tour to showcase its culture. It currently operates an 18-hole minigolf course set in native bushland. A round is $3.50/1.65 adults/children and it's open 1 to 5 pm daily, except Tuesday and Thursday when it's open 9 am to 5 pm. During these times the Yadgalah Aboriginal Corporation also sells locally produced Aboriginal art. Darren Capewell from the corporation is happy to suggest local tour operators.

The interesting **Boolbardi walk** runs along the shore from Denham to the Town Bluff – the two rows of curved rocks are believed to be an Aboriginal fish trap.

Yinggarda Country

Gascoyne River Area

CARNARVON

There is a strong community of Aborigines in this region, but they are still developing their public presence with ventures like the New Vision Aboriginal Art Gallery. Like in many communities, addressing social issues has come before establishing their public face.

Information

Tourist Office The helpful Carnarvon Tourist Bureau (☎ 9941 1146) is at 11 Robinson Street (in the Civic Centre). At the time of writing the town's Aboriginal community was beginning to build an Aboriginal Cultural Centre – ask at the tourist bureau to see if it's open.

Radio The Yamatji Aboriginal Media Association Incorporated can be heard on 6LN 66AM, or on 99.7FM.

Organised Tours
Outback Adventure Tours (☎ 9943 0550) operates from Mt Sandiman Station (some 25km north-east of Carnarvon). It is flexible in its tours and it's best to call beforehand to discuss tour options. You'll need your own reliable 4WD for these tours.

New Vision Aboriginal Art Gallery
To learn about Carnarvon's Indigenous history, the place to visit is the New Vision Aboriginal Art Gallery (☎ 9941 3778) at 344 Robinson St (across the road from the Dalmatians Club). This organisation assists artists to advance their talents, and it has plans to establish a cultural centre and precinct in the town centre. The art varies, but includes paintings, sculptures and emu eggs. It's open 8 am to noon Monday to Thursday.

Maia & Malgaru Country

Kennedy Range

This spectacular plateau lies 150km east of Carnarvon. Extending north from Gascoyne Junction, the Kennedy Range forms the boundaries for the Maia and Malgaru peoples' country. Maia land extends north covering about 12,000 sq km north of Carnarvon to the western slope of the Kennedy Range.

Malgaru country extends from the nearby Lyons River east towards the Gascoyne River.

KENNEDY RANGE NATIONAL PARK
While much of the area's Aboriginal history has remained unrecorded (ie, undocumented in books), this national park has over 100 sites indicating occupation, ritual observance and land use that extends back some 20,000 years. There are a number of artefact scatters

on the western side of the range, near the freshwater springs. Stone tools were made from the semiprecious coloured chert rock that forms the range's outcrops. Many of the park's sites are sacred, for example within the park is a March Fly *thalu* site where ceremonies were conducted to enhance the land's spiritual forces (see also the boxed text 'Aboriginal Sites in WA', earlier). Access to these places should be gained through a tour company (see Organised Tours in the Carnarvon section earlier) and unfortunately there are no local Aboriginal tour guides.

Baiyungu & Thalanyji Country

Exmouth Gulf Area

The Aboriginal history of the country extending from Coral Bay to Exmouth is not well known to the general public. Depending on your sources, the languages spoken in this area range from Thalanyji (around the Exmouth Gulf) to Malgana (also spelt 'Malkana') in the Shark Bay area.

A helpful organisation to contact regarding this area is the Yadgalah Aboriginal Corporation (see the Denham section earlier); also useful are the Yamaji Language Centre (see the Geraldton section earlier) and the Wangka Maya Pilbara Aboriginal Language Centre in Port Hedland (see later).

The earliest evidence of Aboriginal occupation in this area is from the Mandu Mandu rock shelter on the North West Cape, where a 30,000-year-old shell necklace was found, along with the remains of a meal of marine shellfish.

CORAL BAY
Organised Tours
ATV Tours (☎ 9942 5873, **e** coralbayeco tours@bigpond.com) runs four-wheeler motorbike tours from Shop 4, Robinson St, Coral Bay – just look for the bikes out the front. Although this is not an Indigenous cultural experience, tours are run by Aboriginal tour guide Grantley Cooyou, who can give you a good insight into the cultural lifestyles of his people. Motorbike tours start at $50 per person for the discovery tour (two hours) and go up to $75 for snorkelling and fishing tours (four hours).

Bikes are supplied and there's a maximum of nine people per tour.

Station Stays

At the time of writing, Murlanda Enterprises at **Cardabia Station** (☎ 9942 5935), about 5km north of Coral Bay, was developing station stays that will include day tours, bush tucker meals and camp site accommodation. For further information contact the station direct, or contact Grantley Cooyou at ATV Tours (see Organised Tours earlier).

EXMOUTH
Information

The Exmouth Tourist Bureau (☎ 9949 1176), on Murat Rd, has the wonderful local publication *The Wreck of the Bargue Stefano off the North West Cape of Australia in 1875* by Gustav Rathe ($22; published by Hesperian Press). The text details the experiences of a shipwrecked sailor and his relations with the local Aboriginal people.

Ngaluma Country

Roebourne Area

The Ngaluma have occupied the area around Roebourne for up to 30,000 years. Their traditional land covers 6400 sq km of flood country from the Peawah River in the east and the Maitland River in the west, and includes the modern towns of Dampier, Karratha (meaning 'good country' or 'soft earth'), Wickham, Cossack and the Burrup Peninsula (Murajuga). There were three divisions of this grouping: two were west and east of the Harding River and the other occupied the Burrup Peninsula and were known as the Jaburrara.

Numerous shell middens remain, including a number just on the outskirts of Karratha. The Ngaluma constructed spinifex fishing nets and etched symbolic motifs into thousands of rocks.

From the 1860s the white invasion increased. In 1865 the Colonial Secretary's Office in London (England) proclaimed that no convicts were permitted to work north of the 26th Parallel, so the early settlers used Aboriginal labour to establish their land holdings and pearling fleets. They employed the Ngaluma as labourers and shepherds and paid them with goods. Introduced diseases, such as smallpox and measles, soon took their toll.

There were a number of massacres and in one clash in 1872, known as the Flying Foam Passage Massacre, at least 60 Aborigines were killed in retaliation for the spearing of four settlers. The Aborigines who remained were forced into working on pastoral leases, and others were forced to dive for pearlshell.

In the 1930s several neighbouring Aboriginal tribes, including the Yindjibarndi, Banjima and Martuthunira, were moved into reserves in Roebourne and Onslow. The main groups today in the Roebourne area are Yindjibarndi and Ngaluma. The

CHANGES IN THE PILBARA

The Pilbara region has been occupied by Aboriginal people for at least 30,000 years. This diverse area has more than 20 Aboriginal languages, with numerous dialects making up five main language families. There are four *skin groups* (relationship classifications) in the Pilbara. The region extends from Port Hedland in the north, to Newman in the south and east to the NT border. There are about 5200 Aboriginal people living permanently in this area.

European settlement of the Pilbara dates back only 100 years or so. Since the early 1600s Dutch sailors were thought to have mapped these shores (and were at times shipwrecked), although their influence was not as traumatic as the later British settlement of the area. It wasn't until 1861 that the first recorded land-based expedition of the Pilbara was recorded.

It was soon after this that the end of the ancient tribal systems began. Aboriginal people were moved into camps and reserves, and Aboriginal traditional life was changed forever.

The Pilbara – Cradle of an Ancient Civilisation ($19.80) is a visitors guide available from the main tourist offices in the region.

Jaburrara are gone but their curious etchings survive.

KARRATHA
Karratha is recognised as the administrative centre of the Pilbara (meaning 'freshwater fish') region.

Information
The Karratha Tourist Bureau (☎ 9144 4600, ℮ tourist.bureau@kisser.net.au) on Karratha Rd sells *Jaburrara Heritage Trail* brochures ($2) – see later. The helpful staff have a decent background on the Aboriginal history of the area and can direct people to the petroglyph rock engravings on the Burrup Peninsula, about 25km west (see the Burrup Peninsula section later). They also stock the free 'Central Pilbara Coast' brochure which has a tiny bit of information on the Burrup Peninsula, or you can fork out $22 and get the excellent *Pocket Guide to the Pilbara*, which has a few pages of information. The office is open 9 am to 5 pm weekdays, and 10 am to noon on Saturday (September to April), plus 9 am to noon Sunday during the peak season (April to September).

The helpful Karratha National Parks Office (☎ 9143 1488) on the corner of Mardie and Anderson Rds is open 8 am to 5 pm weekdays. It can advise on road conditions to Karijini National Park, which is five hours' drive south-east of Karratha. It also has free brochures on Karijini that are worth picking up for information on the park's general features.

Jaburrara Heritage Trail
This 3.5km self-guided walk highlights sites of cultural importance to the Jaburrara people, including rock engravings, grindstones, etchings and middens, and discusses the impact of the white invasion of the 1860s.

Jaburrara (pronounced 'yabura') is the name of the original inhabitants of the Karratha region. Tackle this walk in the early morning or in the evening. It will be more rewarding if you take the brochure from the tourist bureau with you (see Information earlier).

Aboriginal carvings along the ridge were created with chert and dolerite tools and are estimated to be 5000 to 6000 years old. Flat rocks adjacent to one of the creeks on the trail were used for grinding spinifex and other seeds. The thalu site that features on the trail is related to the Warramurrangka (Giant Fruit Bat or Flying Fox) and forms the mythical path of this spiritual being. See also the boxed text 'Aboriginal Sites in WA' earlier.

Allow two to three hours to enjoy the full trail at a leisurely pace.

BURRUP PENINSULA
In 1861, the explorer FT Gregory landed at the Burrup Peninsula, originally known as Murajuga, and explored the Pilbara lands. This was 'the beginning of the end' for the traditional lifestyles of the Aboriginal people here. The mining boom of the 1960s dramatically changed the landscape of the region. The Burrup Peninsula is 20 minutes' drive west of Karratha.

Rock Art Sites
Murajuga is considered to be one of the largest rock art galleries in the world, containing 10,000 Aboriginal rock engravings depicting creatures including fish, turtles, euros and wallabies at over 700 sites. Contact the Karratha Tourist Bureau (see earlier) for information about this amazing area.

ROEBOURNE
Information
At Roebourne Tourist Bureau (☎ 9182 1060, ℮ roebourne_tourist@kisser.net.au) on Queens St you can view the videos *Our Land Our Life – People, Places and Culture* and *Exile and the Kingdom*. There is also a *History of the Gaol* available ($2) that tells the story of the Aboriginal people who were interned in chains and the horrific slavery practice known as 'blackbirding'. This involved non-Indigenous people using Aborigines as slaves. Once they had finished with one 'service' they were shipped to a local island to await another slave driver, who would boat them back to the mainland to be used again.

The tourist bureau is open 9 am to 3 pm weekdays and 9 am to noon on Saturday from November to April. From May to October it opens from 9 am to 5 pm weekdays and from 9 am to 4 pm on weekends and public holidays.

WESTERN AUSTRALIA

Yindjibarndi Country

South of Roebourne

MILLSTREAM-CHICHESTER NATIONAL PARK

Occupying an area of 2000 sq km, Millstream-Chichester National Park (Ngarrari) lies 150km south of Roebourne. It can be accessed by a gravel road from the North West Coastal Hwy, designated by a signpost 27km past Roebourne.

The area is of great significance with many references to the Dreaming. The **Deep Reach Pool** is the resting place for the Great Snake, the protector of the waters in the area. The **Chinderwarriner Pool** was an important meeting area for local clans. The visitors centre (☎ 9184 5144) has an interpretative display on the area's Aboriginal heritage and is open 8.30 am to 4.30 pm weekdays.

Kariyarra, Ngarla & Njamal Country

Coastal Western Desert Area

PORT HEDLAND

The area surrounding Port Hedland is the traditional country of the Kariyarra, Ngarla and Njamal people. Aboriginal lifestyles were largely unaffected by European invasion until the pastoral industry developed in the region in the late 19th century. After this disruption, Aboriginal people worked on the stations as stockmen and around the homesteads.

The quality of life for Aboriginal people on these stations was at times barely endurable. In 1946, conflict developed between the Aboriginal workers and station owners, and a demand for better conditions led to a widespread walk-off of Aboriginal workers. The strike brought about the establishment of many Aboriginal-run communities on a number of surrounding stations, and in turn led to the beginning of improvements in the social circumstances of the Aboriginal people in the Port Hedland area.

Although there are numerous cultural sites in this region, many are not accessible to the general public.

Information

Indigenous Organisations The Wangka Maya Pilbara Aboriginal Language Centre

(☎ 9172 2344), Lot 5812, Leake St, South Hedland, has local-language books available for purchase. It's open 8.30 am to 4.30 pm weekdays.

If you intend to travel through any of the Aboriginal communities in the Western Desert region, first call the Western Desert Puntukurnuparna Aboriginal Community (WDPAC; ☎ 9172 3299, fax 9172 3132) on Roche Rd, as the communities are not always accessible to the general public.

Another helpful Aboriginal organisation is the AAD, which has an office (☎ 9173 1066) in the Boulevard Shopping Centre, on Wilson St. It's open 9 am to 5 pm weekdays. Its Web site (www.aad.wa.gov.au) is particularly useful as it outlines registered sites, access, regional offices and useful contacts within the department.

Tourist Office The Port Hedland Tourist Bureau (☎ 9173 1711, ℯ phtbinfo@norcom .net.au), 13 Wedge St, has seasonal opening hours. During tourist season (around April to September) it's open 8.30 am to 5 pm weekdays, 8.30 am to 4 pm Saturday and 10 am to 4 pm Sunday. At all other times other times it's open 8.30 am to 5 pm weekdays and 8.30 am to 1 pm Saturday. It stocks free, informative brochures on the Two Mile Ridge Engraving Site (see later).

Dalgety House Museum

The new Dalgety House Museum, (☎ 9173 4300, ℯ dalgety@kisser.net.au), on the corner of Wedge and Anderson Sts, houses a pictorial display and information relating to the lifestyles of the local Aboriginal people. Admission is $3/2 for adults/children. The museum is open 10 am to 3 pm weekdays.

Two Mile Ridge Engraving Site

This protected area on Wilson St has engravings depicting the lifestyles of the traditional inhabitants of the area. *Kartarrapika* (whales), *kurlpanarri* (dugongs) and other coastal creatures can be viewed. To access the site you will need to collect a key (and one of the 'Two Mile Ridge Engraving Site' brochures) from the AAD (☎ 9173 1066).

Shopping

Behind the tourist bureau, in the court house at 16 Edgar St, is a local Community Arts Centre (☎ 9173 1059) that is 50%

Aboriginal-owned. It sells beautiful Aboriginal-made textiles (printed silks, fabrics and T-shirts) and paintings. At the time of writing it was in the process of relocating to the court house, so phone for details and speak to Rose Murray.

Bunjima, Gurrama & Innawonga Country

Hamersley Range Area

KARIJINI NATIONAL PARK
This park was renamed in recognition of its significance to the traditional occupants of the area – the Bunjima to the north-east, the Gurrama to the north-west and the Innawonga to the south-west; it was formerly known as Hamersley Range National Park. There are about 28 dialects from the Pama-Nyungan language that are used in the area. The Pama-Nyungan nation encompasses the towns of Port Hedland, Newman and Tom Price.

Information
Within Karijini National Park is an impressive, newly established visitors centre (☎ 9189 8121), which has Aboriginal interpretative displays along with a shop selling Aboriginal arts and crafts. The centre is in the north-east end of the park, on Banjima Drive. It is run by members of the Karijini Aboriginal Corporation (☎ 9188 1852), based in Tom Price, 45km west of the national park. It can inform of road conditions into Karijini National Park. Information on Karijini is also available at the Karratha National Parks Office (see the Karratha section earlier).

Martu Country

Western Pilbara

While the term Martu may seem like a wonderfully uniform title, the Martu people are actually divided into many different language groups such as the Mangala, Kokatja, Walmajarri, Ildwaongga, Keiadara, Potidjara, Kartudjara, Wanman, Ngolibardu, Njangamarda Iparuka and the Njangamarda Kundal. You'll need to contact WDPAC (☎ 9172 3299) if you wish to visit any of the communities in the area. See the Port Hedland section earlier for full details.

ORGANISED TOURS
There are plans to begin tours of the area with the traditional owners showing people their country with storytelling, bushwalks and bush-tucker tours, to be called Desert Queen Baths Outback Adventure Tours. Contact the WDPAC (☎ 9172 3299) for information regarding the progress of this venture.

NEWMAN
Information
The Newman Information Centre (☎ 9175 2888, fax 9175 2964, e newmantb@norcom .net.au) is on the corner of Newman Drive and Fortescue Ave.

Organised Tours
Newman has no Aboriginal guided tours available. The only way to see the rock art sites in the area is to join Joe and Maria Furulyas on a Pilbara Iron Country Tag-a-long Tour (☎ 9175 1715, e pic_tour@norcom .net.au). You will need to provide your own food and supplies and an off-road 4WD for the day. Easy day tours cost $75. Full-day tours for moderate/experienced drivers cost $90/120 per day and per vehicle (depending on your itinerary). Contact them before you reach Newman as tours are dependent on roads being accessible. See its Web site at www.norcom.net.au/~pic_tour for more details.

WANNA MUNNA & PUNDA ART SITES
Aboriginal rock engravings feature at the Punda and Wanna Munna sites, which are close-to-permanent shaded water supplies. Both these sites are protected so take care, otherwise you could cop a fine! These sites are accessible by 4WD only, and only when road conditions are suitable.

Information
Both the Newman Information Centre (see earlier) and the Nullagine Roadhouse & Superstore (☎ 9176 2012, fax 9176 2025) on Walter St, Nullagine, have the informative brochure 'Waterhole Circuit – Newman' which contains a map locating Wanna Munna and Punda. Both these places can

WESTERN AUSTRALIA

inform you about the current road conditions, as it's dangerous to travel here after heavy rain.

Wanna Munna

This protected area rock art site is 76km west of Newman (not signposted), and a further 2km north off the Great Northern Hwy. The rock carvings feature images of humans, animals and water symbols. It's suggested you walk the last 1km, as the road has a huge hole and is not accessible all year by 4WD.

Punda

This rock art site is on land 'owned' by BHP so to access the area you will have to get a travel permit, obtainable from the Newman Information Centre. Unless you are an experienced and skilled 4WD user, do not attempt to travel out here, as the 5km of road are extremely rough. After rain, it's virtually impossible to access.

RUDALL RIVER NATIONAL PARK

The remote and breath-taking Rudall River National Park (originally known as Karlamilyi) is an area that spans some 15,000 sq km. It is 260km north-east of Newman and is considered an oasis with its permanent water supply. Occupied by the Wanman, Mandjildjarra, Ngolibardu and Gardutjarra language groups, the park has some great stories involving songlines and Dreaming tracks.

Within the national park, Lake Dora is the place where two Creator Being Snakes disappeared underground and so the mouth of the lake (near Lake Blanche) holds special significance. South of Lake Dora is Lake Disappointment, a salt lake that is a taboo area. It offers little in terms of resources for living, and is best avoided anyway due to the fearful Ngayurnangalku Beings that live underneath the lake – they are said to be able to pull aircraft from the sky to crash on the lake's surface; consider yourself warned! The park is accessible only by 4WD and it's worth browsing CALM's Web site (www.calm.wa.gov.au) for further tips on remaining safe in these remote areas; it even offers a recommended course ($295 for three days, held in Fremantle) on dealing with Australia's Outback regions.

Jukun & Yawuru Country

Broome Area

BROOME

Aboriginal people living in Broome tend to come from one of five local language groups: Yawuru, Bardi, Nyul Nyul, Nimanburr and Jukun.

In the 1860s investigations into a convict's claim of a gold find in the area proved fruitless, so sheep were introduced instead. The Aboriginal inhabitants of Roebuck Bay resented the intrusion of the pastoralists, especially their fencing of traditional water holes. In November 1864 three members of a pastoralists' expedition were murdered by Aborigines, which resulted in open conflict (see also the boxed text 'Massacre Sites', later). The pastoralists withdrew in 1867 only to be replaced by pearlers, working north from Cossack, in the 1870s.

As with elsewhere in the north, the pearling and pastoral industries had a devastating effect on the local populations. People were made to leave their traditional lands and children were forcibly removed from their families. The traditional structures and known practices that survived for thousands of years eroded and changed as people tried to survive while keeping true to their Aboriginality.

But local Aboriginal people are welcoming and friendly to visitors. In fact, one reason that Broome has developed so quickly as a tourist destination is its special, friendly multicultural mix.

Information

Tourist Offices The Broome Tourist Bureau (☎ 9192 2222), on the corner of Broome Rd and Bagot St, is an excellent source of information on tours, festivals, road conditions and local maps but be prepared for long waits if visiting in June, July or August. Check the notice boards outside Wings Store (Carnarvon St, Chinatown), the old Seaview shopping centre in Saville St and shops throughout town for flyers on Indigenous events.

Books Magabala Books (☎ 9192 1991, ℮ magabala@tpg.com.au), at 2/28 Saville St, is the first Aboriginal publishing house

BOOKS ABOUT THE KIMBERLEY
Trudi Ridge

The Kimberley is a huge area of northern WA encompassing 421,451 sq km (almost twice the size of Victoria) with a resident population of 27,716. Aboriginal people make up over 50% of the population.

There are a number of books available that will give you a deeper insight into the Aboriginal heritage of this fascinating and remote region of Australia.

Raparapa – stories from the Fitzroy River Drovers is a collection of stories from nine Aboriginal men who worked as drovers in the Kimberley, published by Magabala Books.

First published in 1992, *Tjarany* by Gracie Creene, Joe Tramacchi and Lucille Gill, is a delightful children's publication. The Kukatja people from Malarn, Yaka Yaka and Wirrumanu communities have allowed the Dreaming stories of their people to be shared in this book.

Another good title, *Moola Bulla – In the Shadow of the Mountain* by the Kimberley Language Resource Centre, is published by Magabala Books. It is a collection of personal histories and Dreaming stories told in local Kija, Djaru and Kriol languages (from the Halls Creek area), with an English translation.

in Broome. The company name is the Yawuru word for the bush banana, which disperses its seed across the land.

It has an extensive book list with a range of over 50 titles, including children's stories, language books and Aboriginal historical references to the region, all written by Aboriginal or Torres Strait Islander peoples. It is open 8.30 am to 5 pm weekdays.

Libraries Broome Library (☎ 9192 1635), in Hammersley St, has an excellent collection of material on the history of the area and is also a great place to beat the heat if you're visiting over the Wet. It's open 10 am to 5 pm Monday, Wednesday and Friday, 10 am to 7 pm on Tuesday and Thursday and 10 am to noon on Saturday.

Radio & TV Goolarri Media Enterprises (☎ 9192 1325, e goolarri@gme.com.au) on Blackman St provides an opportunity for Aboriginal and Torres Strait Islander people to broadcast their work through Goolarri radio (99.7FM) and GME TV Channel 35. The Broadcasting to Remote Aboriginal Communities Scheme (BRACS) radio organisation is also stationed here. BRACS operates in 13 remote communities throughout the Kimberley/Pilbara region.

Organised Tours
Stephen 'Baamba' Albert (☎ 0417-988 328), a local Aboriginal actor, storyteller

and entertainer, runs Baamba's Chinatown Tour. Starting from Sun Pictures, these walking tours are packed with anecdotes of Broome's past and Baamba's life story. Two-hour morning tours cost $25 and 2½-hour evening tours – with a few songs thrown in – cost $30. You can book through the tourist bureau if Baamba is not in town.

Once a year in winter (usually July), you can join the Goolarabooloo people (☎ 9192 2959) on their Lurujarri Dreaming Trail. It's a nine-day, 80km walk along the coast north of Broome from Minyirr (Gantheaume Point) to Minarriny (Colomobo Point). It follows in part the traditional song cycle of the local people. You camp in the bush and learn about culture and country. The cost is $1200 ($600 for students or pensioners). There can be up to 200 'family' members and visitor numbers are limited. The organisers are the Rowe family from Coconut Wells up on the Dampier Peninsula. This is one of the best tours of this kind available.

Mamabulanjin Aboriginal Tours (☎ 9192 2660), at 640 Dora St, offers insights into the local area, past and present. Full-day tours including food and water cost $88/38.50 for adults/children. It is also an excellent source of information on remote outstations where you can interact with individual family groups.

If you would like a personalised tour of Broome or the coastline east of Cable Beach, contact Jumbarr Ngunjul Aboriginal

WESTERN AUSTRALIA

THE KIMBERLEY

THE KIMBERLEY

Corporation (☎ 9192 5067, 0419-836 781) for Neil Mckenzie, a Yawuru tour guide. Full-day tours incorporating local mythology and modern-day history cost $90 (minimum of four) – call ahead.

Broome Historical Museum
The Broome Historical Museum on Saville St near Town Beach is run by volunteers from the local historical society and is well worth the $3 admission. Here you can sift through the archives to have a look at Broome's early history, with several files of information dedicated to Aboriginal people. The museum is open 10 am to 1 pm daily during the Wet. During the Dry it's open 10 am to 4 pm weekdays and 10 am to 1 pm weekends.

Special Events
Local artists highlight 'fringe arts' in June at the Broome Fringe Arts Festival with Aboriginal art exhibitions, markets, art installations and workshops.

During October the fantastic two-day Stompem Ground features local Aboriginal bands, along with big-name acts such as Christine Anu and Midnight Oil. Also in

October is the National Indigenous Art Awards. Goolarri Media Enterprises (☎ 9192 1325) has details of both events.

While ostensibly a town festival, there is usually Aboriginal input into the stalls, float parade and activities of the 10-day Shinju Matsuri Pearl Festival. You'll get the best curry and rice this side of Kuala Lumpur at the night markets. Dates vary as it is held in line with the full moon.

Local crowds come out en masse for the Broome Cup in July, and in August for Broome Rodeo at the Jack Knox Arena and the local Australian Rules Grand Final (see Spectator Sports later).

Entertainment
Events such as film launches, and band and karaoke nights are held at the GME Bar on Blackman St. Call the organisers, Goolarri Media Enterprises (☎ 9192 1325), for details of upcoming gigs.

Spectator Sports
Many Broome locals (both Aboriginal and non-Aboriginal) are actively involved in sports. Football is played on the weekend during the Dry season (May to October) at

WESTERN AUSTRALIA

MASSACRE SITES

In 1865, there was a massacre near La Grange Bay, south of Broome. It was depicted as an attack by 'treacherous natives' on the explorers Panter, Harding and Goldwyer who were looking to claim land for the Roebuck Bay Pastoral Company. Newspaper reports at the time stated that trusted Aboriginal people murdered the three men in their sleep. Following the deaths of these invaders, a punitive party was sent out to find the Aboriginal people responsible. The resulting massacre claimed the lives of about 20 Aboriginal men and women of the Karajarri people.

What was not reported at the time was that there was sufficient evidence to suggest that the explorers had desecrated a sacred site and ignored warnings to leave the area. A group of about 70 men, women and children were sighted by the punitive party. Twenty-five fighting men tried to defend the camp. Armed with spears and other traditional weapons they fought against the whites who were armed with rifles and revolvers and were mounted on horseback. The only damage sustained by the punitive party was a wound inflicted on a horse's head.

In 1913 a monument was erected in Fremantle, near Perth, to honour the deaths of the three white men.

This could be any story you read about any massacre site in the country – but this one is our story and happened to my own family.

We don't have a monument erected at the massacre site; we know where it is. There are children of the survivors of this slaughter still alive today (and now grandchildren and great-grandchildren).

We don't have cemeteries or headstones in place for these areas. Not all massacre sites are known to the general public and we don't want everyone to be able to access these areas. If you do come across a burial site, please treat it with respect, just as you would behave in a considerate

Trudi Ridge

My mother has a European ancestry and her father comes from Karajarri and Yawuru language groups from the country south of Broome. My skin group is Karimba and I embrace both the contemporary lifestyle that I live, and a respect of the traditional Aboriginal culture of my father's people.

My lifestyle, beliefs and thought processes are a rich mix of both the old and the new – complementary whilst at the same time understanding and respectful of my strong Aboriginal heritage.

I have travelled throughout Australia – my non-Aboriginal family live on the east coast and my Aboriginal family are mainly Broome-based.

Contributing to this publication has been one of the most fulfilling realisations of my life to date. What a fantastic opportunity to show visitors what we as Aboriginal people have to offer. Working in tourism and especially with my people has been really fulfilling. My life to date has been an interesting mix of all the good the bad and the ugly that can be served up to Aboriginal people. But, this is who I am, and I'm proud of that and what my people can show you about who we are and what we have to offer.

There are too many people I'd like to thank – most know who they are, but special thanks must go to my son Joel Arthur Ridge who inspires me to be more than I can be, Neil Coulthard, Karl Plunkett and Richard Agar. These guys have not only been an inspiration to me, but to the many Kimberley Aboriginal people who are either starting up or now involved in the tourism industry.

manner on any holy ground. Remember that, like any final resting place, someone will feel upset if the area is desecrated.

For this reason we don't want to see these areas open to the general public to be trampled over, with no thought to the actual events that took place there.

In all my writing, I have failed to show where massacre sites are located – this is in respect to the event, my people, my culture and on a personal note, to my own family.

In recent years, a plaque has been erected at the monument in Fremantle stating:

This plaque also commemorates all other Aboriginal people who died during the invasion of their country.

MAPA JARRIYA-NYALAKU. LEST WE FORGET.

the oval in Frederick St opposite the Action Supermarket. Many a skilled Aboriginal footballer has entered the ranks of the WA Football League and the Australian Football League from the West Kimberley Football Association. It's well worth a look. Also during the Dry, a day at the races is popular with regular meets at the racecourse near Gantheaume Point, although the annual rodeo is more of a showcase for skilled local stockmen.

Shopping

There are plenty of opportunities to purchase locally made art and crafts. Ganada Aboriginal Art & Craft (☎ 9192 7272) in the Paspaley Centre in Chinatown features local and interstate traditional and contemporary Aboriginal arts, crafts and giftware. It's open 9 am to 5 pm weekdays, 9 am to 1 pm Saturday and 10 am to 1 pm Sunday. Short St Gallery (☎ 9192 2658) on Short St is a small gallery with excellent exhibits of Indigenous artists. It's open 10 am to 4 pm Monday to Saturday.

More upmarket is Pearlers Row Gallery (☎ 9192 6330), 34 Dampier Terrace, which features changing exhibitions of Kimberley and other Australian artists. It also has a small but good selection of Aboriginal artworks such as bark paintings. It's open 9 am to 5 pm weekdays and 10 am to 2 pm weekends.

Monsoon Gallery (☎ 9193 5881), next door to Matso's Store (a good restaurant that brews its own beer), on Hammersley St, has a small selection of Kimberley Aboriginal art.

Jarndu Yaruwu Aboriginal Corporation (☎ 9192 5039), Lot 2099, Clementson St, is a women's workshop that teaches silk-screening, sewing and ceramics to local women. Visitors can watch the works in progress which are displayed and sold at the attached shop along with other artworks and jewellery. Bring a T-shirt and they will screen-print it for you. The centre and shop are open 8 am to 4 pm weekdays.

Burrguk Aboriginal Community Art & Crafts (☎ 9192 1021), also on Clementson St, has a small selection of locally produced ceramics. It is open 9 am to 4 pm weekdays.

Simply Broome (☎ 9192 8054), 29 Dampier Terrace, has a range of arts crafted by all kinds of local people. It's open 10 am to 4 pm weekdays.

Bardi Country

Dampier Peninsula

The original inhabitants of the Dampier Peninsula are the Bardi people. While it's a hike from Broome (220km from the turn-off 10km out of Broome to the lighthouse at the tip of the peninsula), it's worth the drive for the scenery and being shown around by country-proud Aboriginal guides. Many communities occupy the peninsula, some with well-refined tourism ventures that are definitely worth the visit. The area is best accessed by 4WD as the sandy road becomes impassable in the rain. Check road conditions with the Broome Tourist Bureau (☎ 9192 2222) before setting off.

WESTERN AUSTRALIA

A TRADITION CARVED IN MY MIND

Many memories of my childhood remain very clear in my mind, like the one of my Nyami (grandfather) carving a pearlshell. This is something he has been doing all his life and it is a tradition that was passed onto him from his father – a Bard man of the Dampier Peninsula, just north of Broome.

Nyami comes from a long line of pearlshell carvers who are the only people that have traditionally carved secret/sacred designs as well as open *stories* on these special shells.

I can remember my grandfather wading through the turquoise saltwater just up to his knees. Bending down he picks up a large flat shell. 'Here my girl! This the one now!' he shouts as I patiently wait for him to show me what he has in his hand. He walks towards me holding out a big pearlshell. Sitting cross-legged on the ground in front of me he smiles, never saying anything – because it's all about looking and learning.

He pulls out a pocketknife and splits open the shell and slips the knife under the pink and black flesh of the pearlshell meat.

darangah

I was born in Broome in 1964. I have lived most of my life in the Kimberley, moving to Sydney in 1983 to take up dance with the Aboriginal Islander Dance Theatre (which is no longer in operation). I moved into acting with a role in the Bruce Beresford film *The Fringe Dwellers* and then decided after a few years of acting that the media industry looked pretty exciting. I began as an on-air presenter at the Special Broadcasting Service (SBS) – the first black Aussie – and got serious with the Australian Broadcasting Corporation (ABC), starting a career in television journalism. I have worked in radio broadcasting as a producer/presenter for the ABC and Indigenous radio, and in the last five years I have moved into making documentaries for television. In between all this, when there is time, I write children's books.

BEAGLE BAY

Driving north from Broome on the road to Cape Leveque and the Dampier Peninsula will bring you to the Beagle Bay Aboriginal Community (118km).

In 1890 a mission was established by French Trappist Monks at a time when European pearlers, pastoralists and property owners would have killed the local Aborigines without hesitation. In 1901 the mission was relinquished to the German Pallotines.

Information

The community office (☎ 9192 4913) is open 8 am to noon and 1.30 to 4 pm daily, except Sunday, and is the first building you see as you arrive in the community.

Things to See & Do

A $5 permit fee will allow you to drive through the community and visit the **Sacred** Heart Church, completed in 1918 by the local Aboriginal people and the German Pallotines. The building was constructed entirely of local materials and the altar is exquisitely adorned with pearlshell and other local shells The local women, under the guidance of the Pallotines, collected local shell for the construction and decoration. The altar is made with inlays of pearlshell and sea shells. Tribal symbols of the Nyul Nyul, Ngumbarl, Jabirrjabirr and Bardi people decorate the church in conjunction with symbols of the Christian faith. The church now stands as a representation of Australia's multicultural past, bringing together Indigenous and European spiritual symbols under one roof.

Shopping

The Beagle Bay Women's Centre, behind the community's general store, has artwork

I hope that maybe…but no, there is no pearl in this shell. Scraping off the slime and weeds, he begins to smooth out the shell. It will be a long day.

As the tide slowly comes in, I get up to greet the waves as they touch the shoreline close to where we have been sitting... Enough swimming – time to check on the shell! It is smooth and Nyami has just begun to trace a design on it. 'No don't touch!' he warns, 'This is only for men, it's for *our* dance and ceremony'.

I remember feeling sad for not having been born a boy, because in my culture boys are allowed to do more things than me, a little girl. 'This pattern,' he says, 'is for the ceremony we men go to.' I study the pattern. 'It looks like a map Nyami!' I reply. 'Yes that's true – I have drawn all the sites for ceremony from here down the coast, so I remember what the places are to me. I carry this during ceremony and dance time so people know who I am,' Nyami explains.

Mimi (grandmother) has caught a big blue bonefish, so I collect wood and start the fire. We cook the fish on the coals and eat it with damper, washing it down with sweet billy tea. Nyami takes a break to eat with us and shows us the carved shell. My eyes trace over the tracks and I imagine all the places and stories my grandfather has danced for ceremony. I stare at its beauty and power. 'Not finished yet my girl, gotta put that red ochre in it!' While humming away, I think how ancient my Nyami is, wishing that he will be here forever to share his culture with me.

I collect bait so Mimi can catch fish on the outgoing tide. Nyami is still busy carving his pearlshell. He grins as I run up to him. I wish I could hold the shell just for one time – but I can't – this is how it is and always will be. I look down at the design, not fully under-standing its real story. But simply seeing it carved by Nyami makes it a precious memory, and that in itself has kept this tradition alive. *'Galla!'* (It's finished!) Nyami announces, as the sun slowly sinks in the west.

See also the Visual Arts special section.

on display and for sale. It can be contacted through the Beagle Bay Aboriginal Community.

MIDDLE LAGOON
Middle Lagoon is 33km off the Cape Leveque Rd, 180km north of Broome.

Places to Stay
Middle Lagoon's spectacular camping ground (☎/fax 9192 4002) is run by Aboriginal couple Tracey and Peter Howard and offers fantastic swimming, snorkelling and fishing. Camping costs are $16.50 per person per night (powered site). Double cabins, with fantastic views, refrigerators, water, table and chairs, are $110 per night. Day visitors must pay $5 per person. Nude bathing and removing shells are not allowed. You will need to bring your own food and drinks from Broome or Beagle

Bay. See the Web site at www.users.bigpond.com/pindan.

MADDARR ABORIGINAL COMMUNITY
The local Maddarr Aboriginal Community is on the eastern side of the peninsula, 190km north of Broome.

Organised Tours
Offered as a package through 'Best of the Kimberley' tourism (☎ 9192 6070, 1800 450 850 toll free), the Barramundi Moon Cultural Experience includes a host of activities with the Manado family, who are part of the local Maddarr Aboriginal Corporation. Visitors are invited to do as much, or as little, as they please. Bush-food walks, cliff/reef/cave walks, spear making, story-telling and more are offered. There's a maximum of 10 people at a time so you are

assured of personalised service. Three-day packages (for up to four people) are $450/ 282 per person with/without a 4WD. You have to take your own food and drinks for all meals, as well as ice and other personal items. Call to book or book online through its Web site: www.kimberleytravel.net, under the 'Adventures' link.

LOMBADINA ABORIGINAL COMMUNITY
About 20km from the tip on the Cape Leveque Rd is Lombadina Aboriginal Community.

Information
The community office (☎ 9192 4936) is open 8 to 11 am and 1 to 4 pm weekdays.

Organised Tours
Lombadina Tours (☎ 9192 4936, e lombo@ comswest.net.au) operates the recommended Bushwalking – the Aboriginal Way of Life Tour ($55 per person, minimum of two). The walk gives an insight into traditional and medicinal plants of the area, their English and Aboriginal names, and includes damper and tea refreshments. It's best to go during the June to September period when beautiful wildflowers bloom in the area.

Things to See & Do
The **church** at Lombadina is clad in corrugated iron, lined with paperbark and supported by bush timber.

Throughout the year the Djarindjin Lombadina School hosts **market days/evenings** for the local community and visitors to the peninsula; check with the community office for dates and times.

Places to Stay
Lombadina offers four-bed backpacker units for $38.50 per person. Fully self-contained units, sleeping four, cost $132 (linen and towels provided). Camping is not permitted.

KOOLJAMAN AT CAPE LEVEQUE
Bardi Aboriginal people from the One Arm Point and Djarindjin Communities make up the board of directors at Kooljaman (☎ 9192 4970 e leveque@bigpond.com), a 'wilderness 4WD camp' 220km north of Broome. Mainly set up as a camping ground for non-Aboriginal tourists, the

views and swimming are spectacular. It can only be accessed by 4WD or plane (transfers from Broome are $320 return).

The restaurant at Kooljaman is open April to October, and the store (with basic products) is open year-round for limited hours daily. The reception also sells local Aboriginal art and crafts that are worth a look. Browse the Web site at www.kooljaman .com.au for more details.

Organised Tours
Bush-tucker and mudcrabbing tours, and fishing charters are available at Kooljaman, although most of the staff are non-Aboriginal.

For sea-bound tours check out the Ultimate Experience Boat Tours. These are full-day tours and involve visits to the Sunday Island Mission, cultural history talks, snorkelling and fishing. Costs are $143/88 (adult/child) and include morning tea, lunch and afternoon refreshments; maximum 12 people.

Places to Stay
During peak season (April to November) accommodation at Kooljaman for a safari tent is $176 per night, cabins are between $110 and $121 and powered tent sites are $16. Bookings are essential.

ONE ARM POINT
About 5km from the Cape Leveque lighthouse is the One Arm Point Community (☎ 9192 4930).

Note that while you can look around or purchase goods at Aboriginal communities around Cape Leveque, most communities won't want you to stay on their land. Permission to visit other areas must be obtained in advance. Having said that, the mob at One Arm Point are very keen to show people around on an organised tour.

Organised Tours
If you'd like an insight into the culture of One Arm Point, members of the Mudnunn Community (the Angus family) can provide interpretative commentary and bush-tucker tours. You can contact them through the One Arm Point Community.

Another family-based tour company is Bardi Culture Tours. Irene Davey and her family conduct tours of up to five days with fishing, storytelling and spear making, or

TRAVELLING IN THE KIMBERLEY

Trudi Ridge

It is advisable to contact the Main Roads Department for an updated road condition report before travelling within the Kimberley region, especially from November to June (the Wet season). The Dry season is a magical time to travel but during the Wet the days are hot (35°C) and the nights warm (23°C). Heavy rain at this time of the year can cause flooding, affecting access to outlying communities and making roads impassable for long periods of time. After heavy periods of rain it is advisable to contact the local police stations or the Department of Main Roads (☎ 1800 013 314 toll free).

one-day cultural tours around their community that give insight into the area's Aboriginal history. Prices start from around $30 per person for the day tours, and go up to $100 per person per day for longer tours. Again, contact them through the One Arm Point Community.

Nyikina Country

Derby Area

ORGANISED TOURS

Jarlmadarngah Burru Enterprises (☎ 0417 922 335, e granjoe@tpgi.com.au), 40km off the Derby-Fitzroy Crossing Hwy on Mount Anderson Station in the Grant Ranges, runs J-BAC Bush Adventures. The highlight of coming to this pretty area is taking a camel trip into the surrounding area for $120 per day. All-inclusive overnight trips cost $150 or it's possible to simply come for a visit with the friendly host family and stay in one of their basic units for $15 per person. For those without their own transport, a community bus runs from Derby – call ahead for details.

DERBY

Derby is part of the largest shire in Australia – 102,706 sq km – and over 45% of the population is Aboriginal. Mowanjum ('settled at last'), on the outskirts of Derby, was one of the first independent Aboriginal communities established in the Kimberley.

Information

Tourist Office The Derby Tourist Bureau (☎ 9191 1426) on Clarendon St is open 8.30 am to 4.30 pm weekdays; on weekends between April and September it opens 9 am to 4 pm and between October and

March it opens from 9 am to noon on Saturday only.

Books *Jandamarra and the Bunuba Resistance* by Howard Pederson & Banjo Woorunmurra, published by Magabala Books, was awarded the best WA published book for 1996. Reading like an adventure story, this book places authentic oral history beside the 'official' history of the struggles of the charismatic resistance leader Jandamarra (Pigeon), set against pastoral settlement around the gorge country near Fitzroy Crossing. See also the boxed text 'Jandamarra ('Pigeon')'.

Pigeon Heritage Trail

This self-guided trail takes you to important sites in the life of Aboriginal outlaw and Bunuba hero Jandamarra. It includes places around Derby and the Napier Range, all covered in the 'Pigeon Heritage Trail' ($1.50), which is available from the tourist bureau.

Yuriny Aboriginal Cultural Centre

Yuriny Aboriginal Culture Centre (☎ 9191 1712), in the Winun Ngari Centre opposite the Boab Inn on Loch St, maintains Aboriginal culture in the area. With a small selection of paintings and carvings available for sale, it's open 9 am to 4.30 pm weekdays.

Old Derby Gaol

Part of the Pigeon Heritage Trail, the 1880s gaol has two cells where Aboriginal chain gangs were shackled overnight.

PC Richardson's Grave

PC Bill Richardson and Jandamarra were friends and part of a three-man police unit for years. The details of what happened are suitably vague but in 1894 Jandamarra, sick

WESTERN AUSTRALIA

JANDAMARRA ('PIGEON')

Windjana Gorge, Tunnel Creek and Lillimooloora were the setting for the legendary exploits of the outlaw Aboriginal tracker Jandamarra, nicknamed 'Pigeon'. As a teenager Jandamarra, a member of the Bunuba tribe, was a highly skilled stockman working on the Lennard River Station. His skills eventually led him to become an armed tracker working with the local police to capture Aborigines who were spearing sheep.

In October 1894, Pigeon's tribal loyalty got the better of him – he shot a police colleague at Lillimooloora, freed his captured tribesmen and escaped to lead a band of dissident Bunuba people who evaded search parties for almost three years. Despite being seriously wounded in a shootout at Windjana Gorge only a month after his escape, Pigeon survived and continued to taunt the settlers with raids and vanishing acts.

During this time Pigeon killed another four men. In 1897 he was finally trapped and killed near his hide-out at Tunnel Creek. He and his small band had hidden in the seemingly inaccessible gullies of the adjoining Napier Range.

For the full story, get a copy of the 'Pigeon Heritage Trail' from the Derby or Broome Tourist Bureaus ($1.50), or the more detailed *Jandamarra and the Bunuba Resistance* by Howard Pedersen & Banjo Woorunmurra.

---

of the persecution of his people, shot Richardson and released some Bunubas that he had previously helped capture. It was the turning point for Jandamarra, who spent the rest of his days as an outlaw. Richardson's grave is in the Old Derby cemetery on Villiers St.

Joonjoo Botanical Walk
About 7km from Derby on the Broome road, this interpretative 3km self-guided walk of the Wanganut Land System shows plants and animals and discusses Dreaming stories of the Nyikina. You can obtain an interpretative brochure and trail map from the tourist bureau.

Boab Prison Tree
On the opposite side of the highway from the botanical walk, this mighty boab tree is reputed to be around 1500 years old, with a girth of 14.7m. This a registered Aboriginal site; the hollow trunk was used as a prison for the Aboriginal chain gangs travelling the region.

Shopping
Ngunga Designs (☎ 9191 1128), on Stanley St, is an Aboriginal women's group specialising in traditional art, especially silk-screen printing and hand-painted material, clothing and vibrant traditional and modern

textiles. It also sells carved boab nuts and paintings. Ngunga means 'coming together to talk'. It's open 9 am to 4.30 pm.

Special Events
The two-day Moonrise Rock Festival held on the June full moon features many local musicians. Call ☎ 9191 1013 for line-ups and details.

MOWANJUM ABORIGINAL COMMUNITY
About 15km south-east of Derby, Mowanjum Aboriginal Community (☎ 9191 1104) is home to three main tribes – the Ngarinyin, Worora and Wunumbul groups. These groups are the custodians of the Wandjina (the supreme spirit beings) and many Dreaming stories. It is their responsibility to upkeep and repaint the hundreds of Wandjina rock paintings in the Kimberley and this centre emerged to encourage the youth to maintain their heritage. With some established artists the community was given a huge boost when Donny Woolagoodja was asked to provide a Wandjina image for the opening ceremony of the 2000 Olympic Games in Sydney. It's possible to visit the artists' studio on weekdays to take a look or purchase some art – there are usually a few people around painting or sculpting pearl-shell. Always call beforehand.

Special Events

In June, the two-day Mowanjum Festival displays major Wandjina art and attracts Aboriginal artists and performers from all over the west Kimberley.

Ngarinyin Country

Gibb River Road Area

The rugged Gibb River Rd (GRR) crosses the traditional lands of the Ngarinyin people. This is Wandjina country, where the mysterious mouthless ancestor spirits have left their shadows on the rock in the form of the world-famous rock paintings (see the 'Visual Art' special section for more information).

The GRR is impassable in the Wet; do not attempt it from December to April. The best time to go is from May to November; ring the Department of Main Roads (☎ 1800 013 314) for up-to-date information on road conditions.

ORGANISED TOURS

An initiative of the Ngarinyin Aboriginal Corporation, the Bush University (☎ 9193 1513) is one of the very best cultural experiences available. It offers an opportunity to explore the glorious gorge country of the north-west Kimberley with Ngarinyin guides who have chosen to share and explain their

Dambun (homelands) to visitors. Six-day tours, including air transfers from Kununurra/Derby to the camp, run from June to September and cost from $1950 to $2145. There is a woman-only tour midway through the season and bookings should be made well in advance through Wedgetails Tours (☎ 03-5593 9266, fax 5593 9208, e info@wedgetailstours.com.au), 850 East Hill Rd, Camperdown, Vic 3260. Web site: www.wedgetailstours.com.au

GALVANS GORGE ROCK PAINTINGS

Horseshoe-shaped Galvans Gorge is less than 1km off the GRR at the 286km mark. The rock paintings here include one Wandjina head.

MT BARNETT ROADHOUSE

The Mt Barnett Roadhouse (☎ 9191 7007), 306km from Derby, is owned and run by the Aboriginal Kupungarri Community. A small general store has groceries and is open 7 am to 5 pm from May to September. There's an entry fee of $4 per person and camping costs another $7 per adult.

KALUMBURU ROAD

The road to Kalumburu is a natural earth road that traverses rocky, isolated terrain. To travel it, you must be self-sufficient and well prepared. It is recommended that you obtain a permit before entering the Kalumburu

---

█ KIMBERLEY ART

The Kimberley is one of the greatest ancient art galleries in the world. Many different styles of rock art are scattered through this area, but two of the better known are the Wandjina and the Bradshaw.

The Wandjina paintings, with their large mouthless figures in headdress, are among the most famous of Aboriginal images. The Wandjina are the shadows of ancestors, imprinted on the rock as they pass by. Each Wandjina traditionally had its own custodian family and, to ensure good relations between Wandjina and people, the images should be retouched annually. The sites hold a great deal of significance for Aboriginal people, so if you stumble across one treat it with respect and don't touch the paintings.

The Bradshaw figures (some 10,000 to 30,000 years old) are much older than the Wandjina, but both their source and their significance have largely been lost. The paintings take their name from Joseph Bradshaw, a European who explored the area in 1891.

The best way to see examples of Kimberley art is with a guide from one of the stations. Drysdale River Station (☎ 9161 4326), Theda (☎ 9161 4329) and Mt Elizabeth Station (☎ 9191 4644) run tours.

Aboriginal lands. Call ☎ 9161 4300 (fax 9161 4387) from 7 am to noon weekdays.

Organised Tours

The Drysdale River Homestead (☎ 9161 4326) is 1km off the Kalumburu Rd at the 59km mark. The homestead offers scenic flights and 4WD tours – including trips to see examples of the ancient Bradshaw rock art (see the boxed text 'Kimberley Art').

Around 198km from the Gibb River Rd, Theda Station (☎ 9161 4329) is 1km off the road. It offers tours of Bradshaw art sites and scenic flights.

Gamberre & Miwa Country

Kalumburu Area

KALUMBURU

The Kalumburu Aboriginal Community (☎ 9161 4300) is 267km from the GRR and about 5km from the mouth of the King Edward River and King Edward Gorge. The picturesque mission is set among giant mango trees and coconut palms, and accommodation is available. Entry is $25 per vehicle and an additional fee is levied to camp at McGowan's Island and Honeymoon Beach. The store is open 8.30 to 10.50 am and 1.30 to 3.50 pm weekdays (except Tuesday), plus 8.30 to 10.50 am Saturday.

Fishing, trekking and scenic flights with members of the community can be arranged here. The surrounding Mitchell Plateau is well known for its Wandjina paintings (see the boxed text 'Kimberley Art').

Bunuba Country

Fitzroy River Area

FITZROY CROSSING

Aboriginal people have lived in this area for many thousands of years and more than 34 Aboriginal communities still exist in the Fitzroy valley. The Bunuba in particular put up strong resistance to pastoralists and adopted European fighting methods, causing so much trouble that in 1900 one-quarter of the WA police force was based in the Kimberley.

Many Indigenous people ended up here following the granting of equal pay to Aborigines and the subsequent claim by pastoralists that they could no longer afford to keep Aboriginal staff. The town later grew into a service centre as health and government workers came to work with the communities. Many businesses are now at least partly Aboriginal-owned and six stations within the area have been sold back to the traditional owners.

Information

Tourist Office The Fitzroy Crossing Tourist Bureau (☎ 9191 5355) has good information and a selection of local paintings available for sale. It's open 9 am to 6 pm daily April to September, and 9 am to 5 pm weekdays and 9 am to 1 pm Saturday October to March. The library next door has good local information and is open 2 to 5 pm weekdays and 9 am to 1 pm Saturday.

Radio Wangki Yupurnanupuarra Aboriginal Corporation broadcasts 6FX on 936AM.

Organised Tours

A 1½-hour tour along the Fitzroy River leaving from the Fitzroy River Lodge introduces the local vegetation and its traditional uses for $15 per person.

Darlngunaya Aboriginal Corporation (part of the Junjuwa community), in collaboration with Headwaters (☎ 03-9478 9414, e paddlesports@paddlesports.com.au), offers six-/seven-day white-water rafting trips on the Fitzroy River (Grades 5 to 6) for $1680/1960. The first trip covers the upper Fitzroy gorges passing rainforest, rock art and waterfalls, ending with a helicopter ride out of Moll Gorge. The second trip from Milliwindie station to Dimond Gorge is much more adrenalin-pumping, also with a helicopter ride to finish. Trips operate in the Wet, January to March, and Bunuba guides are on hand to explain the passing landscapes.

Places to Stay

Darlngunaya Backpackers (☎ 9191 5140) on Russ Rd (in the old post office) is Aboriginal-owned. It's about 4km from town and has beds starting at $15 and wombles (self-contained houses) for $90/120 for two/four to six people. It also has bikes and canoes for hire. Pick-up from the Greyhound bus (which stops outside the tourist bureau in the middle of the night) costs $5. Swollen waterways can make Darlngunaya inaccessible by car, so it closes in the Wet.

The Crossing Inn (☎ 9191 5080, fax 9191 5208) on Scuthorp Rd is the oldest pub in the Kimberley. More or less a tin shed, it's been decorated with paintings by local students and is a lively place to meet some locals. Motel-style rooms with verandahs overlooking the river cost $82/100/110 and meals are available in the pub.

Special Events

The Garnduwa Amboorny Wirnan Festival (☎ 9191 5227) in April is a chance for the youth of the Kimberley to show their singing, dancing and athletic skills.

Shopping

Mangkaja Arts (☎ 9191 5272, fax 9191 5279) next to the Tarunda supermarket has ceramic tiles, etchings, paintings, didjeridus and other works for sale. It also has workshops in outer communities and there are often artists milling around. It's open 9 am to 5 pm weekdays.

BUYULU ABORIGINAL COMMUNITY

Visitors are welcome to use the general store and fill up on fuel at the Buyulu Aboriginal Community, about 12km south of Fitzroy Crossing. There are also a few artists there who are happy to show and sell their work – ask at the store.

GEIKIE GORGE NATIONAL PARK

The magnificent Geikie Gorge, cut through the Devonian Reef by the Fitzroy River, is 18km north of Fitzroy Crossing on a sealed road. Part of the gorge is in a small, sandy national park only 8km by 3km. During the Wet, the river, home to freshwater crocodiles, stingray and swordfish, rises nearly 12m and in the Dry it stops flowing, leaving a series of waterholes. There are a couple of short walks and some good swimming spots. The park is open year-round (although not always accessible) from 6.30 am to 6.30 pm.

Darngku Heritage Cruises (☎ 9191 5552), has two Aboriginal interpretative tours/cruises of Geikie Gorge. The 5¼-hour cruise includes lunch ($105 per person); a three-hour cruise is $44 per person. Tours

leave Geikie Gorge Jetty at 8.15 am Monday to Friday from April to November and can be booked through the Fitzroy Crossing Tourist Bureau (see earlier).

WINDJANA GORGE & TUNNEL CREEK NATIONAL PARKS

You can visit the spectacular ancient rock formations, used as hide-outs by Jandamarra, in Windjana Gorge and Tunnel Creek from the Leopold Downs Rd, off the Great Northern Hwy between Fitzroy Crossing and Derby.

Organised Tours

Bungoolee Tours/Fitzroy Crossing Charter Tours (☎ 9191 5355) has a full-day tour taking in Fitzroy Crossing, Windjana Gorge and Tunnel Creek. A local Bunuba guide provides a cultural interpretation of these sites and will acquaint you with the story of Jandamarra ('Pigeon'), an Aboriginal man who evaded police for three years, and his impact on the development of the region (see the boxed text 'Jandamarra ('Pigeon')'). You will also have the opportunity to see the land, traditional hunting grounds and watering holes, and hear stories of the country from an Aboriginal perspective.

Tours leave at 7 am on Sunday, Wednesday and Friday between May and October and a full day with meals costs $85/50 for adults/children. At the time of writing, overnight camping trips were being planned for the future.

Windjana Gorge

The near-vertical walls of the 3.5km-long Windjana Gorge soar 90m above the Lennard River, which rushes through in the Wet but becomes just a series of pools in the Dry. There are also a few short walks including the **time walk** which studies fossilised marine life forms. Also within the park is **Lillimilura Police Outpost** where Jandamarra worked, and which he later raided to steal munitions. Camping is available at the park.

Tunnel Creek

Tunnel Creek is a 750m-long tunnel cut by the creek through a spur of the Napier Range. The tunnel is 3m to 15m wide, and you can walk all the way along it. You'll need light but sturdy shoes; be prepared to

WESTERN AUSTRALIA

wade through very cold, chest-deep water in places.

Near the north entrance to the tunnel are **cave paintings** and at the other entrance is the black dolerite and basalt that was fashioned by Aborigines into stone axes. A cave near the tunnel was used as a **hide-out** by Jandamarra between 1894 and 1897.

Djaru & Kija Country

Halls Creek Area

Prior to European settlement, the town that is Halls Creek formed the boundary between the traditional country of the Djaru and Kija people. This area was a meeting place for tribes as far away as Broome (to the south) and Newcastle River (in the NT) – they travelled here to trade and for ceremonies. Djaru people lived near six waterholes within the southern section of Halls Creek shire and the traditional land of the Kija people extended west to Fitzroy Crossing, east to Turkey Creek (Warmun) and north between the Tablelands and Mount House station

Halls Creek become a European settlement in 1885 due to the discovery of gold. When first sighted, Europeans (known as *gardiyas*, 'white people') were thought to be *gugurr* (ghosts).

The invaders brought about many changes and massacres of the local people were rife. In 1886 a miner named Merriot was murdered and it is thought that as many as 100 Djaru and Kija people were killed in retaliation. Many retribution massacres occurred after pastoralist Alf Barret was speared to death in Kija country. In 1924 the Bedford Downs Massacre occurred when an attempted spearing of the station owners resulted in the owners serving poisoned stew to all Aboriginal people living nearby.

HALLS CREEK

The Shire of Halls Creek covers 143,000 sq km with a population of just 3339, 65% of which is Aboriginal. There are 65 Aboriginal communities within the shire, and most have adopted a 'no-grog' policy. Please respect this if you visit their communities.

Information

Tourist Office The Halls Creek Tourist Office (☎ 9168 6262) on the Great Northern

Hwy is open 8 am to 4 pm weekdays from April to October; it's closed during the remainder of the year. The office is to be relocated in 2001. Ask here about the Heritage Park Trail that is being developed.

Books & Videos *The Human Race* is a documentary featuring a German, an American and a local Halls Creek Aboriginal man walking 500km from Kandimala to Halls Creek over 26 days. You can learn more about this mammoth effort at the tourist office. *Moola Bulla – In the Shadow of the Mountain*, by the Kimberley Language Resource Centre, is a collection of stories from the area – see the boxed text 'Books about the Kimberley' earlier in this chapter for more information.

Radio The Aboriginal organisation PRK Media broadcasts 6PRK on 98.1FM.

Kimberley Language Resource Centre

The broad objective of the Kimberley Language Resource Centre (☎ 9168 6005) on Terone St is to maintain language and promote local Aboriginal languages. It has some excellent resources including explanations of local Dreaming stories, language kits/cassettes and books both for reference and sale. There are also regular language courses. The centre is open 8.30 am to 4.30 pm weekdays.

Shopping

Yarliyil Art Centre (☎ 9168 6460) on Duncan Rd is a community-based outlet founded for local artists. All proceeds from the sales of paintings are injected back into developing the centre. All art is sold with cultural information about the artist. The centre also hosts an artist-in-residence, with work space available to the public. It's open 9 am to 4 pm weekdays, or after-hours on demand.

WOLFE CREEK CRATER NATIONAL PARK

The 835m-wide and 50m-deep Wolfe Creek Crater, originally known as Kandimala, is the second-largest known meteorite crater in the world. It is estimated to be about 300,000 years old.

In the Dreaming, two Rainbow Serpents weaved their way across the desert leaving behind their prints (in the form of riverbeds) and one snake raised his head at Kandimala leaving behind this crater.

The turn-off to the crater (the Tanami Desert Rd) is 18km out of Halls Creek towards Fitzroy Crossing and from there it's 112km by unsealed road to the south. It's easily accessible without 4WD in the dry season (April to November). Check road conditions with the Halls Creek shire office (☎ 9168 6007).

PURNULULU NATIONAL PARK

The 350-million-year-old **Bungle Bungle Range** at the Purnululu National Park is an amazing spectacle: impressive rounded sandstone towers, with an exterior crust striped in bands of orange (iron oxide) and blackish-green (cyanobacteria). The range is a plateau that rises more than 200m above the surrounding plain and at its edges are the curious beehive domes.

Traditionally the land of the Kija and Djaru people, who still live in settlements in the east Kimberley, the park contains Aboriginal art and a number of burial sites, though these are not accessible to the public. Tourists did not start visiting the 'Bungles' until after the area was filmed by a TV crew in 1982. By the end of the 1990s, visitor numbers were approaching 15,000 annually.

There are Aboriginal rangers on site who will interpret the history of the Kija people. **Rock art** is found near seasonal/permanent waterholes. Access to the park is difficult and the park is officially closed from 1 January to 31 March. Visit the CALM office at the entrance to the park (53km from the highway) before venturing in.

LUMUKU

North-west of Purnululu is the Lumuku Aboriginal Corporation, also known as Osmond Valley. There is a community-owned family camping ground (☎ 9168 5073, or leave a message on ☎ 9168 6049 or 9168 6204). Guests must come fully equipped as there are no store facilities on site. The Osmond Valley lies on the western edge of the Osmond Range. It is a tropical oasis on the fringe of Purnululu, with fresh springs and various walking tracks. There is also a historic homestead from the early pioneering days located on the property.

WARMUN

Warmun, or Turkey Creek (☎ 9168 7881), is 167km north of Halls Creek on the Great Northern Hwy, and has a population of about 620 people. Access is restricted, though you can visit the arts centre (see later) if you call in advance for permission.

Daiwul Gidja Cultural Centre

Opposite the Turkey Creek Roadhouse the Daiwul Gidja Cultural Centre is an interpretative centre well worth visiting. It offers half- and full-day bush tours as well as a two-day Aboriginal cross-cultural awareness course that is accredited nationally. There are also visual displays and artworks (most available for sale). It is generally open 9 am to 5 pm weekdays.

Kelarriny-Warmun Arts Centre

Warmun artists are renowned for their distinctive and original work which embodies traditional and contemporary Kija culture. A number of Warmun artists are widely recognised as being among Australia's leading contemporary artists.

Visitors are welcome at the centre (☎ 9168 7496) during weekdays although you must call for permission to enter the community.

Miriwoong Country

Kununurra Area

KUNUNURRA

In the Miriwoong language the region is known as Gananoorrang ('meeting of the waters') – Kununurra is the European translation of this. As in most parts of the rugged Kimberley, Aborigines have occupied the area for thousands of years.

Information

Radio Waringarri Media broadcasts Aboriginal programming on 6WR (693AM).

Organised Tours

Triple J Tours (☎ 9168 2682) has collaborated with Bell Springs Aboriginal Community, 20km south-east of Kununurra, to offer fun trips. Tours start with a short cruise along the Ord River followed by a horse-drawn carriage ride to the community where

WESTERN AUSTRALIA

there are opportunities to talk to community members. There are rock paintings nearby. Trips leave Monday, Wednesday and Friday from April to October and cost $55/35 for adults/children.

Arnie's Fishing Adventure (☎ 9169 1820, fax 9169 2604, ⓔ arniesfishing@wn.com.au) specialises in fishing trips throughout the north-east Kimberley. 'Barramundi man' Arnie uses traditional methods to find the best fishing spots and takes anglers to areas they would otherwise not have access to. He explains local history and culture and passes on bush survival tips. One-day trips cost $210, while overnight camping trips are $360 per person; both are available year-round.

Hidden Valley

About 2km from the town centre, Hidden Valley in Mirima National Park is of great significance to the Aboriginal people. A wonderful area, it has a steep gorge, great views, short walking tracks and ancient **rock art** and **axe-grinding grooves**. The banded formations are similar to the Bungle Bungle and are of great spiritual importance to the Miriwoong people, as part of their Head Lice Dreaming. A very short walk features valley plants and their traditional uses. It costs $9 to take a car into the park.

Shopping

The Waringarri Aboriginal Arts Centre is a bit of a trek out of town on Speargrass Rd. You get a certificate of authenticity with any painting purchased, and biographies of artists are available. It also sells carved baobab nuts. It is open 8 am to 5 pm in the Dry and 8.30 am to 2 pm in the Wet.

Doreen's Flowers in the Coles centre has more local paintings, mainly in dot work. Red Rock Art (☎ 9168 2607) is another gallery with local art, on the highway.

EL QUESTRO WILDERNESS PARK

El Questro Wilderness Park (☎ 9169 1777), 16km off the GRR at the 614km mark, offers 4WD and boat trips to the Chamberlain Gorge (starting at $37), which include a look at some Wandjina paintings.

WYNDHAM

Presented to Wyndham by the Jarook Ngarni Aboriginal Community for the Bicentennial, the town's brilliant **Dreamtime Statues** are not to be missed. They are dedicated to 'those who prepared us for today' and represent a family unit and their animals sculpted from bronze and wire. The father proudly towers above the surrounding grass searching for new hunting grounds while a mother and child rest nearby. The locals are justifiably proud of the statues and a nearby plaque states 'Aboriginal spirits will always survive in this timeless beautiful land'.

Organised Tours

Kimberley Dreamtime Tours (☎ 9161 1288, fax 9161 1408, ⓔ kimberleydreamtime@bigpond.com) is run by a husband-and-wife team offering a variety of tours from Wyndham and Kununurra. All offer insights into local culture by those who live, it taking in a range of sights around Wyndham and the GRR. Half-day tours start at $70 per person and overnight trips complete with campfires and singalongs start from $295. There are a whole heap of other itineraries included and they can be customised to specific interests – call for details.

Warntarri Purlumanupurru

Canning Stock Route

Named after Alfred Canning, the Canning Stock Route (CSR) passes through at least 10 Aboriginal nation's territories. In the north, the CSR (or *warntarri purlumanupurru*) crosses the traditional lands of the Walmajarri and Wangkjunga people (the Great Sandy Desert, between the Percival Lakes and Lake Gregory). North of Lake Disappointment is Manyjilyjarra country (Manyjilyjarra is spoken at Punmu and Jigalong Aboriginal Communities).

The CSR runs south-west from Halls Creek to Wiluna. It crosses both the Great Sandy and Gibson Deserts. You should only travel along the route in a well-equipped party, and careful navigation is required.

INFORMATION

If you wish to travel to any of the outlying communities, you need to contact the Kimberley Land Council (☎ 9168 6274). Access

BLOOD IN THE DESERT

bryan Andy

The Canning Stock Route's 1700km were 'first' surveyed in 1906, a feat that would not have been possible had it not been for the assistance of Aborigines at the time. But it wasn't all happy, reciprocal relations; far from it in fact. Alfred Canning and his men were known to chain their Aboriginal guides up at night (sometimes even during the day) to restrict their chances of escape. Many of the guides that were used would only offer their know-how in their own country, so once they reached their nation's border they would call it quits, receive a token payment (food, clothing, a mirror perhaps) and a small piece of metal inscribed with a thank you – a kind of medal, supposedly.

In April 1907 a member of Canning's party, Michael Tobin, was speared by an Aborigine (who remains unknown), whom Tobin shot dead before dying himself the next day. Tobin's grave is near Well 40 on the route; you'll notice that the marble cross is edged in metal, a measure taken to prevent Aborigines chipping away at the headstone in order to make spearheads. The Aborigine who was shot was buried in an unmarked grave, said to be about 2.5km west of the well.

When the party arrived back in Perth on completion of the initial survey, the cook (Edward Blake) who accompanied the trek made known the mistreatment of Aboriginal men and women by Canning's men. A royal commission was established in 1908, and in the end they were rebuked only for using chains to bind their guides.

to communities can be restricted at certain times of the year.

While you travel the CSR, leave all things as you find them, from gates to signs. You could jeopardise someone else's life by tampering with the signs. And remember, if you take it in, take it out; there's nothing more unattractive than litter in this beautiful region.

WELLS

The route is dotted with numerous water wells (54 altogether). Not all provide suitable drinking water and it's not good etiquette to taint wells with detergents or soaps – use a basin well away from the water supplies. Don't remove anything from the wells as they're part of the area's heritage, both Indigenous and non-Indigenous.

SITES

Along the route you can find evidence of Aboriginal occupation, particularly in the stone country where there are greater numbers of semipermanent waterholes. Camping places are quite common, with stone scatters further emphasising Aboriginal occupation. The ancient practice of firestick farming was used in the area to promote new growth and encourage greater animal

numbers, and these days you can see how the lack of this burning-off dictates the numbers of marsupials that gather in the area. Not only do the Durba Hills offer amazing views (at Biella Spring), rock art can also be found at **Canning's cairn** and **Killagurra Springs**.

Biella Spring

Painted in ochre you'll see very clear pictures of what appear to be men surrounded by snakes.

Tobin's Grave

Michael Tobin's grave is at Waddawalla, Well 40.

LAKE GREGORY

Lake Gregory is close to the Aboriginal community of **Mulan-Paraku** (community office ☎ 9168 8939), about 336km south of Halls Creek. The lake region (Sturt Creek and Paraku) has significant cultural importance to the Aboriginal people of the Tjurabalan native title claim, which looks like it will be accepted, given the lack of opposition to it. Mulan is home to about 180 people, comprising three main family groups. At the time of writing they were establishing a camping ground with basic facilities in the area. Call

WESTERN AUSTRALIA

the community prior to arriving to get permission to enter.

BILLILUNA-MINDIBUNG ABORIGINAL COMMUNITY

In Walmajarri country, the Billiluna-Mindibung Aboriginal Community (community office ☎ 9168 8988) at the northern end of Lake Gregory is home to about 150 to 200 people, comprising five main family groups. They're at the top end of the CSR, some 180km south of Halls Creek.

The community's **Kururrungka School** (☎ 9168 8932) has a culture centre with displays of historical records and artefacts, as well as arts and crafts for sale. Access to the school is only during school hours (7.30 am to 12.30 pm throughout the school year). Entrance donations are appreciated, as is a phone call to gain permission to enter the community.

BALGO-WIRRIMANU

Balgo-Wirrimanu Aboriginal Community (community office ☎ 9168 8900) is a former Pallotine Mission on the edge of the Tanami Track and Great Sandy Desert, 290km from Halls Creek. It lies at the crossroads of numerous tribal/language groups, with Kukatja being the dominant language. Other languages include Djaru, Ngardi, Walmajarri, Warlpiri, Wangkjunga and Pintubi.

Limited motel-style accommodation is available ($50 per night per person).

Warlayiriti Artists

The world-renowned Warlayiriti Artists Aboriginal Corporation (☎ 9168 8960) promotes over 200 artists whose work can be viewed at the art centre. Their paintings reflect the traditional stories of their homelands, and the Balgo painters are renowned for their vibrant colours and incredible variety of expression. See the 'Visual Art' special section for more details. Warlayiriti Artists is housed in a purpose-built art centre, providing a gallery for the works, modern facilities and expansive areas for the artists to work.

Ngaanyatjarra Country

Warburton & Surrounds

WARBURTON
Tjulyuru Cultural & Civic Centre

This amazing gem is in one of the remotest communities in Australia. It's north of the town of Warburton (about 500m from the Warburton roadhouse). The centre (☎ 8956 7966, fax 8956 7959, ℮ info@tjulyuru .com) has exquisite artworks from the local community. It was initiated in the spirit of self-determination and has over 300 pieces on display from the nationally prized **Warburton Arts collection**, a collection that is Aboriginal-owned and -controlled. The centre is open 8.30 am to 4.30 pm weekdays (weekend hours were being considered at the time of writing). The centre also houses an information centre, cappuccino bar and a native plants garden. Also worth trying are the art activities for children – call ahead to get exact times for these or browse the Web site at www.tjulyuru.com for further details.

PUTJARR ABORIGINAL COMMUNITY

About 243km north of Warburton (off the Old Gunbarrel Hwy) is the Putjarr Aboriginal Community (☎ 8956 7900). This remote location is accessible by car or plane (it has its own airstrip). The community is made up of Pintubi and Ngaanyatjarra people who offer local Aboriginal tours, giving an insight into their bush-tucker collection techniques, their environment and Dreaming stories. A one-hour tour is $10 per person (minimum of two) and a five-hour tour costs $50 per person. Bookings (essential) can be made through the community office. The office also sells locally produced art and crafts.

You will need a permit to access this community. These are available from the Ngaanyatjarra Aboriginal Land Council (☎ 08-8950 1711), 58 Head St, Alice Springs. Permits are free and are processed upon application.

Glossary

Prior to colonisation, there were hundreds of languages spoken in Australia and therefore there are many Indigenous words that describe the same thing. For example, the Yamitji word (in the Pilbara) for goanna is *bungarra*, while the Nyoongar word in the Kimberley is *barni*. Wherever possible we have indicated the source language or region. See also the Language sections in the regional chapters.

Note that many of the definitions in this glossary are drawn from non-Indigenous understandings of terms. For a full description of many concepts, turn to the contributions from Indigenous authors in the main chapters.

AAD – Aboriginal Affairs Department (WA)
AAV – Aboriginal Affairs Victoria
Aboriginality – Aboriginal identity
acacia – name for many varieties of wattle tree found across Australia, providing nutritious seeds, and gum for beverages and medicine
AIATSIS – Australian Institute of Aboriginal and Torres Strait Islander Studies
ANTaR – Australians for Native Title and Reconciliation
assimilation – a pre-1970s government policy that involved the subjugation of Indigenous culture to the culture of white Australia
ATA – Aboriginal Tourism Australia
ATSIC – Aboriginal and Torres Strait Islander Commission

balga – grass tree (WA)
bardi grubs – larvae of *Cerambycidae* beetles; a nutritious source of food that can be eaten raw or cooked
beanie – close-fitting knitted hat
Biame – a Creator spirit in NSW
billabong – isolated body of water once part of a river, lake or marsh; a haven for birdlife and a great source of bush tucker
blackbirding – the practice of kidnapping people to sell them into slavery
black tracker – Aboriginal person working for the police
boomerang – traditional weapon made of hard wood; returning boomerangs are the most famous (their special curved shape means that when thrown they fly in an arc and return to the thrower); however boomerangs are also used as hunting clubs or tapped together to make music
bora – initiation of young boys (NSW)
bora ground – circular area ringed with banked earth used for ceremonial purposes, created mainly in NSW and south-east Queensland
bora ring – see *bora ground*
boyoo – fruit of the poisonous zamia palm, which must be treated with salt water before being eaten (WA)
Brownlow Medal – highest individual honour that an Australian Rules football player can achieve, awarded annually to the best player in the Australian Football League
bullroarer – secret instrument comprising a long piece of wood swung around the head on a string, creating an eerie roar; often used in men's initiation ceremonies
Bunjil – a Creator Spirit of south-eastern Australia
bush tucker – food; especially traditional foods, such as kangaroo, shellfish, tubers, nuts and honey

CAAMA – Central Australian Aboriginal Media Association
CALM – Conservation and Land Management (WA)
CDEP – Community Development Employment Program
che-ka-ra – melo shell pendants
cherrabun – Kimberley word for *yabby* (freshwater crustacean)
CLC – Central Land Council (NT)
clapsticks – important percussion instrument used in Aboriginal societies throughout Australia, either sticks (one or two) or a pair of boomerangs
clever man – shaman
coolamon – wooden carrying dish
corroboree – festival or gathering for ceremonial or spiritual reasons; from the Dharug word *garaabara*, a style of dancing

damper – bush bread made of flour from ground seeds and water (these days baking powder and wheat flour is often used) and cooked in the coals of an open fire

dance machine – decorated accessory used for dancing in the Torres Strait Islands, such as hand-held clappers or feather wands

deadly – fantastic, excellent

didgeridoo – see *didjeridu*

didjeridu – wind instrument made of a branch hollowed out by termites, traditionally used only by the communities in the Top End, where its Yolngu name is *yidaki* ('didjeridu' was probably coined by Herbert Basedow in 1926 to describe the distinctive sound of the instrument)

dilly bag – woven carry bag, usually made from natural grasses and often dyed with natural bush dyes

djilki – Nyoongar word for *jilgy*, or *yabby*, a small freshwater crustacean

DOGIT – Deed of Grant in Trust; in Queensland, a special form of title that allows community-level land trusts to own and administer former reserve lands

donga – makeshift shelter, often portable, such as a caravan

Dreaming, the – see *Dreamtime* (Dreaming is often the preferred term, as it avoids the association with time)

Dreamtime – complex concept that forms the basis of Aboriginal spirituality, incorporating the creation of the world and the spiritual energies operating around us (so termed by anthropologists Baldwin Spencer and Frank Gillen in the late 19th century as an approximate translation of the Arrernte word *altyerrenge*, which means something like 'belonging to the Dream'); Dreaming is often the preferred term as it avoids the association with time

Dry, the – dry season in northern Australia (April to October)

dry community – community where the possession and consumption of alcohol is banned, usually by the local Indigenous community council

dry day – day on which the sale of alcohol is banned

firestick farming – technique of controlled burning used to keep land clear in order to prevent uncontrolled bushfires and attract game to the tender regrowth

gnamma hole – rockhole (WA)

gong stones – musical stones from the caves and cliff faces of the Great Australian Bight area

Goori – collective term used to identify Aboriginal people from the mid-north coast and north-western regions of NSW

gubba – non-Indigenous Australian (used by Kooris in NSW)

humpy – temporary hut, traditionally made of handy materials such as bark or tree branches

increase ceremonies – ceremonies to encourage the generation of species, such as fish or animals, sometimes by repeating their name or depicting an abundance of them

jilgy – Western Australian word for *yabby*

keeping place – cultural centre, or place used for activities that help to maintain and strengthen Aboriginal culture (perhaps including meeting rooms, workshops, library or theatre); a place used to keep secret and special items, or protect human remains

Koori – collective term used to identify Aboriginal people from NSW

Koorie – collective term used to identify Victorian Aboriginal people

kulups – Torres Strait hand-shakers made of large seeds tied together

kupai omasker – Torres Strait Islander expression used to describe the traditional system of adoption

lap-lap – waistcloth or loincloth

lava lava – Torres Strait Islander *lap-lap*

law, the – fundamental guiding truths, often grounded in *the Dreaming*; actions carried out in accordance with the responsibilities of members of the society

Lore – see Law

Mabo decision – 1992 High Court decision, in the case of Eddie Koiki Mabo and four other Mer Islanders, that overturned the legal concept of *terra nullius*

Macassans – traders from Sulawesi in modern-day Indonesia who visited Indigenous communities from the 17th century for trepang, or sea cucumber, a marine delicacy

maireeners – shell necklaces (Tasmania)

marron – freshwater crustacean (WA)

mia-mia – *humpy* (WA)

midden – collection of discarded bones, shells, stone artefacts, etc, indicating a settlement of some duration

migloo – non-Indigenous Australian (Queensland)

milbayarr – spear-thrower (in Queensland)

Mimi – spirit people, depicted as slender figures in the art of the Arnhem Land plateau

moiety – system of classification originating in the *law*, according to which interpersonal relationships are organised

Murri – collective term used to identify Aboriginal people from Queensland

NAIDOC – National Aboriginal and Islander Day of Celebration; or sometimes National Aboriginal and Islander Day Observance Committee

nation – community of Indigenous people based on tribal, cultural, linguistic and/or land identification; the territory associated with a nation group

NLC – Northern Land Council (NT)

NPWSA – National Parks & Wildlife South Australia

NPWS – National Parks & Wildlife Service (NSW)

NTPWS – Northern Territory Parks & Wildlife Service

nulla-nulla – club used primarily for hunting or fishing

Nunga – collective term used by some Aboriginal people from parts of South Australia to identify themselves

Nyoongar – collective term used by some Aboriginal people from southern WA to identify themselves

Palawa – collective term used to identify some Tasmanian Aboriginal people

pituri – highly sought-after narcotic, requiring careful preparation

poison relationship – see *taboo relationship*

pukumani poles – tall carved and painted tree trunks used by Tiwi Islanders to mark grave sites

PWS – Parks & Wildlife Service (Tasmania)

quandong – small tree with edible fruit, sometimes called native peach

QPWS – Queensland Parks & Wildlife Service

Rainbow Serpent – Creator Being found in many parts of Australia, always serpentine in shape and often associated with sources of water

rarrk – cross-hatchings designs used in Arnhem Land paintings and body art

renewal ceremonies – see *increase ceremonies*

rockhole – water catchment in rock that collects and stores rainwater

scarr tree – a tree from which bark has been removed and treated to make canoes, dishes, shields or other items; sometimes also called scar tree, scarred tree or canoe tree

settlers – non-Indigenous people

shame job – embarrassment or shyness caused by standing out, or being singled out, in a crowd

sistergirl – term of endearment often used between women; a person who identifies as transsexual (in the gay scene)

skin name – person's name as determined by their *moiety*

songlines – *Dreaming* tracks

sorry business – funeral rituals

Stolen Generations – generations of Indigenous children forcibly removed from their parents

Story – *the Dreaming* (Cape York)

story – tale from *the Dreaming* that taps into the concepts of legend, myth, tradition and the law, and is meant to carry much more weight than the average historical account (given the importance of oral traditions in Aboriginal and Torres Strait Islander cultures); the words 'story' and 'stories' are italicised in this guide to signify and acknowledge the credibility of these oral traditions

story place – place where special *Dreaming* events occurred

taboo relationship – relationship sometimes occurring between relatives (perhaps mother-in-law and son-in-law) in which the parties cannot communicate in any way or even be in each other's presence

TAC – Tasmanian Aboriginal Centre

TALC – Tasmanian Aboriginal Land Council

terra nullius – legal concept that Australia was uninhabited at the time of British colonisations

thalu site – site where *increase ceremonies* take place (WA)

Tjukurpa – the *Dreaming* or Creation Time (central Australia)

totem – symbol of the complex relationships between people, ancestors and environment, embodied by elements of the natural world (animals, objects or phenomena); the word derives from a Native American word said to mean 'he/she/it is a relative of mine'

TSRA – Torres Strait Regional Authority

Wagyl – huge Serpent Ancestors (WA)
Wandjina – powerful spirits of the Kimberley region often depicted in rock paintings
Wet, the – rainy season in the north (November to May)
wiltja – shelter made from a mulga tree (SA)

woomera – Dharug (Sydney region) word for spear-thrower, usually with a barb at one end and a handle at the other that attaches to the end of a spear (when thrown this increases the leverage and therefore the speed)
wurrung – 'language' in Melbourne region

Yamatji – collective term used to identify some Aboriginal people from central WA
yabby – freshwater crayfish
yawilyu – women's law
yidaki – the original Yolngu name for *didjeridu*

LONELY PLANET

You already know that Lonely Planet produces more than this one guidebook, but you might not be aware of the other products we have on this region. Here is a selection of titles that you may want to check out as well:

Australia
ISBN 1 86450 068 9
US$24.95 • UK£14.99

Outback Australia
ISBN 0 86442 504 X
US$21.95 • UK£13.99

Australian phrasebook
ISBN 0 86442 576 7
US$5.95 • UK£3.99

Cycling Australia
ISBN 1 86450 166 9
US$21.99 • UK£13.99

Walking in Australia
ISBN 0 86442 669 0
US$21.99 • UK£13.99

Healthy Travel Australia, NZ & the Pacific
ISBN 1 86450 052 2
US$5.95 • UK£3.99

Sean & David's Long Drive
ISBN 0 86442 371 3
US$10.95 • UK£5.99

Islands of Australia's Great Barrier Reef
ISBN 0 86442 563 5
US$14.95 • UK£8.99

Watching Wildlife Australia
ISBN 1 86450 032 8
US$19.99 • UK£12.99

Australia Road Atlas
ISBN 1 86450 065 4
US$14.99 • UK£8.99

Diving & Snorkeling Australia's Great Barrier Reef
ISBN 0 86442 763 8
US$17.95 • UK£11.99

Also available regional & city guides; maps & *Out to Eat* guides

LONELY PLANET

Guides by Region

Lonely Planet is known worldwide for publishing practical, reliable and no-nonsense travel information in our guides and on our Web site. The Lonely Planet list covers just about every accessible part of the world. Currently there are 16 series: Travel guides, Shoestring guides, Condensed guides, Phrasebooks, Read This First, Healthy Travel, Walking guides, Cycling guides, Watching Wildlife guides, Pisces Diving & Snorkeling guides, City Maps, Road Atlases, Out to Eat, World Food, Journeys travel literature and Pictorials.

AFRICA Africa on a shoestring • Cairo • Cairo City Map • Cape Town • Cape Town City Map • East Africa • Egypt • Egyptian Arabic phrasebook • Ethiopia, Eritrea & Djibouti • Ethiopian Amharic phrasebook • The Gambia & Senegal • Healthy Travel Africa • Kenya • Malawi • Morocco • Moroccan Arabic phrasebook • Mozambique • Read This First: Africa • South Africa, Lesotho & Swaziland • Southern Africa • Southern Africa Road Atlas • Swahili phrasebook • Tanzania, Zanzibar & Pemba • Trekking in East Africa • Tunisia • Watching Wildlife East Africa • Watching Wildlife Southern Africa • West Africa • World Food Morocco • Zimbabwe, Botswana & Namibia
Travel Literature: Mali Blues: Traveling to an African Beat • The Rainbird: A Central African Journey • Songs to an African Sunset: A Zimbabwean Story

AUSTRALIA & THE PACIFIC Auckland • Australia • Australian phrasebook • Australia Road Atlas • Cycling Australia • Cycling New Zealand • Fiji • Fijian phrasebook • Healthy Travel Australia, NZ & the Pacific • Islands of Australia's Great Barrier Reef • Melbourne • Melbourne City Map • Micronesia • New Caledonia • New South Wales • New Zealand • Northern Territory • Outback Australia • Out to Eat – Melbourne • Out to Eat – Sydney • Papua New Guinea • Pidgin phrasebook • Queensland • Rarotonga & the Cook Islands • Samoa • Solomon Islands • South Australia • South Pacific • South Pacific phrasebook • Sydney • Sydney City Map • Sydney Condensed • Tahiti & French Polynesia • Tasmania • Tonga • Tramping in New Zealand • Vanuatu • Victoria • Walking in Australia • Watching Wildlife Australia • Western Australia
Travel Literature: Islands in the Clouds: Travels in the Highlands of New Guinea • Kiwi Tracks: A New Zealand Journey • Sean & David's Long Drive

CENTRAL AMERICA & THE CARIBBEAN Bahamas, Turks & Caicos • Baja California • Belize, Guatemala & Yucatán • Bermuda • Central America on a shoestring • Costa Rica • Costa Rica Spanish phrasebook • Cuba • Dominican Republic & Haiti • Eastern Caribbean • Guatemala • Havana • Healthy Travel Central & South America • Jamaica • Mexico • Mexico City • Panama • Puerto Rico • Read This First: Central & South America • World Food Mexico • Yucatán
Travel Literature: Green Dreams: Travels in Central America

EUROPE Amsterdam • Amsterdam City Map • Amsterdam Condensed • Andalucía • Austria • Baltic States phrasebook • Barcelona • Barcelona City Map • Belgium & Luxembourg • Berlin • Berlin City Map • Britain • British phrasebook • Brussels, Bruges & Antwerp • Brussels City Map • Budapest • Budapest City Map • Canary Islands • Central Europe • Central Europe phrasebook • Copenhagen • Corfu & the Ionians • Corsica • Crete • Crete Condensed • Croatia • Cycling Britain • Cycling France • Cyprus • Czech & Slovak Republics • Denmark • Dublin • Dublin City Map • Eastern Europe • Eastern Europe phrasebook • Edinburgh • England • Estonia, Latvia & Lithuania • Europe on a shoestring • Europe phrasebook • Finland • Florence • France • Frankfurt Condensed • French phrasebook • Georgia, Armenia & Azerbaijan • Germany • German phrasebook • Greece • Greek Islands • Greek phrasebook • Hungary • Iceland, Greenland & the Faroe Islands • Ireland • Italian phrasebook • Italy • Krakow • Lisbon • The Loire • London • London City Map • London Condensed • Madrid • Malta • Mediterranean Europe • Mediterranean Europe phrasebook • Moscow • Munich • Netherlands • Normandy • Norway • Out to Eat – London • Out to Eat – Paris • Paris • Paris City Map • Paris Condensed • Poland • Polish phrasebook • Portugal • Portuguese phrasebook • Prague • Prague City Map • Provence & the Côte d'Azur • Read This First: Europe • Rhodes & the Dodecanese • Romania & Moldova • Rome • Rome City Map • Russia, Ukraine & Belarus • Russian phrasebook • Scandinavian & Baltic Europe • Scandinavian phrasebook • Scotland • Sicily • Slovenia • South-West France • Spain • Spanish phrasebook • St Petersburg • St Petersburg City Map • Sweden • Switzerland • Tuscany • Ukrainian phrasebook • Venice • Vienna • Walking in Britain • Walking in France • Walking in Ireland • Walking in Italy • Walking in Spain • Walking in Switzerland • Western Europe • World Food France • World Food Ireland • World Food Italy • World Food Spain
Travel Literature: After Yugoslavia • Love and War in the Apennines • The Olive Grove: Travels in Greece • On the Shores of the Mediterranean • Round Ireland in Low Gear • A Small Place in Italy

LONELY PLANET

Mail Order

Lonely Planet products are distributed worldwide.They are also available by mail order from Lonely Planet, so if you have difficulty finding a title please write to us. North and South American residents should write to 150 Linden St, Oakland, CA 94607, USA; European and African residents should write to 10a Spring Place, London NW5 3BH, UK; and residents of other countries to Locked Bag 1, Footscray, Victoria 3011, Australia.

INDIAN SUBCONTINENT & THE INDIAN OCEAN Bangladesh • Bengali phrasebook • Bhutan • Delhi • Goa • Healthy Travel Asia & India • Hindi & Urdu phrasebook • India • Indian Himalaya • Karakoram Highway • Kerala • Madagascar • Maldives • Mauritius, Réunion & Seychelles • Mumbai (Bombay) • Nepal • Nepali phrasebook • Pakistan • Rajasthan • Read This First: Asia & India • South India • Sri Lanka • Sri Lanka phrasebook • Tibet • Tibetan phrasebook • Trekking in the Indian Himalaya • Trekking in the Karakoram & Hindukush • Trekking in the Nepal Himalaya
Travel Literature: The Age of Kali: Indian Travels and Encounters • Hello Goodnight: A Life of Goa • In Rajasthan • Maverick in Madagascar • A Season in Heaven: True Tales from the Road to Kathmandu • Shopping for Buddhas • A Short Walk in the Hindu Kush • Slowly Down the Ganges

MIDDLE EAST & CENTRAL ASIA Bahrain, Kuwait & Qatar • Central Asia • Central Asia phrasebook • Dubai • Farsi (Persian) phrasebook • Hebrew phrasebook • Iran • Israel & the Palestinian Territories • Istanbul • Istanbul City Map • Istanbul to Cairo • Istanbul to Kathmandu • Jerusalem • Jerusalem City Map • Jordan • Lebanon • Middle East • Oman & the United Arab Emirates • Syria • Turkey • Turkish phrasebook • World Food Turkey • Yemen
Travel Literature: Black on Black: Iran Revisited • The Gates of Damascus • Kingdom of the Film Stars: Journey into Jordan

NORTH AMERICA Alaska • Boston • Boston City Map • Boston Condensed • British Columbia • California & Nevada • California Condensed • Canada • Chicago • Chicago City Map • Florida • Great Lakes • Hawaii • Hiking in Alaska • Hiking in the USA • Las Vegas • Los Angeles • Los Angeles City Map • Louisiana & the Deep South • Miami • Miami City Map • Montreal • New England • New Orleans • New York City • New York City City Map • New York City Condensed • New York, New Jersey & Pennsylvania • Oahu • Out to Eat – San Francisco • Pacific Northwest • Rocky Mountains • San Francisco • San Francisco City Map • Seattle • Southwest • Texas • Toronto • USA • USA phrasebook • Vancouver • Virginia & the Capital Region • Washington, DC • Washington, DC City Map • World Food New Orleans
Travel Literature: Caught Inside: A Surfer's Year on the California Coast • Drive Thru America

NORTH-EAST ASIA Beijing • Beijing City Map • Cantonese phrasebook • China • Hiking in Japan • Hong Kong • Hong Kong City Map • Hong Kong Condensed • Hong Kong, Macau & Guangzhou • Japan • Japanese phrasebook • Korea • Korean phrasebook • Kyoto • Mandarin phrasebook • Mongolia • Mongolian phrasebook • Seoul • Shanghai • South-West China • Taiwan • Tokyo • World Food Hong Kong
Travel Literature: In Xanadu: A Quest • Lost Japan

SOUTH AMERICA Argentina, Uruguay & Paraguay • Bolivia • Brazil • Brazilian phrasebook • Buenos Aires • Chile & Easter Island • Colombia • Ecuador & the Galapagos Islands • Healthy Travel Central & South America • Latin American Spanish phrasebook • Peru • Quechua phrasebook • Read This First: Central & South America • Rio de Janeiro • Rio de Janeiro City Map • Santiago de Chile • South America on a shoestring • Trekking in the Patagonian Andes • Venezuela
Travel Literature: Full Circle: A South American Journey

SOUTH-EAST ASIA Bali & Lombok • Bangkok • Bangkok City Map • Burmese phrasebook • Cambodia • Hanoi • Healthy Travel Asia & India • Hill Tribes phrasebook • Ho Chi Minh City • Indonesia • Indonesian phrasebook • Indonesia's Eastern Islands • Java • Lao phrasebook • Laos • Malay phrasebook • Malaysia, Singapore & Brunei • Myanmar (Burma) • Philippines • Pilipino (Tagalog) phrasebook • Read This First: Asia & India • Singapore • Singapore City Map • South-East Asia on a shoestring • South-East Asia phrasebook • Thailand • Thailand's Islands & Beaches • Thailand, Vietnam, Laos & Cambodia Road Atlas • Thai phrasebook • Vietnam • Vietnamese phrasebook • World Food Thailand • World Food Vietnam

ALSO AVAILABLE: Antarctica • The Arctic • The Blue Man: Tales of Travel, Love and Coffee • Brief Encounters: Stories of Love, Sex & Travel • Chasing Rickshaws • The Last Grain Race • Lonely Planet ... On the Edge: Adventurous Escapades from Around the World • Lonely Planet Unpacked • Not the Only Planet: Science Fiction Travel Stories • Sacred India • Travel Photography: A Guide to Taking Better Pictures • Travel with Children

Index

Abbreviations

Text

Bold indicates maps.

Boxed Text